Frank,
Tracie & I hope
you enjoy this
untold Cincinnati saga.
Starting with the
(4 page) introduction.

Rusty McClure

CROSLEY

TWO BROTHERS AND A BUSINESS EMPIRE
THAT TRANSFORMED THE NATION

RUSTY McCLURE with
DAVID STERN and MICHAEL A. BANKS

CLERISY PRESS

CROSLEY

For further information, contact the publisher at

CLERISY PRESS
1700 MADISON ROAD
CINCINNATI, OH 45206

Edited by
JACK HEFFRON

Cover and interior designed by
STEPHEN SULLIVAN

Photos Courtesy of:
**ELLEN CROSLEY MCCLURE/CROSLEY FAMILY ARCHIVES,
THE CINCINNATI REDS,
MICHAEL A. BANKS, GETTY IMAGES, PHOTOFEST
AND THE WISCONSIN HISTORICAL SOCIETY**

Library of Congress Cataloging-in-Publication Data
McClure, Rusty, 1950-
Crosley : the story of two brothers and the business empire that transformed a nation /
Rusty McClure; with Michael Banks and Dave Stern.

p. cm.
Includes bibliographical references and index.
ISBN-13: 978-1-57860-291-9
1. Crosley, Powel. 2. Crosley, Lewis.   3. Businessmen-Ohio-Cincinnati-Biography.
4. Industrialists-Ohio-Cincinnati-Biography.
I. Banks, Michael. II. Stern, Dave. III. Title.

HF3023.A2M33 2007
338.7'6838092277178--dc22
[B]
2006029503

PRINTED in the USA
1   2   3   4   5   6   7   8   9   10

To enabling freedom and entrepreneurial
courage, served by those whose ability and
conviction make achievement possible,
we *dedicate* this book.

ACKNOWLEDGEMENTS

Collectively, we would like to thank those who shared their memories of Powel and Lewis Crosley and their times, their respective friends, families, and co-workers. Ellen Crosley McClure, first and foremost, Renny Runck, our own co-author Rusty McClure, Bill DeWitt, Clifford Coors, Neill Prew, Laura Chace, and Charles Stinger. To those who chose not to share their recollections and experiences, it is the sincere hope of the authors that you will feel we have done the Crosley brothers and their legacy proud.

There were many others who helped flesh out the story behind the story—the years of the Great War, the Roaring Twenties, and the Depression. A particular debt is owed to Thomas White and his wonderful website www.earlyradiohistory.us. We thank him for cogent explanations on several complex issues regarding the development of American broadcasting and for continually pointing us toward books and articles that helped illustrate the points he was making.

Right by our side as we wrote the bulk of this book were copies of Erik Barnouw's *Tower of Babel* and *The Golden Web*—the first two volumes in his three-book history of American broadcasting, books packed with so much style, so many memorable anecdotes, and so much information that it was hard not to crib entire passages.

It was a pleasure and a treat to speak with a man who figured so prominently in that second volume, Norman Corwin, whose own brief time at WLW proved so pivotal and who proved such a pivotal part of broadcasting history himself.

It was a similar treat to talk at length with Lawrence Lichty, and we thank him not just for his insights and reflections on the Crosley brothers and their times, but for his 1963 interviews with Lewis Crosley, the recordings of which provided much valuable information. It's a toss-up, in fact, as to which was more valuable; those interviews or his thousand-page, three-volume thesis on 'The Nation's Station,' a treasure trove of information and cogent analysis. We have to thank Steve Scherer for loaning us a copy of Professor Lichty's thesis, and we apologize again for the coffee stains on the cover of volume one.

Diane Coleman did yeoman-like research work at the Public Library of Cincinnati and Hamilton County, the University of Cincinnati and the Cincinnati Historical Society; Elizabeth Pickard was of great help in obtaining information on Powel Crosley, Sr.'s years at the University of Michigan Law School. Others who assisted us in researching were Alison Estes, Jenny Fichmann, and Amy Wallhermfechtel.

Betty Smiddy gave graciously of her time and voluminous knowledge regarding College Hill; her history of the village—the collected wisdom of the College Hill Historical Society—was another invaluable resource regarding the Henshaws, Aikens, Utzes, Cummings, Crosleys, et al. Thanks also to Gail Diebler Finke and her more recent book on College Hill; thanks as well to Kate and Marty Weldishofer.

Shaun Hardy at the Department of Terrestrial Magnetism was our primary source of information on the proximity fuze and all material related to Merle Tuve. Thanks, Shaun, for your feedback and for gathering together so quickly the relevant documentation on that weapon's development.

At the National Archives, appreciation and gratitude to Mitch Yockelson for unearthing the memos/correspondence of the 28th Engineers. Thanks also to Jodi Foor and Deborah Agee of the Archives staff. At the FBI, thanks to Section Chief David M. Hardy.

Thanks also to Paul, Anne, Elizabeth and 'Big Nick' Gambal for their gracious hospitality while researching in Washington D.C.; thanks to Momma Pisarick in Cincinnati for same.

Thanks also to Chuck Howell at the National Association of Broadcasters Library for helping track down minutes/memoranda from those critical early NAB meetings, as well as so much other primary source material for us to pore over.

We would also like to thank Amanda Belden and Leanna James-Blackwell for their help in obtaining reference material.

Caryn Radick at the University of Rutgers was gracious enough to provide material from the university's archives for our use; similarly, we wish to acknowledge the help of the good people at the Baseball Hall of Fame for providing copies of press releases and other materials related to Powel Crosley's ownership of the Reds.

Thanks also to Stephen Headley, Jesse Carmichael, and Marcia Wright of the Magazines and Newspapers Department of the Public Library of Cincinnati and Hamilton County; Norman Luppino and Steve Belack of the Crosley Estate Foundation; Jim Bollman and Dave Anspach of the Crosley Automobile Club; George Babyak, Bill Barber, Michael Broadhead, Bruce Cooper, Jim Fearing, John Huston, Gwendolyn Johnson, Tom Lewis, George McCloy, Dave Milenthal, Bob Scharf, Don Shackelford, Nancy Shawcross, Chuck Berndt, Sister Marta Aiken, Doctor George Gumbert, Ed & Mary Swearingen of Sarasota and from the Cincinnati Reds, Greg Rhodes and Chris Eckes.

And though we don't know their names, the people who run baseball-reference.com deserve our thanks and support, as they deserve the support of all baseball fans everywhere, for the voluminous amounts of information they've put up on their web site, freely available to all.

Finally, a caveat; we bear all responsibility for the interpretation of the information so graciously provided by the above-mentioned people. In other words, if there are stones to be cast...

ACKNOWLEDGEMENTS

~ Individual appreciations ~

Rusty McClure would like to thank Amy (Anderson) McClure, who was the first person to suggest that this book should be written, many years ago. Also, thank you to my daughters, Kaci and Haileigh, who traveled with me to Crosley car shows, the mansions, and the Cincinnati Reds baseball games. And, thanking my mother Ellen Crosley McClure, she and I, together share our gratitude to all who helped make this book possible.

Dave Stern would like to thank his family—that's inclusive of Cleo and Toni, as well as Jill, Maddy, and Caleb—for their patience, forbearance, assistance, and nudging to write faster, already. A passel o' thanks to the staff at Clerisy Press, and former staffers at Emmis Books as well, and of course, most of all, gratitude and acknowledgements to my two co-authors.

Michael Banks offers thanks to Dee, Mick, and Debbie—for new perspectives.

CONTENTS

INTRODUCTION

"If it hadn't been for my brother, I swear I'd have been in jail several times....He kept me on the straight and narrow."

~ Walt Disney, talking about brother Roy, who managed his business empire.

They were as different as two people could be.

One restless, always in motion, consumed by the search for the next big thing—a dreamer, a visionary, the very prototype of the American entrepreneur.

The other, a practical man, an engineer by trade, the consummate manager, rooted in work and family, home every night at five o'clock for supper with his wife and children.

One owned eight homes, half-a-dozen yachts, fourteen airplanes, the finest automobiles.

The other stuck with the same old Buick year after year, until it wore out, and did the same with his suits.

As boys, one dreamt of building a motor car. The other longed to be a farmer.

They were brothers, born two years apart—Powel (the visionary) and Lewis (the farmer). Their story, and that of the business empire they built, the empire that bore the last name they shared—Crosley—is the story of America itself during the first part of the twentieth century. The story of a rural people, a nation of farmers transformed by an unprecedented wave of technological inventions and innovations into an industrial colossus. For a quarter-century, from 1921 through 1946, from their Cincinnati, Ohio, headquarters, Crosley Corporation stood at the heart of that transformation, as radio manufacturers, broadcast pioneers, kings of the refrigeration industry, and maverick auto makers.

Powel was the public face of that empire, one of the most admired businessmen of his time. At the dawn of the radio era, he sat beside Herbert Hoover and David Sarnoff to set industry policy for decades to come. At the peak of the Roaring Twenties, he hobnobbed with the Ringlings and the Fleischmanns and rubbed elbows with Charles Lindbergh and Howard Hughes; in the depths of the Depression, he purchased his hometown Cincinnati Reds and led them to a world championship. He saw the shape of the future to come, the rise of the consumer culture, and rushed headlong to embrace it, building and bringing to market the products that culture wanted, some of which—the refrigerator, radio-FAX systems, the compact car—were years, often decades, ahead of their time.

A giant of a man—six foot four at a time when the average American male was five seven—he used his height to inspire, to dominate; he was impatient with those who didn't share his vision, or his brilliance; he berated those who didn't perform to his lofty expectations.

Lewis was the only man who could stand up to him.

Unlike Powel, the younger Crosley preferred to work behind the scenes. He ran the factories; he hired and fired the workers. Post WWII, when steel was in short supply, it was Lewis who climbed into a plane and went to find it. When the unions came to Crosley, when striking workers barred the gates to the factory and violence flared, it was Lewis who crossed the picket lines each day and negotiated an eventual settlement. When the elder brother wanted to diversify, it was the younger brother who figured out how.

Powel dreamt it; Lewis made it happen.

A story from their childhood sums up the brothers and their relationship and proved to be a seminal moment in their lives:

In August of 1899, Powel, all of thirteen years old at the time, decided he wanted to build a car.

In the bedroom of his College Hill home, he drew up plans. The body would be an old buckboard wagon belonging to their grandparents, the engine, an electric motor of his own invention. The buckboard's original seat was left in place; the steering tiller connected to a custom-designed linkage. A sketch Powel made from memory some years later shows a small wagon with a decorative wooden cowling at the front and a boxlike structure over the engine at the rear.

The boy shared the idea with his father, who promised him ten dollars—an enormous sum of money at the time, a month's rent on an apartment, half a week's wages for the average working man—if the car would run a block. The money seemed more like a bet, even a dare, than a reward, a way for his father to suggest that the car would never make it. Powel took the dare and prepared to build the car. He lacked only one thing.

Money.

The visionary had none. The earnings from his summer jobs, his various chores, had all gone toward the equipment that littered his bedroom, the generator he had designed to power electric lights for the family, and a hobby train for himself and Lewis. But down the hall, in the bedroom of that younger brother, the careful manager...

There was working capital to be had.

Lewis reluctantly but willingly offered the cash he had saved. And then, together, the two of them began working to realize Powel's vision. From the electrician at Pike's Theater in downtown Cincinnati (a building their father held the lease on), they obtained batteries; down the street, on the Hamilton Turnpike, Larry Deininger, the blacksmith who shod their grandparent's horses, built the custom parts Powel had designed. And after a few false starts, a few weeks of trial-and-error...

The first Crosley Car was ready for its maiden voyage.

In later years, when the story was told over and over again, in first the local, and then the national press, it was always 'Powel Crosley' who built the car. But in fact it was built with Lewis, who, the lighter of the pair, actually drove the vehicle his brother had imagined, rode it down to the College Hill Post Office at speeds upward of five miles an hour and back, at which point Powel collected the money from his father, repaid Lewis the capital he invested, and split the remaining profits with his brother.

The Crosley boys were in business. Throughout their lives, they would return to the notion of building a car. Something about this childhood episode—the urge to succeed as a carmaker, the need to prove himself to his father, or, perhaps, the desire to return to that moment of innocent triumph—reverberated within Powel until he died. Even after achieving extraordinary success, surely beyond what the brothers could have hoped for as boys growing up in College Hill, Powel needed to build a car. Late in life, a millionaire many times over, he still had something to prove.

The partnership of Powel and Lewis would endure for over fifty years, spanning the two world wars, from the rise of the horseless carriage to the dawn of the nuclear era. The arc of their story reaches from the depths of obscurity to world renown, from professional triumph to personal tragedy. The tale ends with the two brothers buried side-by-side in Spring Grove Cemetery, on a plot of land chosen for its view of College Hill and the boyhood neighborhood they shared.

It begins, as do the lives of all young men, with the story of their father..

PART I

✦ BIRTH ✦

*"If I were giving a young man advice as to how he might succeed
in life, I would say to him, pick out a good father and mother,
and begin life in Ohio."*

~ Wilbur Wright

CHAPTER ONE

I n the last half of the eighteenth century, in the land that was to
become the United States of America, Ohio was the Frontier, the
border between the English colonies and French possessions, the
dividing line between civilization and 'native' territory. It was virgin
forest, prime farmland, a glittering jewel beckoning both speculators
and land-hungry immigrants to the New World. The Ohio Country—
comprising what is now the states of Ohio, Indiana, Michigan, Wisconsin, Illinois, and Minnesota east of the Mississippi River—was
where the English colonists, crammed together on the Atlantic sea-
board, dreamed of settling. It was the American West, and like the
West that was to come, its wide-open spaces, its larger-than-life
heroes and villains—"not Geronimo but Tecumseh, not Calamity Jane
but Rachel Jackson, not 'Buffalo Bill' Cody but Davy Crockett"—
captured the hearts and minds of an entire generation. In spite of
the law, in spite of the threat of Indian attack, by the middle of the
eighteenth century those colonists had arrived in force on the banks
of the Ohio and settled in for the long haul.

The inevitable result was the French and Indian War, with King
George's troops and the colonists on one side, and the French and
their native allies on the other. The war lasted seven years and ended
with British dominion over the lands east of the Mississippi. But the
war had been expensive, and the colonists, who King George saw as
the cause of that expense, were going to pay for it.

He decreed taxes on sugar, stamps, and other commodities. He
passed laws restricting the colonists power, denying them their own
currency, the right to free trade with other countries, demanding that

they quarter British troops at any and all times. And in order to avoid further bloodshed with the natives, he proclaimed settlement west of the Appalachians strictly prohibited. Moreover, he declared, those colonists who had settled in the Ohio must return east. Shortly thereafter, the colonists entered into a new war with their erstwhile masters.

Among those who took up arms was a young man named Moses Crossley, whose ancestors had come over from England in 1700 and settled down to farm the land in New Jersey, Pennsylvania, and Maryland. Moses fought for seven years in the Maryland Militia until Cornwallis surrendered at Yorktown, and the land beyond the Appalachians opened up for settlement once more.

Moses promptly mustered out of the army, and cut a farm into the Ohio wilderness, near what is now Dayton. In 1810, his son William did the same, staking out land in an area that would soon become Warren County. William's boy Moses (the fourth in the family line to bear the name), like his father and grandfather before him, came of age and purchased twenty-six acres in the town of Springboro, Montgomery County, in the southwest corner of what was now the state of Ohio. He married a woman named Sally Ann Eulass in 1836. They had eleven children, the eighth of whom was a son named Powel (with one 'L'), who came into the world on Christmas Day, December 25, 1849.

From a very early age, he had no desire to be a farmer.

Perhaps Powel's feelings had something to do with the earliest recorded incident in the young boy's life, an event that took place when he was barely more than a year old. The family lived in a log cabin, well away from any neighbors, most likely a single great room, perhaps with a sleeping loft, a house constructed to allow firewood to be brought inside easily, even during the cold winter months.

Powel was sitting on his father's lap when his eldest brother, Marion Crosley, sixteen years old at the time, rode into the house on horseback, dragging behind him a log for the fire. Moses tried to push it into the fireplace while holding Powel; the baby slipped from his father's grasp, and fell headfirst into the flames.

CHAPTER 1

Powel landed with his hands outstretched, his palms pressed into the live coals, where they stayed for the few interminable seconds it took Moses to leap forward and pull him from the fire. The scars stayed with him till the day he died.

More likely, though, Powel's desire to turn his back on farming as a way of life had to do with what he saw as he grew, the routine of Moses Crossley's day-to-day existence. Up before sunrise to milk the cows, clean the barn stalls, slop the hogs, and water the livestock. Breakfast at five a.m., then out to the fields for the day's labor; break for noon dinner, back to the fields for a few more hours, back home for an early supper, household chores, and to bed. Rise, and repeat same. Day after day after day after day, unto the grave.

It was hard manual labor, drudgery, the same life that peasants across the world had led for centuries, despite the fact that by the time Powell was a boy, hand implements like the sickle and scythe were giving way to machines like the reaper, the thresher, the seeder, and the hayloader. Those devices had little impact on the Crosley farm, however, because Moses's principal crop was tobacco, and producing a good tobacco crop required a number of very specific, very labor-intensive practices. Years later, Powel could still feel the ache in his back when he tended to that crop, how he was forced to stay bent over down the entire row of plants until he reached the end, able to straighten only for a second before beginning all over again.

Planting was only the beginning of his tasks in the tobacco fields. A bed of wood, laid to the height of a man, had to be spread over the planted seed, and allowed to burn for an hour and a half. In the face of the smoke, and the soot, the worker had to take an iron hook, pull the plant-bed fires, and roll the ground. In spring, when the seedlings approached a half-foot in height, they had to be continually covered and then uncovered, checked for worms and other infestations. And when the plants were fully-grown, they had to be harvested—topped, primed, suckered—and then the leaves transferred to the drying house to be cured. Temperatures well in excess of 120 degrees were required; beyond the heat, when the leaf was ready, it had to be bound, and brought to market, at which point it was time for the next season's plantings. Tobacco was hard on the soil and a thick, thorough coating of fertilizer was required to replenish the dirt before seeding could begin.

And fertilizer in those days smelled no better than it does now.

His forefathers had crossed the ocean to be farmers, driven by a burning desire for a plot of land to call their own, a place to build a home and raise a family.

Something different burned inside the young Powel Crosley.

At mid-Century, Ohio was no longer a wilderness; canals had been cut through the land, stretching from the Ohio River in the south to Lake Erie in the north; the railroads were moving west, knitting together the great cities of the East with the still-expanding frontier. Ohio was the hub where all came together.

Change was in the air, and young Powel longed to be part of it.

The boy joined his neighbors and playmates in Springboro's one-room schoolhouse, where early on he 'evinced a love for books.' His 'close application and his studious disposition' quickly set him apart from the others. Studious disposition in a one-room schoolhouse was no mean feat; children of all ages, abilities, and inclinations shared that single room the entire day long, five-year-old girls alongside nine-year-old boys, twelve-year-old boys with no desire to learn squeezed next to each other for hours on end. Attention span was one problem, discipline an even bigger one.

Comfort was a problem as well. The children sat on benches that were no more than thick planks of wood, eight inches wide, eight feet long. Their desks were planks as well, fastened onto the wall, held in place by supports, on which the children kept their copy books and an inkwell. Lessons were by rote; lessons were serious business. There was no discussion; there were no questions allowed. The teacher took the copy books in the morning, inscribed the day's lesson along the top, and returned them to her pupils, who spent the day 'striving to imitate' their instructor's hand.

Those lessons were drawn from McGuffey's Reader, a volume of stories and poems designed to inculcate in students the values that their compiler, William Holmes McGuffey of Cincinnati, saw as the very bedrock of American civilization. A sense of fair play, the importance of honor in your dealings, of duty to country, to family, and above all, the importance of hard work, of persistence. The word 'quit' was not in the McGuffey vocabulary; if fate dealt you a bad break, if life knocked you down, there was only one thing to do. Get back up and try again. That particular lesson, Powel Crosley absorbed very well indeed. He absorbed all of his schooling with a ready ear and eye; in 1861, when the *Cincinnati Gazette* began carrying news of the Civil War to the citizens of Warren County, it was Powel who stood on the tallest tree stump in his father's yard and read aloud accounts of the great battles to the neighboring farmers.

And after the farmers left, the boy would read the rest of the paper too.

From it, he learned of life in the thriving metropolis a bare forty miles south of his Springboro home. Cincinnati was the sixth-largest city in America, a place where 'steamboats pointed their prows at public landing' and 'hogs grunted their way to the slaughterhouses.' He read of the Queen City's industrial might, now turned wholeheartedly toward the war effort, its foundries converted to munitions plants, its immense factories engaged in refitting old boats to warships and turning old muskets into percussion-lock rifles.

He read of things besides the war as well: of stores 'as spacious and well stocked as those of New York or London' that sold 'sweetmeats from Havana' and 'oysters from Philadelphia'; he read of grand hotels, of theaters such as the National and the newly constructed Pike's Opera House, where the well-to-do went to hear famed Swedish soprano Jenny Lind sing and showman P.T. Barnum brag. He may even, perhaps, have read of a new game two gentlemen named Matthew Yorston and Theodore Frost were at that very moment introducing to residents of the city, through sporting clubs such as the Live Oak, the Buckeye, and the Excelsior, a sporting contest whose growing popularity back east had already led popular lithographers Currier and Ives to dub it 'the national game.'

The game, descended from the English rounders, was called baseball.

Young Powel Crosley read of the city that had embraced this new game, a city grown so big that getting around it on foot was no longer possible, and thus a thing called public transportation, in the form of horse-drawn cars, had come into being. He read of the gaslights that had replaced oil lamps, of regular trash collection and street-cleaning, of libraries and picture galleries, restaurants and bookstores. He read of all these things and countless others like them, and the contrast between life on the farm in Springboro and life as it was lived in Cincinnati could not have been any clearer.

> While they're riding in their coaches fine
> Or lounging on soft rugs
> The country boys are pulling weeds
> Or mashing tater bugs

So went a popular verse of the day; so too, went the refrain in the mind of young Powel Crosley—and indeed, in the minds of thousands of other boys his age in Ohio and every one of the Union's states. To the dismay of their elders, an entire generation of young men was leaving behind the farm, lured by the excitement and opportunity that urban life represented.

Change was in the air, its currents sweeping the nation. Powel did not have a final destination in mind, but the road ahead of him pointed in one direction—away from Moses Crosley's tobacco farm and outward to a frontier all his own.

In those times, when a child had learned his letters, his sums, his handwriting, perhaps acquired 'a slight knowledge of Peter Parley's Geography,' he (or she, though in those days it was thought that girls 'did not possess the faculty for learning that boys did') was considered to be educated, done with book learning, and ready to return to the farm. The only exception being those who decided to qualify themselves to become teachers.

Powel Crosley took his first steps away from Springboro along that path; he continued his schooling, becoming one of the first students to attend the city's new high school. Working on his father's farm until the age of seventeen, he left to become a teacher in Warren County. He traveled among the schools there, teaching his pupils as he had been taught, disciplining as he himself had been disciplined.

At one of his postings, he had trouble with a group of boys. He beckoned the ringleader of the group to the front of the room and "thrashed him" in front of the others; no more trouble was had.

He began a system of self-education with the aid of the few books and magazines he could find. He grew a mustache and a goatee, which helped him look older than his years. He grew to maturity, five foot ten, a quiet, unassuming man, with a "sturdy fixedness of purpose," a bookworm on the surface, perhaps, but one with a core of steel.

He moved east, to neighboring Clinton County and taught in the graded schools of Clarksville, a small village located on the Cincinnati & Muskingum Valley Railroad. The town revolved around the hog business; farmers from all parts of Clinton County drove their herds there for slaughter, as many as 50,000 in a season. This made Clarksville somewhat of a boomtown, and by 1868 a special school district had been established for its pupils.

By 1870, Powel Crosley, at twenty-one years old, was principal of that district, earning upward of fifty dollars per year.

A success, by some standards, but not his. He wanted more.

He moved on.

In 1872, he quit teaching as a profession and accepted a job as a bookkeeper for a large mercantile house in St. Joseph, Missouri, a growing settlement on the Kansas border, at the edge of the new frontier. The city was the jumping off point for hundreds of thousands of settlers heading West. They came down the Missouri river by steamboat and filled the city streets searching for the supplies they needed for the long journey. St. Joseph's mercantile trade exploded to fill their needs. Powel was the right man in the right place at the right time; his education served him well. Within a year, he had risen from bookkeeper to manager of two flourishing mercantile agencies.

But he wanted more.

In 1873, he left behind St. Joseph's for the road, joining the largest army of traveling salesmen in the world—the Singer Sewing Machine men. Over the next year, by rail and stage, by horse and buggy, he traveled a vast territory that included Missouri, Kansas, and Nebraska, extolling the virtues of Isaac Singer's wondrous 'hand-cranked' machine to any and all who would buy it. The railroad tracks back then were freshly laid steel, slick with grasshoppers; the roads were the old Indian trails, rough and rutted; the land was raw, and still wilderness in many places.

It took him little time to discern that this life was not for him either.

It was now 1874. Powel Crosley was twenty-five, past the age men of his era usually married. He had as of yet no fixed course in life, no specific purpose other than a desire to be part of the vast wave of change sweeping across the country, not just as one of the many caught up in that transformation, but as one of the few directing the current's course. He took stock of himself, his strengths and weaknesses, and then made one, final transformative leap.

He pooled his entire life savings and paid the tuition fees necessary to enter the University of Michigan law school.

The course of law was a three-year study then; a college degree was not required. Discipline was, and Powel had that in spades. To further hone that ability, he joined the Webster Literary Society, a group of students who met weekly for readings, orations, and debates on the burning issues of the day. They argued about U.S. territorial expansion, republican vs. democratic governments, the wisdom of protective tariffs, and immigration reform vis-à-vis Chinese laborers in California.

They debated concerns practical—how much to spend on carpet for the residence hallways and whether or not to fine society members who missed meetings—and philosophical: Was a counselor at the bar 'morally justified in trying to prove his client innocent' when he knew that client to be guilty? Was national character and a man's character influenced more by physical or moral causes?

In Ann Arbor, as in the one-room schoolhouse in Warren County, Powel excelled, distinguishing himself, in particular, by "his ability in argument." Not a demonstrative man by nature, he nevertheless possessed the ability to harness his thoughts and feelings and present them in a logical manner, traits that formed the very definition of the legal mind. In 1875, his second year of school, he was appointed President of the Webster Society.

A year later, he graduated with the highest honors.

And in 1876, at the age of twenty-seven, his course in life set at last, Powel Crosley moved home, or rather, as near to home as he would get for the rest of his days, paying his first visit to the city he had read about as a boy, Cincinnati, where he took up what was to become his life's work.

. . . . . .

In the decade since the Civil War, that city's phenomenal growth had continued. More than three thousand manufacturing firms now called the Queen City home, including a soap factory run by two gentlemen named Procter and Gamble, where two hundred thousand cakes of soap a day were turned out. Its population now numbered over a quarter million; over one hundred thousand of those worked in the city's industries. To ferry them to their jobs, railroads and steam-powered trolley lines had risen up in the small villages surrounding the city, places like Eden Park, Mount Adams, and College Hill.

Pike's Opera House had burned down in a spectacular fire; faring better was the game that Messrs. Yorston and Frost had brought to Cincinnati, which had became so popular that in 1866 a group of local noteworthies formed the Cincinnati Baseball Club. In 1867, they started charging admission to their games. In 1869, the club, now known as the Cincinnati Red Stockings, began paying all their players, becoming the first team in the country to do so, making Cincinnati the birthplace of professional baseball.

That team of professionals went undefeated in ninety-two games that year, becoming the first and only baseball team to do so. A year later, the Red Stockings moved to Boston; in 1876, coincident with Powel Crosley's arrival in town, the franchise was reborn as part of a new association of teams, composed entirely of professional ballplayers—the National League.

While the new Reds took up residence at a stadium called Avenue Grounds next to the sprawling city stockyards, the new lawyer took a room at 55 Pike Street, in the heart of downtown Cincinnati. Shortly thereafter, he was introduced to another member of the bar, one George Sage, who in turn, introduced Powel to a man named Ben Butterworth. Butterworth was also a lawyer, in partnership with a man named George Baily; he invited Powel to join the firm as well.

In 1878, Butterworth's name acquired significantly greater value; he was elected to Congress. A year later, Powel himself entered government service, becoming first assistant city solicitor. He endured a baptism by fire—lead prosecutor's chair in the embezzlement trial of former city auditor Silas Hoffmann. It was the first of many such baptisms; often, when he went to court, he went with a revolver in his pocket.

It wasn't much more than half a century earlier, after all, that Ohio had been the frontier; though the law was codified, order had yet to be firmly established. In March of 1884, it broke down completely. Two teenagers had beaten a well-known horse trader to death, and dumped his body in the river; one of the killers was found guilty of manslaughter, rather than murder and received, rather than the death penalty, a twenty-year jail sentence.

Irate citizens gathered in front of the courthouse to protest the decision; the protest turned violent. They broke down the jailhouse door with a battering ram. Five men were killed that day.

On the next, the good people of Cincinnati became an angry, unthinking mob.

The mayor summoned a hundred of the city's most prominent men to help restore order. Powel was one of them. But a hundred could do nothing against the thousands that had gathered outside the courthouse behind a makeshift barricade of carriages and mattresses, holding pitchforks and firearms.

The army was called in. Before the riot ended, the courthouse burned; over three hundred people were wounded; fifty more died. Adding to the senselessness of the event, the convicted man had been moved to a jail in Columbus, Ohio, before the mob ever arrived.

The Courthouse Riots were salt in the wound of an already hard year; a month earlier, the Ohio River had crested at seventy-one feet, overflowing its banks and turning the streets of downtown Cincinnati into canals. Four thousand homes turned into little more than houseboats. Powel Crosley rowed to work in a skiff.

The capper came in April.

The Reds—who by this point belonged to the American Association, having been expelled from the National League in 1880 for the crime of selling beer during their games—were suddenly forced from their stadium by a second Cincinnati baseball team, also named the Reds, who belonged to the new Union league.

The American Association Reds hurriedly built League Park on an abandoned brickyard at the corner of Western and Findlay Avenue.

Too hurriedly—on Opening Day one of the grandstands collapsed.

One fan was killed, dozens more injured.

The two Cincinnati Reds teams became heated rivals; it was, in the words of baseball historian Lee Allen, "a noisy, beery, brawling, summer." Accent on the beery. Not only were both teams still selling beer during games, but residents of Cincinnati—in particular, German residents, who composed half the city's population—were buying it in staggering amounts both at and outside the new park.

Rough estimates put per capita consumption at thirty gallons per year for every man, woman, and child in the city, and considering that women and children tended to avoid saloons in those days…

Beer consumption rose still higher in 1885, though by then, there was only one ballpark to consume it in, as the Union Reds had folded, and the American Association team had the town all to themselves once more.

That same year, Powel Crosley met a young woman named Charlotte Utz. She was the daughter of a local businessman, a graduate of Woodward High School and the Cincinnati School of Design, and an accomplished pianist who had studied at the College of Music.

She was also fifteen years Powel's junior, all of twenty-one when they met.

He was thirty-six, a prosperous, established, prominent member of the community.

Within a few days they were courting, within a few weeks they were engaged, and on October 8 of that year, they were married, the ceremony being performed by Powel's oldest brother, Marion, who had also escaped the Springboro farm and was now minister of a Universalist congregation in Portland, Maine. Powel's wedding was deemed of sufficient importance that the *Cincinnati Enquirer* gave the event several paragraphs the next day and bade the couple an official bon voyage on their honeymoon in New England. They traveled by rail, first to Maine with Marion, then to Boston where they took in the sights before returning home.

A month after the honeymoon, Powel resigned his position with the city in favor of a return to private practice with Congressman Butterworth.

He and Charlotte took up housekeeping, first on Dayton Street in the heart of Cincinnati and then in Walnut Hills to the east of downtown. The young couple soon outgrew their first home and moved to a second at 438 Kemper Lane, on the corner of Curtis Street, a home large enough that Charlotte needed help to run it.

Powel's law firm needed help as well. Business was booming for Butterworth, Baily, and Crosley. They took on several new associates, including a man named Miller Outcalt.

Then Powel, having mastered the law, moved on.

He took out a lease on Pike's Opera House, rebuilt some years earlier. The Chamber of Commerce had long occupied the new building. Powel put the theater back in; his intent to restore the building to its former glory made news nationwide.

He moved on again, becoming President and Treasurer of the A.J. English Company, a manufacturer of vapor (gas) stoves; he invested in the Forbes Diastase Company (diastase was an enzyme used in brewing, among Cincinnati's most active industries), and the Mendenhall Store Service Company, which dealt in retail store fixtures.

In 1891, he ran on the Republican ticket for Common Pleas Court Judge.

He lost the election and began speculating in land, forming a company with his father-in-law, Lewis Utz, and another attorney, Charles Haight. The group's activities included developing city lots and subdivisions in Cincinnati, Akron, and Lima, Ohio, as well as in West Virginia. He acquired interests in oil and gas wells in Indiana and Texas; he was President of the Crosley Park Land Company in Duluth, Minnesota.

He was a wealthy man, a millionaire, in fact. On paper.

And then, in February 1893, the world that Powel Crosley had built came crashing down around him.

.   .   .   .   .   .

All but eclipsed in history books by the financial panic thirty-five years later, the depression of 1893 was nonetheless devastating to everyone who lived through it. Precipitated by the collapse of the Reading Railroad, businesses by the thousands began to fail. The stock market plunged; banks across the country began to panic and called in their loans.

When they called on Powel Crosley, he had not the cash on hand to pay them back.

He went bankrupt.

He lost his house, his money, and virtually all of his property.

Most galling of all, he was forced to move in with his wife's parents.

He was forty-four years old.

A lesser man, shamed by the very public circumstances of his failure, might have slunk into a corner to hide. That wasn't the way Powel had been raised; that wasn't the way he was taught to deal with adversity. When life knocked you down, you got back up.

He did just that. He rose to his feet and vowed in public to repay every one of his creditors, "dollar for dollar, with interest," because that was another thing he'd been taught. You were a man of integrity. Even when times got hard—especially when times got hard—you stood behind your word.

And you never, ever quit.

Those were the lessons Powel Crosley learned as a young boy.

Those were the lessons he now passed along by word and by example to his two young sons.

CHAPTER TWO

They were born two years apart; one in September 1886, one in November 1888. The elder took his father's name, the younger, his maternal grandfather's. Close enough in age to be playmates from the cradle, the boys were inseparable as they grew. Powel was a few inches taller, but when he and Lewis stood side-by-side, you could see the family resemblance instantly. Yet there were differences. The long, sloping line of the elder boy's jaw, the sad, almost mournful caste of his face, marked him as an Utz, whereas Lewis—darker-complexioned, rounder-faced—was more clearly a Crosley.

In temperament, though, the opposite was true. Powel had his father's stubborn streak and strength of purpose, Lewis his mother's calm, reserved manner. They were best friends, and yet that friendship had a definite hierarchy. Powel was the older brother; always, he led, and Lewis followed.

In 1893, when the panic came, they were seven and five—too young to realize the magnitude of the disaster that had befallen their father, too young to do much more than silently watch their home sold, their possessions auctioned off, the last of their belongings loaded onto carriages and driven away down Kemper Lane, heading off in a vaguely northward direction.

All the boys could do was follow.

But they would never forget the experience, which motivated some of their decisions and behavior for the rest of their lives. Though their success was fueled in large part by ambition, fear played a certain role too. They had seen first-hand—and, when they were older, came to know more about—their father's sudden and shocking fall from wealth and social standing to the humiliation of bankruptcy and living with his in-laws. They wanted to avoid anything resembling such a fall and managed their money and holdings to avoid a similar fate. No matter how much wealth they accumulated, it never seemed like quite enough to make them feel secure about escaping the ignominy their father had suffered.

.   .   .   .   .   .

In the early nineteenth century, farmers from Indiana and points north like Springboro drove their hogs south through Ohio on the old Colerain Road by the tens of thousands. They came straight through the heights surrounding Cincinnati to the slaughterhouses and meat-packing factories in the valley below. It was hard going; under the constant pounding of hooves, the rough country roads turned to muck. The mud grew so deep, the traveling so difficult, that the droves were hard-pressed to make more than a few miles a day.

By the 1850s, new roads such as the Colerain and Oxford Turnpike, paved with fresh-quarried stone dug out of the surrounding hills, had been built, and the great hog drives bypassed the old ways entirely, leaving the heights open for development. Businessmen and their families in search of a respite from the increasingly crowded, noisy city, fled upward into those heights, and made them into wealthy residential enclaves with names like Eden Park, Mount Airy, and Pleasant Hill. In 1866, the latter incorporated as the village of College Hill, taking its new name from Farmers College and the Ohio Female College, both located within village limits.

By 1893, although both of those schools were gone (Ohio Female College destroyed in a fire, Farmers College reconstituted as the Ohio Military Institute) the village itself was prospering. Eight miles from the heart of downtown Cincinnati, College Hill was home to roughly nine hundred people. It had its own post office, streetcar line, shopping area, and school system. It was, in short, a small town. In plain sight of one of America's largest cities, the Crosley family took up small-town living.

In College Hill, everyone knew each other, old families like the Averys and the Henshaws, newcomers like the Cummings and the Utzes. On Hamilton Turnpike, the main road into Cincinnati proper, neighbors waved from passing carriages on their way to get the horses shod at Deininger's Blacksmith. Hamilton was also the route traveled by George Dasch's Daily Meat Market, a horse-drawn wagon that clip-clopped its way through a half-dozen residential enclaves, selling choice cuts of meat along the way. For the rest of their groceries, and perhaps a bit of gossip, ladies congregated at Billy Flamm's store on the old Colerain Road (now called Belmont Avenue); their husbands met each morning at the streetcar terminal, bought coffee and donuts at Henry's lunch counter, read their morning newspapers and exchanged the news of the day while waiting for the next car down the hill.

The children went to the elementary school on Belmont, which everyone called the 'Pigeye' because of the gabled window at the front of the little red brick building, learned the three 'r's' from their McGuffey's Readers and their geography from Peter Parley. When they didn't learn, or didn't behave, they received their discipline from the business end of a sapling or a teacher's open hand. Music lessons had been added to the curriculum, and College Hill's sons and daughters were privileged to learn from members of Cincinnati's illustrious Aiken family; first Walter, and then Herbert—both sons of Charles, who had almost single-handedly brought music to the Cincinnati public school system—taught at the Pigeye.

After class, the children might take to the fields to rough out a baseball diamond or climb to the top of the new water tower, from which they could look down and see the entire village; on Halloween, the older boys took garbage cans to the top of that tower, "and let them roll down the spiral staircase to the ground."

At the Town Hall on Larch Avenue, which ran east-west, connecting Belmont and Hamilton, citizens gathered to attend council meetings and church services or enjoy dances and stage plays, leaving the children to play outside on the park grounds surrounding the hall or disappear down the dirt roads and fields off the main streets in search of further mischief.

When Powel, Jr., and Lewis were finished playing, the street they ran back down was Hamilton itself, past number 239, where the village doctor, a gentleman named P.T. Kilgour, lived with his family, ran until they reached the home of their grandparents, Lewis and Henrietta Utz, which was now, of course, their home as well.

The Crosleys may no longer have been rich, but neither, by any stretch of the imagination, were they poor. The panic may have knocked Lewis Utz out of the real-estate business, but his main business, a leather and findings store in downtown Cincinnati, continued to prosper. He had money enough to insure his daughter's family had a roof over their heads and food on the table. Indeed, for his grandsons, life on the whole continued much as before. The silver spoon, as Powel, Jr., would remark many years later, had been yanked from his mouth before he could get used to the taste of it.

The boys walked to school together in the mornings; they did chores in the afternoons. At night, they gathered around the supper table and listened respectfully as their father and grandfather discussed business, their mother talked about her work with the First Universalist Church, and Grandma Henrietta brought them up to date on the discussions of the College Hill Progress Club. To earn spending money, they traveled throughout the neighborhood, knocking on doors in search of odd jobs, filling their Saturdays and vacations with whatever tasks they could find to earn a dollar. Always, Powel led. Always, Lewis followed.

Shortly after the family's arrival in College Hill, Lewis acquired a follower of his own, a baby sister, Charlotte. Space being a little tight in the Utz household, the girl, when she was old enough to be moved from her bassinette, was soon sharing Lewis's room.

The boys had their amusements, of course; they were both big, even as children, and natural athletes. They became fans of the hometown Reds, and so they played baseball. When they were old enough, they played football too, with pads their mother made by sewing old stair pads onto a pair of shorts. Powel inherited his father's love of books and spent hours immersing himself in the great authors of the day, such as Robert Louis Stevenson and Horatio Alger. Lewis found himself drawn to the Utz family garden out back, where the boys had each been given their own little patch of land. He prevailed on his father to teach him the proper way to plant a tomato. He learned how to lay down seed for corn, plant cucumbers and radishes and all manner of flowers and vegetables.

Powel, Jr., also enjoyed the outdoors but for different reasons. Half a mile in any direction from the Utz's he could find a creek to fish in, and once he learned the art of patience and the proper way to handle a rifle, there was game to be found in the woods—squab, wild duck, the occasional turkey.

On hot summer days, he and Lewis might go swimming in one of those creeks or take off for a day trip in a canoe down the old Miami-Erie Canal, which, since the coming of the railroad, was virtually deserted of river traffic.

Or they might hop on the Hamilton Avenue streetcar and head downtown, where amidst the din of the carriages and bicycles, the trolley cars and the shoppers, they could sample the wares from any number of street vendors—hot waffles, pretzels, ice cream. In baseball season, they might stop to peer through a saloon window in the hope of catching the score of the Reds game, which would be chalked up, inning by inning, on a large blackboard above the bar.

But what the boys liked to do best with their spare time was walk over to Fourth Street and visit their father. For in the aftermath of the 1893 panic, one of the few tangible things Powel, Sr. had managed to hold onto (besides some worthless farmland northeast of the city, in Loveland) was his lease on the Pike Building. It was there, in the last years of the twentieth century, in the glory days of vaudeville, that the Crosley boys received a first-hand education in the entertainment business.

· · · · · ·

By the last years of the nineteenth century, the outlines of the twentieth were coming into view. The West had been won; the last of the great Indian chiefs, Sitting Bull, was dead; the last of the great Indian nations, the Lakota, subdued, the last of the great Wild West outlaws, Butch Cassidy and the Sundance Kid, routed from American soil. The stars-and-stripes flew unchallenged from sea to shining sea; already the world's leading manufacturer, by the end of the decade, by virtue of a four-hour sea battle—Dewey's destruction of the Spanish fleet at Manila—America became a major military power.

The 1890s saw the formation of massive new corporations, such as Carnegie Steel, American Sugar, and American Tobacco, saw new fortunes made (and old ones lost) by men named Rockefeller and Vanderbilt, Morgan and Kellogg; and new movements—the labor unions, the socialists, the suffragettes—spring up to combat the established order of things.

It was to be an age of mechanization, of emancipation from agricultural and domestic routine, an age of urbanization, of great, transformative inventions—the automobile, the airplane, the telephone—that would profoundly affect the course of everyday life. The men who conceived those marvels would become the heroes of this era; Marconi and Bell, Tesla and Ford, and most of all, an Ohio-born inventor named Thomas Alva Edison.

Edison's most important invention was the light bulb, a carbonized metal filament vacuum-sealed inside a globe of thin glass. Electric current applied to the filament caused it to throw off visible light. Others had developed similar products, but Edison was the first to transform it from an inventor's toy into a workable item. In 1879, from his Menlo Park laboratory, Edison gave the first public demonstration of his "incandescent lighting system," which consisted not just of the bulb, but the generators, wires, and transmission system needed to light it.

What set Edison apart from the others, was not just his inventive genius, but his salesmanship, his ability to market his product. The 'Wizard of Menlo Park' was a showman, who used the press and the power of advertising to tout the benefits of his new system. For the site of his first power plant, he chose a square-mile area of downtown Manhattan that just happened to include the nation's largest newspapers, as well as the New York Stock Exchange. To financier J.P. Morgan (who in just a few years would pay two million dollars to buy into The Edison General Electric Corporation) he gave the honor of throwing the ceremonial switch that delivered the "miracle of electric light" to New York City.

And he was just getting started; at the Electrical Exposition in Philadelphia, Edison hired a dancer to tap across the convention floor, wearing a helmet that lit up in "rhythm to his feet." Back in New York, he masterminded an "Electric Torch Light Parade," where men by the hundreds, wearing light bulbs on their heads, all wired to a horse-drawn, steam-powered generator, marched through the streets.

Edison's publicity stunts paid off. Cities all across the country began licensing his system and setting up power plants of their own.

The new technology terrified some people. In Washington D.C., the president, Cincinnati-born Benjamin Henry Harrison, refused to shut off the newly installed White House lights at night, leaving that task to his servants. But it inspired others.

Powel Crosley, Sr., for one, was quick to realize the benefits electric light could bring to the shows at Pike's Theater. Electric light was orders of magnitude brighter than gas; electric light was cheaper, and on the whole, safer. Cincinnati's first power stations, however, supplied power via direct current; the lines could only run a few city blocks, not far enough to reach Pike's, an obstacle the elder Crosley overcame by installing his own generator—a massive, coal-fired, steam boiler—in the basement of the opera house. He had power to light the acts that came to Pike's, in particular, the new vaudeville shows that were taking the country by storm.

These programs, family-oriented variety performances, ran from morning till night, one show following right after another without a break in between. You could walk in during the middle of one performance and leave whenever you liked; each show consisted of multiple acts—sometimes as few as two or three, more often as many as a dozen—with no lull in between; there was always something to see on stage. A dancer, a comedian, an acrobat, minstrels (singers in blackface) following on the heels of short dramatic plays; magicians on top of musical comedies on top of live orchestras. To keep the entertainment flowing, every last detail of the production was choreographed with military precision. Each act was on for a preset amount of time; those performances requiring extensive set-up—plays, magicians, orchestras—alternated with those requiring none—comedians and solo musicians, who could play in front of a closed curtain while preparations went on behind it. Each act always entered from stage right, and exited, of course, stage left.

It was, in a way, assembly-line entertainment. The attraction was the format of vaudeville itself. The individual performers were—except for a few transcendent stars—unimportant.

Powel and Lewis paid close attention.

There also were classical music concerts and full-length theatrical plays, many of them performed by the Pike Stock Company, in which villains twirled their mustaches, heroes chewed on their cigars, ladies (perhaps even flashing a bit of ankle, beneath their skirts) waved to their fans coquettishly.

Though they were forbidden from going backstage, Powel, Jr., and Lewis had front-of-the-house seats for each performance they could get to. And they had free rein of their father's office, on the building's fourth floor, where business was conducted, contracts negotiated, schedules arranged, and receipts reviewed.

Powel, Jr., was as interested in how the business ran—which shows made money, which performers received tepid applause, and which ones standing ovations—as he was in the artistry of the performances.

He was also fascinated by the generator in the basement. He snuck downstairs to watch the machine at work, saw the day laborers shovel pile after pile of coal into the boiler's maw, heard the steam hiss, saw the turbines spin, the wires thrum with energy. He became friends with the house electrician and watched the man struggle to keep the entire contraption from blowing up in their faces. The danger of fire was ever-present; the switchboard often got so hot the electrician had to hose it down to keep it cool.

CHAPTER 2

Powel was spellbound.

He went home, and after much trial-and-error, built one of his own.

He did it courtesy of the water tower over on Belmont. Pipes ran from the tower to a holding tank in the Utz's attic; on demand from a house faucet, the water flowed back down. In the small room under the eaves that he had commandeered for his own, Powel took a feed off that high-pressure stream and used it to drive a homemade dynamo, generating enough current to power—courtesy of the flimsy wiring he strung through the upstairs hall—a few light bulbs and an electric train Powel, Sr. subsequently purchased for his sons.

That water, though, came straight out of the Ohio River. Factories upriver had been dumping sludge into it for decades; the offal from the great West End slaughterhouses had been flowing into it even longer. It was unfiltered, unprocessed, a breeding ground for all manner of germs and diseases. Cincinnati's dreadful sanitary conditions were, in fact, legendary; hundreds had died of cholera and typhoid in the mid-nineteenth century.

Medical science had yet to make the connection between good sanitation and good health. The mechanisms of disease transmission were still sadly misunderstood. Effective means of prevention and treatment were decades away, and thus, the epidemics continued.

Many diseases of the era—diphtheria, smallpox, influenza—were particularly hard on children, especially younger children. In 1894, shortly after the Crosleys moved to the Utz house, a minor outbreak of scarlet fever, one of the worst of those childhood diseases, swept through College Hill. Eight-year-old Powel, Jr., caught it. Today we know the disease is caused by a virus akin to strep throat; it can be banished by a simple course of antibiotics.

Back then, all the Crosley family could do was pray.

Scarlet fever hit young children, between the ages of two and eight, particularly hard. It came on with stunning rapidity. Chills, convulsions, and high fever marked its onset; persistent nausea and vomiting followed. And then came the rash, an eruption of inflamed, pinkish skin beginning on the neck and shoulders and quickly spreading all over the body.

Some years the disease was more deadly than others. An 1879 epidemic in Harrison, Ohio, located west of the city, killed dozens of schoolchildren and left one doctor with vivid memories of the fever's gruesome progress:

> ...as the sepsis increases, a cellulitis develops, the cervical glands enlarge, the neck becomes greatly swollen, extending in some cases beyond the ears. The eyes are glued together with a brownish secretion, while the ears discharge the same characteristic material...the extremities become cold, the pulse is small, weak, and rapid, the mind is dull, coma comes on, and the child dies from toxemia.

Powel, Jr., was lucky. His case was relatively mild. He got out of bed after a few days. Two years later, Lewis and Charlotte caught the disease, and this time it was more serious. For days, brother and sister, ages six and two, lay side-by-side in the little room they shared; eventually, Lewis recovered.

Charlotte died.

Lewis was devastated; in his mind, he wondered if he'd given his sister the disease that had killed her. He mourned her death for the rest of his life, haunted by the question of why he was spared and his sister taken.

Powel, Sr.'s mood was dark indeed. It was his failure that had forced the family's move to the Utzes, had forced his two youngest children to share a room; in his mind, his failure had killed his little girl.

In those times, families formally grieved for months; mourners clothed themselves all in black, wore armbands of the same color, and absented themselves from all forms of entertainment. That was not how Powel Crosley, Sr. was raised to deal with adversity.

Life knocked you down, and you got back up.
Within a few days, he was hard at work.

.   .   .   .   .   .

By 1897, Powel, Sr.'s fortunes had turned enough that he could afford to move his family into a home of their own. They didn't go far. College Hill was their home now, and their new house was just down the street at 5809 Lathrop Place, a narrow lane that ran just off Belmont Avenue. Their new home had nine rooms. Powel and Lewis each got one of their own, as did newly arrived Edythe, born just before the move.

During the summer between eighth and ninth grade, Powel shot up another few inches. He was thirteen years old, a few inches shy of six feet tall, a long, skinny beanpole of a boy with a long, skinny face. His hair stuck up every which way. He looked like a drowned waterfowl.

The neighborhood kids took to calling him Chick.

Two of those kids were Charles and Garfield Kilgour, sons of the village doctor. The Crosleys and the Kilgour brothers became fast friends. Now it was four boys riding the streetcars downtown to catch a show, four boys sneaking down to League Park in the West End, trying to peer over the fence to watch the Reds play, four boys putting canoes in the old canal and paddling north, out past the hills, sometimes traveling all the way to Dayton before turning around and heading for home.

These were long, leisurely trips. They might pass another canoe or the occasional boatload of tourists in a converted canal barge still being towed by a team of mules clomping down the muddy path alongside the waterway, but usually hours would go by without them seeing another soul. They would pull corn stalks from the banks of the canal, roll them into the shape of cigarettes, and smoke them. They had all the time in the world to kick back and watch the scenery, to talk about whatever thoughts popped into their heads. With Powel Crosley, Jr. present, one topic of conversation was certain.

Cars.

The year was 1900.

The age of the automobile was dawning.

CHAPTER THREE

The Duryea brothers—Frank the older, the visionary, Charles, eight years younger, the businessman who turned his sibling's dreams to reality—were the first Americans to build a gasoline-powered car. They did their work in Springfield, Massachusetts, starting in 1886, when Frank first conceived the idea of plopping a gasoline engine onto a carriage frame. In November 1893, their horseless carriage, which looked exactly as its name suggested, like a buggy with four tall wooden wheels and a slightly larger cab than usual, made its first successful test run.

Others weren't far behind. Ransom Olds, who in 1886 had built and driven a steam-powered vehicle, was hard at work on a gas engine, as was a young man named Henry Ford, who spent his days working as an engineer for Detroit's Edison Illuminating Company and his nights experimenting in his kitchen with internal combustion engines of all shapes and sizes.

Americans had very mixed feelings about autos. Some saw the wave of the future. Others saw an annoyance, a passing fad, a dangerous contraption, certainly not a machine with any sort of commercial potential. "You can't get people to sit on an explosion," said Colonel Albert Pope, America's largest bicycle manufacturer.

"They spoil the bicycling and the horse driving; people just seem to hate them," wrote Booth Tarkington in his novel *The Magnificent Ambersons.*

Some looked at the car and fled in terror. Some simply had no idea what it was they were looking at. But by 1900, the sight of an automobile on Cincinnati's streets was no longer rare. Many of those cars were, in fact, built within city limits. The automobile industry was in its infancy, and there were literally hundreds of companies trying to capture a piece of the market. According to *The Hub*, the magazine of the carriage-building industry, Cincinnati, in 1901 was "the greatest manufacturing point in the whole world for vehicles," though that referred to unpowered vehicles; but the city had its share of 'horseless carriage' makers as well. At the turn of the century, mixed in amongst the streetcars, horse-drawn buggies, and steam-propelled fire engines, you could find automobiles made by local firms like Haberer, Emerson-Fischer, and Schacht.

In that summer of 1900, Powel, Jr., decided to take a crack at the task himself. His fledgling attempt, mentioned earlier, sparked the wager with his father, who promised the boy ten dollars if he could succeed in making the car run.

By day, he and Lewis worked repairing telephone receivers. By night, back home in his bedroom at Lathrop Place, he sketched a design for his own version of the horseless carriage. For their phone company work, he and Lewis earned three dollars a week, out of which they had to pay streetcar fare and lunch money. By the end of the summer, Lewis had saved eight dollars, all of which Powel needed, because his own earnings had all been spent when it came time to actually build the car.

The vehicle's successful run was the talk of the town for days. The brothers no doubt were bursting with pride in their accomplishment and all the attention it drew. For Powel, it was a crucial moment in his life, one he would return to again and again. It somehow embodied the innocence of that time in his life as well as his boyhood aspiration to be a rich and famous carmaker. Though he would become both rich and famous in other industries, the memory of building that car—and thereby proving himself to his father and becoming the talk of the neighborhood—and the urge to do it again on a national scale never fully faded from his mind.

By the time he graduated high school the following spring, America's car craze was in full blossom. Newsstands featured magazines like *The Horseless Age* and *The Automobile*. The National Auto show, now all of two years old, had filled New York City's Madison Square Garden the previous season; Ransom Olds' latest car, the Curved Dash, which looked like nothing so much as a one-horse open sleigh perched atop four bicycle tires, had grabbed headlines across the country, courtesy of an endurance run from the Oldsmobile factory in Detroit all the way to New York City.

Other manufacturers staged auto races as a way of publicizing their cars, running them on horseracing tracks, straight across open country, on private estates. One of those racers was Henry Ford, who earned national notoriety in October 1901 for taking on the country's top racer at the time, Alexander Winton, in his brand new two-cylinder car.

Powel, Jr., looked on in admiration and envy; he yearned to be part of it, not unlike the son of a Springboro tobacco farmer who yearned for life in the big city. The heroes of Horatio Alger's books—*Struggling Upward, Young Salesman, Young Bank Messenger, Luck and Pluck, Sink or Swim*—were all about his age, young men left penniless and orphaned by fate, who took the hand life had dealt them and played it, somehow managing to find the fortitude, the drive, and the desire to take on the world and ultimately triumph.

Powel saw no reason he couldn't do the same.

In his bedroom, at night, he continued to sketch plans for an auto of his own design; he pressured his father to buy a car for the family.

What he didn't do was his schoolwork. Though he could coast through English class—he read constantly for pleasure and had become an excellent writer—he barely made passing grades in math and science. His father, the ex-schoolteacher, was not pleased.

The elder Crosley understood his son's fascination with the new technology. Powel, Sr. had been one of the phone company's earliest subscribers, back when no one considered it anything other than a rich man's toy. And in 1901, when Guglielmo Marconi succeeded in transmitting the letter 'S' via wireless telegraphy across the Atlantic, Powel, Sr. was one of the first to buy shares in the newly formed American Marconi Corporation.

Still, Powel, Sr. found his eldest son's energies scattered; he thought the boy undisciplined. Fortunately, there was an easy solution at hand.

In the fall of 1902, he enrolled Powel at the Ohio Military Institute.

.   .   .   .   .

Lewis remained at the Pigeye.

Unlike his older brother, the younger Crosley couldn't coast through any of his classes. He was not a reader like Powel; fiction he found of little interest; writing was not to his taste either. He had to work for his grades, in English as well as math and science. But unlike his brother, he had inherited his father's dogged persistence. Lewis could sit himself down at a desk and go to it until the job was finished. In fact, he had a hard time doing things any other way— unable, by his nature, to leave anything half-finished.

Lewis had also inherited something else from the Crosley side of the family: a love of the land. While his brother tinkered with cars, he tinkered in the garden, out back.

And both boys loved the Reds.

Those were hard years for the team and their fans. By 1901, the Reds were back in the National League, but despite Wahoo Sam Crawford's twelve inside-the-park home runs, and pitcher Noodles Hahn's twenty-two victories, the Reds finished last among the circuit's eight teams, thirty-eight games out of first. They were apparently hard years to be a Reds owner, too; in the middle of the 1902 season, the team was sold to a group of local investors that included businessmen Julius and Max Fleischmann of the famous Fleischmann's Yeast company, and Garry Hermann, of the infamous Cox political machine, which had been running Cincinnati (into the ground, most agreed) since the Gay '90s.

The team also had a new stadium that year, the Palace of the Fans, built on the remnants of old League Park, which had been badly damaged in a fire. That year, the Reds rewarded their new owners by moving up in the standings to fifth place. Wahoo Sam only had three home runs, but he did manage twenty-two triples, which was the true power hit in the deadball era. The next year, Sam was gone, traded to Detroit in the rival American League.

And Lewis joined Powel at OMI.

.   .   .   .   .   .

"A boy here lives among good associates, under capable masters, in healthful, comfortable surroundings. He cannot be where the conditions are more likely to make him a manly, courteous, educated gentleman."

So read a turn-of-the-century ad for the Ohio Military Institute, located at the intersection of Belmont and Hamilton in College Hill. The school had taken over the grounds of old Belmont College in 1890; a new building, Belmont Hall, had been built on the campus as a dormitory to house the incoming cadets, the majority of whom boarded at the school during the academic year. Not so Powel and Lewis, who lived little more than a half mile away; the Crosleys, along with the Kilgour brothers, Charles and Garfield, were day students, arriving at 8:00 a.m. for classes, leaving before afternoon dress parade and the evening meal.

The rector of the school was the Reverend John Hugh Ely, who was also pastor at Grace Episcopal Church up the road. W.L. Siling was headmaster, in charge of the curriculum; among those assisting him was Major Albert Henshaw, of the College Hill Henshaws, one of the city's most prominent families. The major, himself a graduate of the Cincinnati Military Institute, had charge of the military drills run at the school.

OMI though, was not strictly a military academy. Powel wasn't sent there as a punishment. It was a three-year college preparatory school, with a classical liberal arts curriculum that included courses in mythology and ancient history, geometry and trigonometry, civil government and literature, to which cadets added electives of their choosing. Powel was in his second year when Lewis arrived, at his father's urging. The elder Crosley boy followed a vocational course of study, concentrating on subjects that would help him in business. Again, as at Pigeye, he did well in English, poorly in the sciences.

Of course, academics were only part of the boys' days at OMI; the school also provided military instruction. Cadets, in fact, dressed in uniform at all times—dress cap, dress grays, blouse with belt and buckle insignia; shoes had to be shined, spit-polish black. There were daily calisthenics, dress parades, and drills, 'yes sirs' and 'no sirs' and 'how high, sirs?'; the boys learned to handle a firearm and march in a column.

Powel, Jr., considered the time well-spent; the string bean still needed some filling out; at sixteen he stood slightly over six foot two but weighed just 185 pounds. His height was still a problem; he seemed unable to decide whether to stand up straight or hunch forward to accommodate those around him. His long legs were difficult for a boy his age to move gracefully. He was, as they say, still growing into his body.

Nevertheless, he played baseball and football during his years there. In fact, his height served him well as a pitcher. Lewis, a few inches shorter than his brother and more solidly built, found himself particularly suited for, and drawn to, the gridiron. He was the more natural athlete of the pair. His last year at OMI, he was named team captain. A team photo shows Lewis in the center, holding a football and wearing a hint of a smile and a look of determination.

The game they played bears virtually no resemblance to the game as it is played now. Football resembled rugby more than anything else; touchdowns were five points; the forward pass was illegal; on most plays, the offense simply formed into a wedge and bulled the ball forward. Padding was minimal; helmets, when boys bothered to wear them, were barely more than leather caps. The game was a contest of brute force; it was downright dangerous.

People—high school boys among them—died playing it, fourteen in one year alone.

The gridiron, in fact, resembled a miniature battlefield, complete with casualties. While baseball at the turn of the century had already staked its claim to being the national pastime, football was literally seen as a dress rehearsal for war, although war, of course, was the furthest thing from anyone's mind in those times. Nicholas II, Tsar of Imperial Russia, had recently held the first Hague peace conference; he and Kaiser Wilhelm of Germany were cousins; the Kaiser and King George of England were cousins as well, both grandchildren to England's Queen Victoria. War? When the nations of Europe were more than ever a brotherhood, an interdependent whole, locked together by economic forces growing stronger with each passing year? The idea was absurd.

Lewis Crosley certainly didn't picture himself training for battle. Football was a game, nothing more. A game at which he excelled.

Powel's passion during his school years, however, remained the latest wonder of the era—the horseless carriage.

There was rarely a time during his school years when Powel wasn't working on an automobile design, usually with a friend named George Godley. Powel particularly enjoyed illustrating the intricacies of engines and transmissions; Godley was an excellent draughtsman.

The country's interest in cars hadn't lessened either. Two Curved Dashes sped across the Great Plains and up the Rockies in the first cross-country road race, though road was perhaps stretching the term a bit, as both cars spent a good deal of time digging out of the mud. The winning entry finished with a time of forty-four days, or roughly three miles per hour, significantly slower than the world record, held at that time by Henry Ford himself, who the year before had whizzed across the ice on Michigan's Lake St. Clair at ninety miles per.

Lest any locals take a leaf from Ford's page, the city government of Cincinnati established a hard-and-fast speed limit in 1905: seven miles per hour within city limits, fifteen in the suburbs.

By then Powel, Jr., was one of those drivers; after graduating from OMI he'd taken a job as a part-time chauffeur in Avondale, a wealthy Jewish suburb. A chauffeur in those days did more than drive; Powel was responsible for keeping the car in shape too, no small task, when past city limits the roads changed from macadam to muck.

Chauffeurs like Powel had to dress for the part—full-length dusters and racing goggles—and equip their car for the perilous journey into the countryside. That meant bringing a gas can (five gallons at least, as stations could be far apart), a bucket for water to fill the radiator, a block and tackle to help free the car from the mud, and most important of all, tools to change and patch the tires, because if there was one problem your car was almost guaranteed to have during the drive, it was a blowout.

It was, invariably, dirty work; Powel often came home covered with mud and grease—and grinning from ear-to-ear.

His father stewed.

Powell spent the summer driving and repairing—as well as pitching for a local amateur team, the College Hill Belmonts. In one game he struck out sixteen batters.

When fall arrived, Powel, Jr., began classes at the University of Cincinnati. Powel, Sr., foresaw his son joining him in the practice of law; but a few weeks before school started, Charles Kilgour, who was also entering the university as an engineering major, convinced his friend to do the same. The boys also joined the same fraternity, Phi Delta Theta.

A few months into the academic year, Powel realized he was in over his head. His grades reflected it: he got an F in math, he got an F in machine shop; he got an F in geometry.

After that first semester, he was put on probation.

It didn't make any difference.

His passion for things mechanical was genuine, but his academic background was sorely lacking. Charles Kilgour stepped in and started to tutor him. That didn't help either.

On April 13, 1906, he was dismissed from the program.

He spent the summer working for the Philip Morton Company in Cincinnati, and returned to school in the fall of 1906, taking up the study of law full-time, as his father wished.

For the next two years, he went through the motions of being a college student.

There is no record of him playing baseball for the college team; he did, however, return to the gridiron for the football team's woeful, winless 1906-1907 season. They put him on the line, at tackle, where he played with enthusiasm if not distinction. He was one of the tallest players on the team and starting to fill out, to grow into his height a bit, the youthful skinniness turning into the lean look of a young man. He remained a member of Phi Delta Theta, posing for the fraternity's formal portrait in tux and white tie, taller than anyone else in the photo, still a bit awkward-looking but with his eyes focused keenly in the distance, as if looking at a future only he could see.

In the fall of 1907, Lewis joined Powel at the university; in that same freshman class was a young girl named Gwendolyn Aiken, daughter of Walter, their College Hill neighbor. She was pretty, petite, and bright, vice-president of her high school class, the highest office girls were then permitted to hold. She and Powel had seen each other around town; they'd even been in a dance class together as children. At the university, they renewed acquaintances.

If only for a short while.

In Detroit, Henry Ford's Model N, was selling briskly; Ford was already dropping hints about producing a new machine, "a motor car for the great multitude," not just the rich man. In Indianapolis, a man named Carl Fisher, who had patented carbide headlamps for the auto, was making a fortune selling them to rich and poor men alike. In Colorado, an eleven-year-old boy named Floyd Clymer had his own automobile dealership.

Eleven years old.

Powel was twenty-one, taking his first steps down a career path he wanted no part of. His frustration boiled over.

He protested that the allowance he was being given was inadequate; his father's response was: "If you want anything else, son, why don't you earn it?"

The young man thought that sounded like a good idea.

He took his first halting steps into the wider world.

CHAPTER 4

He started out by taking office space in the Johnston Building—the same building where his father's law firm had their offices. One can imagine that he'd have preferred to be in any other place in the city than under the watchful gaze of his father, who more than likely was paying the rent on the office to keep his restless, and thus far underachieving, son nearby. For the father who had worked his way through law school at the University of Michigan, the son must have been a source of great disappointment, particularly given his obvious intellect. Proving himself to his father became one of the great motivators in Powel, Jr.'s life. In some ways, he never stopped proving himself to his father, even after Senior was long dead.

At twenty-one, Powel, Jr. was just coming into his own, anxious to make his mark in the world, desperate to step forth from his father's shadow, and at the same time, still in college, still reliant on his parents for the roof over his head, and the food on his table. Always both blessed and cursed with a large ego, Powel wanted to show the world that despite his failure in school that he could—and would—be a success. Still, that success remained elusive. He radiated supreme confidence in his abilities one second, and nervousness the next.

He then went to work part-time as a bond salesman for a Cincinnati investment firm, Rudolph Kleybolte and Company. He'd been through some of the nervousness the summer before, while with the Philip Morton Company, where he had been responsible for acquiring and renewing billboard leases. On his first call, he'd paced up and down the corridor outside the client's office for a full five minutes before mustering up the courage to knock. When the door opened, things went from bad to worse.

"My knees were knocking together, my heart was missing badly, and I'm sure my face was as pale as paper," he recalled later. Somehow, he managed to squeak out what he'd come for; somehow, he even managed to make that sale.

For Kleybolte, he sold securities to the businessmen of downtown Cincinnati. As the months passed, he improved at the job—his tongue untied, he allowed his natural way with words to surface. The gangly young man straightened up, and stood tall. He was now six foot four; when he walked into a room, people took notice.

He worked not only on his sales pitch, but his speaking voice, striving to eliminate his Midwestern twang. He soon sounded more like someone from upstate New York than from Cincinnati. People, more and more, listened to what he had to say; he found he had a knack for persuasion.

He also found he had zero interest in selling bonds.

The work provided Powel, Jr. valuable insight into the business world, but he didn't want to be a cog in Rudolph Kleybolte's machine anymore than he wanted to join his father's law firm.

He wanted to build a car.

He spent his days hitting the books and selling Kleybolte's bonds. Most nights, he stayed late in his office, sketching plans for his own auto. By summer, he had a finished design and a name to go along with it—the Marathon Six.

He decided to quit Kleybolte, and turn his plans into a finished product.

.   .   .   .   .   .

Thirteen years after the Duryea brothers' gasoline-powered car chugged down the streets of Springfield, there were more than two hundred companies producing cars in the United States. Following the lead of Claude Cox's 1902 Overland, manufacturers had all moved the engine from under the seat to the front. Cars thus began to look less like carriages and more like modern automobiles. They rode closer to the ground, had smaller wheels, and a lower center of gravity. They had metal bodies, Fisher's carbide-powered headlights, and sometimes roofs, but they were still called by names like touring cars and tonneaus, surreys, and runabouts.

At the high end of the market was Charles Duryea's Double Victoria, a six-cylinder touring car, priced at $2,500; at the low end, Henry Ford's Model N runabout, four cylinders and $500. Powel's Marathon Six—'Marathon' for strong, long-lasting runner, 'Six' for the car's six-cylinder engine—was designed to hit smack dab in the middle of the market. He wanted to sell it for about $1,700, several hundred less than Duryea's or any other six-cylinder. His plan was simple: offer customers a small price and a large engine. But before he could sell it, he needed a prototype. And to build that prototype, he needed $10,000. At the age of twenty-one and with no track record, where was he going to get that kind of cash?

Years later, he made it sound simple; "I interested some men with money in the venture," he said. He never named those men. Lewis later characterized them as "friends who had money." Powel's friends, though, were still in college. It's unlikely they had $10,000 to hand out at a time when ten dollars a week was a good salary. Whose friends were they?

Undoubtedly, his father's.

Powel, Sr. looked at his eldest son and saw himself all over again: the drive to succeed, the restlessness. He was going to give his son the hand-up that he'd never gotten, the chance to make his dreams come true without the suffering.

Powel, Jr. took the money his father got him and incorporated the Marathon Motor Car Company. He named himself president, set his salary at $12.50 per week and rented factory space in Connersville, Indiana, a small town about fifty miles northwest of Cincinnati. And then, with the help of local laborers, he set to work on the prototype.

Cars back then were built the way carriages had been: one at a time. The factory was for assembly only; every piece of the auto—the body, engine, wheels, running gear, and so on—was purchased from other sources. In some places, each auto remained in one place while workmen added parts to it; in others, they were pushed from one assembly station to another. The hardest part of the job was fitting and altering the various parts to the designer's sketches.

Building the Marathon Six involved a lot of trial and error. Still, by early fall, Powel finished his prototype. He showed the car around and landed advance orders—six of them, enough money to replace his working capital. The investors were happy; he was thrilled. He began planning his expansion—more workers, more cars. The sky was the limit.

And then the sky came crashing down.

.   .   .   .   .   .

All but eclipsed in the country's history books by the depression that followed twenty-two years later, the Panic of 1907 started in October, with a precipitous decline in the price of Westinghouse Electric stock, which had risen high in the corporate world following its acquisition of Nikola Tesla's patents for AC (alternating current) power distribution.

In the wake of Westinghouse's fall, the entire market followed. There was a nationwide run on banks, as panicked depositors demanded their money. Investment capital dried up; scores of businesses went under for lack of funds. The Marathon Motor Car Company was one.

As quickly as he'd gotten into the car-building business, Powel Crosley, Jr. was now out of it, with only the plans and the now-worthless prototype to show for his efforts. The failure left him numb. He had built a car. He had orders and deposits. He had held success in his hands, and it was taken from him by forces out of his control.

"[It] was the greatest disappointment in my life," he said later. "I have never counted on anything so surely and taken a reverse to heart the way I mourned that automobile."

It wasn't just the loss of the car that disappointed him. He had let down his father—albeit through no fault of his own—and his father's friends. Proving himself to them had surely been, at some level, part of his motivation in starting the company. Nevertheless, he didn't mourn for long; that wasn't the way he was raised.

When life knocked you down, you got back up, and tried again.

While the Marathon Six may have died, Powel's dream of working in the automobile industry lived on. If anything, the initial success redoubled his enthusiasm and his confidence in his own abilities.

It was now time to test those abilities to the full.

Ford and Oldsmobile were based in Detroit, but it was Indianapolis that seemed poised to establish itself as the center of the automobile industry, with dozens of Indy-based manufacturers—Stutz, National, and Lexington among them—turning out cars.

At the tail end of the year, in a brand-new Ford coupe his father bought for him, Powel Crosley, Jr., finished at last with university life, headed north to join them.

·   ·   ·   ·   ·

The stock market crash wasn't the only panic to occur in 1907.

In January, the Ohio River flooded again, the river cresting at sixty-five feet, its highest level since the flood of 1884. The levee broke in Lawrenceburg, Indiana, and residents fled the area. The levee had been built by the Army Corps of Engineers, which, since the early nineteenth century, had charge of the Ohio River as well as all the country's arteries of commerce—waterways, rail lines, and roads, though the corps had very little to do with the latter, as roads were not considered of high importance, before the coming of the car.

On the Ohio, the corps' work focused on channelization—surveying, deepening, damming, removing obstacles to riverboat commerce. In the summer of 1908, in the aftermath of the flood, Lewis Crosley joined them in that task.

Lewis had completed his first year at the University of Cincinnati.

He'd joined the same fraternity, Phi Delta Theta, as Powel. He chaired the freshman dance. He took courses in rhetoric and composition, English and algebra, and French; his grades were marginally better than Powel's. French, in particular, gave him difficulty. He reacted by bearing down, improving his first-term D to a C.

The summer after working with the corps, Lewis decided to concentrate on courses that would let him pursue a degree in civil engineering. His grades improved. Civil engineering wasn't just about numbers and chemical reactions, it was getting out into the real world, getting your hands down into the soil, and building things.

Lewis arrived at a propitious time to do just that, as the university's engineering department was undergoing a rapid expansion. The year before, in fact, a co-op program had been started, one that allowed students to combine their studies with practical experience. Lewis wasn't a formal part of that program, but his work for the Army Corps of Engineers amounted to the same thing, a chance to apply what he was learning to the real world. Over the next few summers, his work with the corps would involve heading out along the river to do survey work, measure and gauge bridges, and lay out dams. He worked as far east as Parkersburg, West Virginia, and west past the levees at Lawrenceburg.

Lewis enjoyed those months, enjoyed being part of a team, pulling together to accomplish things. And the money was good, providing him with pocket cash during the school year.

And yet, like his brother, albeit in a much quieter way, Lewis held tight to his own childhood dream. To the outside world, to his father, he was a budding engineer.

In his heart of hearts, Lewis Crosley was a farmer.

Meanwhile, brother Powel had arrived in Indianapolis, where he'd run smack-dab into a character straight out of a Horatio Alger novel.

. . . . . .

Carl Graham Fisher, owner/operator of the Fisher Automobile

Agency, president of the Prest-O-Lite Company, was the proverbial poor-boy-made-good. When his father, an alcoholic, abandoned Fisher's mother, twelve-year-old Carl promptly dropped out of school and sold newspapers to support his family. (To boost sales, Fisher flashed photos of naked women under his apron, a detail Alger would never have included.)

In his twenties, Fisher made his mark with bicycles, as a dealer and a racer. He shot to prominence as a cross-country balloonist, and when cars came along, he raced those too, to a world record in the two-mile in 1904. When he was thirty, he went to an ophthalmologist for the first time and discovered he'd been born with barely fifty percent vision in both eyes. He bought glasses and then went back to living the only way he knew: on the edge.

He and Powel were polar opposites; Fisher cursed like a sailor, drank like a fish, and not only smoked cigars but often chewed tobacco while doing so. Powel talked in the proper, eastern English he'd taught himself; he did drink, and he did smoke, but after the fashion of the times, in a civilized manner, rarely in mixed company. The two men had only one thing in common: cars. It was enough.

Fisher hired Powel as a floor hand at his dealership, at $12.00 per week. Young Mr. Crosley cleaned autos on the showroom floor and cleaned the showroom too. He drove cars to Fisher's customers and fixed little things when they went wrong. The job, on the one hand, was a giant step backward; Powel went from president of his own company to low man on the totem pole, little more than a glorified chauffeur/janitor.

On the other hand, it was the best possible thing that could have happened to him. Working for Carl Fisher, Powel crossed paths with everyone who was anyone in Indianapolis, including most of the big names in the city's auto industry; Fred and Augie Duesenberg, racers Barney Oldfield and Johnny Aitken, industrialists James Alison, Fisher's Prest-O-Lite partner. Fisher knew them all, and now Powel met them too.

And then there was Fisher himself. The man was unlike anyone Powel Crosley had ever known. If Edison was the king of the spectacular publicity stunt, Fisher was the emperor of the outra-geous. Back in the Gay '90s, to sell bicycles, he'd stretched a tightrope between two buildings and rode a bike across it. After he set up the Fisher Automobile Agency, he thought up an even more impressive rooftop stunt; he dropped a white Dayton-Stoddard car off the top of a three-story building and then drove it away.

In October of 1908, he attached that same Dayton-Stoddard car to a hot air balloon, climbed into the driver's seat, and rose high up into the air. He landed balloon and automobile two hours later, seven miles outside Indy, and drove back. The stunt drew national press—never mind that the Stoddard attached to the balloon had been stripped of its motor and that after landing, he drove a differ-ent, albeit identical, white car back to town.

The New York Times—America's paper of record then as now—reported it as news, which it was, but Powel couldn't help notice it was something else as well. Publicity. A kind of salesman-ship Philip Morton and Rudolph Kleybolte would never have dreamed of engaging in. But then Morton and Kleybolte were hard-ly household names, a fact the young Mr. Crosley carefully noted.

Powel was not always as careful with his attention; right about that time, he was cranking the starter on a customer's Maxwell when it kicked back on him, breaking his arm and leaving him unable to fulfill his duties at the dealership.

The accident occurred at the end of the year, near Christmas and his father's birthday, and so Powel decided to head home; he parted ways with Fisher, who was surprised that Powel didn't ask for compensation for the accident. Not that Fisher dwelt for any length of time on his ex-employee's injury, or his ex-employee for that mat-ter; Fisher was, as always, already on to the next thing, actually the next two things, one of them being a combination race/testing track he and Alison were thinking about building in the area, the other being a young girl named Jane Watts. Young girl, as in fifteen years old, as in twenty years Fisher's junior.

Few people were surprised, much less scandalized, least of all Powel, who went back to College Hill and started chasing after a younger woman of his own—Gwendolyn Aiken.

She was eighteen when he returned home that Christmas from Indy, a young tycoon on the rise. Powel talked about the cars he was going to build, the money he was going to make; he promised Gwendolyn a Rolls Royce and a chinchilla coat. She didn't care that Powel had yet to settle down and make something of himself.

Her father most certainly did.

Walter Aiken viewed the young Powel Crosley as a ne'er do well, a failure two times over. That winter, Powel made it three; he went to work as a salesman for a few months, renting an office in downtown Cincinnati, but again had no success.

In summer of 1909, he kissed Gwendolyn goodbye (chastely, of course), climbed into his Ford coupe and headed back to Indy once more.

On arrival, he talked himself into a job as assistant sales manager for David Parry's new automobile company. A decade earlier, Parry had been the largest carriage manufacturer in the world, but he was smart enough to see the writing on the wall. In 1906, when Claude Cox and his Overland were in dire financial straits, Parry stepped in with a much-needed infusion of cash and saved the company, buying himself a large piece of it in the process.

In 1907, when the panic hit, it was Parry who ran short of dollars; this time, John Willys, a car dealer out of Elmira, N.Y., bailed out Overland and took control. Parry managed to hold on to his stock in the company; by 1909, thanks to Willys's hard work, it was worth a quarter-million dollars. Parry sold it and used the money to jump right back into the car business.

He incorporated the Parry Automobile Company in July of 1909; within a few months, he was shipping cars to dealers. It was Powel's job to visit those dealers and inspect operations, help them generate excitement, promote sales.

He had his work cut out for him. Contemporary ads for the Parry featured a young man and woman dressed in their Sunday best, out for a picturesque ride in the countryside. Puffy white clouds, gleaming chrome, smooth, unrutted roads, all of which, by this point in time, the American consumer recognized as pure bunk. People knew pretty much what they could expect on a drive out in the country, and it wasn't a 'thrill to the funny bone,' as Parry's ad claimed.

Parry's were decent cars, at a decent price—four cylinders, thirteen to fifteen hundred dollars, depending on whether or not you wanted the runabout or the touring car—but they were nothing to get excited about.

As always, the real excitement in Indianapolis had to do with Carl Fisher.

In February of 1909, Fisher and Alison, along with partners Arthur Newby of National Motors and Frank Wheeler of Wheeler-Schebler Carburetor, had bought a few hundred acres northwest of the city and begun construction on their racetrack, which was to be called the Indianapolis Motor Speedway. It was a two-and-a-half mile rectangle, with turns of a quarter-mile each, fifty feet wide on the straightaways, sixty on the turns, all of it paved with a mix of tar and crushed stone.

The Speedway's inaugural races took place August 19; forty-two events were planned over a three-day period. It proved a little more exciting than even Fisher intended. Under the constant pounding by the drivers and their cars, the track's roadbed deteriorated. Stone and gravel flew everywhere. So did some of the autos. Five people died.

Fisher called an early halt to the festivities.

He ripped up the existing surface and had the entire track repaved with bricks—over three million of them. On December 17, the Speedway reopened for business.

Powel began spending a lot of time there, promoting Parry's car and talking with anyone and everyone who would listen—drivers, mechanics, the press, Duesenberg, car maker Harry Stutz. "He never shut up," one observer said. He was constantly offering opinions and advice—some of it worthwhile, according to Duesenberg, whom Powel helped with a crankshaft balancing problem—some of it pure bluster. Some people thought him arrogant; really, he was just excited. The tall, gangly, twenty-three-year-old was the proverbial kid running through the candy store, sticking his hand in every jar he could reach. Powel wanted to build cars, he wanted to repair them, he'd even decided—after watching the drivers take on Fisher's speedway—that he wanted to take a spin around the track himself, and become, in the slang of the day, a 'racing pilot.'

He became friendly with Ernie Moross, who Fisher had brought on as the Speedway's publicity manager. The older man was Barney Oldfield's manager; now he took Powel under his wing as well. Moross started referring to young Crosley as "one of his boys." Powel's hopes heightened. If he could earn a few big purses, grab some headlines...maybe he could leverage his way back into manufacturing his own automobile.

But he was in the wrong place at the wrong time. So were the rest of them. Indy got its share of headlines, but the big news in the car industry that year came out of Detroit, where Henry Ford had at last brought to market the new auto he'd been dropping hints about for some time. He called it the Model T.

It was the car the whole country, without knowing it, had been waiting for.

First of all, there was the price. Four cylinders for under a thousand dollars—$850 that first year, to be exact, which went down to $750, then $440, and finally $360 as economies of mass production kicked in. It was cheap, but there were cheaper on the market.

There were none better built.

The car used a special steel alloy, vanadium, throughout, an alloy that Ford had discovered in Europe, and brought to this country. It was lightweight and tough. Ford used it in the crankshaft, the springs, the axles, and gears. The car had an entirely new kind of transmission system, more reliable and easier to operate in cold weather. It was built for the real world, too; it rode high off the ground, so that the rutted country roads wouldn't damage the underside. And when something did go wrong with the car, it was simple to fix. That first year, Ford sold over ten thousand of them; demand was so high he had to stop taking orders in May.

For years the debate had been about whether or not the car would ever become more than a rich man's toy; now the debate was over.

The horseless carriage was ready to replace the horse.

. . . . . .

There was other news in 1909, too; the wireless industry was exploding. Amateurs all across the country were communicating with each other via the ether. A great many of them were school-boys, who had built their own sets, constructing working apparatus "out of all kinds of electrical junk." These boys had a whole new generation of heroes to emulate; fictional ones like boy inventor Tom Swift, star of books like *Tom Swift and His Submarine Boat*, *Tom Swift and His Electric Runabout*, *Tom Swift and His Aerial War-ship*, and real-life ones like twenty-six- year-old Jack Binns.

Binns was a crewman aboard the White Star liner *Republic*, one of the great passenger ships of the day. On the night of January 23, 1909, cruising twenty-six miles off the coast of Nantucket in a thick blanket of fog, *Republic* was rammed by another ship and began to sink.

On board were over seventeen hundred American tourists, heading for the Mediterranean. Hope seemed lost, and would have been, but for Binns and the machine he operated—Marconi's wireless, which by 1909 had been installed on many seafaring vessels.

Republic's accident had crumpled the metal walls of the ship's wireless cabin, opening it to the elements; nonetheless, drenched with spray, hands numb with cold, Binns stuck to his instrument, "sending, sending, sending the hurry call of the sea—CQD! CQD!"—until help arrived. All seventeen hundred lives were saved. Binns and Marconi's machine were the heroes of the day.

Binns' heroics sparked another surge in amateur wireless activity. Before long, there were so many of those amateurs clogging up the airwaves that the U.S. government had to start issuing licenses. The first of those went to one George Lewis of Cincinnati.

Those amateurs, like Marconi, used radio waves sent out in interrupted bursts to mimic the dots and dashes used by telegraph operators. Others had found the waves could be used to a similar, but different effect. Properly modulated, they could act as carriers of information. They could capture sound at the point of origin and reproduce it across a great distance.

They could transmit the human voice.

One of Edison's Menlo Park assistants, Reginald Fessenden, was the first to see the possibilities. Right behind him was an inventor named Lee DeForest. By 1910, the technology was far enough along that DeForest was able to make plans for a live transmission from New York City's Metropolitan Opera House; the greatest singer of the day, Enrico Caruso, was among those scheduled to perform.

Meanwhile, in Europe, other kinds of plans were being made. War plans, which was nothing new, except that these plans were being made not by soldiers in the field in response to an unfolding battle situation, but in advance of hostilities, by military tacticians completely divorced from political reality. The French had drawn up Plan XVI, the Russians Mobilization Schedule 19, and the Germans The Great Memorandum, which envisioned a lightning-quick strike into France through staunchly neutral Belgium, diplomatic niceties be damned. Fortunately, France's Plan XVI anticipated such an event and called for reserves to be mobilized; unfortunately, the French soon decided that no civilized nation would pursue such a brutal course and moved on to Plan XVII.

Back in Indianapolis, Powel was moving on as well, from a sales position with the Parry Company to a similar post with Arthur Newby's National Motors. It was a smart decision, A few months after Powel left, investors forced Parry out of his own company, having discovered that every one of the nine hundred or so cars he shipped that year were sold at a loss.

Unlike the Parry auto, National's cars had carved out their own niche in the market; they were unapologetically performance machines, rich man's cars for the customer who didn't give a hang about price. The company's 1910 models were the '40', four cylinders, $2500; the '50', six cylinders, $4200; the '60', an even more powerful six cylinders at $5000. Newby's sales brochures crowed about their success in the inaugural Speedway races, making particular note of driver Johnny Aitken, who'd "burned it up" on the track with a National '60', setting world records in the fifty, seventy-five, and hundred mile mark. Aitken, the matinee idol of Indianapolis, was one of racing's most popular drivers, in part because of his good looks.

Within a few weeks of starting with National, Powel was working with Aitken and the rest of the company's racing team on publicizing the cars. In June of 1910 he wrote about his experiences in a piece the *New York Times* picked up: "I stepped forward with an on-my-way to the dentist sort of a smile on my face," the article began, and went on to describe a ride around the Speedway with Aitken at seventy miles an hour.

(Alongside that piece was another titled "Autos for Army Service," which discussed "the possibilities of the motor car in military operations," in purely hypothetical terms, of course)

The gist of Powel's piece was that the car's speed had terrified him, which of course was pure hype; Powel loved speed, he had a reputation for it around the track, so much so that manufacturers warned their drivers not to let him anywhere near their cars.

That kind of over-the-top flair, though, was what editors and audiences of the day expected. Powel was good at it, so good that after a few months at National, he left and went to work for *Motor Vehicle* magazine. He didn't get to do much writing though; he spent more time selling advertising than anything else, much of it to the automobile aftermarket companies, which were starting to make big money on accessories for Ford's Model T.

Powel lasted no more than a couple of months in the magazine business before returning to automobile manufacturing, moving from Indy to nearby Muncie, Indiana, for a job with the Inter-State Automobile Company. Inter-State's cars were designed by Claude Cox, who had left Overland at the same time Parry did. Among its directors were several members of the Ball family, makers of the famous Ball Mason jars. One of those Balls, Edmund, had married a Crosley, Bertha, daughter of Powel, Sr.'s, brother Marion, and thus, Powel's first cousin, a fortuitous set of circumstances he used to his advantage.

With Inter-State, he moved up from assistant sales manager to distributor, responsible for selling to dealers in the twenty-six northern Indiana counties. He had to do a lot of driving. He moved his things back to College Hill, using his parents home as a base, making the seventy-mile journey home every weekend to see them, and of course, Gwendolyn. Infatuation had turned into something a little more serious.

On October 14, 1910, she drove back up to Muncie with him. That afternoon, they got married.

Walter Aiken was not happy.

Neither was Powel, Sr.

"He said that I was a rolling stone," Powel, Jr. recalled. 'When,' he demanded 'are you going to settle down and make something of yourself?'"

The new Mr. and Mrs. Crosley made a stab at doing just that. They moved into the newly built Glenwood Apartments on Hamilton Avenue in College Hill, a few blocks north of Belmont Avenue. Powel, though, still spent most of his time in Indianapolis. On top of his work as a distributor, he started handling publicity for Inter-State's racing team. He began hanging around the Speedway again. He was still hoping to be a driver himself, particularly after Carl Fisher announced that for 1911, instead of a series of races over the Memorial Day Weekend, there would be only one, a test not only of speed but endurance—The Indianapolis 500. Five hundred miles around the track, with the winner to collect $25,000—the fattest purse in racing history.

Drivers from around the world came for a shot at the money. Spencer Wishart entered for Mercedes, Billie Kipper and Bob Burman for Benz, Leo Frayer (with a nineteen-year-old reserve driver named Eddie Rickenbacker) for Firestone, Arthur Chevrolet for Buick, Johnny Aitken and Charlie Mertz for National. Inter-State put two drivers on the card as well; neither one of them was named Powel Crosley, Jr.

Powel went to friends and former employers, hoping for a way into the crowded field. Carl Fisher said no. Arthur Newby said no. Fred Duesenberg wasn't entering a car, but told Powel to call Stutz; by the time Powel got to Stutz at his factory, the man had already signed up someone else.

Powel watched the inaugural Indianapolis 500 from the cheap seats.

He was disappointed, doubly so when Inter-State decided at the last minute to race only one of the two cars they'd brought to the Speedway. That entry was driven by Harry Endicott, who finished sixteenth.

But by then Powel had other things on his mind.

Gwendolyn was pregnant. Two months after the race, on July 10, Powel Crosley III was born.

It was 1911, four years since Powel, Jr. had dropped out of college to find his place in the automobile industry, to become part of the vast wave of change sweeping across the country, not just as one of the many caught up in that transformation, but one of the few directing the current's course. The papers in Indy and Detroit were going to write about him the way they wrote about Fisher and Ford, the way they'd written about Duryea and Olds. It had been his dream since he was a boy.

But he wasn't a boy anymore. He was twenty-five years old, a husband and a father, and while he wasn't quite prepared to let go of his dream, he couldn't ignore reality anymore.

His place wasn't in Detroit or Indianapolis; it was back in College Hill, in the Glenwood Apartments, with his wife and child.

He had responsibilities. The car business would have to wait.

CHAPTER 5

I n 1903, the Pike Opera House, for the second time, burned down. The fire was spectacular, the most destructive, to that point, in the city's history. It started in the basement of a grocery that shared storefront space with the theater; liquors stored there exploded, sending flames all the way up through the roof of the six-story building. It was a total loss.

Powel, Sr., sold his interest in the property; shortly thereafter, the Sinton Hotel was built on the site.

By then, Powel, Sr. was on to other things; he was, for a time, president of the Baltimore and Cleveland Railroad; he stayed active in the law and in politics; he dabbled in stocks, and oil, having interests in the latter down in Texas. He had other interests in Texas as well—land near Houston that he had the notion of turning into a citrus farm. He decided to send Lewis south to see if that notion had any merit.

His younger son was amenable to the idea, having a lot of time on his hands in the spring of 1910. Lewis had withdrawn from the university by then.

He'd suffered a nervous breakdown.

In those days, people didn't talk about such things publicly. The term used was 'nervous exhaustion,' or perhaps simply, 'exhaustion,' implying that the root cause was not mental but physical—the retreat from day-to-day routine necessitated by overwork.

In Lewis's case, that may indeed have been true. He had his father's work ethic but his mother's disposition. When there was a job to be done, he stepped up and did it. And he did it without complaint. When he encountered difficulty, he bore down. When he needed to let off steam, he didn't yell or stomp; he went into the garden, put his hands in the soil, and tried to relax.

At some point during the spring of 1910, that approach stopped working.

No one now living knows exactly when, where, or how the breakdown came or how Lewis's exhaustion manifested itself. What we do know is that he was back on his feet within a few months— too late to receive his diploma with the rest of his class but in time to carry out his father's wishes to travel south to set up a citrus farm in Houston. (Lewis did eventually finish his remaining courses and receive his diploma.)

On arrival in Texas, he settled into a little house on the outskirts of town and set about planting. It was a harsh life; it was an isolated life. Houston was a little cow town back then; neighbors were few and far between. Lewis had to scrabble to get by and didn't even have a horse for getting around. What he had was a little pack mule he took into town to buy groceries. What he ate, mostly, were sweet potatoes that he grew in the garden. He ate so many during that for the rest of his life when someone offered him a sweet potato he'd turn up his nose.

It didn't take the whole year for him to see that his father's notion of a citrus farm wouldn't work. Frost came too hard to that part of the country. He wrote to his father and explained the situation.

Stick with it, the father told the son.

Lewis bore down. At some point he bore down a little too hard, winding up back in bed, not because of nerves this time, but because of disease. He'd caught malaria. His mother came down to Houston; she bought him a steak dinner. Charlotte soon saw for herself that citrus farming in Texas was not going to work out.

She and Lewis finally convinced Powel, Sr. of the fact. Charlotte returned to Cincinnati directly. Her son followed, albeit along a slightly more roundabout path.

Lewis went via the town of Ada, Oklahoma, where he stopped at a farm owned by Salome Johnson. He was there to see Salome's daughter Lucy.

Actually, he was there to propose to her.

The two of them had met a year or so earlier in College Hill, at a party that Lucy and her older sister Ellen had both attended. Ellen, it turned out, lived just down the street from the Crosleys (Powel, Sr. and Charlotte) with her husband Edward Henshaw, whose brother Albert, now commandant at the Ohio Military Institute, was married to Nancy Ely, who was the daughter of Reverend John Hugh Ely, who, in addition to being rector of OMI, was pastor at Grace Episcopal Church, the point being that even in 1910, College Hill was still a small town, although no longer an independent village, having been absorbed by Cincinnati proper that summer. Powel, Sr., had been one of three commissioners appointed by the village to take charge of the incorporation.

There were ten children in the Johnson family. Lucy was the third youngest, born May 1, 1888, in Louisville, Kentucky. She hadn't had an easy time growing up. Her father had been a banker who'd lost almost all his money in a series of bad investments and then died the day before her high school graduation, leaving his family nothing save the farm in Oklahoma. Lucy's mother, Salome, took her three youngest children—Lucy, Bonnie, and Steven—west and made the best of it. She worked the farm; she took the clothes her children had outgrown and sewed them into coffin liners for the reservation Indians nearby; she did whatever necessary to make ends meet.

Lucy inherited her mother's practicality. She worked her way through Oklahoma A&M, graduating with the intent of going on to medical school and becoming a doctor, an almost unheard-of calling for a woman at the time—a dream that died for lack of money.

She was working as a teacher when she and Lewis met at the party in College Hill. Actually, she met Powel at the party first. The two of them didn't hit it off. Lucy—all of five foot one and a "pistol," according to those who remember her best, a sparkplug of a woman—thought the elder Crosley brother too full of himself.

Lewis, she liked immediately.

He felt much the same way, hence the stop in Ada. He stayed

in town several days, courting. There wasn't much variety to their dates; there were no fancy restaurants or art galleries in that part of Oklahoma or on the Johnson farm for that matter.

What they had was a big old stump in the front yard; when Lewis came calling, that was where he and Lucy would talk. By and by, the talk led to other things.

On November 4, 1912, the two of them were married. The wedding took place back in College Hill, at the Grace Episcopal Church, in front of Henshaws, Crosleys, Johnsons, Aikens, and Utzes, with Reverend John Hugh Ely officiating. Afterward, the very practical young couple, instead of honeymooning, went off and did something very impractical indeed.

Lewis and his new bride moved to Loveland Ohio, to the land that his father had managed to save from the creditors in the panic of 1893, and became farmers.

Powel, Sr. must have thought the whole world had gone mad.

His older son had flunked out of engineering college and then left school without a degree, lost ten thousand dollars of his and his friends' money, eloped, and couldn't hold a job. His younger son did get a degree and married a college graduate in an Episcopal church but now had turned his back on the twentieth century to live in the nineteenth. It was the life he and brother Marion had run from thirty years ago.

Lewis and Lucy threw themselves into it wholeheartedly. They drove a horse and buggy to the new property and began work. The plan was, of course, to raise enough crops to generate income to live on. In March 1913, their plans took a hit when the Ohio River flooded yet again, cresting this time at sixty-nine feet. The flood wreaked havoc throughout the Ohio Valley and all the way into the Mississippi. The great canals, nearly a century old, were wiped away. In Portsmouth, hundreds of homes were swept before the raging waters. The Great Miami River, one of the Ohio's principal tributaries, flooded near Dayton, killing 454 people and leaving 40,000 homeless. As the waters receded, cows and horses were found smashed into the sides of downtown office buildings.

In Cincinnati, at the Army Corps of Engineers offices, Assistant Chief Engineer R.R. Jones took notice. So did his higher-ups in Washington. For half a century, it had been corps policy that levees, and levees alone, were enough to protect citizens and their property from flooding by the country's great rivers; clearly, that policy needed to be changed.

Residents of Loveland could surely attest to that. The little town was twenty miles north of the Ohio, on a tributary called the Little Miami River; which had overflowed that same March, destroying buildings and homes that had stood for generations.

Lewis's farm survived the flood, but each trip he took downtown showed him the destructive power of the river. There was water everywhere, as far as the eye could see.

It was an omen of things to come.

.   .   .   .   .   .

Back in the Glenwood Apartments, Gwendolyn Aiken Crosley was seeing a few omens of her own. Powel had come back from Indianapolis, but he hadn't exactly come home. He'd taken a job with the Blaine Thompson advertising firm, drawing $20 per week against commissions; he was also taking in extra work on the side, writing copy for some of the agency's clients. And he'd taken an office in the Johnston Building, where he'd set up "The Powel Crosley, Jr. Company." The staff consisted of Powel Crosley, Jr., President, who in addition to his executive duties sold advertising specialties—buttons, caps, aprons, pencils, anything that could be imprinted with a company or product name—and acted as a manufacturer's representative for several lithograph companies.

He was, in other words, as restless and driven at age twenty-six as he'd been at twenty—or, for that matter, thirteen. Having a wife and son hadn't changed him a bit; nor did the arrival of a daughter, Martha Page Crosley, born September 6, 1912. Powel had a vision of who he was going to be and what he was going to build, and he decided he didn't need to be in Detroit or Indianapolis to do it.

Cincinnati would do just fine.

He set up another office, on 1625 Blue Rock Road, in the city's Northside section and plunged back into the car business. He lined up Kleybolte as an investor—Albert, son of his ex-employer Rudolph—and incorporated the Hermes Automobile Company. Kleybolte was president, Powel secretary and treasurer. They planned to build a six-cylinder machine, like the Marathon Six. They constructed a prototype.

They ran out of money and closed up shop.

Powel tried again.

The latest craze of the day was cycle cars, small-scale open automobiles built low to the ground, designed to carry two people at most, sometimes just one, driver and passenger sitting either side-by-side, or front and rear, bicycle-style.

Powel lined up an investor, G.A. Doeller, and incorporated the De Cross Cycle Car Company. They constructed a prototype, using an air-cooled, two-cylinder engine; the De Cross was a little out of the ordinary, in that the driver sat behind the passenger, in an elevated seat. Powel took the car for a test drive in November; his sister Edythe went along for the ride. They drove from Cincinnati to Hamilton and back, forty-five miles on a single gallon of gas. "I rode with Powel," Edythe would later say, "and the car went like the wind."

A little later the company went too—lack of capital. Powel tried again, this time with another six-cylinder car. Another failure.

He stepped back and thought a minute.

He was persistent, but he wasn't stupid. He kept relying on other people's money to bring his ideas to fruition; that was exactly, he realized, how his father had gotten in so much trouble. Counting on money he didn't have control of; counting on money that wasn't in his bank account, in his name.

He would not, Powel vowed, make that mistake again.

.   .   .   .   .   .

Meanwhile, back in Loveland, spring had come; the floodwaters had receded, and Lewis and Lucy were hard at work. Lewis virtually lived in the fields. When he wasn't tending to the crops, he was using his training as an engineer to make improvements on the property, building, repairing, grading the land where necessary. In the dead of winter, he rose before dawn to milk the cows, to bring water from the well for the livestock to drink, and back to the house for Lucy to wash and cook with. By the time the sun rose, he was out in the fields; when it set, he was asleep in bed, so he could start all over again. Day in, day out, seven days a week, his routine never varied.

Lucy's day wasn't any less full. She saw to the poultry house and the vegetable garden and a seemingly never-ending list of household chores, the cleaning, the cooking, the wash, canning vegetables, churning butter. All of it had to be done without the aid of modern appliances. There was no electricity on the farm, no washing machine, no refrigerator or vacuum cleaner. Clothes were boiled in a tub and hung out to dry. Meals were started from scratch, every day, three times a day, and not just for herself and Lewis but the farmhands they hired to help work the fields. She baked the bread they ate and sewed the clothes they wore. She did it all by herself; in fact, in 1913, their first year on the farm, she did it while pregnant, right up until a few weeks before the beginning of fall, when the baby was due.

Her sister Ellen came to help with the birth; right away, it was clear something was wrong. The baby was breech, positioned feet-first, with delivery posing a danger to both mother and child. They had to send for a doctor, who got there just in time to deliver a baby girl—who they named Charlotte—safely into the world.

It was a hard and isolated life for two college graduates. College Hill, a little more than twenty miles away, was a trip measured in hours, not minutes. Even downtown Loveland, where there was a grocery, a dry goods store, and a post office was an expedition. The roads leading to the farm were no different from the roads Moses Crosley's horse and buggy had tromped half a century earlier, though that was beginning to change. Paved roads were sprouting up across the eastern half of the country.

Some people wanted to accelerate the process.

Carl Fisher was one of them.

"There should be a highway across the North American continent," he wrote in the December 6, 1913 issue of *Collier*'s magazine and went on to discuss in detail both route and rationale for such a road. People had been talking about building a transcontinental road for a long time, but Fisher was the first to do more than just talk. By the time the article appeared, he'd already put together a nationwide organization and raised funds for the Lincoln Highway, which would stretch from New York to San Francisco, serving not just as a way to get from point A to point B, but "a real modern road to act as a model for other highways sure to be built in the future."

Those highways were not just for the benefit of carmakers like Ford or Chevrolet, Fisher wrote. They would be important to farmers like Lewis and Lucy. Good roads, Fisher wrote, would not only make it easier for farmers to bring their crops to market, it would connect rural America with the rest of the country in a way that the canals and railroads had never been able to do.

Though by 1914, more and more residents in the country's heartland were getting connected by the other great invention of the age, the wireless. Two such residents were South Dakota schoolboys Merle Tuve and Ernest Lawrence, who'd started off talking to each over a homemade telephone line and switched to wireless when Lawrence moved away.

By then several hundred wireless organizations had sprung into existence across the country; those groups represented the dawn of a new era in communication, declared the press; "a new epoch in the interchange of information," which may indeed have been so, but what they also represented was chaos.

There were too many amateurs. Some abused the system, particularly when it came to dealing with the Navy. Ships reported receiving faked distress calls, orders for phony missions, and false weather reports. They reported their own signals drowned out by the amateurs' incessant chatter, though to be fair to the amateurs, that was as much a problem with the technology as anything else. Transmitting apparatus of the day was crude. The signal it sent out covered today's entire frequency spectrum and more, which meant that operation was possible only on a single frequency, which meant that a more powerful apparatus could always drown out a weaker one, and the amateurs often had better equipment than the professionals.

The professionals were not above reproach either. In 1909, after Jack Binns had saved the *Republic*, *Harper's* magazine had crowed that, "no longer need the passengers of a wrecked ship scan the horizon hopelessly while the sea pours into the hold and, inch by inch, Death gains his footing." There was now, the magazine declared, "an invisible network of ethereal communications" that united all ships at sea. Except that even in the wake of the *Republic* disaster, this wasn't necessarily true. Neither wireless apparatus nor its continuous monitoring were required for ocean-faring vessels.

Shortly before midnight on April 14, 1912, Cyril Evans, the wireless operator aboard the *California*, went to bed, having been chased off his machine by the wireless operator from a nearby ship, Jack Philips, who was less concerned with receiving Evans's reports of large icebergs nearby than sending out the stack of wireless messages at his elbow from his ship's wealthy passengers. About half an hour later, Philips's ship, the White Star liner *Titanic*, struck one of those icebergs. Philips began signaling frantically, but Evans couldn't hear it from his bunk.

California was only ten miles away.

·　·　·　·　·　·

Back in Loveland, Lewis Crosley was facing a grim reality of his own. The first year's harvest barely paid for the upkeep on the farm; all that work, and they had nothing to show for it. The second year looked to be even harder. Charlotte Jeanne was a small child, thin and sickly, and to Lucy's long list of chores now fell her care as well. Sister Ellen and Lewis's mother came as often as they could to help. Charlotte (the elder) brought fabric for her daughter-in-law to make some much-needed new clothes, fabric she'd gone to the trouble of choosing

CHAPTER 5

herself, white fabric with colorful flowers, except that Charlotte at five
foot ten saw things on a different scale than did Lucy at five foot one.
Held up against the elder woman's frame, the flowers were a decorative element; held up against Lucy, they were perfectly enormous.

Lewis's wife bit her lip and accepted the fabric gratefully. Her
mother-in-law was trying to help, after all, and she and Lewis needed
all the help they could get.

But Johnny Appleseed himself couldn't have saved them.

Part of the problem was the land. In the nineteenth century,
Loveland had advertised itself as the Switzerland of the Miami Valley.
It enjoyed moderate climate and rich soil and was perfect for farming.
After a hundred years of heavy use, though, much of that soil had
turned to clay. Lewis's best efforts weren't good enough.

But the real reason had nothing to do with soil, or baby Charlotte, or roads or the lack thereof. The truth of it was, they were simply in the wrong place at the wrong time.

All across Ohio and the Northeast, the day of the family farm
was ending. By the turn of the century, the Great Plains had become
the nation's breadbasket. The farms were bigger, could grow more
crops, could afford the machinery necessary to seed, harvest, and sell
those crops cheaper. The farmers in Ohio and the Northeast just
couldn't compete.

From the time Lewis Crosley was old enough to think for himself, during all those hours he'd spent in the Utz's garden, all that time
he'd spent canoeing on the canal with Powel and the Kilgour brothers, grinding his way through the engineering program at the University of Cincinnati, working on the Ohio River, he'd had a vision of
himself, a dream he held in his heart. Like his father's father, he was
going to work the land. He was going to be a farmer. It was all he'd
ever wanted to do.

But he was twenty-six years old now. He had responsibilities to
face, a wife and child to support. He had to be practical; he had to
stop dreaming.

He had to get a job, and he knew one place where the door was
open for him already.

He went to the Army Corps office in Cincinnati, and called on R.R. Jones.

.   .   .   .   .   .

In Europe, war was on the horizon. In June of 1914, Serbian terrorists had shot and killed the Austrian emperor's nephew. Austria wanted to retaliate. Germany was Austria's ally. Russia was bound by treaty to Serbia. France and Russia had an alliance, too, and Britain's interests aligned with France's, as did the Italians' with the Germans, and the Sultan and the Kaiser saw eye-to-eye as well, the point being that in Europe, everybody knew each other, their economies, their peoples, their fates were intertwined. Nobody wanted to go to war, and yet...

On August 1, Germany mobilized. On August 4, they marched. For the rest of that month, they massacred.

Pushing through Belgium, and then France, they murdered priests, razed villages, burned universities, libraries, and anything that would take the torch. They raped and pillaged and looted, killing men, women, and children alike, assembling them in the town square, shooting them first, then running the survivors through with bayonets. In Frameries, they marched the townspeople in front of them as they went, prodding them forward with bayonets as they drove on British positions. The British motioned the civilians to move aside; the Germans fired on any who did.

The world was aghast; the Germans quickly countered. "Upon Russia we lay all the blame," Count Von Bernstoff, the Kaiser's American ambassador, told the *New York Times*, neatly dodging all questions about the atrocities in Belgium and France. German-Americans held demonstrations nationwide supporting the Kaiser and condemning the American press. In Chicago, New York, Pittsburgh, Toledo, and of course, Cincinnati, crowds gathered by the thousands to press President Wilson to maintain impartiality in the war.

"We do not beg for sympathy; we demand justice," declared Reverend Hugo Eisenlohr in a speech to an overflow crowd at Cincinnati's Music Hall in October of 1914. Demonstrations, speeches, songs, and marches in defense of the Fatherland continued throughout the year.

In downtown Cincinnati, Powel Crosley, Jr. marched as well.

Though he was still working for Charles Doughty (and keeping a few freelance clients on the side), he spent most of his time pounding the pavement in his size nines, peddling novelties to the businessmen of Cincinnati. He was bringing home close to twenty dollars a week—not a bad salary, but the chinchilla coat he'd promised Gwendolyn, the Rolls Royce he'd promised himself, and the million dollars he'd bragged about earning before his thirtieth birthday seemed impossibly far off.

But he kept going. Day after day, up and down stairs, getting doors slammed in his face, getting 'no' thrown at him over and over again. He had no quit in him.

His father thought him a ne'er do well. His father-in-law thought worse. On the face of it, they were right, obviously. Nothing he'd tried to date had worked. But Powel Crosley, Jr. believed in himself. And Gwendolyn believed in Powel.

All through that year and into the next, as the war raged in Europe, as the German advance stalled in France and the two armies dug trenches along the battle line and settled in for the long haul, he kept going, and found glimmers of hope.

He sold a big order of calendars to the Fleischmann Yeast Company. He and Gwendolyn went out to dinner and splurged on a bottle of wine.

He did a particularly nice bit of work for one of his freelance clients, a man named Ira Cooper, who operated a chain of wholesale auto accessory stores. Cooper had a gasoline additive he thought the world of but couldn't sell. Powel brainstormed a new advertising campaign for it and cleared out most of Cooper's stock.

This seemingly minor success was an omen of things—much better, much bigger things—to come.

CHAPTER 6

The problem back then, Carl Fisher to the contrary, wasn't just the roads. The problem lay also in the automobile, and more specifically, in the pneumatic tire. Those on cars were patterned after those on bicycles; they consisted of an inner tube filled with air, surrounded by a casing of fabric-reinforced rubber. They were narrow, spindly things, inflated to a pressure of seventy-five to eighty pounds per square inch. They had an average life span of just a few thousand miles; they blew out all the time. Other than gasoline, they were the single largest expense involved in the upkeep of a car.

Changing a tire involved a colossal expense of time as well. After a blow-out, you had to jack up the car, pry the casing from the wheel, patch the tube with a piece of rubber called a 'reliner,' pump up the tube, and pray it would hold.

There was big money in the tire business, and Ira Cooper, having recently bought into the Giant Tire Company of Findlay, Ohio, had a piece of it. Giant's primary business was molding new tread to old tires and reselling them. But out of the thousands of used tires Giant bought each month to retread, hundreds were unusable, too old, too torn, too worn, to hold new tread.

They had a lot of wasted rubber lying around. Cooper wanted to do something with it. He had the thought of making reliners, but he was looking for an angle, a way to distinguish his product from what was already a crowded marketplace. Powel had done a good job with the gasoline additive; now Cooper dropped this problem in his lap as well.

Powel thought about it for a few days.

He thought about it while he sat at his desk, doing work for Doughty and while he sold his calendars, stickers, and window displays. He thought about it on the streetcar home to the Glenwood Apartments, at dinner, while Powel III and Page played around him, while he lay in bed next to Gwendolyn.

Reliners, he thought. Thousands of them were sold every year, mostly to Model T owners, because by 1916 there were over a million Model T's on the road. Powel pictured a Model T, saw it banging down a dirt lane, spattering mud and dust all over itself and its coat of shiny black paint, black being the only color the Model T came in. Powel pictured that car, and the driver behind the wheel, going up one hill, and down another, and—

Blam. A blowout.

He knew what came next from his own experience as a chauffeur and car owner—get out of the car, get out the jack, get the car up off the ground, get out the tire irons, pry the tire off the wheel, find the hole in the tube, patch it up, put the tire back on, pump it back up, jack the car back down, and get back on the road. Go another few miles, and—

Blam.

Do it all over again.

People used a lot of reliners, Powel thought. People spent a lot of time fixing blowouts. Cooper was right. It was a huge market.

He thought about it and thought about it.

He slept on it, he woke up, and shaved, and put on his long johns, and his suit and hat, and walked over to the car barn on Hamilton, and waited for the streetcar with all the other College Hill commuters.

His salary was a little more than twenty dollars a week. If he stayed with Doughty, he'd be due for a raise soon; another one would come a few years after that, and so on, and so on, and so on. He and Gwendolyn and the kids would find a bigger apartment, maybe even a house, though it was likely he'd have to borrow money to buy a house, probably from his father. Perhaps his father-in-law.

He thought about Powel Crosley, Sr. then, standing over him, shaking his head, and he thought about Walter Aiken, frowning, and he thought about Ira Cooper, the first man to show faith in him in a long, long time.

Time.

We take all those unused tires and make reliners out of them, Cooper said. People used reliners every day of the week. A blowout here, a blowout there, reliner after reliner after reliner. People spent a lot of time putting in reliners, Powel thought. An awful lot of time.

And then he smiled.

It was his first million dollars, right there. That Eureka moment that Edison had in Menlo Park when the lights went on, that Ford had up in Detroit when he took that first Model T for a spin around the block. Powel's breakthrough wasn't on the same scale, but it amounted to the same thing. He'd thought up a product to make people's lives easier, a product that would save them time and money, a product for which the average working man would happily lay out his hard-earned cash.

He went to Cooper's office and laid it out for the older man.

The real problem isn't what to do with all that unused rubber, Powel said. The real problem is all those wasted hours people spend taking the tires on and off their cars. The real problem is the whole, time-consuming process.

What if, he said to Cooper, you only had to put the reliner in once?

Cooper frowned.

Powel went on. You put the reliner in, he said, before you have that first blowout. You put the reliner in, he said, to protect the whole tire, all at once. The reliner isn't just a patch, it's this, he said, and took out a drawing.

What Powel proposed looked like a tire without tread. It was made up of four layers of rubber stripped from those unusable tires, alternating with four layers of fabric from the same source. It strengthened the tire while protecting the inner tube from the road. It could even be used with tires missing part of their outside casings.

Powel proposed treating the reliner too, so that it would vulcanize itself to the inside of the tire, which was how he'd thought up a name for the product:

Insyde Tyres.

The British spelling, Powel said, for the associations it conjured up, at least in his mind (which was also, in its own way, a portent of things to come). He estimated they would add several thousand miles to the life of most tires.

And Cooper smiled too.

The two men made a deal. Powel would patent Insyde Tyres in his name; Giant Tire would manufacture it. Powel would run the sales and marketing operation from his office; Cooper would pay Powel's office and advertising expenses. The entire operation would be a division of Cooper's automobile accessories company; Powel would get twenty percent of the net.

They shook hands. Cooper took Powel's design to Giant's production people and geared up to manufacture it. Powel geared up to promote his brainchild. He started working every contact he had in the automobile industry. He lined up editorial mentions in magazines like *MoToR*, *Automobile Dealer and Repairer*, *Hardware Dealer's Magazine*, *Garage and Accessory Journal*, *Automobile Trade Journal*. He bought advertisements in those magazines too, as well as in others like *Motorist* and *Popular Mechanics*.

The ads, like the reliner, were a little different.

At the end of every one of them was not a coupon to order the product, but a notice: "distributors, dealers, and agents wanted," with the promise of an extra discount if you qualified as a dealer. The trick was, Powel wasn't going to say no to anyone who wrote in and asked for the discount. He knew some would just buy his product for themselves, but a few, he thought, might actually try to resell them. Powel believed in the Insyde Tyres and that anyone who used it would believe in it too. His best salesman, Powel reasoned, would be a satisfied customer.

He turned out to be right.

His 'agents' quickly began generating more sales than would

have been possible from his efforts alone—hundreds, then thousands, of units. Their enthusiasm knew no bounds. They went to all sorts of lengths to demonstrate the new product. One man cut three-inch holes in the sides of his tires, inserted reliners in them and drove around his town trolling for prospects. Another placed homemade covers over the wheels of his Ford bearing the message "Look At My Insyde Tyres!"

Business grew so fast that Cooper decided to set up a separate organization to market the product. It would be called the American Automobile Accessories Company. In April of 1916 he offered Powel a half-interest in the new concern for an investment of five hundred dollars. It was a great deal, Powel realized. A once-in-a-lifetime opportunity. There was only one problem.

Where was he going to get five hundred dollars?

.   .   .   .   .   .

Not from the brother who financed his first foray into the car business, that was for certain. Not in April of 1916. Lewis Crosley was working for the Army Corps of Engineers as a surveyor for the princely sum of ninety dollars per month. R.R. Jones had hired him as part of the corps' effort to channelize the Ohio River and to get data on the big river and the tributaries that fed it.

Lewis went into the Ohio backcountry to do so, and into all the surrounding states, going up hills and down valleys, carrying the equipment he needed. He set up gauging stations and hired local crews where necessary to help. The corps was after flow curves for each of those rivers, data that would give them information on the critical relationship between river stage and rate of discharge, a fancy way of saying exactly how high the water could get before overflowing its banks. Taking those measurements was tricky work. Lewis had to get out in the middle of the river, and measure not just how deep it was but how fast it was going. Not just at one point in the river but several, sometimes taking dozens of different measurements.

In Waverly, Ohio, on the lower part of the Scioto River, he had to take them hanging off a railroad bridge, scurrying on and off with the equipment when the big coal trains passed by.

On the Licking River in the Kentucky foothills, he had to dodge the big logging rafts that floated down the river bound for the sawmills.

In West Virginia, out on the Big Kanawha, Lewis had to dodge the locals who thought he might be a 'revenooer,' come to collect the recently instituted Federal Income Tax.

It wasn't his dream job, but it was good steady work. Still, in April of 1916, right about the time Powel was looking for his five hundred dollars, Lewis began wondering if perhaps, his services might be of more use elsewhere.

Across the Atlantic, the war that had started over a single assassination had engulfed an entire hemisphere. Fighting had spread through Europe, down into the Middle East, and south into the African colonies.

On June 3, 1916, the U.S. Congress passed the National Defense Act, reorganizing the army, merging the states' National Guards, the Army Reserve, and the Regular Army into a whole. In August, Wilson appointed his Secretary of War, Newton Baker, to head up the new "Council for National Defense."

War hadn't been declared yet. But clearly, it was coming.

Hundreds couldn't wait. They joined the French Foreign Legion or the Escadrille Lafayette (an all-American air squadron); they volunteered as drivers in the ambulance corps. Hundreds more enlisted in the army, and the reserves.

In 1916, Lewis Crosley joined them.

His application to become a second lieutenant in the army went through in mid-year, accompanied by letters of recommendation from Captain W.A. Johnson ("his character is of the best") and Major George R. Spalding ("he would make a splendid officer in the mobile army or the artillery"). While he waited for a response, he worked the river.

And Powel worked the only money connection he had left.

His father.

. . . . .

In the end, really, there was nowhere else to turn for the five hundred dollars. No bank would take a chance on Powel Crosley, Jr. with his track record.

Son brought father the books on Insyde Tyres. Powel the younger spoke of the growth of the automobile industry, especially the aftermarket. He pointed to the revolutionary nature of his reliner design, to the confidence Ira Cooper had shown in him.

Powel, Sr. listened, and frowned, and thought: Failure.

My oldest son, my namesake, the boy I worked and sacrificed and sweated for, the boy I made sure had every advantage in the world, is a failure.

I paid his way through college, and he flunked out.

I got him ten thousand dollars to build a car, and he lost it all.

And now here he is again, thirty years old, and still running to daddy for a handout.

Powel, Jr. imagined himself a character out of a Horatio Alger novel, a Fisher or a Ford in the making, but he was wrong. It was Powel, Sr., who had made his way up from nothing, who'd studied by candlelight every evening after doing his chores on the farm, who'd used his brains and his fists to become a principal at twenty-one years old, who'd ridden railroads and stage coaches halfway across the country to sell sewing machines, who'd paid his own way through law school, who'd come to the big city and made a name for himself as a lawyer, made a fortune in real estate before losing it all and still, even after fate kicked him in the teeth and left him penniless, took his youngest daughter, his home, his money, still, still managed to get back on his feet and make something of himself.

It was Powel, Sr.'s life that was the rags-to-riches story—and both of them knew it.

When are you going to settle down and make something of yourself, father had asked son ten years earlier?

The answer seemed to be never.

When Jr. finished talking, Sr. spoke his piece.

Nobody was in that room but the two men.

Nobody knows what was said, and left unsaid, between them.

Powel, Jr. walked out with his five hundred dollars.

While he lived, though, he never, ever spoke of where it came from—or what he'd had to do to get it—again.

. . . . . .

On May 23, 1916, incorporation papers for the American Automobile Accessories Company listing Ira J. Cooper and Powel Crosley, Jr. as partners were filed with the State of Ohio.

Powel's borrowed five hundred dollars went into advertising and office overhead, the cost of packaging and shipping Insyde Tyres. Cooper's investment was in the form of materials and manufacturing.

Powel bought mailing lists and sent out illustrated circulars packed with testimonials from satisfied customers. Like his ads, these small flyers and brochures did not mention prices but encouraged inquiries. The inquiries were put on a list of qualified prospects, whom Powel deluged with a carefully planned series of sales letters. He kept detailed records of the results of his advertising and mailings; he learned that ads in *Popular Mechanics* drew the greatest number of responses and that one-inch ads were the most effective. Ads and letters that didn't bring in orders were tossed out; Powel constantly fine-tuned the pitches. He mastered the science of mail-order.

The orders continued to come in fast and furious. By August the new company had grown to the point where Powel had to move out of the Johnston building and down the street to larger quarters. He hired a secretary to deal with the clerical work.

He quit his job with Doughty and stopped peddling novelties. He repaid Powel, Sr. very quickly.

And then disaster struck.

Winter came, and people—as they did in those days, rather than deal with the snow, and the ice, and the cold—simply put their cars away. They stopped driving them.

They stopped getting blowouts.

They stopped ordering Insyde Tyres.

The company teetered on the verge of insolvency. Powel teetered right along with it.

Once more, Ira Cooper came to the rescue.

He advanced Powel money—well over a thousand dollars by the time spring rolled around—to keep American Automobile Accessories afloat. As the winter of 1916-17 ended, cars began returning to the roads. Orders picked up again, even stronger than before.

Powel looked at those orders, considered his situation, and decided to throw the dice.

In February of 1917, he bought out Cooper for fifteen hundred dollars worth of notes.

"I was optimistic," he would say later.

Lewis had a different word for it.

"My brother," the younger Crosley said later, "was a gambler."

The gamble Powel took was that sales, so strong during the spring and summer, could be kept going once the cold hit again. He quickly saw a way to do that; if he could sell his product to retail outlets, who placed their orders for the spring season in the dead of winter, he'd have money to tide him over come the next year, when the mail-order business slowed.

He began by calling on auto accessories wholesalers and retailers in Cincinnati and Indianapolis. They were impressed with the product; they ordered in quantity.

Next, he diversified his product line. First up—retread tires from Giant. But these weren't typical retreads. Powel installed an Insyde Tyres in each one, and guaranteed the tires "serviceable."

Next came another gadget for all those Model T owners. Ford's car came factory-equipped with a waterproof textile cover; several manufacturers had come out with a hard-shell limousine top that could be bolted on to the car in the other's place. The limousine top, though, didn't reach all the way down the windshield. There was a gap of an inch or so.

Powel put together an inexpensive add-on, a fabric extension that clipped to the limousine top and the windshield, called it an 'Anti-Draft Shield,' and added it to the product line.

He sold thousands of them.

He devised the 'Litl Shofur,' a gadget that helped return the steering mechanism on those same Fords to a straight line after they'd struck a rock or a rut. That was a big seller too.

Next came a self-vulcanizing tire patch he called 'Treadkote,' a waterless car-cleaning compound he named "Dri-Klean-It," and a gasoline additive he dubbed "Kick."

In addition to flyers for individual products, Powel put together a fifty-page illustrated catalog, two colors on newsprint, that offered the company's full line. He offered the same "dealer discount" (fifty percent off "list price") that had worked so well for Insyde Tyres on all merchandise.

Business continued to boom.

Now he could buy Gwendolyn that house—a gracious four-bedroom home on Davey Avenue in College Hill, next door to Edgar Cummings, who ran the Northside Bank and was president of the College Hill Building Association, which met in the Town Hall just down the street. The new home had indoor plumbing, a finished attic, and an attached garage, as well as a large swimming pool for Page and Powel III.

And then he set his eyes on the big prize—an order from the grand-daddy of all mail-order catalog companies, Sears, Roebuck.

In November of 1917, he took a train to Chicago to meet with the automotive products buyers at Sears. They were taken with the inventor; they were taken with his invention. They placed an order.

A substantial order—an order bigger than Powel had dared dream, an order not in the hundreds or thousands but in the tens of thousands of units. Powel realized that the gamble he'd taken six months earlier was going to pay off: Americo was going to make it.

He was going to be rich.

Not that his problems were over or that being rich meant you couldn't be poor again, but his days of scrambling for five hundred dollars were over—forever, he hoped.

He got back to College Hill and told Gwendolyn, and then, in short order, her father, and then his father, and then his old friend Charles Kilgour.

And in between the congratulatory handshakes, Powel pulled each of those men aside and made a confession. The Sears order was too big for Americo to handle as it was currently constituted. He needed to expand. He needed money to do that. He wanted them to back that expansion.

All three men said yes.

After Powel combined his own cash with that of his investors he had ten thousand dollars—enough to beef up Americo to the degree necessary to fulfill the Sears order.

On December 10, 1917, new articles of incorporation for the American Automobile Accessories Company were filed, listing Powel Crosley, Jr., Gwendolyn Crosley, Powel Crosley, Sr., Charles E. Kilgour, and Walter H. Aiken as officers.

"Said corporation," those articles read, "is formed for the purpose of manufacturing and selling automobiles."

The papers, of course, also mentioned the auto accessories the company was manufacturing, but the point was, new business or not, it was the same old Powel.

Come hell or high water, he was going to build that car.

But first he had to insure that his investors' faith and money hadn't been misplaced. He had to get American Automobile Accessories on a firm financial footing. The first step was to find a bigger building for the company. Powel chose a two-story at 365 Gulow Street in Northside, an industrial area a couple of miles northwest of downtown.

And he had to get a handle on managing his business, which by winter of 1917 employed several dozen people. He found it difficult to delegate responsibility, to trust his staff to do the jobs he'd given them without peering over their shoulders. He micro-managed. Instead of passing on work to his employees, as he would later relate, "I went into every detail myself."

His actions were understandable, given what was at stake,

given how long it had taken him to achieve success, but he found himself with less and less time to devote to what he did best—develop new ideas. He desperately needed a competent general manager he could trust to handle all those details, somebody who understood his idiosyncrasies, could work with him and for him.

Fortunately, there was an easy solution at hand.

He called the Army Corps of Engineers and offered the position to his brother.

At the time, however, Lewis was otherwise occupied.

CHAPTER 7

I n late December, 1917, the fourth year of the World War I, Lewis Crosley set out across the frozen Ohio River to join the fight. He had a rucksack on his back and held a long wooden pole over his head to keep himself from falling completely through the ice if it cracked or shifted beneath him.

Behind him was Vevay, Indiana, some fifty miles from the Indiana/Ohio border, the location of Dam 39, where he'd spent most of 1917 with his family as engineer-in-residence. Ahead lay Warsaw, Kentucky, and the train that would take him back to College Hill for a few days before he headed south to Camp Lee in Petersburg Virginia, site of the Army's Third Engineer Camp.

To his left and right, as far as he could see, the river was frozen, a jam one hundred miles long from Vevay to Rising Sun, where construction would soon start on Dam 38. The two dams were part of a planned fifty-four along the Ohio, numbered sequentially from the river's headwaters at Pittsburgh down to its junction with the Mississippi at Cairo, Indiana. Louis Prell, assistant engineer, had official charge of Dam 39, but Lewis Crosley ended up supervising much of the work that year, thanks to the numerous changes in corps personnel that had occurred because of America's entrance into the war. Lewis's commission had been activated on June 17, and he'd spent his twenty-ninth birthday in Cincinnati, taking the Corps' Junior Engineer Examination. In December, he'd requested formal transfer to that office to prepare for his departure, a move that Mr. Prell, who had a reputation on the river as a taskmaster, acceded to, as long as Dam 39 was not charged with Mr. Crosley's time once he was gone.

In the winter of 1917 snow fell in record amounts, in feet rather than inches. The roads were not only impassable but invisible. Lewis put Lucy and Charlotte on a horse-drawn sleigh and sent them back to College Hill ahead of him, but by mid-December, the only way out of Vevay was across the frozen river.

By Christmas he'd reached College Hill, where he reunited with the entire family—Crosleys, Henshaws, Aikens, and Utzes—for the holidays. Home-cooked meals, Gwendolyn playing the piano, Charlotte and Powel III and Page toddling out in the snow. Lewis was able to relax for a few days, talk about business with his brother and father, talk about government service with Lewis Johnson Henshaw (Ellen's son, nineteen years old and anxious to enlist), and avoid talking with Lucy about mustard gas, machine guns, and what exactly service in the Army Corps of Engineers might entail.

The war was topic number one on everyone's mind, of course. The Council for National Defense had mobilized industry nationwide for the war effort. The Navy seized control of all the country's wireless apparatus, amateur and commercial alike, including a huge new two-hundred-kilowatt transmitter built by the General Electric Company out in New Brunswick, New Jersey. The transmitter, intended for the use of the Marconi Corporation, had been designed by a GE engineer named Ernst Alexandersson. Those two hundred kilowatts could send a signal strong enough to reach across the Atlantic.

In Indianapolis, Carl Fisher built hangars, a flight tower, and floodlights at the Speedway, and lent it to the government for use as an aviation school. In Vevay, Mrs. C.S. Tandy and a committee of town women knit thirty-seven sweaters and sent them off to the Navy.

Some efforts were of questionable strategic value; a nationwide campaign succeeded in renaming sauerkraut Liberty Cabbage, and the hamburger 'Salisbury Steak.' In Cincinnati, the city council ordered the names of thirteen streets anglicized—German Street became English Street; Berlin, Woodrow; Bismark, Montreal; Bremen, Republic—and then voted to remove all German-language books from the library shelves. The propaganda got ugly. German-

Americans, the vast majority of them loyal to a fault, became the targets for vicious abuse.

In Virginia, meanwhile, on January 4, Lewis reported to the quartermaster at Camp Lee. He was handed, among other things, a barrack bag, three wool blankets, two wool breeches, collar ornaments, two dress shirts, two pairs of field shoes, five pairs of socks, a slicker, an overcoat, a Springfield 30/30 rifle, a Colt .45 automatic, a knife, a spoon, a fork, a canteen, and canteen cover, and then set to work.

He learned the right way to dig a trench—skin the sod off, pile it in front for a firing parapet, and then dig a hole six feet deep, three feet wide, making sure to cut out traverses (curves) in the line, so that exploding shrapnel fire wouldn't take out a whole squad of men at a time. Then he learned how to build fortifications—fascines, battlements, gabions—to help protect the entrenched soldiers from incoming shells, and how to clear brush and barbwire from the fields in front of those trenches to provide the soldiers inside a clear field of fire. He learned how to build pontoon bridges, how to put up buildings quickly, and how to knock them down even faster to bar the enemy's way forward.

He even found time to pass the civil service examination for Junior Engineer.

But he wasn't there just to refine his engineering skills. He was there to train for war. His old OMI drills came back to him—close order, marching in formation, training with rifles, training in physical combat—only this time, it was for real, because General Pershing, commander-in-chief of the AEF, had made it a priority, every man in the service, engineers included, had to know how to use his weapon.

Lewis took target practice every day for an hour, with particular emphasis on the Springfield rifle, twenty-two lessons under the watchful eye of seasoned regular Army instructors. Then they put a bayonet on the business end of that rifle and showed him the right way to use that too.

In the middle of February, engineer training ended, and

Lewis's orders arrived. He was assigned to the 28th Engineering Regiment, two hours up the road in Camp Meade, Maryland, right outside Annapolis.

The 28th was a new regiment, formed in late 1917 out of the 23rd, when the U.S. government began to realize the scope of the task it had taken upon itself by joining in the war effort. Reports back from Europe—from General Pershing and Herbert Hoover, who had led American relief efforts to feed starving civilians in occupied France and Belgium—revealed the toll four years of war had taken on France. A massive rebuilding of the nation's infrastructure was required before the three million American troops Pershing wanted could be landed, much less fed, housed, and supplied, and those troops needed a way to the front as well. France's arteries of transport were strained to the limit already; new track had to be laid for the railways; the track bed itself had to be improved. And France's roads were largely macadam—made up of clean broken stones, all about the same size. Those near the front had been pulverized by artillery fire or ripped up by the stress the new motorized vehicles of war—tanks and motor transports in particular—put on them.

For the army to move on these roads, they had to be repaired, resurfaced, and rebuilt, time and time again. Rock was needed in huge quantities, rock quarried from the French hillsides, dug up from deep in the earth or taken from the rubble of hundreds of France's shattered villages. It was the job of the 28th Engineers to get out that rock.

They were the Quarry Regiment, organized into six companies, A through F, two hundred and fifty men and enlisted officers in each, and on his arrival at Camp Meade, Second Lieutenant Lewis M. Crosley, assigned to Company C, became one of them.

At the officers' barracks, he met First Lieutenants Baird, Cappelman, Cronemeyer, and Stock and renewed acquaintances with Second Lieutenant Thomas H. Townsend, a fellow veteran of the Third Engineer Training camp. He learned specifics of the planned quarry work, the equipment they would use, a coal-powered, steam-driven plant of one thousand yards daily capacity, one plant to a company, parts interchangeable to facilitate repairs, equipment including churn drills, steam shovels, McCully Gyratory Crushers, jackhammers, piston drills, and belt conveyors, all equipment that the company would take with them overseas because there was none to be had in France.

By and by, he met the men of Company C—Private Montague the company barber, Master Engineers Whentzle and Morrill, Sergeants Laughlin and Kennedy, Corporals Dean and Gerber, Privates Gianetto and Gerard. He took another crack at learning French, courtesy of the YMCA, which supplied textbooks for the entire company, and Private Hirsch Hootkins, who helped teach the lessons. Lieutenant Stock taught a course on demolition, and Lieutenant Homer Cappelman on knots.

When they weren't learning, they were drilling, and when they weren't drilling, they were marching—ten-mile hikes sometimes, in the hills surrounding the camp, steep, wooded hills that must have reminded Lewis of the Mill Creek Valley and home.

Lucy and Charlotte were there to remind him too.

They had come east, moving from sister Ellen's house in College Hill to sister Mary's in Philadelphia. Lucy found a job at a girl's boarding school as a dormitory counselor; but thanks to an epidemic of measles, Lewis and Company C were in quarantine till the end of March, and he was unable to take leave to see them.

On March 31 they enjoyed time together, and then it was back to camp for more drills, more training; the gas masks came out, along with a little instruction card titled "Correct Use of Gas Mask Equipment."

It was all getting suddenly, frighteningly, real. Lewis filled out the proper insurance forms, designating his beneficiaries.

In Europe, it was getting frighteningly real for the Germans too, who saw the Americans arriving daily by the thousands and knew that they had to strike before the AEF was fully engaged.

On March 21, operation Kaiserschlacht (Kaiser's battle) was launched, a ferocious bombardment of artillery—over six thousand guns firing at once—against British positions in Northern France.

Lewis and Powel; the partnership, just out of infancy.

Credit: Ellen Crosley McClure/Crosley Family Archives

The Crosley siblings: Edythe, Lewis, and Powel, circa 1900.

Sister Charlotte, who died of scarlet fever at the age of three.

**Young Lewis Crosley: captain of the '06 OMI football team;
Army Corps of Engineers Officer (inset).**

Lewis, newly wed, with Lucy, riding to the farm in Loveland.

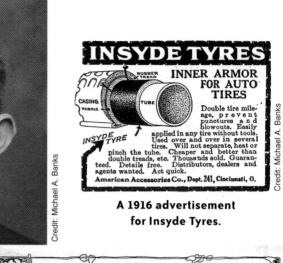

A 1916 advertisement
for Insyde Tyres.

In 1916 Powel Crosley
established himself as
an auto accessories
manufacturer.

An Americo catalog
from 1919.

Sample applause card, one of several included with every Crosley radio. More direct mail innovations, from one of the field's unsung pioneers.

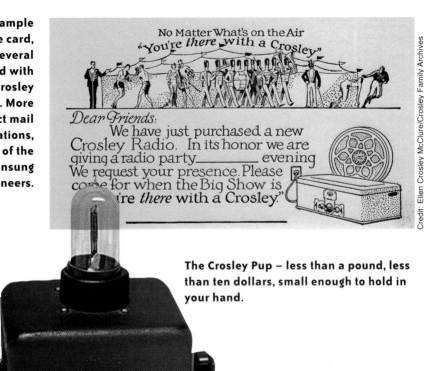

No Matter What's on the Air
"You're *there* with a Crosley"

Dear Friends:
We have just purchased a new
Crosley Radio. In its honor we are
giving a radio party_____ evening
We request your presence. Please
come for when the Big Show is
're *there* with a Crosley."

The Crosley Pup – less than a pound, less than ten dollars, small enough to hold in your hand.

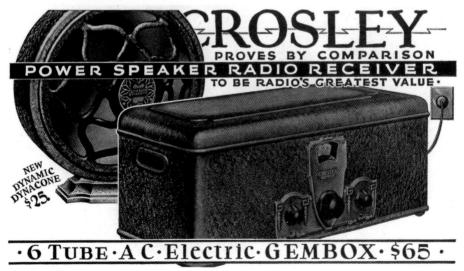

CROSLEY
PROVES BY COMPARISON
POWER SPEAKER RADIO RECEIVER
· TO BE RADIO'S GREATEST VALUE ·

NEW DYNAMIC DYNACONE $25

· 6 TUBE · A C · Electric · GEMBOX · $65 ·

The Gembox. AC power, at last; 'the Golden Age' of radio.

Powel and two unidentified Crosley managers consult Lewis.

Credit: Michael A. Banks

Lewis – figuring out how.

Credit: Michael A. Banks

"I adopted a plan for getting away from the office...." The Boss and Gwendolyn, relaxing after a fishing trip in Sarasota Bay.

Powel Crosley, three generations worth: Sr., III, and the radio tycoon. Circa 1926.

The Germans took back one hundred square miles of territory on the first day of the attack. The British reeled; the French reinforced. On March 28, General Pershing, who had been determined that Americans should fight together as an army, not just serve as reinforcements in the field, for the first time offered AEF troops for use in combat.

In Camp Meade, Company C reported ready for departure. They had to wait their turn for transport overseas. While they waited, it was more of the same. French lessons, target practice, lectures on first aid and personal hygiene and two-arm Semaphore signaling, bayonet drills from Lieutenant Cappelman, a talk on the Engineers in the War from the company's new commander, Captain Frederick S. Cook, and on Wednesday afternoons, athletics, a tug-of-war, relay races, competitions in the running and standing broad jump, and of course...

Baseball.

Company C had uniforms all its own, purchased courtesy of the Clark Griffith Baseball Fund and the company funds. They played among themselves, splitting the company into four platoons and conducting a tournament. The best players took on teams from throughout the area, including the 311th Field Artillery and the 27th Engineers and "made a respectable showing," which had to remind Lewis even more of home.

In 1918, for the first time in a long while, the Reds looked good. The improvement came about in large part due to a blockbuster trade made in 1916; the Reds sent Buck Herzog and Wade Killefer to the New York Giants in exchange for three future Hall-of-Famers—a canny infielder named Bill McKechnie, a fierce young outfielder named Edd Roush, and a pitcher whose best days were long behind him, a pitcher who in 1916 came out of retirement to win his three hundred and seventy-second and final victory before setting down his glove and sitting down on the bench to manage the team.

"Soldiers in France calling for Matty," the papers read, the gist of the piece being that two years after throwing his last pitch, Mathewson was still the single most popular player in the game. In April, the soldiers had asked for, and the government formally requested, Mathewson leave the Reds and come to France to promote baseball among the American soldiers, who needed all the morale boosting they could get, as the Germans had followed their March offensive with another in April, and then another in May, as a result of which the lines of battle, for the first time since 1914, had moved in a significant manner, albeit in the wrong direction for the Allies.

Company C, however, didn't move at all. They stayed in Maryland waiting for the call. They dug trenches; they played cards, they wrote letters home. They built a rifle range. They had a dance.

On May 19, Lewis took five days of leave in Philadelphia; Charlotte had caught the flu. He went back again to see her on May 31 and June 15, and then again for one final time on June 22, because the call at last had come through. Company C was bound for France. On June 28, their new commander, Captain Frederick S. Cook, marched his men onto a train bound for Hoboken, New Jersey.

On the next day they sailed for France.

·   ·   ·   ·   ·   ·

In Cincinnati, Powel, Gwendolyn, and the children did their part as well. They bought war stamps; they set aside space in the yard for a war garden. Powel set aside plans for his new six-cylinder automobile; instead, he thought up a flag holder that clamped onto automobile (read: Model T) radiator caps and displayed five miniature American flags at a time. It sold, he would recall later, "like a cool drink in an arid desert." The success was due in no small part to Sears featuring it in their catalog.

He was a ne'er do well no more. In fact, it seemed that nothing he did could go wrong. Despite wartime strictures, the American Automobile Accessories Company—Americo—continued to prosper.

With Lewis unavailable, he hired another member of the family for the summer, sister Edythe, putting her to work as a secretary. She made the mistake of hanging her coat up in Powel's office; he set her straight on the proper place for her outerwear—and herself. If upbraiding one's own sister for such a thing seems a bit high-handed, it was, nevertheless, quintessentially Powel. A legacy of failure like Powel's might have made another man diffident or, perhaps, bitter, but Powel's large ego would not allow him to indulge such attitudes. When success did come, he saw it as simply what he had always deserved. He'd already developed the regal bearing and the strong personality—which could be both charismatic and formidable—of someone with far greater accomplishments.

By 1918, the young tycoon was feeling his oats. Self-confidence oozes from the pictures taken of him at this time. He seems—like his company, like his country—on the verge of something great. Charles Kilgour came to work with him at about this time, and the two were soon busy on a new automobile ignition system as well as other engineering projects. Both were tall, lean, smart-looking men, smart in every sense of the word, though neither man was classically handsome, Kilgour's face too narrow, his chin too sharp, Powel's brow a shade too high, his face perhaps a shade too full.

Kilgour and Edythe weren't Powel's only new hires. The company grew to nearly a hundred people. The building on Gulow Street began to get crowded.

They moved to another, at 1601 Blue Rock Street in the Northside neighborhood, into a building modeled after the Flatiron Building in New York.

Company C was crowded too; crammed aboard the *U.S.S. Mongolia*, a mail steamer refitted for troop transport. Though the ship was designed to hold 1,818 passengers, 4,061 troops squeezed aboard in Hoboken for the two-week trip to France.

It was tight, to say the least.

The food was terrible; the smell was worse. On the bright side, Second Lieutenant Crosley got to know his men even better, and they got to know him.

Lewis wasn't Powel. His brother was like a star, the biggest, the brightest, usually the most exciting person in a room. He had an undeniable presence, a magnetism that drew people to him; Powel led, and others followed.

Lewis was different.

A practical man by nature, an engineer by trade, he was now a leader by default. By this point a physically imposing man himself—six two, two hundred and ten pounds—he nonetheless preferred to avoid the spotlight, to stay in the background, and do his job. But he was a leader now, one of only six officers among two hundred fifty enlisted men in the company. He was twenty-nine years old, married with a wife and child; a lot of the men under him were just kids, twenty, twenty-one years old. He was the big brother.

Lewis's leadership style was different from Powel's. He was calmer, quieter. Unlike Powel, Lewis was patient, and he was known as a good listener. While Powel's quicksilver mind jumped from one idea to the next—and he expected those around him to make the jumps as quickly as he made them—Lewis was methodical. He led mostly by example. He had a folksy Midwestern voice that relaxed the people around him. He could make and take a joke as well as the next man.

But he could be pushed only so far.

Underneath that patience was a core of steel.

He would need, as it turned out, both those qualities over the next few months.

CHAPTER 8

As the 28th Engineers crossed the Atlantic, the AEF entered the battle full-scale. Four years of war, the Allied ship blockade, and resulting food shortages had pushed the Germans to the edge. The Americans arrival was about to tip them over, though as the *Mongolia* arrived in Brest, the Kaiser's armies remained, for the moment, on the offensive.

Company C disembarked, caught a breath of fresh air, and was promptly crammed into a train headed south to the port of St. Nazaire, one of five base camps that had been set up in France for American troops. Even before the first soldier landed, the AEF's services of supply had devised a simple formula. For every man at the front, there had to be ninety days worth of supplies available. Forty-five days at one of the base camps, thirty days at intermediate storage facilities, and fifteen days near the battle lines. They figured on fifty pounds per day per man, which at three million men worked out to over a five hundred million tons of supplies a week, which worked out to a non-stop stream of cargo coming in to St. Nazaire and a similarly non-stop stream of construction. In order to house those supplies—food, clothing, ammunition, weapons, medicine, vehicles, horses, and so on—hundreds of structures had to be built. Docks, wharves, barracks, storage depots, engine terminals, hospitals, refrigeration plants, remount depots, repair shops....

Lewis stepped off the train and into that whirlwind of activity without a chance to draw breath.

At St. Nazaire, he saw ships coming in, ships going out, cargo going on and off, cranes going up and down, men walking here and there in groups, some regular army, some obviously French civilians, carrying logs or saws or hammers, talking in French that sounded nothing like the language Hirsch Hootkins had been speaking, men carrying logs off ships or leading donkeys down a gangplank, carrying a section of railway here, a log there, sawing, hammering, smoking, standing around in front of one of the long low buildings that seemed to be everywhere.

The company split up and went to work.

First Lieutenant Stock took sixty-one men to work at a nearby quarry. First Lieutenant Cappelman was put in charge of construction at Base Hospital No. 101. Lewis was named Engineer Officer at St. Nazaire's Camp No. 1, in charge of construction and camp maintenance. It wasn't just the men of Company C working for him; he had combat troops, rotating in and out of duty, in his command as well, anywhere from five hundred to a thousand men every day, working on sewage, water supply, plumbing, lighting, repair, construction, land grading, everything and anything to do with keeping the small city that was Camp No. 1 in good running order.

There were problems, of course, of the usual—and unusual—kind, which demanded solutions both usual and unusual.

Private Montague, the company barber, couldn't find any springs for his double-zero shaver and had to ask permission to have six sent over from the States.

Privates Giannetto and Gerard were lost to the company for a few days while they spent time in Venereal Guard House Number One, having succumbed to the temptations commonly associated with French women, an occurrence which resulted in memos from Captain Cook and a later directive from Colonel Sewell of Base Section No. 1 which declared (Article III, paragraph 1) "all houses of prostitution, licensed or unlicensed" off-limits to the AEF, and furthermore required "conspicuous posting" of plans showing locations of same in each company.

Lumber came in continuously, usually logs that were sawed down to size in camp, but in August a ship filled with boards already cut arrived from Norway. The pieces weren't cut to specifications;

no two, of them, in fact, were the same size. Lewis had his men sort the hundreds of tons of wood by eye, putting pieces that approximated two by fours or two by sixes alongside pieces of similar size, and then built a new remount camp, a horse facility, with them.

It was military engineering—accuracy in execution yielding to the imperious demand for results.

It happened more than once.

Sometimes, the wood or the pipes or the wire he needed didn't come in as requisitioned. Sometimes nothing came in, and Lewis had to find a way to make do with what he had. Some of his men, he learned, could work that way, and others couldn't. Some of them, he learned, could go out on their own and get what the camp lacked and didn't mind doing so, having operated on the wrong side of the law in civilian life.

Lewis learned, by and by, to count on them to deliver when no one else could.

After a time, he formed them into a little regiment of their own—nothing on the record, just a group of men he could count on to bring back the material the camp needed.

In August, he took over construction at Base Hospital 101, when Lieutenant Homer Cappelman was sent up the lines to take charge of a quarry at Villaneuve; Homer took with him a detachment of Company C men, though the bulk of the work at the quarry was done by German prisoners-of-war, a group whose number was rapidly growing, because August was also the month of the British attack at Amiens, where thirty thousand German troops, exhausted, starving, and weakened by an encounter with a new, deadlier strain of the flu, surrendered en masse.

The entire American First Army attacked near the St. Mihiel salient, a bulge in the battle lines some one hundred eighty miles west of Paris, and on September 12 attacked German positions entrenched for four years. St. Mihiel was over in a day, thanks to the ferocity and determination of AEF forces, as well as the fact that the Germans had been in the middle of a planned retreat when the first American shells fell.

Nonetheless, it was an inspiring victory. News spread down the line, and overseas as well. Patriotism swelled; enlistments continued. In College Hill, two Henshaws joined up—Ellen's son Lewis, and her nephew by marriage, Edward.

So did Christy Mathewson. He and Ty Cobb went overseas at the end of the season. At a training field southeast of Paris, they were assigned to a special regiment, training hundreds of recruits in the use of a new charcoal-filtered gas mask. The training involved simulation of actual combat conditions, right down to the use of real mustard gas in some of the drills. Of course, a clear warning signal was given before the gas was released.

Except one day, it wasn't.

The drill took place inside an airtight chamber; on the release of the gas, panic ensued. Bodies piled up inside the chamber; Cobb and Mathewson barely made it outside. Eight men died that day; many more were crippled.

Ty Cobb had a hacking cough and a colorless discharge from his chest for weeks; Mathewson had to be hospitalized and shipped back home.

The war raged on.

On September 18, Lewis and Company C were told to put down their hammers, pack up their equipment, and head east to join in the fight. In the cramped rail car, heading toward the front lines, Captain Cook shared what he knew of Company C's orders with his officers. They had been formally attached to the First Army; they were headed, obviously, in the direction of St. Mihiel.

Beyond that, anything else was speculation.

If some of his fellow officers felt they needed to know the plan, Lewis did not. Like the men around him, he was a cog in an enormous machine, but was fine with that situation. He was comfortable with that way of working: a specific task was put in front of him, and he focused on completing that specific task. What the machine was doing—where it was headed, what it would do when it got there—was irrelevant to him. In other words, unlike his brother, Lewis was content to be a passenger. He felt no need to drive.

On September 23, they continued pushing east, passing by Paris, and then on to the Marne. Lewis began seeing first-hand signs of the war's devastation: the bombed-out remnants of villages, barbed wire marking the old trench lines, a bomb crater here, a toppled building there. He saw the wounded and the shell-shocked heading back from the front, and men by the thousands heading toward it, mud-spattered doughboys in ponchos, marching in two columns. He saw roads crammed with supply convoys, horse-drawn wagons with soldiers literally hanging off the sides, a procession of men and animals that looked like nothing so much as one of the old wagon drives headed out west, and nowhere better could he see the strange confluence of old and new technology that the war had become in 1918 than on those roads, because alongside the horses and mules laden with demolition supplies were trucks and cars and motorcycles and up above were planes and observation balloons, and in the distance could be heard the occasional rumble of artillery fire.

As Company C drew closer to the theater of battle, it grew clear that a major offensive was taking shape. The battle that followed is now known as Meuse-Argonne, the former name drawn from the nearby French river, the latter for the thickly wooded forest that the Allies advanced through to meet their objectives.

On the 26th, the attack began.

That first day, everything went exactly as planned. The Germans fell back, the Americans advanced. Company C, two hundred forty-nine men, seven officers, detrained in Clermont and immediately went to work on the Clermont-Varennes road that played a key role in the Allied plan. It had been almost completely obliterated by the last four years of shelling. As the advance moved forward, so did Captain Cook and his men.

They broke down to smaller detachments, split the road into sections to work more efficiently. They repaired carefully, with rock, of course, tamping it into place with motor driven steam shovels, and hand tools.

"The enemy is in retreat," Pershing wrote that evening to the Commanding Generals of I, III, IV, and V Corps. Units, he declared, were to push forward with all possible energy. Any officer who "failed to show in this emergency those qualities of leadership required to accomplish the task that confronts us," he added, was to be relieved on the spot.

But Meuse-Argonne was not to be like St. Mihiel. On the 27th, German resistance stiffened. The advance slowed. As Company C moved up behind the lines, deeper into the forest, they found out the road was not only ruined, but mined. Their advance slowed as well.

They sipped water, tightly rationed, during breaks, gas masks at the ready, and catnapped fitfully through the night.

The German artillery began firing back. Traffic along the road slowed to a crawl, sometimes stopping altogether. German POWs were added to the road crews.

On the morning of the 29th, American lines along the Aire River were pounded by heavy fire. At the back of the line, on the Clermont-Argonne road, Lewis and the men of his detachment took fire as well. Shells exploded all around. The sky filled with what they all could only hope was rock dust and smoke, and not worse.

Some of the POWs broke for freedom; Lewis ordered them back into line.

All through the day, the bombardment continued.

At 4:10 p.m, General Craig of Oklahoma phoned I Army Corps headquarters: German forces had come in on their left. They needed help.

It couldn't get there.

Along the Clermont-Varennes road, the shelling continued.

The POWs broke ranks again; again, Lewis ordered them back to work.

When they broke a third time, when resistance turned to outright revolt, Second Lieutenant Crosley, a patient man by nature, had had enough.

As he later told one family member, he ordered two of the revolt's ringleaders marched from the ranks, and brought up on the road in plain view of the other POWs.

And then he had them bayoneted where they stood.

He made it clear that if the prisoners bolted again, he would take two more men from their ranks and repeat the demonstration. Again, and again, if need be, until the message was clear.

Work on the road resumed, uninterrupted.

. . . . . .

The Americans inched forward through the Argonne, one bloody kilometer at a time.

On September 30, Company C was ordered off the Clermont-Varennes roady to Grange-la Compte, six kilometers to the southeast. They marched on foot; once there, they began the work they'd come to France to do—getting the rock. They opened quarries throughout the area; on October 10, Lieutenant Cappelman took a detachment of the 1st platoon to one on the Montfaucon-Avecort road; on the 18th, Lieutenant Stock took the 3rd and 4th platoons and opened two on the Avecourt-Very road. The same day, Lewis and the 2nd platoon opened one a mile north of Varennes.

Officers and men stayed in place the rest of the month as Meuse-Argonne stalled; Pershing reorganized his forces, forming the American 2nd Army, and resumed the attack.

It wasn't only the Germans slowing the AEF down now; by this point it was the flu as well, which had crossed the battle lines and was now attacking American troops with the same ferocity it had shown the Germans earlier. Seventy thousand were infected during the first three weeks of Meuse-Argonne; over twenty thousand of them died. People recognized that this was no ordinary flu.

It was a full-blown epidemic.

It spread across the entire planet; in Alaska, entire villages were wiped out. In India, five percent of the population, an estimated seventeen million people, perished.

In Indianapolis, racecar driver Johnny Aitken died.

In South Dakota, Merle Tuve, who had lost his wireless to the Navy the year before, now lost his father to the pandemic.

In Philadelphia, Lucy stood at the door to the mess hall of her boarding school, refusing to let any student who appeared even the slightest bit sick into the room.

In Ohio, the Department of Health issued bulletins recommending the wearing of gauze masks when in a sick room.

In Cincinnati, Edward Henshaw caught the disease a month after enlisting.

So did Powel Crosley, Jr.

Henshaw died. Powel got out of his sickbed after a few weeks and returned to work.

Meuse-Argonne resumed October 18, though by then Germany was already collapsing. Civilians in the Fatherland were starving; soldiers deserted their posts and made their way home to be with their families.

They found Woodrow Wilson—or his words, at least—waiting for them.

The president had already used the two-hundred-kilowatt transmitter in New Brunswick to transmit his Fourteen Points, the planks on which he thought a just peace could be arrived at between the Allies and the Germans. After St. Mihiel, he used that Alexanderson alternator again, this time to make a direct appeal to the German people to remove the Kaiser from power.

The Germans, who only a few weeks earlier seemed to be winning the war—declined. Not that their actions made much difference one way or another; by the end of the month, all of their allies—Bulgaria, Austria-Hungary, Turkey—had surrendered.

On November 10, the Kaiser simultaneously accepted the terms of an Armistice dictated to him by the Allies and abdicated, running across the German border to Holland, where he took refuge in the castle of Count Von Bentinck.

On the eleventh hour, of the eleventh day, of the eleventh month, the guns, at last, stopped firing, and the World War was over.

· · · · ·

Lewis, though, stayed in France another six months.

With the end of the war, the quarries were officially closed; First Lieutenant Crosley (he had been promoted on November 8) now turned in his equipment, including 256 shovels, 124 picks, 85 stone forks, 59 stone hammers, and 35 wheel barrows to corps headquarters, and moved, along with the rest of Company C, to the town of Vraincourt. He spent the entire month of December reliving his time at Camp Meade—days of drilling and target practice, nights of French lessons and lectures, reveille at seven, supper at 4:45, lights out at ten. In short, he sat around and waited.

While he waited, the American 3rd Army – the Army of Occupation – came into being, to assist in the reconstruction of the devastated Belgian and French countryside.

There was a lot of unfinished business from the war to take care of: in particular, the matter of the Kaiser. The Allies wanted him put on trial for crimes against humanity. The Dutch refused to consider it; the Kaiser had come to them seeking asylum, they had granted it, and that was that.

In January, on the eve of President Wilson's arrival in France for peace talks, Colonel Luke Lea of the all-Tennessee, all-volunteer 114th Artillery Battalion, who just happened to have been a United States Senator before the war, decided he would take matters in his own hands. He went to Sergeant Larry MacPhail, also of the 114th, and asked for his help. Lea and MacPhail recruited six other men from the battalion. The eight of them took two cars across the border, arriving at Count von Bentinck's chateau with papers authorizing their presence in Holland. They had urgent business with the Kaiser, Lea declared, which they could discuss only with him.

The senator and his men were ushered into the count's library, where they waited and waited.

A butler appeared, bearing a silver tray with port and cigars.

MacPhail noticed a bronze ashtray embossed with the Kaiser's crest on a table and pocketed it. They heard raised voices, German voices, coming from the next room. But the Kaiser himself never showed; Dutch soldiers, however, did, appearing in the courtyard below the library.

Lea recognized a cue when he saw one.

He and his men barely managed to get back in their cars and across the border; the Colonel escaped with a stern reprimand from Pershing.

MacPhail made off with the ashtray. His path would cross the Crosleys' within twenty years.

.　.　.　.　.　.

The AEF's 3rd Army finalized plans for reconstruction in the devastated portions of France and Belgium. Quarries in the Meuse-Argonne sector were reopened, and Company C went back to work, digging rock for road repair. Lewis was given one Number 3 Good Roads Crusher and returned to Varennes to supervise efforts there, but he was restless.

On February 10, he wrote to the Director of Construction and Forestry, asking to be relieved of duty with Company C and reassigned to St. Nazaire for construction work.

"I feel that I would be of considerably greater value to the Service," he explained, "if placed upon work the nature and extent of which I am already familiar."

The request was refused.

In March he was named American town mayor for the village of Triaucourt-en-Argonne, a ceremonial honor, and athletic officer for the Company.

He procured uniforms; "C" began playing baseball again.

In April, he received a letter from R.R. Jones at the Cincinnati district office of the Army Corps of Engineers.

"My dear Crosley," wrote the Mr. Jones. "Are you likely to be home in the near future?" he asked, going on to outline a planned reorganization of the Corps offices along the river, and a potential job opportunity.

Work was beginning on Dam 38, at Rising Sun; Mr. Prell was in charge, but if Lewis wanted it, second place at the dam was available—"at your old rate ($100)," of course, bureaucratic rules not allowing for an immediate jump in pay scale.

"My dear, Mr. Jones," Lewis wrote back, thanking him and Mr. Prell "for remembering me." He expected to be released from duty in May, and "upon my arrival in the States I shall get in touch with you and we can talk things over."

In June Lewis sailed for America, carrying with him mementoes of his service from the men of Company C: the end table they'd built for him at St. Nazaire, and two matching shell casings they'd turned into vases.

He arrived in Ohio in August and went first to Columbus, to his mother's sister Molly's house, where he waited for Lucy and Charlotte to return from Philadelphia. He'd been away a little more than a year; he came home ten pounds lighter, wearing a uniform so worn that it disintegrated into rags the first time he tried to wash it, and immeasurably wiser in both the ways of the world and his own abilities.

Lucy and Charlotte came home too. Together they moved in briefly with her sister Ellen. Lewis went to see Mr. Jones about the job at Dam 38, but the conversation was anticlimactic, because really, his mind had been made up since the first letter.

His old job? At his old pay?

At St. Nazaire, he'd had charge of a thousand men. At Clermont-en-Argonne, he'd stood tall under enemy fire.

He was not going back to hanging off bridges and dodging logging rafts.

Thanks, but no thanks, he told Mr. Jones, and then went to see his brother and visit the offices of the American Automobile Accessories Company.

Powel showed Lewis the newest catalog, the company's newest offerings, and then repeated the offer he'd made before the war. Americo was growing. Powel needed someone to manage the inventory and the workers, their relations with suppliers and customers, someone to actually run things so that he could chart a course for further expansion, dream up new products.

Lewis was the man he wanted.

Lewis agreed.

He took Powel's offer, and the brothers, who had been apart since Powel's last year at OMI, were together again.

As if to celebrate, the Reds went to Chicago that October, and for the first time in their fifty-year history, won the World Series.

CHAPTER 9

Henry Ford built cars; he didn't balance books. That task fell to his partner, James Couzens, a ruthlessly efficient businessman who kept the Ford Motor Company solvent during its early years and put it in position to capitalize on the Model T's success later on. Couzens, unlike some of Ford's other early associates, had no interest in telling the great man how to design automobiles. That wasn't his role in the business; it wasn't his area of expertise. He knew that, and so did Ford, and that was why the two of them worked so well together. They were a team, as were Carl Fisher and James Alison, one the visionary, the other the brilliant industrialist, who pooled their respective talents to build Presto-Lite, the Empire Car Company, and the Indianapolis 500. Fisher got all the press, but his success came because he had Alison— as Fred Duesenberg had younger brother Augie, the master craftsman, who could build anything, as Frank Duryea had brother Charles, as Powel Crosley, Jr. now had Lewis.

The older sibling's drive, his ambition, and his ability to anticipate the market for products ahead of consumer demand, married to the younger's ability to get the job done, come hell, high water, or exploding mortar shell. It was to prove a formidable combination, though there were a few practicalities to take care of, a few kinks to work out, before the Crosley brothers could charge ahead full steam.

Lewis's readjustment to civilian life, for one. Almost the first thing Powel put him in charge of was payroll: Lewis handled it like he was still at war. Every Friday he picked up a wad of cash at the

Northside Bank & Trust, a few blocks west of the plant, and brought it to Blue Rock to distribute to the employees. A man with a loaded .44 pistol walked behind him each step of the way.

It took a few months, but Lewis finally realized he could skip the trip to the bank and just write checks to America's employees.

Lewis and his family also needed a place to live. That one was a little easier to handle: College Hill, of course, the Glenwood Apartments, as Lewis, unlike his older brother, was anything but a rich man. Powel, meanwhile, needed a vacation. Somehow he'd gotten it in his head that the only reason he'd caught the flu was because he was working too hard, and so as soon as Lewis came on board at America, Powel headed to a log cabin on the Miami River where he got in a little hunting and fishing before returning to work.

When he got back, there were serious matters to attend to. The company's primary moneymaker—Insyde Tyres—was in trouble. In 1919, the cord tire was coming onto the market, and with its arrival, the average lifespan of a tire jumped from about three thousand miles to fifteen thousand. The writing was on the wall for Powel's brainchild, and it was obvious to him that sooner, rather than later, the company needed to diversify.

With Lewis running the factory, Powel had time to step back, take a look around, and think about how to do that. He'd made his fortune selling accessories for the Ford Model T, the people's car, and as he looked around at other things people were buying in 1919, one item stood out: the phonograph, or "Victrola," in popular parlance. It brought recorded music into the home for those who had neither the time nor money to go to concerts, the theater, or opera—in other words, the vast majority of the American public.

The average phonograph in 1919, though, sold for about a hundred dollars. With the country in the middle of a brief postwar depression, with the salary of the average working man at twelve dollars a week, that was too much money to ask customers to spend, especially all at once, especially considering that even after buying the phonograph, they still had to buy discs to play on it.

Powel sensed an opportunity.

He looked into the situation a little further and learned that not only had an important patent held by Victor recently expired, but that anti-trust actions in Federal court had broken the monopoly the "big three" phonograph manufacturers—Victor, Edison, and Columbia—had maintained for twenty years.

He talked to Lewis, and the brothers made their move.

Charles Kilgour owned a woodworking shop on Vandalia Avenue that made phonograph cabinets. Powel bought it. Lewis ordered mechanisms from an outside manufacturer and reorganized the woodworking shop to assemble complete machines. By the end of the year, they'd put their first phonographs together.

The first ads for Crosley's "Amerinola" went into the January 1920 issue of *Talking Machine Dealer*. The phonograph offered much the same styling and features as other machines of the day, a rectangular wooden cabinet that stood upright on four feet and played Victor's talking discs.

The ads, though, offered a little something different: phonographs on credit. Customers could get an Amerinola for one dollar down, followed by forty-eight similar weekly payments. Forty-nine dollars for the whole unit, plus shipping—about half the cost of comparable machines.

Powel had clearly identified his target market: the masses, not the classes.

To help him reach that market, he bought the National Label Company, which not only let him print his own catalogs and other sales and advertising materials, but take on outside jobs as well. The Crosley diversified business empire was beginning to unfold, but Powel never lost sight of his main objective.

The car.

In the house on Davey Avenue, he turned the upstairs billiard room into a workroom, where he began, once more, laying out plans for a new auto—the lightweight, six-cylinder car whose development the war had interrupted.

A brief postwar recession aside, it was a good time to be in business. The best of times, as it would turn out, because the transformative inventions of the past few decades—Edison's incandescent lights, Ford's car, Fisher's highways—were about to combine with the era's great social changes—the five-day work week, women's emancipation, and even, in an odd way, Prohibition—to create a mobile, cosmopolitan, thrill-seeking society the likes of which the world had never seen. A nation of consumers, eager for the latest, the coolest, the hippest thing, be that thing music (jazz), fashion (the flapper), or time-saving technological toy.

Powel was just like them.

"He wanted to know the new way, not the old way, of doing things," his sister Edythe recalled of that winter of 1919, and the time when Powel asked her to the house on Davey Avenue to teach him, and Lewis, the latest dances, like the fox trot and the tango.

Powel broke the dances into their component steps, and then he practiced, practiced, practiced until he had them down cold. "He wouldn't settle for anything inferior," Edythe said, and that was as true of his fun as of his business endeavors.

In the decade to come that approach was to be rewarded handsomely.

There was to be joy.

There was to be money beyond his wildest dreams.

But first, there was heartache, at least for Powel, Lewis, and a great many other Cincinnati baseball fans.

It turned out, some claimed, that the Reds hadn't won the World Series after all.

.   .   .   .   .

"Say it ain't so, Joe," went the legend, but it was so, and even though a jury later found Chicago White Sox outfielder Shoeless Joe Jackson and seven of his teammates innocent of throwing the 1919 World Series, the fact was that gamblers had gotten to some members of the team, that the Sox had lost (at the least) three games under suspicious circumstances, and the national pastime faced a crisis. Its integrity had been called into question; something had to be done.

The owners decided to appoint a Board of Control to oversee all aspects of the sport, a tribunal to be composed of prominent men of unquestioned character, men whose mere association with the game would restore the public's confidence in it. Men like Judge Kenesaw Mountain Landis, who the owners asked to chair the board; Landis thanked them for their offer and made a counter-proposal.

Forget the tribunal, he said. Put me in charge.

The owners agreed and appointed Landis baseball's first commissioner. He promptly banned the eight accused White Sox for life, forever tarnishing the Reds championship, never mind that in the opinion of many, Cincinnati had the better team and would have won anyway.

That's what Christy Mathewson thought, at least, and he'd said as much time and time again in the national press before the 1919 fall classic, though Mathewson, admittedly, was biased toward the Reds, having helped put the team together. Mathewson was back home by then, seemingly on the mend. By October, he'd recovered enough to get to the Series, where he wrote the articles praising the Reds.

He also spoke out in praise of baseball's newest star, New York Yankees outfielder Babe Ruth, whose team, city, name, and face were about to become synonymous with the decade that lay ahead.

.   .   .   .   .   .

There was another team that came together at the start of the Roaring Twenties, courtesy not of Christy Mathewson or shared bloodlines, but rather the United States government. A team not of individuals but companies, or more specifically, certain assets of certain companies—companies like General Electric, AT&T, and American Marconi, companies that were circling with increasing interest the ever-growing, ever-developing wireless industry and eying the profits to be made from same.

In 1919, President Wilson returned the vast majority of wireless assets the government had seized in 1917 and lifted the ban that had been established on private use of the ether. Marconi immediately put in an order to General Electric for twenty-four more Alexanderson transmitters like the one Wilson had used to reach Germany during the war.

The order made a lot of Americans, not just those in uniform, snap to attention. Marconi was controlled by its British parent; the order, if filled, would give a foreign corporation virtual monopoly on all overseas communication.

GE's president Owen Young raised concerns in a letter to Assistant Secretary of the Navy, Franklin D. Roosevelt. Roosevelt saw Young's point. If there were any monopolies to be established, clearly, they ought to be American. What was needed, then, was a domestic corporation to stand in American Marconi's stead. In October 1919, Young, with the backing of the Navy and President Wilson, formed the Radio Corporation of America—RCA, for short—with himself as chairman.

British Marconi was then 'invited' to sell the new company its American assets; they had little real choice in the matter, as the government made it quite clear that those assets—the majority of which President Wilson, rather foresightedly, had kept under government control—would never be returned to a foreign corporation. Marconi obliged, consigning its American stepson to oblivion. GE purchased stock in the new concern and signed agreements granting RCA exclusive rights to sell wireless equipment using its products. The new company, with the stroke of a pen, went from a paper tiger to a real-world one.

On March 1, 1920, the Radio Corporation of America inaugurated international wireless telegraphy, at the rate of seventeen cents a word—dot-dot, dash-dash, the new, more powerful technology put to the same old purposes.

That piece, however, was only half of the wireless puzzle. The other piece—the transmission of the human voice itself via radio wave, or radio telephony, as it was being called by then—was substantially more complicated.

The problem was Edison's light bulb or, rather, the improvements that had been made to it over the years.

Back at the turn of the century, a Marconi scientist named Fleming, using Edison's own research, had discovered that the light bulb could act as a radio wave detector. Fleming added a valve to control the flow of current in the glass vacuum tube, for which the Marconi company received a patent. In 1905, Lee DeForest added a third element, a grid, immeasurably increasing the detector's effectiveness. DeForest christened his new invention the Audion; he received a patent for it in 1906. By 1914, he'd sold that patent to AT&T.

In 1916, things got messy.

The courts ruled that DeForest's Audion infringed on Fleming's valve, meaning that Marconi, not AT&T, owned the rights to produce vacuum tubes. Except...

The courts also ruled that DeForest's grid was protected by patent; so AT&T, not Marconi, had exclusive right to manufacture that part of the tube.

Nobody could manufacture a practical vacuum tube radio receiver.

The outbreak of war broke the patent logjam temporarily. The Navy seized everything wireless, including the relevant patents, and so, at its order, sets were produced en masse for military purposes, but with the war over, the logjam returned.

The newly formed RCA now owned Marconi's patents. To get the rights to DeForest's, which AT&T controlled, Owen Young invited AT&T to do as GE had done—buy into RCA and assign it the right to sell equipment produced using its respective patents. That deal was struck in early 1920; vacuum tube production started again.

The amateurs hadn't waited, of course.

Some of them ignored the patents and built their own tubes; some used tubes they'd brought back from the war. The majority, though, made do with a different kind of radio-wave detector, the crystal. It was cheaper, less precise, far less powerful, but still capable of picking up signals, provided the transmitters were close or powerful enough.

Early in 1920, one of those amateurs, a Pittsburgh man named

Frank Conrad, began sending out a regular series of programs from his garage. Conrad got local musical talent to play on the air; he got a local music store to supply phonograph records in return for an on-air mention. He got the attention of a local department store, Joseph Horne, who on September 20 ran an advertisement in the *Pittsburgh Sun* mentioning the broadcasts, and the fact that oh, by the way, radio sets, complete ones, made by Mr. Conrad himself, were available for purchase in the store so that you, too, could listen to the latest wonder of the age.

The sets were priced at ten dollars each.

Harry Davis, president of the Westinghouse Electric Company, paid particular attention to the ad and all mentions of Conrad's broadcasts because Conrad, in addition to being an amateur wireless enthusiast, was also a Westinghouse engineer. A light bulb—figuratively speaking—went on above his head.

Wireless sets for ten dollars.

People in the big corporations who owned the patents saw radio telephony as just an extension of the telephone, or telegraph: a way for two people to talk to each other or send messages without having to run cable. Maybe, Davis realized, they'd been thinking about it the wrong way. Maybe the future of radio wasn't in supplying a means for private conversation but a medium for public entertainment. Not narrowcasting, but rather, broadcasting.

He called Conrad into his office, and the two of them started talking.

. . . . .

The phonograph business slumped; Insyde Tyres sales leveled off. To make up for the slack, Powel found new products to sell: folding canoes, paint, soap, custom-built phonograph cabinets. He always used cash on hand to expand. He and Lewis always discussed exactly how much money they were willing to risk on the new enterprise before calling it a day. A legacy of their father's bankruptcy, a lesson learned from Powel's own bitter experiences, a business principle

Lewis operated by.

None of the new products moved in the quantities Powel wanted, but that was as much a function of the still-stagnant post-war economy as anything else.

As 1921 dawned, he was still casting about for the next big thing.

Lewis and family were settled in the Glenwood Apartments; Charlotte Jeanne was at the Pigeye, being eyed suspiciously by Miss Maybelle Brown, who, in Lucy's hearing, assured the little girl that she was as dumb as her father and her uncle, for that matter, had been.

I'll bet you wish you were dumb like Powel, Lucy snapped back, and hustled her daughter away.

Across town, on Davey Avenue, Page Crosley had just turned seven. She was a beautiful, doe-eyed, dark-haired little girl, the apple of her father's eye. Powel III was nine, a chunky, introspective boy, more Aiken than Crosley in appearance and temperament, hardly surprising, given how hard his father had worked, how often Powel, Jr. had been away during his son's formative years.

On Tuesday, February 22, though, the two of them were home together, commemorating George Washington's birthday, which by 1921 was a federal holiday and meant that all children had the day off from school, and all fathers had the day off from work.

Powel III came to his father with a request.

He'd been on an overnight stay at a friend's house and seen something amazing there—a wireless set. He wanted one too. He was, in fact, desperate for it, in the way that only children can be desperate for the newest, latest toy.

Powel, Jr. looked down at his young son and smiled.

He'd heard of wireless, of course. It was part of the wave of change sweeping across the country, the wave that Powel was, as always, trying to catch, to climb on and direct. It had been his dream since he was a small boy. The papers in Indy and Detroit were going to write about him the way they wrote about Fisher and Ford, the way they'd written about Duryea and Olds.

As it turned out, he was right.

PART II

➤⋙ B O O M ⋘◄

"Horatio Alger's books conveyed a powerful message to me and many of my young friends~that if you worked hard at your trade, the big chance would eventually come."

~ Groucho Marx

CHAPTER 10

The Golden Age of Radio. The American family gathers around a console receiver—a large, wooden piece of furniture—to listen to their favorite programs. News, soap operas, variety shows, and comedies fill the room with a sweep of a single dial. The children smile; father smokes his pipe; mother does her knitting.

Erase that image from your mind.

Radios in 1921 were boxy, awkward-looking things. They ran on batteries that weighed forty pounds, batteries that had to be recharged, batteries that sometimes leaked, that stained the carpet, that burnt holes in the floor. Most sets lacked the power to drive loudspeakers. You had to use headphones to listen. Tuning was a complicated affair; good signals were tough to pull in. Still...

By early 1921, wireless sets were all the rage, thanks in large part to Westinghouse's Conrad and Davis, who had set up a radio station of their own, KDKA, and used it to broadcast the results of the November 1920 presidential election. Newspapers reported the event with disbelief: breaking news right there, in your own home, as it happened. Could such a thing be possible?

It was. Suddenly, everyone had to have a wireless. Manufacturers rushed to fill the demand: radios appeared in department stores and hardware supply outlets across the country.

In Cincinnati, one of the stores with wireless sets for sale was Precision Equipment of Walnut Hills, where on the afternoon of February 21, 1921, two members of the increasingly curious general public walked through the front door and straight into history.

Precision was not just a retail outlet, but a manufacturer and broadcaster as well, under the auspices of amateur station 8XB. When Powel and son walked in, 8XB was on the air. A salesman offered to demonstrate Precision's sets with a live program. He hooked up the batteries, attached the antenna, and handed over the headphones.

Music filled Powel's ears. He listened a moment, then inquired about price. The set, he was told, was a one-tube model, the cheapest in the store. Powel could have it for a hundred and thirty dollars—sans batteries, headphones, and antenna.

Powel was stunned. He looked at the set again. It was a wooden box with circuitry inside. Phonographs came in nicer boxes for far less money.

A hundred and thirty dollars. About what the average workingman made in a month. Too much to spend on a child's toy.

Powel thanked the salesman for his time. He and Powel III left the shop, the boy disappointed, the father angry.

Back home, Powel paced, hands behind his back, mumbling to himself. A hundred and thirty dollars. A third the cost of a Model T. The least expensive set in the shop. Finally, he exploded.

"The idea of charging that much for that little thing," he said. "I could build that set for half that price!"

And so, eventually, he did.

Powel's decision to build a radio would transform the Automobile Accessories Corporation and Insyde Tyres to a footnote in the Crosley saga, would put the Crosley name alongside those of the industry's founding fathers—Marconi, DeForest, and David Sarnoff, general manager of RCA, who had seen the radio boom coming back in 1916, had written his superiors at Marconi of the possibilities of a device that could "bring music into the house by wireless."

His plan never got off the ground. Wireless to the Marconi Company in 1916 involved big transmitters sending radio telegraph messages. They didn't understand broadcasting anymore than did the bigwigs at AT&T. Westinghouse lead the revolution. Everyone else was playing catch-up.

CHAPTER 10

Powel was further behind than the others, though not for long. He hadn't left Precision empty-handed. He purchased a twenty-five-cent pamphlet called *The A.B.C. of Radio*. After reading it, he decided he and Powel III would build their own crystal set. Soon enough, father and son were the proud parents of their own wireless. Initially, they picked up only the dah-dit of telegraph transmitters, but after adding an Audion to the circuit one night, they heard Precision Audio's 8XB, seven miles away.

Powel was hooked. He had Midwest Radio build a three-tube set and had the woodworking shop build a cabinet for it.

He had an idea.

Manufacturers were churning out sets as fast as they could build them, and they needed cabinets to go with those sets. Powel talked to Grebe Radio in Brooklyn, one of the largest independent set manufacturers, and within a few weeks, he was supplying their needs. Soon after, he was advertising cabinets for sale to the general public. By mid-1921, the woodworking shop was bringing in more money than ever before.

Powel began researching, talking to others about the state of the radio industry. Sets were too expensive; so were radio parts. Everyone complained, but no one was doing anything about it.

He sensed another opportunity.

The tubes on his new-three tube set got very hot; the sockets, which were made of a molded composite material, often cracked. Powel brought out a porcelain socket, which he sold for sixty cents. It achieved instant popularity among radio manufacturers and hobbyists. "It is better," advertisements for the socket declared, and it was also cheaper, by about a dollar, than competing products.

"Better—costs less" became Crosley's new slogan.

More parts followed: a tap switch, an improved radio tuning condenser. Powel was on to something here. He sensed it. In his office by day, in his workroom at night, sometimes with Powel III, sometimes with Lewis, sometimes on his own, Powel Crosley's interest in radio grew into an obsession.

It was 1907 and the car all over again, a fascination with the newest, latest, technology, only this time, he wasn't twenty-one years old, trying to play catch-up with the Fishers and Fords of the world. He was thirty-five, a seasoned businessman. He could do whatever he wanted, and what he wanted now, Powel decided, was to build a radio. A set everyone could afford.

Unlike in 1907, events were conspiring in his favor.

. . . . . .

In June of 1921, Westinghouse joined the RCA cross-licensing pool. They brought along the patent for the regenerative circuit, invented back in 1913 by Edwin Howard Armstrong. The circuit amplified the incoming radio signal several-fold, making DeForest's Audion immeasurably more useful as a detector.

DeForest himself had actually built a similar circuit, at roughly the same time as Armstrong but had no idea what made it work. Nonetheless, he sued for patent infringement. The Navy's seizure of wireless assets in 1917 interrupted the court battle, but when the war ended, it picked back up again.

Because DeForest had sold his patents to AT&T, they financed his end of the lawsuit. Armstrong was on his own. In early 1920, to pay his increasingly high legal bills, he sold rights to manufacture radio sets incorporating his circuit to seventeen companies, such sets to be sold to 'amateurs only.' In 1921, Westinghouse gave Armstrong $335,000 for exclusive 'commercial' rights to the regenerative circuit. Joining the patent group transferred those rights to RCA.

The government-engineered corporate colossus now had control of the vacuum tube, the regenerative circuit, and the largest radio manufacturing plants in the country. It began to walk, and talk, and design radio sets of its own.

That colossus, however, was a four-headed beast. GE, AT&T, Westinghouse, and RCA sometimes had trouble agreeing on which direction to move in. And when they moved, they moved slowly, hobbled by the immense bureaucracy of four separate companies.

Circumstances everyone and his brother—Powel and Lewis included—were about to exploit.

. . . . . .

The decision having been made to build a radio, Powel called a meeting. Lewis was there, as was Charles Kilgour, among others. Powel told them about the set he'd built, the stations he'd pulled in, the music he'd heard, right through the air, no wires necessary. Radio was on the verge of becoming unimaginably popular, he said. But first, it would have to have a popular price.

That was what Crosley was going to do: build a set for the workingman, a radio for the masses, not the classes.

Powel gave everyone marching orders, and then headed across town to the University of Cincinnati. Fifteen years ago, they'd kicked him out of their engineering program; he was returning now not just as a successful businessman, but an inventor, with multiple patents to his name.

From the engineering co-op program he pulled two students, Dorman Israel and Elmer Hentz, and set them to work building the first Crosley radio.

Over the next few weeks, the receiver took shape. Its first public unveiling came at the College Hill Town Hall, its second at the Cincinnati Rotary Club. In September, the Crosley Crystal Receiver went on sale, advertised in QST, the monthly magazine of the radio amateur, for seven dollars, phones and aerial extra. It was more radio for less money than virtually anything else on the market.

Powel dubbed the set "Harko," from the old English word "hark," to listen. His job, in a sense, was over. Now it was up to Lewis.

When the younger Crosley brother joined Americo in 1919, it was a mail-order business. By 1921, it was a full-fledged manufacturing concern. He'd recently retooled the woodworking shop to make radio cabinets; now he retooled it yet again, clearing out space to make the Harko. The man in charge was a German named Muller, but after a few days, it was clear that modern assembly-line production was beyond him.

Lewis decided to bring radio production to Blue Rock. He took a handful of workers and cleared out a floor in the rubber plant. They wired a long row of tables for electrical work, then went to the woodworking shop and loaded all the radio manufacturing equipment onto two small trucks.

By Monday radios were coming off the line. Lewis stood over the men and watched them work.

Powel, of course, was already on to the next thing.

. . . . .

In 1921, there was no regular radio programming. There were a handful of commercial broadcast stations, all of which transmit on exactly the same wavelength. Their programs consisted of a few civic-minded lectures and a lot of record playing.

Then there were the amateurs, who broadcast on a largely haphazard schedule as well. Their programs also consisted of a few civic-minded lectures and a lot of record playing. It was difficult, therefore, to tell the difference between the amateur and the professional. Nobody got dime one for broadcasting, not even Westinghouse, who had started KDKA not as a many-making proposition, but as a way to help sell radios.

The description of amateur certainly fit Powel Crosley Jr., who in July added a transmitter to the pile of equipment in his workroom and became a broadcaster himself.

The new toy fed Powel's radio obsession, allowed him to connect with 1921's wireless-happy world. Thousands of other amateurs across the country were doing the same thing—buying parts, assembling their own transmitters, and sending signals into the ether. It was chaos. Nobody had control of the situation.

AT&T—in particular—was not happy.

The four members of the RCA patent pool had joined the consortium not just to share patents but to acquire certain rights. GE and Westinghouse got the right to build receivers; RCA got the right to market them. AT&T received the right to build and sell transmitters, but transmitters back in 1920 had meant big machines, using Alexanderson alternators. By 1921 anyone could build a `radio telephone,' thanks to developments that allowed DeForest's Audion to be used as a transmitter as well as a detector. Anyone could become a broadcaster.

AT&T's grumbling grew louder.

All Powel cared about was the transmitter, and the license he needed to broadcast with it. The latter came through on July 1, 1921, from the Department of Commerce and newly appointed Secretary Herbert Hoover. The Crosley Manufacturing Company had been granted the call letters 8XAA.

Right on its heels came the finished transmitter—a four-tube, twenty-watt model. Powel set it up in the workroom and started playing records. Mostly one record: "The Song of India." He'd move the microphone next to the phonograph's horn, let the song play, then give his name and telephone number over the air, and ask anyone receiving the signal to call him. Then he'd play the record again.

He got a lot of calls and a lot of post cards. He made sure everyone knew what he was doing, giving sets to Gwendolyn, and Lewis, and even his parents. He went next door and invited Edgar Cummings to see his 'studio.' Cummings' daughter Dorothy tagged along. She watched Powel speak into the mike and ask anyone listening to call. Almost immediately, the phone rang.

"I could not understand how any such thing could possibly happen," the young girl was to write much later, an attitude a lot of people shared, young and old alike.

One was Alfred Siegel of the *Cincinnati Post*. No wires attached to any of the equipment? The whole thing was a fraud, he decided. "Let's bust up this racket," he told the paper's sketch artist, Manny Rosenberg. The two men headed to Precision to do just that.

Powel happened by; he and Rosenberg knew each other. The artist asked Powel point-blank: was the broadcasting business on the level?

"Oh," Powel said, "Manuel, this is the real McCoy."

CROSLEY

8XAA was soon on the air three evenings a week, with live music as well as records. Powel had moved the transmitter from the workshop to his living room, crowding out the family furniture but keeping Gwendolyn's baby grand front and center. He brought in pianist Marjory Garrigus to perform; he brought over Robert Stayman, Crosley Manufacturing's advertising manager, to help run the transmitter, and take a turn on the microphone from time to time. Lewis dropped by to do the same. All three mentioned the forthcoming Harko as often as possible.

By this point in time, RCA was getting in on the broadcasting boom too.

Their station WJY broadcast the July 2 Dempsey-Carpentier heavyweight fight. Not be outdone, Westinghouse and KDKA came back in August with the Pirates/Phillies game. The Pirates thrashed Connie Mack's team 8-5, on their way to a second-place finish.

The Reds didn't fair so well. The team plummeted to the second division. The big excitement in Cincy baseball that year, in fact, was an appearance by Babe Ruth in a July exhibition game, where he whacked two thundering home runs, one the first ball to ever clear the center-field fence, the other the first ever hit into the right-field bleachers.

Babe also found time to autograph a baseball for a Christy Mathewson benefit being held at the Polo Grounds. Mathewson had been moved to a sanitorium in upstate New York after developing tuberculosis as a result of complications from his gassing.

The disease was life-threatening; doctors had decided on a treatment called compression therapy, in which one of Mathewson's lungs would be collapsed in order to allow it time to heal without strain. The treatment was controversial; a long sharp needle had to be used, and used with great care, to collapse the lung. For Mathewson, the procedure was a success. In years to come, it would be used again, with far less success, and change Powel's life forever.

·   ·   ·   ·   ·

Right alongside radio, the twenties roared. The economy boomed; music swung, and bootleggers flourished. Times were good for Henry Ford and his Model T, for Carl Fisher and the new resort town he'd just finished building, a small spit of land just off Miami that he'd christened Miami Beach.

Elsewhere, times were less kind. There were labor troubles at the mines of West Virginia, in the steel mills in Pittsburgh, and in the shoe factories in Cincinnati, where workers, most of them women, were marching for better pay as well.

For Lewis Crosley those strikes came at an opportune time.

In September, orders for the Harko began coming in—five thousand dollars worth. Lewis put out the word: he needed more workers. By and by, a lot of women who'd been agitating at the shoe factories came to Crosley. They turned out to be good with the detail work radio production required. And they were speed demons at putting the sets together, a good thing because as the end of the year approached and Christmas orders began to come in, the Harko's sales continued to accelerate.

Powel's broadcasting efforts accelerated as well. He moved the transmitter from his house down to the plant at Blue Rock; he had Dorman Israel set to work on a new, more powerful transmitter, to reach even more people with their broadcasts. To sell even more radio sets.

They were moving out of mail order now, and into retail, which meant dealing with distributors, and sometimes directly with retail outfits, particularly when there was a complication. Like with the L.T. Milner Electric Company in Cincinnati, which was run by L.T. Milner himself, who shared Alfred Siegel's feelings about radio: he couldn't believe it. He thought there was some of trickery involved.

One afternoon, Powel and Elmer Hentz set up the transmitter by the store's main entrance. Hentz went to the rear with a Harko. When the broadcast began, customers gathered around, some fascinated, some unsure of what it was, exactly, they were seeing.

Watching the excitement in their eyes, Powel knew.

What he was seeing was the future; the American family gathered together around a radio—his radio—listening to all manner of entertainment pour into their house at the flick of a switch.

The future was coming clearer to AT&T too, and for the most part, they didn't like what they were seeing.

They were supposed to have exclusive rights to build and sell transmitters, but the amateurs had gotten in on that act. They were supposed to have exclusive rights to the commercial exploitation of radio telephony, but by the end of 1921, Westinghouse, RCA, and GE all had radio stations, and while they might not have been making any money from broadcasting, their actions were clearly contrary to the spirit, if not the letter, of the agreement.

There was, however, one asset AT&T had that was proving, in the ever-changing technological landscape, to be of increasing value: telephone lines. Physical cable, strung all across the country. By terms of the patent alliance, no one, not even their RCA partners, was allowed to tie-in to those lines for the furtherance of 'radio telephony.'

On December 21, 1921, AT&T's chairman wrote a letter to Westinghouse's, reminding him of that fact. It was an attempt to bring order to the broadcasting chaos. A few days later, Secretary Hoover took even more decisive action: he banned the amateurs from broadcasting altogether.

On New Year's Day, 1922, Crosley Manufacturing's 8XAA, like hundreds of other stations across the country, had to stop playing records and cease all mentions of the company's products, most pointedly, of course, the Harko.

Powel was none too pleased.

There was a connection between his broadcasts and the Harko's sales, and it didn't take a genius to see it. If he and Crosley Manufacturing were prohibited from broadcasting as amateurs, there was, clearly, only one thing to do: apply for a commercial license.

He sent along form 761 to the regional Department of Commerce office in Detroit. He also sent a letter, noting his company's service to the rural customer and the new radio—an Audion detector—that they were about to bring to market.

The year 1922 was, in fact, one of new ventures for the entire Crosley family. Edythe acquired a new beau, Albert Chatfield. Lewis and Lucy welcomed a new daughter, Ellen, and Powel, through a series of fortuitous circumstances, suddenly found himself on to the next thing yet again.

As the New Year began, he was, all at once, a toy manufacturer.

Powel was walking home one night, turning the corner onto Davey Avenue, when a man came out of the College Hill Town Hall and stopped him. It was James Carroll, the building's maintenance man, also a College Hill resident, who Powel had known for years.

Carroll asked Powel if he had a minute. Powel said yes.

Then I have something to show you, Carroll said, and produced a piece of paper with a crude sketch on it.

It was a design for a baby walker, a ride-on toy, with wheels in the back, casters in the front, and a seat with a chest-high supporting ring. The seat was low enough for the child's feet to touch the floor.

Carroll's walker, Powel saw instantly, meant that a baby who couldn't walk could sit upright and move around safely.

He sensed an opportunity.

He showed the sketch to Lewis, who saw not only the walker's sales potential, but recognized that the toy could be constructed almost entirely of scrap wood from the phonograph shop.

Powel went back to Carroll; they made a deal. The walker would be patented in Carroll's name and manufactured by the Crosleys. Carroll would get a percentage of each one they sold. A prototype was built, and Lewis took it home for baby Ellen to try. He strapped her in, and she scooted across the apartment floor like a pint-size Barney Oldfield, squealing and laughing with delight.

"She was on this thing and kicking herself all over the floor," he remembered fifty years later. "She just didn't want to stop!"

Powel christened the walker the "Go Bi-Bi." He dusted off his mail-order skills to market the new product, purchasing mailing lists of new and expectant mothers, circularizing them when the baby reached five or six months old, when the child was ready to use the walker and the mother was happy to set her burden down for a few minutes.

Powel by then had developed his own way of setting down the burdens associated with being the chief executive officer of a growing industrial concern. In 1918, when he'd caught the flu, he'd been convinced that part of the reason was because he'd overworked himself. It was certainly true that having a business to attend to prevented him from recovering as fast as he would have liked. Powel at thirty-six was no different than Powel at thirteen, or twenty, or twenty-six; he couldn't stand sitting still, and the idea of bed rest was anathema to him. The idea of sitting at a desk was in some ways anathema too.

When Lewis arrived, Powel was finally able to break free of the confines of the office and put into practice his own method of 'relaxation.' He developed the habit of getting away from the office every few weeks for a block of uninterrupted "outdoor time," as he put it—golfing, fishing, hunting, anything to get the blood circulating. The first place he went was a little cabin up the Miami River, near Venice (what is now Ross, Ohio), a place he rented for the grand sum of twenty-five dollars a year. Sometimes he brought along Gwendolyn and the children, and sometimes Lewis and his family joined them, but more often than not it was just Powel and his hunting dogs. Powel's favorite sport was quail hunting, and by the winter of 1921, he was taking regular trips down to Mississippi, usually after the Christmas holidays, to engage in that sport.

He was able to take such frequent trips because he knew the company was in good hands when he was gone, hands he could trust in a way that few other chief executives could trust their own principal deputies. Powel hunted; Lewis held down the fort.

There wasn't all that much hunting being done in the spring of 1922, though; Powel's and Lewis's energies remained focused on radio, on the twin efforts of set-building and broadcasting.

The Harko Sr. hit stores in March 1922, going up on shelves next to RCA's first sets and models from smaller manufacturers like Grebe in New York, Tri-City out in Davenport, Iowa, and Precision Equipment in Cincinnati. The latter three companies were among the original seventeen Armstrong licensees. Like RCA, their sets incorporated the Armstrong regenerative circuit, which put the Harko Sr. at a competitive disadvantage, although in the spring, with sunspot activity at a minimum, that was less of a concern than it might have been otherwise. Crosley, in any case, offered a two-stage amplifier to go with the Harko, Sr., in a matching cabinet, which allowed the signal to be amplified enough to drive a loudspeaker, never mind that a large part of what was being amplified was noise, rather than the broadcast itself.

The Harko Sr., too, began to fly off shelves.

Lewis hired more workers. The company stopped making phonographs and phonograph cabinets altogether. Sales on the Harko crystal set, now dubbed the Harko, Jr., slowed while sales on the Senior picked up. Soon they were turning out 250 units a day.

On March 2, they got back into the broadcasting business with the arrival of a limited commercial license (#62) from Secretary Hoover and the Department of Commerce. Crosley Manufacturing Corporation was authorized to broadcast at 360 meters. They were given the call sign WLW.

That night, the whole family gathered at Davey Avenue to celebrate. Edythe and Powel danced the new dances. The next morning, the brothers were back at the Blue Rock building, hard at work.

Hoover was hard at work as well. March 2 was the last day of the National Radio Conference, called at President Harding's suggestion to deal with the increasingly crowded airwaves and the exploding broadcast industry. Hoover had summoned thirty or so of the leading figures in the radio movement. Edwin Armstrong was there; as were representatives from each member of the RCA patent consortium, and the amateurs, and the Navy, and a select few others. The group spent close to a week talking, and at the end managed to agree that the situation was chaos and that some sort of regulation was needed. That was about as far as they got. No one liked the idea of government stepping in and laying down the law, including Hoover, who wasn't even sure he had the power to do anything, at least under the Radio Law of 1912, which was as sadly out of date as the terminology Hoover used during the conference—"radiotelephones" instead of "transmitters," "receiving stations" instead of "radio sets."

Hoover was pro-business, but despite grumblings from AT&T and RCA about patent infringement, he made clear his support for the amateurs; it was, after all, "the genius of the American boy" that had started the radio boom. Their rights had to be respected too. The American public's rights overall, in fact, he considered paramount. The airwaves belonged to the general citizenry. Any regulation of same should keep the public interest in mind, first and foremost.

The airwaves were, in a way, like roads, the secretary declared.

By that time, the last two members of the patent alliance were pulling onto the broadcast highway—GE with station WGY, out of their Schenectady, New York, plant, and AT&T, which was building a state-of-the-art radio transmitter in downtown New York City, right on top of the building where all their long-distance lines came together. The phone company was at last going after the prize promised them by the terms of the patent alliance: the commercial exploitation of radio telephony. It was time for them to cash in on the radio boom. But whereas Westinghouse, GE, and RCA were making their money off radio sets, AT&T intended to profit in an entirely different way.

They were going to build a state-of-the-art radio station—in fact, a series of state-of-the-art radio stations, thirty-eight in all, and rent those facilities to the public. Their stations would have free use of the company's long-distance lines. Anyone who paid AT&T's fee could walk into the broadcast booth, step up to the microphone, and address the entire United States of America.

Although no one knew it at the time, that was the true shape of things to come.

. . . . .

Powel watched the goings-on in Washington with one eye.

With the other, he focused on his new radio station.

WLW, commercial broadcast licensee #62, would be transmitting on the 360 meter wavelength, sharing time with licensee #29, WMH, owned and operated by Precision Audio, who had received their commercial license back on December 31. One of the engineers who'd helped set up Precision's station was named Russell Blair. Powel, recognizing that there was no substitute for experience, hired Blair away from Precision and made him WLW's first full-time employee.

They set to work on their own state-of-the-art station, erecting twin forty-foot towers on top of the plant, stringing four long wires between the two masts to maximize the new transmitter's reach. They took a 20 x 12 room on the second floor of the plant and turned it into a makeshift broadcast studio, laying down heavy Persian rugs, lining the walls and ceiling with thick black curtains (made with a fabric sometimes called "monk's cloth") for soundproofing. The little second floor studio had a piano, a phonograph, and a new morning-glory microphone with a horn three feet across. The room had two windows, which had to be kept closed at all times for further soundproofing. Not that keeping the windows closed helped when a train went by. The building was thirty feet from the Baltimore and Ohio railroad tracks, a good location for shipping, far less so for broadcasting. Every time a train passed, it could be heard throughout the factory.

They bought new tubes for the transmitter. WLW had been authorized to broadcast at fifty watts, twice the power 8XAA had been using, and Powel wanted every watt of that power working at peak efficiency to reach as many listeners as possible.

Hours before the station's first broadcast, Powel had a sudden attack of nerves. He was afraid WLW's reach would be no more extensive than 8XAA's. He was afraid the towers weren't tall enough. Relocating the transmitter to the factory, after all, had put the antenna farther down in the Ohio River valley than in his College Hill backyard.

Dorman Israel assured him he was wrong, that from an engineering standpoint the broadcast antenna was perfect. Lewis concurred. Still, Powel fretted.

It occurred to him that, even though they weren't on a hill, they could still move the antenna higher. All they had to do, he realized, was make the towers taller. Could it be done in time for the broadcast?

Lewis told him it could be done and then rounded up a group of employees from the factory before heading for the roof. They added a twenty-foot section of downspout to each tower, increasing the antenna's height to sixty feet, and added a counterpoise to help balance the new structure; problem solved.

The show went on.

WLW's first program featured violinist William Morgan Knox and pianist Romeo Gorno backing up Gorno's brother, Giacinto, who sang the prologue from the opera *Pagliacci*. Powel Crosley, Jr. held the big microphone in place as the three played, a smile on his face.

They had to stop once for a train going by and then pushed on.

The station's "grand opening" program was set for March 23. Powel ran full-page ads in the *Enquirer* and *Times-Star* a day before, ads that with suitable pomp and lots of capital letters announced that on March 23, "WLW, Cincinnati's Great Radio Broadcasting Station, Erected and Located at the Crosley Manufacturing Co. (Radio Division)...Inaugurates a Regular Broadcasting Program Schedule of News, Lectures, Information, and Music, And All Forms of Audible Entertainment."

The page gave complete details of the planned broadcast: Powel was to serve as master of ceremonies, of course, and his special guest was to be the mayor of Cincinnati, George P. Carrel, who planned a few words of welcome on behalf of WLW and the city. There would be singers, a player-piano performance, and a jazz band sent by Capitol Theater, a real concession to listeners, as Powel hated jazz.

The ad also noted that the Milnor Electric Company of 129

Government Square, a newly appointed Crosley distributor, planned to set up huge amplifiers and speakers, which would "magnify the music and talk to such proportions that the entertainment will be heard at any place on Government Square."

The ad encouraged readers to install a wireless receiving set in time for the program, and of course mentioned the full line of Crosley radios, with photos, prices and descriptions. The ad prompted a few critics to cite the broadcast as nothing more than a scheme to sell Harkos.

The critics were right.

The scheme worked.

Come April, Crosley sets were flying off the shelves even faster than before, thanks in no small part to the new station's extended reach.

WMH had been broadcasting mostly in the afternoons, and so WLW took to the airwaves three nights a week, 7:00 to 10:00 p.m. on Tuesdays, Thursdays, and Fridays. The new station also broadcast phonograph music one morning half-hour that WMH wasn't on the air, records selected, played, and announced by an engineer named Robert Cooper, who had joined the station's staff. Evenings they featured live entertainment, experienced performers from places like the Cincinnati Symphony Orchestra, the College of Music, and the Conservatory of Music, who were all willing to lend their talents, as Powel said, "for the glory of appearing on this new medium." Other, less accomplished entertainers appeared as well—Maurice Dambois, who operated the 'reproducing (i.e., player)' piano, Cincinnati business man Robert Alter, an expert on the musical saw, a seven-year-old girl singer accompanied by her mother on piano. To fill the schedule they read articles from the newspaper and quoted current hog prices. On the first Sunday after they went on the air they broadcast a "radio chapel service" from the Mount Lookout Methodist Church.

Whoever was broadcasting—Powel, Lewis, Cooper, Stayman, Blair, a guest lecturer—had to literally put his head into the large end of the microphone horn to talk or sing on the air. To broadcast recorded music, the horn was placed against its twin, the large end of the phonograph speaker. When musicians and singers were performing, a technician held the microphone in what he judged to be the best spot for sound pickup.

They were, in short, making it up as they went along.

"We didn't have what you would call a broadcasting department at that time," Lewis recalled. "Some of us took turns as announcers, somebody else took turns lining up talent or getting people to volunteer to do this or do that—all for free."

WLW's early entertainers were surprised to find the studio located in the middle of a busy factory. They would be led across the factory floor to a set of stairs at the back of the building, then up and through a warren of dimly lit hallways to the studio, which to some looked like a storeroom or workshop.

As spring turned to summer, problems with the little studio developed.

Heat from the transmitter turned the room into an oven. Worse, the heavy curtains held in the heat. Performers and staff had to suffer in silence during broadcasts.

Overheated and often outgunned by the railroad, WLW pushed on.

The station added road reports from the Cincinnati motor club and a contest not unlike *Name that Tune*—a Mr. C.H. Devine, of the Aeolian Concert Company, would play the choruses of ten well-known songs, without announcing the names; listeners called to identify the songs. Lessons were given in bridge, French, Spanish, swimming, dancing, and drawing. The little room began to seem very small.

So did the factory. As orders continued to swell, it became clear that Blue Rock's forty-six hundred square feet was inadequate. Powel and Lewis looked around town for larger facilities.

The broadcast band was getting crowded as well; on March 1, 1922 there had been sixty-five broadcast stations. By May, there were 217. In July, there were 378, all of whom had to share that same, single 360-meter wavelength.

Interference began to be a problem.

Not enough of a problem, however, to slow the broadcast boom.

Newspapers added radio-only columns to their daily features and began printing program listings as well. Magazines devoted to covering the new industry sprang up by the handful, among them *Radio Broadcast* and *Popular Radio*.

Sets continued to sell as fast as manufacturers could produce them; faster, even. Companies everywhere reported being unable to fulfill their orders. People stood in lines four and five deep at the radio counters, hoping for a set. Many of them went away frustrated.

In New York, Gimbel's ran full-page ads in the *Times*:

The Almost-Impossible-To-Find: FOUND!

Meaning that they had come across another group of Grebe receiving sets.

In Los Angeles, Robinson's Department Store announced that demand for sets was greater than the supply and strongly suggested their customers order in advance.

Customers weren't the only ones feeling frustration. RCA— and David Sarnoff, in particular—were frustrated too. The back cover of the very first issue of *Radio Broadcast*, dated May 1922, featured an apologetic advertisement from RCA.

"If the demand for radio sets and apparatus had grown normally," the copy read, "the well-equipped and highly organized factories supplying the Radio Corporation of America would now be producing an excess over the market requirements." But the market hadn't grown normally; the market had exploded. And the patent alliance had misread the signals from day one.

Westinghouse had a leg up on everyone in 1921 but had no tube sets for sale in early 1922. At the February Radio Conference, one top GE official had characterized the broadcasting boom a 'fad.' David Sarnoff was still, for all intents and purposes, the lone voice in the dark among the top echelon of the patent alliance. But he and RCA had no factories; they were dependent on Westinghouse and

GE for all their sets, the manufacturing of which, again, by the terms of the patent alliance, was set forth in explicit detail. GE was to make 60 percent of RCA's receivers, Westinghouse 40 percent. Both were huge corporations, though, with huge work forces, and complicated production schedules. Time on their production lines had to be planned in advance. Sarnoff, in fact, had been forced to place his orders on sales potential, to guesstimate the market for his products months in advance, so GE and Westinghouse could build them. He'd done amazingly well. RCA sets grabbed about a fifth of the market in 1922.

But that left four-fifths for others to split. Anything the others could make and get in stores, the first issue of *Radio Broadcast* pointed out, "could be sold before the varnish was scarcely dry."

The public didn't care whose name was on the set.

A large majority of them didn't even care whether or not their set had the regenerative circuit; the important thing was that they were available in stores, to purchase, right then, right there.

Accuracy in execution, in other words, meant less than results, results in this case meaning sets at the counter, or in the storeroom, or in the supply chain.

And Crosley was turning out sets by the truckload.

By May, they'd found their new plant, a brick-and-stone structure at the corner of Colerain Avenue and Alfred Street, two miles south of Blue Rock. It was three stories tall and had thirty thousand square feet of space.

Back in 1921, Lewis had taken a weekend and wired up the assembly stations for the radio workers at Blue Rock himself.

Now, at the Colerain Avenue plant, he stood back and supervised his production managers as they put in an assembly line that stretched from one side of the building to the other, from one floor to the next. The line began on the second floor, where the first parts were added to the bare radio chassis. Radios rode a conveyor belt through various departments on the second, then the first floor. At the end of the line the sets were boxed for shipping.

By June, they were turning out five hundred a day.

By then, Powel had diversified the product line. Crosley now offered the Harko Senior Model V, model X, and model XV. Crosley's ad in that first issue of *Radio Broadcast* claimed you could "listen to the world," "no technical knowledge or wireless experience necessary with the simplified Crosley outfits."

In the second issue of *Radio Broadcast*, Powel offered proof.

The company's ad that month included a facsimile of a telegram from one H.H. Buckwalter of Denver, Colorado, who reported receiving GE's WJZ all the way from Schenectady, New York, without benefit of the two-step amplifier.

"Crosley Radio Apparatus," the ad declared, "is proving to be the equal of any on the market, regardless of price."

And as far as price went...

Crosley sets were among the cheapest on the market, though customers would be mistaken, the second issue's ad went on to say, if they mistook the low prices for an indication of cheap merchandise. "Crosley Radio Goods are quality goods," "Parts are substantial, well made, and finely finished." "Quantity production" (i.e, the assembly line) was "responsible for the "reasonable prices" at which the sets sold.

Quantity was by that point an understatement.

That first issue of *Radio Broadcast* had discussed the manufacturing boom, mentioning set-makers such as Grebe in New York and AMRAD in Massachusetts, Remler in Chicago, and Colin B. Kennedy in San Francisco as companies "depending chiefly on the radio business." Now the Crosley brothers, a year and a half removed from that fateful walk through Precision's doors, were right up there with them, one of the leading manufacturers in the industry.

The sky seemed the limit.

And then the sky came crashing down.

CHAPTER 12

The Golden Age of Radio. The prototypical American family—mother, father, two small children—gathers around a console receiver, a large, wooden piece of furniture not unlike an early television set, to listen to their favorite programs.

All they can get is static.

In summer 1922, as the number of stations sharing the 360 meter wavelength multiplied, as sunspot interference peaked, the brothers Crosley received a nasty surprise.

Harko sets nationwide suddenly stopped working.

The problem was the regenerative circuit—or lack thereof. It now became clear why Harry Davis of Westinghouse and those seventeen independents before him had paid cash for Armstrong's invention; the regenerative circuit made for a vastly more sensitive receiver, a radio capable of tuning in a signal past the normal summer static and the increased radio interference.

Crosley's two-step amplifier was a poor substitute. Sets that had once been able to tune in, say, distant Pittsburgh, or Schenectady, could no longer accurately bring in those stations. Dissatisfied customers began returning their sets to dealers; dealers started returning them to Crosley.

The sets began to pile up in the warehouse.

The company's bottom line took a noticeable turn in the wrong direction.

It wasn't a catastrophe—not yet. Sets were still going out the door faster than they were coming in. But it was an omen of things to come. If the company couldn't find a way to make a more sensitive receiver, or somehow obtain an Armstrong license...

The Crosleys' rise to the top of the radio industry had been spectacular; their fall would be just as quick.

In the meantime, though, as Lewis and Dorman Israel and Russell Blair and every one on staff with a lick of engineering expertise considered the ticklish issue of interference and how to best overcome it, Powel headed to Washington D.C. to have a few words with the nation's foremost radio buff: President Warren Harding.

.   .   .   .   .   .

He went with a group of other radio manufacturers, who had gathered in New York in late May to form the national Radio Chamber of Commerce, for the purpose of convincing the public that radio was "no longer a toy or a freakish mechanical contrivance." Dozens of them descended on the Capitol on Wednesday, July 26, including Cincinnati native George Lewis, holder of amateur license #1. Lewis, a trim compact man, with a trim compact mustache, had been chosen temporary secretary of the organization: Arthur Lynch, the editor of *Radio Broadcast* was there as well, as was Dr. Lewis Clement of Philadelphia, who gave the keynote address in Secretary Hoover's stead.

After Clement finished talking, Powel rose and said a few words himself.

Thursday morning, he and the rest of the delegates reviewed the chamber's proposed constitution and by-laws; Thursday afternoon, they were off to the White House to meet President Harding. They posed for pictures for the *Washington Post*; Powel stood at one end of the group, hat in hand, leaning slightly in one direction, yet still managing to tower over the other half-dozen men in the picture.

On Friday, the chamber elected officers to serve the rest of the year: George Lewis was confirmed in his post. Powel was voted one of the group's district vice presidents.

The chamber set as its avowed purpose "adequate stocks of dependable instruments" for the American public and improved broadcasting services.

Powel hadn't been back in Cincinnati more than a few days when he made a good start on the latter.

A man named Fred Smith walked into his office for an eleven a.m. appointment. Smith, a balding, genial man in his early thirties, had just returned from eight years abroad, studying in Europe and working as a ship's helmsman. He had a feel for languages; he was a classically trained musician as well. He obviously had something on his mind. Just as obviously he was nervous, pacing around the office, not meeting Powel's eyes directly.

Powel asked him to relax, take off his hat and coat, and speak his peace. Smith kept the hat and coat to himself but shared his opinions.

He'd been listening to WLW for some time, he told Powel, and was sorry to say that he found some of the programming, to be frank, amateurish.

Powel asked him to elaborate.

Your programs sound, Smith went on, like they're being made by technicians, or mechanics.

Powel saw no need to respond, since Smith's observation wasn't far from the truth. He did, however, ask Smith again to take off his hat and coat. Finally, the man relented and sat down.

They talked for four hours.

Smith walked out of the room as WLW's first director of programming, at a salary of forty-five dollars a week. He also took over as the main voice of the station. It would be incorrect to say that ratings soared, as there were no such things as ratings back then, but Smith had a natural way with words, a relaxing manner on the microphone. He talked like a regular person: "hello, hello, good evening" was his standard greeting each night. He talked to the listener, as opposed to at them, like Powel, who often sounded like he was reading a prepared speech (even when he wasn't), especially when he was extolling the virtues of the latest piece of Crosley radio apparatus.

Women listeners, in particular, were taken with Fred. The station began receiving quite a bit of fan mail on his behalf.

Smith had more than a pleasant voice, though; he quickly proved himself worthy of the job Powel had given him. The new WLW studios were on the third floor of the Colerain Avenue plant, alongside the executive offices. Smith moved in, took hold of the programming chaos, and began to organize it. He expanded daytime efforts to a full five days a week, putting Cooper on the morning shift—an hour of record-playing, financial reports, weather and agricultural market updates, starting at ten o'clock—and taking the afternoons for himself, from 1:00 to 2:00 p.m., and then again from 3:00 to 3:30.

He began broadcasting records of entire operas on Saturdays, filling the dead air with a summary of the operatic 'story so far' while Cooper switched disks.

He created theme nights, such as Radio Party Night (for families with sets to invite those without), Hoosier Night (featuring guests artists from Indiana), and Hotel Sinton Night (talent supplied courtesy of the establishment built on the ruins of the old Pike Theater).

He even played a few jazz records, though he didn't care for the new music any more than Powel did. Smith's efforts at WLW were repeated nationwide; as radio schedules began to solidify, listeners began to look for, and anticipate, their favorite programs, and announcers.

Powel began to disengage from WLW's day-to-day operations. He didn't feel slighted in the least; like most successful businessmen, Powel was well aware of the importance of surrounding himself with capable, competent men, and letting them do their jobs. That was what he'd done with Lewis, in a way; it was what he did now with Fred Smith.

. . . . . .

The company's most urgent need remained finding a way to overcome the interference dilemma. Crosley wasn't the only radio manufacturer aware of the regenerative circuit's importance in the scheme of things. An Armstrong license in 1922, was a precious commodity. One (unnamed) company in possession of such a license ran an ad in the *New York Times* offering a "substantial interest" in their concern for thirty thousand dollars. Another (unnamed) manufacturer placed a notice seeking to buy an Armstrong license in the same paper to build receivers "for amateur use."

That disclaimer was, of course, a legal formality; in fact, by that time it was a joke. Similar disclaimers went on every set sold by the seventeen original Armstrong licensees, companies that were making a more-than-healthy living off the regenerative circuit.

RCA steamed. In July, Sarnoff summoned representatives of the seventeen license-holders to his New York office and asked them to accept a cap on their sales as a percentage of the radio business. They refused. Behind closed doors the legal department recommended lawsuits, targets to be chosen at Sarnoff's discretion.

RCA's anger over the regenerative circuit was nothing, however, compared to the way they felt about the vacuum tube.

In 1922 alone, they sold well over a million and a half of those tubes, ostensibly for use by amateurs (whatever 'amateur' meant at this point) or as replacement parts for their own sets. In reality, however, the majority of those tubes went into other manufacturers' sets.

Because every single radio receiver sold in the country in 1922 except those that bore the RCA brand name went to market sans tube, the expectation being that (wink) the consumer would simply purchase the appropriate RCA part for insertion on their own. It was unfair, a clear violation of patent law, in RCA's opinion.

In August 1922, the company's patent policy committee held a meeting. Decisions were made. RCA informed a number of their distributors—specifically, those who sold only RCA tubes—that the company would begin dealing only with distributors who sold RCA sets as well as parts. RCA's lawyers began sharpening their pencils, preparing for battle on the patent front.

Meanwhile, AT&T was on the hunt as well, not just for patent infringers, but for profits from the radio boom. In August, their new broadcast station, WEAF, opened for business. For most of the month, the phone company anxiously awaited their first customer—anyone willing to pay cash on the barrelhead for the privilege of utilizing AT&T's state of the art facilities to deliver a personal message to the American public.

They waited and waited and waited.

On August 28, shortly after 5 p.m., a Mr. Blackwell of the Queensboro Corporation stepped up to the microphone and spoke for ten minutes on the virtues of a series of new, tenant-owned apartment homes in Jackson Heights. He paid AT&T fifty dollars for the privilege of doing so.

As the phone company began, at last, collecting dollars for their radio telephony rights, they also started to make inquiries—some surreptitious, others less so—regarding same. They weren't making plans to sue anyone, not just yet, at least. But they were curious. Who, exactly, was broadcasting? And whose transmitters were they using? AT&T's or units manufactured by others? Were local Bell systems allowing stations use of their telephone lines for remote broadcasting?

Not in New York, at least: Westinghouse was once more rebuffed by AT&T, this time for a request to tie-in to the phone company's lines to broadcast the World Series. The company went to Western Union instead and asked permission to use the old telegraph lines for a remote broadcast of the fall classic; happy to be part of something other than nineteenth century technology, Western Union granted permission immediately.

The series itself was somewhat anticlimactic. Ruth's Yankees had been expected to clobber McGraw's Giants (who won the NL title over Pat Moran's recovered Reds by seven and a half games), but just the opposite happened. The Giants beat the Bombers in four straight; well, actually three straight, as game two of the series was played to a draw, the contest called due to a purely unexpected condition.

Night began to fall. In the tenth inning, it got too dark to see the ball.

Judge Landis, in attendance with his wife, was treated to an unfortunate display of Yankee partisanship upon the game's premature conclusion. A little later, he treated Yankee fans to a dose of their own medicine, banning Babe Ruth for a portion of the following season for conduct detrimental to the national pastime.

Up in Saranac Lake, Mathewson, once more, rose to the Babe's defense, declaring Ruth 'more sinned against' than 'sinning.' By that point, Christy was back on the mend, back up to 204 pounds from the 150 his weight had fallen to a few months earlier, and anxious to find a way back into baseball.

In Washington, Secretary Hoover decried the broadcasting chaos once more and attempted to do something about it, setting up another broadcast wavelength, 400 meters, and a second class of station, the Class 'B' station, which would be given only to those concerns that had a minimum transmitter power of five hundred watts. The idea was to make sure that stations supplying a higher quality of programming could be heard over the din of the rabble.

Powel Crosley was most certainly going to separate WLW from that rabble. He applied for a Class B license and set Dorman Israel to work on a new transmitter (four tubes, five hundred watts). Lewis supervised construction of a new antenna.

The new set-up extended WLW's reach tremendously. By November, listeners reported picking it up consistently from coast to coast, in forty-two states and in countries all across the Western Hemisphere.

There was a reason for that, one Powel and his engineers didn't share with Department of Commerce authorities. The new transmitter operated, more often than not, at a thousand rather than five hundred watts. The brothers had cleverly set up the broadcast equipment rack so that four extra tubes were mounted above the transmitter itself, ostensibly as "backups," in case any tubes on the transmitter should fail. Their location allowed them to be easily tied in to the transmitter circuit, doubling the power. And they could be just as easily disconnected, should a radio inspector happen by.

Meanwhile, the hunt for the regenerative license continued.

Sister Edythe and Albert Chatfield sent out wedding invitations; Powel sent out the first issue of a new magazine, the *Crosley*

Radio Weekly, covering news of the company, its broadcast station, and of course, its radios. Robert Stayman was the editor. A young man from Philadelphia, an amateur magician named Alvin Richard Plough, had been hired as Powel's publicist and became Stayman's assistant. The magazine went to Crosley dealers, to the public at large, to trade magazines such as *Radio Broadcast,* which included a column called "Do You Know Them?" featuring prominent personalities in the radio business.

WLW adopted a new slogan, dubbing itself "the broadcasting station of the Queen City of the West." Fred Smith continued to diversify programming. On November 9, he and Stayman joined author Mary MacMillan in a dramatic reading of Miss MacMillan's one act play *A Fan and Two Candlesticks.*

That same week fire broke out on the Ohio River waterfront, causing millions of dollars in damage. Four riverboats burned. Cincinnati papers ran extra editions to cover news of the blaze.

WLW's listeners didn't have to wait; Smith had reports relayed from the scene and broadcast the story as it happened. Breaking news, on the radio, as you listened, another omen of things to come.

On November 24, the station broadcast a full-length drama, the play *Matinata.* Fred, once again, took part in the reading. This time Powel joined in the cast as well, taking a trip down the hall from his third-floor office to the third-floor broadcast studio to make his acting debut.

Lewis stayed at home with his family and blew out the candles on his birthday cake.

In December the two got a chance to celebrate together.

Powel entered into an agreement with Tri-City Manufacturing in Davenport, Iowa, to make sets for Crosley. Tri-City was one of the original seventeen Armstrong licensees. Having them manufacture Crosley sets was as close as the company could get to owning a license themselves.

Lewis packed up parts for a thousand sets and shipped them off to Tri-City for assembly. The new receivers were called the Crosley

Model V. Each set that came off the Tri-City line carried a metal face-plate that bore the following statement:

CROSLEY REGENERATIVE TUNER
Manufactured exclusively for
CROSLEY MANUFACTURING CO., Cincinnati
by Tri-City Radio Electrical Supply Co., under
license under Armstrong U.S. Patent No.
1,113,149, October 6, 1914, for use by Radio
Amateurs for use in radio amateur stations; to
Radio Experimenters and Scientific schools or
Universities for use in experimental and scien-
tific school or university radio stations.

The company was defensive for good reason. Tri-City was also manufacturing receivers for the Montgomery Ward chain store, or rather, they were subcontracting manufacture of said sets out to a third company, Briggs and Stratton of Chicago.

RCA's legal department was by this point in on the joke. Their pencils, in fact, were not only well sharpened, they were flying across the pages of yellow legal pads and in-house memoranda, scribbling notes in the margins of legal documents. They were writing down the names of those companies David Sarnoff planned to take legal action against.

At the top of his list was Tri-City. Grebe was on there as well, as were tube-makers like Perfection and La France.

So, too, was Crosley Manufacturing.

Powel knew none of this as 1922 drew to a close. He and Lewis and every one of the countless men and women in the three Crosley factories were congratulating themselves on an incredible year, one in which the current of events had swept them along from a mid-size manufacturer of automobile accessories to one of the largest radio manufacturers in the world.

Powel more than anyone else had cause to celebrate. He owned Crosley Manufacturing, lock, stock, and barrel. He'd bought out his father, Charles Kilgour, and Walter Aiken long before. His radio hobby had grown into two full-fledged businesses; right alongside Crosley Manufacturing, WLW's studios and programming efforts continued to expand.

The blueprints for that lightweight automobile he had been hoping to build lay forgotten in the upstairs billiard room at Davey Avenue.

They would lie there for some time to come.

A combined Automotive Accessories and Radio Exposition was held at the Cincinnati Music Hall, starting November 22 and running through November 29, the first show of its kind in the area. Crosley radios and components were well represented, as were Americo's products.

Powel finished the year in New York, with the rest of the Radio Chamber of Commerce and Crosley's sales managers, at the American Radio Exposition in Grand Central Palace. He unveiled the news about Tri-City and displayed the company's newest models. He left for Cincinnati to spend the holidays with his family, to share his good fortune with Gwendolyn, and Powel III, and Page. To wish his father Merry Christmas and happy birthday, and give Powel, Sr. a good look at how far the currents of change had taken his oldest son.

Powel was soon to discover those currents weren't finished with him yet.

The family would be together not just for Christmas, but Edythe's wedding, which was set for December 30.

It was to prove a momentous day for all concerned.

CHAPTER 13

By the end of 1922, there were close to six hundred broadcasting stations. Hoover was beside himself: he wrote a little piece for *Radio Broadcast* titled "The Urgent Need for Radio Legislation." "The present state of broadcasting," he declared, "is intolerable."

AT&T wasn't exactly thrilled either; they'd stopped fulfilling orders for radio transmitters a few months before, hoping to send 'radio telephony' business WEAF's way, but the expected rush of customers to their station had failed to materialize.

While the phone company contemplated its next move, set manufacturers enjoyed the lull before RCA's lawsuit storm, though lull is probably the wrong word; they were enjoying the sales from fiscal year 1922, sixty million dollars on the books, in the aggregate.

Christmas shopping season had provided a last bit of oomph for the bottom line. Manufacturers made a strong pitch for the consumer dollar that holiday season; "Let there be a radio under your electrically lighted Christmas tree," one dealer's ads suggested.

Precision Equipment's holiday ad urged parents: "Don't disappoint that boy! If you are planning on pleasing him with a Christmas Radio Set—Get It Now!"

To those in the know, it was as if they were talking about Powel's (Jr. and III) trip to the store two years earlier. Referencing the Crosley name without saying it out loud. The connection between Precision and Crosley was about to be made a little more explicit.

.   .   .   .   .   .

At the chapel, Powel, Sr., now seventy-three years old, stiff-legged, his hair gone white, the goatee he'd grown to make himself look older still firmly in place, walked Edythe down the aisle and thought, more than likely, of the sister she'd never known, little Charlotte, the daughter he'd lost, the wedding day she would never have.

He presented Edythe to Albert Chatfield and took his seat in the front pew of the church, next to his wife. Crosleys and Chatfields who hadn't had a chance to get acquainted during the pre-nuptial planning smiled and nodded at each other across the aisle.

Edythe and Albert said their vows and then left the church, headed for the reception. Powel and Lewis, their own families in tow, trailed behind.

After the food, after the toasts—dry, of course, as this was Prohibition—came the dancing. Powel and Edythe did the latest steps; Lewis twirled his baby girl in his arms; the Crosleys Senior, Powel and Charlotte, looked on with pride.

As the party continued, William Chatfield, the groom's brother, a securities broker, approached Powel. Could I have a minute of your time, Chatfield said, or words to that effect.

Powel nodded.

You've heard of Precision Audio, of course, Chatfield said.

Of course, Powel answered.

I have news regarding the company, Chatfield continued.

As the celebration swirled around them, the two men began to talk.

.   .   .   .   .

All through 1922, as the radio business exploded, Precision continued to make its radio sets in the same building Powel had visited in 1921, the same building WMH had been broadcasting in since its days as 8XB. The ACE line of radio receivers, however, were not made on the assembly line, but one at a time. A dozen or so people sat at a long row of tables, assembling sets piece by piece. It wasn't a factory, really. It was a boutique store, catering to the radio amateur.

But radio manufacturing was big business now. The days when a small concern could compete effectively were at an end.

As 1922 drew to a close, Precision's president, William Gates, could see the writing on the wall.

Gates, Chatfield told Powel, was interested in selling the company. If Powel was, perhaps, interested in purchasing it, Chatfield felt certain he could arrange terms.

Powel smiled.

He sensed an opportunity.

He was interested, he told Chatfield; he had his own ideas, in fact, regarding terms of the sale.

He pulled out a pen, and turned over a napkin.

As the two of them continued talking, Powel began to write. The remainder of the wedding reception went on without him; Powel had business to attend to.

Gwendolyn and the children, as always, made do.

.   .   .   .   .

Powel's terms, sketched on the back of that napkin, became the foundation for the formal deal, agreed to a few days later. Powel paid forty thousand dollars (personally, out of his own pocket) for Precision, including Gates's station, his store, and his remaining stock, none of which Powel cared about at all. What mattered was the Armstrong license.

The regenerative circuit was at last, well and truly, his.

That license in hand, Powel severed his previous arrangement with Tri-City. He sent Lewis to Precision to do the dirty work of closing down the company.

Lewis interviewed the engineers and the station personnel and ended up hiring some of them, including two technicians, Jack Gray, and Dave Conlan, and a singer named Grace Raine, who doubled as a vocal coach.

That done, he padlocked Precision's doors. Powel notified the Department of Commerce that he was returning Precision's commercial broadcast license as well.

WMH was, for the moment, off the air, a small but meaningful bonus of the acquisition: WLW now could usurp the time when WMH had broadcast its programming.

At the factory, Lewis set up another assembly line. This one was simpler than most. At one end were the stacks of sets that had been returned to Crosley Manufacturing the summer before, the non-regenerative sets. Into each of those sets the regenerative circuit—a coil that "looked like a spider," as Lewis recalled—was inserted. The set was sealed, a new nameplate attached, and then shipped back off to dealers.

The nameplate contained the exact same legalese that had gone on the Tri-City sets, with the exception of the manufacturing notice, which alerted consumer and dealer alike that the set was made by Precision Equipment Company, of Cincinnati Ohio, Powel Crosley, Jr., President.

Powel's name went on the ads for the new sets as well, the first of which, a full-page announcement regarding his acquisition of the Precision Equipment Company, appeared in the February 1923 *Radio Broadcast*. The notice was a shrewd marketing move, a way of letting the consumer know that there was something different about Precision receivers now. They were Crosley quality; built with Crosley parts, in the famed Crosley factory.

Better—costs less.

Powel Crosley, Jr., President.

The Crosley Radio Corporation's first letterhead carried the word "Crosley" four times. A striking black silhouette of Powel's profile appeared at the top of the *Crosley Radio Weekly*'s first page—very reminiscent of Henry Ford's silhouette in early Model T ads. He wrote a column over his signature in each issue, a half-page of commentary giving his views on the state of the industry, and in particular, his company's products. He was interviewed by the staff, named and/or quoted in numerous articles.

He was the public persona of the Crosley operation by default and by design. Lewis was not comfortable speaking to the media; he avoided publicity. But Powel reveled in it. He was so closely identified with the company that newspaper stories frequently used "Powel Crosley" interchangeably with the "Crosley Manufacturing Corporation."

As his profile rose, Powel's social sphere enlarged. His companies did business with many of the well-to-do merchants and industrialists in Cincinnati. Those same people began inviting Powel and Gwendolyn to dinners and other social gatherings. He became associated with names such as LeBlond, Fleischmann, Kroger, Longworth, and other leaders of local society—most of them fellow industrialists or Republican politicians.

Already a Rotarian, he became a member of the College Hill Masonic Lodge and Cincinnati's Syrian Shrine temple as well. He was also accepted into the exclusive Queen City Club and the Cincinnati Commercial Club, both bastions of big business and big money. He joined the Cincinnati Polo Club in 1923, which counted among its members a number of the social elite of his generation, including Julius Fleischmann, one of the Reds owners. He bought several polo ponies and kept them at the Camargo Club on the western edge of Indian Hill, where the club played.

He and Gwendolyn began to think about moving.

The Davey Avenue house had everything he and his family needed (even if the bird dogs did find their kennels somewhat cramped), but for someone of his rising social status...

Well, there was Hyde Park, where the old money lived; Avondale was the center of the wealthy Jewish community, and Indian Hill was just beginning to draw the nouveau riche seeking to establish country estates. But College Hill was Powel's hometown, it was where his parents, his brother, and his sister all lived. It was where he'd grown up.

He decided to stay.

In 1923 they began buying acreage for an estate along Kipling Avenue, in a rural area called Mt. Airy. It was to be a huge estate, but Powel could certainly afford big.

His company had grossed twenty million dollars in 1922, a

number that translates into more than a quarter-billion 2005 dollars. The profit on that sum was nearly two million dollars, close to two hundred thousand dollars every month.

As ACE receivers began to leave the Alfred Street factory by the thousands in the early weeks of 1923, those numbers continued to rise—the number of radios ordered, the number of radios shipped, the money coming into the company, the money going into Powel's pockets.

And the radios were only the tip of the product iceberg; the three Crosley factories turned out tube sockets, switches, and other components by the tens of thousands. Down the street at the wood shop, some radio cabinets were still going out the door to other manufacturers, but most of the production was earmarked for Crosley sets.

And then there was Insyde Tyres, an afterthought by now, but still a profitable one. And the Go-Bi-Bi, though by this point the Crosley brothers were locked in a messy lawsuit with a man named Taylor, a Phi Delta Theta fraternity brother from the University of Cincinnati who had started off as a distributor for their product, stolen the idea, and started manufacturing Taylor Tots in his home basement coal bin. Powel told Lewis he was ready to move on from this breakthrough Crosley product. "We are going to sue him," Powel said, "win the case, and make him buy the business from us."

The radio industry's leading manufacturers in the early days were companies like AMRAD, and Remler, and Colin Kennedy. But they had fallen back in the pack. So, too, had RCA, as well as other independents such as Paragon, Midwest, and Tri-City.

In 1923, in fact, the leading radio manufacturer in the world was a privately owned company a in mid-sized city, a concern that had come rather late to the wireless industry, but by concentrating on the low-priced market, by means of efficient production, marketing and promotion, had risen to the top of the heap.

The Crosley Manufacturing Company of Cincinnati, Ohio, was number one. Its two top executives were brothers, one who had intuitively sensed the coming demand for low-priced radios and conceived the products to seize that market, the other who had the ability to turn out those products by the thousands, come hell, exploding mortar shell, or malfunctioning tuning apparatus.

The elder was a multimillionaire.

The younger was living in a fourth-floor walkup at the Glenwood Apartments.

Lewis didn't care. The way he saw it, Crosley Manufacturing was his brother's company. He'd come back from the war, and Powel had given him a job, cut him in for a piece of the profit. He had no complaints.

His wife did.

Lucy saw Lewis running the factories, solving the problems on the line, hiring and firing the workers. She saw Powel going hunting, going to Washington and New York on business trips, buying fancy clothes and fancy cars, getting all the credit for the work the brothers did together.

She lugged Ellen's baby stroller up and down four flights of stairs every day, multiple times a day, and steamed.

.   .   .   .   .   .

RCA meanwhile, was finished steaming.

On February 10, 1923, preliminary injunctions were granted in lawsuits against the tube manufacturers La France and Perfection.

They sued Tri-City; they sent letters requesting information relevant to the manufacture of regenerative sets to Crosley and several other manufacturers.

AT&T was done steaming as well: the patents for broadcasting were all in their name, they were supposed to have all rights not just to commercial exploitation of radio telephony, but sale of broadcast transmitters. And that was far from the case. Barely five percent of the stations on the air were using their transmitters

The company now informed the others that they were in violation of its patent rights. Rather than sue, AT&T initially adopted a more magnanimous approach. Somewhat. In February, it offered to grant broadcasters nationwide 'license' to continue using the airwaves, the fee for that license to be based on a station's wattage. That fee amounted to a few hundred dollars a year, generally. As a perk, those stations who anted up received the opportunity to utilize the phone lines for occasional remote broadcasting.

AT&T itself had utilized those lines quite recently to great, and even revolutionary, effect. On January 23, their New York station, WEAF, and Boston's WNAC had jointly broadcast a saxophone solo by Mr. Nathan Glanz. This event was the first time 'chain broadcasting' had occurred, though the terminology used to describe the event would soon change, and what WNAC and WEAF had done would shortly be referred to as a 'network' broadcast.

After considering AT&T's magnanimous licensing offer, the hundreds of stations, in the words of broadcast historian Erik Barnouw, "did not rush to comply."

Not only did they not comply, they began to grumble. Those grumblings were echoed in the popular press. Did AT&T presume to claim ownership of the air itself? The stink of monopoly was in the air. The Federal Trade Commission, at Congress's request, began an investigation into the issue.

Lewis, meanwhile, ordered a new transmitter for WLW. A five-hundred-watt, AT&T-approved transmitter. It was shipped from Western Electric (AT&T's manufacturing arm) in a rail car bound for Cincinnati in March of 1923. In the same car was a second, identical transmitter, bound for Cincinnati as well, though not intended for WLW's use.

The second transmitter was for the new radio station in town, WSAI, owned and operated by the United States Playing Card Company, the world's largest maker of playing cards, headquartered in Norwood, an incorporated town within the Cincinnati city limits. Company management had decided radio was the perfect medium to promote their wares. The new station planned to air bridge tournaments, with noted players such as Sidney S. Lenz and Milton Work commenting on the games.

There would be other entertainment as well, but the primary

purpose of the new Cincinnati station was the same as that of the old one; WSAI, like WLW, wasn't in the broadcasting game to make money. They were in it to sell their products. U.S. Playing Card's decks would be used in the on-air bridge games and mentioned frequently. The point was to familiarize as many people as possible with the name, hence the state-of-the-art transmitter.

Powel did not want to play second fiddle to a newcomer. Whoever got on the air first would be among the most powerful broadcasters in the country.

A game of "race to build a transmitter" began.

Other games began that month as well. At Redland Field, the Reds opened the season by beating the Cardinals 3-2, en route to a second consecutive second-place finish, behind (once more) the Giants. Meanwhile, to the delight of baseball fans everywhere, ex-Giant, ex-Red Christy Mathewson re-entered the national pastime, not as a player, or coach, but president of the Boston Braves new ownership syndicate; his baseball know-how was augmented by the financial resources of Judge Emil Fuchs and James MacDonald.

Powel augmented his team, too, hiring as his assistant George Lewis, secretary of the Radio Chamber of Commerce, holder of amateur radio license #1. He came aboard just in time to celebrate WLW's victory in their race to erect the five- hundred-watt transmitter with WSAI.

With the new transmitter in place, the station was given the coveted "Class B" rating by the Department of Commerce. Its frequency was changed from 360 meters to 400, moving them away from the interference caused by the multitude of stations at the lower end of the spectrum.

Along with the new power, though, came a new rule, one forced through by the musicians union, who saw radio threatening their membership's livelihood: WLW, as a Class B station, could no longer play records. All broadcast music had to be performed live.

Luckily, a few months earlier, Fred Smith had hired on a violinist named William Stoess to take charge of the Crosley Orchestra. That orchestra now began to supply more of the station's programming. Grace Raine, who'd come over from Precision's WMH, chipped in her talents more frequently.

Smith continued to experiment with programming. The station broadcast a musical comedy called *When Madam Sings*, written by the *Crosley Radio Weekly*'s associate editor Alvin Richard Plough; an original drama of Smith's own, called *When Love Wakens*; and the station's first sporting event, a blow-by-blow recount of a local boxing match. Robert Stayman was at the fight. Smith was in the studio, on the other end of a phone line, broadcasting the action as Stayman relayed it to him.

When there were lulls in Stayman's reporting, Smith fell back on the phrase "the men are dancing around the ring." He repeated it over and over. At some point, a listener called in to say he wished the boxers would quit dancing and fight.

They were, all of them, doing their best. They were making it up as they went along.

The new transmitter multiplied WLW's signal ten-fold. Local newspaper headlines proudly proclaimed the station's new power and greatly extended reach. Powel received congratulatory telegrams from the governors of several states as well as from President Harding.

He took in the applause and then headed north to Chicago, accompanied by George Lewis, for a trade show. At two o'clock on the afternoon of April 25, the two men walked through the door of the Drake Hotel, and straight into history.

. . . . . .

It was money that brought Powel and George Lewis to the Drake Hotel. The money was being sought by a group known as the American Society of Composers and Performers—ASCAP, for short. The society had petitioned the first Radio Conference for consideration of its members in the radio boom; after all, the members had composed the songs being played. Shouldn't they profit too?

Broadcasters pointed out that no one was actually profiting from the new industry. If you looked at every station's bottom-line, broadcasting was a losing proposition. What money was there to share with ASCAP? None. Besides, weren't broadcasters doing composers a favor by playing, and thus popularizing, their songs?

ASCAP didn't exactly see things that way. By mid-1923, they were finished asking; their lawyers began sharpening pencils.

The society went to the one station that was (theoretically, at least) making money off broadcasting: WEAF. Happy to once more separate themselves from the pack, the phone company's broadcast outlet struck a deal, offering a one-year license fee of five hundred dollars. As WEAF began proudly trumpeting their new arrangement with ASCAP, the rest of the country's six hundred or so stations began grumbling.

RCA's station, WJZ, announced it would stop playing the society's music altogether.

Powel sensed an opportunity.

He had a musician on staff, didn't he? Fred Smith? Perhaps, he thought, Crosley should get into the music publishing business itself.

Smith took a break from his duties as program director and sometime playwright to compose a song called "Steerin' for Erin," the lyrics of which are unfortunately lost to posterity. The new Crosley Music Publishing Company also acquired a song called "Somebody Else Is Stealing My Sweety's Kisses."

Two songs, however, did not an evening's entertainment make.

It became clear that a more pro-active stance was necessary, clear not just to Powel, but to a number of other broadcasters, including Eugene MacDonald of WZN, Thorne Donnelly of WDAP, and William Hedges of WMAQ. Powel joined them, as well as a handful of others, at a series of informal meetings during that April 1923 Chicago Radio Show, and then, on April 25 in the studios of WDAP at the Drake Hotel, where they formalized the arrangement they had been discussing earlier in the week.

That arrangement called for the founding of a new organization to represent the interests of radio broadcasters, specifically in regard to ASCAP, but with an eye toward other dealings as well. The group was to be called The National Association of Broadcasters.

MacDonald was appointed president, Powel, treasurer.

Radio Broadcast ran a profile of the new organization in its August 1923 issue; mention was made of Crosley's music-publishing activities. A photo was included as well, featuring six of the group's founding members.

Powel was not among them.

He had little cause for complaint, however; an article elsewhere in the issue cemented his place in broadcast history.

The article was called "The Henry Ford of Radio."

It was about Powel.

It was written by one of his employees, Alvin Richard Plough.

Large portions of it were even true.

CHAPTER 14

O n the other side of Belmont Avenue, across from the house belonging to Lucy's sister Ellen and her husband Edward Henshaw, there was a long, deep lot, with room enough not only for a house, but a substantial garden behind.

As Powel continued buying acreage for the estate out on Kipling Road, Lewis took the money he and Lucy had saved by moving from the first floor to the fourth of the Glenwood Apartments, plunked down the asking price for that deep Belmont Avenue lot, and began planning a house of his own.

Lewis was not able to devote as much time to those plans as he would have liked. Radio production at the plant was up to a thousand sets per day, the factory day consisting of the same single shift of workers that factories since the 1800s had used. Powel claimed that the lines could run all day and all night if he wanted them to, but he did not—at that point, at least—believe in night work.

Neither did his brother.

Lewis believed in ending the workday at five o'clock, a practice he followed religiously so that he could be home in time for dinner with Lucy and his daughters. Ellen was toddling; Charlotte Jeanne was still at the Pigeye. She'd made it past Maybelle Brown but now had other problems. She'd developed mastoiditis, a painful ear infection, and had to take the streetcar downtown several times a week to have it drained.

Beyond his family, Lewis's primary focus remained radio manufacturing. Keeping an eye on the line seemed like a never-ending job. Every week the Crosley factories went through three million

screws, five million nuts, six tons of bus wire, sixty thousand bind-
ing posts, half a million square inches of Formica, fifteen thousand
sockets, six thousand audio transformers, and one railroad car full
of cardboard cartons.

And it wasn't enough to meet the still-growing demand for sets.

In the fall of 1923, Powel informed his brother that he wanted a factory capable of turning out five thousand radios a day. Lewis
nodded dutifully and began the process of finding yet another new
location for the Crosley Manufacturing Company.

That was, after all, how the division of labor between the two
of them went. Powel imagined it; Lewis built it.

Lewis had not, since he came to work for Powel in the fall of
1919, taken any time off for a vacation, at least not anything more
than a day or two at a time. He never complained about it. If he had,
Powel would have been the first one to put a fishing rod, or a
bathing suit, or a what-have-you in Lewis's hand and tell him to disappear for two weeks. Powel knew better than anyone the importance of winding down now and then. But there was work to be
done. Lewis couldn't imagine doing anything other than hunkering
down and getting to it. That was his nature. That was how the division of labor between the two of them went. Powel imagined it,
Lewis built it—or made sure it got built.

That was how it had gone since they'd made that first car out
of their grandfather's old buckboard, since those days when Powel
had dropped out of college to become part of the vast wave of
change sweeping across the country. Back then, he'd dreamed that
the papers in Indy and Detroit would write about him the way they
wrote about Fisher and Ford.

Now he was in a position to make sure of it.

. . . . . .

No one knows who came up with the phrase; perhaps it was suggested by one of *Radio Broadcast*'s editors. Perhaps it was Alvin
Plough's idea. Perhaps it was Powel himself who devised it; he, after

all, was a genius at naming things. Why not name himself?

"The Henry Ford of Radio."

That headline appeared just above Powel's picture in that August 1923 issue of *Radio Broadcast*, just above the article that began with Plough writing, "The other day I visited two large radio plants" [as if he hadn't been employed at those plants for a year] and continued on with Plough being ushered into the president's office, where he met a man "much younger than I expected" [as if he hadn't been seeing Powel on an almost daily basis for that same year], a man "whose youth" impressed him [as if Powel had missed his earlier compliment] and whose ability to grasp big ideas and make quick decisions Plough marveled at [as if, perhaps, Powel might give him a raise right on the spot].

The article went on to tell about that fateful trip the two Powels made to Precision Audio, noting that Powel now owned Precision. It relayed the story of Powel's early business career, stressing the lesson he learned during those years, "to never again attempt to operate on other people's money."

It added that those who knew him as "a rolling stone" were now "glad to hand it to him as a sound business man."

It was the classic rags-to-richest story, a Horatio Alger tale come to life.

The main point of the article was to pound home the message that Powel had been trying to get across to consumers since the day the first Harko Jr. had rolled off the line—that just like Henry Ford, Powel had used the economies of mass production to bring to market a low-priced product that was every bit as good as ones costing significantly more.

The article was as interesting for what Plough left out as for what he (or, perhaps, Powel) put in. It didn't mention Ira Cooper. It didn't mention Powel, Sr., or the borrowed five hundred dollars. It didn't mention Lewis, which was, of course, just fine with the younger Crosley. Lucy might have wanted him to step up and claim credit, but as far as he was concerned, it was his brother's company, built on his brother's ideas.

That summer, however, Lewis had a thought of his own that would have consequences as far-reaching as any of Powel's ideas.

He took a trip to Redland Field.

He took a microphone with him.

.   .   .   .   .   .

By summer of 1923, in search of programming variety, WLW had begun to do shows by remote, tying into the phone lines to transmit from locations outside the studio. The earliest such broadcast was done from Cincinnati's Hotel Sinton, where Paul Whiteman and his Café de Paris Orchestra performed on Thursday evenings.

Shortly after that broadcast, Lewis took his trip across Colerain Avenue to the stadium on Western Avenue.

As he would explain later to a family member, he'd been looking for an opportunity to further field-test the station's remote equipment. He chose Redland Field to do this, for reasons that are now lost to us. Perhaps the ballpark, on the western edge of town, provided a unique set of transmission difficulties. Perhaps station engineers had other variables they were determined to solve. Perhaps Lewis simply wanted an excuse to take in a ballgame.

Regardless of the reason, he was there, with all the apparatus required, and after a relatively simple set-up, he sat down behind the microphone and called balls and strikes for the fifth, sixth, and seventh innings. Then, having established to his satisfaction that everything was in working order, Lewis pulled the plug on the broadcast, packed up his equipment, and returned to the Crosley plant.

Where the phones, he found, were ringing off the hook. WLW listeners demanded to know why the station hadn't aired the rest of the game.

Lewis began wondering the same thing.

He and Powel talked it over. Lewis made a phone call to Reds owner Garry Herrmann, and plans were made for a closer association between the Crosley brothers and their hometown team.

Fred Smith, meanwhile, was making calls of his own regarding WLW's programming. One of those calls went to Helen Schuster Martin, director of the Schuster Martin Dramatic School in Cincinnati. Smith hired Martin to direct all the station's plays, which Robert Stayman had dubbed 'Radarios.' A company of fourteen actors came aboard at the same time; the group was dubbed (unsurprisingly) the Crosley Radarians.

The term didn't last, but the players did.

Another call went to the Cincinnati Zoo, which held opera performances every summer. Fred made arrangements to broadcast those shows. He not only ran lines to the studio, he hid three microphones in the footlights. "Sitting beneath the stage," as WLW historian Lawrence Lichty wrote, "he narrated the story of the operas."

In August, the station broadcast the wedding of William Mains and Alice Hazenfield. In October, Smith, Robert Stayman, and Albert Plough gathered around the microphone to review local plays for the benefit of the Cincinnati literati. The WLW staff was still, even in late 1923, making it up as they went along.

The station was still operating at a loss, of course. Lewis put the figure at a few thousand dollars a month. Both he and Powel regarded those dollars as well spent. The station existed, after all, to sell Crosley radios, to provide programming for its customers to listen to on those radios, not to make money on its own.

Not that either of the brothers were anxious to throw away money. By this point, with the broadcast day growing ever longer, they'd managed to convince a few companies to help sponsor (read: underwrite) the cost of providing programming. Stock quotations, for example, came courtesy of Westheimer and Company; financial reports came through the good offices of Fifth-Third National Bank. Pianos were supplied by Baldwin, dance orchestra by the Hotel Sinton, and despite being snubbed by Powel/Plough in the 'Henry Ford' article, I.J. Cooper placed ads for his new 'storage batteries' in the *Crosley Radio Weekly*.

The National Association of Broadcasters was casting about for direction as well. Subsequent to their initial April meetings, they'd had further get-togethers in Chicago, and appointed an executive chairman, a man named Paul Klugh, who'd already fought ASCAP on behalf of player-piano manufacturers and was happy now to take up NAB's cause. Klugh had set up offices in New York and ran ads in the trade papers asking for songwriters to submit their material directly to the group, for performance and subsequent broadcast. By mid-June, they'd gotten three hundred submissions, of which a hundred were usable, of which a grand total of six—by the estimation of the group and the man in charge of their new music bureau, an experienced songwriter named Raymond Walker—were potential 'hit' material.

Clearly, they had their work cut out for them.

ASCAP wasn't going to make NAB's job any easier. By that point they were monitoring the big stations for any potential copyright infringement. It didn't take them long to find their first target: WOR in Newark, New Jersey, which infringed, according to the society, by playing a recording of "Mother Machree." The publisher of said song, M. Witmark, an ASCAP company, filed suit. The courts came down on the side of the composers; WOR was told to cease and desist.

Score one for ASCAP.

In October, the composers' second target presented itself.

The Crosley Manufacturing Company.

.   .   .   .   .   .

The supposed infringement occurred on or about October 22, between the hours of nine and ten p.m., when one of WLW's orchestras played a song called "Dreamy Melody." The song's publisher, Jerome Roenick, claimed the broadcast of the song by WLW constituted a public performance for profit and that WLW should pay a royalty or cease broadcasting the song.

Powel begged to differ.

In the first place, he said, the performance was 'inadvertent.'

In the second place, he—through his attorneys, Allen & Allen—argued that the broadcast performance was not "public" because it was not presented to a large audience gathered in one place. Instead, Powel maintained, the performance was received by individuals, each with an individual receiving set, which made it a private affair. The attorneys further argued that radio was not covered by the intent of the 1909 Copyright Act and pointed out that WLW charged no admission for the performance.

U.S. District Judge Smith Hickenlooper listened to both sides make their arguments and retired to his chambers to consider the case.

Powel, meanwhile, was on to the next thing, that next thing being the new Crosley manufacturing facility. Lewis and he had settled on a four-story, one-hundred-thousand-square-foot stone building, the former home of the Corcoran Lamp Company, one-time manufacturers of automobile lamps. Located at Colerain and Sassafras Streets in the heart of a burgeoning industrial district, alongside Procter & Gamble, Drackett, and the Andrew Jergens Company, the building offered the size they needed and was served by its own railroad siding.

The factory was purchased with cash on hand—one hundred and fifty thousand dollars. As Lewis planned the upcoming move, Powel and George Lewis returned to New York for the first annual NAB convention.

By this point, the NAB meetings weren't just about business. Powel had made some genuine friends among the broadcasters and manufacturers in the group, chief among them Eugene MacDonald. The two were kindred spirits, men who loved the outdoors, driven businessmen who liked to play as much as they did work. MacDonald had recently renamed the manufacturing arm of his corporation Zenith. By late 1923, he and Crosley were among the top names in the radio business.

And business was still booming. Total retail sales would reach a staggering one hundred and thirty-six million dollars before the year was out, which worked out to about eleven million dollars a month.

Alongside established firms such as Grebe, and Crosley, and of course, RCA (which planned to introduce for 1924 a new type of radio receiver, the super heterodyne, another Edwin Armstrong invention), there were plenty of new companies jostling for a share of those consumer dollars.

The biggest of those newcomers was Atwater Kent, founded by an electrical and automobile parts manufacturer of the same name. Kent entered the market with a splash, spending a half-million dollars in advertising his first year. Early Atwater Kent radios, called 'breadboard sets,' were sold without cabinets to show off the components. They had style. They appealed not just to the masses, but to the classes as well, who were interested in more than just low prices. To them, the radio set was a piece of furniture and should be presented as such.

By the end of 1923, Kent had passed Crosley as the leading set manufacturer.

Not that the Crosley brothers were complaining.

Everyone associated with the Crosley Radio Corporation had reason to celebrate as the year ended. Powel had hosted a convention for his distributors earlier in the year, a party to renew/make acquaintances with the men selling his radios.

Around Christmas, he decided to share his good fortune with those less fortunate. He rented Cincinnati Music Hall, hired clowns, musicians, and a Santa Claus, bought candy and fruit and toys, and then invited all the children "who could possibly attend" to celebrate the holiday season.

For Christmas Day, of course, he was home with his own family.

And as the New Year began, he was, once more, off hunting.

By this point, his trips to Mississippi to hunt bobwhite quail were being augmented by expeditions to more remote country. He went to Wisconsin, where he fished Bear River in an ice storm, and to Northern Minnesota and the Flambeau River. He explored Florida and Canada, too, traveling by rail to the town nearest his destination, and then by auto and horseback for the expedition itself. Sometimes the family came along for part of the trip. Sometimes he took Lewis, or Robert Stayman. Sometimes he traveled with only a local guide.

Always, he returned energized, eager to dive back into work, eager to move on to the next thing.

Always, Lewis watched over the old thing for him.

In January 1924, on his return to the factories, Powel folded Precision Equipment into the Crosley corporate umbrella; the entire concern now became known as The Crosley Radio Corporation. That same month the company closed the deal for its new manufacturing facility. The building, however, would require a hundred thousand dollars worth of improvements and several months of hard work before it was ready to be occupied.

While construction began in Cincinnati, in New York, the patent wars continued. RCA sued Grebe for violating its set patents; AT&T sued New York's WHN for violating its radio telephony rights.

Both companies were condemned for greedy, grasping policies. *Radio Broadcast* made note of the fact that consumers spent four million dollars in 1923 on tubes and that three years after securing its patent position, RCA was still adding a 'cost of development' line into the retail price of its vacuum tubes.

Of more concern to the patent pool partners was the Federal Trade Commission's report, released to the press in late January of 1924.

"Monopoly in Radio" the commission charged, citing all parties concerned—RCA, Westinghouse, GE, and AT&T. Secretary Hoover saved his ire for the phone company, declaring that while he could not comment on ongoing investigations by the Federal Trade Commission, he himself thought it would be "most unfortunate" if a single company controlled all the nation's broadcast outlets.

AT&T, undaunted, pressed on.

By this point, its makeshift broadcast network comprised some half-dozen stations. Sponsors were paying an increasing premium for the right to be heard not just in their local area, but across wider regions of the country. Some of those sponsors continued to broadcast direct appeals to the consumer. Some of them simply attached their names to certain programs.

With more money in hand, AT&T could afford to pay not just ASCAP but a better quality of performer. New York was then the entertainment capital of the country. The big stars, the big singers, the big-name conductors and their orchestras all gravitated toward the big money.

RCA and its other patent partners—GE and Westinghouse— owned radio stations of their own. Though primarily set-makers, they, like Crosley, felt broadcasting an essential part of their business. They were not going to take AT&T's dominance of the airwaves lying down.

They began to put together a network of their own.

Use of the phone lines to transmit programming was out, of course, but Western Union was, once more, happy to cooperate. In early 1924, linemen began stringing new telegraph wire along New York City's elevated railway lines, connecting studio to broadcast outlets throughout the entertainment district.

AT&T was not pleased, and tension between the erstwhile partners simmered; behind closed doors, a war of words and letters, begun the previous year, threatened to boil over.

The two giant corporations, tired of attacking the smaller fish in the radio pond, had turned upon each other.

Lawyers heard the call to action and began sharpening their pencils.

Back in Cincinnati, meanwhile, another call went out.

"Play Ball."

It was April 15, Opening Day of the 1924 baseball season. The first game of the year, as always, was played in Cincinnati, home of the first professional baseball team. This year, it was the Reds against the Pirates.

And this year, the game was on the radio.

.   .   .   .   .   .

Lewis's phone call to Garry Herrmann the previous summer had resulted in WLW being granted permission to broadcast on Opening Day, as well as a handful of other contests throughout the year. Engineers from the station set up a microphone and power amplifier on top of the grandstand, right alongside several hundred other fans. It was crowded, it was hot, it was noisy, and the excitement was palpable, not just in the stands, but everywhere a radio signal could be picked up in the Cincinnati area. Thousands tuned in. Receivers went on in Cincinnati's City Hall, and in the Department of Health, and across the river in the county sheriff's office located across the river in Newport, Kentucky.

WLW's broadcast started at noon with Alvin Plough at the mike. He entertained listeners by "describing interesting events that transpired in the park." It seems likely that the words Crosley crossed his lips more than once as well. At game time, 2:45 p.m., Robert Stayman took over for Plough and did his best to describe the action as it occurred. The art of baseball play-by-play was not much more evolved than that of ringside commentary. Nonetheless, the broadcast was a smashing success and ended on a high note, with the Reds beating the Pirates 6-5.

The rest of the year didn't go so well for the Cincinnati team, which finished in fourth place. The untimely death of manager Pat Moran just before the season began cast a cloud over the club the entire year, which ended in the same terrible way, with the death of first baseman and team captain Jake Daubert shortly after the team dispersed.

WLW was running into problems too.

In early May, another Cincinnati radio station had come on the air—WFBW. Department of Commerce officials had assigned it the same 309 meter wavelength that WSAI and WLW were already on.

Powel steamed.

He vented his ire to Department of Commerce officials. They moved WLW up to 423 meters on the dial, where it would now share time with WBAV in Columbus, Ohio.

On May 12, Powel got more good news from the government.

Judge Hickenlooper announced his verdict in the "Dreamy Melody" case. He found that the broadcast of a song in no way constituted a public performance.

He found for Crosley and dismissed the case.

Score one for the NAB.

While ASCAP prepared to take another turn at bat, filing an appeal, Powel declared that even with the court victory, he would play no more of the society's copyrighted music.

"In view of the unfriendly attitude of the society," he told reporters, "we have no desire whatsoever to advertise their publications."

What Powel wanted to advertise, as always, were his radios.

That summer, the advertising went upscale. Crosley supplemented the usual trade ads (*Radio Broadcast*, *Radio Digest*, *QST*, etc.) with a full-page splash in the July 26, 1924, *Saturday Evening Post*, promoting the company's latest radios: The Trirdyn, Trirdyn Special, and the Crosley model 50, 51, and 52. *The Post*'s circulation at the time ran into the millions. The company's ad rates reflected those figures.

The full-page cost nearly seven thousand dollars.

The fact that Powel was willing to spend that kind of money let Crosley distributors and Crosley retailers know that he and the parent corporation were committed to bringing customers into the stores, committed to hammering home the Crosley brand name, and of course, the Crosley message:

Better—costs less.

The message continued to be hammered home even after the customer made a purchase. Inside the operating instructions that came with each set, customers found a dozen postcards. Some were 'applause cards,' intended for listeners to send in to their local radio station (WLW, perhaps?) declaring their favorite programs. Others were meant for radio buyers to send to friends, to invite them to a listening party. At the bottom of each card was printed, "P.S. We Own a Crosley Radio."

Another item packed with each radio was a small paperbound book titled *The Simplicity of Radio*. Published by (who else?) the Crosley Publishing Company and carrying Powel's (who else's?) byline, the book explained how radio worked, as well as how to operate and even build a receiver, though of course, the company's preference was that you buy a Crosley of your own.

By mid-summer, those sets were, at last, coming off the line at the new Colerain street facility.

A year and a half earlier, when they'd moved the assembly line from the woodworking shop on Vandalia to Blue Rock, it had taken two small trucks to transport the manufacturing apparatus, such as it was, from one plant to the other.

This time it took fifty large trucks.

Powel had asked for a facility that could turn out at least five thousand radio sets per day. The Colerain building could do that and more by the time the production lines were in place. Radio assembly was done on the second and third floors; the first floor housed the shipping and receiving departments. Corporate offices, the engineering department, and experimental labs shared the top level of the new building with WLW's offices and two new, state-of-the-art studios.

The company had spared no expense when it came to the new broadcast facilities. The larger of the two studios, equipped with furnishings such as a Baldwin concert grand piano and xylophone, could accommodate a complete orchestra or choral group. The smaller studio, meant for soloists and lecturers, contained a Baldwin grand piano as well. Monk's cloth covered the walls in both rooms; hung like drapes, it could be moved to adjust the acoustical qualities of the room as the engineers desired. A triangular control room between studios allowed directors and technicians to see into either room. Special microphones helped smooth switching between the two. The words "Prepare" and "Broadcast" on them could be lit from the control room, to signal performers when to get ready and when they were on the air.

Next to the studios was an enormous auditorium, one wall of which was lined with plate-glass windows so visitors in a large lounge area could watch performers as they broadcast.

The furnishings, the furniture itself, gave the studio an aristocratic appearance. WLW, according to one report, had 'wrapped itself in red plush.'

Powel's offices went the studio one better.

His workspace was outfitted with the most expensive and

luxurious appointments, courtesy of Closson Galleries of Cincinnati. Dark wood paneling covered the walls, a deep pile carpet the floors. The room's antique furnishings—a massive desk, sideboard, bookshelves, and plush chairs—were impressive, but the highlight was the wood-burning fireplace that took up most of one wall. Above it, Powel had placed the Crosley coat of arms and motto, carved into a block of oak.

The office housed what Powel referred to as his "radio relics," among them his first factory-made receiver, and Precision Equipment's 10-watt 8XB transmitter, which had gone into service in 1919.

Photos on the walls displayed moose and other big game Powel had bagged and a large muskellunge that he landed up on the Bear River.

Other fourth floor offices were similarly well appointed. Tapestries and paintings hung from the walls. Persian rugs covered the hardwood floors. All the woodwork was mahogany. Overstuffed sofas and chairs lined the corridors. The furniture was a mixture of Spanish and Italian, some of it centuries old.

And then there was Lewis's workspace.

He had a desk. He had a chair.

He had a coat rack, filing cabinets, and a telephone.

There was a framed photo on the wall: him on a fishing trip, with a particularly big catch.

It was one of the few personal touches in the office. For Lewis, personal touches weren't necessary. He didn't identify with work. Work wasn't who he was. Work was what he did.

His brother was different.

Powel was the Henry Ford of Radio. He'd spent his whole life preparing for the role, and now that he had won the audition, so to speak, he was going to play it to the hilt.

In the first act, he had been one of many leading characters in the broadcasting drama.

Now he was going to take center stage.

CHAPTER 15

That fall of 1924, Powel was everywhere. He was in Washington, to meet with the Department of Commerce, on behalf of the Radio Manufacturer's Association, where Secretary Hoover sent him an invitation to attend the upcoming Third Annual Radio Conference

He was in New York, for the second annual NAB convention, where he was once more elected the group's treasurer, and chosen by Eugene MacDonald, Klugh, Hedges, "et al.", as the broadcasters' official delegate to that same conference.

Then he was back in Cincinnati to see his family, to visit the studios, and his office, back to DC, for the radio conference, where he sat on subcommittee number three, alongside Edwin Armstrong, Atwater Kent, Paul Klugh, David Sarnoff, et al, and joined those gentlemen in recommending that, among other things, the government grant some of their Class B station licenses to experiment with so-called superpower—broadcasts in excess of the current thousand-watt limit.

He was in the national press; in *Radio Broadcast*, and of course, the *Crosley Radio Weekly*, where piece after piece mentioned his name, showed his picture, profiled his doings, told his life story, and referred to him as the Henry Ford of Radio.

One of those pieces appeared in the October 8, 1924 issue. It carried Fred Smith's byline. It was headlined "The Genius of Powel Crosley Junior." It depicted a man in constant motion, a man who, in addition to being the "biggest single figure in radio today," was possessed of a keen intellect and an unerring vision, a man who had used his early years in business to train himself to think "logically, clearly, and all the time more and more rapidly." A man "whose story was only beginning."

The article was, to use the modern phrase, a "puff piece." Many newspaper pieces back then fit that term. In the 1920s, reporters usually steered clear of questions about the personal lives of politicians, their families, their private peccadilloes and pet peeves. But even in a puff piece, there's a difference between exaggeration and out-and-out falsehood. An example of the former:

"On that Washington's Birthday I wondered how other men on salaries as small as mine could afford to buy radio sets at the prices I was asked."

The quote is from the *New York Mail-Telegram*. The speaker is Powel, talking about the day he took his son to Precision Audio. At the time, he was owner of the American Automobile Accessories Company. He could have paid for that tube set.

He didn't want to.

Exaggeration.

Another example:

"When the great Indianapolis Speedway was opened, the company [the Carl Fisher Company] selected me for one of their entries. A few days before the race I broke my arm cranking an automobile and was thus unable to drive."

The quote is from a second *Radio Broadcast* piece on Powel, which appeared in November 1924.

Powel was indeed there when the Speedway opened, and it's true that he wanted to drive a car. But that wasn't when he broke his arm. And no one—not Fisher, not Stutz, not Duesenberg—had entered him as a driver in any Indy race.

Falsehood.

Others were to pop up in the portrait of the Henry Ford of Radio, as his story began to be told in places like Philadelphia, and New York, and points radiating from Cincinnati.

The question is why.

Powel deserved every bit of publicity he got. He was the one who'd not only glimpsed the potential for a radio in every home but realized the only way that was going to happen was if those radios were cheap enough for every home to afford them. He was also the one who realized that people who bought those sets had to have something to listen to, and so created WLW. He continually pushed to boost the station's wattage because the more powerful he made his radio station, the easier it would be for people to hear and the cheaper he could make those sets.

Sell a lot on a little margin, he'd make a big profit. Just like Ford.

The comparison was an apt one—even if he made it himself.

But for some reason, it wasn't enough.

There was something in Powel that craved not only attention but control.

"Here is my story," he said, in so many words. "As I want it told. Now tell it."

That story was an amalgamation of truth, exaggeration, and out-and-out lie.

It was a myth his employees were assigned to perpetuate. Powel was, after all, the boss.

Reporters did the same. Many were writing from publicity releases, of course. Writing puff pieces. Even those who tried to go deeper, however, often faltered. Powel was six foot four. He spoke in a deep, measured, some might say intimidating voice. He had a powerful gaze and a more powerful glare. He could wither people with his eyes. He had a commanding presence and the type of personality the average person doesn't try to cross.

He wore custom-tailored suits and silk ties embossed with the Crosley family crest. He was long past the point of feeling awkward and self-conscious about his height. He was becoming—deliberately so—a larger-than-life figure.

In creating his own legend, he eliminated the parts that he saw as flaws, even though many were testaments to his willpower, his determination.

He was doing something else in the process, however.

He was separating himself from the marketplace he was serving.

He was making products for the masses, not the classes, and yet he was no longer one of them.

It was a disconnect Powel would never realize.

It was not an omen, or a sign of things to come; it was happening right then, right there, in 1924. It was a problem.

In the end, it would turn out to be his downfall.

· · · · ·

The FTC began taking testimony in the radio antitrust case. WHN settled its suit with the phone company out of court, and paid them the usual license fee.

AT&T backed down a bit from its demands. It softened its rhetoric, reduced its license fees, and began to offer leased lines to all stations, regardless of whether or not they were using Western Electric Transmitters.

WLW took the offer. In mid-1924, they made arrangements with the phone company to carry the Republican National Convention, live from Cleveland, and then the Democratic one, from New York City's Madison Square Garden.

AT&T wasn't giving the service away, of course. The cost to rent those lines for both conventions came to just under five thousand dollars, and that was most definitely an omen of things to come.

Another omen: an appearance that spring by the Tweedy Brothers, a jazz band out of West Virginia, on WLW, which had now taken up the slogan "The Station With A Soul."

Music still composed about three-quarters of its programming, but popular tastes—the tastes of the masses, as opposed to the classes—were shifting.

Powel paid little attention. He was, once more, on to the next thing, the newest thing, the latest, fastest thing.

In 1924, he bought himself an airplane.

. . . . . .

It was the Wright Brothers—Wilbur the elder, the visionary, Orville the younger, the engineering genius—who in 1903, working from their home in Dayton, Ohio, and a proving ground at Kitty Hawk, North Carolina, brought the miracle of powered flight to the world.

By the mid-1920s, a fledgling airline industry—jump-started by the U.S. Post Office's decision to use airplanes to deliver the mail—had sprung up. Interest in air travel, particularly among the well-to-do, began to grow.

Powel was among the first of those early air travelers. He started out by chartering a Buhl Air-Sedan when he had to be in two cities on a schedule that railroads couldn't accommodate. He grew to like the convenience and decided to buy an aircraft of his own.

Actually, he decided to buy two.

Both were Curtis JN-4D "Jenny" biplanes. Hundreds had recently been retired from Army service. Powel had the Crosley Radio logo (complete with lightning bolt) painted on the undersides of the wings, and "Crosley Radio" put on the fuselages.

He hired a pilot and off he went.

In September, he was in New York, for the NAB's second annual meeting. Most stations, despite the organization's stance against ASCAP, had by this point given in and were paying the society a modest license fee. RCA and Westinghouse were on the fence; Powel urged an education campaign; fight on, was his message.

He took it to Chicago for the fall Radio show. Then he was back in New York for the Radio World's Fair.

While his brother traveled about the country, Lewis stayed put.

The house on Belmont Ave was ready by this point. With four bedrooms and one and a half baths, it was plenty big for his family and any guests who might drop by. And then there was the backyard, big enough not just for his daughters to play in, but for his garden.

Every morning, before he went to the factories, Lewis slipped on overalls and a t-shirt and went to work in the soil. Every night, when he came home, after he ate dinner with the family, he did the same. By then Ellen was old enough to be given a few kernels of corn and to be shown the right way to plant them.

He was busy at home, he was busy at work, too. He had yet to take a vacation. No hint of one loomed on the horizon; Powel's latest push for more power had succeeded. Super-power—in the form of a new five-thousand-watt Western Electric 'radio telephone'— was coming to Cincinnati.

Hoover and the Department of Commerce had authorized, per subcommittee three's recommendation, superpower transmission on an experimental basis. Powel was anxious to start the experiment because once the new transmitter was on-line, his station would be, once again, the most powerful in the world.

Five thousand watts, however, was a lot of power. To minimize interference engineers decided to locate the transmitter well outside of town. An extensive survey of the counties surrounding Cincinnati had to be undertaken.

Luckily, the station had a civil engineer on staff.

The boss's brother.

After considering all factors, a site was chosen: a knoll outside Harrison, Ohio, twenty-five miles west of Cincinnati, on the Indiana border. Programming would travel from studios to transmitter over leased telephone lines. The transmitter itself would be remotely controlled from the studios, a first in broadcasting.

A transmitter with that type of power required a substantial antenna. Engineers drew up plans for a three-hundred-foot one, supported by twin two-hundred-foot towers. Each would be topped by a warning light for aviators; the north tower's beacon was red, the south's green.

Power requirements forced substantive additions to the local electric company's distribution plant. The cost of the new lines, transmitter, and antenna came to a bit over one hundred and fifty thousand dollars.

As always, the Crosley Corporation paid with cash on hand.

They forked over even more cash for an inaugural broadcast celebration on January 27, 1925. Actually two celebrations: one on the air, one in the studio at the WLW auditorium. The guest list for the latter included some of the most important people in the radio industry, as well as local celebrities and politicians. Powel arranged to have two luxury Pullman cars placed on Plant One's rail siding to accommodate them all.

Liquor was (discreetly) served.

Powel himself opened the broadcast. Other speakers, instrumental soloists, and a seemingly endless series of dance bands and orchestras (the latter including all five of WLW's own orchestras) followed.

Eugene MacDonald couldn't be there, but he sent a telegram: "Most sincere congratulations to 'The Henry Ford of Radio' on his latest accomplishment."

So did Edwin Armstrong: "Believe that the higher the power of WLW the greater will be your success."

And so did Secretary Hoover: "Experiments which you and others are conducting are of the greatest interest."

There were other experiments of great interest to the radio public going on as well, though at the time, few were aware of them. In the nation's capital scientists were puzzling the secrets of the skywave. The term referenced that part of the radio signal that bounced around the atmosphere, a very, very weak part of the overall signal, but one that by 1925, was of increasing concern to manufacturers, listeners, and broadcasters worldwide. By 1925, new receiving sets—such as RCA's super heterodyne, and ones incorporating the newly invented Hazeltine circuit—were orders of magnitude more sensitive. They were picking up the skywave, no matter how distant the originating signal.

Locally, WLW shared the 423-meter wavelength with Columbus station WBAV; they split the broadcast day. There was no interference.

There were dozens of other stations using that same wavelength, however. Those stations weren't in the same part of the country, but with the skywave, location didn't matter. People in Cincinnati and in every other town across America began to pick up more and more skywave signals. No one knew exactly how the wave propagated, what happened to it once it went up in the sky.

Scientists at the Department of Terrestrial Magnetism, interested in the electric properties of the upper atmosphere, decided to find out.

One of those scientists was Merle Tuve. The ex-farmboy by this point had moved on from South Dakota. No longer solely a radio amateur, he had a degree in physics from Princeton and by early 1925 was assisting in experiments at the Department of Terrestrial Magnetism in Washington relating to the skywave and associated electrical phenomena.

By summer, Tuve and his colleagues were front-page news—in the science journals, at least—for having puzzled out not just the mechanics behind the skywave's transmission, but the physical structure of the ionosphere itself.

It was the first time—however obliquely—the path of Merle Tuve and the Crosley Corporation were to cross.

There were more encounters to come.

· · · · ·

Science marched on at WLW as well.

Engineers installed permanent microphones in a variety of Cincinnati venues: Music Hall, the city and county courthouses, and the Hotel Sinton ballroom. Remote broadcasts became an integral part of the broadcast programming.

The studio upgraded again, installing an elaborate pipe organ in the big room. Made by Cincinnati's Rudolph Wurlitzer Company, it was a limited-production, state-of-the art instrument that cost in the neighborhood of ten thousand dollars.

Rumor had it Powel dedicated the organ to his mother.

Talent began showing up at the studio doors, looking for work. Soloists, musicians, instrumentalists. One band came in looking to show its stuff, accompanied by their own vocal backing group. The band was ordinary; the singers were anything but.

There were four of them, brothers, out of Piqua, Ohio, just north of Dayton. First names, Herbert, John, Don, and Harry; as fast as a pen could be found they were signed to a contract.

Grace Raine pitched in to fine-tune their act. The group, which had been playing at various nightspots as "Four Boys and a Kazoo," went to work for WLW under a variety of names. On Sunday evenings, they were the Tasty Yeast Jesters, in a program paid for by Fleischmann Yeast. Other nights, they were the Steamboat Four. And some nights, they were just themselves.

The Mills Brothers.

Fred Smith continued to experiment with programming. His approach went from the sublime (daily updates on the stages of the Ohio River) to the ridiculous ("Musical News," the day's headlines accompanied by appropriately themed organ pieces).

At five thousand watts, the programming reached virtually nationwide, no skywave necessary. WLW found itself competing for listeners in Cleveland, Indianapolis, Chicago, New York, Baltimore, and just about every city east of the Mississippi.

In February, more in-town competition arrived. The call letters WMH had been reassigned to a new concern at 423 meters. Now WLW, WBAV, and WMH had to work out an equitable division of the available broadcasting time.

But Powel was the number one figure in radio. His station was the most powerful in the country. He didn't want to give up a single minute of the broadcast day. His definition of equitable and WMH's diverged. Both stations began broadcasting Monday and Wednesday nights at the same time. The situation brought a whole new meaning to the word 'interference.'

It was chaos; it went on for weeks.

Secretary Hoover was reluctant to get involved, but at last, he sent two men from Washington to settle the problem. The settlement: WLW gave up early Wednesday evenings and agreed to split Wednesday nights from eight to ten p.m. with WMH. For a month.

The following month, 423 meters would belong to WLW solely, from eight till ten. But WSAI, on 309 meters, agreed to split their

Wednesdays from eight till ten with WMH, who switched broadcasting frequencies for that portion of the day, that one night a week, for every other month. It was confusing, to say the least.

Monday night arrangements were even more complicated.

By the end of the year, the broadcast band was so crowded that Hoover simply stopped issuing licenses. Those on the outside looking in, businesses, individuals, and educational institutions desiring to utilize the new medium for their own purposes, steamed.

At the same time, conclusions of more lasting import were being reached at the federal courthouse. On February 7, the United States Circuit Court began hearing ASCAP's appeal in the "Dreamy Melody" case.

On April 10, they overturned Judge Hickenlooper's verdict. The court declared the copyright law did cover radio broadcasting. Radio broadcasts were legally considered public performances.

Score two for ASCAP.

Powel's lawyers began preparing an appeal of their own.

Powel put on knickers and an overcoat and headed to Redland Field, where he climbed to the top of the grandstand and called the first few innings of the Reds 1925 Opening Day game himself.

The Reds beat the Cardinals, 4-0. Powel shared the microphone with Stayman, Plough, and a retired semi-pro player named Carl Scholl.

In College Hill, on Belmont Avenue, Lewis was sharing too. Lucy's older sister, Laura, was coming to stay with the family, and so they opened up the spare bedroom and began preparing for her arrival.

At this time, Powel was developing an open-door policy. Despite the troubles with the Go Bi-Bi and the ongoing lawsuit with Frank Taylor, Powel was always on the lookout for new ideas, always on the hunt for the next big thing.

One day a thirty-one-year-old inventor named Charles W. Peterson, stepped into his office with an idea for a new kind of speaker—a conical piece of parchment that would reproduce sound by means of mechanical vibration, an infinitely superior method than the one utilized by the tinny horn speakers then in use.

Powel put Peterson in Charles Kilgour's hands and sent both men down the hall to the engineering labs to start experimenting.

They were experimenting on the factory floor, too.

Sales were way down on the Model 50. The one-tube set was—in this day of the super heterodyne and Hazeltine circuit—on the way out. The factory, however, had already manufactured thousands of cabinets and radio parts for new Model 50 sets. Lewis had come up with a plan to package amplifiers in the already-produced cabinets, but the "guts" of thousands of radios still remained.

Powel sensed an opportunity.

He wondered if those guts could serve as the basis for a different kind of radio, a small one that could retail for under ten dollars.

He asked his engineers how small a cabinet they could fit the parts into. They came up with a little box that measured 3-3/4" x 4-1/8" x 4-5/8", small enough to fit into the palm of a person's hand. The receiver's single tube was mounted on the top, outside the cabinet. Each of four sides had a control or connector mounted on it. The whole thing weighed less than a pound.

Powel nicknamed it the 'Pup.'

It went out at $9.75—sans (of course) tube, batteries, headphones and aerial.

It was more radio for less money than anything else on the market.

It was a unique product. To sell it, the company came up with a whole new advertising campaign, featuring a little dog, a Skye Terrier, wearing headphones while listening to the new, smaller (Better—costs less) Crosley radio.

They brought WLW in on the promotion too, introducing a female singing group called the Crosley Skye Terriers. With the canine theme established (perhaps modeled on RCA's famous Nipper), Crosley marketing people elaborated.

In-store promotions were introduced, featuring Bonzo, the creation of British cartoonist George Studdy, a clownish, pudgy little creature with big feet, big blue eyes, and a smiling, crinkled face.

Tremendously popular in Europe, by 1925 Bonzo had crossed the Atlantic to North America. There were Bonzo books and Bonzo Toys as well as promotional "glamour shots" of the little dog with movie starlets.

The character's popularity was still on the rise when it became the Pup's official emblem. Crosley dealers were provided with fourteen-foot papier-mâché Bonzo figures wearing Crosley headphones. Newspapers were given publicity photos of the dog listening to the new Crosley radio.

Powel was in the picture as well, smiling down at the half-asleep pooch.

That marketing campaign targeted the low end of the market. For the high end, the company turned once more to *The Saturday Evening Post*.

An elaborate four-page ad appeared in the magazine's September 12, 1925, issue, accompanied by stunning artwork that portrayed the full Crosley line. The ad cost twenty-eight thousand dollars.

A six-page version appeared in *Radio Digest*'s October 31 issue.

Powel was the centerpiece of the new campaign, which praised him almost as much as Crosley radios. He was the "Master of Mass Production." His radios were "the Crowning Accomplishment in a Career of Radio Leadership." *The Saturday Evening Post* ad drew comments from several financial papers, among them the *Wall Street Journal*.

Crosley radios had already drawn local attention for another publicity stunt they'd pulled back on June 29, during a game between the Reds and the Chicago Cubs.

Eric Matchette of the Milnor Electric Company and reserve outfielder Tommy Griffith of the Cubs (a Cincinnati native who was about to retire and open a radio store in Norwood) spent the first two innings of the game setting up a Crosley Trirdyn receiver in one of the boxes at the ballpark. Griffith then beckoned to Cubs teammate Cliff Heathcoat and, as several thousand fans looked on in astonishment, sold him the complete set-up.

The radio didn't help the Cubs, who lost 6-2. The Reds club

**Crosley Corporation
Board Meeting, ca. 1939.
Lewis, Powel, and Powel III
at the head of the table.**

Make ICE from Heat

at a Cost of only 2¢ a Day

**Cold from heat, refrigeration
without electricity.
The most profitable product in
the corporation's history:
The Icyball.**

Pinecroft, as it exists today: a Franciscan retreat and holistic health center.

A boat party at Seagate in the early thirties. Revelers take to the lawn: that's Powel on the right, sitting cross-legged, playing with a camera. Neill Prew is the boy to his left. Eugene MacDonald is the man standing behind him, holding his hat in hand. Gwendolyn is in the center of the page, in the dark coat and hat. Standing in the rear, off to the left are Powel Crosley, Sr. and Powel Crosley, III (white jacket and cap).

The Aviation Pioneer with John Paul Riddle, who flew Powel's WACO in the 1927 Air Tour.

12 CROSLEY

Powel with the Crosley WACO flown in the 1927 National Air Tour.

Gwendolyn.
She was there every step
of the way.

Charlotte Jeanne, Powel III, Page,
early nineteen twenties.

Powel III. Trapped.

The Arlington Street facility: assembly-line radios, refrigerators, and broadcasting. The executive tower is on the right. WLW's studios were on the eighth floor.

Credit: Michael A. Banks (Both images this spread)

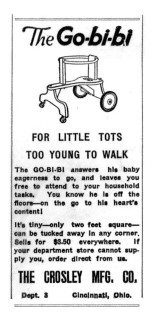

Go Bi-Bi advertisment

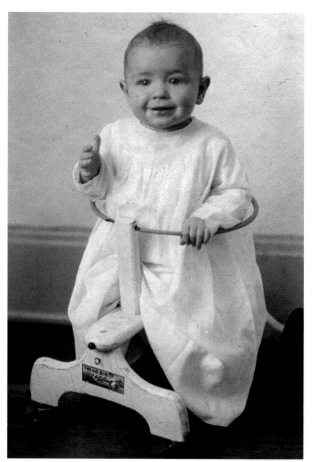

Ellen on the Go Bi-Bi – "she just didn't want to stop!"

1924, transmitter dedication ceremony. Powel and Lewis, Ellen in between with flowers.

went on to finish the season six and a half games behind the Giants, fifteen back of the Pirates, who, under manager Bill McKechnie, an ex-Reds infielder who would play a significant role in the team's success down the road—beat the Washington Senators in the World Series, four games to three.

Flags flew at half-mast throughout the games.

They flew in honor of Christy Mathewson, who had suffered a relapse that summer. The gas, the tuberculosis, and the strain of trying to run a ball club had gotten to him.

He died on October 8, opening day of the series.

Back at Plant Number One, Lewis added a night shift.

And the Twenties roared on.

CHAPTER 16

Powel was in New York for the NAB's third annual meeting, where he was elected vice-president. Then he was in Washington for the fourth annual radio conference, where he and David Sarnoff sat together on committee four and considered the general problems of broadcasting. Then he was back in Cincinnati for the holidays, and then off to Mississippi to hunt and back in Ohio again in time for WLW to celebrate its fifth anniversary.

They commemorated the event with a thirty-hour marathon broadcast. Powel hosted part of the show from his Davey Avenue living room, just like the old days, courtesy of a special Cincinnati Suburban Telephone and Telegraph hook-up.

The station's staff numbered seventeen at this point. Fred Smith was still in charge, Robert Stayman was now (officially) publicity director, Rudolph Stoess musical director, Grace Raine, vocal coach.

WLW was broadcasting forty or so hours a week, some of it old, some of it new. Talk shows were becoming an integral part of the broadcast schedule as were religious programs. There were weather forecasts, market reports, reports on the stages of the Ohio River. Most daytime shows featured piano or organ music.

They were still making it up as they went, and Smith was still innovating as fast as he could. In 1926 he scripted a multiple-part adaptation of a story published in *Radio Digest*, titled *The Step on the Stair*, giving birth to the mystery serial. Fred made other additions to the station's repertoire: Saturday night dramas, children's action-adventure shows, interviews, and even a hillbilly variety half-hour.

Fred's boss added to his repertoire as well.

Powel bought a yacht, the *Muroma*, a forty-foot vessel based in Miami. He bought the clothes—white slacks, blue blazer, ascot, and officer's cap—to go with it. In February, he and Gwendolyn took a month-long cruise along the Florida coast to break in the boat.

He bought more land on Kipling Road.

He bought DeForest Radio of Canada, giving the company a presence north of the border.

He hired away the Columbia Phonograph Company's foreign sales representative, Charles S. Hopkins, to run a powerful network of retailers and distributors in Europe, Africa, and the Middle East.

He bought AMRAD, giving him the Neutrodyne circuit.

He saw a new fuel, oil, replacing coal in home heating and sensed a market opportunity. He decided to build an oil burner. He went to Lewis, because of course, when the older brother wanted to diversify, it was the younger brother's job to figure out how. As always, when Powel came to him with a new idea, Lewis had a question.

That question was not about projected consumer demand for the new appliance. It was not about engineering considerations or available factory space. It wasn't about marketing strategy or competing products. It had nothing to do with whether or not Lewis thought the idea was a good one. That wasn't his role in the business. His job wasn't thinking of the idea; it was making the idea work. It was making the idea profitable.

The question Lewis asked was the same one he'd asked back when they had talked about getting into the camera business and when they first thought about building radios, canoes, and phonographs:

How much money are we going to put into this?

How much money are we prepared to lose before calling it a day?

For the new home heating appliance, they came up with a ballpark figure: eighty thousand dollars.

Then they came up with the Crosley Oil Burner—guaranteed clog-proof, equipped with electronic ignition, guaranteed not to cause radio interference.

It was on the market by fall.

And it was gone shortly thereafter.

That fate was fine, in a manner of speaking, by both of them. They'd done their jobs.

Powel dreamt it; Lewis built it.

They had been in business together for going on eight years by that point. Powel was nearly forty that summer, Lewis approaching thirty-eight.

"I'm glad I have someone around here who keeps me down," Powel always said about Lewis.

Lewis was one of the few people who could stand up to Powel, who could get Powel to consider the full ramifications of his actions before he flitted off again. Something about Lewis's solid, patient nature balanced Powel's hyperactive one, made the older brother slow down and think an idea through to the end. It was a nearly perfect synergy. If Lewis did not have Powel he would have lacked the force of personality and imagination to achieve greatness. He would have been mildly successful, perhaps, at a job offering far less responsibility. Without Lewis, Powel would have run the company into the ground, scattering his resources in pursuit of one idea after the next. Together they were far more effective than either man could have been alone. As partners, each knew his role and felt comfortable with the situation.

It was not to stay that way forever.

. . . . . .

By mid-year, the plants were turning out nearly seven thousand sets a week. The Musicone was flying off the shelves as well. Powel got an offer from unnamed Eastern bankers to purchase the Crosley Radio Corporation for six million dollars.

He turned it down.

. . . . . .

They needed more room. The brothers thought about moving again, but instead decided to build a six-story addition onto the Colerain Avenue plant, which would add 120,000 square feet of manufacturing space.

The need for sales literature had grown exponentially as well; Powel and Lewis bought a new, bigger building for National Label, moving it from downtown Cincinnati to Colerain Avenue, around the corner from Plant number one.

They paid for everything, as always, with cash on-hand.

While Crosley Corp expanded, AT&T downsized.

In mid-1926, after much heat from the press over its 'monopolistic' ambitions, after much behind the scenes battling with RCA over tubes, radio sets, and transmitters, and after much consideration of its own overall corporate goals, the phone company concluded it no longer wanted to be in the broadcasting business. AT&T made arrangements to sell WEAF and its entire network of stations. RCA's board of directors, led once more by Owen Young, created a new concern to purchase that network, the National Broadcasting Company.

The brand-new radio network was co-owned by the old patent pool partnership: RCA (50 percent), Westinghouse (20 percent), and GE (30 percent). NBC made its debut in November 1926 with not one but two broadcast chains—the Red Network, the old WEAF web of stations, and the Blue Network, RCA's old WJZ chain, each named after the color-coded lines AT&T engineers used to distinguish its circuits. One of the first things they did on incorporation was issue an additional fifteen thousand shares of stock, at one hundred dollars each, to provide operating capital.

Almost immediately, cries of monopoly were heard.

GE was adding to its repertoire as well. The continuing electrification of rural America—the spread of AC power plants and power lines across the country—had created a huge new market for electric-powered household appliances, washing machines, irons, refrigerators, and so on. GE dove into the business headfirst, finding particular success with the Monitor-Top Refrigerator, which quickly became the best-selling model in the industry.

Allegations of monopoly still dogged RCA. Tired of the FTC's questions about their intents and tired of paying lawyers, the company set up a simple licensing policy regarding its basic patents, a royalty to be paid on every set sold using their patented inventions.

The first two companies to purchase the new RCA licenses were Zenith and Crosley. Powel and Eugene MacDonald were at the forefront of another deal as well, the one between NAB and ASCAP. Crosley's appeal to the Supreme Court had failed. The judges sided with the composers, affirming that the broadcast of ASCAP songs was "public performance for profit."

Strike three for the NAB.

At the organization's 1926 meeting (which Powel chaired), an argument broke out between Powel and a man named George Coats, a music promoter, regarding the situation. Coats thought the broadcasters were fools for knuckling under. Powel pointed out that the courts had given them no choice, adding that he had no problem paying ASCAP a reasonable fee, but ASCAP's definition of reasonable seemed to change from moment to moment, from station to station. They agreed to disagree on the matter. Coats, his blood boiling, walked out of the NAB meeting and straight into history, though that history would not be written for some months to come.

MacDonald was at the center of another controversy that year. He had a Class B station of his own, WJAZ in Chicago. Like Powel, he had to share airtime, but whereas the Commerce Department allotted WLW forty hours of broadcast time a week, they were far less generous with WJAZ.

They received two—a grand total of a hundred twenty minutes.

MacDonald wasn't having it.

He moved his station to another frequency, one that had been reserved for Canadian broadcasters. Hoover told him to move back. He refused. The case went to court, which sided with MacDonald. The commander's station stayed put on the dial.

The radio industry, however, shuddered.

Hoover had been begging Congress for meaningful radio legislation since the Radio Conference of 1922. He'd led broadcasters as much as his powers allowed under the Radio Act of 1912. But the court decision gave him no power of regulation whatsoever. The industry was now—had always been, in fact—free to do whatever it wanted.

All hell broke loose.

Hoover had issued no new licenses since the Radio Conference of 1925; two hundred new stations now took to the airwaves. Old stations jumped frequencies; interference problems multiplied; sales of radio receivers, for the first time that decade, fell.

The industry's shudder turned into a full-fledged spasm.

In Florida, the real-estate business, which had been booming ever since Carl Fisher dredged Miami Beach, shuddered as well. A series of reversals had struck the Gold Coast; land that had gone from worthless swamp to priceless beachfront almost overnight was suddenly without value once more. The capper came September 18, 1926, when a hurricane struck Miami Beach. Carl Fisher, who'd been trying to repeat his success in Miami on Long Island, at a planned Montauk development, hurried home to try to save the city he'd built.

But his luck, at last, had run out.

Fisher lost everything—his fortune, his house, and Jane Watts, the fifteen-year-old girl he'd married sixteen years earlier.

North of Miami, in Sarasota, the real-estate market collapsed as well. John McGraw, who'd lent his name to a real-estate development that featured a Christy Mathewson Drive was among those hit. Hit harder were the Ringling brothers, John and Charles, who owned mansions next to each other along the coast and who'd been instrumental in building Sarasota from nothing.

The *Muroma*, Powel's yacht, was based out of Miami. He and Gwendolyn's cruise had given them a "bird's-eye view" of the real-estate boom, and the news about the bust hit them hard.

But neither event—the fall of the gold coast, or the Commerce Department's failed attempts to regulate the broadcast band—could stall the Crosley brothers.

For both, the twenties roared on bigger and better with each passing year.

.   .   .   .   .   .

On Davey Avenue, Powel's family was growing. Powel III was sixteen; Page two years younger. Both of them, at Powel's insistence, were riding, Page somewhat reluctantly, They kept their horses in the Cummings stables next door. In return, they let Dorothy Cummings use their pool.

Powel was a dark-haired, quiet boy, with a ready smile who still tended toward chubbiness. Page, meanwhile, had blossomed into a stunning young woman who was—in Dorothy Cummings's words—"boy crazy." The Cummings family had bought a handsome new Lincoln town car and hired a handsome chauffeur to drive it around. Page, in turn, took every opportunity to follow the driver.

Dorothy Cummings's mother found the young Crosley girl an annoyance.

It was not destined to last too much longer.

Nor was NBC's monopoly on network programming.

George Coats, who had stormed out of the NAB meeting after his argument with Powel back in September, was intent on showing those composers what for and decided that the broadcasting business need not just a program bureau, but an entirely new source of programming—a network independent of the Radio Corporation's tentacles. By and by, he obtained financing for his new enterprise, first from Bettie Fleischmann Holmes, late of Cincinnati, then the Columbia Victor Phonograph Company, then Jerome Lochheim of Philadelphia, and (finally) a young man named William S. Paley, whose family owned the Congress Cigar Company.

By and by, the Columbia Broadcasting System was born.

And while Coats built his network, Powel, at last, built his dream house.

.   .   .   .   .   .

CHAPTER 16

Henry Ford had Fair Lane—a thirteen-hundred-acre estate on the outskirts of Dearborn, Michigan.

William Randoph Hearst had La Cuesta Encantada ('The Enchanted Hill'), a fifty-six-bedroom, sixty-one-bathroom castle halfway between Los Angeles and San Francisco.

John Ringling had Ca'd'Zan in Sarasota. Atwater Kent had estates in Maine, Florida, and Pennsylvania.

And now Powel Crosley, Jr. had Pinecroft.

The name came from the stands of pine trees that dotted the property he and Gwendolyn had accumulated. It had a vaguely British sound to it, which suited the home to be built there, though in years to come, the name would be seldom-used by anyone but the press. Powel, and his family, usually referred to Pinecroft as "the big house."

And big it was—13,300 square feet, though it wasn't so much the square footage of the main house that impressed as the estate as a whole, which was styled in the manner of an old English country home, with certain Powel-specific additions.

A landing strip for his airplanes. A garage big enough to hold his ever-increasing collection of cars. Formal gardens, of course, on two levels, and an Olympic-size swimming pool. A bathhouse with a half-dozen changing rooms and a fireplace. A short golf course. Tennis courts, which were flooded when winter came to make an ice-skating rink. A stable for his polo ponies and bluegrass fields for them to graze on. Kennels for his dogs. A pigeon loft. An orchard and a vineyard. A vegetable garden that took up an entire acre of the property. Cattle. A milking parlor. A chicken coop. A greenhouse complex. A man-made lake five acres wide, filled with bass and bluegill.

And then there was the house itself, designed by a New York City architect named Dwight James Baum, who came to Powel through Sarasota and John Ringling's Ca D'Zan, which Baum had also worked on. The architecture was English Tudor, brick and stone with a slate roof. Parts of the second floor were half-timbered, with brick and simulated wattle and daub between the wood timbers. Much of the stone was brought from the Cotswold region of England, and several artisans came with it to work on the construction.

The main entranceway was roofed, enclosed on two sides by half-timbered walls. To the right of the entrance, a circular tower topped by a crenellate displayed the Crosley coat of arms and the family motto, "Per Cruceum Con Fido" ("In the Cross We Trust"), etched in stone. Etched above the motto were Powel's initials.

A massive wooden door opened into the home's foyer. The first thing visitors saw on entering was a deluxe Skinner organ similar to the one in WLW's studios. On the newel post of a stairway that faced visitors entering the hall was a life-size carved monkey wearing headphones, listening (presumably) to a Crosley radio. That stairway led up a half-flight to a long, windowed landing, and then up another half-flight to the second floor, to Powel and Gwendolyn's bedroom suites on the south end of the house, each with its own bath, fireplace, and walk-in closet.

Powel's room was done in dark oak, Gwendolyn's in softer woods. The bathrooms were done in marble, with Rookwood tile; down the hall, Page had a suite of rooms of her own, with another bath. Powel III's room was opposite hers.

Powel's office was upstairs as well. The windows in it were of stained glass and featured several designs, among them the shield of his (almost) alma mater, the University of Cincinnati.

Downstairs, the kitchen included stainless steel fixtures and the latest in appliances. There was a freezer big enough to accommodate six men lying on the floor. Six fireplaces served the home, venting heat through three pairs of twin brick chimneys, done in a stunning spiral pattern. Additional heat was provided by two automatic coal burners, the manufacturer of which subsequently featured photos of the house and Powel in product advertisements.

There was a butler's pantry, a formal dining room, and a library, which doubled as a family room. An elaborate radio aerial ran across the top of the house.

There was a basement with a game room, dominated by landscape paintings on the walls and heavy carpet on the floor. High windows on one wall admitted light via window wells. There were stained glass windows too, decorated with scenes that reflected

Powel's interests—an angler landing a trout, a hunter in a field.

There was a workshop, with the newest and most expensive power tools available. There was an exercise room. A cupboard door in the kitchen concealed a room-size walk-in safe, where the silver was stored. In the basement, off the game room, a second hidden chamber—tucked beneath a stone spiral staircase, and protected by a thick steel door with a combination lock—was big enough to hold a party in, which was no doubt the idea. It included racks for liquor and wine bottles.

The south end of the house featured an enormous walled outdoor entertaining area, with entrances from the house and the front garden. Two garages were built into the north end of the manor: a separate building housing a two-car garage with chauffeur's quarters above faced them across a paved parking apron.

The estate's main entrance was guarded by a gatehouse. Above was an elaborate stone façade, guarded by two stone lions, presented by two dragons rampant clutching snakes on either side of a shield.

A Cincinnati builder named Edward Honnert handled most of the construction.

A Cincinnati civil engineer named Lewis Crosley served as general contractor on the project, conducting preliminary surveys, letting contracts, and doing much of the hands-on landscaping for his brother's five-acre lake.

By mid-year, work on Pinecroft was completed. It cost roughly $750,000, exclusive of furnishings—a significant sum of money in a time when a new, well-equipped three-bedroom house on a nice lot in a good neighborhood sold for five thousand dollars.

At Pinecroft, Powel didn't really have any neighbors. He had a staff—a chauffeur, a gardener, a gatekeeper, a maid, a cook, and a housekeeper.

His days of running into the town hall maintenance man were over.

On Belmont Avenue, Dorothy Cummings ran into Lewis Henshaw, the son of Lucy Crosley's sister Ellen, who lived across the street. Sparks flew. The two young people were soon wed.

Lucy's other sister, Laura, who had been staying with her and Lewis, took ill and died. Lucy and youngest daughter Ellen took a train to Philadelphia and fetched another one of Lucy's sisters, Mary, whose husband had recently passed on. Mary took up residence in the spare bedroom.

Lewis and Lucy, stirred to action, built an addition onto their home. A whole new wing of the house that added space upstairs and down. While watching the men at work on her family's new patio through her bedroom window, Ellen, now five years old, decided she wanted to become a bricklayer when she grew up.

Charlotte Jeanne, who recently turned fourteen, held a taffy pull for her friends.

Babe Ruth hit sixty home runs and led the 1927 Yankees to the pennant and a World Series sweep of the Pirates. The Reds finished in the second division, eighteen and a half games back, another bad year for the team and a worse one for Garry Herrmann, who had served as president of the club for almost a quarter-century. Herrmann was sixty-eight and losing his hearing. He retired. The team's board of directors chose a man named C.J. McDiarmid, who had been the club's secretary, to replace him.

Changes were afoot in Washington as well. Congress had, at last, stirred to action, and passed the Radio Act of 1927, codifying in legislation the basic principles Herbert Hoover had declared back in 1922. The government owned the airwaves, as a public trust. License to broadcast over those airwaves was granted at the government's discretion. The government was now exercising that discretion. All existing broadcasting licenses were hereby declared null and void, said directive to take effect in sixty days. Congress had, in effect, decided to start all over again.

So did Powel.

He entered the refrigerator business.

CHAPTER 17

He and Lewis began looking into the idea of refrigerators early in 1927. One of the first things they did was hire a young engineer from Toronto named David Forbes Keith to help them investigate electric-powered absorption technology. One day Keith mentioned an idea he'd patented in Canada, a design for an absorption refrigeration system that required no electricity. He showed some sketches to Lewis, who was intrigued by the design's simplicity.

It was a metal cabinet and a dumbbell. The dumbbell was actually two hollow nine-inch balls, connected by a hollow tube four inches in diameter. One ball held a mixture of water and gaseous ammonia. You heated it on a stove for about an hour, until the mixture evaporated and moved to the other ball, where it condensed into a liquid.

Then you put the dumbbell into the metal cabinet, which was actually an insulated chest; there was a slot in the cabinet for the hollow tube. The hot ball stayed outside the chest, the cool one in.

Over a day's time, the liquid in the cold ball evaporated and flowed back into the hot ball, carrying with it the heat it had absorbed, cooling the interior of the chest. The 'refrigerator effect' lasted about a day, at which point you pulled the dumbbell out of its slot, and repeated the process again.

And that was it. There were no moving parts. There was nothing to break. There was nothing like it out on the market. Lewis talked to Powel, and they decided to build a prototype.

Their big concern was product safety; ammonia was highly flammable, even mixed at 40 percent strength, as per Keith's design specifications. They feared the contents of the dumbbell might explode. They tried everything they could to generate that worst-case scenario but couldn't.

They decided to bring the product to market. Lewis still insisted on carrying product liability insurance, on the one-in-a-million chance that some customer might produce an explosion.

Keith filed for a U.S. patent in June of 1927 through Crosley's attorneys, licensing the invention to his employers on a royalty basis.

Powel of course, named the product: the "Icyball."

As always, Lewis and Powel set an undisclosed dollar amount they were prepared to lose on the product. Engineers modified Keith's basic design to better suit it for mass production. The company laid out another chunk of cash for production lines at a building a few blocks down Colerain Avenue.

The non-electric refrigerator taken care of, they turned to the electric-powered radio. The acquisition of the RCA patent license, along with the maturation of technology allowing sets to run off AC current as opposed to those heavy batteries, allowed Crosley to mass-produce, and bring to market nine new radio models, including the Bandbox and its companion models, the Jewelbox, Gembox, and Showbox, which were actually one radio, the Bandbox receiver placed in differing cabinets.

The company continued to expand overseas, adding a distributor in Hong Kong and introducing two sets designed expressly for the European market. Orders from abroad created a new level of complexity to the manufacturing process. New tuners and dials had to be fashioned to accommodate foreign frequency ranges, and new tubes and sockets were needed because of differing power requirements. Wherever possible, cabinet and dial designs were standardized. But some American styles weren't popular overseas, and sometimes there was outright resistance to importing American products.

No matter their eventual destination, all Crosley radios were built in Cincinnati. Radio and speaker cabinets were still made at the old wood shop, parts and components at the building on Alfred Street. National Label ran off tens of thousands of instructional manuals, applause cards, product brochures, and catalogs daily from its new location on Colerain Ave. Everything came together at the newly expanded Plant Number One, where two shifts of workers assembled, tested, and shipped radios to the four corners of the earth.

Each of those workers received a copy of the Crosley Corporation Employee Handbook, which emphasized they were part of the Crosley family, They were instructed to say they worked *with* Powel, not *for* him.

But he was rarely there to work with. They might read about him in the papers or the *Crosley Radio Weekly* (now renamed the *Crosley Broadcaster*), but Powel to most of the line employees was an abstract symbol, a larger-than-life figure akin to other symbols of the time—Babe Ruth, Henry Ford, even President Calvin Coolidge. They rarely saw him. He was the public face of the corporation, but Lewis was the face everybody knew on the factory floor. He was the man they saw everyday, walking the floor, watching the production lines. He was always there, in fact; he never took a vacation.

They noticed. So did Lucy and Charlotte Jeanne and Ellen. They also noticed that the stress was beginning to show. Lucy thought the problem was Powel, who she saw as demanding and ungrateful.

"Your brother's taking advantage of you," she would tell Lewis. "You ought to get a new job."

Lewis would smile and head into the garden to see how the tomatoes were doing.

Whether or not the problem was Powel, Lucy was right that the daily grind of running the factories, of overseeing WLW, of being responsible for the company's bottom line was like a bubble growing inside him.

Sooner or later, it was going to burst.

.   .   .   .   .   .

In early 1927, a new name joined the ranks of the larger-than-life figures that ruled the Roaring Twenties. Charles Lindbergh was a twenty-seven-year-old pilot who contracted for the U.S. Post Office. On May 20, he climbed into a plane he'd christened *The Spirit of St. Louis* and began a one-man, twenty-seven-hour flight across the Atlantic, intent on reaching Paris and claiming a twenty-five-thousand-dollar prize offered by a New York City hotel owner.

The money would prove to be chump change.

When reports reached America of Lindbergh's safe arrival in Le Bourget airfield, the entire country went mad with triumph and relief. Lindbergh became the biggest celebrity of the era. Newspapers describing his feat sold out nationwide; the *New York Evening World* printed 114,000 extra copies of the edition announcing his landing.

When Lindbergh arrived in the States, there was a parade in Washington; there was one in New York; there were parades nationwide. Thousands of people sent congratulatory telegrams. A town in Texas renamed itself in his honor. He was offered millions of dollars to tour the world by air. He received the Congressional Medal of Honor, and the Distinguished Flying Cross. He was commissioned a Colonel in the United States Army.

Lindbergh's feat set off a boom in the aviation industry.

Up in Troy, Ohio, the Advance Aircraft Company cashed in. They produced a new airplane, the Waco 10, a sturdy, open-compartment biplane that proved wildly popular. Nearly a third of all aircraft sold in that boom year of 1927 were Waco 10s.

Powel bought one too.

He had the Crosley logo painted on each side of the fuselage aft of the wings, next to the airplane's entry number, 12. "Cincinnati" appeared on the forward part of the fuselage and beneath the two-seat passenger compartment was the image of a stork carrying a Crosley Bandbox radio.

He nicknamed the plane "The Crosley Stork," and entered it in Edsel Ford's National Air Show tour.

The entry was a publicity stunt, of course, designed to promote the new Bandbox. The tour was scheduled to start in Detroit and head east to Buffalo. From there, stops were scheduled in (among other places) Schenectady, Boston, New York, Dayton, Cincinnati, Dallas, Wichita, and Omaha, before ending in Grand Rapids, Michigan.

Alvin Plough visited every stop a month ahead of time. He made contact with Crosley distributors and dealers, as well as the local press. The plan was to have the plane met by those dealers, and photographed by newspapers and magazines whenever possible. Receptions were set up at local venues, and the company sent out a barrage of press releases before, during, and after the tour.

John Paul Riddle, of the Embry-Riddle Company (who'd finished fifth in the previous year's tour) was the pilot; Crosley sales manager Harry Sherwin was the passenger. Powel flew to Detroit with them the day before the tour started to kick off the promotion onslaught and to party with the Fords—Edsel and his son Henry II— as well as other aviators and various aircraft builders.

He flew the Buffalo leg of the race in the Stork. On arrival, he was met by distributors, who'd bused in scores of Crosley dealers and potential dealers for the event. There was a big reception that night. The next day, Powel returned to Cincinnati. Riddle and Sherwin flew on, finishing the tour in sixth place, which Powel considered a bonus.

The real reward, of course, was the crowds they drew at every stop. Thousands of people got a look not only at the Stork but the new Bandbox set and heard, for the first time, the company's new slogan:

"You're there with a Crosley."

The promotion cost nearly twenty thousand dollars. It was the first of many such campaigns centered on aviation.

Beyond radios, the company moved briefly back into the phonograph business. In early 1927 they introduced the Merola, a device that converted the mechanical output of a conventional phonograph into an electrical signal, one that could be reproduced through a radio's speaker. The market was temporary; record players with built-in amplifiers were on the way. But while the market was there, they served it.

Meanwhile Congress had passed along the work of reorganizing the broadcast band to a bipartisan committee, the Federal Radio Commission. The five-member group created by the Radio Act received a year's charter to deal with the chaos. It was complicated, difficult work, in the words of broadcast historian Thomas White, "a high-pressure assignment."

Two of the five appointees died before the group started; new members had to be confirmed, and appointed. The sixty-day license extension granted all stations had to be extended several times. As the committee set about its business, they ran smack into the same questions Herbert Hoover had been dealing with since 1922.

The airwaves were owned by the government, to be regulated and used to serve the public interest. But what, exactly, was the public interest? Some thought more small stations with local programming would provide the best service. Others believed superpower—stations that could reach to the far corners of the continent and the wide-open spaces in between—was the way to go.

Powel was most definitely in the latter camp.

Superpower for him served two purposes: one, he felt an obligation to provide the people who'd bought his radios something to listen to, and superpower let him reach more of them; Two, the more powerful he made his station, the cheaper he could make his radios.

He was at five thousand watts now and wanted to take the next step up. Actually, he wanted to skip the next step.

He wanted to go to fifty thousand watts.

He'd been planning the jump for some time, having placed an order for a new Western Electric transmitter several months earlier. As the FRC sorted out the broadcast band, engineers prepared the transmitter site in Harrison for the hike in power.

In June, the FRC moved WLW from 710 on the dial (kilohertz, not meters; new nomenclature to replace the old) to 700. They shared time there with two much smaller stations, WMAF in Massachusetts and KFBU in Wyoming. The commission began the hard work of weeding out undesirables—those who in its judgment were not serving the public interest—from the broadcast band.

The number of radio stations in Cincinnati went from twenty-one to four.

In College Hill, Grace Episcopal Church moved to a new building, a brand-new Gothic Revival structure. They were anxious to attract new members to help finance the new structure. Lewis—not a particularly religious man, more of a Universalist himself, in fact, in the mode of his uncle Marion, a man of faith but no particular creed—joined the vestry, at Lucy's behest, to help in the recruiting process, press the flesh, and manage the church's affairs.

Lucy was an active member of the congregation. She and Gwendolyn both, in fact, were members of the Junior Cooperative Society, a group that, working through Grace Episcopal, helped raise a lot of money for the Cincinnati Children's Hospital. The two of them were not only relatives, they were friends.

Their children—the older three, at least—were friends as well. Ellen, however, traveled in more limited circles, having recently outgrown the Go Bi-Bi; Powel III was the proud owner of a new Ford Model A, the second one off the line to arrive in Cincinnati.

Powel had bought it for him.

He'd bought himself a little something too: a farm.

It was at the northern end of Colerain Avenue, about six miles from the plant. It was a working farm with an orchard, and there was a farmhouse on the property occupied by a farmer and his family. The farm wasn't for Powel as much as it was for the Crosley Radio Corporation. He planned to use it as the new site for the company's picnics and distributor conventions.

Those conventions were becoming ever more elaborate. To reward the people who sold his radios to dealers, Powel arranged not just picnics, but formal dinners. He took them (and their wives) on riverboat cruises and bought them tickets to Reds games.

The company's meteoric rise over the past seven years, however, had been mirrored by a concomitant rise in the number of distributors. Lewis took on the hard work of thinning their ranks. By the time he was finished, there were only eighty distributors nationwide handling Crosley products. It was "a terrible job," he said later, but when your point of comparison was recalcitrant German prisoners of war…

One of those still selling the Crosley line of products after Lewis's purge was a man named Henry Hulse, who'd run a garage in the town of Vernon, Indiana, just over the Ohio border. Powel was a frequent visitor to the garage. Before building Pinecroft, he'd kenneled his hunting dogs with a breeder in the area, which was rich with game birds, particularly quail. The fishing in Jennings was excellent too.

He started buying land in the area early in the year—and stopped when he reached about four thousand acres. Then he built himself a little hunting lodge on the property—eight bedrooms, four baths, big kitchen, screened-in porch—that, by and by, acquired the name Sleepy Hollow.

Over time he put in an airstrip. He put in new roads. He built a bridge over the Muscatuck River, which flowed through the property. He built a dam on the Muscatuck too, to provide deeper water fishing. He built a second dam to back up one of the creeks that ran through the property. He built a two-story boathouse—fireplace, kitchen, bedrooms, full bath—over the fifteen-acre lake that ran through the property, which by and by, acquired a new name: Crosley Lake.

They tore down abandoned buildings, ripped up old fences, grew pasture land, built kennels and outbuildings, brought in and raised cattle, hogs, sheep, and of course, game birds.

Birds by the thousands—bobwhite, partridge, pheasants, and quail.

Powel would call ahead when he wanted to hunt; his staff would have the dogs ready, the birds turned loose.

There were more than a dozen members of the staff.

There were no neighbors.

.   .   .   .   .   .

By mid-1927 there was another NBC network: the Pacific, which now joined the Red and Blue in supplying programs to stations across the country.

By September, CBS—now firmly under the direction of William S. Paley, George Coats having dropped out of the picture entirely—was up and running as well.

Chain broadcasting, network broadcasting, was clearly the wave of the future. The best entertainment money could buy, reaching out from a central hub to spokes scattered beyond.

With the networks supplying more and more programming, the answer to the other great question that had dogged radio since its beginnings, who was going to pay for broadcasting, began to come clear as well.

The answer was advertising.

Hoover and others had rejected that possibility at the first radio conference, but now everyone saw it as the only solution for the increasing expenses of talent, license fees, equipment, and technical staff necessary to run a radio station. At WLW there were three station announcers, three secretaries, three studio operators, and three assistant engineers. There was Joe Chambers, the technical director, Fred Smith, William Stoess, Grace Raine, and there was also a man named John Clark, newly appointed commercial manager of the station.

WLW was by this point taking programming from the two original NBC chains, the Red and Blue. With that programming came some of those network sponsor dollars, which helped defray some of the costs of running the station, which Powel, of course, considered a necessary adjunct to his radio business. But he and John Clark began to discuss advertising as a way to supplement the station's bottom line.

In the fall Powel headed off to New York for the fourth annual Radio World's Fair at Madison Square Garden. The show was bigger and better than ever, and Powel, "the biggest single figure in radio today," was everywhere. On the convention floor, mingling with competitors and customers alike, giving a speech to Crosley distributors, giving a talk to the National Association of Broadcasters. Giving four thousand dollars to AT&T to pay for the long-distance lines that would enable the Radio Industry Association dinner to be heard over sixty stations, the largest chain radio broadcast up to that time.

He served and was in turn, served himself, by the De Forest Radio Company of New Jersey, which he'd bought into a few months back (distinct from DeForest Radio of Canada, which he already owned). He hoped to turn around the company that bore the name of one of radio's founding fathers.

By then he'd figured out another way to supplement the corporation's bottom line. The twenties, after all, were roaring, and the stock-market soaring. He decided to take the Crosley Radio Corporation public.

The initial offering was forty-eight thousand shares at twenty-five dollars; those shares were to be sold on the Cincinnati Stock exchange only. Actually, the initial offering was three hundred thousand shares, but Powel held onto the others. He had no intention of losing control of his company.

He was out of town when the news broke. He returned from Mississippi with a brace of quail to find himself on the front page of the *Cincinnati Enquirer*.

By February the stock was up to 26-1/8; the corporation declared a 4 percent dividend, plus an initial dividend of one dollar per share. Powel received a few dividends of his own; for one, his salary, now a matter of public record, was increased to seventy-five thousand dollars per year, exclusive of bonuses.

For another, the United States Playing Card Company decided it wanted to get out of the radio business. They didn't need to own a radio station to advertise their products anymore. They could simply buy time on a network.

Powel got the news of their change of heart from Charles Sawyer, whose law firm represented both WSAI and WLW. A radio station license in 1928, as the FRC continued winnowing the broadcast band, was clearly a precious thing.

He signed an agreement to lease the station for a year, with the option to buy at the end of that time. WSAI staff and management moved into the WLW studios, which began to feel a bit cramped.

Bandbox orders were up; a new speaker, the Dynacone, was out, and production space was tight.

Lewis and Powel looked at each other, and realized that, unbelievable as it seemed, they were going to have to expand again.

It wasn't just the radios now. It was the Icyball, too, out on the market and making a big splash, particularly in rural, still unelectrified America. Full-page ads appeared in magazines like *Farm Mechanics* and *Country Gentleman*, promising "ice for two cents a day," that being the cost of the fuel required to heat, or "charge" the Icyball. Farmers, the ads suggested, could use it to store milk. The factory turned out super-sized cabinets for that purpose, ones that fit two or even three Icyball units.

The standard Icyball retailed for eighty dollars; it was soon obvious the company had a hit on its hands. Distributors and retailers went for it in a big way. Some attached an Icyball cabinet to the rear of an automobile, so they could demonstrate it to customers at their homes. Powel had Cincinnati's health commissioner provide a product endorsement. An engineer named Russell Smith came up with a way to use the Icyball to cool office water fountains. Lewis patented a device that regulated and extended cooling inside the Icyball's cabinet.

Advertising expanded, moving beyond the farm market, suggesting myriad places the machine could be used: in restaurants and retail locations, among street vendors, on golf courses.

More than twenty thousand were sold the first year of production. The foreign market would eventually prove to be huge, with thousands sold in Africa and South America. American missionaries adopted the device as their own. It was literally a lifesaver, the only way of keeping perishable medicines cool in remote regions of the globe.

The Crosley name was going places where few American companies had gone.

Powel wanted to push it out even farther. He was itching to get that fifty-thousand-watt transmitter on line. He had a few other ideas as well, as always, and went down the hall to tell Lewis. But his brother wasn't there.

He wouldn't be there for some time to come yet.

He'd had a nervous breakdown.

The term they used was "nervous exhaustion." The treatment prescribed for Lewis was the same as it had been for his breakdown in 1910—a retreat from his day-to-day routine. This case seems to have not been as serious as the earlier one, at least not as long-lasting. By mid-February of 1928, Lewis was back on his feet, well enough to make his way down to the Cincinnati train station, climb aboard a southbound railroad car, and take, at long last, a well-deserved holiday.

The March 15 issue of the *Crosley Broadcaster* featured a picture of Lewis posed at his desk over the headline: "Mr. Lewis Crosley has just returned from Florida where he has been for a much-needed vacation."

Even on vacation, however, he couldn't entirely get away from the factory. As he prepared to leave, one of the office managers passed him a package, telling him not to open it until he reached his destination.

Lewis couldn't wait.

Lucy was with him, of course. The two of them opened the package together. It turned out to contain a dozen or so letters from his co-workers at the factory. Lewis sent back a telegram immediately, telling his friends "you can count on us doing many things suggested in your masterpiece of foolishness."

It's doubtful one of those letters was from Powel. There is little doubt, however, about what his older brother felt seeing Lewis collapse from the strain of running the factories. Guilt—and no small measure of it. From the time Lewis returned to work after his holiday with Lucy, Powel made it a point to take his brother with him on trips.

He didn't lessen his brother's workload, but Lewis wouldn't have stood for that anyway. Lewis might not have had Powel's affinity for the spotlight, but he wanted to stop being at the center of things, to have other men take over the jobs he'd been doing for almost a decade. But Powel did change his brother's routine. Lewis, at his doctor's suggestion, did the same. He brought in a couch, told his secretary no calls, shut his door, and lay down for an hour after lunch to rest. It was a prescription he followed for the rest of his working life.

By May, Lewis was back at it full-time, with the new office furniture in place and looking at a survey conducted by Bell Laboratories Engineers regarding the two transmitter sites Crosley owned—WLW's, and WSAI's. The FRC granted him approval to take WLW to fifty thousand watts. By this point, Crosley had control of not only WSAI but its transmitter in Mason, north of Cincinnati. WLW's transmitter was in Harrison, west of the city. Lewis commissioned a comparison survey of the two sites. WSAI's proved to have better ground properties, and so they decided to install the new transmitter and supporting facilities there. Several acres adjacent to the property were purchased.

The FRC authorized construction to begin in late May. Powel, by that point, was already on to the next thing.

He was, all at once, an airplane manufacturer.

.   .   .   .   .   .

First, however, he had some unfinished business with Frank Taylor; the courts, unsurprisingly, had found in favor of Powel's side in the Go Bi-Bi case. Powel cut a deal with Taylor, selling him the Go Bi-Bi patent and the company's remaining inventory and split the profit with James Carroll, the town hall maintenance man who'd created the idea. Taylor continued to sell his Taylor Tot for another half-century.

The airplane business came to Powel through his polo buddy, Julius "Junkie" Fleischmann (the nickname resulting from Junkie's ardent collecting of antiquities and anthropological specimens). Planes back then were made of wood and fabric, but recent developments in metal alloys had opened up new possibilities. A Cincinnati businessman named Thomas Halpin was one of the first to see those possibilities. Halpin had developed what he thought was a viable design for an all-metal machine—a plane with a framework of steel tubing covered by an aluminum alloy skin. He needed investors to build a viable prototype.

Powel, who'd been there at the dawn of the auto industry, sensed an opportunity.

On May 1, 1928, he put an undisclosed amount of cash, as did Fleischmann and a few others, into a new concern incorporated as the Metal Aircraft Company. Junkie and Powel were first and second vice-presidents, respectively. The company immediately built a one-hundred-thousand-dollar brick factory next to the airport and started work.

In Mason, Powel turned over the first spoonful of dirt at groundbreaking ceremonies on June 25 for the new concrete-and-steel building that housed the transmitter. New power lines were run, miles of grounding cable were buried ten inches underground around the perimeter of the property. Four massive holes were dug, and four concrete piers sunk into the ground. Twin three-hundred-foot towers were erected to support the new antenna.

When the first phase of work was complete, engineers from AT&T Laboratories arrived to install the huge fifty-thousand-watt transmitter; the main circuit panels alone stretched on for forty feet. Lumber from the crates the transmitter arrived in was used to build a structure beneath the antenna called a tuning house. The entire project cost a quarter-million dollars.

The Crosleys, however, could afford it. Their stock had risen to fifty-seven dollars a share. Trading on the Cincinnati exchange was brisk, to say the least.

In New York, it was even brisker.

RCA was over two hundred dollars a share and climbing. AT&T, GE, Westinghouse, and General Motors were all heading toward unprecedented highs, and suddenly everyone was anxious to get in on the new 'bull' market. Volume leapt up to unheard-of, undreamed-of levels. Five million shares traded in a single day.

.   .   .   .   .   .

The stock-market boom did not reach all the way down the assembly line. In the late 1920s workers at the Crosley Radio Corporation made about eleven dollars for a thirty-five-hour week. They were paid three times a month. If they were productive employees they received time-and-a-half after forty hours; non-productive employees were not paid overtime until after forty-four hours.

The definition of productive was an arbitrary one, provided by a particular employee's foreman at his discretion.

Women, of course, were paid less.

Radio work was still seasonal, and there were no guaranteed jobs, per se. Many of the women on the line, with families to take care of, were happy to work nine months out of twelve.

Many weren't.

There were other rules in the employee handbook that, viewed through the workers' eye, could have been seen as arbitrary. There were unwritten rules on the factory floor as well. Talk of unions was strictly, to borrow a phrase, *verboten*. That was Powel's rule, learned at the feet of David Parry, one of the most famous anti-union men of all time. Both he and Lewis considered the corporation a family. You didn't work for the Crosleys, you worked with them. They sat at the head of the table, passed the plate around, and everyone got their fair share.

Shut up and eat.

Workers in the late 1920s were inclined to do just that. The tenor of the times was far less confrontational than it had been at the beginning of the decade.

The times, though, were soon to be changing.

.   .   .   .   .   .

In June 1928, the company did another promotion tie-in with Edsel Ford's National Air Show. The pilot this time was Charles Myers, a Crosley sales representative. A veteran of the WWI Canadian Air force named William B. Baldwin was radio operator and announcer. Alvin Plough went out ahead of the tour again to stir up the troops. Dealer receptions were arranged at many stops, and Baldwin gave pep talks to the assembled "Crosley men."

Powel took a little tour of his own—a month-long cruise to Europe with Gwendolyn. Mr. and Mrs. Harold van Ardal of College Hill accompanied them. Mr. Van Ardal also happened to be general sales manager for the Crosley Radio Corporation.

The trip, thus, mixed business and pleasure.

They visited—among other places—France, Scotland, Belgium, and England, where they toured some genuine English country homes, many of which, to Powel's interest, were run by butlers.

They met Crosley distributors and retailers for various luncheons and dinners. Powel heard a lot of complaints regarding the radio manufacturing industry in England. The vacuum tube patent was controlled by a corporation that demanded a royalty equivalent to $2.50 per set, more than the manufacturing cost of the receiver itself. A lot of people were simply building their own radios.

It all, no doubt, sounded vaguely familiar to him.

He returned home in July, wrote an article on the subject for the *New York Times*, and hired a butler to run Pinecroft, a Rumanian fellow by the name of Michael Rutcher. Gwendolyn found her house being run by someone else. She had, no doubt, mixed feelings. On the one hand, everything was taken care of for her. On the other, she had very little to do.

Lucy, whose opinion of Powel had never been very high anyway, thought it another black mark on his character, another sign of his pretentiousness and lack of concern for anyone but himself. Lewis saw only Powel's good intentions.

Gwendolyn looked around for more charity work.

On the business side, Powel settled the DeForest lawsuit and joined that company's board of directors.

The stock market fell briefly, and then began climbing again, even faster, even higher than before.

John Clark, WLW's commercial manager, continued to crunch numbers, zeroing in on a figure to charge advertisers for broadcast time.

The station partnered with the State of Ohio to create the first system of public education courses delivered via radio: the Ohio School of the Air.

Fred Smith brought in another idea for a news program; a ten-minute daily round-up of the day's top stories, picked up from *Time* magazine. Called *NewsCasts*, the program was an instant success. A little while later, Smith and a *Time* executive, Roy Larsen, came up with another program called *NewsActing*, which featured dramatizations of the day's top events, complete with actors and sound effects.

Time liked the idea so much, Smith and Larsen were hired to produce it for them. He packed up his things and headed for New York. A man named Ford Billings was hired to replace him. By and by, the program was refined and developed further and went nationwide under a new name: *The March of Time*.

By 1928, WLW was on the air over a hundred hours a week, all day, every day—except Fridays, when they had a staff meeting from 2:30 to 3:15 in the afternoon, proving that, to some extent, they were still making it up as they went along.

The station's new transmitter went on the air for tests in early October. The formal dedication was Monday, October 29. Nearly five hundred dealers, distributors, and dignitaries were bussed from Cincinnati to the Mason site, where lunch was served. Then it was back to Cincinnati for a tour of the factory and downtown to the Hotel Gibson for an on-air celebration starting at nine that evening.

Powel gave a speech, threw a gold switch, and the fifty-thousand-watt transmitter was on the air.

Special programming followed until three in the morning. A thirty-five-piece orchestra in New York presented a concert, courtesy of NBC, that was transmitted by telephone line to WLW for rebroadcast. There were numerous live performances from the Hotel Gibson Ballroom. Vaudeville star Walter Kelley emceed the second hour of the broadcast in character as "The Virginia Judge."

Broadcasting at fifty thousand watts, the show could be heard in every state in the union. Powel was owner, once more, of the most powerful broadcast outlet in the world. Staffers soon came up with a new motto, befitting WLW's new status: "The Nation's Station."

John Clark came up with a number of his own: six hundred dollars an hour. That was what advertisers would have to pay, primetime, for their programs to continue broadcasting. They paid with little complaint. The audience was out there, after all. Gathered around the set, listening.

The money rolled in.

The twenties roared on.

CHAPTER 18

February 14, 1929, will be forever known in American history for the St. Valentine's Day Massacre, in which members of Al Capone's mob gunned down seven of Bugs Moran's men in Chicago.

In Cincinnati, that day was notable for other reasons. Crosley corporation stock, which had split the month before, increasing the total pool of available shares to well over half a million, was admitted to the New York Stock Exchange. Sales volume immediately doubled. The price climbed briefly above two hundred, before dropping as part of an overall market slump.

Also happening in New York that February was the National Air Show, where Powel and the Metal Aircraft Corporation unveiled their new plane to the world. The Flamingo offered the well-to-do air traveler the last word in style and convenience. It held up to eight people inside, in wicker chairs, with an on-board lavatory included. Removable seating allowed the interior to be quickly altered to carry freight. The company immediately provided one for the use of famed aviatrix Elinor Smith as a publicity stunt.

Powel received congratulations from all concerned on the new plane's elegant design.

And then moved on to the next thing.

Television.

On February 19, the FRC issued Crosley Corporation a license for an experimental television station, experimental being the key word. Though many in the communications industry, David Sarnoff among them, had been predicting the arrival of a viable voice and image transmission method for years, the new broadcast technology was still some time away.

Which was just fine with Powel; he had his hands full with the old broadcast technology.

He'd sold eighteen million dollars worth of radios in 1928. In the boom year of 1929, he expected that business to double. They had fourteen active assembly lines, each over a hundred feet long.

It wasn't enough.

They bought two square blocks adjacent to the Colerain factory, fronting Arlington Street, Drawings were done for a new eight-story building. When finished, it would add two hundred thousand square feet of production space.

WSAI had shifted to 1360 on the dial. They were still broadcasting at five thousand watts, on the same antenna they'd been using since 1925, though they had a new slogan now: "Cincinnati's Own Station." Their programming focus was regional.

WLW's was national, one of a dozen or so stations across the country with fifty thousand watts of power. Broadcasting from close to the geographic heart of the country, they were an integral part of one of the most revolutionary developments in human history.

Radio—the first true mass medium in the history of the world. Through its power to connect Americans wherever they lived, there was coming to be a single, common, recognizably American culture, one in which every boy's hero was Babe Ruth, every girl squealed over Rudy Vallee, and everyone's favorite radio personalities—with a single, qualified exception—were Amos'n'Andy.

Radio provided common ground for urban and rural America, connecting the isolated family on its farm in the middle of Kansas with the apartment-dweller in New York City. Whether through the phone lines and network programming or through the airwaves and superpower, those rural communities—still, by decade's end, comprising roughly half the country's population—were being drawn by radio into the country's social fabric.

To a great many of those communities, radio was WLW, at 700

on the dial. Powel knew it. So did others. The governor of Kentucky, on behalf of his grateful citizenry, appointed Powel Crosley an honorary colonel for bringing the world to their doorstep.

And though WLW's programming focus was national, their reach was global. Listeners in the West Indies, in the Caribbean, and in Central America found 'The Nation's Station' came in clearer than their own local broadcast outlets.

Through myriad innovations, from the radio to the car to the airplane, the world was shrinking at an ever-accelerating rate. Thanks to the Wright Brothers, in fact, the day when you could be in Germany one day and America the next was just around the corner.

Powel looked around that corner and saw that day coming.

He was part owner of one airplane company already, an executive vice-President at Metal Aircraft, but he was used to being the number-one figure.

He decided to start an airplane company of his own.

.   .   .   .   .   .

Though it wasn't formally incorporated until May, Crosley Aircraft operated for several months in secret, in a building at Blue Rock Road and Turrel Street, just around the corner from the original Crosley factory. Unlike all of his other ideas and enterprises, he did not involve Lewis.

Powel started the company by borrowing two engineers from the radio corporation—Herb Junkin and Karl S. Fuller, both of whom had experience with airplanes. Late in 1928 they began to design the company's first airplane, an open, three-seat monoplane that soon acquired a typically catchy Crosley name, most likely courtesy of Powel:

The Moonbeam.

Powered by a one-hundred-and-ten-horsepower engine, the plane was twenty-six feet long. Its single wing, mounted on struts high above the fuselage, spanned forty feet. Two passengers could ride side-by-side in front of the pilot. Powel's intent was to produce it in sufficient quantity to allow a retail price of five thousand dollars.

The initial prototype, the Moonbeam C-1, was completed in April 1929. It was then disassembled and trucked to Lunken Airport, in the southeast area of town, where it was reassembled and flown for the first time. Satisfied with his new toy, Powel had it flown to Pinecroft in early May, where it landed on the polo field in the middle of the seventh annual Crosley distributors convention.

At the same time, Powel's engineers were working on other Moonbeam aircraft: the C-2, a closed-cabin monoplane with seating for four; and the C-3, a biplane that came in both open and closed cabin configuration.

The C-3, in particular, featured a number of innovations. The landing gear's brakes were actuated by the throttle control. The control surfaces (ailerons) on the lower wings were operated by a patented system of torque tubes. Both airplanes were equipped with self-starting motors and could fly and operate at remarkably low speeds.

Powel's intent—with his planes, as with his radios—was to produce a product for the everyman, at least everyman who could afford one. The airplane business was new, and no one understood the rules yet or the potential size of the market.

The public first learned of Powel's new company on May 4. Management at Lunken Airport expressed the hope that Crosley Aviation would locate its factory there. But Powel had other ideas. He bought a 193-acre tract of land in Sharonville, just north of Cincinnati, and built his own airport.

Crosley Airport had three runways, one of which was thirty-five hundred feet long, big enough to accommodate the largest aircraft of the time. In the large hangar, Powel could accommodate all of his planes, with room to spare. The airport also included a factory building as well as a farmhouse for the caretaker and his family.

Then Powel moved on to the next thing.

The Crosley Autogym.

The new device was an electric motor mounted on a pedestal, with a broad leather belt attached to it. The user placed the belt around his or her waist, switched on the machine, and stood there while the belt vibrated.

Instant workout.

"The Crosley Autogym," boasted the advertisements, "brings, with consistent daily use, the same satisfactory results as out-of-door physical exercise. Systematic use of the Crosley Autogym improves digestion of food and elimination of waste, makes the muscles firm and hard, stimulates circulation of the blood, and reduces flabbiness and fat in any part of the body!"

One ad featured a young woman clad in a skimpy bathing suit, smiling for the camera as the Autogym worked its magic.

Powel had an Autogym delivered and set up in the basement at Pinecroft for his own use, though his initial enthusiasm for the device soon petered out.

Around this time, a Cincinnati man named Earl Metcalf sold Powel on his idea for a health tonic called "Peptikai." Lewis later recalled that Powel was "a great guy for remedies and medicines—he had a room full of them." Powel set up a business to sell the tonic with his own money, providing office and manufacturing space in the Arlington Street building separate from the Crosley operations. The Peptikai operation, however, didn't last long.

Powel was on to the next thing.

Fish.

A particular kind of fish, actually: Tarpon. Which were, Powel soon learned, very big fish that could weigh up to a hundred pounds, fish that roamed the waters of Florida in schools up to an acre in size.

Powel had been invited to see those Tarpon—and to, if possible, catch one—by Bob Ringling, who, despite the real-estate bust, still lived in Sarasota, in the mansion his recently deceased father Charles had built, just north of the estate, called Ca'D'Zan, his uncle John still owned. Bob had found his own way into the entertainment business. Some years back, he'd run away not to the circus, but the opera. He was a world-famous baritone, who'd sung numerous radio concerts, which was how he and Powel had met.

Bob wanted Powel to come to Sarasota as well, for the second International Tarpon Tournament, an event being co-sponsored by the Sarasota Chamber of Commerce for reasons that had nothing to do with fish and everything with the price of local real estate, which had not greatly appreciated since the bust. The chamber was hoping a little publicity might do the town's reputation some good, hence the invitations to prominent people like Powel, who was himself just hoping for a good day's fishing.

All concerned were going to get more than they bargained for in the deal.

Powel flew down on May 17. The following afternoon he went with Bob Ringling and a guide into the waters off Siesta Key, an island in the bay near Sarasota. Near a spot called the Point of Rocks, Powel landed a 102-pound Tarpon. He fought it for an hour and ten minutes. It was an exhausting, exhilarating experience, one he later wrote about in detail. He described the fight, his struggles with the reel, and the tarpon, the numbness in his hands, the ache in his back; "for the first three quarters of an hour at least, I did almost everything wrong…it was a toss up as to which was the more tired, the fish or I."

At the end, when he brought in the fish and released the rod, his left hand was useless, "so stiff and numb that I could not move my fingers." He was thrilled. In fact, he was more than thrilled.

"For once in my life," Powel wrote, "I was satisfied."

It's difficult to imagine higher praise from Powel. For someone who seemed to be perpetually feeding an inner hunger, seeking (and not finding) fulfillment in business, hobbies, possessions, even people, to feel "satisfied" was a rare thing indeed.

He was so satisfied, in fact, that he decided that night to build himself a winter home in the area.

He got a little carried away.

He ended up with another mansion.

On May 23, he bought a sixty-three-acre parcel that fronted Sarasota Bay. To the north was Ca'D'Zan as well as Bob Ringling's home. Powel got the land cheap, through a local real estate broker named Maurice Prew. It had been owned by developers who had planned to build a subdivision called Seagate, but when the mid-

1920s boom went bust, the development was abandoned. The developers had paid $365,000 in 1925 for the property; in 1929, Powel was able to buy it for around thirty-five thousand dollars.

Prew introduced Powel to a local architect named George Albree Freeman. Though recently retired, Freeman agreed to design Powel's (second) dream home. He came up with a three-story, eleven-thousand-square-foot Mediterranean-style mansion. Powel wanted it done by December 1, so that he and the family could be in for the winter season.

Paul Bergman, the general contractor, had crews at the site working nine hours a day, less than a month after Powel caught his fish. The first thing to go up was the house's frame; Freeman and Powel had decided on a steel superstructure. Maurice Prew's six-year-old son, Neill, thought it looked "like a skyscraper going up."

Powel left Bergman and his men to raise the rest of the building and headed back to Cincinnati, where the wheeling and dealing continued.

He and Julius Fleischmann started an airline.

They called it Mason & Dixon Airline. Their plan was to offer weekday service between Cincinnati and Detroit, via Dayton, to enable prosperous businessmen to do an afternoon's work in another city and be back home in time for dinner.

Articles of incorporation were filed on June 19, 1929. The company ordered several Flamingo airplanes (at about twenty-three thousand dollars apiece) from the Metal Aircraft Corporation.

Regularly scheduled flights began in July. At the same time the company had a deal in the works to acquire Johnson Airplane Supply, a Dayton firm, for a reported five million dollars. Johnson was one of the oldest parts manufacturers in the still-young airline industry. They also owned Vandalia Airport outside of Dayton, which would provide a perfect base for flight and maintenance operations.

Mason & Dixon had other deals in the works, such as agreements with airlines based in the American Southeast for connecting flights, agreements with airlines serving Central and South America too. The intent was to make Mason & Dixon international in scope.

Powel was arranging connections as well—connections in his old business, rather than the new. He and Crosley Radio engineers mapped out a plan for a network of commercial shortwave stations in Central and South America.

He and executives from WOR in Newark and WLS in Chicago formed a mini-network of their own. Programming efforts started small. The first show, which each station would broadcast simultaneously, was a talk by Powel on the subject of broadcast technology titled, "The Big News in Radio."

Powel gave that talk, stood back a moment, and then took stock.

Shares of Crosley Radio Corporation were selling at ninety-five dollars, which was higher than RCA and still climbing. Projections looked for radio sales in 1929 to exceed those of 1928 by more than two million dollars.

In Sarasota, the Crosley winter home was halfway to completion, as was the new factory on Arlington Street. But something about the latter building wasn't quite right, to Powel's eyes, at least. He decided to add a one-hundred-and-fifty- foot tower to the northwest corner of the building.

Perhaps still under Sarasota architect Freeman's influence, Powel wanted the tower to be finished in a Mediterranean style. It would have an executive dining room and several conference rooms. Reflecting Powel's new aviation interests, large frescos of winged shields displaying the letter "C" decorated the tower's base on two sides and above the building's main entrances.

The addition of the tower took the Arlington Street Building to ten stories and took the price tag to $750,000.

Lewis made an addition to the expanded factory complex as well, a slightly more utilitarian one: a one-story building measuring 580 feet by 100 feet to go in directly across Arlington Street. Referred to as "Building K," this edifice would house the final assembly department and railroad-loading shed. The two buildings were to be connected by an enclosed second-story bridge, through which the completed radios would pass on a conveyor belt, down to the loading shed.

Building K and the connecting bridge cost half a million dollars.

CHAPTER 18

From the new complex, company workers would be able to pack and ship thirty railroad boxcars filled with radios every day.

. . . . .

Powel wasn't the only one wheeling and dealing that summer of 1929.

In Cincinnati, a man named Sidney Weil was surreptitiously buying shares in the Reds. C.J. McDiarmid didn't know it, but his days of running the club were officially numbered.

On Wall Street, stocks were soaring higher than ever before. Millions of people had been bitten by the investment bug. Stocks split, and split again. The more shares available, the lower the price per share, the more people could buy in.

Crosley stock continued to be bought. With the new transmitter in operation, with the new building going up, with the Icyball and the Dynacone and the Showbox selling faster than the workers could churn them out, the Cincinnati company was a good buy.

Powel and Gwendolyn owned 52 percent of Crosley Corporation stock, which made them, on paper at least, worth well over twenty million dollars.

Powel's other businesses continued to boom as well.

Mason & Dixon Airline officially announced its intent to serve most of the southeastern United States. Metal Aircraft sold Mason & Dixon six tri-motor versions of the Flamingo, priced at approximately thirty thousand dollars each. Metal Aircraft also sold four Flamingos to Great Southern, the first airline to offer flights between Los Angeles and New York. They sold several single-engine Flamingos to individual customers as well.

Construction at Crosley Airport was finished. In the Crosley Aviation factory, work proceeded apace on two new Crosley Moonbeams.

In Sarasota, Paul Bergman hired on a second crew. Men were working night and day to finish Powel's mansion by his December 1 move-in date.

On Arlington Street, the Crosley Radio Corporation was hiring new employees to fill its new building. There was a line of people outside the construction gates looking for work, a line of such size that people stopped to gawk. One of them asked Lewis how many people were employed at the factory.

"I don't know," he answered. They were taking on new hires so quickly he didn't have time to count them.

Hundreds of those new employees were at work already on the first four floors of the Arlington Street building, even as concrete was still being poured for the seventh and eighth, which would house company offices and WSAI and WLW studios, respectively.

The company payroll stood at five thousand. Crosley was now Cincinnati's largest employer.

The wheeling and dealing continued.

Powel sold his interests in Mason & Dixon and in Metal Aircraft. He struck a deal with the Huckins Yacht company to have Crosley radios installed as standard equipment on their boats.

He began looking for a new yacht himself.

Picking up on the success of the Ohio School of the Air, WLW partnered with neighboring Indiana and Kentucky as well to create the Central States School of the Air, broadcasting, to start, five hours of programming per week.

Back in College Hill, Ellen started attending the Pigeye herself.

September gave way to October, and stock prices began to slip, ever so slightly at first, and then faster. Another bump in the market, experts felt. Ride it out, they assured investors, and all will be fine.

But just around the corner, though not even Powel could see it coming, was the fall.

CHAPTER 19

I t began in early October. Crosley stock slid to eighty-six on the tenth, to seventy-nine a week later. GE fell even more precipitously, from above four hundred to barely three hundred. On October 24, a Thursday, the panic began.

Almost thirteen million shares changed hands that day. In the morning session, stocks plunged so fast that as soon as prices posted they were out of date. The ticker, the stock boys with their handwritten cards, the telephone, the broker's clerk calling out prices on the floor could not keep up with the slump. RCA fell twenty points in the span of a few hours. Montgomery Ward thirty. GE slipped below three hundred and kept falling. Crosley hit fifty.

At noon, in the face of the accelerating panic, six men—the heads of First National, Chase, and Bankers Trust among them—rendezvoused in the offices of J.P. Morgan, and pledged forty million dollars from each of their respective institutions to shore up the market.

It worked—for Friday.

But on Monday, "the rout was underway once more." GE fell forty-seven points, Westinghouse thirty-four. Crosley stock, unlike most, held for the moment, sticking close to fifty.

And then came Tuesday, October 29, Black Tuesday and the stock market crash, in the wake of which came a panic that obliterated memory of every panic that had come before. Everyone was suddenly selling at whatever price anyone would offer, except no one was buying. The average price of the top fifty stocks fell close to forty points. Crosley plummeted to twenty-eight. A company called

White Sewing Machine, which had reached forty-eight only a few weeks earlier, plummeted toward single digits. Someone put in a bid of one dollar a share, which was happily accepted.

One broker simply stashed a group of sell orders he received into a desk drawer. They turned up later, unfilled. Not that it mattered, save for the purposes of this book, for those unnoticed slips of paper are, in their own way, an omen of things to come.

There was another meeting at noon that Tuesday, this time a conference among the stock exchange's forty governors, who debated shutting the exchange's doors. Ultimately, they decided against it.

The plunge, nonetheless, continued—throughout that day and the remainder of the month and on into the middle of November, when prices at last hit rock bottom.

Crosley bottomed out at 19.

Billions of dollars were gone. Worse than the vanished money was the change in the country's mood. The gleaming future, in which poverty was a barely remembered myth, in which ever-newer, ever-shinier consumer goods were within reach of all, was suddenly revealed to be a myth itself. While the twenties roared, while the stock market soared, while the good times went on like they would never end, people spent like there was no tomorrow. They bought on credit—new cars, new furniture, new homes. In the wake of the stock market crash, credit dried up, and the bills, all at once, came due.

Few could pay them.

The panic was over. The Great Depression, the single most catastrophic economic downturn in the history of western civilization, had begun.

The scope of the disaster was too much for some people. Newspapers everyday were filled with reports of suicides. In Cincinnati, Sidney Weil, who had only just taken control of the Reds, was forced to surrender his shares of the club to the Central Bank and Trust. Though Weil continued to run the team, any move with financial implications had to be approved by the bank.

Weil also owned a minor league franchise in Columbus, Ohio. He sold that as well, to ex-Sergeant Larry MacPhail, who right after World War I had been part of the group who tried to assassinate Kaiser Wilhelm. MacPhail had the gift of gab. Though the Depression hit him as hard as anyone, he was nonetheless able to sweet-talk a group of local investors into backing his bid for the Columbus franchise.

In Europe, unemployment soared from England to the Rhine. Germany, in particular, was hit hard. The voices of reason in that country, who had spoken out in favor of Owen Young's amended repayment plan, were increasingly drowned out by extremists—the Communists, on the left, the Nazis, on the right.

In Sarasota, Florida, John Ringling lost control of the circus his family had founded.

But up the beach, at the old Seagate site, nothing changed.

Paul Bergman's men remained hard at work raising the roof on the new mansion, struggling to meet that December 1 completion date.

For Powel Crosley, the twenties roared on.

.   .   .   .   .   .

It would be incorrect to say the crash didn't touch him—or Lewis, or the Crosley Radio Corporation, for that matter.

Radio sales slowed dramatically. There was, for the first time in company history, a glut of production space in the factory. But no banks called in their loans. Powel's fortune didn't vanish overnight. The Crosley Corporation operated on a cash basis; they didn't owe anyone a red cent.

Powel and Lewis had learned that lesson long ago, when their father lost everything and had to start over again from scratch. Back in 1893, they were too young to understand why the silver spoon was being yanked from their mouths, why their belongings were being loaded on wagons and driven away, but by 1929 they knew exactly what had happened to them and why.

Their father had overextended himself. When the banks came calling, he didn't have the cash on hand to pay them back. So they'd had to move in with their grandparents, and make do with those football uniforms made from old stairpads. Lewis had to squeeze into a bedroom with his baby sister because the fancy house they'd lived in before the move wasn't actually theirs; the bank owned it. Their lives were, literally, in someone else's hands.

Powel, Jr. had learned it the hard way, too, from his own failures—the Marathon Six, the DeCross cycle car, the Hermes. More than once, his dreams had gone up in smoke because he'd been dependent on other people's capital to run his business.

Lewis always appreciated the value of a dollar even more than his brother. He was the one whose savings Powel used to build that buckboard car, way back when. He'd scrimped and saved to make the farm work. He'd moved his wife and children up four flights of stairs to put together the cash for a down payment on the house he wanted. All through the glittering twenties, while the stock market soared and the good times rolled, he kept driving the same old Buick because if there was nothing wrong with it, why spend the money to get a new one?

Powel was careful with his money when caution was called for, but Lewis always pinched every one of his pennies. In fact, Powel counted on his brother's frugality. No doubt aware that he took after his father much more than did his younger brother, Powel needed Lewis to keep him in check, to provide the cautionary advice that tempered Powel's grandiose ideas. Every time Powel wanted to jump into a new business, Lewis would ask him how much they were prepared to lose.

They never spent more than they agreed on, and they never borrowed to expand faster than their sales would allow. Throughout the difficult decade to come, a decade of personal, corporate, national, and international triumph and tragedy, they never strayed from those principles. While other companies foundered and folded, Crosley survived, morphing, mutating, and changing along the way.

.   .   .   .   .

Christmas of 1929 was a special one for reasons that had nothing to do with stock prices or radios. Powel, Sr., born on December 25, 1849, turned eighty years old. He was still working—or, at least making the trip to his office a few times a week. He was gardening, in the backyard of the house his sons had bought him in College Hill, sometimes by himself, sometimes with his grandchildren. On Christmas Day, at the big house his son owned, the entire, extended family—Crosleys, Utzes, Johnsons, Averys, and Aikens—gathered to celebrate. They passed around the December 25, 1929, issue of the *Cincinnati Enquirer*, which featured a full-page profile on Powel, Sr., reviewing his childhood, education, and law career, and retelling the growing legend of his namesake. The son was, of course, the reason the father was in the paper.

The son was also getting full-page coverage in Florida. Paul Bergman ran a series of spreads in the Sarasota paper advertising his progress on the mansion and thanking his subcontractors for their help on the project: Sarasota Builders Supply Company, Benkendorf Electric, Sarasota Cement Company; J.B. Green Plumbing, Downs Paint, Smith and Branham, who did the sheet metal, and Jack Crawford, who did the swimming pool. When the mansion was finished, the local economy no doubt shuddered.

But Powel's new home, on completion, provided yet another showpiece for the community, right alongside Ca'd'Zan. The exterior was Mediterranean in style, and the house was the first in the state constructed with steel framing and a concrete foundation. The floors were all laid in tile, while the ceilings featured exposed cypress beams, each hand-decorated with colored patterns of flowers and vines.

The main entrance, facing east, opened into a living room measuring twenty-four feet by forty-six feet. There was also a music room, with grand piano, pantry, refrigerator and safe. The south wing contained the dining room, servants' hall, kitchen, butler's pantry, and a circular breakfast room. In the north wing, a stairway rose to a second floor guest room, with a bath and a small side entrance hall. An elaborate porte cochere extended from the main entrance over the curved driveway. A loggia stretched across the back of the residence, a decorative fountain set into the outside wall punctuating the space between its twin sets of entrance doors. The loggia opened onto a walled patio with an antique Spanish fountain in the center.

An outdoor staircase led to the second floor and large, inset balcony overlooking the patio and lawn. From that balcony, two sets of entrance doors led into a gallery that ran the width of the house. At the north end were Powel and Gwendolyn's bedrooms, at the south, Powel's office. Gwendolyn's room featured a small balcony of its own and an intercom-telephone system, which could be used to contact the house's staff in the service wing. Four more bedrooms opened onto the gallery opposite the balcony.

A back staircase and servants' rooms lay beyond Powel's office, which was called the ship's room. It was the most striking chamber in the house, paneled completely in wood, including the high, beamed ceiling. Brass-framed portholes set above the room's narrow windows gave it the feel of a cruise ship's stateroom, except that it was circular, and fifteen feet in diameter. A weather vane on the room's roof connected with a moving steel pointer set in the ceiling of the room. The stylized pointer moved against an inlaid wood pattern depicting all sixteen points of the compass. Powel only had to look up to see the wind direction at any time. Just outside the ship's room a small curving staircase led downstairs.

Nearly one hundred feet of lawn lay between the house and the Bay. A stone's throw from the patio was a terrazzo swimming pool that measured thirty by sixty feet; Jack Crawford had also built a sea wall to protect the lawn, which extended six hundred feet along the eleven hundred feet of Crosley property that fronted the bay. A few yards to the north of the house was a yacht slip, with four landing stages. It could accommodate yachts or fishing boats up to one hundred feet long. The channel was seven feet deep, and ran sixteen hundred feet into the bay. An enormous turning basin was dredged outside its entrance.

The final, advertised cost of the mansion was $350,000—nearly five times that of Pinecroft. The real cost—when overruns, overtime, and other factors were added up—was closer to a million.

Lewis was alternately amazed and angry—amazed that his brother was spending that kind of money, angry that those extra expenses had been permitted. Powel wouldn't have stood for that kind of waste of the company's money, and Lewis, though bayoneting Bergman and his subcontractors would not have been an option, certainly would have taken them to task.

But Lewis hadn't been involved in Sarasota. Powel was spending his own money.

And he was spending a lot of it.

The only thing Seagate didn't have was a beach. So Powel bought a beach house on nearby Siesta Key.

Problem solved.

.   .   .   .   .   .

After the holidays, Powel and Gwendolyn flew down to Sarasota and moved in. They began entertaining almost as soon as they occupied the new house. There were dinners, cocktail parties, and Sunday picnics on the lawn. Guests included out-of-towners like Eugene MacDonald and Charles Deeds, the vice-president of Pratt & Whitney; Bob Ringling and Maurice Prew, who brought along his entire family, including children Neill and Ann, were frequent visitors.

Powel started looking for a new yacht to replace the *Muroma* and found a seventy-five-foot cruising houseboat named the *Argo*. He bought a car too, an American Austin, a $445 midget auto that he used to get around the grounds (on drives Jack Crawford had laid out for him as part of the mansion's construction) and for quick trips into town. The car's miniscule four-cylinder engine developed all of twelve horsepower, but it could do over forty-five miles per hour if it wasn't heavily loaded and sometimes got as much as fifty miles to the gallon.

Powel was impressed.

In March, he and Gwendolyn returned to Cincinnati for the opening of the new WLW/WSAI studios on the eighth floor of the

Arlington Street building. Isolation and soundproofing techniques had improved from the days when the old Baltimore & Ohio Railroad passed by Alfred Street and drowned out Romeo Gorno. During construction of the new building, the entire eighth floor had been structurally isolated; steel girders and concrete floors rested not on each other, but on a surface of felt.

There were five studios in all, the largest of which was sixty-three feet long, thirty-nine feet wide, and had ceilings thirty-nine feet high. It was a little symphony space unto itself. The décor was high deco, with wood paneling, open-beam ceilings, and parquet floors. There was a bandstand for the organ, with a massive inlaid-wood design featuring stars and bolts of electricity emanating from gargantuan images of microphones.

Though March was the move-in date, June was the official dedication. As always, Powel turned it into a media event. The governor of Ohio, Myers Y. Cooper, attended, as did about ten thousand others, all told. Manuel Rosenberg mingled among them, doing sketches of a handful of top Crosley executives for the *Crosley Broadcaster*. He drew his friend Powel, of course, hairline receding slightly, and Lewis, going gray at the temples, just below him, as well as Ralph Haburton, the station's new program director, and John Clark, now director of both WLW and WSAI.

Refreshments were served in an office adjoining the new studios, and then the entertainment began, courtesy of the "Nation's Station."

WLW offered, by that time, top-notch programming. Powel heard a young singer named Jane Froman, who had recently graduated from the city's Conservatory of Music, sing at the home of a mutual friend, and asked her to come to the studio for an audition. She was hired immediately—and would go on to national stardom in the .starred) in a comedy program called *Doodlesockers*. The station did a thirty-minute 'rural drama' called *Centerville Sketches*. A stock company of players—the Crosley Theater of the Air—was formed. Each week, the group performed a new play, live on the air; not just once, but three times: Thursday late night, Saturday evening, and Sunday afternoon. The innovation was the brainchild of production manager

Edward Byron, who thought a single airing of a play, after so much preparation, wasteful.

Then Powel had a brainchild of his own.

He loved organ music, and his mother loved it even more. And the studio had that big, beautiful Wurlitzer. What if, he said to Byron one day, we could do a late-evening program, with organ music and poetry?

What if indeed, Byron thought. Certainly it was possible, he allowed.

Excellent, Powel replied, or words to that effect. Have it ready tomorrow night.

Byron, no doubt, gulped.

Powel was the boss, though, and so Byron went off and did what most executives in his shoes would do—repair to a local speakeasy for a few beers.

Inspiration struck; he began to write a poem of his own. What came out was this:

Down the valley of a thousand yesterdays
Flow the bright waters of Moon River
On and on, forever waiting to carry you
Down to the land of forgetfulness,
To the kingdom of sleep,
To the realm of Moon River

It went on like that for a bit—not quite Shakespeare, but not half-bad either. A good night's work, all in all, and with the poem came the title of the program Byron was supposed to put together for the boss: *Moon River*.

It went on the air the following evening, opening with Byron's poem, read by announcer Bob Brown, set to dreamy organ music. The program was an instant hit.

It would be on, more or less continuously, for the next thirty years.

Powel was no doubt pleased with the new WLW program; he

was even more pleased with the new WLW bottom-line.

In fiscal 1930, for the first time ever, the station turned a profit; $43,464, thanks to increased advertising revenue and income courtesy of the NBC Blue Chain network, which by that point was supplying roughly a third of WLW's programming.

The radio manufacturing division, surprisingly enough, was also making money, even in the midst of what was now clearly much more than a mere economic downturn.

The company was, by this time, focused on producing console receivers. Looks and style were important too, as important, in some ways, as price. New 1930 models, called the Companionship Series, were all cabinet-style radios, with names like The Buddy, the Pal, the Mate, the Director, and the top-of-the-line Arbiter, at $137.50, which combined cabinet, radio, and electric phonograph. All were AC-powered. The day of the forty-pound radio battery was gone, except in rural, still-unelectrified America, for which the company also produced a wind-powered battery recharger. Powel never forgot the farm market.

It wasn't those models that made money in 1930, however.

The manufacturing division of the Crosley Radio Corporation made a profit largely because of a new product, one that, in retrospect, it seems surprising Powel hadn't come up with earlier, combining as it did two of his great passions.

The new product was called the 'Roamio,' and there is little doubt who came up with that name.

It was a car radio.

.   .   .   .   .   .

It wasn't the first. People had been installing radio sets—homemade jobs, largely—in cars since the early 1920s, and the Motorola, short for "Motor Victrola," was already on the market when the Roamio appeared.

But of the big radio firms, Crosley was there first and, as had happened almost a decade earlier with the Harko Senior, they were able to grab a big slice of the emerging market for themselves. It wasn't quite as big a market as had developed in the early radio boom, largely because radio and the automobile didn't fit together as smoothly as they would in the years to come.

Installation, moreover, was a nightmare. You needed to hook up the set to the car's six-volt battery, and the set required three additional batteries, which were typically installed beneath the car's back seat, which was typically where the receiver and amplifier were placed too. The control panel was a separate unit, which you had to attach to the bottom of the dashboard. In some models, the speaker was built into that panel; in others, it had to be installed separately.

Much wire, and effort, was required.

And then there was the antenna, which required even more wire—several dozen feet more. Trailing a retractable wire (as was done in airplanes) was impractical, so the antenna wire was carefully looped and placed either on the car roof or just underneath it.

The process of installation usually took about three hours.

Nevertheless, the Roamio sold well. By the end of the year, the factory was turning out three different models, ranging in price from $37.50 to $75.00.

One of Powel's businesses, however, wasn't doing so well. Crosley Aviation was just about finished. The last of the Moonbeams, the C-4, was built in May 1930, to compete in the National Air Races. In keeping with Powel's trademark of innovative design, the high-wing monoplane had overhead control sticks and folding outer wing panels.

Powel was hardly finished with airplanes, however. He bought a new Sikorsky amphibian, the S-39, a "sport amphibian," designed specifically for men like him, wealthy men who wanted to expand their destination choices. It was a single-engine aircraft with seats for four passengers, plus the pilot and co-pilot. The airplane had a top speed of one hundred and twenty miles per hour, and could cruise at one hundred miles per hour. The nominal range was four hundred miles on a tank of fuel, which meant the S-39 could make the trip from Cincinnati to Sarasota in three hops. The price tag was twenty thousand dollars.

He had a dock built for it in front of the Sarasota house.

He flew it to Florida for the first time that same month, for the 1930 Tarpon Tournament. Powel was now President of the Sarasota Anglers Club, and he planned, perhaps as another boost for the local economy, to publicize the event by broadcasting it over WLW. A special kind of boat was required—so special, in fact, that one had to be built from scratch. A thirty-foot fishing boat was outfitted as a floating radio studio, though perhaps the term 'fishing boat' gives the wrong impression, as in addition to a shortwave transmitter, the boat was also equipped with a bar, kitchen, and salon.

After the tournament and broadcast, which went off without a hitch, Powel flew back to Cincinnati. It was summer. The children were out of school, and in fact, no longer children. Page was seventeen, set to make her debut the following spring. A lot of boys were following her around, and it wasn't only because her father was the richest man in College Hill (though that hardly hurt matters). Though still a teenager, she already had the kind of beauty that simply tied tongues.

Powel III had someone following him around as well. Back in the spring, a young woman named June Huston Smith, came from Canada to visit her grandmother in Cincinnati, where they met. They spent a great deal of time together during the Easter Holiday, taking several long drives across the river into Kentucky. Unfortunately for Powel III, June, at her parents' insistence, attended a girls school in England.

He was looking forward to his last summer at home before college. In the fall, he planned to attend the University of Cincinnati. The young man had a hard act to follow. The newspapers reminded him of it everyday, with every quote from Powel, Jr., every ad for Crosley radios and WLW.

But he had no desire to follow in his father's footsteps. He had no single burning desire at all, at least not at the moment. Powel III wasn't like his father—or his grandfather, for that matter. They were driven men. Powel III wasn't. He had interests; he had hobbies. He played the piano; he liked to tinker. Over the last few summers, he'd developed an interest in speedboats.

That August, he took his hobby a step further, when he and a friend named Tom Johnson tried to break the existing speedboat endurance record. They stripped a fourteen-foot runabout, equipped it with a new two-cylinder engine, and started cruising the Ohio River between the Queen City Boat Club and the Cincinnati Suspension Bridge, a distance of about five miles, over and over again.

They were at it for four days, sleeping in shifts. A few hours shy of the record, a spark plug malfunctioned, and they came up short.

Powel, meanwhile, was buying another airplane—a Lockheed Vega. This one, however, was for the company's use—for publicity purposes, to ferry executives to and fro, although of course, more often than not the executive it would be ferrying was Powel. He had it repainted (the fuselage red and the wings a cream color), and christened the 'New Cincinnati.'

Along with the plane came one of its former owners, William Brock, who started work for the Radio Corporation as the company's official pilot. Brock's first job came August 15, when he flew Powel to Indianapolis to meet with Fred Duesenberg. On the way, Brock set a new record for the journey: forty-three minutes. He broke that record by five minutes on the return flight.

Crosley engineers soon installed a one-hundred-and-fifty-watt radio transmitter and a retractable seventy-five-foot trailing wire antenna: instant mobile radio station.

The New Cincinnati flew in the 1930 National Air Races, finishing fourth, then served as official radio ship for the remainder of the show's events, some of which were rebroadcast on NBC. Powel hired well-known aviatrix Elinor Smith (who Metal Aircraft Corporation had lent a Flamingo in 1929) to handle the mike for part of the festivities.

On Labor Day, the Vega was in Cleveland to cover the International Balloon Races. From September 11 to 27, it flew the National Air Tour, thirty cities in those sixteen days, with, once again, promotional events for Crosley dealers at each stop.

The next-to-last stop on the tour was Cincinnati's Lunken Airport; a weekend celebration was held there, after the tour finished, to rededicate the airfield, as the Lunkenheimer family, who had owned and operated the facility for better than a decade, had decided to donate it to the city to serve as a municipal airport.

It was a gala the likes of which Cincinnati had not seen for some time. Aviation was still, even in the midst of the worsening depression, the newest, hottest, latest thing.

Charles Lindbergh himself had been scheduled as the principal guest, but at the last minute he was unable to attend. Howard Hughes was there, however, along with Jean Harlow, star of the about-to-be-released film *Hell's Angels*. Powel was there, as was the last Crosley Moonbeam, featured in a round of exhibition flying on Friday and Sunday. At a banquet Saturday evening, Hughes awarded cash prizes to winners of an aerial contest. Powel, with him on the dais, gave away Crosley radios.

Powel was back at Lunken a few weeks later, on October 15, for another celebration. The occasion this time was the first transcontinental "through" flight from Atlanta to Los Angeles. The plane had a half-hour stop scheduled in Cincinnati. The passengers, many of them celebrities, took the time to debark and mingle.

One of those passengers was a young woman named Ruth Nichols, who had a little more than mingling on her mind. Nichols was a pilot herself, a friend of Elinor Smith's, a resident of Rye, New York, a Wellesley College graduate, who'd been bitten hard by the flying bug early on. She turned in her life as a socialite for that of an aviatrix, hence her nickname, "The Flying Debutante."

The debutante was deadly serious about her flying career. She and her friend Amelia Earhart were co-founders of the pioneer women pilots club, the Ninety-Nines. Nichols had also recently set several aviation records; now she had another goal in mind. She was going to follow in Lindbergh's footsteps and be the first woman to fly the Atlantic alone. But she needed a sponsor, someone to provide an airplane and cover her expenses.

Enter Powel.

CHAPTER 19

The meeting at Lunken was arranged by Nichols, who made her pitch brief, and to the point. "I suggested," she said later, "that it might be a great idea if I used the plane to try for new transcontinental altitude and speed records as publicity for the Crosley company."

The plane she wanted was the Vega, which was, for the moment, sidelined, as William Brock was in a Cincinnati hospital, having an appendectomy.

The idea intrigued Powel. He and Nichols agreed to talk further.

Off she went to Los Angeles.

A month later, she was back in Cincinnati, though not for long. She took off again from Crosley Airport in the Vega, heading for New York as fast as she could fly. Her goal was an inter-city speed record for the Cincinnati-New York trip. It was the first of several record attempts she and Powel had planned. She hadn't said a word to him yet about a trans-Atlantic flight. She was saving that pitch until she'd proven herself to him.

Her plan hit a snag when she had to make an emergency landing in the fog, well short of her goal. Coming down, she broke the Vega's propeller.

Powel—or rather, the company—paid to fix it.

Nichols tried again on November 24, leaving from NY, headed to LA. This time, she (and the Vega) arrived in one piece. On the way she set a new women's record for the trip: sixteen hours, fifty-nine minutes. Both pilot and airplane were lauded by the press and photos of the Vega, with CROSLEY boldly lettered on the fuselage, appeared in dozens of papers across the country.

The return trip got even more attention. Not only did Nichols break the women's record for the west-to-east cross-country run, in the process, she topped Charles Lindbergh's time for the same flight. She was interviewed nationwide and wrote articles for several high-profile magazines. To the press, she often mentioned that the Crosley radio installed in the New Cincinnati had been vital to her success, enabling her to keep abreast of weather conditions along her route.

Powel immediately gave her the go-ahead for an attempt on

the women's altitude record.

And he and Lewis made preparations for a new venture of their own.

After taxes and depreciation, 1930's profit was $223,994. It was, all things considered, a good year.

But...

Crosley sets now accounted for less than 13 percent of all radios sold. The company had slipped to fourth place among radio manufacturers. They knew it was time to move on to the next thing. And they knew exactly what that next thing was going to be.

The Icyball had shown them the way.

It was time to break into the refrigerator business big-time.

CHAPTER 20

O
n March 6, 1931, Ruth Nichols took off from Roosevelt Field and climbed to an altitude of close to thirty thousand feet, breaking the record previously set by Elinor Smith in her borrowed Flamingo. When she landed, she sent out a telegram:

HAPPY TO ADVISE BOTH ALTIMETERS SHOWED OVER THIRTY THOUSAND FEET THUS BREAKING IN CROSLEY RADIO PLANE BOTH THE WOMENS ALTITUDE AND ALSO THE WORLDS RECORD FOR MEN AND WOMEN IN COMMERCIAL SHIPS WISH TO EXPRESS MY DEEPEST APPRECIATION TO MR POWEL CROSLEY WHO MADE IT POSSIBLE
RUTH NICHOLS

As 1931 began, Powel was receiving 'hails' and 'farewells' from other corners as well. The Mills brothers said goodbye, moving on to New York and CBS. WLW signed up another group, the Four Riff Brothers (formerly the Percolating Puppies and later the King, the Jack, and the Jester), to fill their shoes. By and by, the new group appeared on WLW programs such as *The Rhythm Club* and *The Crosley Club*. By and by, they followed the Mills Brothers to New York, where they became known by yet another name: The Ink Spots.

Fred Smith was in New York too, developing a stock company of actors to work on *The March of Time*, but to some members of the Crosley family that particular month, it didn't seem like time was marching on at all.

It seemed as if time was bending back on itself, repeating the events of some twenty years ago. The news (part of which broke to the world on the front page of the February 25, 1931, *Cincinnati Enquirer*) was this:

Powel Crosley had eloped.

Powel Crosley had moved into the Glenwood Apartments with his new wife.

Powel Crosley was flunking out of the University of Cincinnati.

The Powel Crosley in question, though, was not Junior or Senior, but Powel III.

It seemed as if one of those drives over the river to Kentucky the previous Easter had been to a justice of the peace.

Powel III and June Smith, as it turned out, were married.

·　·　·　·　·

In 1919, when Powel, Sr., learned that his son had driven across state lines to elope, he raged.

"When," he'd demanded, "are you going to settle down and make something of yourself?"

When Powel, Jr., heard what his son had done...

He arranged for wedding announcements to appear in the local papers.

He sent the young couple on a belated honeymoon to Sarasota.

And he arranged for Powel III—having problems at the University of Cincinnati—to attend Miami University, in Oxford Ohio, starting in the fall.

He was not going to put his boy through the same treatment he'd received.

Part of his motivation was, no doubt, a feeling of guilt. He'd spent the last ten years building an empire. The boy who'd been there at the beginning with him, the boy whose desire for a radio set had really gotten the Crosley Radio Corporation its start, was suddenly a man. He'd missed huge portions of his son's childhood, and he wanted to make up for that.

Powel was soon to discover, however, the truth behind the

adage: all the money in the world could not buy him, or those he loved, happiness.

. . . . . .

In March, she'd gone for height; in April, Ruth Nichols went for speed. The morning of April 13, the New Cincinnati raced across the skies of Grosse Isle, Michigan at 210.685 miles per hour—twenty-five miles per hour faster than the old mark, which had been held by her friend Amelia Earhart. Triumphant, Nichols flew back to Crosley Airport that afternoon and took a taxi over to Arlington Street.

The time had come, she decided, to talk to Powel about the trans-Atlantic flight. The meeting didn't start out well; he turned her down flat. I do not wish to take the responsibility, Powel told her, of risking a woman's life.

Nichols had heard that one before.

"I pointed out the injustice of making different roles for women than for men," she related in her autobiography. "I recount-ed all the difficulties and the desperate efforts entailed in establishing the three world records I now held, for his plane."

Powel was unmoved.

Nichols was unstoppable.

She wouldn't take no for an answer. She talked about the publicity she'd already brought to Crosley and the additional publicity that a trans-Atlantic flight would bring. She talked again and again about the potential benefits of the flight and her ability to see it through.

Powel had rarely met someone willing to argue with him so strenuously.

In the end he spread his hands in a gesture of resignation and smiled.

Go fly the ocean if you must, he told her. With my blessing.

. . . . . .

Nichols spent the next six weeks thoroughly preparing for the attempt. She flew training flight after training flight, made adjustments, consulted with other flyers, including Charles Lindbergh. She lined up additional sponsors to help finance the venture, which would end up costing more than one hundred thousand dollars.

She had the interior of the plane gutted and extra fuel tanks installed. She had the Vega's standard landing gear replaced with a specially designed lightweight set. She had the instrumental panel redesigned, the shoulder of the wing lowered to improve visibility and reduce drag.

The entire airplane was repainted, white with gold wings, "Crosley" curving across the leading edge of the rudder, "Crosley Radio Plane" on the nose. She renamed the plane *The Akita*, a Native American word meaning "to explore," and on June 22, 1931, she set off from New York to do just that.

She headed for Nova Scotia, her official North American point of departure. Her official destination was Ireland. Weather conditions were favorable; more than favorable, in fact, they were friendly. An unexpected tail wind put her in Portland, Maine, ahead of schedule for a refueling stop. She decided to push on to the St. John airport, her jumping-off point. She had never been there herself, but another flier had assured her it was large enough to accommodate the Vega.

As it turned out, the other pilot had never been there either.

The St. John airport was smaller than she had been led to believe—much smaller. She overshot her touchdown point on the runway. She tried to take off again, but the airplane's tail hit the treetops. The engine stopped. The plane nosed down and crashed.

Nichols lay stunned a moment.

When she recovered her wits, she saw oil oozing from a tank beneath her seat and gasoline pouring from a broken fuel line. She shut off the engine, undid her safety belt, and reached for the hatch above her head.

Excruciating pain nearly paralyzed her. Somehow she managed to crawl out of the plane and onto the wing.

CHAPTER 20

Rescue workers took her to a nearby hospital. She had five broken vertebrae and would be bed-ridden for several months, in a plaster cast, and then a steel brace. She was, all things considered, lucky to be alive.

But before she even allowed doctors at the hospital to check her over, she dictated two telegrams. One went to her mother, the other to Powel. She advised him of the crash and her intent to repair the Vega with insurance money and make another try as soon as possible. She hoped for his consent in the attempt.

He gave it, no questions asked, because if there was one thing Powel understood, if there was one character trait he appreciated, it was persistence. If at first you didn't succeed, there was only one thing to do.

Try again.

The Vega was dismantled, crated, and shipped off for repairs.

Powel didn't miss it a bit. By then he'd bought another airplane, a Douglas Dolphin 3, the latest in amphibious aircraft, with all the leading-edge technology aviation had to offer in 1931. The plane flew at two hundred and fifty miles per hour and had a range of over six hundred. Powel's was the first off the line. The Vanderbilts picked up two afterward, and the Rockefellers got one for Standard Oil.

Powel's came with a bar and a sofa in the passenger cabin, which meant that it only seated six, instead of the usual eight, so he held onto the Sikorsky as well, just in case, keeping that down in Sarasota.

The new plane cost him thirty-five thousand dollars. He named it the *Le'sgo* and got himself a new pilot to go along with it, a man named Eddie Nirmaier, who had worked for Al Capone, which meant he knew where liquor might be easily obtained, knowledge which was to prove quite handy come winter, when Powel and Gwendolyn resumed throwing parties in the Florida house.

Powel had the same distinctive emblem painted on the nose of the plane that he'd put on his yacht's flag: a blue triangle with a white "C" inside it, crossed by a red lightning bolt.

Powel returned to Cincinnati, where he learned he was going

to be a grandfather.

June Huston Smith Crosley was pregnant. Powel decided to give the young couple an early Christmas present; he made plans to build them a house across the road from Pinecroft, so that the family could stay together, so that he and Gwendolyn would be there to help them if they needed it.

The impending arrival of the next generation gave him pause.

He and Lewis bought a plot of land in Spring Grove Cemetery, up the road from the Crosley Radio Corporation headquarters. Prominent Cincinnati names such as Garfield, Taft, Kroger, and Seasongood could be found throughout the landscaped grounds. Now the Crosley name would join them. The plot was not just for the brothers, but their families as well, the land to be evenly divided between the two.

The first thing Lewis did was move his baby sister Charlotte, now thirty-five years gone, and have her re-interred on his side of the lot.

Down the road, at the Arlington Street factory, the focus was on the future not the past. The focus was on refrigerators; Crosley engineers were finalizing designs. Lewis was there with them. He was focusing on the door seals, which were especially tricky. They'd paid a Canadian inventor named James West ten thousand dollars for patent rights to a seal he'd developed. Lewis offered a few (later patented) designs of his own to the engineering team.

Powel, meanwhile, focused on cost. His goal was refrigeration for the masses, not the classes. He was adamant that the refrigerator retail for under one hundred dollars. But an analysis of projected production costs showed the unit would have to sell for $187.50 to generate an acceptable profit.

Powel called in the team, held up the design they'd been working on for the better part of a year, and told them it was useless.

"Throw it in the ash can," he said. Cut costs. Find a shortcut. Make it cheaper.

The engineers, no doubt, gulped.

Then they did what most other engineers would do in their

shoes, went back down the hall, and back to the drawing board.

Powel went out to shop the marketplace. He found another company had beaten him to the punch and were already selling a refrigerator for less than a hundred dollars. Powel bought one and had it delivered to Arlington Street. That afternoon, he had it disassembled and the parts laid out on a large table in a conference room.

The next morning, he brought the engineers in again.

Here is our competition, he said, or words to that effect. Our job is to build a refrigerator for less than this.

The engineers tried not to look dubious.

Powel picked up a compressor and asked how much it would cost to buy.

Five dollars, was the answer. In quantity.

Then we can build it ourselves for less than two, Powel said.

The engineers didn't know what to say to that.

So it went for the rest of the day, as Powel went over one part after another, looking for ways to cut costs. In that room the first Crosley refrigerator was designed, unnecessary components eliminated, cheaper ones substituted. They decided which parts to manufacture in-house and which to outsource. When they were finished, Powel told his team to come back in two weeks with what he wanted.

The engineers, alternately inspired and terrified by the boss, delivered right on schedule. They brought Powel a design for a 4 1/2 cubic-foot box with a compressor on top that could retail for under one hundred dollars.

He was pleased.

He went down the hall to the marketing department and hovered over their shoulders, making suggestions until he was satisfied with the ad copy. In a way, it was inspiring for the staff to have the boss right there with them. In a way, it was terrifying.

In every way, it was unusual.

Powel wasn't the Crosley who ran the factories; that was Lewis's job. Whenever Powel upset or interrupted that routine, it made even more work for his brother. Lewis never took work home, but he couldn't help expressing his frustrations to Lucy when he got there.

"You ought to get a new job," she would tell him.

That was unlikely to ever happen, and Lewis would seek solace in his garden. But the stress was beginning to show: the stress of running the factories, of overseeing WLW, of managing thousands of workers in the middle of a rapidly growing depression when he was responsible for the company's bottom line and at the same time aware that every dollar earned by every worker in the factory was precious.

It was like a bubble growing inside him.

Sooner or later, it was going to burst.

.　.　.　.　.

Ruth Nichols was ready to fly again. Repair work on the Vega wasn't finished until early September, too late in the year for an Atlantic crossing. She decided to tackle a different record: the women's non-stop distance flight, then at 1,810 miles.

She started in Oakland, California, on October 24; she landed some fourteen hours later in Louisville, Kentucky. Total mileage: 1977. It was not only a new record but a greater distance than the trans-Atlantic crossing would require.

She sent a telegram to Powel and then caught a few hours sleep at a friend's house. The next morning, after a radio broadcast for WLW, she headed to the airport to see that the Vega was properly refueled and serviced. It looked okay to her.

But it wasn't.

A small fuel dump valve had been improperly adjusted; the next day, as Nichols started to taxi down the runway for take off, gas began spewing from the front of the plane. Engine exhaust ignited it.

Nichols managed to escape through the airplane hatch; an instant later, a gas tank exploded.

The fire burned for a good long while.

She called Powel and gave him the bad news; he told her to ship the Vega's remains back to Cincinnati.

She told him no.

She wanted another chance; she needed another chance. She

was going to be the first woman across the Atlantic, and she'd raise the money to rebuild the Vega herself. All he had to do was let her fix his plane and let her try again.

There was only one thing Powel could say to that.

The Vega was shipped by rail to Roosevelt Field in New York, where numerous mechanics set about the task of rebuilding it.

Nichols set to work raising the money she needed.

. . . . .

Another year came and went. On Christmas Day 1931, Powel, Sr., turned eighty-two. In January 1932, Powel, Jr., rather than travel to Mississippi to go quail hunting, took part in another Aviation Country Club racing event. He and Eddie Nirmaier, who piloted the Douglas Dolphin won the trophy, competing against such notables as William Randolph Hearst, Jr., Miss Alice du Pont, and Powel's Indiana cousins, Edmund F. Ball and Frank E. Ball.

In early February, Powel flew back to Cincinnati to help with the introduction of the Crosley refrigerator. The company and its distributors began a campaign urging every one of the seventeen thousand Crosley retailers in North America to stock the refrigerators. Shipping began in earnest that March, simultaneous with advertisements in magazines, newspapers, and, of course, radio.

It was, in some respects, just like old times. At $99.95, the Crosley refrigerator cost around fifty dollars less than comparable, competitive, models. Once more, they were there first, with the cheapest. Before long, there was a backlog of orders. Lewis expanded the production lines. Soon they were shipping more than a thousand refrigerators per month.

One of the reasons Crosley refrigerators cost less was because they were a bit smaller than their competitors. Market analysis soon convinced Powel that the company could succeed with larger refrigerators as well. The new models were in full production by summer. They cost correspondingly more than the original, but they were still cheaper than comparable models from Frigidaire, GE, and other manufacturers.

Upstairs, in the WLW studios, new fingers were tickling the keys of the 'Moon River' organ. They belonged to Thomas Wright "Fats" Waller, a twenty-seven-year-old jazz singer-pianist with a string of show scores and hit tunes to his credit. He was given his own program, *Fats Waller's Rhythm Club*, in addition to his Moon River responsibilities. Also working on the latter at the time was a young singer/actor named Eddie Albert. Waller, Albert later recalled, had a hard time staying within the confines of *Moon River*. Soothing organ music was not his style; he tended to jazz things up now and then.

Another new arrival at the station was an announcer named Peter Grant, who came aboard to read news headlines provided courtesy of the papers and the wire services. The days of the old media providing the new those free-of-charge services were rapidly coming to an end; soon enough, radio stations would be responsible for gathering their own news, a development that would have significant consequences for all concerned.

Other talent came and went. Jane Froman departed, as did the singers soon to be known as the Ink Spots. Powel and Lewis gave station management the go-ahead to recruit large numbers of East Coast entertainers on a "trial" basis. Singers, musicians, and even writers were given free transportation to Cincinnati and a salaried, trial run on WLW. If they proved to be popular, they were signed to a contract. If not, WLW paid their train fare back home.

Audience response determined who stayed and who got the hook. It was just like the old vaudeville days at the Pike Theater.

"A perfect radio program should, I believe, put a one-hour vaudeville show on the air," Powel had told a reporter once, and that was how he and Lewis ran their radio station.

And just like the old days, there was always another show coming to town. If one star left, someone just as capable would be waiting right around the corner.

· · · · ·

Ruth Nichols wrote magazine articles. She gave speeches, and served as a flying goodwill ambassador for the National Council of Women. She collected funds from the Life Savers candy company, as well as individuals. She sought money anywhere she could find it to finish repairing Powel's airplane.

She was determined to follow in Charles Lindbergh's wake, to become the first women to cross the Atlantic Ocean.

But on the night of March 1, 1932, Lindbergh himself was wishing he'd never made that flight. His celebrity had forced him and his wife, Anne, to seek seclusion from the press and a never-ending stream of admirers. They'd purchased a house in the isolated Central New Jersey township of East Amwell, not far from Anne's parents. They had one child, Charles, Jr., and were expecting another.

And then that one child was gone.

Sometime between eight and ten p.m. someone broke into the mansion and kidnapped the little boy, who was eighteen months old. The kidnappers left a ransom note asking for fifty thousand dollars.

The Lindbergh kidnapping was in the headlines for weeks, months, even years to come. It was the Crime of the Century. When the press first caught wind of it, they descended on the house in such numbers that the crime scene and potentially valuable evidence was obliterated.

In the midst of the furor, another child was born.

Powel Crosley IV, the would-be heir to his grandfather's empire, arrived on March 19, 1932; very shortly thereafter, Powel Crosley III, following in his father's footsteps once more, dropped out of Miami University, whereupon Powel, Jr., like his father before him, arranged a job for his son with the Proctor-Collier advertising agency.

At the same time, the hunt for the Lindbergh baby continued. A thousand leads were followed, all leading to dead ends. Numerous would-be intermediaries with the supposed kidnappers came forward. None proved real. On May 12, a truck driver walking in the woods near his home stumbled across a toddler's body. It was Charles, Jr., who had died, most likely the very night of his kidnapping, of a skull fracture. The shock and sorrow and rage were palpable nationwide;

who could have done such a thing?

Among the wealthy, there was fear as well.

These were desperate times. The question for them became who might be next.

. . . . . .

Ruth Nichols was once more ready to fly. Powel himself gave her the last thousand dollars she needed for the repairs. She prepared herself and the plane for her flight across the Atlantic. On May 19, she met with Amelia Earhart to discuss the hazards of ocean flying. The two women were neighbors, both residents of Rye, New York, and were friends. But they were also competitors, a fact both were well aware of that night. Earhart concealed a secret as they spoke: she was ready to go, right then, right there.

She took off from Newfoundland the next day. Landing in Ireland fifteen hours later, she became an instant celebrity, basking in Lindbergh's reflected glory. She entered the pages of history; Ruth Nichols became a footnote.

But she refused to give up.

Her friend was first across the Atlantic, all right. That was over and done. But there was another possibility. She could be the first woman to fly the Pacific, from Hawaii to California.

That trip would require additional funding, and Nichols made arrangements to raise it from the Republican Party. She would undertake a cross-country flight, dropping Hoover-for-President leaflets along the way.

On the morning of November 3, she prepared to leave Chicago for Los Angeles. Taxiing down the runway, one of the landing gear snapped. The Vega slewed sideways and began spinning, a ruptured fuel line spewing gasoline across the runway. Nichols killed the engine immediately, but it was too little, too late.

The Vega was done.

It was disassembled and shipped, once more, to Roosevelt Field in New York, presumably sold later for parts. Exit Ruth Nichols, stage left.

CHAPTER 20

. . . . .

Nichols wasn't the only one having a string of bad luck. Sidney Weil had had nothing but bad luck since gaining control of the Cincinnati Reds in the last days of the stock market boom. The 1932 team, despite the presence of Babe Herman and a young catcher named Ernie Lombardi, who had both arrived that spring courtesy of a blockbuster deal with the Dodgers, was on its way toward a second consecutive last-place finish. Attendance was down. Talk was that Cincinnati, the birthplace of professional baseball, was no longer capable of supporting a major-league franchise.

A hundred or so miles north of the Queen City, Larry MacPhail and Weil's old minor-league franchise were doing just fine. The Columbus club was now an affiliate of the major-league Cardinals. MacPhail ran it like it was a major-league team itself. He built a new ballpark and built himself a handsome new office. He ran incessant promotions, generating a handsome profit. He dealt with Cardinals owner Branch Rickey like an equal, a fact the other man found infuriating. Their relationship was not destined to last much longer.

Another relationship, one of considerably longer standing, was about to fall apart as well. RCA, Westinghouse, and GE, prompted by yet another round of monopoly investigations by the government, had at long last agreed to dissolve the union Owen Young had forged in the aftermath of the Great War. As part of the deal, the Radio Corporation was given manufacturing plants belonging to the other two companies. RCA, at long last, was able to make its own receiving sets.

David Sarnoff, by then president of the company, made plans to move his entire organization into a vast new complex of buildings being built by the Rockefeller family in midtown Manhattan.

Powel was making plans too, of similarly grand scope.

He wanted to take WLW to five hundred thousand watts.

It was broadcasting power at a level that had never been attempted. But to Powel, it was the next logical step. Extending the station's range enabled him to reach more people. It enabled him to sell more radios. And the more powerful the station, the cheaper he could build those sets.

To reach five hundred thousand watts, however, much of the design and engineering would have to be experimental. He thus applied to the FRC for an experimental license; permission was granted in June 1932.

Broadcasting magazine made an official announcement to the trade in its June 15 issue: the coming of a "New Radio Giant," was to take place within the year. Hours of operation were set between one and six in the morning.

The grumbling began at once. Some said that the transmitter's powerful signal would blanket the entire broadcast band. Others immediately applied for permission to build their own five-hundred-thousand-watt transmitters. The FRC refused.

The license granted was experimental; only one such case study was needed. The government's interest was, as always, how to best use broadcasting to serve the public. Superpower was one possibility, but this was superpower of an unprecedented scope. No one knew the ramifications—technical, cultural, economic—such an experiment might have.

The license had to be renewed every six months. That stipulation would cause no little problem for Powel and WLW later on.

For the moment, however, he had other concerns.

His daughter had eloped.

And his father was dying.

. . . . . .

Powel, Sr., had been sick a long time, and had told no one, not even his wife. The first clue came in the spring, after Lewis had given his ten-year-old daughter, Ellen, a handful of tomato plants from their garden to take to his father. Later that day, he'd checked in with her.

Nellie, he said (his nickname for Ellen). Did you do as I asked? Did you give your grandfather the tomato plants?

Yes, she told him. But they're not going to grow.

And why is that, Lewis asked.

Because he didn't plant them the right way, Ellen said.

The smile dropped from his face.

Powel, Sr., was as much a gardener as Lewis. Something, obviously, was wrong. Lewis went to his father's house, where he learned that the older man had not been feeling well for some time. The family finally convinced him to go a doctor. It was too late.

Powel, Sr., had cancer.

On September 18, 1932, he passed away, missing his granddaughter Page's wedding—but he wasn't the only one.

Page, like her brother and father before her, had run to a justice of the peace, sans family, to marry. Her accomplice was a young man named Gilman Shelton. Powel, Jr., knew little of him, but what he did know he didn't like. Nonetheless, he gave Shelton a job and gave the young couple a hand-up financially as well.

Powel's money did not solve their problems.

.   .   .   .   .   .

In Washington D.C., Merle Tuve was also experimenting with superpower—on the order of two million volts. Tuve was formally attached to the Institute of Terrestrial Magnetism, and his work now had nothing to do with radio. Tuve was interested in those high voltages as they could be used to help accelerate the elementary building blocks of matter, as they could be used to explore the inner workings of the atom.

His boyhood friend from South Dakota, Ernest Lawrence, who had moved on by that point from the crystal radio to theoretical physics, shared his interest. Through the years, the two men had continued the correspondence they'd begun as children In September 1932, Lawrence developed a device he called the cyclotron. The power it generated, close to four million volts, provided both he and Tuve ever more precise tools for probing the atomic nucleus. Those tools would soon prove of cataclysmic importance, not only to physicists but to every human being on the planet.

The presidential election of 1932, held less than two months later was more than anything else, a referendum on Herbert Hoover, one of the most competent, selfless leaders in American political history. He simply had the great misfortune of taking office at exactly the wrong moment. He now exited, stage left, bound for the pages of history.

The Great Depression continued, unabated. The unemployment rate ballooned to twenty-five percent. In Washington D.C., WWI veterans set up a shantytown. They wanted bonus money promised them for their service during the Great War. The Army evicted them with bayonets, tear gas, and tanks.

In New York, police repeated the action with a group of homeless squatters in Central Park. The group had built themselves a shack of fruit and egg crates in the center of their makeshift village. On top of it was an American flag. In the center of that shack was their single most important communal possession—a radio.

It was a symbol of the times.

In the twenties, it stood for the boom. In the thirties, it was a source of light—one of the few remaining in ever darker, ever more disheartening times. In homes all across the country, people gathered around their sets each night, waiting anxiously for their favorite programs to begin. With a sweep of a single dial, entertainment of every conceivable variety filled the room.

It was, at last, the Golden Age of Radio, that moment in time when both hardware and software—receiving set and programs— came of age, when the stars of the past, the great vaudevillians and actors of the traveling stage circuit, came together with the stars of the future, the names that would become as big on the hardware to come, the television set, as they were now on the broadcast dial.

And as the company's new slogan promised, no matter what was on the air, you were "there with a Crosley." The director series models like the Arbiter or the Buddy were handsome pieces of furniture that were the centerpiece in living rooms across the country.

The company had led the way in the twenties with the Harko, and the Model V, the first mass-produced, truly affordable radios, and their sets would be there in the thirties as well, although the company name was to carry far more weight because of its association with radio station WLW.

At fifty thousand watts, its signal reached metropolitan areas in most of Ohio, Indiana, and Kentucky, rural areas in those states and half a dozen others as well. It was, in the words of *Broadcasting* magazine, "perhaps the most widely heard broadcasting station in North America."

At Powel's proposed five hundred thousand watts, it would be, in fact as well as name, the Nation's Station.

Along with that power, however, would come an awesome responsibility.

"The use of this magic multiplier of yours, the microphone," Ohio Governor Cooper had told Powel at the dedication ceremony two years earlier, "makes of you a newspaper magnate, a magazine publisher, a superintendent of schools with half the nation as your district, a leader of industry, and even a leader in things religious."

The words were part flattery, no doubt.

But in no way were they exaggeration.

Radio in the 1930s was more than entertainment. More and more, it shaped public opinion, convinced people what to buy, what to think, what was hot, and what was not. That power was terrifying to some people. Who could tell, listening in the comfort of their home, what was truth and what was fiction?

The lines, in the years to come, would blur more than once.

CHAPTER 21

I n the winter of 1932, Crosley engineers began finalizing designs for the 1933 refrigerators. Tooling was completed when James West, the engineer who'd earlier sold them the patent for a refrigerator seal, which turned out to be ten thousand dollars down the toilet, asked once more for a moment of Powel's time.

Powel, who was always open to new ideas, agreed. The inventor, it turned out, had another idea. Actually, it was his wife's idea. Constance West, like every other housewife across the country, had enjoyed the benefits of refrigeration for the last several years but always found herself short on space when it came to storing food. She'd looked at her refrigerator one day and realized something interesting.

When the door was shut, the inside of that door was part of the refrigerated environment. Why not, she thought, take advantage of that space. Why not put shelves on the inside of the door?

Constance West had just come up with an idea that was about to make millions of lives a little bit easier. She'd shared the idea with her husband, who immediately recognized its importance. He'd elaborated on the basic concept, received a patent for it, and then gone to all the major players in the refrigerator business—Frigidaire, Kelvinator, and GE among them—intent on cashing in on what seemed to him a bulletproof product.

No one was interested.

West began to think he and his wife were crazy, that maybe the shelves-in-a-door concept wasn't such a great one after all. Crosley, not a major player in the business, represented one of his last few chances to make a sale. West made his pitch.

Powel sensed an opportunity.

More than that, he sensed the same thing West did: a bullet-proof product. He asked the inventor for a price.

Twenty-five thousand dollars, the man shot back.

Powel brought Lewis in on the conversation.

Lewis saw the same potential in the product his brother had seen. He couldn't figure out why the other companies had passed on it. He and Powel urged West to take five thousand dollars in cash and a royalty of one dollar on every unit.

The inventor demurred. He wanted twenty-five thousand.

Powel and Lewis showed their hand, just a little bit.

The refrigerator market was booming, Powel told West. He felt certain that the company could sell well over twenty-five thousand units in the first year. West would be selling himself short if he settled for a lump sum.

A lump sum, West insisted, was what he wanted.

Powel frowned.

He and Lewis tried again; West wouldn't budge.

Powel saw there was no moving the man. Lewis pulled his brother aside, and reminded him of the ten thousand dollars they had lost on West's failed refrigerator seal patent.

Powel saw his point. If you insist on cash here and now, he told West, we'll insist on deducting that ten thousand dollars. That leaves you with fifteen thousand. A one-time-only payment. Is that really what you want? No royalty, on what I assure you is a sensational product?

That's what I want, West said.

Powel sighed, and buzzed in the lawyers.

An agreement was quickly drawn up. West got his check; the Crosley Radio Corporation got his patent. The brothers set up meetings with the company's refrigeration engineers, product designers, and marketing people and began a crash program to get a refrigerator with shelves in the door into production.

Lewis and the engineering department soon ran into a major

problem: to meet shipping deadlines for the new appliance season, the new units had to come off the line by a specific date. There was no time to retool the equipment, to reshape the cabinets and the doors to accommodate the patent. The existing cabinets were shaped to fit a flat door, with flat hinges. They couldn't be changed.

Lewis came up with the solution but didn't like it.

"We bumped out the door," Lewis explained, "just like a little pan, and designed the shelves to go into that." Making the inside of the door concave provided just enough room for usable shelves. The following year's model would have much deeper shelves.

Powel named the new refrigerator the Shelvador.

It hit in February of 1933, priced at $99.50. Distributors, retailers, and consumers everywhere immediately began clamoring for it. By May the company was back-ordered, a hundred and forty railroad cars worth.

Powel, en route to the Sarasota house to rejoin Gwendolyn, arranged a quick meeting with several Crosley dealers at Chandler Field in Atlanta during a refueling stop. Someone tipped off the newspapers that he was coming to town. A Crosley distributor, a factory rep, several dealer representatives, as well as reporters and photographers from the *Atlanta Journal* and the *Atlanta Constitution* showed up to meet him. Powel, wearing a natty snap-brim hat and full-length chinchilla coat, spoke briefly on the state of the radio business and on business trends in general. Given the bleak economic times, the distributors were ecstatic to have a new product that people would buy. The newspapers were eager to publish some good news for a change. Powel, in his imperial tone, gave them all what they wanted and basked in their adulation. And then he was off to Florida. Knowing that the Shelvador was already generating spectacular sales and his bank account would continue to fill, he planned to buy more toys— yachts and airplanes—when he got to Sarasota. He would leave to his brother the details of how all of those orders for refrigerators would be filled. He had things to buy and fish to catch.

Lewis, meanwhile, was back at the factory trying to figure out how to fill those railroad cars with new refrigerators. He pulled workers and production space away from radios, and kept the new refrigerators coming.

Crosley engineers redesigned the door to provide more shelf space. They increased effective storage space by putting a slide-out bin between the legs of the refrigerator, and then extended the sides and the door down to an inch above the floor. (The bin was called the Shelvabin.) Shelves were added to the part of the door that extended to the floor.

The new model was called the Tri-Shelvador; it sold almost as well as the original. More improvements, more options followed. Before long, Shelvador buyers had their choice of exterior color—white with black trim or green. They also could choose among an array of new features, such as the Shelvatray, Shelvabasket, and Stor-abin. Crosley came out with a larger Shelvador and a small counter-top model with two cubic feet of storage space. A chest Shelvador, the counter-top model with the door on the top, followed (the door had shelves, of course).

Other manufacturers tried in vain to follow suit.

A company called Fairbanks-Morse added a second door inside the refrigerator and lined it with shelves. Consumers didn't buy it. Philco tried the novelty of a door that opened from either side. That didn't work either.

Most manufacturers simply advertised their refrigerators with the door closed or with a model standing in front of the open door. That was the best they could do. Crosley had a patent, which, like the one for the regenerative circuit, was good for seventeen years. No one else would be able to put shelves in the doors of refrigerators until 1953.

The new refrigerator's success proved conclusively to Powel and Lewis that the market for home appliances was growing everyday. They jumped in with both feet. The company introduced ironing boards in May. They followed with an industrial-size ironing machine called the Crosley Moto-Iron and a washing machine, both of which they branded with the name Savamaid. Next came the Temperator, a space heater with a fan, for two-season comfort.

They came out with new refrigeration products, such as the "Kool-Rite" bottle cooler, a flat chest on spindly legs that was marketed to grocery stores, barber shops, restaurants, auto repair shops, and anywhere cold soft drinks might be popular. They also devised a vending add-on for the unit. A streamlined version called the "Koldrink" followed, featuring a water fountain option. Next came the Crosley "Kool-Draft;" a combination cooler/dispenser that sold for two hundred dollars and accommodated a half-barrel of beer, the 3.2 percent version of which had been newly legalized under the Blaine Act of February 1933. Prohibition itself was soon to be repealed; it was an omen, perhaps of good times to come.

.   .   .   .   .

A few months later, in May of 1933, RCA went to work for the Crosley Corporation. Its job: build the five-hundred-thousand-watt transmitter the FRC had approved. The radio corporation got the assignment because they had some of the brightest engineering minds in the country on staff, but they weren't manufacturers—or rather, they'd only been manufacturers a few months. They had to subcontract a lot of the work, which went right back out to their old patent pool partners Westinghouse and GE.

The new transmitter required a new antenna. Construction on one began at the Mason site in March, and finished up in June.

It was a skyscraper unto itself.

The foundation rested on pilings driven seventy feet into the ground. The tower was built from 136 tons of steel, built to withstand winds of up to 112 miles an hour. It stretched up 831 feet into the air, taller than the Washington Monument, taller than most skyscrapers. Shaped like an elongated diamond, it came to a point at the top and bottom, widening to thirty-five feet near the middle.

A neon-lit sign with "WLW" in ten-foot high letters was stretched across the south side of the tower about 350 feet above the ground. The sign alone weighed a ton.

The new antenna went into service that month, in conjunction with WLW's existing fifty-thousand-watt transmitter. It provided an increase in signal strength comparable to doubling the transmitter's power.

At the station's studios, new talent came and went, as always. A young man from Florida arrived to audition for an announcer's job wearing a white linen suit he'd bought especially for the occasion. Both he and his clothes made quite an impression. He won the audition, returned south to pack, only to learn a few weeks later the situation had changed, and there was no job for him after all.

His name was Red Barber, and he would be back soon enough.

Programs making their debut that year included a detective series called *Dr. Konrad's Unsolved Mysteries*, a quiz show called *Doctor I.Q.*, and a new kind of program aimed at housewives, a weekday offering patterned after the fiction serials then popular in magazines and newspapers.

It was called *Ma Perkins*. Because it was sponsored by Procter & Gamble's Oxydol soap, the show—and other programs like it—would eventually become known as "soap operas."

WLW aired shows for the rural audience as well; one of those was *The R.F.D. Hour*, R.F.D. standing for "rural free delivery," which was how the mailing addresses of most members of the audience began. The hour-long program, hosted by George "Boss" Johnston, featured country music performances and Johnson's tall tales of the numerous characters who had been a part of his rural upbringing. Johnston also told stories of his hunting and fishing exploits, He was a man after Powel Crosley's own heart.

Gilman L. Shelton was not.

Page Crosley's new husband had turned out to be what was then called "a bad seed." He was a heavy drinker. He beat his new wife, more than once. She fled to Sarasota and the arms of her parents.

She didn't come alone.

She was pregnant.

The baby was born on September 18, 1933, in Sarasota. It was a boy. By this point Powel had succeeded in getting the marriage annulled, but neither he nor Page nor Gwendolyn wanted the child to carry Shelton's name. The infant's grandparents formally adopted him.

They named him Lewis.

When Neill Prew and his sister Anne came over one day to see the new baby, they noticed some new personnel at the Crosley home. Powel had hired armed Pinkerton guards to watch Page and the baby. He was afraid he hadn't seen the last of Gilman Shelton.

As things turned out, he was right.

· · · · · ·

Sidney Weil's run of bad luck continued. The 1933 Reds fared no better than the 1932 club, finishing last for the third year in a row. Weil resigned in November. Meanwhile, in Columbus, Larry MacPhail had gotten on Branch Rickey's nerves one too many times. Despite the fact that his Columbus team won the pennant by fifteen games, he was fired.

The stars aligned. Central Bank and Trust appointed MacPhail to run the Reds.

The first thing he did was ask waivers on every single player on the team, to gauge interest around the league. That done, he promptly made a half-dozen moves to better the club.

Then he went for broke.

In December, he asked the Yankees for permission to talk to Babe Ruth. What he had in mind was not a trade but a job offer. He wanted the Babe to come manage the Reds. Ruth by that point was slowing down, although his slowing down was still better than most players could do operating at peak efficiency. MacPhail's offer no doubt intrigued him, because he wanted to stay in baseball when his playing days were over. It was, after all, the only life he'd ever known. Managing the Reds would have provided great—and much-needed—publicity for the Cincinnati club as well. It was a favorable scenario for both men.

But the Yankees wouldn't let the Babe go; worse yet, they made him take a pay cut. He steamed.

CHAPTER 21

MacPhail moved on. Cincinnati was a good fit for him. He was a believer in young blood, and the town was anxious—desperate, really—for change. Real change, however, required real money. He needed a farm system, improvements to the ballpark, top-dollar money to lure top-dollar players. Bankers tended to watch every dollar, he knew. They'd be leaning over his shoulder each time he made a move toward the checkbook.

It was a relationship inherently fraught with tension; MacPhail began to think about ways that he might alter it.

. . . . . .

Page and Gwendolyn stayed in Sarasota with the new baby while Powel commuted back and forth to Cincinnati as needed. One day, Boss Johnston showed up in his office with a bunch of letters from listeners who had responded with interest to Johnson's talk about having an "old-time" shooting match with muzzle-loading rifles. Johnston thought Powel might get a kick out of seeing the correspondence.

He was right.

See if you can't put on a rifle match for these old fellows, Powel told Johnston, and thus was born the Powel Crosley, Jr., Muzzle Loading Rifle Championship, which became legendary among enthusiasts of the sport. The first match was held two days before Christmas, in the yard of an old-fashioned schoolhouse in Friendship, Indiana.

At the same time, up in Mason, the five-hundred-thousand-watt transmitter neared completion.

It was, in every way imaginable, big: fifty-four feet wide, seventeen feet deep, and thirteen feet tall, so tall that a catwalk had to be run along the main panels to afford access to upper-level components. The tubes in it were five feet high and weighed thirty pounds. The transmitter required twenty of them, at a cost of $1,625 each.

Those tubes got monstrously hot when operating. To cool them, distilled water, moving at the rate of seven hundred gallons per minute, was pumped around their base. That newly heated water then had to be cooled, which was done by pumping it outside to a newly built pond seventy-five feet square and several feet deep, where the heat dissipated and the water pumped back in to cool the tubes again.

All that equipment required a lot of electricity; the bill was expected to come in at about one million dollars a year.

There was, of course, a significant upside to the new transmitter.

Engineers calculated it would increase WLW's coverage to an area twenty-five times greater than the fifty-thousand-watt transmitter, a giant circle roughly five thousand miles across. Under favorable conditions, it would not just be the Nation's Station, it would be the world's. On December 31, 1933, experimental transmissions, under the call sign W8XO, began.

By then Gilman Shelton had returned.

He'd shown up at the Florida house, first asking to see the baby, and then demanding it. He was refused, of course, and ordered to leave. But he would not be brushed off so easily.

He threatened to come back and kidnap his son as well as to get Page. If he couldn't have his boy, he would kidnap the next youngest Crosley child—Lewis's daughter, Ellen.

Powel sent him off but kept the guards. He sent word to Lewis, who thought the threat to Ellen minimal. Despite the furor among the well-to-do caused by the Lindbergh kidnapping, Lewis considered Shelton's words, at least as they concerned his daughter, mostly bluster. Lewis also felt that if Shelton did show up on his doorstep, he'd be quite capable of handling the situation.

Nevertheless, he knew he couldn't always be home to protect the family, at least, not before dinnertime, and so he decided to get a dog. Powel sent him a German Shepherd that promptly threw up its dinner and hid under the couch.

Lewis sent it back.

. . . . . .

In Mason, the engineers began to run into problems—one after the other after the other. The experimental designation had been made for good reason; no one had ever built anything like a five-hundred-thousand-watt transmitter before. The biggest problem was those five-foot vacuum tubes, which had a habit of burning out nearly every time the new transmitter was used. The tubes were made by GE, who told Crosley to cease and desist testing until their lead engineer could arrive to correctly diagnose and fix the problem.

A few days later, he was there. Rolling up his sleeves, the man turned the set on and five of those tubes, at a cost of $1,625 each, promptly blew out.

Testing continued.

. . . . . .

Lewis and Lucy went down to Sarasota for the holidays. Powel and Gwendolyn took them to a party hosted by John Ringling at Ca'd'zan, an elaborate affair where the food was served by footmen in full-dress costume. The kidnap threat came up as a topic of conversation. Ringling offered Lewis a pedigreed German Shepherd pup from his own kennels, one that (presumably) would not run and hide under the couch when trouble threatened.

When Lewis and Lucy went to the kennels to look at the available pups, one of them jumped into her arms. Husband and wife looked at each other, and decided that, guard dog material or not, this one was a keeper. They took him back to Powel's house and made arrangements to ship him north with Powel's hunting dogs in a few weeks. They picked a name for him, too: Dutch.

After returning home, Lewis went into the factory, pulled a few of his friends on the woodworking line aside, and asked them if they wouldn't mind doing him a favor. Soon enough, the first doghouse ever built by the Crosley Radio Corporation rolled out of the factory, headed for Belmont Avenue.

Powel continued to fly back and forth from Cincinnati to Sarasota. It was a stressful time for him. There was Shelton's threat, and baby Lewis, and Powel III, who by this point had left the advertising agency and gone to work as a Crosley salesman. June was expecting again, she and Powel III were fighting, and there was, as always, the next thing to attend to, that being a new idea he'd had for a kind of individual air cooler—a bed canopy with a refrigeration unit attached, which not only cooled the air inside the enclosure but filtered it as well, making the device beneficial to those with allergies. Powel named it the Koolrest.

There was also the matter of a lawsuit, initiated by General Electric in Canada regarding the Shelvador patent, which the Crosley Radio Corporation would, much to Powel's surprise, eventually lose. There were the ongoing transmitter tests in Mason, and in the midst of all this, he received a call from a friend of his named Reamy Field, who wanted to set up a lunch for him with a man named Larry MacPhail.

He wanted Powel to buy the Reds.

CHAPTER 22

Powel said no. He told MacPhail he would be happy to back him as president of the club and even would buy a large block of shares to insure it.

MacPhail said no.

Larry was a baseball man, a promotion man, an idea man. He wanted to be on the field, or at least as close to it as he could get, not in the boardroom.

Powel was an idea man too, and he could appreciate that. But he wasn't a baseball man. He was a fan, all right, but he had no idea how to run a team.

That's my job, MacPhail said. I'll handle that.

And so it went, on and on, for several hours.

MacPhail, as has been noted, had the gift of gab.

He also had a couple trump cards. The first appealed to Powel's wallet. Owning the Reds would offer numerous opportunities for promotional tie-ins with the Crosley corporation and, in particular, its two radio stations, WSAI and WLW.

The second appealed to Powel's wallet (again) and also, to his ego. MacPhail suggested Powel rename the ballpark, currently called Redland Field. What did Powel think of the name Crosley Field?

One can almost hear MacPhail suggesting it had a nice ring to it.

As the two men continued talking, Powel found himself considering an even more important factor. The Reds were his team. They'd been his team since the days of Wahoo Sam and Noodles Hahn. MacPhail made it clear there was a real chance they would end up leaving town if he couldn't find a wealthy backer in Cincinnati. Forget the miserable attendance the last few years, MacPhail said, the team was lousy, and just imagine the effect on the city if the Reds leave, which was a distinct possibility, particularly with a bank owning the club, because a bank was in business to make money, and baseball wasn't only about money it was the National Pastime, for gosh sakes. And the birthplace of professional baseball was right here, in Cincinnati. You don't want to see the game's birthplace without a team, do you?

Powel came to realize he most emphatically did not.

He tentatively agreed to MacPhail's suggestion: shortly thereafter, Lewis and the Crosley Radio Corporation's controller visited team offices to look over the operation, including the books. What they found—an organization MacPhail had taken firm charge of in a very short span of time—impressed them greatly. It impressed Powel too.

There began several weeks of negotiations.

·   ·   ·   ·   ·

Rumor had it that other negotiations were going on at the time.

The Pinkerton guards were still at the Florida house. Page dressed in bulky clothing and a veil whenever she went off the grounds, and whenever she left Sarasota, Powel had her travel in a private railroad car.

The situation was untenable.

He met with Shelton and reportedly gave him a million dollars in return for an agreement never to darken his doorstep—or that of his daughter or grandson/adopted son—ever again.

Dutch, meanwhile, arrived in College Hill.

He did not throw up on arrival. Quite the contrary. He made himself at home—too much so, for Lewis's taste. In the beginning, the dog had to be chased off the furniture more than once.

Developments with Shelton had made his presence unnecessary, but Dutch and Ellen nonetheless became constant companions. When he was old enough, she looped the handle of a basket around his neck and took him shopping down at Boland's grocery store. He made himself at home there, too. In fact, he made himself at home in the entire neighborhood. One day Ellen walked into the five-and-dime to buy something; she was surprised to see Dutch coming through the back door like he owned the place.

Get out of here, she told him. Get back home.

The store owners asked her not to speak to the dog that way; he was a regular.

He was her dog, primarily, but Lewis became fond of him as well. One day, he came home with a collar for Dutch, a custom-made leather harness with colored buttons. He started taking Dutch for walks in the evening, and he trained the dog to fetch his hat.

It was a good way for him to relax. Lucy approved. Despite the naps after lunch, despite the fact that Powel was now not only allowing Lewis to take vacations but insisting on it, to the point of sometimes dragging him along for a weekend of hunting and/or fishing, to her mind the relationship between the brothers was still weighted unfairly. As she saw it, Powel dashed into town, made a bunch of arbitrary decisions, and dashed back out again, leaving her husband to clean up the mess, to get things running right again. To rub salt in the wound, Powel was making millions, while she and Lewis had to get by on far less. Your brother doesn't appreciate you, she told Lewis. You should get out in the market, see what your skills and experience are really worth. Get a new job, she told him.

At some point, up in the executive offices at Arlington Street, Lewis shared those sentiments with his brother.

Get a new wife, Powel snapped.

Lewis looked at his brother and laughed.

Then he went back to work.

.   .   .   .   .   .

The deal for a syndicate led by Powel Crosley, Jr., to assume control of the Cincinnati Reds was announced on February 4, 1934. Powel put up $240,000 to buy thirty-two hundred of the six thousand shares outstanding. He was given a two-year option to buy a controlling interest in the team.

He didn't say much at the news conference. MacPhail was an able man and could speak for himself. MacPhail had convinced him to buy the team, and MacPhail would run the team. The baseball people would make the baseball decisions, Powel declared. He did make one promise, however: the Reds would remain in Cincinnati as long as he was in control.

The number one figure in radio was now the member of another, very elite fraternity. In the 1930s, professional baseball was not just the National Pastime, it was the only game in town. The NBA didn't exist. The NFL had yet to draw a lot of interest. The NHL? Hockey was a Canadian game, first of all; second of all, it was a cold-weather sport, and they didn't have cold weather down south.

If you followed professional sports, baseball was it. The owners were like kings; the players, bound to their clubs by the reserve clause, were mere serfs. There were sixteen of those owners, for the sixteen teams, and now Powel was one of them.

At the 1933 owners meeting in Manhattan, he met his new mates: Judge Fuchs of the Braves, Charles Stoneham of the Giants, National League President Ford Frick, grumpy old Commissioner Landis, and the others. Powel was at this point forty-eight years old, thicker in body, hairline receding even further, but no less vigorous, still possessed of the same boundless energy that catapulted him from room to room, from conversation to conversation, that often caused people to shave years off his age. *Time* magazine, reporting on his presence at the owners conclave, described him as a tall young man, "with good clothes and an earnest, slightly bewildered expression." He was excited, no doubt, and nervous.

Back in Cincinnati, he left the baseball to MacPhail, as promised. But Powel was a promotion man himself, and he had a few ideas in that regard.

Redland Field became Crosley Field, as agreed.

A model of a giant Shelvador refrigerator went up on top of the scoreboard.

Cries of profiteering and rampant commercialism went up as

well. One of them came from a young man MacPhail had brought down from Columbus to serve as the team's press officer: his name was James Reston. Reston thought Powel should not have put the Shelvador model on display, never mind changed the name of the stadium. He said so, in earshot of several people, and word got back to Powel. Reston was gone to New York shortly thereafter. He eventually ended up at the *New York Times*, where he received awards for speaking his mind.

Lewis and the broadcasting staff decided WSAI, Cincinnati's own station, would be a better choice than WLW to broadcast the Reds games. The station didn't have anyone on staff, however, who could call the games.

Chet Thomas, one of the men present, then remembered the auditions they'd held the previous summer. The young man who'd won, who they'd been ultimately unable to hire, had done sports before.

"You mean the boy who wore that beautiful white linen suit?" Lewis asked.

"That's the one," Thomas said.

"Send for him," Lewis said.

Re-enter Red Barber, stage right.

Larry MacPhail was hard at work, too.

He made developmental arrangements with six-minor league franchises. He made more player moves, letting go of some old fan favorites, such as pitcher Eppa Rixey, and bringing in some fresh blood, both young and old.

He hired new coaches, new front-office staff. He had the ballpark repainted and got the ushers new uniforms. He brought in cigarette girls "so cute they made the customers want to smoke themselves to death."

None of it made any difference.

The Reds lost Opening Day, 6-0. They lost ninety-eight more times over the course of the year, finishing last for the fourth season in a row. Attendance dropped to barely two hundred thousand for the entire season.

Clearly, something more drastic needed to be done.

Powel and MacPhail talked about what that something might be.

. . . . . .

Transmitter tests continued throughout the early spring of 1934, now taking place in the daytime as well as at night. Other broadcasters' fears about WLW blanketing the AM dial seemed thus far to be groundless.

But strange things were happening up in Mason.

A large neon sign at a motel a couple of miles from the tower went on, and wouldn't go off. Light bulbs in nearby houses and barns glowed all day and night. Farmers reported hearing WLW through wire fences, barn roofs, gutter downspouts, and screen doors.

Lewis sent engineers to do what they could: they ended up rewiring a number of houses in the area, at WLW expense. They would end up having a crew of two or three engineers who spent most of their time for several years running down cross-talk that developed from downspouts and different parts of buildings.

On April 17, the FRC granted WLW permission to run the transmitter during regular broadcast hours. All that power was about to go into operation.

All that power was about to pay off.

WLW planned to increase its advertising rates by ten per cent on July 1, by another ten or so percent in October. That would put the cost of time at well over a thousand dollars an hour. It would put revenues in the neighborhood of three million dollars per year.

Cries of profiteering went up almost at once.

Those cries paralleled others being heard at the same time, cries directed not just at WLW or Powel Crosley but at the whole rotten system, the brokers and the bankers and the businessmen who'd played around with the stock market and brought it crashing down, the rich men who now seemed to be—even in the midst of the Great Depression—getting richer, while the poor continued to stand on breadlines and spin their wheels.

Those men on the breadlines began to grumble.

They began to get angry.

They began, once more, to organize.

. . . . . .

June Crosley wasn't happy either. She was twenty-one years old, and the entire course of her life seemed laid out before her. She was a mother of one baby, there was another on the way, and she was trapped in a town she barely knew with a husband who she'd married on what looked now like a bad impulse. There were perks to being a member of the Crosley family, obviously, but June missed her family and friends. She felt somehow cheated out of her life at school in England and didn't quite know whom to blame.

She ended up taking out her anger on Powel III.

The marriage continued to deteriorate.

. . . . . .

Lewis, meanwhile, was basically happy. He had a good job, a good marriage, two good kids, and a dog that was good most of the time, though the German shepherd in Dutch had come out the last time someone had tried to deliver a package to the house on Belmont Avenue. But there was something bothering him. Something was missing. From the time he was old enough to think for himself, during all those hours he'd spent in his grandparents' and then his parents' garden, through all the energy and sweat he'd expended down in Houston for his father, and then out in Loveland, and even now, Lewis Crosley had a vision of himself, a dream he held in his heart. He was going to work the land. He was going to be a farmer. It was all he'd ever wanted to do. He was forty-six years old, and it was, he decided, about time to make that dream come true.

He crossed the Ohio into Kentucky, and began scouting farmland. It was the middle of the Depression; farms were failing almost too fast to count. Lewis soon found what he was looking for: a run-down property, no water to speak of, and rocks everywhere he turned. One of the centerpieces of FDR's New Deal was a series of relief programs designed to help out the small farmer. Lewis signed up for a five-year program that enabled him to hire on men to mend the fences, clear the land, and plant crops. To get at the bigger stones, the boulders, they had to bring a rock crusher. Lewis started going down every other weekend to help out as he could.

It was, in a way, just like old times.

. . . . .

In Mason, the testing was done. The big tubes were ready to officially fire up. WLW was going to half a million watts, and to celebrate, Powel pulled out all the stops.

The big moment was set for Wednesday, May 2, 1934, at 9:00 p.m.

Guests began crowding into the formal dining room at the Netherland Plaza Hotel a couple hours ahead of time. David Sarnoff was there, as was Thad Brown (vice-chairman of the FRC), and Ohio Governor George White, along with Cincinnati Mayor Russell Wilson. Powel and Lewis were present of course, along with Gwendolyn and Lucy and some five hundred others, among them the cream of Cincinnati's civic and business leaders, as well as other notables from the radio and broadcast industries.

The Crosley Symphony, under the direction of William Stoess, provided music while the Crosley Glee club, under the direction of Grace Raine, sang for the crowd. There was food (Louisiana shrimp cocktail and beef filet), and there were, inevitably, speeches. Peter Grant introduced the speakers as they came to the dais: Sarnoff of RCA, Governor White, station manager John Clark, and of course Powel ("with this greater and greater audience has come greater and greater responsibilities"), among others.

And then came the main event.

At 9:03, President Roosevelt 'turned on' the transmitter from the White House by pressing a golden telegraph key, the same key

President Wilson had used back in 1918 to open the Panama Canal. WLW, "the Nation's Station," went on the air at full power.

Almost.

The problem was, once again, those big tubes. They took a long time to warm up. They were still warming when Roosevelt hit the key. It was a detail everyone had forgotten about when planning the event. But by 9:30 the big antenna was pushing every one of those watts into the air.

Congratulatory telegrams came in from Albert Einstein, CBS President William S. Paley, and Roosevelt himself.

Guglielmo Marconi sent one as well:

It affords me genuine pleasure to be present in spirit at the inauguration of your powerful broadcasting station …we cannot but feel more and more united as radio waves encircle our globe, bringing us tidings of friendship and good will.

Marconi, however, was wrong. By mid-1934, those radio waves were being used for purposes other than an exchange of good wishes. The Third Reich had begun broadcasting a series of programs aimed directly at the United States; *Reichsender* (German Overseas Radio) programming consisted largely of innocuous entertainment, classical music, and operettas, but there were subtler elements to the broadcasts, such as the station's repeated statements of its reason for existence: "We wish to safeguard the eternal foundations of our existence and of our nationality" and began to encourage group listening sessions across the United States.

Tidings of friendship were the last thing on Adolf Hitler's mind.

.　　.　　.　　.　　.　　.

Other developments in the broadcast industry that month presaged a cataclysmic battle yet to come—a fight not between countries, but individuals, representing different points of view regarding radio's proper fit in the American cultural landscape.

One of those individuals was Powel Crosley.

The other was a man named George Henry Payne.

Payne was one of seven men appointed to the newly formed Federal Communications Commission, created by an act of Congress in July 1934 to succeed the FRC. Payne, although a Republican like Powel, and generally pro-business, nonetheless had some strikingly different views on a number of topics. Soon enough, the two men would come into bitter conflict.

In the meantime, Powel was in the middle of another battle, one he'd been fighting, and losing, for a number of years.

At forty-eight, he was losing his hair.

Enter Dr. Andrew E. Cueto, stage right.

Cueto was a member of the University of Cincinnati's medical school faculty. Sometime in 1933, he noticed that a device being used to treat gangrene patients at Cincinnati's Holmes Hospital had an unusual side effect. The device was an airtight glass boot worn around the affected limb. It used alternating bursts of vacuum and high pressure to induce increased circulation.

As gangrene therapy, it proved useless.

But wherever the boot was applied, hair grew. On people's arms and legs, admittedly, where it was nothing to get excited about.

If, however, Cueto could induce a similar effect on the human scalp...

He took out a patent on the idea and went to work building a device.

Cueto was a doctor, though, not a mechanic. After a short time he gave up, and went to Powel, who by that point was getting quite a reputation in the scientific community as an industrialist with an open-door policy, no matter what the idea. Powel called in Lewis—

whose hairline was receding as well.

Coincidence or not, Cueto made a sale. Crosley bought the patent.

Lewis made some design improvements, Powel dubbed the device the "Xervac," and they contracted with a Chicago company to manufacture the machine.

Powel bought a few other things that summer as well. One was an island on McGregor Bay in Canada—ten acres with a ten-room house. He dubbed it "Nissaki," Greek for "little island."

He also bought a new plane, a Northrop Delta, for forty thousand dollars. It had seating for six, a top speed of 225 mph, and a range of fifteen hundred miles. He was now one hop away from just about anywhere he wanted to go.

In the fall, he helped start a new network, the Mutual Broadcasting System (MBS), an affordable alternative to the big networks for smaller stations.

He oversaw the second annual Muzzle-loading contest, in Rising Sun Indiana, the site of Ohio River Dam 38, where Lewis had worked before the war.

He accepted John Clark's resignation as manager of WLW and WSAI and hired a man he could trust—his brother—as chief executive of the broadcasting department.

Lewis continued taking his naps and his every-other-weekend trips to the farm in Kentucky, where he made further improvements to the property. Lucy began to go with him. There was a house on the property with a nice porch, where she could sit and look at the farm, till the flies got to be too much for her. She asked Lewis if they could screen in the porch. He said he'd think about it.

Lewis had a lot of other things on his mind, such as the big transmitter. A problem had come up—not the tubes this time, the skywave. Canadian station CFRB at 690 on the dial was experiencing a great deal of interference at night from that portion of the signal, bouncing around the ionosphere. CFRB took up the problem with the Canadian government. Canadian authorities carried the complaint to the U.S. Embassy, which handed it off to the Federal

Radio Commission. WLW was told to take action immediately or risk losing its license.

The engineers got to work.

They built another pair of specially designed towers to block transmission of the skywave. The new job was even harder than the original, because components for the two new antennae had to be grounded at all times and raised with block and tackle and old-fashioned rope. Metal guy wires couldn't be used; the five-hundred kilowatt transmitter lit light bulbs for miles. Any metal close to its signal picked up a considerable charge, one so powerful that workers who inadvertently touched metal components of the new antenna during construction were burned.

All went well, however: no one was killed, the design worked perfectly, and CFRB had no more reason to complain.

But there were problems on Arlington Street, too. The issue of production space reared its head once more. Shelvadors continued to sell as did radios. Many of the other appliances were moving too, and General Motors had just put in a big order for a batch of car radios.

Lewis's first thought was to move the WLW and WSAI studios. This would free twenty thousand square feet. He began a search for appropriate quarters. Powel got involved. The brothers announced they would build new studios in Mount Adams. Plans were quickly drawn up, and just as quickly scrapped. They ended up moving WSAI back to the old studios at Plant number two, leaving the entire eighth floor of the main building for WLW.

That freed space on the factory floor but not enough.

They bought a building in Indiana in the small town of Kokomo, about forty miles north of Indianapolis. Fittingly, it was an old automobile factory, from the days when Indy, not Detroit, was king of the car industry.

Lewis enlarged the plant and set up a production line devoted solely to turning out those car radios General Motors needed. This freed up more space on the factory floor but still not enough. He contracted with out-of-town companies to produce Shelvador cabinets, and that did the trick.

Lewis and Powel meeting
with Ahmed A. Faselbhoy,
distributor for Crosley
Shelvador refrigerators in
Bombay, India, and
A.G. Lindsay, manager
of the export division.
Cincinnati, 1937.

CROSLEY
SHELVADOR

A catalog entry for
a Shelvador.

Crosley (nee Redland) Field;
corporate sponsorship decades
before it became fashionable.

The lights go on; Ethan Allen of the Phillies waits for a pitch during the first night game in major league history.

The young man in the white linen suit – Hall of Famer Red Barber.

World Champions! Commissioner Landis celebrates with Bill McKechnie (center) and Warren Giles (right).

Powel mixes with the boys. The owner shaking hands with Warren Giles; kudos to all for a job well done.

Superpower comes to Cincinnati: the big tower, in Mason.

Promotional booklet for the Nation's Station, printed in 1935.

THE WORLD'S MOST POWERFUL BROADCASTING STATION

A TRIP THROUGH WLW

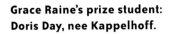

Grace Raine's prize student: Doris Day, nee Kappelhoff.

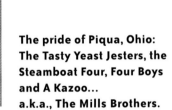

**The pride of Piqua, Ohio: The Tasty Yeast Jesters, the Steamboat Four, Four Boys and A Kazoo...
a.k.a., The Mills Brothers.**

Powel and Lewis, at the dedication ceremony for the 50,000-watt transmitter and its new building, October 29, 1928.

Problem solved.

Meanwhile, Powel and Larry MacPhail broke their huddle, and revealed their plan to restore the Cincinnati Reds to profitability.

Night baseball.

CHAPTER 23

Purists thought it was sacrilege. Players thought it was dangerous. Some saw it as pure show-biz. Some saw it as profiteering. To Powel, playing ball under the lights was just simple, old-fashioned common sense. The minor leagues did it, and he saw no reason why the majors shouldn't as well.

The idea had been floating around for some time. It had, in fact, come up back when he and MacPhail had first talked about the Reds. MacPhail had seen the benefits of night baseball first-hand. He'd installed lights in Columbus a few years back and found that it opened up the game to whole families, to workers who couldn't afford a day off, to women anxious for a night out with their husbands.

But in the big leagues? The owners would never go for it, MacPhail assured his boss. It was messing with tradition.

Powel wasn't so sure. He had come aboard too late to put the matter before the other owners prior to the 1934 season, but he wanted it put in front of them now. The entire league needed night baseball, he felt, not just the Reds. The 1934 season hadn't been good for anyone. Of the eight National League teams, only the Cardinals had finished in the black. Powel wanted MacPhail to make the same arguments to the other club owners he'd made to him.

In December 1934, those owners got together at New York City's Waldorf Astoria Hotel for their annual winter meeting. Powel had the topic put on the agenda. Its presence there was no secret. In the days before the meeting, opposition to the idea coalesced, not just from the National League owners, but their American League counterparts, and other big names in baseball.

"Not in my lifetime," said Commisioner Landis.

"I'll never vote for [it]," said Charlie Stoneham, owner of the New York baseball Giants.

"Bush league stuff," said Clark Griffith, owner of the Washington Senators.

"Sure I know it would draw," said Joe Cronin of the Red Sox. "So would football on roller skates."

The American League as a whole wasn't having any of it; item number one on their agenda was Babe Ruth. The situation with the Yankees had gone from bad to worse. Their not letting him go to Cincinnati was a part of it, so was the pay cut, and so was the fact that the Great Bambino felt like baseball owed him a shot at managing, after all he'd done for the game.

While the AL owners wrestled with the thorny question of how to placate a living legend, the National League got down to business. The first day of meetings, the owners tended to the inauguration of new league president Ford Frick. Then came the contentious issue of greyhound racing: Christy Mathewson's old partner, Boston Braves owner Judge Emil Fuchs, had gotten himself in deep financial trouble. Fuchs wanted permission from the owners to build a racing track in the Braves Stadium and have his team play its home games at Fenway Park.

Everyone decided to sidestep that one for the moment.

The owners broke for dinner, and then retired for the evening.

On the second day, they turned to night baseball.

Powel and MacPhail came to that session with a forty-page brief that included technical details on the kinds of lights they planned to install. Powel broke down the Reds 1934 attendance figures. He pointed out that of the two hundred thousand fans who had shown up at the ballpark that season, over 70 percent of them had come during only fifteen playing days—on Opening Day, Sundays, and holidays.

The facts supported only one conclusion. Day games weren't working. Not only weren't they working for the owners, the fans weren't getting the chance to see their teams play. The National Pastime, Powel said, was losing its audience.

The old guard—Stoneham, Griffith, Frick, Landis—didn't buy his arguments. Not initially, at least. Part of the reason was tradition; part was concern over player and spectator safety. Stoneham predicted "all manner of injuries to athletes playing in semi-darkness, riot-provoking rulings by futilely peering field officials, and wails of anguish from fans unable to follow the meanderings of the horsehide pellet." MacPhail, who'd had considerable experience with night ball up in Columbus, thought those points ill-informed. Stoneham wouldn't budge.

The other owners eventually did.

In the end, everyone but Stoneham voted to allow the Reds to put lights in Crosley Field, albeit on a trial basis. There would be seven night games scheduled, one with each of the other teams in the league.

Powel and MacPhail congratulated each other on a job well done. MacPhail went back to Cincinnati, where he would talk to Lewis about installing the new lighting system. Powel wanted Lewis to oversee the project to ensure it was done the right way. Given the vote of confidence of the other owners, he knew that he had to deliver a quality performance.

Powel stayed in New York for a meeting with Walter Chrysler. No doubt they touched briefly on the auto business, but the primary focus of their meeting—a meeting also attended by two dozen or so other prominent business and government leaders—was to draw attention to what they saw as an increasing threat to one of the country's most precious natural resources. Out of that conclave of avid sportsmen, hunters, and fishers came another new group: the American Wildlife Institute.

Back home, Powel bought himself a 1935 Duesenberg sedan. Fred Duesenberg was dead by this point, but Augie had continued on, making the cars his big brother had imagined. By now the name Duesenberg stood for luxury. It was the ultimate status symbol, the ultimate sports car, owned by movie stars and maharajahs. Powered by a massive straight eight-cylinder engine with a supercharger, it could do well over a hundred and twenty-five mph. It was Powel's pride and joy.

Lewis didn't understand the attraction. The car spent a lot of time in the shop, from what he could see. Lucy didn't get it either. She kept calling the car a Duesenberry, which incensed Powel.

Get a new wife, he told his brother.

Powel drove the Duesenberg when he was in Cincinnati, mostly out to Sleepy Hollow Farm. He drove the Austin down in Sarasota. The Austin's maker had by this point gone bankrupt, but the little car continued to impress. It was no Duesenberg, but for short hops here and there, the Austin did just fine.

The wheels in his mind began to spin; the gears, ever so slightly, to shift.

He was, consciously aware of it or not, getting ready to move on.

.   .   .   .   .   .

He bought a house in Havana, where there was good fishing, legal gambling, and the cost of labor to maintain the property when he wasn't there was ridiculously cheap. There were no unions in Cuba.

He threw another party at Cincinnati's Music Hall for needy children, this one bigger and better than all the others combined. Fifteen thousand kids attended. Powel might have looked a profiteer to some, but he was always generous with his money, particularly with friends and family. Too generous, some might say.

Powel III might have been one of them.

The heir to the Crosley throne was by this time working his way through a series of jobs inside his father's company, being prepped to assume greater responsibility. He'd been in sales, and marketing, in the studios, and even in the engineering department. He'd been given stock and a seat on the corporation's board of directors.

None of it meant anything to him. None of it was what he really wanted. He wasn't the businessman like his father; he was his mother's son, a musician, a singer. Not only that, it was as obvious to Powel III as it was to everyone else that he hadn't earned his position. He was twenty-three years old, and the entire course of his life seemed laid out before him.

Back in 1927, when he was still in high school, playing the saxophone and singing in the glee club, he'd asked his father for a position in WLW's programming department. He wanted to be a musician, an entertainer, he said.

"You can go to work in the shipping room packing radios," Powel, Jr., told him.

Father wanted son to follow in his footsteps; father envisioned no other role in life for his son, for the Powel Crosley that was to follow him. It had been true back then, and it was true now. Though Powel loved his son, and his entire family, he was known to be controlling of all of them. He felt he knew what was best for them and expected them to follow his advice to the letter.

Powel III, the father of two children of his own, felt trapped: in a job for which he had no passion, in a house he hadn't really wanted, with a wife as unhappy as he was. He felt smothered by it all. There were perks to being Powel Crosley III, obviously, but there was something missing from his life, something he couldn't name. He found himself heading down to Sarasota as often as he could. Things were simpler there, away from the office: June would go off by herself, his mother would play with her grandchildren, and he was free to walk down to the water and look at the bay, at the yachts and motorboats moored up and down his father's slip.

It gave him a sense of peace.

It felt, far more than Cincinnati, like home.

. . . . .

Lewis was having family problems too.

Some of those had to do with Dutch.

Not only had the dog marked the whole neighborhood as his territory by this point, he'd begun following the neighborhood children home as it struck his fancy, which was fine in and of itself, but the problem was that once he followed them there, he didn't always know how to get back to Belmont Avenue. More than once, Lewis or Lucy or Ellen had to go get their dog and bring him back.

Lewis had other family problems as well, considerably more serious ones.

Those had to do with his work family: with the women and men on the lines at the Crosley Radio Corporation.

The unions had come to town. There was a union for the machinists, and a union for the metal polishers, and a union for the radio and refrigerator workers. Officers for the latter group, after organizing factory workers, immediately demanded higher pay, recognition of seniority, paychecks weekly instead of three times a month, mandatory overtime pay for anyone who worked over thirty-six hours, and a guarantee of a half-day's pay for employees who were called in but were not put to work.

Lewis said no.

In March 1935, the union called a strike. The vote wasn't unanimous. There was dissension among the employees, as some wanted the work stoppage and some didn't. Twenty-five hundred of the union's four thousand members ended up walking out. Tension seethed throughout the factory. A worker from the machinist's union (which wasn't striking) was beaten up the first day of the walkout when he went out for lunch. Several men and women applying for jobs at the factory were assaulted as they left the premises.

The strike came at the worst possible time for the company. The refrigerator season was just gearing up, with nine models in production and tens of thousands of back orders. Every hour the lines weren't rolling cost the Crosleys big money.

Lewis sat down at the bargaining table with the union leaders. Powel remained at Pinecroft. There were times when he came to the factory—and managed mostly to disrupt routine, changing the systems and micro-managing details he knew little about—but this was not one of them. Given the delicate, even potentially violent, nature of the situation, Powel was no doubt grateful that employee relations fell into Lewis's territory.

Powel's presence at the bargaining table would only have

exacerbated tensions. He was a poor listener and too impatient to sit for long in any one spot. He also was quick with an acerbic response and just as quick to lose patience. By this time he'd developed a reputation for having a temper, and he very much liked to have things done his way. There also was an imperious quality about Powel that could have rubbed the union leaders the wrong way. Though Crosley literature and the employee handbook offered much talk about the employees working *with*, rather than *for* him, in truth he kept them at a distance, preferring they address him by "Mr. Crosley" rather than by his first name. It was better that he stayed away.

Lewis's temperament was a much better fit for this type of negotiation. He knew the workers well, and they knew him. He was known as a good listener, as a methodical person who heard all sides of an argument before reaching a conclusion. Lewis also had a somewhat folksy manner that would put the union representatives at ease. He was, at heart, a farmer.

The brothers agreed that Lewis should handle the situation.

Every night, however, they talked strategy.

On March 25, they offered the unions a compromise proposal. The deal, approved by a commissioner from the U.S. Department of Labor, gave a little something to both sides. Workers would be paid weekly, overtime pay would be granted for anyone who worked over forty hours in a week, and employees who were called to work but did not get to work would receive two hours' pay.

Lewis delivered the company's offer over a public-address system that reached into all the Arlington Street buildings. He wanted to be sure that the offer was relayed accurately by the union leaders, who were furious, feeling he'd gone behind their backs.

They decided to continue to picket; the picketing turned violent.

Union representatives started fights with Crosley workers leaving the plant. Cincinnati police were called in. Seven thousand people filled the streets that afternoon. Authorities succeeded in scattering the warring factions, but the next morning, and for several mornings thereafter, Lewis had to drive through a daily gauntlet of rock-throwers to get into the plant.

Meanwhile, down at Crosley Field, the lights were going up. The system and new lighting plant Lewis put into place was designed, by GE, to be bigger and better than anything built before. Ken Rad Lamp Works, who built tubes for the Crosley Radio Corporation, worked for weeks on the bulbs for the new system. They were designed to provide twice as much illumination as those used in the minor leagues, designed to be so bright you could read a newspaper by them four blocks away.

Ford Frick was convinced the experiment was going to be a success, a moneymaker, for sure, though not quite as much of a moneymaker as another attraction the National League would be bringing to its fans that season.

Babe Ruth was coming to the senior circuit. Judge Fuchs had brought him back to Boston, where he'd started back in 1914 with the Red Sox. Ruth was returning not just as a player but an assistant manager, and vice-president of the team. Ruth's presence on the field, Frick estimated, would mean an additional five hundred thousand fans passing through the turnstiles that year. Babe was happy, Fuchs was happy, and Frick was thrilled, as were the rest of the NL owners, including Powel.

A couple weeks later, Powel was even happier.

Lewis and his negotiating team came to terms with the union. They yielded on few points. A minimum wage of forty-four cents per hour was instituted for men, while the minimum for women workers was thirty-three cents. The average wage was a bit higher—fifty-seven cents for men, and forty-four cents for women.

A few weeks after that, the company declared its annual dividend: twenty-five cents per share. Lewis received $1,098.50. His daughter Charlotte Jeanne received a brand-new Ford Coupe from Powel, his way of saying thanks to his brother for resolving the strike.

Powel and Gwendolyn, who owned 283,509 shares (52 percent of the corporation), received a dividend of $70,877.25.

There were, of course, cries of profiteering.

There were other cries of protest issuing that month as well. Some came from Europe, where in March 1935 Adolf Hitler revealed to the world that the German Reich possessed, quite contrary to the letter of the Versailles Treaty, an air force of considerable power and sophistication.

Some came from inside WLW's Arlington Street studios, where a recently hired announcer named Norman Corwin was surprised to discover the following memo on his desk when he came into work the morning of May 20: "No reference is to be made of strikes on any news bulletin broadcast over our stations."

Corwin thought the memo a bad idea. The company had a suggestion box on the floor for its employees. Into it he put a slip of paper, noting that if any other station or newspaper got wind of WLW's policy, the station would be subject to accusations of censorship. He suggested that, if nothing else, the station at least cover any strikes that were likely to become headline news.

No reply came for several days. In the meantime, another cry went up down at Crosley Field.

Lights on.

·   ·   ·   ·   ·

It was May 23, 1935. That evening the Cincinnati Reds and Philadelphia Phillies played the first night game in major league history.

Except it didn't quite work out that way.

Instead of baseball, the fans got rain.

The rain (a reminder of things past, an omen of things shortly to come again) did nothing to dampen the anticipation, the growing excitement at Crosley Field.

It was a good time to be a Reds fan again. The team was winning. Not a lot, but as the first month of the season passed, the Reds were flirting with the .500 mark for the first time in years. Attendance was inching up too—planned as well as actual, for by the middle of May, over twelve thousand fans had already made reservations for that first night game, proving that MacPhail and Powel were right about night baseball's profit-earning potential, as a comparable daytime contest could expect to draw roughly two thousand people.

As game day approached, MacPhail pulled out all the stops. He arranged for a fireworks display, a drum and bugle corps, a series of marching bands. It was going to be a spectacle.

Powel pulled out all the stops, too.

He got word, once again, to FDR, who agreed to press a button in the White House to light the ceremonial first bulb. (Larry MacPhail got the honor of throwing the switch to illuminate the entire field.) Commissioner Landis even agreed to show up and throw out the ceremonial first pitch.

The one-day rain postponement didn't change anything, except that because Landis had business elsewhere the next day, Ford Frick was named to throw the first pitch.

On May 24, things went off as planned. FDR lit the first bulb, MacPhail lit the rest, Frick threw his pitch, and best of all, the Reds won the game, 2-1, their third in a row. The contest was noted for sparkling defensive plays and outstanding pitching, in particular by the Reds Paul Derringer, matters that pretty much put to rest concerns about the quality of the lighting. Over twenty thousand people showed up for the celebration, which included MacPhail's marching bands forming a huge C, with 'Reds' spelled out in the middle.

And the next day Babe Ruth came to town.

Babe's victory lap around the National League had started on a high note; on opening day in Boston, he'd whacked a homer off the league's best pitcher, Carl Hubbell, and the Braves beat the Giants, 4-2.

Things went downhill from there. His skills were largely gone and, worse yet, it was becoming clear Fuchs had only hired him as a publicity stunt. He wasn't interested in Babe's thoughts on how to manage the game.

The day before, at Pittsburgh, he'd hit three home runs. The third, number 714 of his career, went over six hundred feet, the first ball ever hit out of Forbes Field.

Cincinnati fans were hoping for more of the same.

What they got was the end of an era.

On Saturday, at Babe Ruth Day in Crosley Field, the Bambino

went 0-4, striking out three times.

In the outfield, he misjudged a ball and fell on Crosley Field's inclined warning track. He took himself out of the game.

A week later, he retired.

·   ·   ·   ·   ·

Norman Corwin received a response to his memo about how to handle the news of strikes. He had been hoping, in his words, for something of a "merit badge."

Instead, he was told his position on staff was redundant.

Exit Norman Corwin, stage left.

Enter Joe Julian, stage right.

Julian was a New York actor who came to WLW in the company of thirty other New Yorkers—actors, writers, directors—hired in the wake of the station's rapid growth. One of those hired was a writer-director named Thomas Ashwell, who pulled Julian aside and told him he had a plan to stand out among the crowd.

He was going to carefully monitor the interactions between Powel and the broadcast staff, Ashwell said.

If they were bootlickers, he told Julian, he'd speak his mind. If they were straight shooters, he'd suck up. After a few weeks, Ashwell decided the program staff was largely composed of bootlickers. He went in to Powel's office and told him the station's programming needed work, and a lot of it.

Powel made Ashwell the new program manager.

Ashwell had to clean some house to live up to his words. One of the first actors he fired was Joe Julian. Julian protested. Ashwell relented, somewhat. He hired Julian to do sound effects.

One of Julian's first assignments was Red Barber.

The young man in the white linen suit had, in a short span of time, established himself as one of radio's premier play-by-play voices. The Reds actually only broadcast a handful of home games because Larry MacPhail was afraid that easy availability of games over the air would cut into home attendance. He did want to broadcast as many road games as possible, feeling it important for fans to be able to maintain a connection with their team. Barber broadcast most of those via re-creation, taking a Western Union ticker-tape summation of the action ("the count was oh and two, Goodman popped up") and embellishing to make it seem like it was happening in real-time.

Sound effects were a critical part of the process. Joe Julian used a record of a crowd cheering and an actual bat and judge's gavel—smack!—to simulate the sounds of the game. It was a harmless bit of trickery, and many fans were aware of what was going on.

Other radio frauds going on at the time were less innocuous.

The Treaty of Versailles had stripped from Germany not just its colonies and weapons but placed the vast coalmines of the Saar, a region of the country that bordered France, under League of Nations rule. The terms of the arrangement expired in 1935. According to treaty, an election was to be held, in which the residents of the Saar would determine which country, Germany or France, they would join.

In the months leading up to that vote, radio broadcasts under the direction of the Nazi Minister of Propaganda, Joseph Goebbels, flooded the province. The Nazis distributed receiving sets by the thousands to those who didn't have them. More ominously, they undertook a campaign of whispered propaganda—*flusterpropaganda*—designed to convince voters that the party knew how individuals were voting.

The final results were not even close.

Big Brother—Big Adolf—was watching.

. . . . . .

In Cincinnati, the big signal was booming, now reaching rural areas in the Midwest, South, and portions of the Great Plains. To hold the interests of these new listeners, the station expanded its Country & Western programming. Before long, fully 10 percent of the station's programming would involve country music, beginning with a 5:45

sign-on program called *Top o' the Morning*.

The station—and the city, for that matter—became something of a crossroads for country music entertainers traveling around the country. Cincinnati was the first big city north of the Mason-Dixon line, a gateway to the industrial North from the rural South. More than a few country music folk were drawn by the prospect of the national exposure that WLW could provide. Listeners soon became familiar with names like Merle Travis, Cowboy Copas, Grandpa Jones, The Duke of Paducah (Whitey Ford), and Lulu Belle and Scotty. Significantly, a number of national sponsors signed on, eager to reach the millions of "home folks" who tuned into WLW's nightly country music shows.

Powel didn't care for "hillbilly music" any more than jazz. He'd made national headlines in October when, irritated that he couldn't pick out the melody in a Tommy Dorsey swing tune, he all but banned hot jazz from both WLW and WSAI. He declared that modern music would be limited to "a reasonable amount." Asked about this by a *Time* reporter, Powel said, "There is a tendency back to the simpler things. Careful surveys have indicated that listeners prefer bands of the Wayne King, Guy Lombardo, and Lucky Strike Hit Parade type."

Careful surveys taken, no doubt, among listeners like Powel and Fred Smith.

Still, he could see what was good for business. As long as programming brought in advertisers, he let the management go their own way.

He let Larry MacPhail go his own way too, though he could see that the man's reputation for difficulty was not unearned. But Reds attendance during 1935 more than doubled. Their record improved, as well, to 68-85, good enough to climb up to sixth place in the National League. The improvement had come at a cost, however. Powel spent roughly four hundred thousand dollars that season to improve the team. As he said at the time, "Building a baseball club is a lot more difficult than building radios and refrigerators."

. . . . . .

That same month, he took one final fling at the aircraft business.

Henri Mignet, a French inventor, had designed a small, radically styled biplane that could be easily built and safely flown by almost anyone. The plane was more commonly known as *Pou du Ciel* (literally, "Louse of the Sky") in France, and *Himmelslaus* ("Sky Louse") in Germany. Enthusiasts had built several hundred in Europe. Powel discussed building one of the airplanes with Eddie Nirmaier, who immediately warmed to the idea. Eddie began work on what became known as the Crosley-Mignet HM.14 on October 3, 1935. He followed Mignet's plans exactly, save for changes in how the frame was welded. The press got wind of the project, and the airplane quickly became known as the "Crosley Flying Flea." The first test flight was scheduled for November 1.

The day before, Walter Aiken, Gwendolyn's father, died in a bizarre accident. He took a spoonful of dog medicine instead of his prescription medication. He was seventy-nine years old.

Powel was forty-nine. In the twenties, when Crosley Radio was just taking off and Powel's millions were freshly minted, Gwendolyn had said of her husband, "I think we've been fortunate that Powel could have had his money while he is young. He seems to enjoy it so."

He was still enjoying it. But death, as always, made him take stock. He wasn't young anymore. He was a grandfather four times over now, as June and Powel III had yet another son, Thomas, in 1935. He had literally everything he wanted, in terms of worldly possessions. He had a wife he loved, a son and daughter he doted on, and every dream he'd ever had in his life had come to fruition.

Every dream, that is, except one—the one that eluded him as a young man.

In December, the Crosley Flea flew at the Eighth International Miami Air Trials. Then Powel had it disassembled, crated, and shipped to Cincinnati, where it was stored in a hangar at Crosley Airport. He kept the airport going, under Eddie Nirmaier's management, but he was finished with the airplane business.

It was time for him to make that one last dream come true, the dream he'd had since he and Lewis had taken their grandparents' old buckboard out of the barn and slapped an electric motor in it.

He'd failed numerous times before, but that was when he was young, inexperienced, when he'd been dependent on other people's money. He wasn't young anymore, and he had all the money he needed.

He was the number one figure in radio.

He ran the most powerful broadcast station in the country.

He owned the Cincinnati Reds.

He could do whatever he wanted, and what Powel Crosley wanted to do now was build a car.

As always, the first person he talked to was his brother.

For the first time, Lewis told him no.

CHAPTER 24

I n 1907, thirteen years after the Duryea brothers' gasoline-powered car first chugged down the streets of Springfield, Massachusetts, there were more than two hundred companies producing automobiles in the United States.

In 1935, there were ten.

Only three of them mattered. Ford, GM, and Chrysler accounted for 90 percent of auto sales in the U.S.

With the market so obviously controlled by the big three, Lewis didn't think a new company had a chance to succeed.

Powel disagreed—particularly because of the kind of car he had in mind. The Crosley car, he told his brother, would be a car for the masses, not the classes. In some ways, it drew on his plans from years before for a lightweight six-cylinder auto. In a lot of ways, it drew on the little Austin he'd been driving in Sarasota.

It would be a very small car. It would be an inexpensive car, one that would retail for under two hundred dollars at a time when the average car sold for seven hundred. It would be, as much as possible, an assembled car, like in the old days of automobile manufacturing, one that depended on ready-made components from other companies. Powel had been thinking about it for a long time, and he wanted to set up an engineering department as soon as possible, to start working on sketches.

He told Lewis others had seen the market potential for a small auto: Nash, for one, William Durant, for another. Small cars were already popular in Europe; Powel felt it was only a matter of time till economics, and common sense, made them popular in America as well. He wanted to move fast. As with radio and refrigerators, he wanted to be first into the low-price market.

He led the conversation around, eventually, to the question his brother always asked: how much money should the company invest in the project before calling it a day?

Zero, Lewis told Powel. Zero dollars is how much I think the company ought to risk on a car-making proposition.

Lewis elaborated: It's too risky. It's not just your company anymore. We're a public concern. We have shareholders. We can't do it.

Powel didn't bat an eye.

We won't use company money then, he said. We'll use mine.

Lewis looked at his brother.

Powel, clearly, was not asking permission. He was going to build the car no matter what Lewis said, which left him only one thing to say: All right then. Let's figure out how.

That was Lewis's part of the job, no matter what his wife said, no matter what his own intuition told him, no matter what the economics of the situation were. They were a team.

They sent a few engineers to the old Flatiron building on Blue Rock Road to start work on some designs, keeping the new project a secret for the moment.

In the meantime, they had their hands full with the old projects.

Refrigerator sales were up 63 percent. An average of two thousand Shelvadors rolled off the lines every day. Refrigerators, in fact, now made up 50 percent of the Crosley Radio Corporation's sales, while radios made up only 30 percent. And despite the strike, the company had made an after-tax profit of over half a million dollars in 1935. The Reds even ended up in the black for the year, for the first time in over ten years, with earnings of $165,000.

As if to celebrate, Powel went out on and made a few additions to his portfolio. He bought another airplane, a Grumman Goose, one of the all-time aviation classics. He paid sixty thousand dollars for it and named it the *Le'sgo II*.

He bought another airplane, a Fairchild 45, which cost twelve thousand dollars. What Powel especially liked about the Fairchild was that he could stand up straight in every part of the cabin, except the cockpit.

He bought another airplane, a Lockheed Electra Junior, a beautiful machine Powel was so proud of that he kept a brass display model of it in his office.

He bought another yacht, a thirty-eight-footer he named the *Pagwen*, a combination of Page and Gwendolyn's names. He had it transported to Canada for use at Nissaki.

He bought another yacht, a one-hundred-foot cruising house-boat he christened the *Sea Owl*. He had it sailed to Miami, where he kept it docked for visits to Palm Beach.

He bought another yacht, a thirty-six-footer he named the *Sea Owl* Too. He sent it to Seagate, where it was used for fishing expeditions and Sunday afternoon cruises on the bay.

He built another house, a vacation home, on an island called Cat Cay in the Bahamas. The island had been set up as a resort for the super-rich. There was an annual tuna-fishing competition held there that appealed to him, as well as an authentic replica of an English pub, called Sir Bede Clifford Hall, where visitors carved their names on the walls' wooden beams.

Powel put his name alongside the Duke and Duchess of Windsor. He brought Lewis and Lucy down for a visit, and Lewis scrawled his name on the beams as well. Lucy didn't. She was annoyed by being dragged along on Powel's vacations and didn't appreciate the demands her brother-in-law placed on her husband's time. She had taken to calling Powel 'Lord Pinecroft'—behind his back, of course, though she made little effort to hide her feelings toward him. Both had strong personalities and opinions, and conflict between them was inevitable, particularly on the subject of Lewis, who loved both his wife and his brother and tried to stay out of the fray.

When Lewis told him to get a new job, he smiled. When Powel told him to get a new wife, he smiled. But Lewis was very much his own person, and he was going to do what he felt he should do. He would keep both the job and the wife no matter what anyone told him.

. . . . . .

Early in 1936, the brothers launched the Crosley Xervac, the device intended to grow hair. It was big news. Articles appeared in *Popular Science*, *Popular Mechanics*, and *Newsweek*, and ads ran in *Life* and *Liberty*, among other magazines.

The company encouraged people to buy the machine for home use from Crosley retailers or straight from the factory. But the marketing plan for the Xervac went beyond direct consumer sales. The machine was sold to barbers and beauticians too, who rented time on the device. "Xervac salons" were set up throughout the U.S. and Canada, in places like Chicago, New York, Detroit, and even St. John's, Newfoundland.

A big salon in Detroit was promptly sued by the Better Business Bureau, which questioned the efficacy of the device until its operator, a former medical student, brought an enormous album of before and after shots of his clients into court. He won the case.

Powel had one of the machines brought to Pinecroft. He'd don the helmet and read the morning newspaper. Lewis got one and kept it in the bathroom at the Belmont Avenue house,

Lucy's sister Mary had by that time moved out and her mother, Salome, elderly and quite frail, had moved in. Lewis got her a Koolrest to help make her comfortable. That spring, he got Reds pitcher Paul Derringer one as well, to help with his allergies. There was a Derringer at Belmont Avenue, too, in Ellen's fish tank, along with eight other fish named after her favorite Reds players.

Page and young Lew were in Sarasota. Powel III was still going to work at Arlington Street every day, though he spent as much time as possible on the Ohio River, experimenting with an outboard boat motor. Every now and again, his father would join him. It was, in a way, like the old days, when they'd worked on that first crystal set together.

Powel, Jr., built another radio that year—or rather, had it built for him. The world's largest radio, the "WLW Model Super-Power Radio Receiver," which had a cabinet five feet tall, three and a half feet wide, and two feet deep. It had thirty-seven tubes, six speakers, and seventy-five watts of power. It also was a public address system. He'd built it mostly to goad Eugene MacDonald, who a few months earlier had come out with the Zenith Stratosphere model, which was four feet tall and had twenty-five tubes and fifty watts of power. The two men, friends since the early days of the NAB, had drifted apart.

In November, Powel hired another acquaintance from those early NAB days, William Hedges, who by this point was in charge of all of NBC's owned and operated stations. Hedges left New York to run WLW and WSAI. It was a coup, of sorts.

It didn't last. Hedges made it all of ten months in Powel's employ before returning to New York after a disagreement between the two men about the scope of his responsibilities.

Powel had a reputation, particularly among the staff at Crosley Radio, for dismissing employees he felt were ineffective or, simply, not a good fit. One of the writers there, a woman named Mary Wood, recalls a time when a program director lasted two months as being 'some kind of record.' She was kidding, of course, and yet...

There was no doubt in anyone's mind that it was Powel's way or the highway.

It was no surprise, therefore, that Larry MacPhail left Cincinnati in 1936. The story in the press said he'd left of his own accord, that he was ready to move on to another challenge having laid the foundation for a successful franchise. Rumors circulated he'd punched Powel during an argument. It was a fact he'd punched a Cincinnati City Detective. MacPhail was a drinker, to be sure. He was loud and argumentative. The truth was that he and Powel made an unlikely pair from the start. Both were strong-willed "idea men," and a clash between them was inevitable.

One reason Powel and Lewis got along so well was because they were so different. Both admired the other's talents, because the talents were different from their own. Lewis did not think himself as creative as his brother; Powel realized he lacked Lewis's managerial skills. Lewis admired Powel's ability to charm a room full of strangers; Powel admired Lewis's thoughtful reserve, his ability to sit still and think through a problem. There was no rivalry between them. As Powel grew more impatient and, some might say, disagreeable through the years, people around him grew more fearful or resentful of him. That was not the case with Lewis, who never quite lost the little brother's love and admiration for the older brother—and the ability of one brother to tell the other exactly what he thinks.

Powel replaced the flamboyant MacPhail with his antithesis, Warren Giles, a suave, tactful man who'd run a minor league franchise for several years up in Rochester, New York, with considerable success. Giles was now president of the International League. He and Powel hit it off right away. Giles brought one of his assistants to Cincinnati with him, a young man named Gabe Paul. Powel hit it off with him as well.

That same year, 1936, the radio union came calling again, this time to Atwater Kent's factories in Philadelphia. Kent was less accommodating than Powel and Lewis had been to the organizers. He handed the keys to the plant to his son and told him to shut the place down.

Exit stage left Kent. Also exit stage left Bruno Hauptmann, executed on April 3 for the kidnapping and murder of Charles Lindbergh, Jr.; Crime of the Century solved. Shortly thereafter, Charles Lindbergh, Sr., was invited to tour Nazi Germany. He came away impressed by Hitler, Goering, and the German air force, which he proclaimed the mightiest in the world. Invincible.

Exit stage left a great many Lindbergh admirers.

It was a bad year for another pilot, Okey Bevins, who accidentally flew his plane into the WLW tower. The tower survived the crash unscathed.

Bevins did not.

It was a pivotal year for Powel Crosley. He had achieved the success he had wanted—broadcast industry leader, owner of the country's most powerful radio station, industrial magnate, titan of refrigerator and radio manufacturing; one of the two dozen or so most powerful figures in baseball, a newly elected director of the National League, an innovator, a savior of the professional game for his home town. He'd rubbed shoulders with presidents, Hollywood celebrities, and industrial giants.

He was, at long last, building his dream car.

For the previous twenty years the arc of his life had moved in one direction—upward. From the Insyde Tyres to the Shelvador, from the Harko Jr. to the Roamio, one success led to the next.

The fall began in 1936.

.   .   .   .   .   .

Lucy's mother fell ill. Lewis sent Ellen and Charlotte Jeanne away for a month to Michigan with his mother. When they returned to the house, Salome Johnson was gone. So was the Koolrest.

Dutch remained, still defending his territory from any deliveryman who dared cross it. Factory workers came from Arlington Street with a new batch of radios, fresh off the line. Lewis, like Powel, kept a sampling of the latest models in his house. Dutch held them at bay for a good long while; Lewis bought the dog a muzzle.

In September, Powel faced the Cincinnati press corps and made the twin announcements about Larry MacPhail and Warren Giles.

In October, he was in New York for the National Radio and Electrical Exposition, where he spoke to the *New York Times* regarding the state of the broadcast industry. Things looked good for radio, he said. Election years always stimulated set purchases. He was less sanguine about television, which he saw as years away. There were a number of technical issues to overcome, and he thought the cost of programming would be prohibitive.

At the end of the month, he traveled to Washington D.C. to testify in front of the FCC. There was increasing controversy surrounding the issue of superpower. Some of the concerns revolved around technical issues, such as interference and clear channel operation. There was, however, increasing talk about the social and ethical implications of one station having that much power.

Smaller stations within WLW's broadcast area complained that advertisers were abandoning their stations for Powel's. There were complaints from other broadcasters, who felt they, too, should be granted license to broadcast at superpower.

The FCC shared those concerns and had others of its own.

Enter FCC Commissioner George Henry Payne, stage right.

He began his questioning by accusing Powel of unjustifiably raising WLW's advertising rates. Powel denied the charge and produced figures showing that the station's increased revenue was more than offset by its increased production costs.

Payne continued.

He accused Powel of refusing to accept advertising from other companies in competition with Crosley. Powel denied the charges.

Payne pressed on.

He accused WLW of censoring the news, particularly when it came to labor disputes. Powel denied those charges as well.

Payne produced a copy of the memo Norman Corwin had received a year earlier:

Our news broadcasts, as you have already been told, and which has been our practice for some time, will not include mention of any strikes.

Powel insisted he'd never seen that memo. It ran contrary to his own beliefs.

Payne, his point made, rested.

WLW's license to broadcast at five hundred thousand watts was extended another six months, but the battle between the two men had just begun.

.   .   .   .   .   .

If, by 1936, life could be said to have fulfilled all Powel Crosley's childhood imaginings (save the one desire he was currently working on bringing to fruition), it had certainly, long ago, surpassed his wife's wildest expectations

She'd married a young dreamer. She was now living with one of the most successful businessmen in the world.

She would have liked for Powel to be with her more, with the family, particularly when the children had been growing up, but that phase of their lives was over. Men in those days went to work. They provided. He'd kept up his part of the bargain, and more.

She had homes all across the continent. She didn't use them the way Powel did, of course, but she went with him a great deal of the time, and when she couldn't go, she had whatever she wanted at her fingertips. She had her grandchildren and her work with the church.

Lately, though, there was something bothering her.

She'd lost her appetite. She had a persistent fever and a cough that wouldn't go away. She was tired all the time and had lost weight. Finally, she went to the doctor. He confirmed what she already knew deep inside. She was sick. Very sick, in fact.

She had tuberculosis.

Today we know the disease is caused by a virus, treatable with a course of antibiotics. Back then, though doctors were aware of tuberculosis's method of transmission, they had no ready cure. Some people got better, some didn't. No one was quite sure why. About all Gwendolyn and Powel and the rest of the family could do was pray.

The commonly accepted prescription was bed rest and isolation. She had to be kept away from everyone—her family, friends, children, grandchildren.

Powel built her a two-bedroom cottage behind Pinecroft and hired a nurse to be with her twenty-four hours a day. He did whatever he could to make her comfortable. He talked to as many doctors as possible, hearing many different recommendations for treatment. Some thought a dry climate therapeutic; others leaned toward seaside air. Still others favored more aggressive therapy, such as artificial pneumothorax, in which one lung was induced to collapse so that the lesions on it could heal without strain.

The treatment was also known as compression therapy, which

had been used, without success, on Christy Mathewson. It remained, roughly two decades after its introduction, a controversial, dangerous, procedure.

· · · · · ·

In December, FCC Commissioner Payne was in New York to give a speech entitled "Is Radio living up to its promise?" His answer, he readily allowed, was no. Commercial interests dominated the airwaves. The public, which owned the ether, got nothing but commercials and programs asking for their dollars. As much as was in his power, Payne declared, he would see things set right.

Payne also came down on the side of the inventors whose discoveries had created the vast broadcasting empires now run by corporations. He noted in his speech that of the forty-three scientists who had contributed the most to radio, only two had made any substantive profits whatsoever.

One of those was Edwin Armstrong, who in selling RCA his super heterodyne receiver years earlier had become for a time the single largest shareholder of the company's stock. In 1936, Armstrong revealed to the world what he'd been working on for the last few years. It was called FM, short for frequency modulation.

It made the regenerative circuit and the super heterodyne a footnote to his personal saga. Forget sunspots, forget frequency interference, forget the skywave, there was no static whatsoever with Armstrong's new type of radio-wave transmission. What you got when you tuned in a station was the station, period. No noise.

Armstrong had made his discovery three years earlier but delayed announcing it because of his ties to RCA. He'd been hoping that RCA would take advantage of his discovery to corner an entire new area of the broadcasting market.

They were prepared to do just that, only not as Armstrong had anticipated.

The inventor and David Sarnoff, close friends for more than twenty years, were about to become the bitterest of enemies, protagonists in an epic battle that would soon make the one between Powel and Payne seem like tiddlywinks.

. . . . . .

Plans for the Crosley car proceeded apace, albeit in fits and starts. Powel made frequent changes to the auto's design, often vacillating on major elements, such as whether the car would have three wheels or four. His initial intent was to make only one model, a two-door sedan. Now he was leaning toward offering a coupe as well. He and Lewis had chosen the Waukesha Engine Company to build the power plant. They had in mind an air-cooled engine plant that could generate 13.5 horsepower—not much by big-car standards but plenty for the Crosley, provided they could keep the car's weight down enough for the engine to move it and four passengers at a reasonable speed.

Powel targeted fifty mph as his goal; he also wanted the car to average fifty miles to a gallon of gas. That would give him an operating cost of a penny a mile, as compared to the three to five cents per mile most cars offered.

Christmas 1936 was held at Pinecroft, as always. Everyone was there: Lewis and Lucy, Edythe and Albert, all the children and grandchildren, and Charlotte Crosley. Powel, Sr., was by this point four years gone, but his absence was manageable.

Gwendolyn's was harder.

She had to stay in the cottage. In addition to TB, she'd developed the flu. She accepted visitors as she could: Ellen and Lucy, among others, brought her presents.

Dutch stayed home.

After the holidays, Powel headed south for a couple days of quail hunting but cut his trip short because of constant rain. He went to Seagate to wait for better weather. Page and young Lew were there. The boy was three. Powel doted on him in a way he'd never doted on his own children, in a way he never doted on Powel III's sons. It was understandable, in some ways. Young Lew was his adopted son and had no father, though Page had, of late, been seeing a man named Robert Jennings.

As understandable as it might have been, it was a source of tension.

Grandfather was a very wealthy man. It did not do for grandfather to play favorites.

Up north, the rain kept falling. Day after day after day.

The Ohio River and its tributaries began to fill, their waters, to rise.

The Arlington Street complex of factories was about a mile away from the riverbanks. When the Crosley Corporation had built Building K—the one-story shed on Arlington Street that abutted the railroad tracks, where the radio sets were packed up and shipped off to distributors—a consideration, naturally, had been the height of that river.

During the floods in 1884 and 1913, the river had reached about seventy feet above the zero gauge mark. Seventy-two feet was generally considered a safe level for foundation construction in the river's immediate area. Lewis, the careful manager who had considerable experience with the vicissitudes of the Ohio, had insisted on a base of seventy-four feet for Building K and a number of other Arlington Street facilities.

Predictions in early January called for the river to crest at around fifty-two feet. So they were safe, in that respect, though by mid-month, Powel had to write off quail hunting entirely. He conducted what business he could from Florida, waiting for the weather to clear. He worked from the round ship's room, with a small desk and a handful of telephones. Neill Prew remembers walking in at one point, and seeing 'Uncle Powel' on the phone, a look of equal parts anger and impatience on his face. He wasn't happy with the situation.

Neither was Lewis.

A violent storm—snow, sleet, ice and hail—hit Indiana. In Ohio, the rain continued to fall. Looking out the window of his office on Arlington Street, Lewis Crosley began to worry.

Perhaps, for once, he hadn't been quite careful enough.

CHAPTER 25

D espite the on-going efforts of George Payne, WLW continued to grow. The "Nation's Station" had close to a hundred
and fifty full-time people on staff by the end of 1936. Most
were musicians. They had a few dozen writer/directors, as well as Peter
Grant and Red Barber and were not only originating programming for
the Mutual Broadcasting network but the NBC Blue and Red chains
as well.

Exclusive of the superpower controversy, broadcasters as a
group were involved in a number of other fights. One of those was
with ASCAP, who were once again making royalty demands the
NAB considered nothing less than extortion. Powel was again
involved in that fight. By and by, the NAB once more formed its own
organization of composers as an alternative to ASCAP. This time,
their efforts were more successful.

By and by, that alternative organization took shape: BMI.

By and by, David Sarnoff's reasons for spurning Edwin Armstrong and FM took shape as well. The new transmission method
was not just an improvement, it was a new animal entirely—"a better mousetrap"—in Sarnoff's words. So much better, in fact, it
would make the old mousetrap (the products, programming, and
services NBC and RCA had spent close to twenty years developing)
obsolete. Sarnoff had a different idea, one that created a new avenue
of business entirely.

Television.

Spurned by RCA, Edwin Armstrong began cashing in vast
shares of his Radio Corporation stock and constructing his own
network of FM broadcast stations.

. . . . .

The rain kept falling. By mid-January, the Ohio River had reached flood stage. By the 24th, parts of downtown lay under several feet of water. That same day, water flowed across Spring Grove Avenue and lapped at the foundations of Building K. Crosley employees at the main plant moved machinery from the first to the second floor as flood waters began entering the building.

The Cincinnati Gas & Electric Company was forced to shut down its generators and emergency power was tapped in from Dayton. Thousands of people had to be evacuated. Water rationing was put into effect.

The next day, with the river more than twenty-five feet above flood stage, disaster struck. Several gasoline and oil storage tanks owned by the Standard Oil Company started leaking, resulting in a layer of oil and gas estimated at two inches thick floating on the floodwaters. A sparking trolley wire on a Northside street set the flammable liquid ablaze.

Fire exploded a quarter mile into the air. Ten tanks went up within twenty minutes and two square miles of floodwater were soon ablaze. As the fire roared toward the block where the main Crosley plant stood, employees fled, using stairways because the elevators weren't working.

The fire didn't reach the eight-story main plant, but Building K went up like a tinderbox. Further down Spring Grove Avenue, the National Label building went up as well. Held at a distance by the floodwaters, firefighters could do little more than watch while keeping the flames from spreading. WLW engineers set up a temporary studio at the Netherland Plaza Hotel. Two days later, WLW moved in with WSAI on the third floor of the old Corcoran Lamp Building, at Colerain and Sassafras Streets.

For the rest of that week, the worst week of flooding, the station stayed on the air for twenty-four hours a day, breaking into regular programming as needed with emergency messages, rescue team directions, and words of encouragement from announcers Peter

Grant, Durward Kirby, and others. The entire broadcast industry mobilized; CBS, NBC, and stations across the U.S. and Canada united to form an emergency response network.

A few miles away from Arlington Street, Crosley Field was a swimming pool. Twenty feet of water lay over the playing surface. The stands and bleachers were half-submerged.

Two Reds pitchers, Lee Grissom and Gene Schott, made their way across the infield and over the centerfield fence in a rowboat; a photograph of them doing so made the papers nationwide.

But the flood was no laughing matter.

It caused over half a million dollars of damage to the Crosley plants. Powel returned from Florida the day after the fire to forge the company's recovery strategy with Lewis. Partial production resumed within weeks, helped along by the fact that most of their refrigerator cabinets were fabricated by sub-contractors in Cleveland and Indiana. By spring the main plant was cleaned up and producing Shelvadors and radios at an almost normal rate.

The flood also postponed progress on the Crosley automobile. A building on Spring Grove Avenue that Powel and his engineers had been using as an automotive "lab" was completely submerged under floodwaters and not ready to use again until April.

And Powel's run of bad luck wasn't over yet.

As the main plant was getting back into production, fire destroyed the big hangar out at Crosley Airport. The Grumman Goose was outside at the time, but the four Moonbeams inside were destroyed. The Crosley Flying Flea was removed from the hangar before the flames reached it.

There was, sadly, more to come.

On July 19, Texas Congressman W. D. McFarlane took to the House floor and accused Powel of profiteering. "Upon receiving your experimental license," MacFarlane said, "you immediately raised the price of your radio advertising time some 50 percent and continued to collect handsome commercial profits on the basis of experimentation... why, I think it is fair to ask, has this unusual concession been handed out and continued in the hands of one of the

700 [radio] licensees?"

Payne had earlier written Powel, asking that he turn over WLW's balance sheet, profit-and-loss statement, and other financial reports so the FCC could get to the heart of the matter. Powel, attempting to smooth things over, wrote Payne and invited him to a Reds game to talk things over.

That only made matters worse.

In August, Payne wrote back, providing the *New York Times*, the *Washington Post*, and other national newspapers copies of his letter.

"On June 30 I received from you an invitation to a baseball game and to a 'small informal lunch'," he said. The invitation, Payne went on, seemed strange to him, as did the offer of 'good fellowship.' "When I recalled, however, that an official letter that I had addressed to you had remained unanswered for over six months, the problem became not one of gaucherie but of defiance of the law."

Powel sent a response of his own through the press. First of all, he said, MacFarlane was wrong. WLW's advertising rates had gone up only 20 percent, though power had been increased ten-fold. He further pointed out that there were numerous other concerns doing business under experimental licenses, and it was unfair to single out WLW for doing the same. Details of the station's operation would be reported to the FCC at the proper time, during hearings for the renewal of its experimental license.

FCC chairman Sykes called a special meeting of the commission the next day, and the *Washington Post* reported that Payne was expected to be "sharply criticized for his one-man fight on Crosley."

That fight was not over yet.

·   ·   ·   ·   ·

The Reds struggled through 1937 along with their owner, losing 98 games and finishing in last place again. One of the only bright spots was Lee Grissom, who led the team with 13 wins, led the league with five shutouts, and finished second in strikeouts. Grissom was voted to the all-star team, as was Ernie Lombardi, who hit .334 with nine homers. Not quite Ruthian numbers, but playing at Crosley Field, known for its cavernous dimensions, made home runs difficult to hit.

Powel and Warren Giles expected better from their team. Even before the season was over, they let manager Charlie Dressen go. While Giles began scouting about for a successor, Powel remained focused on the superpower controversy, which was turning out to be about politics as much as anything else. He added a publicity man from the Democratic National Committee named Charles Michelson to his team, paying him a retainer of ten thousand dollars to give advice on the situation.

Lewis was, as always, focused on production space. It was time to expand again. The demand for Shelvadors and other new appliances was taxing the existing plants. And he had to prepare for the car, progress on which had been slowed by the flood, but which would still, almost certainly within the next year, require production space of its own.

He and Powel decided to solve both problems at the same time. They bought land in Richmond, Indiana, thirty miles northwest and began construction on a long, narrow brick building. Long, as in one-mile long, narrow, as in just wide enough to accommodate two parallel production lines. The first line would be for Shelvadors, the second would turn out the (still hush-hush) Crosley auto, which Powel was still modifying. He'd been playing with the idea of a three-wheel auto, with a single wheel in the rear, but by now he was settled on a more conventional four-wheel chassis with rear-wheel drive.

Powel was tinkering with other new technology too. He'd been following for some time the progress of a radio-FAX system developed by an engineer named William Finch. Finch had perfected a setup whereby FAX images could be transmitted over short distances (say, a hundred miles) to small home-type radio receivers. With the addition of a FAX printing unit, home receivers could be converted to receive news by FAX. Three stations tested the system in 1937 by sending daily "radio newspapers" to subscribers in their cities. Powel liked the idea so much that he not only signed up WLW to participate in the service but also convinced WOR and WGN to conduct experiments with WLW by sending text and images station-to-station. He sensed an opportunity, though in this instance he turned out to be a few years ahead of his time.

He and Lewis were also tinkering with the construction of a new, ultra-modern building to house the combined WLW/WSAI broadcasting operation, which by this point employed close to three hundred people. It seemed, in some ways, ludicrous for the Nation's Station to be run from the top floor of a factory building. The brothers had an architect begin working up plans for a facility in the Clifton neighborhood near the university.

Powel was in Newport, Rhode Island, on August 5, watching the America's Cup races in the *Sea Owl*. He was back in Cincinnati that November to greet WLW's new station manager, James Shouse. About this time, he was also on the factory floor, where after hearing two engineers complain about the difficulty of removing ice cubes from freezer trays, he came up with an idea for a new kind of ice cube tray, one with a removable aluminum grid inside. A lever was attached to the grid; lift it, and the cubes popped right out. Powel got a patent for that bit of tinkering.

At the same time, Gwendolyn's doctors were tinkering with her treatment. The tuberculosis was not responding as well as they hoped. They suggested a change of climate: she and Powel, after some discussion, agreed.

She moved to Sarasota. Once there, she settled into her own suite at the northwest corner of the mansion. Page took up full-time residence in the house with her. So did young Lew. So did Page's new husband, Robert Jennings, though he spent quite a bit of time traveling for business.

Old husband Gilman Shelton, however, was still on everyone's mind. Despite the million-dollar payoff, Powel was concerned about his adopted son. He didn't let young Lew venture off Seagate's grounds unguarded.

In addition to Gwendolyn's nurse, at least a dozen servants lived on-site, taking care of cooking, housecleaning, laundry and other chores. A chauffer was always available. Captain Michaels lived onboard the *Argo*, and Perry, the yacht's steward, moved into one of the garage apartments and took on the duties of gardener.

In Cincinnati, a man named John Dunville arrived to take charge of WSAI. Before long, he would move to WLW as the station's commercial manager. He and James Shouse would, eventually, outlast both Powel and Lewis.

A woman named Dorothea Bauer was Powel's executive assistant. Her desk was located between Powel's and Lewis's offices, on the eighth floor. She became the gatekeeper for anyone seeking access to Powel.

In early 1938 Powel continued tinkering, not just at the Arlington Street factory, but down at Crosley Field, where home plate was moved, on Powel's order, twenty feet out toward the fences, a shift suggested by a column in the *Cincinnati Times-Star*. The move paid off. The team hit more home runs that season than in any previous in their history, though the big excitement was on the pitcher's mound, where Johnny Vander Meer pitched two no-hitters in a row. The first came at Crosley Field, the second four days later in Brooklyn, a team now run by Larry MacPhail.

The most important move of all, however, was made by Warren Giles before the 1938 season started when he brought Bill McKechnie back to Cincinnati to manage the Reds. The Deacon, as McKechnie was known, was a perfect choice to handle the team Giles had assembled, a group of savvy veterans who didn't require a cheerleader so much as a man who knew how to put them in the right positions to use their skills. The soft-spoken, church-going McKechnie brought the team together off the field as well as on it. The entire city's excitement was palpable by season's end. This was a team on the upswing, and everybody climbed on the bandwagon.

The Reds performance would prove to be the highlight of an otherwise difficult year.

Fourteen year-old Doris Kappelhoff, an aspiring dancer from College Hill who had broken her leg the year before in a terrible auto accident, shattered it a second time while attempting to dance, while on crutches, to a record of "Tea for Two." To keep her daughter's mind off her misfortune, Mrs. Kapplehoff paid for singing lessons. Young Doris's first vocal teacher didn't work out.

Her second teacher was Grace Raine, who saw great potential in the young singer. She asked Mrs. Kapplehoff if Doris could come three times a week. Mrs. Kapplehoff, who was a single mother, said she could barely afford the one lesson.

"That's all right," Grace said, or words to that effect. The other two would be free. After more lessons, Grace landed Doris an audition on WLW, then a job singing at a local Chinese restaurant, and finally, a spot with a band led by Barney Rapp at the Hotel Sinton. Rapp, a well-known personality in town, was impressed with the young girl's singing, but her last name....

It was a mouthful. It didn't fit on a marquee. Rapp wondered if she'd consider changing it. He made a few suggestions. She didn't like any of them. The only one she could tolerate was taken from what had become her signature song, "Day After Day." The name that went up in lights—and eventually, on movie screens, and record charts, and into the pages of history—was Doris Day.

That was also the year the Crosley Radio Corporation brought out a modified version of the radio-FAX receiver, which Powel called "Reado." He placed Reados with WLW staffers, family, and friends, and had the WLW newsroom prepare each night's news in a special format for FAXing between midnight and five in the morning.

He had a Reado assembly line set up at the Arlington Street plant; soon, a hundred sets were coming off the line each day. He placed those sets with Crosley retailers in various cities. There was a Reado printer, which came with instructions for connecting it to a home radio set, and a Reado radio receiver. Each sold for $79.95. A ten-dollar appliance timer and replacement rolls of Reado paper were also added to the line.

Consumer acceptance was sluggish at first, but Powel insisted that sales would pick up.
He would be wrong.

That spring, the Federal Trade Commission ruled against Crosley in the matter of the Xervac, concluding that claims being made for the machine were unsubstantiated by fact. They ordered the company to temper its advertising message—a death knell for the product.

It was shaping up to be a difficult year.

The struggle for power is on, declared the *New York Times* on June 5.

The struggle they referred to was not the growing aggression of the Nazis but the one in Washington, where an FCC subcommittee—among whose members, of course, was George Henry Payne—was set to convene.

The subject, once more, was superpower.

The hearings initially focused not on WLW but the further expansion of the program; the granting of additional 500kw licenses. Testimony revealed little doubt, from an engineering standpoint, that the increased wattage would provide service to areas of the country where lower-power stations could not reach.

That service, in the opinion of many, was not the issue.

The issue was the type of service those people could expect from superpower stations. Here the shadow of the 1936 hearings—WLW's rate hikes, its broadcast policies, and other related issues—loomed large. The issue became a political football: what kind of service could people expect from superpower stations? Advertising pablum, in the opinion of men like Senator Burton Wheeler of Tennessee. Superpower stations, Wheeler declared, belonged to no community. They had no local interest to serve, no interest whatsoever save the almighty broadcast dollar.

Superpower, in the Senator's opinion, was dangerous.

"Such operation would tend to concentrate political, social and economic power and influence in the hands of a very small group," Wheeler said, not mentioning any names, but again, he didn't have to. There was only one superpower station.

He went before Congress and introduced resolution 294, declaring that power in excess of fifty thousand watts was against the public interest. The Senate passed it virtually without opposition.

The FCC subcommittee, rumored to have been inclined

toward further 500kw stations, recommended against the issuance of other such licenses.

And then they turned to WLW.

Powel had decided against testifying himself, against confronting Payne head-on and making the issue any more personal. Instead, James Shouse spoke before the subcommittee. He said that the charges of profiteering were unfair; yes, the station was making slightly more money, but they were putting far more of their increased revenue back into programming, exactly the kind of programming rural America wanted to hear, in fact: Country & Western entertainment, Country & Western music, farm reports, news, weather updates. WLW was also subsidizing the Ohio University of the Air, and bringing network programs from both coasts to the heart of the country. And yes, they carried advertising, but what station didn't, and in no way did their advertising hurt the smaller stations serving the same markets, Shouse said, and brought out pages of data to back up his assertion.

Payne said little. He, in fact, asked no questions whatsoever.

It was as if, in his mind, the question was settled already.

The subcommittee finished its hearings and retired to consider its recommendation to the full FCC. In the meantime, WLW's superpower license was renewed for another six months.

Powel tried to focus on other things: the car, first and foremost. By now, he and his engineers had moved beyond the drawing stage to testing prototypes. A bodyless chassis, nicknamed the CRAD, for Crosley Radio Automobile Division, served as a continuing test bed for engines and other components. Powel was often seen driving it on the private roads of Sleepy Hollow Farm.

The early three-wheel design had inspired him to build an odd prototype, with the front wheels forty inches apart, the rear wheels separated by only eighteen inches. The configuration gave the car an odd, triangular look; it also eliminated the need for a differential, a major cost savings.

On the odd-shaped chassis engineers hung an early, hand-made version of the Crosley body, with a high front hood and streamlined fenders tapering back to a narrow, fenderless rear end that had only a tiny bumper and a single brake light. The little CRAD had a push-button starter inside, a lawn-mower style pulley starter out.

There was a single bench seat, big enough for two adults; a small area behind it offered minimal storage. The roof was fabric, with a small plastic rear window. The doors swung on externally mounted hinges and offered sliding plastic panels instead of windows. The headlights were mounted directly on the fenders. The wheels were designed for twelve-inch tires.

They built it small and as cheaply as possible. It was going to be different from anything else on the road.

And then, all at once, it wasn't.

Enter the Bantam subcompact car, stage right.

Roy Evans, a former salesman for American Austin, had purchased that company's assets some time earlier. For the last few years, Evans had been working on an auto of his own. His car, the Bantam, was now revealed to be in production, several months ahead of the Crosley car. On the one hand, it was good news, affirmation of Powel's belief that the U.S. market was ready for a small, economical car. On the other, Evans's car would be out first; the press would focus on it as the pioneering American subcompact.

Powel tried to focus on other things.

By then both NBC and CBS were conducting television broadcast tests, the former from atop the Empire State Building, the latter from the Chrysler skyscraper. Powel, though he still had his doubts about the new medium's profitability, felt he had to keep pace. He requested quotes from RCA, Westinghouse, and General Electric regarding the cost of a television transmitter. The quotes came back too high. Worse yet, none of the companies could promise delivery in less than eighteen months.

As Lewis put it, "Powel wouldn't wait eighteen months for anyone."

He decided WLW's engineers could do the job themselves.

He called in his chief engineer, James Rockwell, gave him a budget, and a deadline: thirty days.

Rockwell did what most broadcast engineers would have done

in his shoes; tell the boss what he wanted was physically impossible, that he needed sixty.

Then he went ahead and did it in forty-five.

As always, Powel's door on Arlington Street was open to inventors and other visitors—those who could get past Dorothea Bauer. That September, a man named Grover Whalen stopped in. Whalen was president of the New York World's Fair committee. The upcoming exhibition was set to open in the spring of 1939, to commemorate the 150th anniversary of George Washington's inauguration as America's First President. But the fair wasn't about the past; it was about the future—the glittering World of Tomorrow. That world was to take shape on three and a half square miles just outside of Manhattan. Structures already were rising, being erected by companies and countries from around the globe to showcase their vision of the future, where technology freed one and all from the routine of day-to-day drudgery and offered entertainment beyond imagining, where poverty and war and struggle were things of the past.

Whalen wanted the Crosley Corporation to be a part of it.

Powel talked to Lewis, and they agreed to become exhibitors and construct a building to showcase the company's wares, at a cost of at least two million dollars.

That same month, at a special stockholders' meeting, the Crosley Radio Corporation officially became "The Crosley Corporation." The rationale offered was that the company's name should more accurately reflect its business activities. *Time* soon devoted two columns to the possibility of a forthcoming Crosley automobile. Powel admitted he'd been experimenting with some ideas and left it at that. By now he and Lewis were well into the process of signing up suppliers for the parts they wouldn't be manufacturing themselves—Autolite for batteries, generators, and starters; Delco for shock absorbers; Goodyear for tires. Work was proceeding in Richmond, the factory moving closer and closer to full-scale production.

Anticipation regarding the Crosley automobile continued to mount.

In Europe, there was anticipation as well, of a far more nervous sort. Hitler's armies stood at the border of Czechoslovakia. While the world watched, British Prime Minister Neville Chamberlain flew to Berlin, and "negotiated" a pact. Britain and France acknowledged German claims to certain portions of Czech territory; Hitler promised a halt to Nazi aggression. Chamberlain flew home wearing a triumphant smile and waving a piece of paper, declaring "Peace in our time" had been achieved.

In October, Martians invaded Earth, landing in the town of Grover's Mill, New Jersey. CBS radio reported the death of untold thousands in the attack. Panicked listeners jammed the streets, towels wrapped around their faces to protect themselves from poison gas. Police were called. A handful of other radio stations picked up CBS's reports and rebroadcast them. It turned out to be an on-air dramatization of a decades-old science fiction novel by H.G. Wells titled *The War of the Worlds*, brought to new and frightening life by the Mercury Theater Company, under the guidance of actors Orson Welles and John Houseman. The panic was a terrifying demonstration of the broadcast medium's power to create the illusion of reality from nothing but smoke and mirrors.

All too soon, Chamberlain's peace would turn out to made of similar stuff.

. . . . . .

There was other demoralizing news that October of 1938, at least as far as the Nation's Station and its supporters were concerned.

On the 17th, Payne and the other members of the FCC subcommittee announced their decision. They felt further extensions of WLW's superpower license unwarranted. They recommended to the full FCC that at the end of the current six-month operating period, the station be ordered to return to transmitting at fifty thousand watts.

They cited three major reasons for their decision:

• Interference complaints by station WOR in New York, broadcasting at 710 on the dial;

- Economic damage, in the form of lost advertising revenue, to smaller stations;
- Four years of 'experimentation' was quite long enough to judge the effects of 500kw transmission.

Not mentioned at all was the question of service to rural areas.

Rumor spread that FDR himself, who had pressed the telegraph key to fire up the big transmitter four years earlier, now saw it as a political albatross, a symbol of profiteering. The word was that he was telling the FCC the same thing as Payne's subcommittee; take the 500kw machine off-line. In the eyes of most observers, superpower was dead.

Powel begged to differ.

Faced with the displeasure of America's chief executive, he did what his father would have done, what his father had taught him to do: fight back.

WLW filed an immediate objection regarding the interference with WOR. Powel's lawyers pointed out there had been a total of eight complaints—individual complaints, not from the station itself—during the four years. Regarding the second point, evidence was submitted discrediting the few witnesses who had come forward to complain of lost revenue. Finally, the lawyers argued that there was plenty of experimentation yet to be done, particularly with regard to the question of sunspot activity.

And most important of all, perhaps, without that transmitter, there would be huge areas where radio service, in the words of the appeal, "in large measure would be destroyed."

They were summoned before the full FCC to make their case: Commissioner Payne didn't even bother to show.

.   .   .   .   .

In November, the Bantam made its debut at the National Automobile Show in New York. It was a stylish little car, ranging in price from $399 for a coupe to $565 for a station wagon. It differed from

Powel's auto on a number of fronts: the Bantam's design was flashy, the Crosley's utilitarian. There were several Bantam models, only one Crosley, which at a planned price of $290 was significantly cheaper.

Reassured, Powel flew to Sarasota for the holidays. Shortly thereafter, he, Gwendolyn, and Page flew to Miami and boarded the one-hundred-foot *Sea Owl*. They sailed to Palm Beach, entertaining friends on the way and returned to Seagate in time for Christmas. Powel III and his family joined them. Gwendolyn, tired out by the travel, remained mostly sequestered in her room.

On December 29, Powel flew to New York to sign the lease agreement for the Crosley Building with World's Fair officials. They held a little ceremony. He posed for the cameras, climbed back in his plane, and returned to Sarasota.

In early January, he was back in Cincinnati, to speak before a convention of the company's distributors. He was optimistic about prospects for the coming year. He didn't talk directly about the car, but the publicity it was sure to spark could only help the other Crosley businesses.

Then he was off to Georgia for camping and quail hunting. Afterward, he returned to Sarasota once more. In early February, the FCC denied the renewal of WLW's superpower license. *Business Week* accused the committee of being pushed around by politicians.

Powel wasn't finished fighting yet. On February 21, the company filed an appeal with the U.S. Circuit Court asking for a stay of the FCC's decision.

"Our duty to ourselves and this listening public dictates the need for this step," he said in a statement issued to the press.

On Saturday, February 25, 1939, he drove to the airport at Bradenton. Gwendolyn came with him. He said goodbye to her and climbed into the Fairchild, with Eddie Nirmaier at the controls. There was still much work to be done on the Crosley car, now nearly ready to be introduced to the public. The 1939 refrigerator business looked to be a real dogfight; everyone was cutting prices. The Circuit Court's decision on staying the FCC's order to cut WLW's power was expected at any moment. Lewis had the factories in hand, of course, and Shouse had WLW firmly in his charge, but Powel wanted to be in Cincinnati nonetheless, for all the above and many other reasons.

The Fairchild rose into the sky; Gwendolyn returned to the Sarasota house. She had treatment scheduled that afternoon. Part of the reason Powel had stayed south so long was to be with her as doctors, dissatisfied with her condition, continued to tinker with her therapy.

She'd been undergoing compression therapy, the procedure in which one of her lungs was deliberately collapsed to allow lesions on the organ time to heal, without strain. It involved the use of a needle to pierce the chest cavity.

Great caution was necessary.

.   .   .   .   .   .

Powel was forced to land in Atlanta because of an unexpected turn in the weather. Rather than wait for the skies to clear, he decided to press on via train to Indiana. A car would pick him up at the station and take him to Sleepy Hollow that night.

He never made it that far. When the train stopped in Louisville Kentucky, he was summoned to the station office.

There was a message waiting for him.

CHAPTER 26

Powel Crosley, Jr., was on the verge of realizing his fondest dream—mass production of the car he'd been trying to build for almost three decades.

He was also living his worst nightmare.

On February 28, he stood on the plot of land in Spring Grove Cemetery that he and Lewis had chosen for its view of College Hill and buried his wife.

She is largely absent from the story, because she, like so many women of her day, was content to be behind the scenes, supporting the work of their husbands.

But she was there, every step of the way.

When he came back from Indianapolis after breaking his arm; when the Hermes, and then the cycle-car failed, when the American Automobile Accessories Company teetered on the verge of bankruptcy, when he came home after the humiliating lecture from his father on the value of a dollar.

She was there that Washington's Birthday in 1921, when her son came back to the Davey Avenue house upset because her husband had not bought him the radio set he'd been promised.

When the Harko Jr. hit stores, when the Harko Seniors started coming back, when WLW went to five hundred thousand watts, when the Cincinnati Reds became part of the Crosley family, Gwendolyn lived every chapter of the story right alongside her husband.

People who knew her commented on her kindness and generosity. Though appreciative of the lifestyle afforded by Powel's success, she did not take it for granted or use it to feel superior to those less fortunate. To Powel she had always been quietly supportive. In some respects, she was similar to Lewis in her personality—quiet, reflective, comfortable with Powel's need to run the show.

The entry in the 1907 Walnut Hills High School Yearbook describes her during her teens: "She is one of the jolly little girls who have a smile and a good word for everyone."

She remained genial as she grew older, though it's difficult to miss the wistfulness, even melancholy, in her face in photographs taken later in life. Perhaps her more sensitive, artistic nature was not perfectly suited to life with a man of Powel's intensity and power. The luxury of their lives also gave her less and less to do as she grew older. When Powel, no doubt with loving intentions, hired a butler to run Pinecroft, she had even less. Seagate was built according to Powel's specifications, not Gwendolyn's. She arrived at the mansion to find it not only built, but furnished.

The momentous discovery Powel made in 1939 was how different the world was without her. On Monday morning, February 27, he drove to Cincinnati's Union Terminal to meet the train from Sarasota. Page was on board. So was Gwendolyn's body.

Something had gone terribly wrong that Saturday night. The cause of death was officially listed as "complications due to tuberculosis," but what actually occurred could have been any number of things. The needle might have punctured one of Gwendolyn's lungs; she might have died from lack of oxygen. A nick in a blood vessel may have led to an internal hemorrhage; the tuberculosis itself might even have killed her at the last.

In the end, it made no difference.

The body went to the funeral home; Powel and Page went to Pinecroft.

In Sarasota, young Lew, who'd been told nothing, waited with his nanny for his mother and 'na-na' to return. In Tampa, Reds players cancelled scheduled spring training workouts in Gwendolyn's honor.

The next day, family and friends gathered at Pinecroft to pay their respects. It was an event that sixty-five years later Ellen Crosley could recall with absolute clarity. Gwendolyn's coffin was in the living room downstairs. Elegant wreaths of gardenias and camellias adorned the walls, and there were pansies—Gwendolyn's favorite flower—everywhere she looked. The gallery upstairs was filled to overflowing with Aikens, Utzes, Crosleys, and Henshaws. A musician had been hired to play Gwendolyn's favorite music on the organ in the foyer. The minute his fingers hit the keys, Powel's mother Charlotte collapsed in tears.

That afternoon, Gwendolyn was buried in Spring Grove cemetery. It was a scene Powel had never imagined in his worst nightmares.

All too soon, he would be back.

.   .   .   .   .   .

That same day the Court of Appeals denied WLW's request for a stay of the FCC's order. The next morning, March 1, 1939, the big transmitter went off the air, and the Nation's Station returned to fifty thousand watts. They lowered their advertising rates accordingly, though not low enough, some said.

Powel didn't hear any of it. He returned to Pinecroft and sequestered himself in the big house, where he would remain for much of that month. Life had knocked him down; he would, of course, get back up.

But not right away.

The world moved on without him.

Hitler marched into Czechoslovakia, and annexed the entire country. He would be there for the next seven years.

Red Barber joined Larry MacPhail in Brooklyn. He would broadcast Dodger games for the next fifteen years before moving across town to work for the Yankees.

At WLW, James Shouse, having cut advertising rates by 10 percent because of the drop in wattage, began sending out a booklet called *The WLW Plan of Merchandising* to advertisers. The move was one of many made to reassure potential sponsors that the station's decreased audience in no way meant that their message would not get across. It was deadly effective; not a single advertiser dropped away.

At the same time, they weren't giving up the fight for super-power. To demonstrate their continued focus on the rural market, Shouse brought over a man named George Biggar from WLS in Chicago. Biggar was one of the single biggest figures in 'hillbilly' (a.k.a. country) music. He'd been instrumental in popularizing a show called *The National Barn Dance*, spotlighting country and western stars. At WLW, he took charge of rural programming.

In Richmond, Indiana, at the mile-long factory building, the first Crosley coupes and sedans began coming off the line. There were a few problems. The first hundred cars lacked the "Crosley" emblem and had to have the name painted on. Worse, employees began to talk among their families and friends about the little auto. More than a few people, by this point, had seen the CRAD proto-type in Northside and around Sleepy Hollow Farm. Rumors contin-ued to circulate. At the Crosley Corporation's annual stockholders' meeting on March 28, one shareholder asked the question point-blank: Is the company building a car?

In his brother's stead, Lewis stepped—reluctantly—into the spotlight.

"It is possible," he said, "that an announcement concerning the development of an automobile will be made in the near future."

Making that actual announcement, of course, would be Powel, who was still at the big house, still getting his sea legs, as it were. Get-ting used to life without Gwendolyn. Young Lew had by this point come north from Florida. Powel spent a great deal of time with his adopted son, who began to call him 'Pops.' They drove the CRAD; they wandered the big house, and the grounds as they could, depend-ing on the weather. Powel was healing. Lew's presence helped.

On April 3 he emerged from Pinecroft to attend the first pub-lic demonstration of W8XCT (the X was for 'experimental,' CT for Crosley Television). The broadcast was simple—one of WLW's female singers performing on a small, brightly lit stage. Reporters pressed Powel for a date when WLW television might go on the air full-time; he denied any such intention. He had no plans for regu-larly scheduled television broadcasts at this time, he said, nor were there plans to build/market a Crosley television receiver.

He remained focused—as focused as he could be, all things considered—on the car.

On April 19, the *Cincinnati Times-Star* ran a story, credited to "an independent source," on the forthcoming Crosley automobile. It was to be "a one-seat, three-passenger car... powered with a two-cylinder air-cooled engine." The rear wheels would be only sixteen to eighteen inches apart, the paper revealed, which would give the auto an almost "triangular suspension."

The Associated Press picked up the piece and ran with it; so did the *New York Times*, which was unfortunate, as the original article was in large part based on publicity material prepared back when the CRAD was first built, outdated material that did not correspond to the car's final design. Some later attributed the leaked material to Powel himself, an attempt on his part to generate additional publicity for his auto.

Powel did release a statement to the press a few days later, promising further details on April 28, at the car's formal unveiling. That unveiling would not take place in Detroit. Nor would it be at the big auto expositions in New York or Chicago. The car would have its first showing, appropriately enough, at the track Carl Fisher and James Alison had built thirty years previous in Indianapolis, the city where Powel had worked so hard, if unsuccessfully, to make his mark in the budding auto industry. The world was to get its first peek at the Crosley Car on Friday, April 28, 1939, at the Indianapolis Motor Speedway, before an audience of select Crosley dealers and press representatives.

Powel had a temporary grandstand built to accommodate the crowd and a podium set up for speeches. Thursday evening, the night before the official unveiling, he had three little cars driven out onto the track and covered with white tarps. Guards remained on scene throughout the night.

Powel arrived at Indy the next morning. Young Lew came with him, not just for moral support but to help in the show. Dressed in miniature white mechanic's coveralls with "CROSLEY" on the back, a racing helmet, and a cape, the five-year-old pulled the tarps from the Crosley cars at noon, and—to a round of applause from onlookers—christened one by smashing a fifty-cc bottle of gasoline on its nose.

And there, at the brickyard where he'd watched from the cheap seats the day of that first Indy 500, Powel Crosley and his car took center stage at last. The little auto wasn't as radical a departure from the norm as the CRAD had been—the norm in 1939 autos being bigger, more powerful, more comfortable—but it was different enough to make everyone in attendance take notice.

First of all, of course, was the size. The Crosley Car was all of ten feet long; the wheels themselves were all of twelve inches in diameter. The gas tank held four gallons, the crankcase two quarts of oil. The entire car weighed a little over nine hundred pounds.

Though the three-wheel idea was long gone, the basic triangular shape was still there, particularly in the front hood, which sloped down to a very definitive nose. The front headlights—affixed close together, directly on either side of the nose, well above the tiny bumper—made eyes, giving the auto what would later be described as "a quizzical expression."

The car came in two models, a convertible sedan or convertible coupe, which could do double-duty as a quarter-ton delivery car. It came in pale blue, gray, or cream (which cost extra). The fabric top was black, the wheel covers red. The thin material on the seats was the only upholstery on the car; the door panels were pressed fiberboard. The windshield wiper was hand-operated, as was the three-speed transmission. The emergency brake consisted of a chain with a small ring for a handle, which came up through the floorboard between the front seats. Available options included an in-dash radio, a second stoplight, and an outside mirror. (There were no turn signals; the driver slid open the window to signal a turn.) The glove box could hold, perhaps, two pairs of gloves.

While the press looked on, Powel tucked himself behind the wheel of the nearest car and posed for photographers. Following the photo session, veteran Indianapolis 500 drivers Wilbur Shaw, Louis Meyer, and Kelly Petillo took the passengers for demonstration rides around the track.

And then Powel stepped to the microphone.

"I have been dreaming of this car for some twenty-eight years," he declared, 'blaming' radio, refrigerators, and broadcasting for getting in the way.

The coupe and sedan retailed for $325 and $350 respectively, exclusive of shipping and dealer prep. Powel had been unable to meet his $290 target, but the Crosley was still the lowest-priced car in the U.S., underselling the American Bantam by $62. It had the best gas mileage in the country as well, at close to fifty mpg.

"I have always wanted to build a practical car that would not only operate at a low cost but sell at a low cost," he said that day at Indy, "and I believe I have it here."

He'd built his dream car at last, a car for the masses, not for the classes.

It remained to be seen how many of them would buy it.

·   ·   ·   ·   ·   ·

Two days after Indy, Powel offered the Crosley Car up to the American people for inspection on a much bigger stage: the 1939 World's Fair. It was billed as "The Car of Tomorrow" for "The World of Tomorrow." The car wasn't the only thing Crosley was showing off at the exposition. They had the latest "Freezorcold" Shelvador on display, alongside the "Radio of Tomorrow," the Crosley Magnetune, a push-button car radio with an improved tuning system, as well as gas and electric ranges, gas and electric washers, irons, and a handful of other household appliances. They introduced the new Crosley Camera, the Press Jr., the latest addition to the company's line of products, on which they would end up risking, and losing, sixty-five thousand dollars.

The fair had been split up into several areas. The Crosley Building, appropriately enough, was at the intersection of the Street of Wheels and the Court of Communications. It was a prime location, a few hundred feet from the Trylon and Perisphere, the fair's architectural and symbolic center, in the path of foot traffic from the fair's most popular exhibit, GM's Futurama. The Crosley Building was actually three separate structures, built on three-quarters of an acre, a curving three-story rotunda anchored on either end by two five-story towers, and styled, like the rest of the fair, in a minimalist, modern design. Within the rotunda was the main exhibit hall, as well as a broadcast studio. Transmissions were made throughout the fair to WLW for rebroadcast.

At the rotunda's center, doors led to a pavilion behind the building, overlooking a landscaped garden, beyond which was a fenced-in area with a short, curving race-rack, where, on opening day, fair-goers were introduced to the new Crosley car by Powel himself. The Crosley Glamor-Gals took the curious for rides.

Motor Age, *MoToR*, *Automotive Merchandising*, and *Commercial Car Journal* ran major features about the car. The Cincinnati papers, naturally, lauded the Crosley; the *Indianapolis Star*, the *New York Times*, the *Washington Post*, and other dailies around the country ran publicity photos and material from Crosley press releases, along with quotes from Powel. *Colliers* included the Crosley in its comparison chart of American automobiles. *Newsweek* made particular mention of the fact that the auto was designed to be comfortable for tall people, like its creator. *Time* called the Crosley "a sleek, rakish, convertible sedan."

Industry sources noted it was the first car to offer four-wheel mechanical brakes. Conventional automobile brakes operated by pressing two "shoes" against the inside of each wheel's brake drum. The Crosley's brake system used an expanding ring that pressed "floating" brake lining against the entire inside of the drum.

The car would be offered through the same dealers that sold other Crosley appliances. Small enough to roll through the front door of most stores, it could be displayed right alongside the new Shelvadors and Magnetunes. The company also decided to offer it for sale through better department stores nationwide.

On June 19, Macy's put one on display in its Broadway window. Over the course of the week some ten thousand people trooped through the store to see it. Ropes had to be used to hold back the crowds. The store sold sixteen that first day alone—the buyer of the first being Mrs. Averill Harriman, wife of the famous financier. They immediately ordered one hundred more.

Across the river in New Jersey, the little car made an appearance in Bamberger's department store. In Ohio, it was at May's in Cleveland. The week of June 26, Powel arranged a special showing for the "home folks" in Cincinnati. He rented Music Hall and displayed four Crosleys—coupes and sedans in blue and gray. He took members of the press and anyone else who would go with him for rides around town, showing off the car's acceleration ("Watch it pass this truck!") and its maneuverability on the hills and crowded streets of Cincinnati.

That same week, the Court of Appeals came to its formal, considered, conclusions regarding the FCC's decision to end the superpower experiment.

They decided they didn't have jurisdiction.

Variety magazine, among others, found their reasoning peculiar and disappointing. They thought the case should have been decided on its merits.

So did Powel.

He decided to fight on. His lawyers began preparing an appeal to the Supreme Court.

A month later, the FCC gave the Crosley Corporation permission to increase power once more. Not with regard to WLW, but WLWO ('O' for 'overseas'), Crosley broadcasting's shortwave station, which was given permission to boost its signal strength to fifty thousand watts and begin commercial operation, meaning they could sell advertising time. Short waves, unlike the ones used in the regular AM broadcast band, could reach literally around the world. The Crosleys expected to use WLWO to break into, in particular, the Latin American Market.

Events would soon alter the station's focus.

Germany attacked Poland with sixty-two divisions—six armored, ten mechanized—along with thirteen hundred aircraft.

The Poles had a single brigade of obsolete tanks and four hundred planes. Europe was formally at war.

And the Reds, for the first time since 1919, were in the World Series.

. . . . . .

They got there behind pitchers Paul Derringer and Bucky Walters, a career year from first baseman Frank McCormick, timely hitting, baseball smarts, and the cheers of almost one million Cincinnati baseball fans.

In the Series they ran into Joe McCarthy's New York Yankees, who had a pretty good pitching staff of their own, anchored by Red Ruffing and Lefty Gomez, and a bunch of pretty good hitters to boot, no Murderer's Row, perhaps, but a dangerous line-up featuring Bill Dickey, Joe Gordon, and a centerfielder by the name of Dimaggio.

The Reds pitchers held their own. The Yankees, who hit .287 for the season, hit .206 in the Series.

Unfortunately, the Reds only hit .203.

Worse than that, whenever the Yankees needed a timely hit, they got it. Whenever the Reds needed to make something happen, they couldn't. Every move McKechnie tried backfired. Derringer pitched the first game, and they lost 2-1 on some bad fielding. Walters pitched the second game, and the team lost 4-0, managing only two hits. The next game, they managed ten hits to the Yankees five, but four of the Yankee hits were home runs, and so the Reds lost again, 7-3.

Sunday October 8 was their last chance. McKechnie sent Derringer to the mound once more. Paul had won twenty-five games during the regular season. McKechnie needed him to pull out one more.

It was not to be.

More bad fielding; more mental errors. More bad breaks. The Reds were ahead 4-2 going into the top of the ninth; McKechnie brought in Walters, who'd won twenty-seven games that season, to get the last three outs. He couldn't do it. Not entirely his fault; the

Reds made one error in the ninth, another in the tenth, and the Yankees came away with a 6-4 win and their fourth World Series victory in a row.

Postseason experience was the difference. The Yankees had it, the Reds didn't. When it counted, the team from the Bronx stood up to the pressure. Powel Crosley's team cracked.

Powel had another bad break a day later—three vertebrae, broken in a riding accident at Sleepy Hollow. He was bedridden for the rest of the month. He spent his recovery time specifying the design of a new yacht, the *Wego*. Designed especially for fishing, it included a fourteen-foot launch powered by a Crosley automobile engine and was rigged to enable a Crosley automobile to be hoisted and stored on deck.

He also watched the launch of the 1940 line of Crosley Cars, which debuted, along with the rest of the industry's new models, at the New York Auto Show on October 16. The new Crosleys included a "deluxe" sedan, a maple-bodied station wagon, a pickup truck, and a delivery truck—all adaptations of the existing Crosley chassis and body. From the doors forward, in fact, they were the exact same vehicle. The pickup truck had an open bed and a fabric top over the passenger seat. It was the first pickup with a fleetside body (i.e., no fender wells). The delivery truck, called the "Parkway Delivery," added a shell that covered only the area over the rear cargo area. The station wagon featured a top and rear sides built up with wood.

A week after the New York auto show, the new cars went on display at the World's Fair. Powel's sub-compact continued to make news. Race car driver Cannonball Baker drove one cross-country and back on only 130 gallons, bearing out the company's fifty miles per gallon promise. Crosley automobiles were driven through country club banquet halls, found perched on third-floor landings, and parked in unlikely places. A Cincinnati policeman, finding four Crosley coupes parked sideways in one space with an expired meter, didn't know whether to write one ticket or four.

Powel continued to make the news too. *The Saturday Evening Post* ran a feature article on the "Crosley Touch—and Go!" devoted to his family history, business philosophy, and Midas Touch, the latter of which he scoffed at, claiming that whoever accused him of that hadn't been keeping score. "If I've batted .300," he told the magazine's reporter, "I've been lucky."

All the publicity, however, translated into precious few car sales.

Part of the problem was organizational: people wanted dealers who were able to service the cars they sold. The company had to begin signing up regular car dealers to handle the Crosley. There were also difficulties on the production end; suppliers unable to deliver material as promised, bugs in the assembly line.

Part of the problem, though, went deeper.

"The market for cars that can be built to sell new below $600 is strictly limited," *Time* had warned back in May, and so far, it seemed, they were right. The American consumer had shown little interest in a sub-compact car. In 1939 the mile-long factory in Richmond produced exactly 2,017 of them.

Powel, however, wasn't discouraged. He'd made a fortune figuring out what the masses wanted, and he believed in his product. He'd experienced hard times before. The trick was not to give up. He was not about to change his modus operandi because of a difficult first few months.

·　·　·　·　·　·

In November, he went back to Sarasota, to the house where Gwendolyn had died. It was the first time he'd been there since the beginning of the year. He didn't go for the Tarpon tournament or to socialize with Bob Ringling or the Prews. He didn't go to relax, or to spend time answering phones in the captain's room.

He went there to sell it.

He paid off the staff, directed the removal of furniture and personal possessions, and put the house on the market.

He never went back again.

In December, the Supreme Court declined to take up the issue of superpower. WLW stayed at fifty thousand watts, though the experimental license allowed them to continue broadcasting at five hundred thousand after midnight.

Powel spent Christmas at Pinecroft with his children and their families; Lewis and Lucy had a party on Belmont Ave. for theirs. Without Powel, Sr.'s, birthday to celebrate, with Gwendolyn gone, the families began to drift apart, though the brothers, as always, remained close.

. . . . . .

In Europe, serious fighting had begun, with the western Allies crumbling before the onslaught of Hitler's army. Radio gave Americans listening across the Atlantic a window on the world at war. From the bomb shelters in London's underground, from the rubble of England's streets, network correspondents from CBS, NBC, and Mutual sent back stories of life under the Blitz, of Britain standing tall against the hordes of fascism.

Among those reporting was a young CBS correspondent named Edward R. Murrow. Among those listening was Merle Tuve, who was still in Washington trying to figure out the atom. Tuve, whose grandparents were Norwegian, whose colleagues included numerous refugees from the Nazi horror, burned to do something to alleviate England's suffering.

One day, after hearing broadcast reports of a particularly devastating Luftwaffe air raid, he had the first inklings of how he might be able to help. Despite the valiant efforts of the British, Luftwaffe planes still managed to break through England's defenses on a nightly basis. And when they reached the skies above London, they were free to do as they willed, because British anti-aircraft fire—all anti-aircraft fire of the era—was woefully inadequate.

It was a matter of point, shoot, and hope for the best.

Nobody dared dream of a direct hit on a plane. Anti-aircraft strategy consisted of determining flight trajectory and speed and then flooding a pre-determined zone of fire with shell fragments in hope that one would bring down the aircraft. Under optimum conditions, it worked, approximately, once every twenty-five hundred times.

What was needed, Tuve realized, was a bomb triggered to explode when it reached a certain, specified distance from its target. Listening to the radio one day, he began to see how such a device might be constructed.

Suppose, Tuve thought, that instead of a timing fuse on a shell, you had something a little more complex. A device that could sense when it was getting close to a potential target, and then, at a pre-determined distance, blow up, all on its own. A smart bomb, in other words.

The way to make it smart, Tuve realized, was to use radio waves.

You would put a radio transceiver—a transmitter and receiver in one—inside the shell. The transmitter would send out radio waves, which would bounce off a potential target, and the receiver would pick them up. At a specified level of intensity, the shell would explode.

You would need to build a new kind of radio tube to make it work, Tuve knew, one much smaller and sturdier than any in existence, one capable of withstanding the incredible g-forces the shell would be accelerated to. The entire 'smart' assembly, in fact, would need to be miniaturized to fit into the tip of a shell. That would require components manufactured to incredibly precise tolerances, components that would need to be made in huge quantities, under very strict security conditions, with all possible haste, because as important as execution of the idea was, what mattered more were real-world results. Experience in mass production of radios and associated electronic components would be critical but just as necessary would be an understanding of the principles of military engineering.

Dreaming up the fuze was, in a way, the easy half of the equation.

The hard part would be finding somebody who could build it.

PART III

⊷ B A T T L E ⊶

"Open the ordinary radio set on your table and try to imagine how you would fit it, equipped with a power plant and a transmitter as well as a receiver, into the nose of Navy 5-inch, 38-caliber shell in a space about the size of an ice-cream cone."

~ James Phinney Baxter, *Scientists Against Time*

CHAPTER 27

I n the 1939 World Series, the New York Yankees taught the Cincinnati Reds what winning baseball was all about. Focus, concentration, determination; every at-bat, every pitch, every minute of every game was potentially win or lose, do or die.

The Reds played the entire 1940 season that way. Fifty-eight of their one hundred fifty-three games were decided by a single run. They won forty-one of those games. Again, it was pitching that kept them in every contest. Paul Derringer won twenty games. Bucky Walters won twenty-two. A young right-hander named Junior Thompson won sixteen. An old right-hander named Jim Turner won fourteen. The team hit in the clutch, led again by Frank McCormick, who won the 1940 National League MVP award. Catcher Ernie Lombardi had a big year as well, hitting .319 with fourteen homers. They played outstanding defense, setting a major league fielding mark of .987. They played the whole year, in fact, like men on a mission, men determined to avenge their 1939 loss to the Yankees by returning to the fall classic.

Not all of them made it.

On August 3, back-up catcher Willard Hershberger killed himself. His suicide cast a pall over every game the rest of the way.

On September 15, with the pennant virtually clinched, Ernie Lombardi sprained his ankle so badly he was finished behind the plate for the year. The only other catchers the team had on the active roster were two rookies. McKechnie turned to bench coach Jimmy Wilson, forty years old, former player-manager of the Philadelphia Athletics. Wilson was, essentially, retired. He'd caught three games in

1938, four in 1939, with a grand total of five at-bats for both years.

Wilson caught sixteen games the rest of the season and managed to hit .243. The Reds beat Larry MacPhail's Dodgers by twelve games for the NL Pennant, making it back to the Series to face the Detroit Tigers, managed by Del Baker, led by sluggers Hank Greenberg and Rudy York, and pitchers Bobo Newsom and Schoolboy Rowe.

The Series went the full seven games, and during it, something extraordinary happened. Forty year-old Jimmy Wilson, who caught six of those games, hit .353. He registered the only stolen base of the Series by either club. In the last and deciding contest, held at Crosley Field, the Reds were down 1-0 going into the final three innings—a pitcher's duel between Newsom, going on one day's rest, and Derringer, going on two.

In the bottom of the seventh, Frank McCormick came up and smacked a double. Outfielder Jimmy Ripple, acquired in mid-season from the Dodgers, smacked another. McCormick scored. Tie game.

Up to the plate stepped Jimmy Wilson.

Newsom, who had won games one and five of the Series for the Tigers already, both complete games in which he'd given up a total of two runs, had no intention of letting this one get away. He bore down.

Wilson focused too—and laid down a perfect sacrifice bunt. Ripple went to third and scored on a sacrifice fly two batters later.

The Reds won the game 2-1 and won the World Series. The crowd, and the entire city, went absolutely crazy. There was no doubt about it this time—no talk of thrown games, no saying it wasn't so, Joe. The Cincinnati Reds were World Champions.

In the stadium, fans tore off cushion seats, and tossed them onto the field. Grumpy old commissioner Landis made his way to the winning locker room, wearing an ear-to-ear smile. He told Wilson "you did our generation proud, Jim."

The celebration lasted all night downtown. It lasted for days in other parts of the city. The streets were so crowded that, as one reporter wrote, " before a gal could cross the street her dress was in danger of going out of style." There were fights, there was drinking, a trolley car was overturned, a billboard defaced, a man drove around with a "McKechnie for President" sign proudly waving from his auto.

Six and a half years earlier, the team was a doormat, a perennial last-place finisher, in danger of being removed from town and sent god-knows-where by the game's powers that be. Now the Reds were champions of the world, the undisputed best team in baseball.

They did it on the baseball smarts of Warren Giles, Gabe Paul and of course, Bill McKechnie, on the guts of Jimmy Wilson and Ernie Lombardi, on the right arms of starters Derringer and Walters and closer Joe Beggs, on the bats of Frank McCormick and Ival Goodman, Billy Werber and Billy Myers, they did it for Willard Hershberger and the fans of Cincinnati, who came out again in big numbers all season long.

They were all able to do their jobs because of Powel Crosley's willingness to do his—spend money. Cash flowed those half-dozen years whenever Warren Giles or Larry MacPhail deemed it necessary. Powel left the baseball decisions to the baseball men. His only concern was fielding the best possible team. He had as much cause to rejoice as anyone else that October.

He just had a harder time doing it.

That year was difficult for Powel. It had nothing to do with the looming shadow of war or lingering grief over Gwendolyn's death. It did, however, have everything to do with tuberculosis, which even as the Reds were celebrating, was, unbelievably, impacting his nearest and dearest once more.

This time, his son had caught the disease.

. . . . .

Powel III had first noticed symptoms that summer; a cough that wouldn't go away, a tiredness he couldn't shake. He felt sure it wasn't anything serious. He was twenty-nine years old; how could he have a life-threatening disease? He was in the prime of his life, had been promoted to vice-president and director of the Crosley Corporation, and even if there were parts of the job that he sometimes felt ill-prepared or unsuited for, there were parts he enjoyed. He liked working on a motorboat engine he'd designed, one patterned after the Waukesha air-cooled power plant being used for the Crosley Car.

The tuberculosis stopped the work in its tracks.

He resigned his post at the Crosley Corporation and began a therapy of bed rest, like his mother before him. He moved from the house across the street from Pinecroft into the small cottage behind it, the building his father had built for his mother. But there was going to be no compression therapy for him. No radical treatment of any sort. Powel III was determined to simply rest and recuperate. He would use the time alone to gather his strength.

All that time alone, however, weighed on the young man's mind. Before long, he had become obsessed with the idea that he had contracted tuberculosis before his mother and had given it to her. He became convinced he was responsible for her death, and the knowledge weighed on him day and night.

Nothing anyone could say could persuade him otherwise.

By summer's end, he'd had enough of the little cottage. He decided to try a change of climate, hoping this would cause a complete cure. Having seen that Florida did little to help his mother, he opted for the dry desert air of Arizona. He and June wrapped up their affairs in Cincinnati and headed west with their children.

They didn't stay long. While Powel III liked the climate, June didn't. Their sons had problems acclimating to the high altitude as well. They kept getting sick, a combination of the hot days and cold nights. Before the end of the year, the family was back in Cincinnati. But they wouldn't remain long; they wouldn't, in fact, remain a family.

Page was having marital problems too.

Robert Jennings was proving to be far less interested in wife and child than in social activities. He had little regard for Lew. He would prefer, he let his wife know, to be in New York. Chicago and Cincinnati, where business primarily took him, "just weren't the same."

They fought.

Pinecroft seemed less and less like a home to Powel and more like a battleground. Meanwhile, he thought of Gwendolyn. With her gone, everything seemed to be coming apart.

. . . . . .

In the election year of 1940, for the first time in history, an American president was running for a third term. FDR's decision to break with long-established political tradition was one of the key issues in the campaign. The war in Europe was the other. Though America was still officially neutral, Britain was already receiving substantial shipments of arms and industrial supplies from its former colonies. And despite FDR's promises during the 1940 election not to involve America in Europe's affairs, many were convinced that sooner or later the U.S. would enter the war on England's side.

Powel and Lewis were among them.

The younger brother began taking one of the little Crosley cars on quick trips to Jeffersonville, Indiana, and Wright Field in Dayton to discuss military production needs, to bring Army and Navy buyers up to speed on the scope and capabilities of the Crosley Corporation.

His route to Wright Field took him by the Mason transmitter facilities. On one trip he noticed a handwritten sign posted nearby, announcing that the farm next door was for sale. WLW had already leased five acres of the property to build the suppressor antennas back in 1935 to eliminate the skywave. The entire spread was 137 acres, a complete, working farm, right there beside the big WLW transmitter.

Lewis, not an idea man per se, had an idea.

Buy the property (which would also guarantee the station room for future expansion, if necessary), and then rather than simply carrying market reports, have WLW staffers work on and report from an actual, honest-to-goodness farm.

On his return from Dayton he explained his idea to Powel, who gave it the green light. The deal for the property was closed within a few weeks.

Shortly thereafter, *Everybody's Farm Hour* was added to the schedule. George Biggar had charge of it, naturally. The program featured Earl and Mame Neal, who lived in the farmhouse. They made several broadcasts each week from a concrete block building known as "the Little White Studio."

Lewis stopped by several times to check on his pet project's progress. On one of those trips, he brought his old pet project, Dutch, with him. The dog, by this point getting on in years, showed he still had a little spunk left in him.

He ran down one of the farm's pigs and killed it.

Needless to say, Dutch never visited the farm again.

Powel, meanwhile, was wondering if the Army could find a use for the Crosley auto. He began sketching some ideas. His concept was a basic Crosley sedan without a top, doors, or sides, a lightweight auto that could move troops and equipment quickly and cheaply. The back seat was a bench on which passengers could ride facing the front or rear, with rails to hold on to. In this configuration, the car could haul four fully equipped soldiers who, not having to deal with doors or other obstructions, could get in or out quickly. Having shed so much metal, the Crosley Army car could carry quite a bit more weight than the standard civilian auto.

He was able to use his influence and contacts to interest the military. The Army requested a prototype, informally dubbed the Mosquito, which was delivered to the quartermaster depot at Camp Holabird, Maryland, in May 1940.

At the same time, the Army was also, not surprisingly, talking to Roy Evans and the American Bantam Company, who supplied them with a series of prototype reconnaissance vehicles, BRCs (Bantam Reconnaissance Cars), as well.

On June 27, 1940, the quartermaster's office released their desired specifications for a lightweight military vehicle to one hundred and thirty-five motorized vehicle manufacturers and invited them to submit plans in a little more than three weeks.

Only four of them bothered to show up at Holabird for the competition. Crosley and Bantam, of course, Ford, and Claude Cox's old company, Willys-Overland, one of the few remaining independent passenger car manufacturers in the country. Only Willys and Bantam actually put in bids to build the reconnaissance vehicle. Of the two bids, Bantam's was the lowest. They received a contract and produced a number of modified prototypes of their BRC for evaluation. Unsure about Bantam's production capabilities, in November the Army made those prototypes available to others to produce vehicles of their own. Willys and Ford produced similar vehicles. The Army eventually went with Willys's BRC-esque prototype, which was soon to become known by another name entirely: the Jeep.

They were still not ready to write off the Crosley Mosquito, or for that matter, the Crosley "Covered Wagon," a military version of the passenger wagon with the wood panels and top replaced by easily removable canvas. The Crosley assembly line produced a number of Mosquitoes and Wagons for shipment to Camp McCoy in Monroe County, Wisconsin.

At roughly the same time, the 1941 model Crosleys began coming off the lines in Richmond. Powel included a civilian version of the Covered Wagon in the new offerings, ads referring to it as a "sport utility vehicle," ideal for camping, hunting, or hauling small loads. The new cars were slightly different from the 1940 models. New engineer Paul Klotsch had added universal joints and shock absorbers, switched back to conventional brakes, and modified the little Waukesha two-cylinder engine to make it more reliable. Prices rose slightly—ranging from $299 to $450—but it was still the cheapest car on the market. Demand for the little cars outpaced supply, driven in part by rumors of impending gasoline rationing, but sales figures and production numbers remained miniscule.

A total of 2,289 cars rolled off the lines in 1941.

Spin it as best as he could for the press, or for the company, or even family members, Powel couldn't hide the fact that the car wasn't working.

Neither was the marriage between Powel Crosley III and June Huston.

Arguments between the two, which had never slackened, intensified on their return to Cincinnati. There were new elements added to the equation: Powell III's tuberculosis, for one, June's boyfriend, for another. By all accounts, she'd recently become very friendly with a man named Elmer Bramlage.

One day she just walked out, abandoning her husband, her three boys, and everything to do with the name Crosley. Powel III, with sole custody of the children, decided to leave Cincinnati again, this time for good. The city, the house, in some ways even his job, held too many memories for him. He wanted a fresh start.

He decided on Florida. The climate was one factor, though his health had improved tremendously in the last few months. Tuberculosis—as he knew all too well—was an unpredictable enemy. He also wanted to be near water. Both he and his father were intent on staying in the boating business, and Florida seemed a perfect base of operations.

Neither father nor son, however, wanted to be in Sarasota.

By the end of 1940, Powel III, his sons, and his boats settled in Coral Gables, just outside Miami. He was working on boats incorporating the new water-cooled Waukesha engine. His new company, the Crosley Marine Company, was also turning out custom marine structures and experimenting with pressed-wood and laminated fiberglass hulls. It seemed, at last, that Powel III had found, if not exactly happiness, his place in the world.

Lewis's oldest daughter had found hers as well.

Charlotte Jeanne had gotten engaged to a local boy named Bud Runck, who she'd known (and according to some, had her eye on) since high school. The Runcks lived toward the north end of Belmont Avenue, in a converted farmhouse. Bud's father was in the construction business. Bud was, more than anything else, into horses, having gone to Texas to work on the King Ranch for a while before returning to Cincinnati to work for his father for a time. By the end of 1940, he and Charlotte were making wedding plans: Grace Church, of course. Henshaws and Aikens, Crosleys and Runcks and Johnsons all received invitations.

Ellen, meanwhile, was still in high school. She spent summers swimming in the big pool over at Pinecroft, with Powel's permission. She also spent time at Crosley Field in the press box or at Lewis's seats along the third-base line. The family by this point had a full-time maid, a laundress, and a new cook—a German cook.

Lewis was suspicious of her.

His feelings no doubt were due, in part, to his experience during WWI. They also were connected to what happened the evening of October 20, 1940, at WLWO's Mason, Ohio, transmitter site.

Nazi saboteurs burned down the station's electrical coupling house.

. . . . . .

At least, that was Lewis's thinking.

The fire in question took place at 6:18. By 9:30 that night, Lewis was on the phone to the FBI. He told them he thought the coupling house had been firebombed.

Special Agent R.C. Suran reported immediately to his boss, J. Edgar Hoover. Hoover reported the incident just as quickly to the State Department official in charge of all Latin American affairs, Nelson Rockefeller. "I thought you would be interested in this matter," Hoover wrote, "particularly in view of the possibility that recent broadcasts transmitted from this station to South American countries may have motivated sabotage."

WLWO, Hoover noted, transmitted on the same frequencies that several German and Dutch stations were using, albeit at far greater power. Hence the reason for Nazi concern: Crosley was drowning out German propaganda efforts in Latin America. The station was expected to be off the air for twenty-four hours, Hoover reported. Total damage was in the neighborhood of six thousand dollars.

While Special Agent Suran and his team began their investigation, station personnel began their repairs.

. . . . . .

Powel spent Christmas with his children and their families at Pinecroft then headed south for business and pleasure—a little hunting and a little shopping. There was a game reserve for sale in South Carolina, a property called Pimlico Plantation, situated on the Cooper River just north of Charleston, twenty-five hundred acres stocked with quail, turkey, and other game birds. After a quick visit, he bought the property almost immediately. He spent quite a bit of time at Pimlico the first few months he owned it, overseeing repairs and furnishing it with antiques borrowed from Page. For him, as for his son, the new place was therapeutic; there were no memories associated with Pimlico.

Gwendolyn had died two years ago now. He was two years older, two years closer to that plot at Spring Grove himself. What would happen to his family when he was gone—not only Page, and Powel III, but his grandchildren, his sister, his brother, all their families?

He wanted them safe and happy and financially secure. He decided to set up a series of trust accounts, to be funded by Crosley Corporation stock. The trusts would be managed by the Fifth-Third Bank, with a percentage of the income from each to be paid out monthly to the beneficiaries. The principal could not be touched by its beneficiaries, but it would be dispersed to his/her descendants twenty-one years after the beneficiary's death.

Robert Jennings was not named in any papers.

He and Page had divorced. To keep her and young Lew near him, Powel had another house built on Pinecroft's grounds, less than two hundred yards from his own front door, Page's new home was a large, two-story brick structure that overlooked Pinecroft's lake.

Lewis, meanwhile, was overseeing some construction of his own.

The FBI had been unable to pinpoint the cause of the coupling house fire. Hoover wrote two follow-up letters to Special Agent Suran, prodding and asking for further information, but there was none. In February, having found no evidence to suggest sabotage, the case was closed. Later that month, however, floodlights, a high metal fence, and a seventy-five-foot guard tower were added to the WLWO transmitter site. Every bit of shrubbery that might obstruct the guard towers' view came down. A twenty-four-hour watch was instituted, handled by a twelve-man security patrol.

The war of words that Hitler and the German *Reichsender* service had started back in 1934 was intensifying. By 1941, German stations were broadcasting fifteen hours a day via shortwave to the Western Hemisphere. Their broadcasts were now in English, and they used American speakers on many programs to reach American listeners, urging them not to get involved in what was, after all, a strictly European conflict.

Lewis called the FBI again after an explosion March 10 at the Richmond plant. He told the FBI it might have been an industrial accident, but, in the spirit of better safe than sorry...

Special Agent Suran, once more, came to take a look. Again, an investigation was undertaken. Again, nothing of import was found.

By April, Lewis's mind was on other things. Bud and Charlotte's wedding, for one. The night before the big event, Powel threw his niece and her new husband a party at Pinecroft. It was a send-off of sorts. A few weeks later, the young couple moved to Washington D.C., where Bud had gotten a job working for the government.

In June, Adolf Hitler tired of trying to break Churchill, and turned on Stalin. Across the Atlantic, President Roosevelt issued a Proclamation of Unlimited National Emergency. "I call upon all loyal citizens," FDR declared, "to place the nation's needs first in mind," to have ready "for instant defensive use all of the physical powers, all of the moral strength and all of the material resources of this nation."

William Knudsen, Chairman of General Motors was appointed head of the government's Office of Production Management (OPM). Knudsen instituted new restrictions on civilian car manufacturers. Production for the entire 1942 model year was to be limited to 50 percent of each firm's 1941 numbers. That meant that Crosley would be allowed to manufacture eleven hundred and fifty cars for the year, if they could find enough materials to reach their quotas.

At the same time, the demand for Shelvadors and other appliances was holding steady. The Richmond plant was already turning out ovens for military use, and Lewis was continuing to search out more government contracts, more military contracts.

In October, one found him.

A call came from the Naval Bureau of Ordinance, telling the company to be on the alert. Within a short span of days, they would be contacted regarding a high-priority top-secret undertaking, which in the phone call was referred to simply as "Project A."

Merle Tuve, of course, knew it by another name entirely.

CHAPTER 28

W hen Adolf Hitler took control of Germany in the early 1930s, many of the country's more prominent Jews saw the writing on the wall and fled. Among those who left were two scientists who, back in 1926, had designed a new kind of refrigerator, one that contained no moving parts, operated soundlessly, and used butane as a refrigerant. They received a U.S. patent for their ideas in 1930.

They did not sell the rights to Powel Crosley.

Instead, the elder man assigned his share to the younger, who lived off the proceeds while working on other ideas. The elder scientist was Albert Einstein. The younger was Leo Szilard. Both were theoretical physicists as well as refrigerator designers, and both were, like Merle Tuve, interested in the inner workings of the atom.

It was Szilard, inspired by a decades-old science fiction novel by H.G. Wells, who first conceived of a chain reaction that could tear apart the atomic nucleus and release the awful energies hidden within. It was Einstein who, in 1939, at his old partner's request, wrote a letter to President Roosevelt regarding the terrible possibility that the chain reaction could be turned into a weapon, and that in the race to do so, the Germans were ahead of the Americans.

By mid-1940, Roosevelt had created the National Defense Resources Council to begin work on that weapon. Merle Tuve was initially assigned to the NDRC's uranium committee, but by August he'd re-focused his energies. At his urging, a new arm of the NDRC was formed—Section T (for Tuve). Their task: construct a working prototype of the radio-wave triggered bomb fuze that Tuve had envisioned after listening to reports of the Blitz, now nicknamed the proximity—or VT—fuze.

By the end of 1940, they were testing specific types of vacuum tubes for durability. By June of 1941, they were beginning construction of circuitry for the fuze. By September, a complete prototype had been built. In October, Lewis Crosley received the phone call regarding Project A.

On October 28, Dr. Lawrence Hafstad, who had helped Tuve uncover the proton-proton interaction and worked with him closely on splitting the atom, arrived at the Arlington Street factory of the Crosley Corporation. In the company of Lieutenant Victor Hicks of the U.S. Naval Reserve, he made his way to the sixth-floor offices of Lewis Clement, the vice-president in charge of research and development for Crosley.

The doors were locked.

The shades were drawn.

Lieutenant Hicks put his gun on Clement's desk.

Clement and two other executives present, Don Nason and W. P. Short, were asked to sign the Espionage Act. That task accomplished, Dr. Hafstad took out a prototype of the fuze Section T had been working on and explained what the government wanted from the Crosley Corporation.

.   .   .   .   .   .

In early December, Lewis and Lucy went to Washington to visit Charlotte Jeanne and Bud. All four went to a football game Sunday afternoon, as guests of an Army officer named Baird Wilson. In the middle of the contest, Wilson, as well as a number of other military personnel, were suddenly paged from the stadium.

Lewis looked at Lucy. Something was happening.

What it was, was war.

The day was Sunday December 7, 1941. An ocean away, the Japanese had attacked Pearl Harbor. WLW was on the air with a program called *Canal Days*, which was interrupted time and again by news bulletins. The news team eventually took over the microphone and, along with the few guests they could round up, tried to bring some order to the chaos.

Norman Corwin, whose suggestion to WLW management had resulted not in a merit badge but an attempted demotion, was on a train heading from New York to Hollywood. He had prospered since his abrupt dismissal from the Nation's Station, having become one of the most respected writer/directors in radio broadcasting. In November 1941, Corwin had been hired by the government to produce a program entitled *We Hold These Truths*, set for broadcast on December 15 and intended as a celebration of the 150th Anniversary of the Bill of Rights.

In the aftermath of Pearl Harbor, it became much, much more than that. The show served as a reminder of what America stood for and by extension, what the war was all about. An all-star cast—Orson Welles, Edward G. Robinson, Rudy Vallee, Lionel Barrymore, among others—was set to participate. Corwin's train was taking him to California to meet and work with his ensemble of players. In the aftermath of the Japanese attack, he assumed cancellation and called to confirm same.

Nonsense, he was told. FDR considered the program more important than ever now.

We Hold These Truths aired as planned on December 15.

It opened with a young corporal, played by actor Jimmy Stewart, giving the radio audience a virtual tour of Washington D.C.. It closed with an address by President Roosevelt. Close to sixty million people, half the country's population, listened to the broadcast. It was the largest audience for a radio drama ever.

Four days prior to the show, Nazi Germany had joined with Japan and Italy and declared war on the United States. With that declaration, the conflict became a true world war.

It was, increasingly, a war not just of armaments, but of words, a fight conducted by both broadcast and bomber. Hitler had a head start in those departments, but by early 1942 America and the Allies were catching up.

Six months before Pearl Harbor, an Army Colonel named William Donovan, alarmed at the extent and sophistication of Nazi propaganda in the United States, persuaded President Roosevelt to establish the Office of the Coordinator of Information. Donovan was soon leading the newly acronymed COI, assisted by a man named Robert Sherwood, one of FDR's speechwriters, as well as a Pulitzer Prize-winning playwright. Sherwood established the Foreign Information Service (FIS) within the COI. It was little more than a paper tiger until the events of December 7 prompted the creation of the U.S. government's first official radio station. Sherwood hired John Houseman—a New York colleague and theater producer, as well as a man with considerable experience in the world of radio production—to take charge of the new broadcast entity.

The station was to be called the Voice of America.

By late January of 1942, Houseman and his staff were creating three daily fifteen-minute segments in German, French, and Italian for broadcast overseas. Those programs went out over the airwaves through existing commercial shortwave facilities. They were also relayed to the European continent via the BBC over standard AM frequencies.

But the BBC edited some of those shows for content. And commercial American shortwave stations—those belonging to the networks, in particular—had their own agendas regarding airtime. Sherwood and Houseman decided the Voice of America needed its own dedicated broadcast facilities.

They turned to WLWO.

Powel responded by not only agreeing to lease the station's transmitter facilities, but by sending a number of station personnel back to New York to assist in the early VOA broadcasts. By March, America's voice was emanating from the shortwave transmitter at Mason, 75kw strong. By May, eleven other stations had joined WLWO in sending the FSI's message across the Atlantic. Houseman and Sherwood received considerable pressure to tailor that message to fit American military objectives. They decided, instead, on a far simpler policy:

The truth.

What the Voice of America broadcast was not music or entertainment but news: roughly seventy-five percent of VOA programming was devoted to providing the European continent and those countries writhing under the jackboot of Nazi occupation with the real story of the war.

The reason for that focus was simple. As one government official told former Cincinnati Reds publicist James Reston, in a piece the latter wrote for the *New York Times*: "Nobody inside Germany is going to smuggle his radio under the bed and take a chance on being shot to hear the "Blue Danube Waltz."

VOA broadcasts differed from those of the BBC and Nazi propaganda. Instead of one announcer reading news, Houseman used multiple voices during his shows to create a sense of excitement, of movement, of individuals united in purpose. His programs, Houseman later related, were modeled after *The March of Time* and the works of Norman Corwin.

By summer, those programs were on the air to Europe continuously, going out over as many different transmitters as possible to insure the greatest possible signal penetration.

The signal most often heard in Berlin—or at least, the one the Nazis complained about the most frequently—was WLWO's.

"No other station in the world is so bad as Cincinnati," declared one German radio official.

"The contemptible creature, the foul slanderer has descended to the very depths of obscene defamation," another complained.

By summer, WLWO had twenty full-time employees and was also able to draw, as needed, on WLW staffers.

There were changes happening over at the Nation's Station as well. A "war program director"—a woman named Kit Fox—had been appointed three days before the Japanese attack. The news staff had been beefed up; there were eight rewrite men, charged with taking the wire service clippings as they came in, and scripting news for the commentators. As much as 85 percent of the material that went out on WLW was prepared at the station. Three foreign correspondents—one in Europe, one in the Pacific, one in the Mediterranean—were soon added to the payroll.

New programs arose. The sitting around and talking WLW newsmen had done the day of Pearl Harbor evolved into a show called *War Front*. In the fall of 1942, the station made arrangements for an exchange of programming with the BBC, news from the real war front, tailored to the Midwestern audience, rebroadcast via shortwave. Listeners tuning in to *Everybody's Farm* heard the hardships of farm life in wartime England. A program called *Consumer's Foundation* reported on the role of British women in the war.

The station added new dramatic programs as well, such as *Your Son at War* and *Camp Wolters Calling*. The soaps incorporated the war's events too: Ma Perkins lost a son, sparking an avalanche of reader mail.

The biggest change at WLW, however, took place because of Merle Tuve's fuze—or rather, the security to attached it. Pilot production on the fuze started with fifteen engineers and six hundred square feet of production space. Security was easy enough to insure in such a limited area. But as preparations began for mass-production, the Navy developed concerns regarding the constant to-and-fro of visitors from the eighth floor studios.

The radio stations, company officials were told, had to move. After considering several locations, the company settled on Elks Lodge number five, in the heart of downtown Cincinnati. The huge six-story structure took up half a block and came complete with a bowling alley in a sub-basement. An architect was hired to remodel the space. Jim Rockwell was placed in charge of insuring the move took place with no disruption of radio service.

The building acquired a new name as well: Crosley Square.

Lewis, meanwhile, had continued meeting with officials at Wright Field in Dayton, building a network of contacts among military buyers and other manufacturers. By spring he was beginning to take on jobs that other companies had contracted for and found they couldn't handle.

One contract involved airplane bomb releases. "They were

paying about thirty dollars apiece for these," Lewis recalled thirty-five years later, "and I gave them a price of about eight dollars. They thought I'd lost my mind, until I delivered the initial run."

Soon enough, Crosley gained a reputation as an outfit that could get things done—quickly and for less. Little wonder; military production required experience in military engineering. The company also produced gun turrets, airplane-tracking radar, Mark XVI anti-aircraft gun sights, gun mounts, briefcase-sized direction finders, military radios, portable generators, coastal radar installations, and several other military products in its Cincinnati and Richmond plants and at the streetcar barn Powel owned in Sarasota, Florida.

With so much work coming in, the demands for tooling and dies multiplied astronomically. They bought the G&G Manufacturing Company, a tool and die maker. Having its own source for dies and templates gave Crosley a big edge over competitors.

Changing to war production was not without extra expenses. The company had been borrowing money carefully for the past couple of years, mainly to insure a supply of ready capital. Before the end of 1942, the debt would rise to $9,650,000—against assets of more than thirty-five million dollars.

Some of Powel's personal assets went to work for the government as well.

The Douglas Dolphin was pressed into service by the Army Air Corps in March. It eventually went to England on the lend/lease program, and ended up in Australia after the war. The Lockheed Electra was also pressed into service. It, too, went to England, served as an airliner in Europe for some time after the war, and made its way back to the United States a number of years later. The Grumman Goose was loaned to the Royal Canadian Air Force. It was the only airplane Powel would get back after the war.

Eddie Nirmaier was pressed into service as well; the Navy recalled him to active duty, and put him to work as a flight instructor.

Powel's yachts were all dry-docked, with the exception of the *Sea Owl* and the *Wego*, both of which went to the U.S. Coast Guard on loan. *The Sea Owl Too* was kept available for use in Miami, as were the various smaller boats at Nissaki, in Canada, but Powel wasn't able to get away to either place.

By then, he wasn't able to get away to Pimlico, either. The State of South Carolina announced a series of major public works projects, and Powel was forced to sell them the property. He made eighteen thousand dollars on the deal but would have preferred to keep the game preserve and the house.

Circumstances forced him, then, to spend a great deal of time in the Cincinnati area that spring and summer. He went to a number of Reds games and attended concerts and parties. He began to socialize. By and by, the inevitable happened.

At one party, he met a young divorcée named Marianne Richards Wallingford. She was thirty years old. A quarter century younger than him. His daughter's age.

He was, if not in love, infatuated.

It would be incorrect to say work took a back seat, but for the first time since Gwendolyn's death, he began trying to fit someone else into his life.

It was, he discovered, hard to do.

.   .   .   .   .   .

At the same time Merle Tuve and Section T were working on a fuze at the Department of Terrestrial Magnetism, British scientists were hard at work on a similar device.

With the U.S. entry into the war, Washington and London began cooperating on both military strategy and scientific research. With regard to the fuze, the priority was anti-aircraft fire: task number one was developing a fuze to fit shells fired from U.S. Navy 5"/38 guns. British Navy needs came second, U.S. Army third, British Army fourth.

In the winter of 1941-1942 Crosley was the only company working on production of the fuze. Lewis Clement had operational charge of the project. He sent an engineer named Burgess Dempster to Washington to liaise with Section T. At the plant, J.D. Reid was engineer in charge. On the organizational chart beneath him, in charge of amplifier design, was Charles Kilgour—a long way removed from the canal and OMI, but still working with his old friends Powel and Lewis.

The company's first job was to copy as exactly as they could the Section T prototype. Crosley was also free to make whatever suggestions they thought might improve the fuze's capabilities.

Kilgour spent some time studying the fuze, and then suggested a small modification, a change in how the antenna series capacitor was mounted.

By January 1942, the first Crosley pilot fuzes had been assembled. Four groups of ten were built. Group one was the duplicate of the section T prototype. Groups two through four incorporated Charles Kilgour's suggested mounting change.

The fuzes were shipped under tightest security to a firing range at Stump Neck, Maryland, where they were tested. Crosley pilot group one achieved the same score as the section T prototype, a success rate of 10 percent.

Group two, with Kilgour's change, achieved 40 percent.

Groups three and four—which incorporated not just Kilgour's modification but a change in fuze material—malfunctioned entirely. Zero percent score.

Merle Tuve was not happy.

One change at a time, please, he wrote back to Crosley.

It was slow, painstaking work. Lawrence Hafstad soon learned the difference between laboratory engineering and mass-production. "I thought," he wrote later, "that all we had to do was put the dimensions on the drawings for these metal parts, and they'd come out that way. Hell, no!"

Tolerances—deviations—had to be engineered into the fuze specifications, a hundredth of an inch here, a hundredth of an inch there. Mechanical error had to be accounted for, as did the weather. The summer of 1942 was a sticky one in Cincinnati; humidity in the factory was found to have a detrimental effect on fuze performance. Air-conditioning was installed throughout the fuze assembly rooms.

Crosley's job, though, wasn't just to engineer the fuze, which was now officially known as the Mark 32. It was to assemble it from components manufactured elsewhere. During the run-up from pilot phase to actual mass-production, they began having difficulties with a certain coil in the oscillator. A company in Chicago was the manufacturer. Clement sent a man to track down the problem. This time cold air was the culprit—drafts from windows left open in the factory. The windows were closed.

In September 1942, production began and immediately ran into further snags. A committee of Crosley engineers and Section T personnel got together and decided on a methodical approach to ironing out the difficulties. Fifty fuzes went on a train to Maryland on Monday night and were fired on Tuesday. Results were telephoned to Crosley that afternoon. Changes were made on the line, and another batch of fifty went out on Wednesday. They were fired on Thursday. Results were given to Crosley that afternoon, changes were made on the line, and...

Two weeks of that schedule, and the fuzes were ready to go into action.

The assembly lines began to roll in earnest in November.

At the same time, full-scale security precautions were put in place. Not just radio personnel but everyone in the company had to submit to them, Powel included.

He was surprised, one afternoon, to find himself barred from entering the plant where the fuzes were being assembled. He identified himself repeatedly to the security officer in charge, who refused to let him through. Like many of the other Crosley plant workers, the guards had rarely seen Powel around the offices, after all. Lewis was the Crosley everyone recognized, the one who arranged the military contracts, who knew all the procurement personnel, who socialized with the officers at Young's Dairy Barn on the way there and back.

The security didn't stop after assembly. Finished fuzes were packed in milk cartons. The cartons were loaded onto milk delivery trucks and taken to Lunken Airport for delivery to various port facilities. Security was just as tight on the other end: not a single person was allowed to leave a transport until each MK 32 was accounted for.

In December, Commander William "Deak" Parsons, one of the Naval officers assigned to the fuze project, reported to Admiral William Halsey, Commander South Pacific Forces. Parsons had with him a supply of MK32s and the required shells. He asked Halsey to send him into action—to send the fuzes where they could be tested in combat. Halsey sent Parsons to the light cruiser *Helena*.

On January 5, 1943, the *Helena* joined with an Allied ship convoy some twenty miles shy of Guadacanal. The sky was clear; the sun was high. Suddenly four Japanese planes, hidden by the glare, swooped down from above. Ships and air combat patrol scrambled to retaliate.

Lieutenant 'Red' Cochrane was at the aft battery aboard *Helena*. He watched one of the Japanese bombers flying off after an attack run—flying in a straight line, taking no note of possible antiaircraft fire. A mistake, on the pilot's part. His last.

Cochrane launched three salvos of the fuzed shells. That was all it took.

The second destroyed the bomber, sending it into the sea in flames.

In that instant, wrote historian Ralph Baldwin, "the history of warfare changed."

The smart bomb—triggered by Merle Tuve's proximity fuze, mass-produced by the Crosley Corporation of Cincinnati—was a go.

.   .   .   .   .

So were Powel and Marianne Wallingford. On January 9, 1943, at Sleepy Hollow Farm, they were married. The honeymoon didn't last long.

When they returned to Cincinnati, the new Mrs. Crosley attempted to make changes in the décor at Pinecroft. Powel told her in no uncertain terms that the house was to remain as it was. A scene ensued.

It was, sadly, an omen of things to come.

CHAPTER 29

L
ewis was having troubles at home too. Some of them concerned the cook. It was nothing he could put his finger on, but he simply didn't trust her. He never brought work home, but he was very conscious of what he said on the phone when he talked business after hours. He found out she was receiving a pension from Germany and decided she was spying on him. The suspicion and ill will were mutual. One day she announced quite simply, that she was leaving. She accused Lewis and Lucy (and Ellen, for that matter), of treating her poorly. You are not nice people, she said, and disappeared.

Shortly thereafter, there was another departure from Belmont Avenue.

Dutch.

The pig incident at Everybody's Farm aside, the German Shepherd had been showing his age for some time. He was closing in on ten years old, a senior citizen, in dog years. He had a chronic cough and a sore that wouldn't heal. He wasn't running around the neighborhood as much as going down to the basement, where it was cool. He wasn't even trying to get up on the furniture anymore.

One Friday afternoon, Ellen came home from school and found him leaning against the wall, asleep. She told Lewis.

Her father didn't say a word.

That Sunday, Ellen and Lucy went off to Grace Episcopal for services. Lewis stayed home.

When the two women came back, Dutch was gone.

.   .   .   .   .

A mile and a half northwest of the house on Belmont, at Pinecroft, there were troubles as well: more arguments between Powel and Marianne. She wanted the two of them to be more involved in the Cincinnati social scene. Powel had responsibilities that not only occupied his time but took him away frequently on business.

Gwendolyn had grown up with Powel's comings and goings, and she'd been accepting of them in a way he'd taken for granted. Marianne, understandably, wasn't. It was becoming obvious—to Lewis, at least, if not his brother—that the two were a poor match.

Page made a better one a few months later.

She married an Army officer named Stanley Kess, who she'd met the previous year at a Reds game. The wedding took place at Pinecroft. The third time for her would turn out to be the charm.

By that point, there was another woman in Powel's life as well. Her name was Ruth Lyons.

Lyons was a force on the local radio scene, the host of WKRC's *Woman's Hour*, one of the pioneer talk shows geared to female listeners, and *A Woman's View of the News*. In July of 1942 Shouse and Dunville offered her ten dollars more a week to work for Crosley Broadcasting.

It would turn out to be the best investment they ever made. Fourteen sponsors followed Lyons to WSAI. She was given a new program patterned after *Woman's Hour* called *Petticoat Partyline*. Station policy required her to write and read from a script for each show; that wasn't how Ruth was used to operating. She was one of the most entertaining on-air personalities in the history of the medium. She was smart, she was honest, and she could think on her feet.

After a week, she dropped the scripts and began ad-libbing again. She expected to get called on the carpet any minute. It didn't happen. Months passed. One day Dunville asked her to see him and bring along the script for that morning's show. "My knees quaking, I went to his office and confessed," Lyons wrote later. Dunville laughed; no contrition necessary. He loved what she was doing; she was given another show, one to air not on WSAI, but WLW. It was called *Morning Matinee*. Lyons soon took over *Consumer's Founda-*

tion as well.

WSAI also hired a new "Voice of the Cincinnati Reds" for the 1942 season: Waite Hoyt, a veteran Yankee pitcher whose gravelly voice would be identified with the team for the next twenty-three years. The team itself had a mediocre year, slipping from third to fourth place in the standings. Crosley Field was designated a defense area; air wardens were notified to stand by in case of attack.

By this point, Doris Day was back in Cincinnati, after a couple years on the road with Bob Crosby and Les Brown and a bad marriage that left her a single mother at age eighteen. Day was hosting a fifteen-minute show called *The Lion's Roar*, which promoted upcoming MGM film releases. By and by, she became the featured vocalist on *Moon River*. She also became friendly with one of the newest singing groups at the station, four brothers out of Wall Lake, Iowa, who harmonized like nothing heard over the WLW airwaves since the Ink Spots. Monday nights at the brothers' house, the sound got even sweeter. While the boys' mother made hot chocolate and baked cookies, the singers rehearsed, with Doris adding her voice into the mix. The band urged her to join them, but she hesitated.

Time passed, and the group left Cincinnati for New York. Day, prompted by their departure, soon left again. By and by, the elder three boys—Bob, Dick, and Don—left their youngest sibling to fend for himself on the streets of the Big City. He did all right.

The group had been the Williams Brothers. The youngest boy, who became a big star in his own right, was Andy Williams.

Station personnel—Shouse, Dunville, Powel, Lewis—had little time to focus on entertainment during the war, however. Shouse had been appointed to the U.S. Board of War Communications, subcommittee six, in charge of international broadcasting. In mid-1942, he was summoned to a meeting in Washington, where government officials queried industry experts regarding the feasibility of building a series of fifty-thousand-watt shortwave transmitters to extend the reach of the VOA and similar programming.

Shouse thought they were thinking small. Germany, he pointed out, already had hundred-thousand-watt shortwave transmitters in operation. He wanted to build one twice that power. The other radio men on the committee protested. Superpower for commercial broadcasting—medium-wave signals, like WLW at 700 on the dial—was one thing. But shortwave power on that scale was beyond the realm of known technological capability. Shouse wasn't so sure.

He called Jim Rockwell back in Cincinnati and asked him if it was possible.

Rockwell, presented with a wartime request from the boss for the unprecedented, perhaps even for the impossible, did what most Americans would have done in that situation.

He said yes. Shortly after that, the government contracted with Crosley to build two of the high-power transmitters.

Even at seventy-five thousand watts, WLWO was still going strong at that point, so strong that Hitler himself was reported to have railed against the station, calling them "Cincinnati liars" to anyone within earshot.

On November 7, 1942, Voice of America announced to the world that the war was about to enter a new phase, one of liberation. It called upon freedom-loving citizens across the globe to assist in the struggle.

In this regard, it was not entirely successful.

The terms of armistice Hitler had imposed on France split the country in two: half was occupied by German forces, half was ruled by a government based in Vichy, a government allied to the Nazi powers. Vichy France also had control of French colonial possessions, and French Army positions, in North Africa.

Those VOA broadcasts on November 7 were specifically directed at Vichy French troops, because on November 8, American forces landed on the beaches in French Morocco and Algeria. They came waving flags in hope the French would surrender. The citizens of Casablanca and Tunis welcomed the Allies with open arms.

The French Army, unfortunately, opened fire.

The battle, thankfully, was brief. Within days, Vichy forces in North Africa had swung over to the Allied cause.

. . . . . .

At the beginning of the war, the FBI had made mass arrests of suspected Nazi saboteurs. In the summer of 1942, eight German agents ferried from Europe via submarine and arrived on U.S. soil. They carried close to two hundred thousand dollars in cash and instructions from Lieutenant Walter Kappe of German Intelligence—the *Abwehr*—regarding various acts of industrial sabotage they were to perform. All eight were captured almost immediately; six were eventually executed. The speed and ease of their capture dissuaded the Germans from attempting any further missions, but Hoover and the FBI remained vigilant.

By that same January of 1943, the Bureau had eighteen informants within the Crosley factories, in place to watch out for, and report on, any incidences of suspected sabotage. In July of that year, a thirty-page report was filed on an incident involving sugar dumped into the gas line of one supply truck. No firm conclusions were reached.

In August, a twenty-page report was submitted regarding a spare electrical cable found within a packing crate. The cause was employee error, which was again found at fault in November of that year, when a worker accidentally opened a box containing spare parts for a Sperry Mark XIV gun sight while looking for something else.

Hoover's suspicions focused not just on German agents but Communist subversives as well. There was a genuine, long-standing alliance between some of the left-leaning labor unions and the Communist party in the early 1940s. Industry and government leaders were increasingly hostile toward such associations. Even as FDR and Stalin were meeting to discuss military strategy during the campaigns of 1943-44, anti-Communist suspicions were on the rise nationwide—in Washington, in Hollywood, even in Cincinnati.

Lewis Crosley started keeping an eye on the more vocal union members. He also combed the trash after union meetings on company premises. He found anti-American Communist newsletters and leaflets, confirming his suspicions about the motivations of certain union leaders. In May 1943, the FBI arrested a Crosley plant inspector on suspicion of sabotage.

There were, of course, many non-nefarious union actions, such as when women at the Crosley plant walked out to protest their lunch period being cut to twelve minutes. Two days later, they were given thirty-minute lunch periods. And a threatened strike by WLW engineers in the spring of 1943 was averted by a long-term agreement that made WLW the highest-paying independent radio station in the nation.

Given the stakes, a degree of vigilance was necessary. The danger came when that vigilance descended into prejudice, against things, and people, of particular racial descent, of particular political beliefs.

In that regard, there was more to come.

.   .   .   .   .   .

The corporation that began life as the American Automobile Accessories Company a quarter-century earlier was, by the middle of 1943, Cincinnati's largest employer.

Over ten thousand men and women worked the lines at Crosley plants. The Cincinnati and Richmond factories ran twenty-four hours a day, seven days a week, turning out untold thousands of items that were shipped to troops on all fronts—gun sights, military radios, proximity fuzes, radar equipment, field cooking stoves, and more. One item they weren't turning out was becoming a hot ticket on the home front as well.

The Crosley car.

With gasoline supplies so limited, it was no longer a matter of saving money. Driving a fuel-efficient car like the Crosley let people go two hundred miles on a month's ration of fuel, instead of just sixty or seventy. Enterprising individuals were buying up entire dealer stocks on the East Coast, and then selling them in the Midwest and on the West Coast for three to four times list price. It was an opening in the market, a chink in the Big Three's armor. Powel sensed an opportunity to establish market position.

Had Crosley been building cars for civilians, it could have sold every one that came off the line. But the lines at Richmond were engaged in military work. There was no civilian auto manufacturing, save for a few trucks and autos being produced for military use stateside by Chrysler.

Powel must have been dying inside, just a little. Still, he wasn't about to let the automotive arm of the company go to waste. The Army had displayed interest in an ultra-lightweight motor vehicle for use in the jungles of the South Pacific and by airborne assault troops. To fit the needs of the latter, the vehicle had to fit into the hold of a C-47 transport plane and be light and durable enough to survive a drop by parachute. While the Mosquito and Covered Wagon were still being tested at Camp McCoy, Powel had engineers start work on his version of that lightweight car, the Crosley Pup.

Officially designated the CT-3, the Pup was a miniature version of the Jeep, based on the Crosley auto chassis and powered by the improved version of the Crosley Waukesha engine. Crosley engineers thus took a minimalist approach in designing the Pup. The body used as little sheet metal as possible. The fenders were made of heavy canvas. A high hood mounted on two upright steel panels enclosed the engine. The car could only carry two men. The passenger sat beside and slightly behind the driver on top of a storage compartment, with legs extended next to the driver's seat. The Pup rolled on fourteen-inch wheels. Fully fueled, it weighed about 1,125 pounds—less than half of a Jeep.

The first one was delivered to Fort Banning, Georgia, for tests in February of 1943. Thirty-six more were delivered before the end of the year. But the Army decided it was too small and stuck with the Jeep.

Powel tried again.

He came up with the Bull Pup, a lightweight scout car, and delivered a prototype. It fared no better. Next up was the Crosley Snow Tractor. Similar in design to modern walk-behind roto-tillers, it used the twelve-horsepower Waukesha engine as a power source and moved on two cleated tracks. Crosley delivered prototypes to Colombian Glacier in Alaska and Camp Hale in Colorado. He went to Hale for several days in conjunction with the tests.

One day, he went for a hike with some officers from the post to scout potential hunting grounds. The group came across a detachment of troops from the 10th Mountain Division. Powel spent most of the afternoon by a campfire, swapping stories with the rangers. When it came time to leave, he gave them a stack of cash and told them to have fun. They drank forty-three cases of beer in his honor.

Despite his largesse, the Army did not order any Snow Tractors.

A series of other small vehicles followed: the Crosley Tug, a dual-tracked vehicle designed to tow artillery on rough or muddy ground; a variation of the Tug called the Crosley Track Laying Mule, whose purpose was to lay out temporary road surfacing on loose or swampy ground; a version of the Tug with special cleats on the tracks for use in snow called, appropriately enough, the Snow Tug; the Self-Propelled Gun Mount, a low-slung version of the Tug with a seat, engine and a fifty-caliber gun.

Each made it as far as a prototype. None was ordered in quantity.

Powel stayed alert to the military's requirements, and in 1943 he got word of a new kind of lightweight gasoline engine that the Navy was testing. Reports of the engine's performance for its size and weight were remarkable. Powel thought immediately of the Crosley automobile. He sent Paul Klotsch to California to meet with the inventor, Lloyd Taylor.

Taylor's engine was as radical as promised. It was made not from cast iron or steel, but one hundred and twenty-five pieces of stamped metal, which were then brazed together with an aluminum crankcase. The four-cylinder engine weighed only sixty pounds.

It produced thirty-five horsepower, running at fifty-six hundred RPM with a nine-to-one compression ratio. It used very little gas.

Powel bought exclusive commercial rights to it immediately.

After exhaustive testing—which included running a sample engine for twelve hundred hours nonstop—the Navy was sold on

Taylor's design as well. They opened a contract for bids to produce thousands of them for power generators. Crosley won the bid. Powel hired Taylor, who moved to Cincinnati for the war's duration, to consult on engine development and production, and of course, with an eye firmly on the future, to help transition the Crosley car from the Waukesha two-cylinder engine to the new copper-brazed—a.k.a. COBRA—power plant.

Lewis wasn't so sure that transition was a good idea. He had a gut feeling about Taylor's engine, which in addition to being lightweight, powerful, and economical, was also water-cooled. The idea of running hot water through all that steel to cool it troubled him. He was worried about corrosion. Powel wasn't. The elder brother went ahead with the deal, the younger, as always, followed along.

Incidental to his war work, Powel was commissioned a Lieutenant Commander in the U.S. Navy. Partly it was a courtesy, partly it was necessity because of the sensitive material he came in contact with on a daily basis. Lewis was given his old Army rank of Lieutenant. Edwin Armstrong became a major once more. David Sarnoff, who had been commissioned a colonel in the Signal Corps in WWI, returned to that rank as well.

The two men set aside their battle over FM broadcasting for the duration of the war. Armstrong freely granted his patent rights to the military and Sarnoff placed the resources of NBC at the government's disposal.

Relations between his company and the FCC were not as cordial.

An FCC report declared that NBC's ownership of two radio networks, the Red and the Blue, was monopolistic in effect. The company, bit by bit, was forced to divest itself of one.

On October 12, 1943, NBC Blue was sold to a group headed by Edward J. Noble, who had made his fortune with the Life Savers Candy Company. A new radio network came into being—the American Broadcasting Company, ABC for short.

Construction, meanwhile, continued apace on the new WLW studios in downtown Cincinnati. Two enormous two-story ballrooms in the center of the building were transformed into studios. The sub-basement bowling alley was converted to a music library. Bit by bit, management, advertising and promotion staff, writers and musicians began planning and executing their respective moves to the new building. Lewis and Powel decided to stay at Arlington Street, a decision that would prove significant in years to come.

Construction on the new shortwave towers in Bethany neared completion as well. Rockwell had been wrong, though, about the feasibility of a two-hundred-watt transmitter. The Bethany array, when finished, would broadcast at seven hundred and fifty thousand watts.

WLWO would be the most powerful radio station in the world, transmitting with sufficient power "to knock a radio set off the shelf in Italy, Germany, or Japan," according to officials.

In the Pacific theater, the Army began a slow march on Japanese strongholds in the Pacific Islands. The proximity fuze played no small part in quickening that advance; without it, as Secretary of the Navy James Forrestal was to say later, "the westward push could not have been so swift and the cost in men and ships would have been immeasurably greater."

Crosley was by that point turning out those fuzes by the thousands daily. Four other companies were engaged in fuze assembly as well—Sylvania, RCA, Kodak, and McQuay-Norris. Close to three-quarters of the country's plastics-molding facilities were involved in making separate fuze components. It was an operation conducted in the highest possible secrecy. Even with so many workers involved, at all those companies, only the key executives knew anything about what was being produced. Security remained so tight people in one room didn't know what was happening in the next. Powel himself was not permitted in areas inside the factory where portions of the assembly took place.

The tight security extended into the theater of battle as well. Use of fuzed shells was restricted to anti-aircraft batteries aboard ships, in the ocean, so that the enemy could not recover unexploded shells. The fuzes were also protected by self-destruct mechanisms. The Allies were determined to prevent the Nazis or the Japanese from obtaining a working fuze and reverse-engineering their own such device. By the spring of 1944, it was obvious that the Axis powers had little time remaining to do so.

Powel stepped up his plans to resume automobile manufacturing after the war. Interviewed on returning from an April 21 conference of automotive executives in Washington, he told reporters that "the postwar Crosley car will be bigger and produce more power but will not be placed in competition with the 'big car' market."

Powel had already put a gifted designer named Carl Sundberg to work on designing that car. The heart of it was Taylor's COBRA engine. The four-cylinder, forty-four-cubic-inch (700cc) power plant cranked out twenty-six horsepower, compared with twelve horsepower from the old two-cylinder Waukesha unit. The cars would still be plain. There were no turn signals. Radios, heaters, and mirrors were options. But they would have a distinctive look, one borrowed from Powel's own experiences in the aviation industry—an all-aluminum body. The metal had proven an ideal material in situations where lightweight, strength, malleability, and corrosion resistance were required, all features Powel wanted for his car. He also felt that an aluminum body would give the car "an aircraft appearance."

He painted vivid pictures of a car that could do sixty miles an hour and get sixty miles per gallon of gas. There would be one model, "built for two persons, but usable by four," an auto "for the man the big manufacturers forgot when they designed their cars." The Crosley would be "a family car that is capable of getting him to work and his family to town... a car that won't cost a fortune to operate."

He had big plans; he had no car to show.

He had no factory either.

What he had was a dream—the same dream he'd had for going on fifty years now.

It would not be enough.

· · · · · ·

After the Allied landing on June 6, 1944, the crack in Fortress

Europe widened. Hitler began to crack himself. He ordered deployment of Germany's newest weapon on the man and the people who he considered the source of all his problems: Churchill, and the citizens of England.

That weapon was the V-1, a high-explosive unmanned projectile that soon became known as the buzz bomb. By mid-June, they began falling not on any targets of military value, but the streets of London. Anti-aircraft fire was of little use. Churchill was given proximity-fuzed shells to help in England's defense.

By August, fuzed shells, fired from ground-based anti-aircraft batteries, were destroying four out of every five V-1s launched toward the city.

Even the fuze, however, was no match for the next weapon out of the Nazi laboratories: the V-2. A guided missile forty-six-feet high, capped by a ton of high explosive, the V-2 rocket launched straight into the air and came back down at four times the speed of sound. When it hit, it destroyed not just buildings but entire blocks. The only way to stop it was to prevent it from being launched in the first place.

As summer turned to fall and Allied troops pushed deeper into the continent, the Germans could see the end coming. But in December, against the advice of his generals, Hitler ordered a massive assault on Allied positions in France. German forces in the Ardennes forest, the same forest from which the Nazis had launched their blitzkrieg in the spring of 1940, punched a hole and moved through, creating a bulge in the lines. This fight, the Battle of the Bulge, was the Germans' last chance to halt the Allied armies before they crossed onto Nazi soil. For the first time, the Allies authorized use of the proximity fuze in land-based combat, where it proved as devastatingly effective an anti-personnel weapon as an anti-aircraft device. By January 1945, the tide of battle had turned. The Allied lines were reestablished, and the advance on Germany resumed.

The fuze, in the words of General George S. Patton, "won the Battle of the Bulge."

That victory came at a high price for the Crosley family. Among those who died was Lucy Crosley's nephew—her sister Bonnie's son Allan. He left behind a wife and an infant son, who soon enough were installed in the spare bedroom at Lewis's house on Belmont Avenue.

The same month, Powel presented the prototype for yet another military vehicle: a tracked amphibious unit called the Crosley Duck. Able to travel on land or water at will, the bathtub-shaped Duck was large enough to carry seven people. A trailer, also on tracks, could be hooked up so the jaunty little craft could tow additional passengers or cargo.

On January 8, 1945, he invited reporters and photographers to Cincinnati's Public Landing to watch it go through its paces. Powel, Paul Klotsch, and an Army captain rode the craft up and down the shoreline and into the Ohio River as a small crowd watched. The steel-hulled craft was powered by a Crosley Cobra engine and featured a wooden ship's wheel at the pilot's post amidships.

The Army, once more, was unimpressed. The prototype joined the other Crosley military vehicles in storage. Powel was undaunted. He continued to plan strategy for the postwar Crosley car.

Lewis, meanwhile, had his hands full at the plant. The problem was racial, and in March 1945, the Crosley Corporation ended up right in the middle of it.

Powel at his desk, the shadow of his father (framed photo at rear of shot) always looming.

Vacationing together.

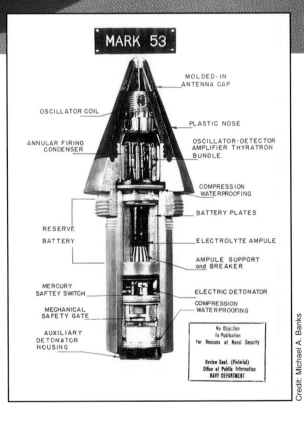

The top-secret proximity fuze that turned the tide of battle in the South Pacific.

MARK 53

MOLDED-IN ANTENNA CAP

OSCILLATOR COIL

PLASTIC NOSE

ANNULAR FIRING CONDENSER

OSCILLATOR-DETECTOR AMPLIFIER THYRATRON BUNDLE.

COMPRESSION WATERPROOFING

BATTERY PLATES

RESERVE BATTERY

ELECTROLYTE AMPULE

AMPULE SUPPORT and BREAKER

MERCURY SAFTEY SWITCH

ELECTRIC DETONATOR

MECHANICAL SAFETY GATE

COMPRESSION WATERPROOFING

AUXILIARY DETONATOR HOUSING

No Objection to Publication For Reasons of Naval Security

Review Sect. (Pictorial) Office of Public Information NAVY DEPARTMENT

Schematic of the proximity fuze

Credit: Michael A. Banks

Frank Lloyd Wright and his wife, Olgivanna, in a Crosley Hotshot. Wright owned a fleet of Crosley cars, which he repainted Taliesen red.

Promotional postcard for the Crosley car at the 1939 World's Fair.

One of the first 1939 Crosley coupes, photographed at Pinecroft's front door.

★ THE ★ CAR ★ OF ★ TOMORROW

AT THE WORLD OF TOMORROW

AS SHOWN AT THE CROSLEY BUILDING AT THE N. Y. WORLD'S FAIR ALSO THE AMAZING FREEZORCOLD Shelvador Refrigerator Feather Touch Electric MAGNETUNE RADIOS

SEE THE NEWEST OF THE NEW IN HOME APPLIANCES AT POPULAR PRICES

CROSLEY

Reado, facsimile radio printing—Crosley Camera, Press Jr. model—Gas and Electric Ranges — Electric and Gas Engine Washers — Electric Ironers — at Crosley Dealers everywhere.

Major Improvements in
CROSLEY for 1951

These make the Crosley the *most improved car* for 1951 — the greatest assembly of improvements ever put into a new Crosley model.

New strut type hydraulic shock absorbers

New, big 9 inch Bendix hydraulic brakes

New heavy duty front axle

New larger, easily adjustable clutch

Cast iron block

New mechanical link clutch release mechanism

New exhaust valve rotators for longer engine life

New full flow oil filter

New seats with improved cushions and pads

New full-fashioned floor mats

New interior upholstery and trim

Turn indicators

New improved hand brake control

Radically new front design combined with late restyling of body

Roll-down windows

New tailored upholstery on door panels

Fold-up rear seats

Folding top (Super Sports)

The Crosley wagon of 1951; despite all the hullaballoo, the end was near.

1951

SUPER STATION WAGON

All steel. Rear seat folds forward or is removable for extra luggage space. Roll-down windows. Seats 4, or 2 with ¼ ton load. New basket-weave design on wagon panels. Deluxe appointments.

His first passion, his last business: Powel with Wally Post (left) and Ray Jablonski, 1955

Powel in 1958 – striving, as always.

Lewis and Ed Kinney at Crosley Field, dedicating a plaque to Powel.

Lewis Crosley (far right) watches as Ival Goodman tosses the ceremonial first pitch to Johnny Bench marking the 40th anniversary of night baseball, May 1975.

Lewis down on the Kentucky Farm: following his own dreams, at last.

CHAPTER 30

I n the early nineteenth century, farmers from southeastern Indiana and points north of Cincinnati, such as Springboro, drove their hogs to market on the old Colerain road by the tens of thousands. By night the road was used for another purpose entirely.

It was part of the Underground Railroad. The Ohio River formed part of the border between the free and slave states, and Cincinnati was an important stop on what was also known as the Freedom Train or Gospel Train, the movement of enslaved human beings within the United States to emancipation. Among those lending a hand in Cincinnati were men like Levi Coffin and Dr. Lyman Beecher, whose daughter Harriet wrote a novel titled *Uncle Tom's Cabin* based on what she had seen of the Underground Railroad.

Springboro, Powel Crosley Senior's birthplace, was also a stop on the Underground Railroad. Two of his older brothers, William and Luken, fought for the Union. William was captured at the Battle of Fisher's Creek and spent the last part of the war in a Confederate prison.

The end of the Civil War meant the end of slavery, but not prejudice. At the height of the broadcasting boom, in a show called *Amos'n'Andy*, two white men, Charles Correll and Freeman Gosden, made fun of the black man's supposed ignorance.

There were, undoubtedly, some who didn't get the joke.

The Crosley Corporation and its immediate ancestors—Crosley Radio, Crosley Manufacturing, the American Automobile Accessories Company—were as guilty of discrimination as the rest. In 1945, out of the company's thousands of employees, only seven were African-American.

One of those was a porter named Cliff Stanfield. He was one of the company's longest-standing employees. His connection to the Crosley family, in fact, went back almost as far as Charles Kilgour's. Cliff was the family's live-in help. Powel, Sr., had hired him shortly after the move to Belmont Avenue, though what Cliff received in exchange for performing chores around the house was not a wage but room and board. He was an orphan. For him, and for the Crosleys, the exchange was more than fair. It was just the way things were back then.

But things were changing.

In 1943, FDR issued Executive Order 8802, which stated "there shall be no discrimination in the hiring of workers for defense industries or Government because of race, creed, color, or national origin." The order also established the Fair Employment Practice Committee (FEPC) in the Office of Production Management (OPM) to investigate complaints and address grievances having to do with violations of the order.

That year, the U.S. Employment Service, responsible for placing workers with defense contractors, began sending black applicants to Crosley for work. The company was Cincinnati's largest employer, taking on job after job for the government, hiring workers as fast as they could.

Not a single applicant the Employment Service sent ever received a job.

A complaint was filed with the FEPC, which began hearings early in 1945 to address numerous such incidences occurring among defense contractors. In the course of the hearings, it was revealed that Crosley's biggest union, the IBEW, was the reason no blacks were hired. The president of the local union testified that members of his union "...would not work with Negroes and had so voted." He further noted that the day before the hearings began he had received 3,755 "complaints" from union workers "voicing their opposition against working with Negroes."

The attorney representing Crosley thus declared that the company was not promoting discrimination. They were simply doing what was necessary to keep the lines rolling, because the IBEW's membership—most of them transplants from Kentucky and Tennessee—refused to work with blacks.

As if to prove the point, the union struck the plant the same day.

In the end the FEPC made plans for cooperative efforts with the Crosley Corporation and four other companies to change hiring practices. The union would eventually replace its leadership. Change would come, but the road ahead was a long one.

Edwin Armstrong was by that point facing a similarly difficult struggle. In early 1945, the FCC reassigned frequencies in the broadcast spectrum. Those originally allocated to Armstrong's FM receivers were given to television. For the inventor, it was a catastrophe of unparalleled magnitude. Every single FM set manufactured before the war was suddenly useless. It would cost an estimated seventy-five million dollars to convert existing equipment to the newly assigned frequencies.

It was even worse than that, actually; RCA soon began using Armstrong's invention in its television sets without paying a penny in royalties. Sarnoff had a policy of cash settlements, and he reportedly offered a million dollars.

Armstrong filed a lawsuit, but RCA had an army of patent lawyers and nearly inexhaustible cash reserves. They insisted on pretrial hearings and stretched those out for a full year. From the first day, their legal strategy was apparent: stall. They hoped that Armstrong would settle.

It would turn out that David Sarnoff didn't know his old friend that well after all.

Powel, meanwhile, had reached two important decisions of his own.

His marriage to Marianne Wallingford was done.

He also concluded, after much soul-searching, that he was finished with an endeavor of much longer standing: the Crosley Radio Corporation.

. . . . .

In March, three hundred thousand American troops laid siege to Okinawa, a rocky island just three hundred and fifty miles off Japan, the perfect jumping-off point for an Allied invasion. It was the Japanese Army's last stand, and they fought accordingly. Fighter planes filled the skies above Okinawa, kamikaze pilots desperate to sink American ships.

The MK32 proximity fuze stopped them dead in their tracks.

"The horizon," according to one official report, "was full of burning planes...there were too many to count."

The destroyers *Hadley* and *Evans* used the fuze to stand off 156 suicide bombers. By the end of June, the battle was done, and the way to Japan lay open.

The war in Europe was already over by then.

. . . . .

WLW employees were by this point settled in to their new downtown studios. WSAI employees were elsewhere entirely. They were reporting to a new owner, Marshall Field of Chicago. The station's change of ownership had nothing to do with Powel's decision to sell the Crosley Radio Corporation; it had everything to do with the FCC's new rules against ownership having more than one commercial broadcast outlet within a designated area.

Soon enough, the organization and Crosley would butt heads once more.

Powel's decision to sell the company he and I.J. Cooper had founded back in 1916 had multiple motivations. On the one hand, he was simply tired of it. As in bored. He'd been there at the founding of the radio broadcast industry. Those were exciting times, the trips to Washington to meet with President Harding and soon-to-be President Hoover, the founding of the RMA and the NAB, maneuvering to get first the Armstrong and then the Hazeltine circuit. But his days as the Henry Ford of Radio were behind him now. He was interested in the car and wanted to spend his time and energy making it the success he knew it could be.

Part of the motivation to sell came from his brother.

If Powel was bored, Lewis was just plain tired. He'd heard what various manufacturers were planning for after the war and felt that just maintaining market share was going to be a dogfight. He, like Powel, had been at the radio business for a quarter-century and the home appliance business for going on fifteen years. Neither of them were young men anymore. They were pushing sixty.

They wouldn't be around forever, and no immediate heir loomed on the horizon. Powel III was no longer involved. Stanley Kess had been a member of the family for less than a half-dozen years and Bud Runck even less than that. Keeping the company intact was another factor the brothers considered.

As was the Shelvador patent. It had a few more years left to run and was worth something now. If they waited, it would be valueless.

The time to sell, both brothers concurred, was now.

At the beginning of 1945, Powel very quietly let a few people know of his intentions. Almost instantly, they were fielding inquiries. The first came from north of the border, from a company called Moffats, Ltd. of Weston, Ontario, manufacturers of commercial cooking equipment. By February, they'd purchased Canadian rights to Crosley radios, the Shelvador, and other products in the Crosley line.

The next inquiry came from a man named Victor Emanuel, a fellow Trans World Airlines board director. Emanuel was also director of AVCO, a conglomerate that during the war had manufactured everything from airplanes and buses to furnaces and aircraft carriers.

AVCO's current domestic product divisions included companies that made ranges and entire kitchens. Buying Crosley would not only expand the company's appliance offerings, but give them a distributor network for these products.

The company initially had no interest in the Crosley Broadcasting Empire. Powel, however, was not interested in parceling out his company bit-by-bit. Gradually, AVCO came around.

Negotiations, headed by Lewis and R.C. Cosgrove, vice-president and general manager of the corporation, began in earnest. While he wanted to focus his energies on auto manufacturing, Powel was not ruling out new business activities, particularly with his son. He and Powel III had begun talking about a "family cruiser" boat, powered by the Crosley COBRA engine. The two had also discussed additional projects, as varied as hearing aids and advanced plastic products.

Powel Crosley III was looking forward to these projects, though at the time the AVCO negotiations began his focus was elsewhere. In March 1945 he'd met a nurse named Betty Taylor. After two months of dating, Powel III proposed, and shortly thereafter, they married.

As he was celebrating his son's marriage, Powel was ending his own. Actually the first move was Marianne's, who filed for divorce, alleging "gross neglect of duty." She asked for restoration of her maiden name. She received that and a lump sum of cash.

Exit stage left, Marianne Wallingford, nee Crosley.

.   .   .   .   .   .

With the war in Europe winding down, American car manufacturers began to resume civilian production. Steel manufacturers announced that by September, they anticipated having material in quantities large enough to supply domestic needs as well as any remaining war requirements.

Powel was encouraged.

The War Production Board then announced that it would continue to be in charge of allocations of steel, rubber, and other vital materials for the foreseeable future. The board was working out its own scheme of allocation, which called for manufacturers to produce cars at a rate determined by a formula based on prewar output. The quotas would be announced by summer.

Powel was disheartened.

He felt that companies like Crosley Motors, with lesser requirements than the likes of GM and Ford, should be allocated materials first. The WPB turned down his requests. COBRA engine or not, the postwar Crosley Car would start off with a handicap. By government decree, its initial splash would be a modest one.

In the meantime, rumors began circulating about the Crosley Corporation's impending sale. The Crosley plant on Arlington Street was hit almost immediately with a strike, the union leaders apparently believing that this could somehow manipulate the pending sale in their favor. The strike, called over vague issues, went on for several days, until the Navy moved in with armed guards to protect its property against vandalism by union members.

The nation's business community took notice. Both *Business Week* and *Time* ran profiles of Powel the last week of June and the first week of July, 1945, respectively. By then the rumors were confirmed. Powel explained his rationale to the media thusly: "My decision to sell was based on personal considerations, one of which is my desire to concentrate on the manufacture of the Crosley auto."

On June 21, he announced that he would offer stock in his automobile manufacturing company—which he would call Crosley Motors, Inc.—to Crosley Corporation stockholders at six dollars per share and would buy all unsold shares himself.

On June 22, he applied to the FCC to transfer his broadcast licenses—AM, FM, TV, shortwave, radio-fax—to AVCO.

Not so fast, the commission said. There were problems with the proposed terms of sale. For one thing, the airwaves were public property. The FCC granted Crosley a license to use that property. It did not grant Crosley the right to sell that license at a profit. For another, the right to that license was extended to qualified applicants only after a hearing process. AVCO had gone through no such hearing.

For a third, if the last dozen years or so of broadcasting had proven anything, it was that possession of a 'magic multiplier' like WLW's fifty-thousand-watt transmitter amounted to possession of enormous power and influence. AVCO was the definition of a commercial conglomerate. Their sole concern was profit. They had no investment in the public interest.

Hearings were scheduled before the full commission for

August 8. AVCO, anxious to close the sale, asked for an earlier date and the FCC agreed.

As the questioning began, it became obvious that a large portion of the purchase price was going to Crosley for the broadcast licenses. AVCO's ignorance of the broadcasting business in general, and of the Cincinnati market in particular, was revealed. All seven commissioners ultimately agreed on those basic facts but differed in how to apply them. Some trusted in AVCO's motivations; others did not. By a four-to-three vote, the sale was allowed to proceed.

Two days before the deal was set to close, Powel incorporated Crosley Motors, Inc., with himself as president and treasurer, and Lewis as vice-president and secretary.

On August 6, the atom bomb was dropped on Hiroshima. In less than two weeks the Japanese surrendered. The war was over.

On August 8, the AVCO sale was consummated, and the Crosley Corporation was no more.

PART IV

⇢≫ B U S T *≪⇠*

"He quit walking. He used to walk my tail off."

**~ Lewis Crosley,
on Powel's reaction to the failure of the Crosley car.**

CHAPTER 31

I n May of 1945, GM and Ford announced they were planning to enter the 'lightweight' auto field. Industry talk had it that customers were ready to economize, that in the postwar era, Americans would be prepared to sacrifice luxury to more utilitarian considerations. The Big Three, two of them at least, were ready to respond to that demand. They delegated engineering staff to draw up plans. GM requested (and was granted) approval to build their car in Cleveland.

Powel, of course, was several steps ahead of them. He had the COBRA engine, he had name recognition as a small car pioneer, he was the Henry Ford of Radio, the person best suited to build a car for the masses. He seemed, once more, to have peered around the corner and glimpsed the shape of the future. And the sale of his other interests gave him the cash he needed to implement his plans quickly.

AVCO paid a total of $15,600,000 for 400,000 of the 548,000 shares held by Crosley family members. Powel's share of this came to about twelve million dollars, which was given to him at a public ceremony in the form of several checks. (He was also given a large quantity of AVCO stock, which made the deal worth quite a bit more than announced.) The transition of ownership of the Crosley Corporation and Crosley Broadcasting took place with a remarkable lack of problems. Most of the existing staffs kept their jobs. Powel was named a director of AVCO and Lewis a vice-president at AVCO Broadcasting.

Powel put three million of the money he'd received to work right away, sinking it into the new concern. In addition to the capital, Crosley Motors owned the tooling for the prewar models and two buildings that weren't included in the sale to AVCO. These were the Crosley Motors Engineering Laboratories and the building at 2530 Spring Grove Avenue, right around the corner from the old Alfred Street plant, where a quarter-century earlier, in the days of Fred Smith and the Armstrong regenerative circuit, of Precision Equipment Company and the National Radio Chamber of Commerce, Powel and Lewis had taken the Crosley Radio Corporation from a local concern to a national powerhouse.

They were hoping, in a way, to repeat history.

There is a picture of Lewis, taken at about this time, sitting at his desk. He poses with a pen in hand, the trace of a smile on his face. His hair, what remains of it, is slicked-back, liberally tinged with grey. He looks, oddly enough, relaxed; he has the aura of someone at peace with himself.

Some family members feel he was ready to retire right then and there. He had the house on Belmont Avenue as well as the farm. He had more than enough money for his own purposes and to see that his family and his extended family remained comfortable, though he still hadn't gotten around to screening in that porch down on the farm for Lucy.

He had, in fact, everything he wanted.

But Powel wasn't finished, and Lewis stood by his brother. It was no longer about money for Powel or about being remembered as a success. It was about finishing what he'd started, what not just this war, but the war before it, and the depression of 1907 before that had interrupted. It was about building the car.

It was, in some ways, about his father. There is a picture of Powel, taken in 1936, sitting at his desk, at the apex of his career, the years of the five hundred kilowatt transmitter, the years of Larry MacPhail, and Seagate and Gwendolyn, of the Shelvador and the CRAD and the promising beginnings of the Crosley car. He sits at his desk, fifty years old, looking ten years younger, looking somewhat bothered, and somewhat impatient at having to sit still for the minute required to snap the picture. Behind him is a stained-glass window; on the ledge in front of it is a Crosley radio.

Next to the radio is one framed picture—his father.

The son never forgot the ten thousand dollars he lost trying to build the Marathon Six or the five hundred dollars he'd had to borrow to get his start. He wasn't going to rest until he proved he was worthy of it—and of his father's praise.

. . . . . .

Production lines had already been set up for the COBRA engine at the Spring Grove facility, and Powel and Lewis planned to set up the Crosley automobile assembly line there too. But it soon became obvious that the building did not have enough room, and Powel began searching in Cincinnati for a larger plant, ideally a single-story building with at least one hundred and fifty thousand square feet of production space.

He couldn't find one.

The huge Wright plant just south of the Crosley Airport, which had built aircraft engines during the war, was too big. A second local plant that appeared to meet his requirements went out for public bid, but Powel lost in the auction.

He wasn't the only one who wanted Crosley Motors to base its operations in Cincinnati. The city fathers wanted to avoid losing the plant and the jobs that went with it to a town like Kokomo or Richmond. The Chamber of Commerce came to Powel's aid, but they couldn't find anything either.

Powel and Lewis started searching elsewhere, at plants as far away as Indianapolis and Louisville. In September, tipped off by a banker friend, they found what they were looking for, a 170,655 square-foot factory in Marion, Indiana, one hundred and forty miles from Cincinnati, the former home of the Indiana Motor Truck Company.

The purchase price was three hundred and fifty thousand dollars. The company planned to put another $1,500,000 into renovations, machinery, and tooling. Powel estimated that the plant would employ twelve hundred workers when production reached its peak and told reporters that he expected cars to be coming off the line at the rate of one hundred and twenty-five per day by December and be in the hands of dealers in January.

Powel felt compelled to express publicly both his frustration and the reason for his decision. "All kinds of plants were supposed to be available after the war was over," he told Cincinnati newspapers after announcing the Marion plant purchase, "but, surprisingly, this was not true.... Cincinnati is my home and it has been good to me, but we simply could not find anything adaptable here."

The delay in finding a factory meant that Crosley Motors would produce no cars in 1945. Anxious to keep the publicity machine going, Powel decided to put together a prototype of his new auto to display for the press.

He ran into more problems.

He couldn't find aluminum anywhere.

The metal was now in demand by more than just aircraft manufacturers. The national housing shortage had inspired aluminum-skinned mobile homes. New applications were being found for it in conventional building and household goods as well.

Powel had to make do with a wooden mockup. A photo of it, with a pretty model posed alongside, was released in January 1946. The press release accompanying the photo detailed the car's performance, size, and advantages:

The post-war Crosley would be faster than the 1939 to 1942 models, capable of going sixty miles an hour.

It would be bigger, more than two feet longer than the pre-war car.

It would have a six-gallon gas tank, with the same fuel efficiency—fifty miles per gallon.

It would have an aluminum body, of course, giving it a high-tech, aircraft appearance.

Most of all, it would have the COBRA engine, weighing only fifty-nine pounds, producing twenty-six horsepower, giving the small Crosley performance equal to that of larger cars.

The COBRA was by that point beginning to get attention from numerous manufacturers interested in using it to power equipment, so much so that Powel had to hire an engineer to negotiate the incoming business for him. Before long, COBRAs were being used to power long-haul truck refrigeration units, material handling equipment, tractors, and a variety of other applications.

Machine Design magazine featured the engine on its cover. *Consumer Reports*, *American Machinist*, and other magazines and newspapers covered it in detail.

Publicity for the engine was publicity for the car—and, by extension, publicity for Powel as well. A December 23, 1945, Gallup Poll listed him as one of a number of non-politicians that Americans thought would make a good president.

He wasn't interested in politics.

He had a car to produce.

In January of 1946, he ran into still more problems. A machinists' strike at Plant No. 1 in Cincinnati lasted from January into early March, pushing back the start of production to May.

The aluminum shortage continued. Powel was forced to abandon plans for his 'aircraft-style' body, and go to all-steel construction. Some might have taken the difficulties for an omen of things to come but not Powel and not Lewis, who, though he maintained his reservations about the little sheet-metal engine, did his best to get the materials his brother's car required.

Steel, however, was in short supply as well. Lewis worked all of his contacts, military and civilian, to try to track down enough for their production needs. He ended up going to Pittsburgh, jumping into a plane, and scouting the train yards by air, searching for unused freight loads of the precious metal.

Finally, on May 9, 1946, the first Crosley auto rolled off the Marion, Indiana assembly line. Cincinnati mayor James Garfield Stewart trumpeted the little auto as the first of "thousands, perhaps millions" sure to roll out of the factory. Page christened it by breaking a bottle of champagne against the bumper. Alice Ruth Cox, wife of a prominent Marion businessman, hopped behind the wheel to drive the car to the Hotel Spencer in Marion where it would be displayed in the lobby. It wouldn't start. She tried again. Still nothing.

The third time proved the charm, and she was able, at last, to drive away.

The new Crosleys, called 1947 cars, were available in one model only: a two-door, four-passenger sedan. The little car retained some of its "quizzical look." It had the same high front end, the same rounded nose. The interior was still plain but far less Spartan, with what were described as "four, luxurious, deep seats, covered with smart pig skin, leather-like fabric."

Press releases emphasized the Crosley's modernity, roominess, and comfort, as well as its "aircraft flavor." They were "the nearest thing to flying on wheels," with "pilot-type" seats, and "smart, aircraft-style sliding windows." The exclusive Crosley "Duv-Gray coloring blends with the wild blue yonder," the releases continued, and at "one-third the weight and half the price" of any other car, the Crosley "virtually glides along!"

The popular press welcomed the car. *Scientific American* called it a much-needed and welcome addition to the marketplace. *Popular Mechanics*, *MoToR* and other publications featured it in roundups of 1947 automobile models. A half-dozen, largely favorable road tests were published.

Advertising resumed, mostly small ads in the backs of magazines like *Popular Science*, *The Saturday Evening Post*, *Field and Stream*, *Outdoor Life*, and *Mechanix Illustrated*. A special logo was created for the company. An interesting mix of old and new, it consisted of the name CROSLEY in rightward-slanting block letters, with a feathered, flint-tipped American Indian arrow through the letters.

The 1947 Crosley was officially introduced to the world on August 27, 1946, at Macy's in New York. Two cars were put on display and drew a crowd of nine thousand people. More than a thousand offered to pay cash for a Crosley, but Macy's was taking only ten orders per day. At that, no cars would be delivered before October 1.

This time around, however, department store sales were to be the exception, not the rule. Lewis had convinced Powel that selling cars through outlets that weren't set up to provide service was a bad idea. Crosley franchises were granted to established car dealers only, although some prewar retailers like Macy's were able to remain Crosley outlets. There were some six hundred of those dealers set up to sell cars that first year. Lewis's long-range goal was a network of three thousand nationwide, but the first six hundred did pretty well. They generated a backlog of thirty thousand orders. Under WPB allowance, the company was authorized to produce only eight thousand, and because production had been so slow getting started, they only managed to turn out 4,979 vehicles by year's end.

Still, the car seemed to be working.

War restrictions defined the new-car market. Buyers faced a year's wait for a new Chevrolet, the most popular car in America. Customers for Ford, Buick, Chrysler and other established makes had to wait almost as long. Crosley buyers, on the other hand, waited only a few weeks between the time they put their money down and took delivery.

And the used car market was tight. Many of those cars had been recycled for steel in the war effort. Families on a budget, families who had to consider gas rationing (still in effect in 1946), found the Crosley not just a smart choice but sometimes their only choice.

Powel and Lewis recognized these factors, but Powel continued to hope that he could carve a niche in the market by appealing to the buyers for whom money would always be a concern. The masses, not the classes.

He depicted the Crosley as the working man's solution to the big corporations' price-gouging: "There are reasonable limits to what many American families or individuals can afford to pay for efficient, serviceable cars, particularly in these times, when the high cost of living has reduced the public's car-buying ability to new lows."

Under Office of Price Administration (OPA) regulations the Crosley was priced at seven hundred and fifty dollars. That was too high for Powel; "I hope to eventually sell the Crosley automobile for five hundred dollars," he said.

Page's husband, Stanley, was put in charge of sales, having been brought into the company on his release from the Army earlier in the year.

As production ramped up, Powel diversified. Announcements of the new Crosley pickup truck and the Crosley convertible appeared in newspapers large and small across the country. Both were put on display at Macy's. He continued to refine his sales pitch. To those who weren't swayed by price and economy, Powel reached out with logic: "You don't use a battleship to cross a river; why drive a big car to work and around town?" The Crosley, he suggested, would make a fine second or third car. Businessmen would better serve themselves by buying a Crosley car or pickup than a full-size truck for delivering small items. The Crosley was ideal for fleet service, where its low operating cost could save companies significant amounts of money in a year's time.

The February 17, 1947, issue of *Life* magazine ran a feature on the car that also portrayed Powel, and his right-hand man, Lewis. Lucy was pleased. At last, the public could see her husband, no longer hidden behind the scenes. At last, he would get a bit of the credit he deserved. Lewis, on the other hand, didn't much care.

By spring, the Marion plant was turning out twenty-seven hundred vehicles each month. In June, the number rose to thirty-five hundred. The icing on the cake was the financial statement at the end of Crosley Motors' first fiscal year: the company had turned out a total of 16,637 cars and earned a net profit of $476,065 on a $12,073,721 gross.

Powel celebrated by buying another island.

This one was in South Carolina, near Hilton Head. Bull Island was seven miles long by four miles wide. It was big enough for quail, game, and whatever other hunting Powel wanted to pursue. It was big enough, in fact, to accommodate all of Powel's existing recreational interests and some new ones he had in mind.

His first activity after taking possession of the island was to have a modern boat dock and large house built. He brought in Delmar

Beach, the gamekeeper at Pimlico, to supervise the property, and prepared to operate it as a wildlife preserve, farm, and breeding station.

Powel had several streams dammed to create marsh-like habitats for ducks. After a barn was built, Powel brought in his own horses. He bred some of the island's "marsh tackies," tough little ponies that had occupied the island for decades, to a Tennessee walking horse. The offspring were what Powel called "fine hunting horses."

August Busch, who owned a herd of miniature donkeys, gave several to Powel. Powel also imported wild sheep from Sardinia and North Africa. He would eventually take up cattle breeding as well. Most of this activity, of course, was overseen by employees. Powel came to the island primarily to fish and hunt duck.

Eddie Nirmaier, now out of the Navy, flew Powel to the island, and elsewhere, in a new Grumman Albatross. Powel had also purchased a Beech Model 18, a twin-engine craft that seated eight and had a range of a thousand miles, suitable for most of his travel needs to land-based destinations like Marion.

While he was in a spending mood, Powel bought 1,439 additional shares of Cincinnati Reds stock (much of it from the estate of a shareholder who had passed away), which brought his ownership stake to 75 percent.

After the highs of consecutive World Series appearances, the team had entered a period of decline. Bill McKechnie had resigned as manager. Jimmy Wilson, who had gone on to become skipper of the Cubs in the wake of his 1940 heroics, had died suddenly, after his son's death in the war. Frank McCormick was traded to Philadelphia in 1946. Pitcher Ewell Blackwell was the team's only bona fide star. In 1947 he came within two outs of matching Johnny Vander Meer's feat of consecutive no-hitters.

Powel spent little time with the Reds, however, his mind being so thoroughly occupied by the car. The July 1947 issue of *Mechanix Illustrated* featured the first comprehensive review. Writer Tom McCahill gave the car fair marks but noted that the only way someone could ride in comfort in a Crosley doing fifty miles per hour was to sit in one loaded on a train going at that speed.

Powel took the critique in stride, and he and McCahill soon entered into a correspondence. By this time, the company had developed its own in-house publicity paper, *CM INK*—Crosley Motors, Incorporated—intended for distribution to dealers and employees. The fifth issue featured a profile of Lewis—Powel's "right hand" since boyhood days, as the paper put it. The story began with Lewis pulling up in front of Cincinnati's Music Hall with a trailer hitched to his car. Inside the trailer was a calf. The Music Hall's doorman—uniformed, stiff-shouldered—told Lewis he was in the wrong place. Lewis told him he wasn't, that he was just waiting for someone. The doorman arched an eyebrow, whereupon a well-dressed woman—Lucy, presumably—exited Music Hall and climbed into the car. Lewis drove off. The direct approach—making one trip with calf and passenger as opposed to two separate ones, the article noted—was Lewis's trademark. It was a quality that Powel greatly appreciated, a quality that led Lewis to mince no words with his older brother about the COBRA engine. He saw problems headed their way because of it.

He was right.

.   .   .   .   .   .

The 1948 Crosleys were introduced at the National Automobile Show the third week in November. Powel, as excited at this rollout as he had been when he presented the first postwar Crosley to America in 1945, took care to emphasize that he was not taking on Detroit. After saying, "I should like to make clear that our ambitions are comparatively unpretentious," he defined Crosley Motors as being "in competition with the used-car market."

The Crosley retained its high nose, but the styling was updated with slightly straighter lines. The slightly hump-backed look of the 1947 models was smoothed out in the new sedans.

And there were now six models. In addition to the sedan, convertible, and pickup truck, the Crosley lineup for 1948 included a panel delivery truck, a sports-utility vehicle, and an all-steel station wagon.

The latter was the company's first honest-to-goodness hit.

Before the year was out, one out of every three station wagons purchased in the U.S. was a Crosley. In response to the demand, Powel sprung for full-page ads in some of the glossy magazines, which also featured the Crosley panel delivery truck (a.k.a. the Parkway Delivery), an altered station wagon with rear seat omitted, the Crosley Sports-Utility vehicle (metal sides and top eliminated and replaced with canvas), the convertible, and of course, the sedan.

It was just as well that Crosley had widened its offerings, for competition loomed on the horizon.

Austin had recently established the Austin Motor Export Company and an American subsidiary. The French carmaker Renault, already assembling cars in Mexico, was likewise eyeing the huge American market and would soon open a sales office in New York. These represented a potential threat because they catered to the same market as the Crosley (unlike other European makes such as Jaguar and BMW). In the U.S. the King Midget made its first appearance, but—much smaller than the Crosley—it was considered little more than a toy. In Germany, Volkswagen was beginning to export cars to other European countries.

In Miami, Powel III was experimenting with designs for new boats to be powered by the COBRA engine. He patented a method of fabricating fiberglass hulls, and, picking up an interest in helicopters from his father, came up with a new kind of fiberglass helicopter rotor. This project was cut short by the catastrophic failure of at least one rotor while it was in use. It shattered just as Powel III and a pilot were about to take off in a chopper equipped with a Crosley rotor. A large fragment of the rotor pierced the cockpit and just missed Powel.

While fiberglass helicopter rotors left something to be desired, Crosley Marine enjoyed some success with both wood and fiberglass hulls. The boats' powerplants attracted as much attention as the craft themselves, and other manufacturers and racers were trying out the Crosley COBRA. The radical little engine would ultimately prove less seaworthy than the two Powels would have liked, however.

Still, it was a good year. The company had enjoyed $17,203,857 in sales in the nine months between August 1947 and April 1948, five million dollars higher than sales during the entire fiscal year of 1947. The after-tax profit was $807,096, or $1.42 per share. Total Crosley production through June 1948 was 42,794 cars.

The Marion property was expanded from forty-one to seventy acres, and additions to the factory were begun. Except for tires, glass, and a few other items that could be bought more economically than manufactured, Crosley Motors was now making all its own parts.

Powel planned to deliver a talk regarding the company's fiscal future before a meeting of the New York Society of Security Analysts on June 15.

The day before the scheduled speech, Powel III woke early in Florida and went into his backyard to work. He was stung by a bee.

He died.

CHAPTER 32

As early as 1947, the COBRAs had started coming back. The problem that Lewis Crosley had foreseen five years earlier had come to pass. Corrosion, the action of the hot water on the stamped sheet-metal engine, was setting in. Tiny holes—the kind you would get, Lewis recalled later, if you used a fine point drill on the metal—were appearing in the engine block. Customers began bringing in their cars, and Crosley dealers began calling the home office with complaints.

Powel and Lewis talked; the younger brother had an idea. They had built some cast-iron engines with a firm in Detroit. Lewis's thought was to replace the COBRA engine entirely with a cast-iron block.

Powel didn't want to have anything to do with that.

The company had sunk a lot of money into acquiring, developing, and marketing the engine. He wasn't about to set all that work aside. Besides, Powel had an idea of his own. We'll galvanize the engine, he told Lewis. Coat it with zinc, to protect the steel. That'll stop the corrosion entirely.

The younger brother wasn't so sure.

They called in a group of chemists. The consensus was the galvanizing procedure would definitely help, but it probably would not solve the problem alone.

Powel was willing to take the chance; he was, as has been noted, a gambler.

Lewis, as always, followed his brother's lead. On June 15, 1948, the day after Powel III's death, he did the same, traveling to

New York to give the speech his brother had written to the Society of Security Analysts. It was a roundup of the history of the Crosley automobile and Crosley Motors, filled with optimism, impressive financial details, and a rosy vision of the future.

Lewis's heart just wasn't in it.

His nephew, his brother's namesake, the boy whose desire for a little wireless set was partly responsible for all the success, was in a coffin on his way to College Hill. Killed by an insect sting.

For Lewis, who'd spent a great portion of his life with his hands in the soil, the whole thing would have been funny—if it wasn't too sad to be believed, if it wasn't reminiscent of what had happened in 1939 when Gwen's sudden death in Florida caused an unexpected summons to Spring Grove Cemetery.

This tragedy was in some ways, even worse than the first.

Gwendolyn had lived nearly half a century. She'd had more than her share of happiness, by her own admission. Powel III's life had seen more downs than ups. The fact that he was taken just as he was beginning to really find his way in the world seemed to Lewis too much to bear.

He could not even imagine what his brother was feeling. Losing Gwendolyn was hard, but for a father to have to bury his son...

Lewis gave the talk as best he could.

A few days later, he was back in College Hill, with his brother and Page, with his mother and Edythe, with Betty Taylor and Powel III's three sons, standing over that plot in Spring Grove Cemetery.

All too soon, they would be back.

.   .   .   .   .   .

Life had knocked Powel down once more. Once more, he got back up, dusted himself off, and pushed forward.

In July, Crosley Motors purchased a five-story building not far from Plant No. 1 for use as a parts depot. The new facilities would enable the company to push production up to thirty-five hundred units per month, and perhaps, to catch up on backlogged orders, which stood at eight thousand units.

In August, the company announced it would add forty-five thousand square feet to Plant No.1, to raise the production of the COBRA engine from five hundred to one thousand units per day.

The increase was necessitated by a growing demand for the COBRA. Powel was generating some of this demand himself, by designing specialized vehicles to use the engine. One was the "gasporter," a fuel tank on wheels, designed around a Crosley truck chassis and powered by the COBRA. It was marketed to airport and marina operators for use in tight spots where larger fuel trucks couldn't fit. It was used by fleet operators for mass fueling as well.

Some of the demand came from outside sources.

In 1948, aircraft engineer Al Mooney began working on a design for a single-seat airplane. He dubbed it "Mooney Mite," and he hoped it would become "everyman's airplane." After examining the dozens of gasoline engines then in production, Mooney decided on the Crosley COBRA. He and Powel had the engine tested and certified by the Civil Aeronautics Administration (CAA) for use in an aircraft. Mooney decided, ultimately, that the engine was too small, the plane underpowered at twenty-six horsepower, and switched to a more robust power plant.

That August, Crosley Motors hit a record production high: 3,857 cars were produced. The car and Powel continued to get good press. Noted newspaper columnist Earl Wilson visited Powel and described a ride in a Crosley. In the article, Powel reiterated how he disliked hearing his car called a midget auto. It was a small car, he insisted.

"People ask me if I'm not afraid of getting hit by trucks," the article continued. "I reply, 'Do you deliberately run over dogs or small children because they're smaller? You give them MORE room!'"

The rest of the column served as a forum for Crosley jokes—many of which, Wilson noted, were recycled Model T jokes. The comparison suited Powel just fine.

.   .   .   .   .   .

You don't just order a Crosley—you get fitted for one.
A Crosley is so convenient you don't park it—you wear
   it at the end of your watch chain.
If you have a Crosley and also have a chauffeur, where
   does the chauffeur sit? At home, probably.

At least one United States Post Office found Crosleys less a joke than a moneysaver. An Associated Press item that fall reported that Los Gatos, California, had become the first post office in the nation to use light trucks—Crosley panel delivery trucks—to deliver mail. The city's postmaster was quoted as saying that the Crosley trucks not only saved money on gasoline and oil but also sped up mail delivery.

This news briefly raised Powel's hopes that he might equip one of the largest fleets on the continent. He was able to convince the postmaster in Cincinnati to try Crosleys as mail delivery vehicles as well, though no orders were placed.

In October 1948, Powel wrote an article for *The American Magazine*, an autobiographical piece titled "50 Jobs in 50 Years." It was a salute to his drive, his determination, to Powel Crosley as the ultimate American entrepeneur, the living embodiment of the credo he quoted in the article: "he who serves best, profits most."

It also summed up his life's purpose, his life's motivation.

He talked about the car he and Lewis had built as boys, and his father's reaction to it. "He thought so little of the contraption," Powel wrote, " that he laughingly offered me $10 if it would run."

When it did, Powel continued, he "gloatingly" pocketed his share of the profits. He'd proved himself then, in some ways, though it's not difficult to speculate that his father's thinking "so little of the contraption" haunted him, especially after the many failures in college and his early career. In some ways, he was still out to prove himself now, nearly half a century later. He was, in his own words, realizing his "lifelong ambition to build a small car within the means of the average wage earner."

He was consciously echoing Henry Ford's sales pitch for the

Model T. He was hoping to repeat Ford's success with the car, and his own with the Harko, by appealing to the low-priced market.

The market, however, was about to move on.

.   .   .   .   .   .

In December 1948, in the wake of the company's record production of 27,707 vehicles, Powel unveiled the 1949 Crosleys. The look leaned in the direction Ford stylists had taken, featuring a chrome-laden grille and wide-spaced headlights mounted along the outer edges of smoothly curving fenders. For the first time, a hood ornament graced the car, and beneath it was the car's new emblem—a modified Crosley coat of arms.

Slight changes had been made, attempts to make the car look bigger. The front and rear fenders carried embossed lines just above the wheels to suggest wheel wells, which gave the illusion of a wider car. The sedans and convertible coupes—tagged the Crosley Deluxe—retained the previous year's sloping backs and had just a hint of a fin at the rear, adding to the perception of length. The Crosley station wagons and pickup trucks still had the same sharply angled rear, while the Sports-Utility Vehicle was gone from the line-up, replaced by a "Sports Sedan."

He began to gear up for a massive advertising campaign, hiring marketing and production men from Kaiser-Frazier and Studebaker, and he hoped to sell as many as eighty thousand cars in 1949.

It was not to be.

The 1949 Crosleys entered a consumer marketplace that had changed dramatically. Rationing was over. Gas was twenty cents a gallon. Economy was no longer an issue, not even for the masses.

People were thinking big once more. So was Detroit. There were dozens of new cars on the market—big, powerful cars, with big, powerful engines, stylish cars with long fins and push-button radios and more styling options, it sometimes seemed, than Crosley had employees. At the same time, prices for steel, rubber, and other materials were rising, making it difficult to hold the line on the

Crosley's price, which had been raised a hundred dollars in November. The higher price edged the Crosley too close to the thousand-dollar line for Powel, who felt there was a great psychological advantage in being able to market a car at under a thousand dollars while basic Fords and Chevrolets were selling at between fifteen hundred and eighteen hundred dollars.

The company had a bigger problem, though, than a changed marketplace, or rising supply prices.

It was the COBRA engine.

Lloyd Taylor's brainchild hadn't been run hard enough or long enough under real-world conditions during the war years. Out on the roads, electrolysis set in after two or three years. The result: the engine leaked coolant and overheated, often cracking the block. Crosley cars were going into the shop, and staying there. Powel's gamble had failed. Galvanizing the engines had only delayed the process, and not for long.

Something had to be done. A team of engineers, led by Paul Klotsch, began working feverishly on a new engine, a replacement for the old.

Orders began to drop.

Right after the New Year, there was more bad news. On January 14, at the age of eighty-five, Charlotte Utz Crosley passed away. Her death was no tragedy. It was the end of a long, fulfilling, life.

But given everything that had happened—given who else lay with his mother in that plot at Spring Grove Cemetery—it was hard for Powel to feel anything other than despair, a sense of events spiraling out of his control, of everything sliding, slowly, inexorably downhill.

The fall was not over yet.

.   .   .   .   .

The new Crosley engine was ready early in 1949. It was uncannily similar to the COBRA. Both engines had a forty-four-cubic-inch displacement, and both put out roughly twenty-six horsepower. This engine, however, had the cast-iron block Lewis had wanted all along. It was twelve pounds heavier. Engineers at Crosley referred to it as the CIBA (for Cast Iron Block Assembly).

Powel announced that Crosley Motors would replace the COBRA engine with a CIBA engine in Crosley cars under a certain age. (To those who weren't covered by the offer, Crosley Motors tendered a forty-dollar changeover kit to convert the COBRA to a cast-iron block.) The logistics would be handled by Crosley dealers.

It was a move the company could not afford. Sales as the new year began continued to plunge dramatically. But Powel felt responsible toward the tens of thousands of Americans who had given him their money and taken his car in return. He'd made, in effect, a deal with them, and he, like his father, was a man of his word.

The engines—corroded and rusted, useless even as scrap metal—began to come back to Cincinnati. The company's bottom line plunged even further.

Powel, however, was far from finished.

The CIBA was, to his way of thinking, an improvement. He decided to make even more improvements on the car. He added hydraulic brakes—disc brakes, the first ones put on an American vehicle.

They were announced in May of 1949 and were immediately the object of several articles in science and automotive publications. Powel naturally needed a special name for the brakes; he called on his advertising agency, the Ralph Jones Company of Cincinnati, to come up with one. The company brainstormed and gave their ideas to Powel. He chose the "hydro-disc," which was the brainchild of the only woman on staff, a young copywriter named Mary Ann Kelly. Powel, when informed who had come up with the idea, found it hard to believe. A woman—and not even a licensed driver?

Times were indeed changing.

He took Mary Ann for a ride in one of the little cars, so she could experience the Crosley first-hand. It was not the most pleasant experience of her young life.

"My bones," she wrote later of the joyride, "denounced the buckboard bounce," which was a copywriter's way of saying the car was not built for comfort.

Nor, really, was it built for speed.

It was built to Powel's idea of what the common man might want in an auto, except that by 1949, the common man was used to better. It was a disconnect—one he still, unfortunately, couldn't see.

"You don't think that he went to the office in one of the little cars," his sister Edythe asked an interviewer some forty years later. "He went in Lincolns and Cadillacs."

When he drove a small car, he often drove one of the new foreign imports, a sports car he'd recently purchased called the Jaguar XK-120. Most sports car owners treated them like thoroughbred horses, as well they might. They were exquisitely engineered vehicles with high prices made even higher by import costs. The owners tended to be well-off financially. Like Powel himself.

But driving around in the little vehicle, which held the road and handled like nobody's business, Powel wondered if there might be a market for a less-expensive version of the Jaguar, if the public might not be interested in a small car for recreation.

With this in mind, he and Paul Klotsch went to work.

They came up with America's first postwar sports car—the Crosley Hotshot.

The car (named, this time, by Powel) was introduced to the public on July 14, 1949. Powel chose a familiar venue for the unveiling: Macy's.

The little car caused quite a stir.

First of all, though Crosley autos were small, the Hotshot was tiny. The low-slung, two-seat auto had a sharply rounded nose and no grille. The lack of a grille was another of Powel's "something different" features. The engine air intake was beneath the front bumper. The center curved down and outward from the hood area just like the fenders, resulting in a "bumped-out" appearance.

The car's headlights were mounted in detachable pods just inboard of the fenders, which gave it a "bug-eyed" look. Access to the engine compartment was through a lockable panel about the size of a baking sheet, which was lifted off the center of what would be the hood in any other car.

There were no doors on the car. Behind the windshield, the body dropped down to less than a foot high, creating openings for the driver and passenger to step through. There was no trunk. The rear deck served as a spare-tire mount, and the space beneath it was accessible behind the seats.

The car had a folding canvas top. The upholstery was imitation pigskin, the instrumentation minimal. Like the other Crosleys, the Hotshot rode on twelve-inch wheels. It had a base price of $849.

It hit the market with a big splash, preceded by a feature in the July 2, 1949 issue of *Life* magazine. *Time* covered it too: the little sports car also received coverage in *Hot Rod*, *Popular Science*, and *Mechanix Illustrated*.

Tom McCahill, once more, reviewed it for the latter magazine, giving it high marks. His review made a lot of friends for the little car. The vice-president of the Sports Car Club of America bought a Hotshot, as did former State Department official, now Governor of New York, Nelson Rockefeller.

The Hotshot's older cousins were beginning to gain acceptance as fleet vehicles. A Memphis company turned out several fleets of Crosley-based ice cream trucks. The Carnation Company used a fleet of modified Crosley wagons for delivery, as did a number of small florists.

The Crosley brothers needed every one of those sales. Two weeks after the Hotshot's introduction, Crosley Motors reported a net loss of $1,030,309 for fiscal year 1948.

Powel remained optimistic. He was convinced that things were going to turn around.

.   .   .   .   .   .

Powel III's youngest son, Teddy, walked out into the backyard that terrible June of 1948 in time to watch his father die. He developed significant psychiatric problems and eventually was committed to an institution.

Powel IV, who had been eight when his mother walked out—the only one of the boys old enough to understand what was happening—developed issues as well.

Betty Taylor, widowed with three boys, did the best she could but eventually made the difficult decision to send her oldest stepson to boarding school.

Within months, the boy ran away. He ended up in Cincinnati, on his grandfather's doorstep. After lengthy discussions between the two Powels, an agreement was reached.

Powel IV would return to school.

He would do it in Cincinnati, in his grandfather's care.

Lew Crosley had been sent to boarding school as well by then, in Massachusetts. He spent large chunks of time each summer with his grandfather, however, traveling to Nissaki, Bull Island, Miami and Cat Cay. And when in Cincinnati, Lew went to many Cincinnati Reds games on a free pass.

The Reds suffered through another hard season in 1949. Bucky Walters by this point had left the pitching mound for the dugout, managing the club for the second year in a row. Warren Giles did his best to supply the team with players but had a hard time getting the boss's attention.

Powel was engaged in a fight for the Crosley car's life. He did everything he could to get publicity for it. He gave the first baby born in a Crosley auto a silver spoon and cup, of all things. He pushed hard for the new engine, too, beginning a campaign to find new applications for the CIBA as he had for the COBRA.

It was used to power bus air conditioners and truck refrigeration units, Navy life rafts, industrial trucks, portable and fixed electrical generators, and several special-purpose vehicles, including the Crosley Tug (used to move materials in factories and on loading docks), the Transitier fork-lift truck, and, in the Pacific Northwest, ten miniature earthmovers belonging to the U.S. Department of Agriculture.

The CIBA was also packaged as the Crosley Marine Engine and found a small but enthusiastic market of boat racers in the forty-eight-cubic-inch class. Powel, of course, thought of his son.

He was reminded of Powel III again that fall of 1949 when he sat down with Powel Crosley IV for a frank discussion of the young man's future. He laid out the boy's options. Powel IV was seventeen years old, and he could go on to college, or he could go to work—Powel could help him get a job at any number of places. But he had to get out into the world.

The young man agreed.

Powel looked at his oldest grandson, and, perhaps, smiled just a little bit. That sort of restlessness, he understood all too well.

They talked for nearly two hours before Powel IV decided what it was he wanted to do. He wanted to join the Marines.

On November 22, 1949, with Powel's blessing, he enlisted. Within days he was off for basic training at Parris Island, South Carolina.

The son was gone. But the grandson—the heir and namesake to the Crosley name—seemed to be on his way toward making a place for himself in the world.

. . . . . .

The 1950 Crosley line was introduced at the New York Auto Show, with Lewis rather than Powel representing the company. Powel had taken ill, a rare occurrence for him, and was bedridden at Pinecroft. He spent the better part of a week reading, doing paperwork, and talking on the telephone from his massive four-poster bed.

Jim Nelson, one of Powel's ad reps at the Ralph Jones agency, came to see him one day. There were gadgets everywhere. It was like, Jones later said, visiting Ben Franklin's bedroom.

The new Crosleys varied little from the 1949 models. Powel and Lewis decided to save money by using the same stamping templates for the bodies, and concentrated on cosmetic and marketing changes. A Crosley "Super" was introduced, with chrome trim and better upholstery. The design elements, they hoped, would capture some of the market the Crosley had lost. The company's sales for 1949 were dismal. When the counting was done, 1949's production came to 8,939 cars and trucks—less than one third the number sold in 1948.

At the Marion plant, several hundred workers had to be laid off.

Powel refused to give up. He kept the new ideas coming.

His first for 1950 was an updated version of the wartime Mosquito, a Crosley station wagon with the top and sides removed and two sideways bench seats in the back. It was a military vehicle. Coincidentally or not, that same summer saw U.S. forces deployed as part of a United Nations force in South Korea, in response to an invasion from the Communist North.

Several of the new Mosquitoes were built under a development contract. They ended up with the U.S. Air Force, which put them to work as personnel carriers at Eglin Air Force Base in Florida.

The large order for which Powel hoped did not materialize.

He looked south, to Mexico.

After negotiations with the government there, Crosley Motors was allowed to ship Crosley car components into Mexico, where they were assembled by a Mexican company, Automotriz Crosley, S.A., a co-owned partnership of Crosley Motors and Equipos Automatrices in Monterey. The foreign version of the car was called the "Crosmobile." Some Crosmobiles were also shipped to Europe.

It didn't take off either.

The second week of January 1950 saw Powel IV return to Pinecroft on leave. Basic training seemed to have done him good, but the two had little time to discuss his experiences. Before long, the eighteen year-old was off again, headed for California where he would join a unit scheduled to ship overseas.

In February, Crosley Motors brought out a made-over Hotshot called the "Super Sports." The engine's compression ratio was raised to ten to one, which increased the horsepower by 15 percent. In a nod to racing rules, the Super Sports had real (removable) doors. The Super Sports also had a flying bird hood ornament, a larger rear window, and a side-mounted (optional) radio antenna. The model displayed at the New York Sportsmen's Show at Grand Central Palace featured imported leopard skin seat covers and carpet.

Tom McCahill put the Super Sports through its paces and did a report for *Sports Cars* magazine in which he called it both "a mechanical roller skate" and "a great American sports car." He found the wheels too small and the brakes uneven in operation but was pleased with the handling. The car held the road so well, the hefty McCahill maintained, that it was liable to flip if a driver pushed it beyond a certain point when cornering. He also derided the doors, which had a tendency to pop open unexpectedly. And, McCahill griped, Powel still hadn't addressed his pet peeve with the car.

"When I tested the Hotshot," McCahill wrote, "I yakked about the lousy placement of the gear shift and pleaded with Mr. Crosley to change it. Last year when I was at Crosley's house in Cincinnati, I brought it up again and understood that something was to be done...but it hasn't."

He went on to describe how shifting into second gear tended to force the driver's knuckles into the sharp edge of the key in the ignition switch. It was a minor point, lost in the shuffle of trying to save not a specific model but an entire company.

It wouldn't have helped anyway.

.   .   .   .   .   .

Nash President George Mason was also fascinated by small cars and, like Powel, considered the small-car market woefully neglected. Mason and Lewis Crosley were well acquainted, as Mason had headed the Kelvinator Corporation before the war. The two were occasional golfing partners in Florida, and through Lewis and other contacts, Mason kept a close eye on the development of the Crosley automobile.

Mason spent several years researching and thinking about small cars before beginning design work, all the while following the Crosley saga. In January 1950, he began showing a prototype small car he called the NXI (for "Nash Xperimental International") to select focus groups in American cities. Those who viewed the NXI were asked to fill out a questionnaire. Before the year was out,

Mason had collected the opinions of a quarter-million people. The data he gathered convinced him that Americans were interested in buying small cars.

The NXI was a stalking-horse for a car already in development. The new vehicle, the Nash Rambler, hit the market in March. Two models were offered, a two-door station wagon and a convertible coupe, both of which sported Crosley design elements. The car, however, was 25 percent longer than the Crosley. It also had a radio, a heater, a six-cylinder engine, and comfortable seats. Nash sold just over eleven thousand units in 1950. He would do a lot better in the years to come.

Henry Kaiser's small auto, the "Henry J," was also introduced in March. It came with a four-cylinder engine that was twice as powerful as the Crosley CIBA. An optional six-cylinder made the car a real hotrod.

The Henry J. had style—a bullet nose, tail fins, rakish lines. The New York Fashion Academy named it the "1951 Fashion Car of the Year."

It sold almost eighty-two hundred units, even with a price tag around 50 percent higher than the Crosley.

The new compacts seriously eroded the Crosley market.

It seemed that, while Americans were interested in saving money, they were not willing to sacrifice a lot to do it. Both George Mason and Henry J. Kaiser had gambled that a compact car just a bit larger than the Crosley was what the market wanted, and they were right.

Powel might have taken the hint, but he didn't.

.   .   .   .   .   .

In June, Powel brought out a "new" line of Super Crosley sedans, station wagons, and pickup trucks. The vehicles were the same as the 1950's lineup, but with the engines modified for high compression operation and automatic windshield wipers standard. The increase to thirty horsepower made the cars livelier.

It did nothing for sales.

There was more bad news on the horizon.

Thorough analysis, testing, and numerous owner reports revealed that disc brakes were not the great idea they had seemed. Road salt and high levels of dirt caused them to lock up, and they wore down faster than anyone had expected. The malfunctioning components were replaced by conventional Bendix hydraulic drum brakes.

Exit the hydro-disc, stage left.

Enter the lawyers, stage right.

The disc brakes' manufacturer, Hawley, sued when Crosley Motors cancelled a contract for twenty-five thousand sets of disc brakes. Powel had to make an out-of-court settlement.

In July, he came out with another new model, one he'd been working on for even longer than the Hotshot. He'd started by sketching ideas for a general-purpose vehicle, one that could be used on the farm, around factories and other commercial operations, and that could be driven on highways and city streets. What he ended up with had a superficial resemblance to a Jeep, with high ground clearance, flat front fenders and a high hood, but the resemblance ended there. This vehicle was short and square, with a sixty-inch wheelbase and a forty-inch tread. It had six forward and two reverse speeds and was powered by a standard Crosley CIBA engine.

It was, in many ways, an updated version of the old Crosley Pup.

Powel named it the "Farm-O-Road." He and Lewis worked up a variety of add-on agricultural implements for the vehicle: extra-cost options like a cutter bar mower, a plow, a hay rake, a cultivator, and a snow plow/dozer.

The basic model had seats for two and a tiny removable cargo box in the rear. To haul more cargo or additional passengers, a larger bed (optional) could be attached and a rear bench seat and grab bars (again, optional) added. The large bed could be used as a dump bed. Canvas tops for regular or long beds were available, as were detachable dual rear wheel assemblies.

The Farm-O-Road and its accessories made their first appearance on July 19, 1950. Two weeks later, on July 31, Crosley Motors announced its fiscal 1949 results; the company had lost $857,687.

Powel was still optimistic things could be turned around. To Lewis's chagrin, he began loaning his own money to the company to pay for tooling, expansion, and day-to-day operations.

Powel sought celebrities to associate with his cars just as he had with Crosley radios. He gave a Crosley to Art Linkletter. He sent a few of them to Hollywood, where producers of the *Abbot and Costello* comedy films used them a few times as sight gags, which was not exactly the sort of exposure Powel had in mind.

One celebrity, however, sought the Crosley automobile on his own.

For some years, architect Frank Lloyd Wright had maintained a small fleet of American Bantam automobiles for use at his Taliesin compounds in Wisconsin and Arizona. When a Willys dealer near Taliesin began carrying Crosley cars, Wright came to see them.

He was impressed, and immediately bought several, indicating those he wanted by whacking them on the hood with his walking stick. Wright expressed a great admiration for Powel's automobiles. According to writer Frank Hockenhull, Wright was heard to tell his students, "It takes a conscience to drive a Crosley!"

Few of them, apparently, were listening.

Sales continued to drop.

Powel diversified again. He designed a fire engine based on the Farm-O-Road, intended for use "where maneuverable fire fighting is needed quickly, such as around airports, refineries, large factories, warehouses, docks, etc." The little fire truck carried an eighty-gallon water tank, along with a hundred feet of heavy hose and an optional ladder rack. A second CIBA engine mounted on a front boom drove a 700-psi water pump. It came with dual rear wheels standard.

That summer, he brought in modernist designer Count Alexis de Sakhnoffsky to help with the design of the 1951 cars. Sakhnoffsky had previously worked on the redesign of American Bantam automobiles, in addition to serving as an art consultant and designer for Packard, Auburn, and other automakers.

There was also a major shuffling of executives. Stanley Kess was named secretary of Crosley Motors on July 5, 1950, and the sales force was reorganized.

By August, the new model designs were complete, and Powel spent the month at Nissaki with Page and Lew.

On October 2, 1950, PFC Powel Crosley IV was traveling with an advance unit of armored vehicles when a squad of North Korean soldiers ambushed his platoon.

He was killed instantly.

CHAPTER 33

T his time, he was more the comforter than the comfortee. It
was Betty's and her boys' loss, the second tragedy in their
lives in as many years. It was June Smith Bramlage's loss as
well. For all that, Powel had grown close to his grandson. What he
mourned in the aftermath of Powel IV's death was not only the boy
he had come to know, but the man who might have been.

What he mourned was the future.

Gwendolyn and Powel III, Charlotte and now Powel IV.

He could not imagine what—or who—might come next.

That would turn out to be a good thing.

.   .   .   .   .

Only 7,612 Crosley cars and trucks were produced in 1950. Production on the 1951 line commenced in September, and the new models were unveiled on November 13. The most visible change was up
front: the grille treatment resembled that of the 1949 Ford, with a
large circle of ornamental chrome at the center of the upper cross-
piece. The effect was that of an airplane viewed head-on; a six-inch
spinning metal propeller could be added if the customer wished.

Nearly all of the models came with minor price increases,
ranging from thirty-three to seventy-seven dollars. One could still
buy a pickup truck or business coupe (formerly the sedan) for under
a thousand dollars. The highest-priced Crosley—and the most popular—was the station wagon, at $1,133.

The new models had little effect on Crosley Motors stock,

which had been trading at about three dollars for months.

The year did end on a positive note: on December 31, 1950, the first Sebring six-hour endurance run was held at a track set up on an abandoned airfield outside Sebring, Florida. Unbeknownst to Powel or anyone else at Crosley Motors, a pair of auto enthusiasts, Ralph Deshow and Fritz Koster, entered a converted Crosley Hotshot in the competition. The little sports car, minus windshield and bumpers, with the number 19 painted on its nose and sides with black shoe polish, went up against a field of Ferraris and Jaguars.

It won.

The Hotshot, able to hold the track tighter through the course's turns than any of the other cars, made only one pit stop during the entire six hours of the race.

At last, Powel had something to cheer about.

"When a bargain sales colt outruns a 'name' three-year-old in a major stakes race," he crowed to the papers, "you've got an upset whether you like it or not. And you've got the same startling kind of reversal when an eleven-hundred pound Crosley costing only $924 takes on a field of two dozen foreign-made sport cars, some of them weighing over two tons and selling for up to $20,000, and whips them at their own type of international endurance driving 'test.'"

It was a mouthful. It was a sales pitch. It was all too little, too late.

.   .   .   .   .   .

Powel himself was racing horses, not cars, in 1951. He'd started a thoroughbred breeding program with some of his horses over the last couple years. Early in the 1951 racing season he had a colt named Democles at Keeneland racetrack in Lexington, Kentucky, and a two-year-old filly named Lady Page at Aqueduct in New York. The racing wasn't about money to him; it was about evaluating the results of his breeding program.

Not so to the Commissioner of Baseball Happy Chandler. To Chandler—as to his predecessor, Kennesaw 'Mountain' Landis—the line between baseball and gambling was an absolute, never to be crossed under any circumstances. Chandler had earlier forced Bing Crosby and John Galbreath to sell their interests in racing stables when they bought into the Pittsburgh Pirates. Now he wanted Powel to do the same.

Powel protested.

"You have to know whether your stock can run, or it is of no value," he said. "That's why I entered them in the races."

The issue simmered throughout the 1951 season. Before it could be decided, Commissioner Chandler retired. National League President Ford Frick replaced him and turned out to be a disciple of Landis's as well. Sell, he told Powel. Warren Giles, former Reds general manager, replaced Frick as National League President and was a little more lenient toward his old boss.

"The question seems to be whether Mr. Crosley is racing his horses as a matter of testing them. I don't see where there's anything wrong with that," Giles told the press.

A protracted argument ensued. Powel didn't win that round either.

He retired from racing.

Right about then, Powel's pilot called it a day as well.

Eddie Nirmaier was sixty-five years old, losing his hearing from having spent so much time near the roar of an airplane motor. He said goodbye to Powel after two decades of service and retired to Florida. Powel searched for an adequate replacement but finally gave up. By and by, he sold his planes and flew commercial alongside the masses.

He introduced a new engine for the Super Sport, a high-compression version of the CIBA. He gave the Ralph Jones agency the task of naming it, and Mary Ann Kelly came up with the winner once more—the 'Quicksilver' engine. It required high-octane gasoline that wasn't commonly available, so Powel had the Thompson Products Company of Cleveland design a water-alcohol injector called the Vitameter. Using this device, and an additive called "Vitane," the engine could be safely run on regular gasoline.

The Quicksilver, as its name implied, came and went.

Another Crosley car modification garnered more positive attention.

Florida import auto dealer Phil Stiles had been chairman of the first Sebring race when the Hotshot won. Stiles was also a driver. His dream was to race in the classic endurance contest held each year at Le Mans, France. There was only one problem: entries had to be factory-sponsored, and Stiles did not know any automobile manufacturers likely to back a relatively unknown driver. Major carmakers typically fielded their own group of carefully chosen drivers and mechanics.

One evening in March 1951 he discussed the problem with his friend and racing partner, George Schrafft, of the New York restaurant Schraffts. Mrs. Stiles, who had heard it all before, had an idea for her husband: why don't you let Crosley build you a car?

Certain that he would be turned down, Stiles nonetheless wrote a letter to Crosley Motors, outlining his racing experience and his desire to enter a Crosley Hotshot in the Grand Prix Le Mans. Powel—knowing a publicity opportunity when he saw one and, perhaps, having in mind his own frustrating experiences at the first Indy 500—approved the request.

Stiles and Schrafft were invited first to Cincinnati to oversee construction of a special Hotshot chassis. They followed the chassis to Indianapolis where a custom body was built, and then journeyed with the car back to the Crosley Motors Plant on Spring Grove Ave., where a number of further modifications were made, in particular to the engine.

Powel gave the duo a boat trailer he wasn't using, and the two men—and their little car—were off.

They landed in Le Havre, France, and made their way to Le Mans. On the trip, they discovered that the Hotshot's headlights were insufficient for nighttime driving, necessary because Le Mans was an endurance race and much of the driving would take place at night.

Several electrical equipment manufacturers were present, and so Stiles and Schrafft made the decision to equip the Hotshot with more powerful headlights. Another problem soon presented itself, however: the more powerful headlights were too much of a power drain on the car's generator. The two men decided to replace that as well. It was, in the words of writer Edward Jennings, "a fatal error."

The race began: George Schrafft took the first turn as driver. The Hotshot astounded spectators and drivers alike by passing Talbots and other larger cars literally at every turn. The road-hugging ability that had won at Sebring and had so impressed Tom McCahill of *Mechanix Illustrated* soon had the little car performing impressively.

Then disaster struck. The generator simply gave out. The car's electric system, running off battery power alone, began behaving erratically. Schrafft was unable to shut the engine off, even for pit stops. Even if by some miracle he could keep the car going, when night fell, things would get worse. He'd have to switch on the head-lights, and that would swiftly use up what little charge might be remaining. The Hotshot wasn't going to win, Schrafft realized. It wasn't even going to finish the race.

Five hours into the twenty-four-hour marathon, the little car finally died.

Had the Hotshot been able to maintain its starting pace, it might very well have won. Even in defeat, the little car—and the way it handled those racetrack turns—made an impression. Soon Hotshots were showing up in races throughout Europe, along with a variety of "Crosley specials," cars built on a Crosley chassis or using a Crosley engine by manufacturers such as Sarti, Nardi, and others.

The racing world in America took to the Hotshot too, and to the CIBA that powered it. The little engine made it into many of the popular midget racers of the 1950s, as well as a variety of homebuilt cars.

A California entrepreneur named Nick Brajevich built a highly successful business supplying "Braje" modifications to Crosley engine owners. The innovations were so effective in increasing horsepower and overall performance that some of them were adopted by Crosley Motors.

But the racing market was tiny.

The public in general continued to ignore the Crosley.

The 1951 model year saw just 4,831 cars produced. Company stock dropped to 2-⅛; on July 31, 1951, Crosley Motors reported a loss for the fiscal year of $846,686.

Macy's, Bamberger's, and the May Company notified the company they would no longer carry the car.

The writing was on the wall. Powel, at last, began to read it.

·　·　·　·　·

The 1952 Crosleys were put on display at Crosley dealerships across the U.S. on November 26, 1951, with little fanfare. There was really no difference between the new Crosleys and the 1951 models other than the serial number plates. The prices remained the same, but a new Federal Excise Tax on automobiles added fourteen to twenty-four dollars to retail prices.

Demand was so low that shortly after the New Year, over half the remaining workers at the Marion factory were laid off. The factory was by this point turning out fewer than a hundred and fifty cars per month. They were losing money on every car.

"Somebody," as Lewis put it two decades later, "had to stop it."

Powel, of course, was the only who could.

He began to consider his options. He could change the Crosley, building a slightly bigger vehicle. Americans seemed to be more interested in those models. But success was far from certain. And producing a bigger car would involve major retooling on the line, a major capital investment.

Powel by that point had sunk millions into Crosley Motors. He wasn't going to risk anymore. Considering the economic climate and the automobile marketplace, he'd have a hard time convincing others to risk theirs either.

So a bigger car was out.

Merger was another possibility. But that seemed unlikely because the car was a losing proposition. The engine was the company's most valuable asset. Besides, a merger would require an established, healthy company run by someone who had the kind of faith in the small car market that Powel possessed. Those kind of people were few and far between.

He could, of course, just shut the company down. But even that would cost a considerable amount of money.

As he weighed those choices, none of which appealed to him in the slightest, as he faced the fact that he was sixty-six years old, and that the dream he'd had since he was a little boy was in fact, not going to come true, he received an inquiry from a man named William O'Neill, who had followed with interest recent developments regarding Powel's car.

O'Neill was President of the General Tire & Rubber Company.

He wanted to buy Crosley Motors.

While Powel considered O'Neill's offer, he pursued another interest of his own, one he had recently made outside the scope of the automobile business.

Her name was Eva Brokaw—Eve, to her friends.

She was to be, as it turned out, exactly who he had been seeking for fifteen long years.

Powel had known Eve since the 1930s. She was a friend of Page's. She'd been, in fact, at Page's wedding to Stanley Kess back in 1943. She was married at the time but now was divorced. Powel saw her again for the first time in early 1952 and saw her a lot more frequently in the months that followed.

Unlike Marianne Wallingford, she traveled in the same circles. She was a member of Grace Episcopal Church, a volunteer who devoted numerous hours to the Church's Junior Cooperative Society and the Cincinnati Children's Hospital. She liked the outdoors; she liked the Reds.

Powel found in her something he had been missing since Gwendolyn died: a true confidante. By all accounts, he was happier with her than he'd been in a long time.

Her presence helped cushion the blow of the car's failure.

She made it easier for him to accept William O'Neill's offer to purchase Crosley Motors, even though General Tire had no intention of manufacturing automobiles. They wanted the CIBA engine business and the factory space for expansion. They also wanted to carry over Crosley Motors' loss for tax purposes.

It was, nonetheless, a bitter pill to swallow.

Negotiations began, continuing through June and on into July. The week of the July 4th holiday, a skeleton crew of workers oversaw the final few cars coming off the production line. Powel and Lewis made the trip out to Marion for that last day, when the last machines shut down, when the last employees clocked out.

At the end, the two brothers stood there, in the silence of the cavernous plant that, in a way, Powel had struggled his whole life to build. No words were necessary, really. Each knew what the unmanned stations along the assembly meant.

They were boys when they started together: Powel and his dream, Lewis and his eight dollars following behind. They made that little electric car work. They made the trip to the College Hill post office and back, collecting a dollar each for their troubles. The car put them in business; the car now took them out of it.

For Powel, the irony was almost too much to bear.

Cars had been his passion for fifty years. He'd dreamed of them, drawn them, taken them from blueprint to boardroom to assembly line, first as a young man and again as a seasoned executive. The Marathon Six had broken his heart. The Hermes and the Cycle Car had taught him valuable lessons.

The Crosley car's failure crushed him.

For half a century, he'd sought his place in the automobile industry, sought to become part of the vast wave of mechanization sweeping across the country, not just as one of the many caught up in that transformation, but one of the few directing the current's course. For a brief moment—those few months in mid-1948, when the Crosley's sales peaked—he'd held the reins in his hand.

But the moment had passed. The car industry had moved on, or rather, stayed in the same place. The small-car revolution Powel had seen coming had failed to materialize.

He'd failed.

What must have eaten at him just a bit was the knowledge that part of the fault was his; he told Lewis as much in the car's final days.

The thing that cooked us, Powel said to his brother, was that sheet-metal block. If we'd started with the cast-iron we would have made it.

It was as close to an apology as he was ever likely to offer. Lewis didn't need it. The two of them were a team. They rose—and fell—together.

For Powel, the end of the car meant the end of his entrepreneurial career. After the sale, he retired.

For Lewis, the end of the car meant, in a way, the beginning. Though he would stay on for another year to help Aerojet General manage the business, he was, from that moment when they shut down the plant, a different man—his own man, no longer tied to his brother's dreams.

He could begin, at last, to pursue his own.

.   .   .   .   .   .

The sale was formally announced on July 17, 1952. Powel received what seemed a paltry sum for his interest in Crosley Motors: the equivalent of about twenty cents per share for 317,077 shares (including those held by Lewis and other family members). But there were other considerations. The deal gave Powel a substantial number of shares in General Tire. Furthermore, after the merger, the directors voted to reimburse Powel some $3,600,000 of his own money he had put into Crosley Motors.

Powel retired. Lewis stayed with Crosley Motors after the buyout, serving as vice-president and treasurer. Lewis was there when Aerojet began to clear up the offices. In a desk drawer he found a number of invoice slips—unfulfilled, unnoticed, orders for Crosley autos. Dozens of them.

Not that it mattered.

Americans in the 1950s, coming off the enforced hardships of war, were not in the mood to economize or sacrifice the comforts they'd fought so long and hard for the right to maintain. They weren't interested in squeezing into a little car to save a few cents worth of gas. The people who bought the car in quantity back in 1948 were people who couldn't afford a new vehicle otherwise. When the used-car market reemerged after war restrictions were lifted, those people preferred to spend their thousand dollars for a used Ford, or Buick, or Chevy.

The Crosley Car was simply the wrong vehicle, in the wrong place, at exactly the wrong time.

Times, though, would soon be changing.

. . . . . .

Powel and Eve spent two weeks at Nissaki. The press was waiting when he returned, with questions about the one business of his that was left: the Reds. One writer wanted to know if Powel's retirement meant he would sell the team.

No, he said.

One wanted to know if the sale meant that he would devote more time to the Reds.

Perhaps, he answered, though, in fact, it would have been almost impossible to do anything else. He'd seen fewer games in recent years than any owner, with the possible exception of John Galbreath, the Pittsburgh Pirates owner who lived in Columbus, Ohio. Other than promoting Gabe Paul to take Warren Giles's place, he had devoted his full attention to Crosley Motors.

His attention in that fall of 1952 was still focused elsewhere: on Eve. Shortly after their return from Nissaki, he proposed, she accepted, and they were off in the *Wego* for a celebratory cruise around the Caribbean. They stopped in Cuba and Cat Cay, did some fishing, did some swimming, and returned to Cincinnati the first week in October.

He seemed—all things considered—to be handling the death of his dream rather well. On Friday the 10th, on the grounds of Forest Retreat Farm in Carlisle, Kentucky, not far from Lewis's farm, Powel and Eve said their vows and then resumed the celebrating.

Lewis, meanwhile, was still at work.

He'd been named vice-president at General Tire, now known as Aerojet-General, which continued to manufacture the Crosley CIBA engine under the auspices of Crosley Motors. The engine, renamed the Aerojet, enjoyed an increasing demand in automotive, marine, and industrial applications.

Rumors that Aerojet-General would put the Crosley automobile back into production began flying immediately after the sale. The first speculation regarding the Crosley being revived came from Lewis himself. He sent a letter to Crosley dealers notifying them that, while Aerojet-General did not want to get into making automobiles, the company was hopeful regarding the prospects of selling the auto manufacturing operation. Soon after, the company received an offer from a former New York Crosley distributor, Service Motors. The deal didn't materialize because Edward Herzog, the owner, couldn't line up financing.

In October, Aerojet-General declared it was not interested in resuming automobile production. Moreover, the rights to produce Crosley automobiles were for sale, along with a $350,000 inventory of chassis and body parts.

In March 1953, Lewis contacted Crosley dealers to inform them that negotiations were underway with a Japanese company that would manufacture Crosley automobiles in Japan and distribute them worldwide. The company intended to buy not only the rights to build the Crosley but also the templates, tools, dies, and machinery used in its manufacture.

The deal fell through.

Another was announced a few months later.

Aerojet-General revealed that an Israeli concern, the Abena Investment and Development Company of Tel Aviv, had arranged to purchase Crosley motors. The plan was for Abena to manufacture the Hotshot and Crosley station wagons and sell part of their production in America. The company's principal, Joshua Ben-Anav, detailed plans whereby Abena would manufacture in Israel everything but the engines, which would come from Aerojet's Cincinnati plant. Payment was to be half of Abena's three million dollars in stock, which meant Aerojet-General would be, in effect, manufacturing automobiles.

That deal broke down as well.

Aerojet management finally decided to scrap the Crosley automobile tools and dies and sell off the parts inventory. An auction was held at the Marion Plant in September. Edward Herzog ended up buying nearly everything. This stock served as the basis of his company, Service Motors, for more than two decades.

The task of putting the last of his brothers' dreams to bed accomplished, Lewis finally called it a day himself, at least as far as desk jobs were concerned.

He had a little dream of his own to attend to yet.

.   .   .   .   .   .

As usual, Powel celebrated Christmas at Pinecroft. But unlike previous years, this time he didn't go hunting afterward. He made no trips to Mississippi, or Bull Island, or Sleepy Hollow, or Florida. He stayed home with Eve, with Lew, who was home for the holidays, with Page and Stanley Kess, and their two children. He and Eve went to the opera; they attended parties. Powel took it easy, or at least, as easy as he could take it.

He made plans for the upcoming summer of 1953.

He'd ordered a new yacht the year previous from the Huckins Yacht company, who way back in 1928 had been the first to install Crosley radios as standard equipment on their boats, an eighty-five-thousand-dollar vessel with four cabins that slept two each, plus every design feature and amenity under the sun. It would be ready by May, and Powel had an extensive shakedown cruise in mind, the type of journey he'd never been able to consider before.

In March he and Eve spent a week in Tampa, for spring training. In April, they were back in Cincinnati, for Opening Day. It was a different team that took the field that afternoon, different in name, at least. Not the Reds, but the Redlegs. The standoff in Korea, the brutal crackdowns by Soviet authorities behind the Iron Curtain, and the arrival of the Cold War had transformed reasonable fears regarding enemy espionage into paranoia. To be "red" was to be Communist, unpatriotic, even a spy.

Entertainers found themselves under particular scrutiny and some found themselves on a blacklist, unable to work. By that point, the radio industry was dying. Television had arrived. Leading the way were NBC broadcasting and RCA television, with sets featuring FM sound, sets using Edwin Armstrong's patents, for which the inventor was still not receiving a dime.

Armstrong's lawyers, and RCA's, were hard at work. They'd moved beyond pre-trial hearings into actual proceedings. RCA's tactics remained exactly the same: stall. They had all the time and money in the world.

Edwin Armstrong was running out of both. He wanted, at last, to settle the suit. After six years there was still no end in sight. It burned him, but he had no choice but to abandon his quest for patent royalties and accept a one-time cash settlement. He asked for $2.4 million; RCA's lawyers made a counter-offer: two hundred thousand dollars.

Armstrong was stunned.

That amount of money wouldn't even cover his remaining legal fees. He was backed into a corner—one partially of his own making, perhaps, but a trap nonetheless. He considered his options.

He had none. His fortune was gone. His wife was gone too, after a bitter quarrel the memory of which ate at him day and night. His decision to fight David Sarnoff's company—to fight for FM against the man who, ironically, had urged him to invent it in the first place—had cost him everything.

Life had knocked him down. Armstrong couldn't see the point in getting back up again. On February 1, the man whose inventions had defined and shaped the broadcasting boom dressed in a coat and scarf, opened the window to his thirteenth-floor apartment, and stepped outside into the cool morning air.

. . . . .

In April, Powel received word that his new yacht, the *Taureau Rouge*, was ready. He and Eve flew to Miami to take it on that shake-down cruise. On the way out, he stopped at the Huckins yards to place an order for another vessel, to be christened the *Sea Flash*. The new craft cost over $140,000. Powel paid Huckins a hefty percent-age of the price as a deposit.

Right away, he had buyer's remorse.

A few days into the *Taureau Rouge*'s shakedown cruise, the yacht developed problems. He had to return it for repairs, and he and Eve spent several unplanned weeks in Miami as a result. By mid-summer, the repairs were done, and they headed out for Annapolis and then Bull Island.

In November, the *Taureau Rouge* broke down again. Powel visited the Huckins offices in person to have a "talk" with company executives. He left with the president's personal assurance the *Taureau Rouge* would be restored to perfect running condition. And it was, at no little expense to the company. Among other things, the Huckins yard installed new engines. The boat was ready just after the New Year.

In February, Powel received the tragic news that Charles Kil-gour had died of a heart attack. His old friend was sixty-seven.

Powel and Eve set out for the Caribbean once more. They enjoyed an extended stay at Cat Cay, using the island as their base for cruises to the Florida Keys, Cuba, and several islands in the Bahamas. Powel spent much of the time fishing. Eve was right with him.

They cruised to Miami at the end of March, then flew to Cincinnati for Opening Day. Eve went to her doctor for a routine check-up, received the all-clear, and then accompanied Powel to Crosley Field for the game.

Riding with his chauffeur in his Cadillac Fleetwood, Powel noticed the heavy volume of traffic around the stadium and was a lit-tle taken aback. People, he saw, were being forced to park a great dis-tance from Crosley Field. The city should do something about the problem, he decided, and made a note to talk with officials about it.

The two of them flew back to Miami after Opening Day. The new yacht was ready. They took it to Bull Island for the month. The last week of May, they boarded a plane at the Savannah airport for Cincinnati.

Eve wasn't feeling well. She went to her doctor, and then, on the afternoon of May 27, checked into Cincinnati's Holmes Hospital.

She had cancer.

Thirty-eight days later she was dead.

CHAPTER 34

His wives. His son. His grandson. His mother. His car. Powel Crosley was sixty-seven years old. He'd just been through half a dozen years of unimaginable pain, disappointment, and tragedy.

But he wasn't stepping out any windows just yet.

What Powel did was get up and move on to the next thing.

Actually, it was the same old thing, albeit dressed in different clothes, so as not to offend. The thing he'd followed since the days of Wahoo Sam and Eddie Roush, the thing he'd bought back in 1934 not to make money but to keep it from leaving town. The only business he had left: the Redlegs.

In the twenty years since Larry MacPhail had prevailed on him to buy the franchise, he'd never looked at the club as a profit-making enterprise. The Redlegs were for fun—for the little kid who'd peered in the saloon windows to see the game scores scrawled on the blackboard, who'd pitched for the College Hill Belmonts.

Lewis Crosley enjoyed the Redlegs too. In fact, he was an even bigger fan than his brother. He was now, at sixty-six, serving as vice-president of the team, signing the checks and keeping an eye, as needed, on day-to-day operations, a job not unlike what he had done for the Crosley Corporation.

He had another business to keep an eye on as well.

Cross Acres Dairy.

Prior to the early fifties, he'd run his Kentucky operation as a hobby, a weekend getaway. When he retired from Aerojet, however, Lewis decided to change the nature of the operation.

He got into the milk business. He bought a bunch of Holstein cows and the necessary equipment, and soon enough he was running a full-fledged dairy. He sold cottage cheese, butter, milk, of course, and every dairy product conceivable to interested locals.

Charlotte and Bud Runck were by this point back from Washington. They had a son named Renny. Ellen had met and married a man named Bill McClure. They had two children, a son and a daughter.

Powel, meanwhile, was downsizing. He'd already given Nissaki to Page. Now he sold the house in Havana, the house on Cat Cay, and put Sleepy Hollow Farm on the market. He sold two of his yachts, the *Taureau Rouge* and the *Wego*. He sold the Grumman Mallard too. As soon as that was gone, he put Crosley Airport on the market.

He began traveling with the Redlegs, often chartering private planes. He spruced up the stadium and began spending more money on players and management. He and Gabe Paul worked closely together. Powel left the baseball decisions to Paul, but he was, as always, not shy about expressing his opinions. His relationship with Paul was different from those with Larry MacPhail and Warren Giles. He and Paul were a generation apart. Paul was the one in his prime now. Powel had watched him grow into the job, move up from traveling secretary to one of the most respected young minds in the business. He couldn't help but feel proud and a little responsible.

By 1956, they'd taken the team that had finished in sixth four years in a row and created a contender once more. But this was a different kind of club from the ones that went to the Series in '39 and '40. Those teams relied on pitching and defense. They scrapped for runs and fought for every out. They were built for speed.

The '56 Reds were built for power.

The most powerful was first baseman Ted Kluszewski, a former football star who ripped the sleeves of his shirts to free his huge biceps. But '56 was an off-year for "Big Klu," as back problems began to hobble him. He only hit thirty-five homers, after smacking forty-seven in 1955 and forty-nine in '54. He finished third on the team. Wally Post, who hit thirty-six after clubbing forty a year earlier, was second.

The man who led the team in homers was Frank Robinson, only twenty years old, only the second African-American to wear a Cincinnati uniform. He hit thirty-eight his rookie season and would go on to hit five hundred and eighty-six before becoming the first black manager in the major leagues.

All that power wasn't quite enough. The Reds fell two games short of the pennant that year, though it was a race till the final days of the season. They ended up in third, a game behind the Milwaukee Braves, two games behind the Brooklyn Dodgers. It was, nonetheless, a thrilling time to be a Reds fan. A good time to be the Reds owner too. The team, for the first time in its history, drew more than a million fans that season.

That year Powel had his own box built over Crosley Field's right-field grandstands. With seating for a dozen or more, it was air-conditioned and featured a bar and kitchen. He began watching games from it as soon as it was finished; Lewis preferred his seats behind the Reds dugout. He couldn't hear the game from all the way up there.

Powel, by and by, started to bring along a guest. Her name was Charlotte Kaye Wilson. She was a New Yorker and thirty years old to Powel's seventy. She was not, as you might expect, a regular at Grace Episcopal Church.

She was, however, good company.

They were married in Cincinnati on October 31. He took her first to Bull Island, and then to Miami, where they made the rounds—receptions and parties at the Miami Yacht Club and aboard the boats of his various acquaintances—before returning to Pinecroft for Christmas. Then it was off to Bull Island again at the beginning of 1957.

Charlotte rode horses and did some target shooting. After a week, she was bored. Life on the isolated island was not to her taste. Powel took her to Miami but was soon exhausted by the social whirl. Though it seemed a bad match, Powel didn't give up on it just yet.

They went to nearby Sea Island, a resort founded by Hudson auto magnate Howard Coffin. Sea Island had golfing, shooting, and plenty of other people for socializing. Powel and Charlotte spent several days there each of the next few months, and that seemed to ease the tensions between them.

In mid-March they cruised to Tampa for spring training. Powel, who once upon a time had donned a uniform himself to work out with the team, was past that point by now, but he still enjoyed the camaraderie, the atmosphere, and stayed in Tampa to cheer the team through every game.

Come April, he and Charlotte journeyed to Cincinnati for Opening Day.

They were greeted by traffic that was worse than ever. Scores of cars were lined up in the no-parking zones on the streets leading to the ballpark.

He and Lewis again attempted to talk to city officials regarding the parking situation. Again, they met with little success.

The Redlegs continued to draw well and to smack home runs at a prodigious pace. Frank Robinson proved no flash-in-the pan, hitting .322, good for third in the league behind Stan Musial and Willie Mays. The Red Scare, unfortunately, proved to have similar staying power. Americans talked of the Cold War, the hydrogen bomb, and of the domino effect. Men were still being drafted into the service.

In October, Sputnik went up. It was a shot heard around the world. New York baseball fans, having been hit hard by a shot of their own several months earlier, weren't listening. The Dodgers and the Giants were heading west, the former to Los Angeles, the latter to San Francisco. That left the senior circuit in dire need of a New York franchise.

That franchise, the press soon reported, was to be the Cincinnati Redlegs.

The move seemed logical and almost inevitable. Cincinnati in 1957 was no longer the sixth-largest city in the country. From the decaying grandeur of Over-the-Rhine to the encroaching slums on the west side, the town was slipping. Its population was the smallest of any city with a big-league team.

Crosley Field was one of the oldest ballparks in the majors, located in the middle of a deteriorating neighborhood where parking was not only difficult to find, but often dangerous. By one count, less than one-third of the desired number of parking spaces (seven to ten thousand spaces) were available within walking distance of the ballpark.

New York attorney William A. Shea made a public offer for the team. The deal would have netted Powel several million dollars, but he wasn't interested in the money. What he was interested in was those parking spaces.

For years, he'd been after the city to do something about the problem. Now he had the leverage to get them to take action. Instead of turning down Shea's offer, Powel let the public speculate as to whether or not he would go for the deal. He even stoked the fire a bit.

"My feelings," he told the *Cincinnati Enquirer*, "are that at no time prior to this has the franchise here been as much in jeopardy as now."

Privately, he had no intention of selling. As he told Gabe Paul, "I dislike the tactic we are using, but I'm convinced that there is no other way I can get the city to give us parking space we badly need."

October and November found Powel with Charlotte dividing their time between Bull Island and Sea Island. Tensions resurfaced. Charlotte tried to extend the length of their visits to Sea Island, while Powel complained about the limited time he was getting to hunt and fish at Bull Island. A visit to Miami did little to improve matters between them.

Christmas was spent at Pinecroft. Back in Tampa for spring training in March of 1958, Powel received word from Lewis that the city had made overtures regarding the parking situation. By mid-April, Lewis and the city manager had worked out an agreement under which the city would spend two million dollars for off-street parking near Crosley Field, if Powel would guarantee that the Redlegs would stay in Cincinnati for at least five years. Powel was happy to make that promise. He signed the agreement on April 28, 1958.

Meanwhile, something interesting was happening in the wider world.

Americans were at last discovering the benefits of the small car.

. . . . . .

In 1932, in a restaurant in Munich, Germany, Adolf Hitler sketched a design for an automobile that every German could afford. Small, cheap, and reliable. Why take a battleship to cross the Hudson, as the Henry Ford of Radio would one day put it, when all you needed was a motorboat? In 1933, after being named Chancellor of the Republic, Hitler met with an auto manufacturer named Ferdinand Porsche (another advocate of small-car designs) and asked him to turn his vision into a reality.

By 1958, that car, now known as the Volkswagen, was taking the world by storm. In fact, a number of European imports began to make a dent in the American marketplace. George Mason's Nash Rambler had also seen a continual upswing in sales during the last half-dozen years. By 1958, the combination of the imports and Rambler accounted for twelve percent of all car sales. The Big Three themselves were rumored to be on the verge of getting into the small car business.

Powel must have been dying inside, just a little bit.

He was hurting in other ways as well.

By summer of 1959, things with Charlotte were getting worse. Fortunately, owning a baseball team was excuse enough to get out of the house just about any time during the season. Powel attended nearly every home game and traveled to several. The ever-popular rumor about the Redlegs leaving town resurfaced, coupled with pointed references to Powel's age.

He was visibly wearing out—his hair almost gone, his body stooped and sagging. He'd been a great one for walking everywhere. Lewis, as part of his job, always tagged along, a step behind. He had a hard time keeping up with his older brother. Not anymore.

Whatever it was that had burned inside Powel Crosley for seventy-odd years was flickering. Whatever it was that enabled him to keep getting up after life kept knocking him down was weakening too.

He was not a happy man. He'd spent his life pursuing one dream after another. Now they were all gone. So were his friends, for the most part, MacDonald and Kilgour, most prominent among them.

What he had left was his family and the Reds. He told the press that he would be leaving the team to his daughter and grandchildren in his will.

Thanksgiving at Pinecroft was a trial, Christmas a torture. The tension between Powel and Charlotte pervaded the holidays so heavily it couldn't be ignored. The inevitable showdown came a few days into the new year. What began as a disagreement over some petty matter escalated into a shouting match and climaxed with Powel ordering Charlotte to leave. She packed her bags and left for her parents' home in Greenwich, Connecticut, with Powel telling her how happy he was to be paying for her airplane ticket.

In March, he sued for divorce on grounds of extreme cruelty. She counter-sued on charges of gross neglect. The divorce was granted on June 20, 1960.

Powel found his way back to Bull Island for a little bit of welcome peace and quiet.

In mid-July he attended the National League meeting in Chicago, where he was obligated to deny yet another rumor that the Reds—no longer the Redlegs, the Red Scare having lessened enough to allow a name change once more—would move after the agreement he signed with the City of Cincinnati in 1958 expired.

Before the meeting, Gabe Paul came to him with a bombshell.

The league was continuing to expand. A new franchise was planned for Houston, Texas. They were interested in having him run it. He wanted, Gabe told Powel, to leave the Reds.

Powel wouldn't hear of it.

He told Gabe he was essential to the team, that the organization would not be the same without him. He talked Paul into holding off his decision until the end of the season. That fall, back in Cincinnati, Powel marked his seventy-fourth birthday by watching the first Kennedy-Nixon debate on television. In October, he returned to Bull Island. He found that he was less interested in hunting than just taking long horseback rides or lounging around the farm, reading and talking with the help.

On October 24, Powel received word that Gabe Paul had received a formal offer from the new team in Texas. He resolved to do whatever necessary to keep his long-time general manager; money was no object. He would go to Cincinnati as soon as possible to talk Paul out of the move. Fortunately, there was a connecting flight to Cincinnati out of Savannah late the next morning, Tuesday. Powel made arrangements to be on it.

Tuesday morning, Powel rode a motor launch to the mainland and took a car to the airport. He hurried into the terminal. Just inside the entrance, he paused.

He felt, all at once, a rush of dizziness and pain.

The next thing he knew he was on the floor.

Within minutes he was in an ambulance and on the way to the local hospital, where doctors quickly confirmed what Powel already suspected: he had suffered a mild heart attack. By mid-afternoon he was resting in a private room, having telephoned Lewis, who contacted the rest of the family and Powel's doctors in Cincinnati.

Most men in that position would have stayed right where they were for a good long chunk of time. Not Powel. He was released after three days and flew to Cincinnati, where he met with Gabe Paul a week later.

To Powel's dismay, Paul was set on leaving. The opportunity to build a team from scratch was a once-in-a-lifetime chance.

Reluctantly, Powel accepted his resignation.

Soon after, Bill DeWitt was named general manager; yet even as Powel was recovering, more rumors about the Reds leaving Cincinnati surfaced. Harry Wismer, who owned the New York Titans football team, had announced that he was forming a syndicate to buy the team. Wismer, however, hadn't even spoken with Powel. As soon as he heard the rumor, Powel got the man on the telephone and made it quite clear that no one—least of all a New Yorker—was buying his team. The Reds were staying in Cincinnati. Period.

· · · · · ·

Christmas came and went; 1960 followed in its wake. The second week of January, 1961, found Powel back at Bull Island. Doctors had told him to avoid strenuous activities—horseback riding included. The hell with that, Powel said. He bought a Studebaker Lark convertible—one of the new compact cars—and modified it to accommodate his hunting gear.

He flew off to Tampa in February for spring training and then back to Bull Island a week or so later. Three days after his return, while walking from the island's dock to the sawmill, he collapsed. A worker nearby helped him to the house and summoned aid. Nobody needed to tell him what had happened this time—another heart attack.

Powel stayed two days in the Savannah hospital and then flew to Cincinnati, where his cardiologist admitted him to Holmes Hospital for tests. By the beginning of March he was back home at Pinecroft, reluctantly recuperating and looking forward to Opening Day.

Doctors had told him to take it easy, but that word was not in Powel's vocabulary. He was out jogging one day along Kipling Avenue. Merle Hutchinson, his chauffeur, drove right behind, just in case.

Lewis drove up alongside his brother.

Powel stopped. Lewis stopped and got out of the car. They talked. Nothing much of consequence: good to see you, how are you feeling, we'll get together soon. Lewis climbed back into his car. Powel watched him drive away, and then started jogging down the road again.

It was the last time the two men would see each other.

.   .   .   .   .   .

Opening Day of 1961 was set for Tuesday, April 11, against the Cubs.

Gabe Paul was in Houston; a great many of the Reds front-office staff were there with him. Bill DeWitt, already putting his own stamp on the franchise, had made a number of trades in the off-season, bringing in new infielders and a number of new pitchers. Powel had a good feeling about the team. He had a good feeling about DeWitt. No surprise, there. That was why he hired him, after all, and if there was one thing the passage of time had proven Powel was good at, it was judging a man's competence.

The morning of Tuesday, March 28, 1961, Powel woke early, as usual. By 6:15 a.m. he was down in the kitchen. The cook was there too, getting ready for the day. Powel walked into the living room, staggered, and then fell.

The ambulance was there in less than five minutes, but it was too late.

He was gone.

.   .   .   .   .   .

Two days later, at Spring Grove Cemetery, friends and family—two hundred or so of them—came to say goodbye. Floral tributes filled the small church on the cemetery grounds. Expressions of sympathy for Page and Edythe, for Lewis and Lew, for the family, came from all across the country.

Warren Giles was there and Bill DeWitt and dozens of others from baseball and Powel's other enterprises. The mayor of Cincinnati came, as did thirty members of the city's Commercial Club, who served as honorary pallbearers.

The Reverend Leroy Hall, of Grace Episcopal conducted services. A brief Masonic observance was held by members of the College Hill Lodge as well. No eulogy was given.

Tributes filled the papers that day and in the days that followed. Many of them came from local sportswriters, expressions of gratitude for keeping the Reds in town when they might otherwise have moved.

The Cincinnati Enquirer ran a lengthy editorial, titled "A Titan Passes," that praised Powel as much for his devotion to the city and his family as for his accomplishments. That devotion was to continue even after his death.

He'd put most of his money in trusts years earlier. His will now provided for the creation of a charitable organization, the Crosley Foundation, to which his after-tax assets—thousands of shares of Aerojet-General, TWA, and other corporations in which Powel had an interest—were given.

The foundation also received the Cincinnati Reds.

Powel's will further specified that profits from the Reds and other Crosley Foundation holdings were to go to "charitable, scientific, educational, and literary agencies and institutions." It urged the foundation to use every means possible to keep the Reds in Cincinnati.

Foundation trustees were Lewis, Edythe, Page and Stanley Kess, Powel's personal secretary, Dorothea Bauer, and his investment counselor, Thomas C. Haydock. Page was named president of the Reds, but Bill DeWitt actually ran the club and handled the baseball end of the business. Lewis was his business partner, signing the checks and overseeing—if not actually seeing to—day to day operations.

In Powel's honor, the players wore black armbands on their uniforms for the entire 1961 season. Behind the hitting of Vada Pinson and Frank Robinson, who won the Most Valuable Player award, and behind exceptional starting and relief pitching, the team won the National League pennant and moved on to the World Series, which they lost in five games to the Yankees. Shades of 1939: Powel would have been elated anyway. Lewis was happy in his brother's stead. He served as the Reds' de facto owner's representative at the New York games. He and Lucy got to taste, if very briefly, the life of baseball royalty. The next season, he was happy to return to his usual seats and to the role of a fan.

In 1962, the foundation sold the club to an ownership group headed by Bill DeWitt. Lewis stayed on to advise for a year. He and Lucy continued golfing, continued taking their trips to Florida. He went to Reds games as often as he could, keeping a meticulous scorecard as always, enjoying the hospitality of the staff he'd come to know over the years, getting to talk with the ballplayers, socializing with old friends, and making new ones. In 1963, a scrappy young infielder named Pete Rose, whose hustle reminded Lewis of old-time players like Edd Roush and Wahoo Sam, joined the team. The two men hit it off instantly. Rose was nothing if not a fan of those same old ballplayers Lewis admired.

It was, in a way, the best of times for him. He had his family; he had his farm; he had no pressure at all to do anything other than relax and enjoy the fruits of his labor. He continued to serve on the board of the Eye Bank and the Crosley Foundation. A member of the same Masonic Lodge as Powels Junior and Senior, he was also active in the organization's charities. He popped in on Bill DeWitt from time to time to offer advice and did the same with Clifford Coors at Northside Trust.

He and Lucy sold the house on Belmont Avenue, and moved to a single-story ranch on Loiswood Drive a few miles away, still in College Hill, of course. It had become too hard for her to get up and down the stairs in the old house. The new house had a long, deep lot, in which Lewis planted a garden. For a while, he continued to run Cross Acres Dairy, but it simply became too hard for Lucy to get down to the farm.

He gave it to Charlotte Jeanne and her husband. He bought Ellen and Bill McClure a home as well. Powel's old home—not just Pinecroft but the majority of the acreage surrounding it—was given to the Franciscan Sisters of the Poor, who established a retreat there. In 1969, a hospital was built on the grounds as well.

Lewis puttered around the garden, and Lucy bought him a riding mower so he could take care of the lawn. On one of their trips to Florida, Lucy suffered the first of what would be a debilitating series of strokes. She began to have trouble remembering things and became snappish and irritable. She'd go to sleep mad at Lewis over some petty infraction and wake up still angry but unable to remember why, which only made her even more upset.

She grew increasingly queasy and had trouble forcing herself to eat. One of the only foods she could stomach was Jello. Lewis called Ellen and asked if she could tell him how to make it.

The directions are on the box, she told him.

That's right, he said after a moment, and then hung up.

At seventy-eight years old, after more than a half-century of being served, Lewis Crosley learned how to cook.

. . . . .

In 1970, the Reds played their last game at Crosley Field. Down-town, waiting by the river, was a brand new ballpark, Riverfront Sta-dium, a multi-use facility with ample seating, parking, and easy access to the highway. The team bid Crosley Field goodbye in style, winning 5-4 on back-to-back home runs by Johnny Bench and Lee May. Lewis was there, of course. Though nervous as always before a crowd, he managed to say a few words, most of them about his brother, by then ten years gone. When the game was over, home plate was pulled up and flown by helicopter to Riverfront.

Two years later, Crosley Field was razed. Pete Rose, Jr., had the honor of sitting behind the wheel of the bulldozer and dropping the wrecking ball on the right-field bleachers.

. . . . .

In 1973, Lucy fell and broke her hip. She went first to the hospital, and then a nursing home to recover. She couldn't. Three months after the break, she was gone.

Lewis pushed on, still hearty, still six foot one, two hundred and ten pounds, the same height and weight he'd been in 1918, at the Third Engineer Training Camp. He had another dream now: he was going to live to be a hundred. He'd taken good care of himself his whole life, always exercised and eaten right. He began taking vitamins and studying the aging process. He'd set himself a task, and now he set out to accomplish it.

. . . . .

The Crosley Foundation put Powel's money to good use. They bestowed a large gift to the YMCA, which established the Powel Crosley, Jr., branch of the organization. The foundation gave to the Cincinnati Art Museum, to the Children's Hospital and Grace Episcopal Church, to the Cincinnati Symphony Orchestra and the

Cincinnati Natural History Museum. They established the Powel Crosley, Jr. Amateur Baseball Fund for Knothole baseball as well, and began work on a large broadcasting studio and operations center for Cincinnati's public television station, WCET. Lewis lent a hand with that project.

The foundation also set up a nature preserve on the outskirts of Cincinnati. Preserve officials soon ran into a problem. There was one patch of land that kept drying up in the summer heat. They'd irrigate it, but that approach made no difference. They asked the foundation for more money to buy land surrounding the preserve, to access other waterways.

Lewis came to the site, surveyed the problem, and made a recommendation.

Dig a hole, he said. A big hole. A big, deep, round hole, and fill it with gravel. When the rains come, the hole will hold the water for a spell, and then it'll leech out slowly and gradually.

Problem solved.

It wasn't necessarily the best solution, but it worked. It was military engineering—accuracy in execution yielding to the imperious demand for results.

.   .   .   .   .   .

In the spring of 1977, Lewis looked in the mirror and frowned. The skin under his eyes sagged so much the blood vessels were visible all the time. He decided to get minor cosmetic surgery to fix the problem.

In the hospital, the doctors discovered he had far worse things to worry about. A blood test revealed he had acute leukemia. They gave him three months, at most, to live. They asked him to consider hospitalization. He shouldn't be living alone. He should have part-time or even full-time care. He could certainly afford it.

The hell with that, he said, or words to that effect. He had a cleaning woman who came in once a week. Ellen asked him if he wouldn't be lonely living by himself. Lewis assured her that word was not in his vocabulary.

He had the surgery and drove himself back home.

. . . . .

In November 1978, a year and a half after Lewis received his three-months-to-live diagnosis, Ellen, about to go pick him up for an early dinner, got a phone call.

Don't bother getting in the car tonight Nellie, he told her. I don't feel well enough to go out.

That's all right, she said. I'll come over, and we'll eat in. So they did. Lewis seemed tired. He agreed that perhaps having someone else around, someone other than the cleaning woman, might be a good idea.

Around 7:30, back home, Ellen got another call.

Lewis was having trouble walking. One foot is kind of flopping around, he told her. He had loaned their in-laws Lucy's walker because they weren't using it anymore, and he wondered if Ellen would mind bringing it to him, so he could get around. Tomorrow would be fine.

I'll bring it to you tonight, she said, and with her husband, she went to pick it up.

They arrived at Loiswood around 9:00. Ellen rang the doorbell. There was no answer.

She went inside and found her father lying on the ground, unconscious, but breathing deeply. She talked to him, but he wouldn't wake up.

She called the operator, who summoned help. Ambulances arrived. Paramedics loaded Lewis onto a stretcher and took him to the closest hospital—Providence Hospital on Kipling Road, on the grounds of the Franciscan retreat that now occupied what had once been his brother's estate.

Lewis had requested no heroics. They gave him a glucose drip to make him comfortable. He never woke up again.

On November 6, 1978, at around 6:00 a.m., in the shadow of

the mansion he'd helped Powel build, not far from where their eight-dollar car had run and the old Pigeye school had stood, in plain sight of the water tower they'd climbed and the town hall where the Harko had been unveiled, where really the whole thing—Insyde Tyres, the Icyball, WLW, and the Crosley Radio Corporation—had begun, Lewis Crosley passed on.

A few days later, he followed Powel one final time, to a plot of land in Spring Grove Cemetery, chosen by the two of them for its view of College Hill and the boyhood neighborhood they shared. There, they were buried side-by-side.

There, the story ends.

EPILOGUE

*"Within a century to come, what diversity of character
will meet within this field of death!"*

**~ The Honorable John MacLean, at the consecration
of Spring Grove Cemetery**

There is no Crosley legacy. The company, for all practical purposes, died that August day in 1945 when Powel sold it to AVCO, subsumed in a corporate shell that robbed it of everything that had made it a success: the ability to spot a market need, apply technology, and to create a consumer-friendly product; the know-how to manufacture and sell that product en masse to the buying public. What they lacked, in other words, was Powel and Lewis. The new Crosley Corporation, a division of AVCO industries, longed for someone with the elder brother's gift of vision, for someone with the younger's can-do attitude.

AVCO ended up hiring twenty-six people to fill Lewis's shoes.

They never found anyone to replace Powel.

They ended up combining Crosley's line of products with those of another manufacturer, Bendix, and incorporating both of them into the home appliance division of the larger corporate structure, which tells you all you need to know about why they needed those twenty-six people to do one man's job.

In 1956, they closed down the Crosley division altogether.

In 1976, one of the original Crosley distributors, Buddy Dixson, started a new line of household appliances bearing the same name. They are made overseas, for the most part. The company later branched into reproductions of the original Crosley radios.

Crosley's broadcasting legacy fared much better: Ruth Lyons repeated her radio success on television, essentially creating the daytime talk industry. Her *50-50 Club* begat Phil Donahue's show, which begat Oprah Winfrey. WLWT is still on the air, as part of Hearst-Argyle Communications.

So is WLW radio, broadcasting at 700 on the dial, right where Powel and Lewis put it. The FCC, however, still limits transmitter power to fifty thousand watts. There never was, nor likely will be, a second Nation's Station, though WLW revived the slogan in the early years of this century.

It wasn't just the company that died in 1945; it was Powel's personal legacy, his legend as well, though it probably would be more correct to say that his legacy died with his son, and grandson, in Florida and Korea. Unlike David Sarnoff, who had his son Robert to carry forward the family name, to take charge of not just RCA but his father's story, there was no Crosley to fill Powel's shoes, to take stewardship of the family legacy.

This book was written, in large part, to fill that void.

In 1988, the Crosley Foundation funded a documentary on WCET, Cincinnati's public television station, titled *Powel Crosley and the 20th Century*. They took a camera inside the Arlington Street building and went into Powel's office, which at the time was being used as a boardroom. The narrator—Bill Nimmo, a WLW alumnus who had gotten his start listening to Peter Grant's broadcasts—reminisced about the glory days of WLW, marveled at the mahogany and cherry wood throughout Powel's office, at the stained glass windows he'd had installed.

It didn't look like much: a faded remnant of an empire few remember.

Edythe was ninety-one years old when the video was made. On camera, with the older brother she taught the fox trot long gone, she revealed at last that it was Powel, Sr., who lent his son five hundred dollars to buy into the American Automobile Accessories Company.

Also appearing in the production were Gabe Paul, Lew Crosley, Elmer Hentz and Tom Muir, Powel III's boyhood friend, who recalled waiting on the Davey Avenue porch when father and son came home from Precision Equipment sans crystal set, way back on Washington's Birthday, 1921. Hentz, for his part, reminisced about the day he and Powel convinced L.T. Milnor of Cincinnati that radio actually worked. Lew Crosley shared fond memories of the man who, for all intents and purposes, was his father, whom he, nonetheless, referred to as "the boss."

The last words—the most moving words—in the entire documentary belonged to Gabe Paul, who said "There aren't many things I regret that happened in the fifty-eight years I was in baseball. I think I regret more than anything having left him."

Paul also felt that Powel would have been happiest if the car had succeeded, which is probably true.

But he wouldn't have been satisfied. Satisfaction for Powel was fleeting. Something different burned inside him—it was his blessing, and his curse. He couldn't sit still. He couldn't help but get up and look around the corner, take a peek at what was coming, see how he might make a place for himself in it.

Lewis suffered no such affliction. He was happy and satisfied with what he had. Work wasn't who he was; work was what he did. Work was the task Powel set in front of him. Where his brother led, Lewis was compelled to follow.

The documentary about Powel was made almost twenty years ago. The Arlington Street building is now falling down. The mahogany is long gone, the stained-glass windows broken and cracked. Pinecroft is a faded memory too, empty of furniture, personality, Gwendolyn's gardens gone, the swimming pool filled in, the lake shrunken, the remains of the estate grounds dominated by the hospital. The house itself seems shrunken somehow, much smaller than its thirteen thousand square feet.

Powel III's house stands across the street as a private home.

Lewis and Lucy's Belmont Avenue home is still there, as is their house on Loiswood Drive.

Powel's Sarasota mansion is now known by the name Seagate once more. It's owned by the county, which rents it out for weddings, balls, corporate events, and other social occasions. One of the highlights of their season is the annual Festival of Trees in December. A large number of Crosley car owners hold one of their regional meets at Seagate over two days of the week-long festival and many examples of Crosley automobiles are displayed in the backyard by Sarasota Bay.

Cat Cay is still a vacation resort, MacGregor Bay still a vacation retreat, a favorite destination for Page's children. Page herself is gone now, as is Stan Kess, as is Edythe, and Lew Crosley too, and Charlotte Crosley Runck. When she died, her father's Cross Acres farm passed to Bud, and when he remarried, to his second wife's family.

Their son Renny has a farm of his own next to it.

There is a plaque where Crosley Field used to stand, in the middle of a parking lot on Western Avenue. It's supposed to represent the location of home plate.

As of this writing, it's in the wrong place.

It's difficult to recapture the past, to know exactly what happened and when and where. And the most difficult question to answer is why. Powel Crosley achieved what is commonly seen as the American dream. He attained fame and fortune, probably to a greater degree than even he had hoped. And yet he could not be satisfied.

If there's a leitmotif for Powel's life, it's the car, his Rosebud.

In the beginning, the car clinched the bet with the father. That bet, of course, was about much more than money. It was about, in part, the son proving himself to the father. For a gifted first-born son, expectations are higher. His character is defined, finally, by achievement.

After the success of the little car, Powel endured his late teens and twenties as his father's problem: unable to finish college; losing ten thousand dollars, a fortune at the time, that his father had gathered from friends; unable to hold a job of consequence for ten years.

When success came, it did not eradicate those failures, and so Powel Crosley created the myth of Powel Crosley, or rather, hired a *New York Times* reporter-turned-publicist to do it for him.

Another motivation that drove him relentlessly was the loss of home and possessions both boys suffered while very young, watching all they knew of life driven away after their father lost everything in the Panic of 1893. The fear of such a thing happening again settled deeply into them, particularly into Powel, for whom no fortune was ever quite big enough to protect him and his family.

And, in some ways, he was right.

His millions could not keep his son safe from a failed marriage or, worse, the deadly sting of a bee. The fortune could not keep his grandson from dying in battle in Korea. The state-of-the-art medical care he provided for Gwendolyn could not keep her alive.

Nor could it ultimately sate the gnaw of need inside him to find, at last, peace and satisfaction. In that way Powel epitomizes a fundamental quality of the American spirit—the hunger to be on the move, the belief in a place just beyond the next bend that holds untold pleasures and will, in the end, be good enough to make us happy. Powel is the America of movement and materialism, of the belief that wealth can satisfy and protect, can calm our fears and restless ambitions.

Lewis, conversely, is the other America, the humbler, practical spirit seeking the simplicity of working the land, of taking pleasure in making things grow and satisfaction in a job well done. His happiness at the end of life and Powel's unhappiness suggest that their story, in a way, is a cautionary tale or, at least, an instructive one. Powel set out to conquer the world and, one could say, did just that, overcoming obstacles and prevailing against moments of doubt to fashion an empire: from the world's largest manufacturer of radios, to the world's most powerful radio station, to the World Series, to the World's Fair, to helping America win World War II.

Somehow, it wasn't enough.

"My brother could never get it out of his head that he had to build a car," Lewis said, and one wonders if he understood the significance of that car to Powel, what it symbolized somewhere deep in his brother's heart. If the little Crosley car had succeeded, as some have suggested, would Powel have been, at last, content? Probably not.

Because the car, by that point, had become something else in Powel's powerful imagination—the embodiment of qualities that exist only in a child's innocent dreams. It would have had to recapture for him the elation of watching Lewis, his beloved brother and most trusted friend, skitter down the road toward the post office, moving, in a miracle they'd built themselves, faster than his father and the rest of the adults had ever moved in their horse-drawn buggies; it would have had to embody the joy of hearing the little engine they'd attached to a buckboard split with a thrilling roar the tranquility of a blue-skied long-ago day, grown more blue and beautiful with every passing year; it would have had to sustain the ecstasy of creating, to the wonderment of a doubting world, a sort of magic. It would have had to be what life, ultimately, can never be for more than a moment. It would have had to be perfect.

Perhaps it's no coincidence that, when given the chance to build a car, Powel chose to make it small. Finding a market niche aside, he envisioned and created a little car, one that still possesses an undeniable charm largely because it is so small. To the modern eye it looks almost comical. It looks innocent. It looks like a car sprung from the mind of a boy—or a man seeking to find something in the past that, while seemingly close enough to touch, is forever lost.

The brothers built their first car in a different world, one not far removed from the days of the horse and buggy, the days before the telephone and the Federal income tax and the page after page of government regulations prospective entrepreneurs now have to wade through to bring their products to market. Powel got a taste of the world to come, and that bureaucracy, when he fought George Payne and the FCC on superpower. He didn't like that fight, but he didn't back away from it. He, like his brother, was his father's son, through and through. If at first you didn't succeed, you tried and tried and tried again.

Back in that world of men with waxed mustaches and ladies in petticoats, Colerain Avenue was a dirt road. When farmers from Indiana and points north drove their hogs south to market along that road, the constant pounding of hooves turned the dirt to muck. The mud grew so deep, the travel so difficult, that the droves were hard-pressed to make more than a few miles a day.

The speed limit on Colerain now is fifty miles per hour. Cars pay little attention to it. It's easy enough to picture Powel in one of them, zooming along in the left lane, impatient to get where he was going. He'd be doing ten other things at the same time, of course—multitasking, to use the current vernacular. Listening to the radio, talking on his cell-phone, planning his next getaway, probably to a remote island somewhere, where the fishing was good. You can see him ending one call, and then immediately making another. Another trip, another product, another way to leapfrog past the competition, undercut them in price and features and value for their money. To make it better. To make it cost less. He'd be talking about one thing, and yet, in his mind…

Already moving on to the next.

You can picture Lewis on the other end of a few of those calls, setting down the phone, and trying to figure out how in the world to accomplish the impossible task his brother had just set out for him, and then rolling up his sleeves and getting to work, knowing he'd find a way. That was his part of the job.

Powel dreamt it, Lewis built it.

They were a team.

THE END

NOTES

PART I
BIRTH

Epigraph: www.nasm.si.edu/Wrightbrothers/who/ 1884/index.cfm

CHAPTER 1

"..larger than life heroes and villains..."—Hurt, *The Ohio Frontier...*

Background information on Ohio—Catton, *The Frontier Republic*; Jordan, *Ohio Comes of Age*.

Background information on Cincinnati's early history—Perry, *Vas You Ever...*Federal Writers Project, all listed guides.

Details on Powel, Sr.'s, boyhood and early career—Lewis Crosley, interview with Elvira Adams; Powel Crosley Jr., interview with Ohio State Archaeological Society; Keller, 'Powel Crosley Jr. And the Dawn of Wireless.'

Importance of McGuffey Readers—Smith, "William Holmes McGuffey..."; McGuffey, *The Annotated McGuffey*; Watts, *The People's Tycoon*.

Details on tobacco farming, farmer's life—Jordan, ibid.

"...evinced a love for books..."—Roe, *Cincinnati: The Queen City*.

"close application and studious disposition..."—Roe, ibid.

"...as spacious and well-stocked...", "sweetmeats...," "oysters..." etc.—Federal Writer's Project , *Cincinnati, A Guide....*

"....while they're riding..."—verse from Jordan, ibid.

Details on Powel, Sr.'s, Law School Years—Bentley Archives, University of Michigan.

"...ability in argument..."—Roe, ibid.

"a noisy, beery, brawling summer."—Allen, *Cincinnati Reds*. "dollar for dollar"—Keller, ibid.

CHAPTER 2

Background on College Hill—Cincinnati Historical Society, *Old College Hill*; Smiddy, *A Little Piece of Paradise...*

"...and let them roll...,"—Cincinnati Historical Society, ibid.

Powel, Jr.'s, Lewis's early years—Interviews with Ohio State Archaeological Society, Elva Adams; Keller, ibid.

Details on Cincinnati Street Life—Seasongood, "Remembrances...;" Perry, *Vas You Ever...*

Background on Edison—
www.pbs.org/wgbh/amex/edison/filmmore/description.html

Vaudeville background—S.D., Trav. *The Book That Made Vaudeville Famous.*

"...as the sepsis increases..."—*The Eclectic Practice of Medicine*, by Rolla L. Thomas, M.S., M.D. (1907), as cited at www.henriettesherbal.com.

Description of Powel, Jr.,—Davis, "The Crosley Touch – And Go!"; Powel Crosley, Jr., interview w/Ohio State Archaeological Society.

CHAPTER 3

Background on Cincinnati Auto Industry—Decamp, "Motown on the Ohio."

Background on turn-of-the-century football—Boemeke, et al, *Anticipating Total War.*

"You can't get people...", "They spoil the bicycling..."—
Waitley, *The Roads We Traveled.*

Powel, Lewis's University of Cincinnati Activities:—*The Cincinnatian*, Various years.

"a motor car for the great multitude..."—www.pbs.org/wgbh/aso/data-bank/entries/dt13as.html

CHAPTER 4

"My knees were knocking..."—*Cincinnati Times-Star*. Opportunity Knocked More Than Once." March 28, 1925.

Background on auto industry: Kollins, *Pioneers...*—Clymer, various.

"I interested some men with money..."—May, "The Story of Powel Crosley..."

"...the greatest disappointment in..."—May, ibid.

Background on University of Cincinnati Co-op engineering program:—http://www.ase.uc.edu/about/history.html

Background on early wireless, Jack Binns, etc.:—Douglas, *Inventing American Broadcasting*.

"...all kinds of electrical junk..."—Douglas, ibid.

Background on pre-World War I War Plans—Keegan, *The First World War*.

"... I was a rolling stone..."—Crosley, "50 Jobs in 50 Years..." —Interview, Rusty McClure.

CHAPTER 5

Lewis Crosley nervous breakdown, years in Houston, courtship of Lucy Johnson—Interview, Renny Runck.

"I rode with Powel..."—Walz, Gene. *Powel Crosley Jr. and the 20th Century*.

Lewis and Lucy Crosley in Loveland—Interviews, Ellen McClure, Rusty McClure, Renny Runck.

Background on Loveland, turn-of-the-century farming practices—www.communitypress.com/LovelandOH/Resources/info history_.html; www.ohiohistorycentral.org/entry.php?rec=1579

"...a new epoch..."—Douglas, ibid.

Telegrams from Tsar Nicholas/Kaiser Wilhelm:—
www.firstworldwar.com/source/willynicky.htm

Details on German massacres in Belgium—Taylor, *The German Terror...*

"Upon Russia..."—Marshall, "Count Von Bernstoff Gives Germany's Point of View."

"We do not beg for sympathy..."—Wittke, *German-Americans and the World War*, p. 26.

CHAPTER 6

Lewis Crosley's Corps of Engineers Experiences:—Crosley, Interview with John Knoepfle; National Archives, Civilian Records Division.

"...his character...," "...he would make..."—Letters in Lewis Crosley's Civilian Personnel Record File.

"I was optimistic..."—Crosley, Powel, "50 Jobs in 50 years."

"My brother was a gambler..."—Lewis Crosley, interview with Lawrence Lichty.

"I went into every detail myself."—Smith, *The Genius of Powel Crosley, Jr.*

CHAPTER 7

War background throughout: Keegan, ibid. Wilmott, *The First World War*.

Details on Lewis Crosley's Corps of Engineers Experience, Corps background: Anderson, Bone, Crosley, interviews with Knoepfle.

Details on Lewis Crosley's/28th Engineers Camp Meade Training: National Archives RG 391.

'made a respectable showing'—ibid.

'Soldiers in France Calling for Matty,'—*The New York Times*, April 25, 1918.

'like a cool drink in an arid desert'—Crosley, "50 Jobs..."

CHAPTER 8

War background throughout: Keegan, ibid; Wilmott, ibid; Gregory, *Argonne 1918.*

Supply/construction statistics St. Nazaire: U.S. Army Center, *The U.S. in World War I, Volume 14, Report of the Transportation Office.*

St. Nazaire reference: U.S. Army Center, ibid: Army Signal Corps Films.

28th Engineers Activities St. Nazaire, Clermont-en-Argonne, etc.: National Archives RG 391.

Details on Lewis Crosley's St. Nazaire Experiences: Interview, Rusty McClure.

Mathewson, Cobb Training Accident: Stump, *Cobb: A Biography.*

28th pushes east reference: U.S. Army Signal Corps Film, National Archives RG 391.

Details on Meuse-Argonne Battle Plans; U.S. Army Center, *The U.S. in World War I, Meuse-Argonne Operations.*

"The enemy is in retreat...," "I am counting..."—ibid. Lewis Crosley's actions at Clermont-en-Argonne—Interview, Rusty McClure.

Lewis Crosley's activities post-armistice—National Archives, RG 391.

Kidnapping the Kaiser—Warfield, *The Roaring Redhead.*

Lewis Crosley letters from/to R.R. Jones—National Archives, L. Crosley Civilian Personnel File.

CHAPTER 9

"He wanted to know the new way..."—Jennings, *Dreams Do Come True...*

Formation of RCA; Wireless Market Conditions—Barnouw, *Tower of Babel*; Archer, *History of Radio to 1926*; Goldsmith, Lescarboura, *This Thing Called Broadcasting.*

Conrad, Davis, $10 Radio Sets—After Barnouw, ibid.

NOTES

PART II
BOOM

Epigraph: http://www.city-journal.org/html/104urbanities-themoral.html

CHAPTER 10

General Radio Background throughout; Barnouw, ibid; Archer, ibid; Goldsmith, Lescarboura, ibid; White, www.earlyradiohistory.us

"The idea of charging that much..."—Walz, ibid.

"I have in mind a plan of development..."—Sarnoff, as quoted in Barnow, ibid, p. 78.

"I don't know whether my son or I..."—May, The Story of Powel Crosley...

Details on Crosley radio ads—QSC, Radio Broadcast advertiser, various.

Details on Armstrong license—Barnouw, ibid; MacLaurin, Invention and Innovation...

Early Harko Assembly-line problems—Lewis Crosley, interview with Lichty.

"They couldn't get anything out right..."—ibid

CHAPTER 11

General Radio Background throughout; Barnouw, ibid; Archer, ibid; Goldsmith, Lescarboura, ibid; White, ibid; McLaurin, ibid; Balk, The rise of radio...

Powel's encounter with James Carroll—Lewis Crosley, interviews with Benningus, Lichty...

"She was on this thing..."—ibid.

Details of Powel's Miami River vacation spot—ibid.

"the genius of the American boy"—after Barnouw, ibid, p. 83.

"for the glory of appearing..."—"Mr. Crosley Recalls..."

"We didn't have…"—L. Crosley, Lichty interview.

CHAPTER 12

General Radio Background: as above.

General background on WLW history—Lichty, *The Nation's Station.*

Background on vacuum tube patent issues—MacLaurin, ibid; Barnouw, ibid; Tyne, *The Saga of the Vacuum Tube.*

Christy Mathewson—Outlook, 'Christy Mathewson;' *Los Angeles Times.* "Mathewson is Long on Ruth," September 11, 1922.

Details on Early WLW broadcasts—Lichty, ibid.

CHAPTER 13

General Radio Background: as above.

Details of Edythe Chatfield's wedding: Walz, ibid; L.Crosley, interview with L.Lichty; May, The Story of Powel Crosley…

Lewis interviews WMH employees—L. Crosley, interview with L. Lichty.

Details re: regenerative circuit assembly—L. Crosley, ibid.

…the largest radio manufacturer in the world—Balk, ibid.

Powel/Lewis/Lucy interpersonal relationships—Interviews Ellen McClure, Rusty McClure, R. Runck

RCA lawsuit details—Barnouw, ibid; WESTINGHOUSE ELECTRIC & MFG. CO. v. TRI-CITY RADIO ELECTRIC SUPPLY CO. et al.; No. 6858; Circuit Court of Appeals, Eighth Circuit; 23 F.2d 628; 1927 U.S. App. LEXIS 3200; December 28, 1927.

AT&T legal policies—after Barnouw, ibid.

"the hundreds of stations"—ibid.

WLW programs, personnel—Lichty, ibid.

"…the men are dancing around the ring." – ibid.

Fred Smith compositions—Lichty, ibid.

Details on formation of NAB, early meetings—Library of American Broadcasting/National Association of Broadcasters Archives.

CHAPTER 14

General Radio Background—as above.

Details on NAB meetings—as above.

Lewis Crosley house purchase, Charlotte Jeanne health problems—Interview, Ellen McClure.

Lewis Crosley First Reds Broadcast—Interview, Rusty McClure.

WLW Broadcasting Efforts, background—Lichty, ibid.

NAB meeting details—NAB archives.

Crosley/Roenick lawsuit—Lichty, ibid; *Crosley Radio Weekly*, "Freedom of the Air is Won..."

RCA Network Development , conflict with AT&T—Goldsmith, Lescarboura, ibid; Barnouw, ibid; Archer, *Big Business & Radio*.

Details of First Reds Broadcast—*Crosley Radio Weekly*, "Listeners Pleased..."

"In view of the unfriendly attitude..."—*Crosley Radio Weekly*, "Freedom of the Air..."

CHAPTER 15

General Radio Background—As above. Also Archer, *Big Business and Radio*; Barnouw, *The Golden Web*.

WLW Background, Personalities, Programs—Lichty, ibid.

Lewis Crosley Personal Life—Interviews, Ellen McClure, Rusty McClure, Renny Runck.

Skywave/Merle Tuve background—Department of Terrestrial Magnetism Archives; Brown, *Centennial History...*

CHAPTER 16

General Radio Background—as above.

WLW Background—as above.

"I'm glad I have…"—L.Crosley, Lichty interview.

Founding of NBC—Barnouw, *The Golden Web*; Archer, *Big Business and Radio.*

GE refrigeration efforts—Nagengast, "It's A Cool Story."

NAB Meeting Details; Powel/George Coats argument—NAB Archives; Barnouw, ibid; Archer, ibid.

Powel Crosley personal life—Henshaw, ibid.

Details of Pinecroft Construction—Jennings, ibid.

Lewis Crosley Personal life—Interviews Ellen McClure, Rusty McClure.

Reds Ownership Changes—Allen, ibid.

CHAPTER 17

Icyball Development—L. Crosley, Lichty interview.

Lewis Crosley personal life—Interviews, Ellen McClure, Renny Runck.

National Air Show background, Crosley Publicity Efforts—*Crosley Broadcaster*, Various issues.

Lewis Crosley on Episcopal Church Vestry—Interviews, Laura Chace, Ellen McClure.

"a terrible job"—L. Crosley, Lichty interview.

Details on Sleepy Hollow construction, outfitting—Jennings, ibid.

Network development—Barnouw, *Golden Web*; Archer, *Big Business & Radio.*

WLW Background, Personnel, Programming—Lichty, ibid.

"the biggest single figure in Radio today"—*The Philadelphia Record*, November 16, 1924.

Lewis Crosley's nervous breakdown—Interview, Renny Runck.

Lewis Crosley's vacation—*Crosley Broadcaster*, March 15, 1928.

Gwendolyn Crosley's feelings—Interviews, Ellen McClure, Renny Runck.

CHAPTER 18

"...a great guy for remedies..."—L. Crosley, Lichty interview.

Details on Powel's Tarpon Fishing—Crosley, "My First Tarpon."

"for the first three-quarters...,"; "so stiff and numb...,"; "for once in my life..."—ibid.

Details on Sarasota Construction—*Crosley Broadcaster*, various issues. Interview, Neill Prew.

Arlington Street Construction—*Crosley Broadcaster*, various issues; Heinl, Off the Antenna.

Reds ownership dealings—Allen, *Cincinnati Reds*.

Stock Market Activity—Allen, *Only Yesterday*; *Cincinnati Enquirer, various issues.*

"...I don't know."—Heinl, Off the Antenna.

CHAPTER 19

Stock market crash, events of October 1929—after Allen, *Only Yesterday*. *Cincinnati Enquirer*, various issues.

"the rout was underway..."—ibid.

Reds ownership dealings, Larry Macphail activities—Allen, *Cincinnati Reds*; Warfield, *The Roaring Redhead*.

Details on Seagate Construction—Jennings, ibid; interview with Neill Prew; *Sarasota Herald*, various issues.

Lewis Crosley's feelings on Sarasota construction—Interview, Rusty McClure.

Construction/details on WLW Studios—*Crosley Broadcaster*, various issues; Lichty, ibid.

WLW personnel/programming—Lichty, ibid; *Crosley Broadcaster*, various issues.

Ruth Nichols background, activities—Nichols, *Wings for Life*; *Crosley Broadcaster*, various issues.

CHAPTER 20

"I pointed out..."—Nichols, ibid.

Spring Grove Cemetery Plot Background—Interviews Ellen McClure, Rusty McClure.

Building the Crosley Refrigerator/"Throw it in the ash can..."— Segal, "One City's..."

WLW personnel/programming—Lichty, ibid.

"A perfect radio program..."—Keller, ibid.

Radio background—Barnouw, *The Golden Web*; Archer, *Big Business &...*

Powel, Sr., and the tomato plants—Interview, Ellen McClure.

Radio as symbol—after Barnouw, ibid.

"The use of this magic multiplier..."—*Crosley Broadcaster*, "Crosley Dedicates..."

CHAPTER 21

Shelvador development—Crosley, "50 Jobs...;" Interview, Rusty McClure.

"We bumped out the door..."—L. Crosley, interview L. Lichty.

Details, antenna construction—Lichty, ibid; Stinger, "The Eminent Years..."; *Crosley Broadcaster*, various issues.

Red Barber's arrival/departure—Barber, *Rhubarb...*

Lew Crosley's birth, William Shelton's intentions—Interviews, Neill Prew, Ellen McClure, Rusty McClure.

MacPhail takes over the Reds/Reamy Field Arranges Lunch—Allen, *Cincinnati Reds*; Warfield, *The Roaring Redhead*.

Details, transmitter construction—L.Crosley, Lichty interview; Lichty, ibid; Stinger, ibid; *Crosley Broadcaster*, various issues; Crosley Corporation, "A Trip Through WLW."

Gilman Shelton Returns/Dutch arrives—Interviews, Ellen McClure, Rusty McClure; Jennings, ibid.

CHAPTER 22

MacPhail/Powel Discussions—Allen, ibid; Warfield, ibid; L. Crosley, Lichty interview.

Shelton/Dutch—Interviews, Ellen McClure, Rusty McClure.

"...with good clothes..."—*Time*, February 19, 1933.

Reston departs/Barber returns—Barber, *Rhubarb...*

"You mean the boy..."—ibid.

"so cute they made the customers..."—Allen, ibid.

Superpower problems/engineering crew—L. Crosley, Lichty interview; Lichty, ibid.

Cries of profiteering—after Barnouw, *Golden Web*.

Lewis Crosley's farm—Interviews, Renny Runck, Ellen McClure.

WLW Super-power celebration/"with this greater and greater audience has come..."—*Crosley Broadcaster*, various issues; Perry, *Not Just A Sound....*

Reichsender Programming/"We wish to safeguard..."—Rolo, *Radio Goes To War.*

WLW personnel/programming—Lichty, ibid.

Skywave Antenna construction—L. Crosley, Lichty interview; Stinger, ibid; *Crosley Broadcaster*, various issues.

CHAPTER 23

Night Baseball at N.L. Meetings—*The New York Times*, various issues; Warfield, ibid.

"Not in my lifetime;" "I'll never vote…;" "Bush league stuff"—Warfield, ibid.

"Sure it would draw…"—*The New York Times*, "Cronin Attacks Night Games as Joke," February 12, 1935.

Babe Ruth Background—*The New York Times*, "Reds Tried to Get Ruth," December 30, 1933; "Ruth Will Draw 500,000 Fans to National League, Says Frick," March 17, 1935; *The New York Times*, various dates.

"…all manner of injuries…"—Cuddy, "Night Ball Wins Favor…"

The Duesenberg—Interview, Ellen McClure.

"You can go to work…"—*Crosley Broadcaster*, "Crosley's Son Reaches Mike."

Union Troubles—Rutgers Archive; Interviews, Ellen McClure, Rusty McClure.

Norman Corwin's tenure at WLW—Interview, Norman Corwin.

Joe Julian's tenure at WLW—Julian, *This Was Radio*.

"flusterpropaganda"—Rolo, ibid.

WLW personnel/programming—Lichty, ibid.

"There is a tendency…"—*Time*, October 25, 1937.

"I think we've been fortunate…"—*Sarasota Herald*, May 1929.

CHAPTER 24

Car Industry Statistics—Luger, *Corporate Power…*

Powel/Lewis Debate The Car—L. Crosley, interview L. Lichty; L. Crosley, interview F. Benningus.

"Lord Pinecroft"—Interview, Renny Runck.

Xervac background—L. Crosley, interview L. Lichty.

William Hedges tenure at WLW—Hedges, interview with Hill.

Powel's reputation/'some kind of record'—Perry, *Not Just A Sound*.

Superpower controversy—Lichty, ibid; Foust, *Big Voices…*

CHAPTER 25

WLW personnel/programming—Lichty, ibid.

The 1937 Flood—*Cincinnati Enquirer, Cincinnati Post, Crosley Broadcaster*, various issues; Harris, *Microphone Memoirs.*

Superpower controversy—Lichty, ibid; Foust, ibid; *The New York Times*, various dates.

"Upon receiving…"; "On June 30…"—"Accuses Crosley of FCC Data Delay." *The New York Times*, August 16, 1937.

Sarasota background, developments—Interviews Neill Prew, Steve Belack; Jennings, ibid.

Reds background, McKechnie hiring—Allen, ibid; Baskin, Wheeler, *The Cincinnati Game.*

Doris Day background—Hotchner, *Doris Day…*

"Such operation…"—Foust, ibid.

"Powel wouldn't wait…"—L. Crosley, Lichty interview.

"…in large measure would be destroyed."—Lichty, ibid.

"Our duty to ourselves…"—ibid.

CHAPTER 26

Gwendolyn's death/funeral—Interviews, Ellen McClure, Rusty McClure; Jennings, ibid; *Cincinnati Enquirer, Post*, various issues.

Crosley Car Development/Initial Publicity—Interviews with Ellen McClure, Rusty McClure; L. Crosley, Lichty interview; Jennings, ibid; Lichty, ibid; *Cincinnati Enquirer, The New York Times*, various dates; *Time*, "Little Fellow."

WLW personnel/programming—Lichty, ibid: *Crosley Broadcaster*, various issues.

"…a quizzical expression."—Gelernter, *The Lost World…*

"I have been dreaming…"—"Two Cylinder, Aviation-Type Car on Market." *Chicago Tribune*, April 29, 1939.

WWII background—Mosley, et al, *The Battle of Britain*; Sulzburger, et al, *The American Heritage Picture History...*; Wernick, et al, *Blitzkrieg* .

Reds in the 1939 series—Allen, ibid; Baskin, Wheeler, ibid.

Radio in WWII—Barnouw, *The Golden Web;* Blue, *Words at War.*

Merle Tuve listening to the Battle of Britain—after Abelson, "Merle Antony Tuve."

Anti-aircraft fire effectiveness—Hartcup, *The Effect of Science...*

PART III
BATTLE

CHAPTER 27

Reds 1940 Season/Series—Allen, ibid; Baskin, Wheeler, ibid.

"...before a gal could cross..."—Baskin, Wheeler, ibid.

Powel III tuberculosis—Interview, Ellen McClure.

"...just weren't the same."—ibid.

Lewis Crosley's wartime activities—Interviews Ellen McClure, Rusty McClure, Renny Runck; L. Crosley, interview L. Lichty, interview F. Benningus; Jennings, ibid; Lichty, ibid.

WLW personnel/programming—Lichty, ibid; *Crosley Broadcaster*, various issues.

Powel's wartime auto plans/Jeep Development—Allen, *Jeep*; Crismon, *U.S. Military Wheeled Vehicles*; Jennings, ibid; Jeudy, *The Jeep.*

Charlotte Jeanne/Bud Runck—Interview, Renny Runck.

Lewis Crosley's cook—Interview, Ellen McClure, Rusty McClure.

Crosley Plant sabotage/FBI involvement—Crosley Corporation FBI File.

"I thought you might be interested in this matter..." Letter of J. Edgar Hoover to Nelson Rockefeller, October 21, 1940 from FBI Crosley Corporation files.

Wartime radio propaganda background—Barnouw, ibid; Blue, ibid; Laurie, *The Propaganda Warriors*; Margolin, *Paper Bullets*; Rolo, ibid; Shulman, *The Voice of America*.

"I call upon all loyal citizens..." Text of FDR's proclamation: http://www.yale.edu/lawweb/avalon/presiden/proclamations/frproc01.htm

CHAPTER 28

NDRC Background/Formation—Rhodes, *The Making of The Atomic Bomb*; http://www.vectorsite.net/ttwiz5.html

Early Development Proximity Fuze/Crosley Corporation—Baldwin, *The Deadly Fuze*; Baldwin, *They Never Knew What Hit Them...*

The News of Pearl Harbor—Interview, Renny Runck; Barnouw, *The Golden Web*; Blue, ibid; Lichty, ibid.

Birth of the Voice of America/Crosley involvement—Interviews Fearing, Stinger; Houseman, *Front and Center*; Shulman, ibid.

"Nobody inside Germany is going to..."—Reston, "U.S. Broadcasts News..."

"No other station in the world...;" "The contemptible creature..."—Shirer, "The Propaganda Front."

WLW Personnel/Programming—Lichty, ibid; *Crosley Broadcaster*, various issues; *Cincinnati Post, Cincinnati Enquirer*, various issues.

"They were paying..."—L. Crosley, Lichty interview.

Proximity Fuze Development/Charles Kilgour involvement—Baldwin, *The Deadly Fuze*; Baldwin, *They Never Knew...*

Proximity Fuze firing tests—ibid.

CHAPTER 29

Dutch—Interview, Ellen Crosley.

Ruth Lyons comes to WLW—Lyons, *Remember With Me*.

"My knees quaking..."—ibid

Doris Day returns—Hotchner, ibid.

WWII background—Sulzburger, ibid; various.

Suspected Crosley Sabotage/Lewis Crosley Actions—FBI Files; Interview, Ellen McClure.

Pup Development/Background—Jeudy, *The Jeep*.

Powel's Beer Blast—
http://homepage.mac.com/galaher/10thMountain/songs.html

COBRA Engine—L. Crosley, Lichty interview.

"to knock a radio set off the shelf..."—*The New York Times*, "Radio Station in Ohio to Muffle Axis." June 12, 1943.

"the westward push.."—Colley, *Deadly Accuracy*...

"won the Battle of the Bulge."—Baldwin, *The Deadly Fuze*.

CHAPTER 30

College Hill/Cincinnati/The Underground Railroad—Smiddy, ibid; Ludwig, "Eighty Birthdays, But Has had..."

Union disputes—*Cincinnati Enquirer*, various.

"..would not work with negroes."—*Cincinnati Post*. March 16, 1945.

Proximity Fuze at Okinawa—Mallon, "Navy Discloses Radio Shell Fuze."

Powel's decision to sell/Lewis's state of mind—Interviews, Rusty McClure, Renny Runck; Jennings, ibid; Lichty, ibid; Cincinnati Enquirer, various.

"My decision to sell..."—"Aviation Corp. Buys Control..." *The Wall Street Journal*, June 20, 1945.

PART IV

B U S T

CHAPTER 31

GM, Ford plan a lightweight car—White, *The Automobile Industry since 1945.*

Crosley Car development/background—L. Crosley, interview L. Lichty; Interviews, Ellen McClure, Rusty McClure; Walz, ibid.

"All kinds of plants..."—"Indiana Gets Crosley Auto Plant." *Cincinnati Post*, October 19, 1945.

"four, luxurious..."—All quotes this paragraph from Crosley Corporation, "Mr. Powel Crosley Announces..."

"There are reasonable..."—Powel Crosley, interview with Ohio Historical Society.

"I hope to eventually..."—"Crosley Auto Price Announced." *Cincinnati Times-Star*, June 11, 1946.

"You don't use a battleship..."—"Millions Are Monotonous." *Cincinnati Enquirer*, December 16, 1948.

Reds background—Baskin, Wheeler, ibid.

Pimlico construction details—Jennings, ibid.

"I should like to make..."—"Not interested in Out-Fording Ford." *Cincinnati Enquirer*, September 29, 1943.

CHAPTER 32

COBRA Engine problems—L. Crosley, interview with L. Lichty.

Crosley Car Press/Earl Wilson material—Earl Wilson's national column, printed in the *Zanesville Ohio Times-Recorder*, December 1, 1947.

Crosley Car development/background—L. Crosley, interview L. Lichty; Interviews, Ellen McClure, Rusty McClure; Walz, ibid; Crosley Motors Incorporated History Booklet.

"My bones..."—Kelly, *The Trouble Is Not In Your Set.*

Powel took ill—ibid.

"When I tested the Hotshot..."—McCahill, "Crosley Super Sport..."

"It takes a conscience..."—"The Crosley Cars of Frank Lloyd Wright." *Automobile Quarterly*, Vol. 29, no. 3 (May, 1991).

CHAPTER 33

"When a bargain sales colt..."—"Automobile History Made by Crosley Car." *Cincinnati Enquirer*, February 4, 1951.

"You have to know..."—*Cincinnati Enquirer*, October 25, 1951.

"The question seems to be..."—*ibid.*

Stiles/Schrafft at Sebring—"Crosley At Le Mans." *Road & Track*, February 1958; Jennings, ibid.

"Somebody had to stop it..."—Sussman, ibid.

Eve Brokaw—Interview with Laura Chace.

The thing that cooked us...—L. Crosley, interview L. Lichty.

Red Channels/Arrival of Television—Barnouw, *The Golden Web.*

CHAPTER 34

Cross Acres Dairy—Interviews Rusty McClure, Renny Runck.

Reds of the 1950s/Franchise Maneuvers—Baskin, Wheeler, ibid; *The New York Times*, various dates.

"My feelings..."—"Crosley Says Redlegs May Leave Cincy." *Los Angeles Times*, December 28, 1957.

"I dislike the tactics..."—"Gabe Paul Sells Stock in Reds." *Cincinnati Post* and *Times-Star*, September 18, 1961.

Auto industry developments, 1950s—White, *The Automobile Industry...*; Editors of Consumer Guide, *Cars of the 1950s...*

NOTES

The last time Powel and Lewis saw each other...—Interview, Renny Runck.

Lewis's last days—Interview, Ellen McClure.

EPILOGUE

Epigraph: McLean, Address delivered on the consecration of Spring Grove...

General background—Walz, ibid; Interviews, Ellen McClure, Rusty McClure.

"There aren't many things..."—Walz, ibid.

SOURCES

INTERVIEWS

Sr. Marta Aiken
Steve Belack
Laura Chace
Norman Corwin
Powel Crosley V
Bill DeWitt, Jr.
Jim Fearing
Dr. George Gumbert
Edward Jennings
Lawrence Lichty
Ellen McClure
Rusty McClure
Neill Prew
Renny Runck
Charles Stinger

ARCHIVES

Baseball Hall of Fame. Cooperstown, NY. Powel Crosley folder.

Cincinnati Historical Society. Cincinnati, OH. Various materials.

Department of Terrestrial Magnetism. Washington D.C.

Federal Bureau of Investigation. Washington D.C.

National Archives, St. Louis, MO; Army Corps of Engineers, Civilian Records of Lewis Crosley.

National Archives, College Park, MD; RG 391, case 1, drawer 4, Records of U.S. Regular Army mobile units; Record Group 111, AEF 28th engineers box 2036 and box 2037.

United States Trademark and Patent Office. Washington D.C.

University of Cincinnati. Cincinnati OH. Transcripts for Powel and Lewis
Crosley. The Cincinnatian (Yearbook)

University of Maryland. College Park, MD. Library of American Broadcasting.

University of Michigan. Ann Arbor, MI. Bentley Archives.

University of Rutgers. Rutgers, NJ. International Union of Electrical,
Radio and Machine Workers. Box 26, folder 24, MC 690, Records of
the President's Office of the International Union of Electrical, Radio,
and Machine Workers.

ORAL HISTORIES

Yeatman Anderson. Interview with John Knoepfle. August 10, 1957.
University of Illinois.

Evan Bone. Interview with John Knoepfle. August 26, 1957. University
of Illinois.

Lewis Crosley. Interview with John Knoepfle. July 3, 1957. University
of Illinois.

Lewis Crosley. Interview with Mrs. Elva R. Adams. April 18, 1975.
Warren County (Ohio) Historical Society.

Powel Crosley Jr.. Interview October 14, 1938. Ohio State Archeological
and Historical Society Library.

William Hedges. Interview with Frank Ernest Hill. March 28, 1951.
Columbia University, Broadcast Pioneers Project.

Manuel Rosenberg. Interview with Len Johnson. April 1, 1963. Columbia
University, Broadcast Pioneers Project.

BOOKS

Allen, Frederick Lewis. *Only Yesterday; An Informal History of the
Nineteen-Twenties*. New York, London: Harper & Brothers, 1931.

Allen, Jim. *Jeep*. St. Paul, MN: Motor Books International/MBI, 2001.

Allen, Lee. *The Cincinnati Reds*. New York: Putnam, 1948.

Archer, Gleason Leonard. *History of Radio to 1926*. New York, N.Y.:
American Historical Society, 1938.

Archer, Gleason Leonard. *Big Business and Radio*. New York, N.Y.: American Historical Company, 1939.

Army War College (U.S.). *Historical Section, Order of Battle of the United States Land Forces in the World War*. Washington: U. S. Govt. Printing Office, 1931.

Atkins, Chet, and Cochran, Russ. *Me and My Guitars*. Hal Leonard, 2002.

Baldwin, Ralph Belknap. *The Deadly Fuze: The Secret Weapon of World War II*. San Rafael, CA: Presidio Press, 1980.

Baldwin, Ralph Belknap. *They Never Knew What Hit Them: The Story of the Best Kept Secret of World War II*. Reynier Press, 1999.

Balk, Alfred. *The Rise of Radio, from Marconi Through the Golden Age*. Jefferson, N.C.: MacFarland & Company, 2006.

Bannerman, R. Leroy. *Norman Corwin and Radio: The Golden Years*. University, AL: University of Alabama Press, 1986.

Barber, Red. *Rhubarb in the Catbird Seat*. Garden City, N.Y.: Doubleday, 1968.

Barber, Red. *The Broadcasters*. New York, N.Y.: Dial Press, 1970.

Barber, Red. *1947, When All Hell Broke Loose in Baseball*. Garden City, N.Y.: Doubleday, 1982.

Barnouw, Erik. *A Tower in Babel*. New York, N.Y.: Oxford University Press, 1966.

Barnouw, Erik. *The Golden Web*. New York, N.Y.: Oxford University Press, 1968.

Baskin, John, and Wheeler, Lonnie. *The Cincinnati Game*. Wilmington, OH: Orange Frazer Press, 1988.

Baxter, James Phinney III. *Scientists Against Time*. Boston, MA: Little Brown, 1946.

Bentley, John. *Great American Automobiles, A Dramatic Account Of Their Achievements in Competition*. Englewood Cliffs, N. J.: Prentice-Hall, 1957.

Bierley, Paul. *Hallelujah Trombone! The Story of Henry Fillmore*. Columbus, OH: Integrity Press, 1982.

Bilby, Kenneth W. *The General: David Sarnoff and the Rise of the Communications Industry*. New York, N.Y.: Harper & Row, 1986.

Blue, Howard. *Words at War*. Lanham, Maryland: Scarecrow Press, 2002.

Boemeke, Manfred F., Chickering, Roger, and Forster, Stig. *Anticipating Total War: The German and American Experiences, 1871-1914*. New York, N.Y.: Cambridge University Press, 1999.

Boyce, Joseph (editor). *New Weapons for Air Warfare*. Boston, MA: Little, Brown, 1945.

Brosnan, Jim. *Pennant Race*. New York, N.Y.: Harper, 1962.

Brown, Louis. *Centennial History of the Carnegie Institution of Washington: Volume II, The Department of Terrestrial Magnetism*. Cambridge, UK: Cambridge University Press, 2004.

Byerly, Carol R. *Fever of War*. New York, N.Y.: New York University Press, 2005.

Catton, Andrew R.L. *The Frontier Republic: Ideology and Politics in the Ohio Country, 1780-1805*. Kent, OH: Kent State University Press, 1986.

Childs, Harwood L. and Whitton, John B. *Propaganda by Short Wave*. Princeton, NY: Princeton University Press, 1942.

Cincinnati Historical Society. *Old College Hill*. Cincinnati, OH: College Hill Historical Society, 1988.

Crismon, Fred W. *U.S. Military Wheeled Vehicles*. Minneapolis, MN: Victory WW2 Publishing, Ltd., 2001.

Clymer, Floyd. *Floyd Clymer's Historical Motor Scrapbook*. Los Angeles, CA.: Clymer motors, 1944.

Clymer, Floyd. *Floyd Clymer's Scrapbook of Early Auto Supplies and Equipment*. Los Angeles, CA: Floyd Clymer Publications, 1944.

Clymer, Floyd. *Treasury of Early American Automobiles, 1877-1925*. New York, N.Y.: McGraw-Hill, 1950.

Consumer Guide, The Editors of. *Cars of the 50s*. New York, N.Y.: Beekman House, 1978.

Consumer Guide, The Editors of. *Encyclopedia of American Cars*. Lincolnwood, IL: Publications International, Ltd., 2002.

Cook, Joe, and Slate, Sam J. *It Sounds Impossible*. New York, N.Y.: Macmillan Co., 1963.

Corbett, Ruth. *Daddy Danced the Charleston*. Cranberry, NJ: A.S. Barnes & Co., 1970.

Crafton, Donald. *The Talkies*. Berkeley, CA: University of California Press, 1997.

Crosley, Powel, Jr., *The Simplicity of Radio*. Girard, KS: Haldeman-Julius Co., 1923.

Dellinger, Susan. *Red Legs and Black Sox*. Cincinnati, OH: Emmis, 2006.

Dixson, C.E. "Buddy" Sr. *The Crosley Legacy*. Winston-Salem, NC: Crosley.

Douglas, Susan J. *Inventing American Broadcasting 1899-1922*. Baltimore, MD: Johns Hopkins University Press, 1987.

Douglas, Susan J. *Listening In: Radio And The American Imagination, From Amos 'N' Andy And Edward R. Murrow To Wolfman Jack And Howard Stern*. New York, N.Y.: Times Books, 1999.

Durant, Pliny A. *History of Clinton County, Ohio*. W.H. Beers & Co.: 1882

Eckhoff, Maria R. *Sharonville and its People*. Mount Pleasant, SC: Arcadia Pulbishing, 2002.

Elson, Robert T., and the Editors of Time-Life Books. *World War II: Prelude to War*. Chicago, IL: Time-Life Books, 1977.

Evans, Harold. *They Made America: From the Steam Engine to the Search Engine: Two Centuries of Innovators*. Boston, MA: Little, Brown, 2004.

Federal Writers Project (WPA), Ohio. *They Built a City: 150 years of Industrial Cincinnati*. Cincinnati, OH: *Cincinnati Post*, 1938.

Federal Writers Project (WPA), Ohio. *Cincinnati: The Childhood of Our City*. Cincinnati, OH: *Cincinnati Post*, 1938.

Federal Writers Project (WPA), Ohio. *Cincinnati: Glimpses of Its Youth*. Cincinnati, OH: *Cincinnati Post*, 1938.

Federal Writers Project (WPA), Ohio. *Cincinnati; Highlights of a Long Life*. Cincinnati, OH: *Cincinnati Post*, 1938.

Federal Writers Project (WPA), Ohio. *Cincinnati: A Guide to the Queen City and Its Neighbors*. Cincinnati, OH: *The Cincinnati Post*, 1943.

Finke, Gail Deibler. *College Hill*. Charleston, S.C.: Arcadia Pub., 2004.

Firestone, Harvey S. *Men and Rubber: The Story of Business*. Garden City, N.Y.: Doubleday, Page & Company, 1926.

Firestone, Harvey S. Jr. *The Romance and Drama of the Rubber Industry*. Firestone Tire and Rubber, 1932.

Fisher, Jerry M. *The Pacesetter: The Untold Story of Carl G. Fisher*. Fort Bragg, CA: Lost Coast Press, 1998.

Fisher, Jane. *Fabulous Hoosier: A Story of American Achievement*. Robert M. McBride & Company. New York, 1947.

Foster, Mark. *Castles in the Sand: The Life and Times of Carl Graham Fisher*. Gainesville, FL: University of Florida Press, 2000.

Foust, James C. *Big Voices of the Air: The Battle Over Clear-Channel Radio*. Ames, Iowa: Iowa State University Press, 2000.

Friedmann, Otto. *Broadcasting for Democracy*. London: George Allen & Unwin Ltd.

Gelernter, David. *1939: The Lost World of the Fair*. New York, N.Y.: The Free Press, 1995.

Giglierano, Geoffrey J. and Overmyer, Deborah A. *Bicentennial Guide to Greater Cincinnati: A Portrait of Two Hundred Years*. Cincinnati, OH: Cincinnati Historical Society, 1989.

Goldsmith, Alfred N., and Lescarboura, Austin C. *This Thing Called Broadcasting; A Simple Tale Of An Idea, An Experiment, A Mighty Industry, A Daily Habit, And A Basic Influence In Our Modern Civilization*. New York, N.Y.: H. Holt and Company, 1930.

Goss, Charles Frederic. *Cincinnati, the Queen City, 1788-1912*. Chicago, IL: S. J. Clarke Pub. Co., 1912.

Grace, Kevin. *The Cincinnati Reds, 1900-1950*. Charleston SC: Arcadia Publishing, 2005.

Graves, Ralph H. *The Triumph of an Idea: The Story of Henry Ford*. Garden City, N.Y.: Doubleday, Doran & Company, Inc., 1934.

Gray, Jack. *Bits of Wireless History*. Cincinnati, OH: Privately printed, 1969.

Greenwood, Harold S. *A Pictorial Album of Wireless and Radio, 1905-1928*. Los Angles, CA: 1961, Floyd Clymer Publications.

Gregory, Barry. *Argonne 1918: The AEF in France*. Ballantine's Illustrated History of the Violent Century. New York, N.Y.: Ballantine Books, 1972.

Greve, Charles Theodore. *Centennial History of Cincinnati and Representative Citizens*. Chicago, IL: Biographical Pub. Co., 1904

Halper, Donna L. *Invisible Stars: A Social History of Women in American Broadcasting*. Armonk, N.Y. : M.E. Sharpe, 2001.

Hare, William Francis, et al. *The Brown Network: The Activities of the Nazis in Foreign Countries*. London: Knight Publications, 1936.

Harris, Credo Fitch. *Microphone Memoirs of the Horse and Buggy Days of Radio*. Bobbs-Merrill, 1937.

Hartcup, Guy. *The Effect of Science on the Second World War*. New York, N.Y.: Palgrave, 2000.

Henshaw, Dorothy Cummings. *College Hill: 90 Years of Memories*. Cincinnati, 1996. Privately printed.

Hotchner, A.E. *Doris Day: Her Own Story*. New York, N.Y.: William Morrow, 1976.

Houseman, John. *Front And Center*. New York, N.Y.: Simon and Schuster, 1979.

Huffman, Wallace Spencer. *Indiana-Built Motor Vehicles, Centennial Edition*. Indianapolis, IN: Indiana Historical Society, 1994.

Hughes, Matthew and Philpott, William J. *The Palgrave Concise Historical Atlas of the First World War*. Hampshire, England: Palgrave, MacMillan, 2005.

Hurt, R. Douglas. *The Ohio Frontier: Crucible of the Old Northwest, 1720-1830*. Bloomington, IN: Indiana University Press, 1996.

Ikuta, Yasutoshi. *The American Automobile: Advertising from the Antique and Classic Eras*. San Francisco, CA: Chronicle Books, 1988.

Ikuta, Yasutoshi. *Cruise-O-Matic: Automobile Advertising of the 1950s*. San Francisco, CA: Chronicle Books, 1988.

Jennings, Edward, and Crosley, Lew. *Dreams Do Come True: The Story of Powel Crosley, Jr.* Pigeon Forge, TN: Privately printed, 2004.

Jeudy, Jean Gabriel. *The Jeep*. New York, N.Y.: VILO, 1981.

Jones, Loyal. *Minstrel of the Appalachians: The Story of Bascom Lamar Lunsford*. Lexington, KY: The University Press of Kentucky, 2002.

Jones, R.R.. *The Ohio River*. Fourth Edition. Washington D.C.: United States Government Printing Office; 1929.

Jordan, Philip D. *Ohio Comes of Age, 1873-1900, v. 5*. Columbus, OH: Ohio State Archaeological and Historical Society, 1943.

Julian, Joseph. *This Was Radio*. New York, N.Y.: Viking, 1975.

Juptner, Joseph P. *T-Hangar Tales*. Eagan, MN: Historic Aviation, 1994.

Keegan, John. *The First World War*. New York, N.Y.: Vintage, 1998.

Kelly, Mary Ann. *The Trouble Is Not in Your Set*. C.J. Cincinnati, OH: C.J. Krehbiel, 1990.

Kienzle, Rich. *Southwest Shuffle: Pioneers of Honky-Tonk, Western Swing, and Country Jazz*. New York, N.Y.: Routledge, 2003.

Kirsch, George B. *Baseball in Blue and Gray: The National Pastime During the Civil War*. Princeton, N.J.: Princeton University Press, 2003.

Kittross, John Michael, and Sterling, Christopher H. *Stay Tuned: A History of American Broadcasting* (Third Edition). Mahwah, NJ: Lawrence Erlbaum Associates, 2002.

Kollins, Michael J. *Pioneers of the U.S. Automobile Industry* (4 volumes). Warrendale, PA : Society of Automotive Engineers, 2002.

Landon, Grelun and Stambler, Irwin. *Country Music: The Encyclopedia*. New York, N.Y.: St. Martin's Press, 2000.

Laurie, Clayton D. *The Propaganda Warriors: America's Crusade Against Nazi Germany*. Lawrence, KS: University Press of Kansas, 1996.

Lessing, Lawrence. *Man of High Fidelity: Edwin Howard Armstrong*. Philadelphia, PA: Lippincott, 1956.

Lewis, Tom. *Empire of the Air: The Men Who Made Radio*. New York, N.Y.: Edward Burlingame Books, 1991.

Lichty, Lawrence Wilson, and Topping, Malachi C. *American Broadcasting; A Source Book on the History of Radio and Television*. New York, N.Y.: Hastings House Publishers, 1975.

Ludwig, Charles. *Playmates of the Towpath*. Cincinnati, OH: *Cincinnati Times-Star*, 1929.

Luger, Stan. *Corporate Power, American Democracy, And The Automobile Industry*. New York, N.Y.: Cambridge University Press, 2000.

Lyons, Eugene. *David Sarnoff*. New York, N.Y.: Harper & Row, 1966.

Lyons, Ruth. *Remember with Me*. Garden City, N.Y.: Doubleday, 1969.

MacLaurin, W. Rupert, with the technical assistance of R. Joyce Harman. *Invention & Innovation in the Radio Industry*. New York, N.Y.: MacMillan Company, 1949.

Man, John. *The War to End Wars*. Pleasantville, N.Y.: Reader's Digest, 2000.

Margolin, Leo J. *Paper Bullets: A Brief Study of Psychological Warfare in World War II*. New York, N.Y.: Froben Press, 1946.

McGuffey, William Holmes. *The Annotated Mcguffey: Selections from the Mcguffey Eclectic Readers, 1836-1920*. New York, N.Y.: Van Nostrand Reinhold, 1976.

Mosley, Leonard, and the Editors of Time-Life. *World War II: The Battle of Britain*. Chicago, IL: Time-Life Books, 1977.

Mulligan, Brian. *The 1940 Cincinnati Reds and Baseball's Only In-Season Suicide*. Jefferson, N.C.: MacFarland & Co. 2005.

Nichols, Ruth. *Wings for Life*. Philadelphia, PA: J.B. Lippincott Co., 1957.

Nolan, William F. *Barney Oldfield; The Life And Times Of America's Legendary Speed King*. New York, N.Y.: Putnam,1961.

Parsons, William Barclay, 1859-1932. *The American Engineers in France*. New York, London: D. Appleton, 1920.

Perry, Dick. *Vas You Ever in Zinzinnati?* Garden City, N.Y.: Doubleday, 1966.

Perry, Dick. *Not Just a Sound: The Story of WLW*. Englewood Cliffs, N.J.: Prentice-Hall, 1971.

Pietrusza, David. *Lights On! The Wild Century Long Saga of Night Baseball*. Lanham, MD: Scarecrow Press, 1997.

Plowden, Gene. *Those Amazing Ringlings and their Circus*. New York, N.Y.: Bonanza, 1967.

Reaves, John S. (ed.) *The Air Pilots Register, 1935*. Hew York, N.Y.: Air Pilots Register Company, 1935.

Rice, Joe. *Cincinnati's Powel Crosley, Jr.; Industrialist, Pioneer Radio Builder*. Covington, KY, 1976. Privately printed.

Richards, J. Stuart. *Pennsylvanian Voices of the Great War: Letters, Stories, and Oral Histories of World War I*. Jefferson, N.C.: McFarland, 2002.

Rhodes, Anthony. *Propaganda. The Art of Persuasion: World War II*. New York, N.Y.: Chelsea House Publishers, 1976.

Rhodes, Richard. *The Making of the Atomic Bomb*. New York, N.Y.: Touchstone, 1988.

Robinson, Thomas Porter. *Radio Networks and the Federal Government*. New York, N.Y.: Columbia University Press, 1943.

Roe, George Mortimer (ed.). *Cincinnati: The Queen City of the West*. Cincinnati, OH: C.D. Brehbiel & Company, 1895.

Rolo, Charles J. *Radio Goes to War*. New York, N.Y.: G.P. Putnam's Sons, 1942.

Sann, Paul. *The Lawless Decade: A Pictorial History of a Great American Transition: From the World War I Armistice and Prohibition to Repeal and the New Deal.* New York, N.Y.: Crown Publishers, 1957.

Sarnoff, Paul, and Sobel, Robert. *The Automobile Makers.* New York, N.Y.: Putnam, 1969.

Scott, Graham. *Essential Military Jeep: Willys, Ford, & Bantam Models 1941-1945.* St. Paul, MN: Motor Books International/MBI, 1996.

Shulman, Holly Cowan. *The Voice of America: Propaganda and Democracy, 1941-1945.* Madison, WI: University of Wisconsin Press, 1990.

Sinclair, James, et al. *Lloyd's Register of American Yachts.* New York, N.Y.: Lloyd's Register of Shipping, 1936, 1941, 1950.

Smiddy, Betty. *A Little Piece of Paradise—College Hill, Ohio.* Cincinnati; College Hill Historical Society, 1999.

Spring, Harry. *An Engineer's Diary of the Great War.* West Lafayette, IN: Purdue University Press, 2002.

Stump, Al. *Cobb: A Biography.* Chapel Hill, N.C.: Algonquin Books, 1994

Sullivan, Mark. *Our Times; The United States, 1900-1925.* New York, N.Y.: C. Scribner's Sons, 1926-35.

Sulzberger, C.L., and the editors of American Heritage. *The American Heritage Picture History of World War II.* U.S.; American Heritage Publishing Company, 1966.

Taylor, A.J.P. *The Second World War: An Illustrated History.* London: Penguin Books, 1976.

Taylor, Rich. *Indy: Seventy-Five Years of Auto Racing's Greatest Spectacle.* New York, N.Y.: St. Martin's Press, 1991.

Teller, Edward, with Judith Schoolery. *Memoirs.* New York, NY: Perseus Publishing, 2002

Thomas, Bob. *Building a Company: Roy O. Disney and the Creation of an Entertainment Empire.* New York, N.Y.: Hyperion, 1998.

Timlin Jr., Robert K. *American Engineers Behind the Battle Lines in France.* New York, N.Y.: McGraw-Hill, 1918.

Toynbee, Arnold J. *The German Terror in France.* New York, N.Y.: George H. Doran Company, 1917.

Trav S. D. *No Applause, Just Throw Money, Or, The Book That Made Vaudeville Famous: A High-Class, Refined Entertainment*. New York, N.Y.: Faber and Faber, 2005.

Tygiel, Jules. *Past Time: Baseball as History*. New York, N.Y.: Oxford University Press, 2000.

Tyne, Gerald F.J. *The Saga of the Vacuum Tube*. Indianapolis, IN: H. W. Sams, 1977.

U.S. Army Center of Military History. *The United States Army in World War I* [computer file]. Washington, D.C.: Supt. of Docs., U.S. G.P.O., distributor, 1998.

U.S. Naval Historical Center. *Radio Proximity [VT] Fuzes* [computer file]. Washington, DC: Naval Historical Center Web site.

Van Dort, Paul M. *1939 New York World's Fair Photo Collection*. Sparks, NV: Privately printed, 2002.

Waitley, Douglas. *The Roads We Traveled: An Amusing History of the Automobile*. New York, N.Y.: Messner, 1979.

Warfield, Don. *The Roaring Redhead: Larry MacPhail—Baseball's Great Innovator*. South Bend, IN: Diamond Communications, Inc., 1987.

Watts, Steven. *The People's Tycoon: Henry Ford and the American Century*. New York, N.Y.: A.A. Knopf, 2005.

Welch, David. *The Third Reich: Politics and Propaganda*. London: Routledge, 1993.

Wernick, Robert, and the Editors of Time-Life Books. *World War II: Blitzkrieg*. Chicago, IL: Time-Life Books, 1977.

White, G. Edward. *Creating The National Pastime: Baseball Transforms Itself, 1903-1953*. Princeton, N.J.: Princeton University Press, 1996.

White, Lawrence J. *The Automobile Industry Since 1945*. Cambridge, MA: Harvard University Press, 1971.

White, Llewellyn. *The American Radio*. Chicago, IL: University of Chicago Press, 1947.

Willmott, H. P. *World War I*. New York, N.Y.: DK Publishing, 2003.

Wittke, Carl. *German-Americans and the World War*. Columbus, OH: Ohio State Archaeological And Historical Society, 1936.

Wixom, Charles W. *ARBA Pictorial History of Road-building*. Washington, D.C.: American Road Builders' Association, 1975.

SOURCES

MAGAZINES

Bulletin of the Historical and Philosophical Society of Ohio. Various issues, 1943-1963. Cincinnati, OH.

Cincinnati Historical Society Bulletin. Various issues, 1964-1982. Cincinnati, OH.

CM Ink, Various issues. Cincinnati, OH: Crosley Motors, Inc.

Crosley Broadcaster. Various issues. Cincinnati, OH.: Crosley Radio Corporation.

Crosley Radio Weekly. Various issues. Cincinnati, OH: Crosley Corporation.

Queen City Heritage. Various issues, 1983-1999. Cincinnati, OH.

QST; Devoted Entirely to Amateur Radio. Various Issues. Newington, CT, etc.: American Radio Relay League.

Radio Broadcast. Various issues. Garden City, N.Y.: Doubleday, Page & Co., 1922-1930.

Radio Service Bulletin. Various issues. Department of Commerce, Washington D.C.

Time Magazine. Various Issues.

ARTICLES

CM Ink. "Meet the Executives: Lewis M. Crosley Has Been Brother's 'Right-Hand' Since Boyhood Days." September, 1947.

Colley, David. "Deadly Accuracy." *Invention and Technology Magazine* (Spring 2001).

Crosley Broadcaster. "Crosley's Son Reaches Mike." April 15, 1928.

Crosley Broadcaster. "Crosley Dedicates The Nation's Station." August 1, 1930.

Crosley, Powel, Jr., "50 Jobs in 50 Years." *The American Magazine* (October 1948).

Crosley, Powel, Jr., "My First Tarpon." Unpublished, May 1929.

Crosley Radio Weekly. "Listeners Pleased with Broadcasting of Opening Game." May 5, 1924.

Crosley Radio Weekly. "Freedom of the Air Is Won by Radio Broadcasters." May 12, 1924.

Cuddy, Jack. "Night Ball Wins Favor." *The Los Angeles Times* (October 31, 1935).

Cushing, Harvey. "Detroit Speaks." *Motor Trend* (March, 1951).

Davis, Forrest. "The Crosley Touch—and Go!" *The Saturday Evening Post* (September 30, 1939).

DeCamp, Graydon. "Motown on the Ohio." *The Cincinnati Enquirer* (May 17, 1981).

Johnston, Maurice "Boss." "'Twas the Day Before Thanksgiving." *Muzzle Blasts Magazine* (May, 1941).

Heinl, Robert D. "Off the Antenna." *The Washington Post* (September 8, 1929).

Hutchens, John K. "This Is America Speaking." *The New York Times* (May 10, 1942).

Keller, Cynthia. "Powel Crosley, Jr. and the Dawn of the Wireless in Cincinnati." *Queen City Heritage* (Summer 1997).

Ludwig, Charles. "Eighty Birthdays—But Has Had Eighty-One Christmases." *The Cincinnati Enquirer* (December 25, 1929).

Mallon, Winifred. "Navy Discloses Radio Shell Fuze." *The New York Times* (September 21, 1945).

Marshall, Edward. "Count Von Bernstoff Gives Germany's Point of View." *The New York Times* (August 30, 1914).

May, Myra. "The Story of Powel Crosley." *Radio Broadcast* (November, 1924).

McCahill, Tom. "1951 Crosley Super Sport Road Test." *Mechanix Illustrated* (June, 1951).

McCarthy, Joe. "The Man Who Invented Miami Beach." *American Heritage* (December 1975).

Nagengast, Bernard. "It's A Cool Story." *Mechanical Engineering-CIME* (May 2000).

New York Telegram-Mail. "The Story of Powel Crosley Jr." 1924, Date unknown.

Outlook. "Christy Mathewson." August 30, 1922.

Outlook. "The Eternal Mucker." October 18, 1922.

Piel, Gerard. "Powel Crosley, Jr." *Life Magazine* (February 17, 1947).

Plough, Alvin Richard, "The Henry Ford of Radio." *Radio Broadcast* (April 1923).

Popular Mechanics. "Making Five Thousand Radio Sets A Day." Date Unknown.

Radio Broadcast. "Radio Repays its Genius." August 1923.

Reeves, Earl. "The Boys Who Made Radio-2." *The Youth's Companion Magazine* (May 20, 1926).

Reston, James B. "U.S. Broadcasts News to Europe." *The New York Times* (October 6, 1941).

Seasongood, Murray. "Remembrances of a Youthful Nonagenarian." *The Cincinnati Historical Society Bulletin 29* (Spring 1971).

Segal, Eugene. "One City's...?". *The Cincinnati Post* (October 9, 1933).

Shirer, William L. "The Propaganda Front." *The Washington Post* (July 7, 1942).

Smith, Fred. "The Genius of Powel Crosley, Jr." *Crosley Radio Weekly* (October 20, 1924).

Smith, William E. "William Holmes McGuffey—Mid-American." *Bulletin of the Historical and Philosophical Society of Ohio, Volume 17* (January 1959).

Stinger, Charles. "The Eminent Years of Powel Crosley, Jr.: His Transmitters, Receivers, Products, and Broadcast Station WLW, 1921-1940." *The AWA Review* (Volume 16, 2003).

Sussman, Larry. "The Crosley Auto Was a Generation Too Early." *The Cincinnati Post* (May 21, 1977).

Time. "Little Fellow." May 8, 1939.

Turner, Leo. "Millions Are Monotonous." *The Cincinnati Enquirer* (December 16, 1948).

The Washington Post. "`Peace-At-Any-Price Propaganda In U.S. Denounced by Roosevelt." July 20, 1915.

Young, Anthony. "America's Forgotten Entrepeneur." *Ideas On Liberty* (October 2001).

"Mr. Crosley Recalls WLW's Start in '21." Cincinnati newspaper, date and provenance unknown.

NEWSPAPERS

The Cincinnati Commercial.
The Cincinnati Enquirer.
The Cincinnati Post.
The Cincinnati Times-Star
The Los Angeles Times.
The New York Times.
The Sarasota Herald.
The Washington Post.
Various dates, all.

VIDEO/AUDIO RECORDINGS

Lewis Crosley, interview with Fred Benningus for "I Remember Radio," 1970.

Lewis Crosley, interview with Lawrence Lichty, 1965.

U.S. Army Signal Corps. Footage of Ohio Flood of 1914; 28th Engineering Regiment; Construction at St. Nazaire.

Walz, Gene. Powel Crosley, Jr. and the 20th Century. Cincinnati, OH: Greater Cinicinnati Educational Television Foundation, 1988.

WLW 25th Anniversary Broadcast, National Association of Broadcasters Library.

SCHOLARLY PUBLICATIONS

Coale, Jr., Alvin Hugh. "Market Analysis of the Crosley Radio Receiving Set." Dissertation: Thesis (BBA), University of Texas, 1925.

Lichty, Lawrence Wilson. "The Nation's Station: A History of Radio Station WLW." Dissertation: Thesis (PhD.), Ohio State University, 1964.

Richards, Amyle P. "The WLW Model Super-Power Radio Receiver." Dissertation: Thesis (Professional Degree), Oklahoma Agricultural and Mechanical College, 1939.

University of Cincinnati Teachers Bulletin. Field Notes in Nature Study, Volume 1, Number 2. Cincinnati OH: University Press, 1905.

MISCELLANEOUS

Abelson, Philip. "Merle Antony Tuve." Biographical Memoir for National Academies Press (www.nap.edu/html/biomems/mtuve.html).

Crosley Corporation Annual Reports. 1929-1945.

Crosley Corporation, A Trip Through WLW. Date Unknown.

Crosley Corporation, Mr. Powel Crosley Jr. Announces The Revolutionary CROSLEY - "A Fine Car - America's Newest, Smartest Automobile." April, 1939.

Crosley Motors Incorporated history booklet. Crosley Motors, 1951.

Crosley, Powel, Jr.. The Crosley Car: A Talk. Cincinnati, OH: Privately printed, 1948. (Bound volume, Cincinnati Historical Society).

McLean, John. Address delivered on the consecration of the Spring Grove cemetery near Cincinnati, August 20th, 1845. Cincinnati, OH: Daily Atlas office, 1845.

Payne, George Henry. "Is Radio Living Up to its Promise?" Address at the University of the Air, College of the City of New York (December 18, 1936).

U.S. Board of War Communications, June 1944 Pamphlet.

WEB SITES

earlyradiohistory.us

www.ominous-valve.com/wlw.html www.pbs.org/wgbh/amex/edison/film-more/description.html

bioproj.sabr.org/bioproj.cfm?a=v&v=l&pid=8621&bid=1070

www.armyhistory.org/armyhistorical

members.aol.com/jeff1070/wlw.html

www.eyewitnesstohistory.com/guernica.htm

www.baseball-reference.com

Crosley Automobile Club: www.ggw.org/~cac/

U.S. Navy Historical Center: www.history.navy.mil/faqs/faq96-1.htm

WLW Transmitter History: hawkins.pair.com/wlw.shtml

http://newton.nap.edu/html/biomems/mtuve.html

INDEX

ABOUT THE AUTHORS

RUSTY MCCLURE, advisor and investor in numerous entrepreneurial projects, has a Master of Divinity degree from Emory University and a Harvard MBA. He is the son of Ellen Crosley McClure, daughter of Lewis M. Crosley, the sole surviving direct descendent of the Crosley brothers. He lives with his wife and children in Dublin, Ohio.

DAVID STERN, author of over two dozen fiction and non-fiction titles, including the *New York Times* bestselling novelization *Blair Witch Project: A Dossier*, has worked on a wide range of titles during his twenty-year career in the publishing industry. He has edited numerous national bestsellers and worked with many award-winning authors. He lives with his wife and children in western Massachusetts.

MICHAEL A. BANKS, author of more than 40 non-fiction books and novels, is a lifelong resident of Crosley's hometown, Cincinnati. He counts classic cars and old radio among his hobbies. Banks is a member of the Crosley Automobile Club and the Antique Wireless Association and has been on the air on WLW radio several times.

The Master Musicians Series

ELGAR

SERIES EDITED BY

SIR JACK WESTRUP
M.A., Hon.D.Mus.(Oxon.), F.R.C.O.

THE MASTER MUSICIANS SERIES

ELGAR

by

IAN PARROTT

*With eight pages of plates
and music examples in text*

LONDON
J. M. DENT AND SONS LTD

FARRAR, STRAUS AND GIROUX, INC
NEW YORK

First published in 1971
© Text, Ian Parrott, 1971

Made in Great Britain
at the
Aldine Press · Letchworth · Herts
for
J. M. DENT & SONS LTD
Aldine House · Bedford Street · London

ISBN 0 460 03109 0

PREFACE

ON THE factual side of Elgar's life the present volume must to a large extent be a summary, as many books are available on the subject. The most valuable early sources are Buckley and Newman, whilst in 1955 appeared the treatments by Dr Percy Young, detailed and thorough, and Miss Diana McVeagh, discerning and imaginative. Dr Young followed up his biography with two valuable collections of letters. Michael Kennedy's *Portrait of Elgar* (1968) sees the composer in yet another light.

Then there are my own views when it comes to assessing the major compositions: these are unaffected by personal friendships and so can be contrasted with those of biographers such as Reed and Maine. I have been able to approach the personalities 'pictured within' the *Enigma Variations* without being tied to existing opinions, which had tended to solidify. I did in fact once meet Troyte Griffith—and was able to confirm the suspicion of others that he was unlike his apparent musical portrait—but, by and large, I live in a post-Elgarian world and know the composer only through his music, through memories of others and, to a fair extent, through visiting many parts of Worcestershire and the cottage, Brinkwells, in Sussex.

The two chapters on the *Enigma variations* contain entirely new material, as does the study in Chapter XII of the sketches of the slow movement of Symphony No. 2. I am indebted to the Right Reverend John Richards, the Lord Bishop of St Davids, who helped me to solve the first part of the enigma, and to Mr Alan Webb, curator of the Birthplace, who has been untiring with his assistance in every possible way.

I am grateful also to Mrs Joyce Crook, Miss Winifred Barrows and Mr A. T. Shaw for much practical help, and to Dr Percy Young for encouragement. For permission to use photographs I am grateful to Mrs Iliffe (Dr Sinclair and Dan), Mr E. A. Butcher

vii

Preface

('Dorabella') and to Messrs Alan Meek and Desmond Tripp, E.M.I. and the B.B.C. My warm thanks to Dr David Harries for preparing the Index. Finally I am particularly grateful to the late Mrs Elgar Blake, not only for permission to reproduce her father's music and to quote from her mother's diary, but also for the friendly personal interest she took in my work.

IAN PARROTT

Aberystwyth.
1971

CONTENTS

ILLUSTRATIONS

CHAPTER I

THE SETTING: THE SALON

IN THE Soviet Union there is a birthplace museum proudly commemorating Tchaikovsky; in Italy they pay similar homage to
Verdi; and in the Germanic countries the habit had already been
formed, so that the 'Beethovenhaus' at Bonn is only one of many
composer museums. In Britain after the seventeenth century no
such custom prevailed. The domination of the German foreigners,
first Handel and then Mendelssohn, was accepted without
question; there seemed to be no native-born composers of standing
in this country, and thus the art of enjoying any relics or associations died out.

By the second half of the nineteenth century Great Britain was
well on the way to commanding the largest empire the world had
ever known and national pride was at its most buoyant. The class
structure, however, had its rigid divisions and all professional
musicians, performers, teachers and creators alike, were expected
to belong if not to the company of 'rogues and vagabonds' at least
to the lowest stratum. In fact they were looked upon as unlikely
and unwelcome amongst the higher strata, the tradespeople and
the landed gentry, who were happy to be amateur performers for
light amusement only and for whom *salon* music was adequate.
The only exception for a British professional musician was to be
associated with the hierarchy of the Church, which then, very
much more than now, occupied a central position in every community. The use of the word 'imperial', not only for colleges and
museums but also for hotels, was natural in those expansive times.
Foreign musicians, who were looked down upon, could come
from anywhere and frequently the best came from Germany. As
there were in fact very few British-born composers of real worth,
this attitude of mind not unnaturally hardened and it has been a

I

long time—about a hundred years—before any change has come
about in the general public's mind.

About three miles west of Worcester on the Bromyard road there
is something which is still unique in Britain: a signpost pointing
the way to a composer's birthplace. Along the side lane in the direction of the signpost there is a cottage half a mile short of the village
of Broadheath. Here Edward William Elgar was born on 2nd
June 1857. More than thirty years after his death this cottage has
become the symbol of a great composer: it is a birthplace museum.

Another, if negative, sign of the slow recognition of genius has
been his changing image. All his life and for many years afterwards Elgar was thought of as the musical embodiment of
imperialism, a jingo who looked like a cross between a squire and
a colonel. Gradually the image has changed as the true facts have
come more and more to light, so that by 1968 a *Portrait* [1] shows
him as a neurotic, withdrawn dreamer, cut off and infinitely sad.
'He encountered snobbery, both social and artistic, and it wounded
him,' says Michael Kennedy. 'Somewhere . . . something or someone wounded him so deeply, so irreparably, that he never fully recovered . . . he buried the secret of this wound in his heart. It showed
itself only in the anguish and solitude of certain passages in his music.'

Edward Elgar was the second son of William Henry Elgar and
Anne Greening. Much detailed information on both families is
given in the opening chapter of Dr Percy M. Young's *Elgar O.M.*
Elgar's father was organist of St George's Roman Catholic Church
in Worcester and also kept a music shop. When the family was
growing the Elgars moved out to the quieter countryside of Broadheath, but a few years later, when Edward was between two and
three, they moved back into Worcester again. What the city could
offer the growing boy was the organ loft, the music and books in
the shop and provincial concerts. His father had introduced him to
the music of Bach by the age of nine; the boy had concocted an
anagram on the name—he had inherited an interest in history and
literature from his mother. Some of his first tunes, later a basis for

---

[1] Michael Kennedy, *Portrait of Elgar* (1968), pp. 3 and 271.

the *Wand of Youth* suites, were written in his early teens.[1] At this time also he was amused by the contradictory statements on the 'rules' of various music theorists.[2]

The Victorian world in which he grew up was rich, confident and stable, but indifferent to artistic values. This became increasingly irksome for a man who, self-taught, knew he had more to offer than was dreamed of around him; contemporary indifference made him more bitter than if he had had to contend with the political up-heavals and the constantly divided loyalties that most European composers of stature had had as both burden and stimulus.

Elgar never lived under the shadow of the atom bomb. He acquired considerable skill in science and later conducted his own private experiments, but he would have shared the view of Rutherford: that the splitting of the atom could have no practical application. Nor did he live in the days of experiment as a substi-tute for creativity.

His schooldays, during which he learnt the violin, were never-theless happy, almost happy-go-lucky, and he enjoyed pranks and jokes as much as anyone.[3] His apprenticeship to a solicitor in 1872 lasted for only a year, after which he turned wholly to music, helping his father at the organ, in the shop and as violinist and conductor of the Worcester Glee Club. By 1877 he could afford to go to London for a few violin lessons. 'Do you compose?' asked Adolphe Pollitzer, his teacher. 'I try,' Elgar replied. Some of his earliest works, music for the Roman Catholic service, date from this time; he also played the violin in the important (Anglican) Festival of the Three Choirs of Hereford, Gloucester and Wor-cester when it took place in Worcester in 1878. His considerable feeling for orchestral instruments grew also from playing the bassoon in a wind quintet in which his brother Frank played the oboe. The next year his appointment as band instructor of the Powick lunatic asylum gave him teaching, coaching and, even

[1] Percy Young, *Elgar O.M.* (1955), pp. 31, 35 and 37.

[2] W. H. Reed, *Elgar* (1939), p. 6; R. J. Buckley, *Sir Edward Elgar* (1905), pp. 11–13.

[3] Diana M. McVeagh, *Edward Elgar* (1955), p. 5.

more important, composing experience. More like a painter than a composer, he wrote part of a symphony, bar by bar, on the framework of Mozart's G minor and considered that it was a very useful discipline.

Visits to both Paris and Leipzig at this time were rewarding, though he did not show the same precocious talent that his fellow-countryman, Sullivan, had displayed in the latter town a quarter of a century earlier. Leipzig gave both composers one lasting influence which was to be fundamental: Schumann. Though Sullivan lost it in a welter of trivialities in his declining years, Elgar, in his 'third' period during and after World War I, was to display this influence in a new and refined light. At this time Elgar also followed Sullivan at the Crystal Palace, with the encouragement of August Manns, but his modest *Sevillaña* lacked the brilliance of the *Tempest* music of the older composer. It was a *salon* piece by a 'provincial' with talent, and the first piece of his to be performed in London.

More pieces were written, some were performed and a few were actually published. Perhaps the most successful of his *salon* pieces was *Salut d'Amour*, written in 1888. Messrs Schott & Co. soon changed the German *Liebesgruss* to the more lucrative French title [1] and by giving the composer the name Ed. Elgar they left his nationality in doubt, much as Simrock had done deliberately with Ant. Dvořák. 1889 was the year of Elgar's marriage to Caroline Alice Roberts, one of his pupils. The daughter of the late Major-General Sir Henry Gee Roberts was thought by her family to have 'married beneath her', according to the strict class code of the time, but she was the right person to help this particular composer on the hard road to recognition—and she had a small income. One of the wedding presents was a copy of *The Dream of Gerontius* by Cardinal Newman, with annotations made by General Gordon,[2] a national hero whom Elgar wished to commemorate in music, though the project was never completed.

[1] Kennedy, *op. cit.*, p. 27.
[2] It was not, however, the copy he had in Khartoum before being killed in 1884 (Young, *op. cit.*, pp. 61 and 336).

THE BIRTHPLACE AT BROADHEATH, where Elgar lived for two and a half years.

BRINKWELLS, near Fittleworth, Sussex (before being rethatched in 1967), where the chamber music was written, 1918–19.

Sketches by Elizabeth Parrott

CHAPTER II

SLOW RECOGNITION: THE CATHEDRAL

NEWLY married, the Elgars settled in London for a while, but in spite of the extra help of a devoted wife the music made little head-way with publishers or concert promoters, though the concert overture *Froissart* was performed at the Worcester Festival and pub-lished in 1890, the year in which their only child, Carice, was born. The important *Serenade* for strings was completed early in 1892. In 1891 they had settled under the massive hills of Malvern and Elgar had to take up again some of the teaching and playing which he had hoped to be rid of for good.

Mrs Norah Parker of Hereford makes it quite clear how Elgar hated teaching. As a scared young girl, she learned the violin from him between 1894 and 1897. He played the piano the whole time, eyed the golf clubs in the corner and showed that 'teaching dread-ful children was the most loathsome thing in life', she wrote.

Between 1842 and 1872 Malvern had been a famous spa under Dr James Wilson and Dr James Manby Gully;[1] in 1876 the latter was involved in the famous Bravo murder mystery (see 'Poison at the Priory' by Elizabeth Jenkins, the *Sunday Times* magazine, 20th October 1968). Elgar was often to be afflicted with headaches and colds but, strangely, he preferred to take the waters at Llandrindod. More visits to Germany meant hearing more music, including a considerable amount of Wagner, another lasting influence on his style. He wrote 'TRISTAN' in capital letters in his diary.[2] The *Tannhäuser* march was first introduced to the Three Choirs Festival in 1883 [3] and Elgar arranged it for piano the same year; similarly the *Parsifal* prelude appeared in Hereford Cathedral

[1] Vincent Waite, *Malvern Country* (1968), pp. 29–43.
[2] Reed, *op. cit.*, p. 36.
[3] Watkins Shaw, *The Three Choirs Festival* (Worcester, 1954).

for the first time in 1891 and a few years later Elgar arranged the Good Friday music for small orchestra. The compositions which followed, however, were not operas: they were cantatas. *The Black Knight* (1893), *From the Bavarian Highlands* (1896) and *The Light of Life* (1896) were given at Worcester, while *King Olaf* was per-formed at the North Staffordshire Festival, also in 1896. It was creatively a very fertile and vigorous period in Elgar's development, and in this 'splendid Saga-ing' (Alice's note on *King Olaf*) there was also the influence of Sullivan's best cantata, *The Golden Legend*, written for the Leeds Festival of 1886, and of Dvořák, whose cantata *The Spectre's Bride* was first given in Birmingham in 1885.

Elgar made many friends, mostly living in or near to Malvern, and some of them were soon to be immortalized in the first truly great work, the *Enigma Variations*. One who did not live locally was August Johannes Jaeger, a German who was a music assistant and eventually a reader at Novello's. He was a true friend and supporter who had much faith in the young composer. In fact it was the German in him that appreciated the real worth of Elgar, who was neither a purveyor of anthems and ballads nor a cathedral organist nor a director of music in a college for boys.[1] Elgar hated more than anything being lumped with these 'mechanical' composers. 'Many a young composer,' said Vaughan Williams, 'has stifled his natural impulses in the desire to be musicianly' [2]—by which he also meant 'mechanical'.

Another good friend was Dr G. R. Sinclair, who gave a per-formance of the first movement of the year-old Organ Sonata at Hereford Cathedral in December 1896. Of a fugue in *The Light of Life* Elgar told Buckley: [3] 'I thought a fugue would be expected of me. The great British public would hardly tolerate oratorio without fugue . . . in short there's enough counterpoint to give the real British religious respectability.' But then turning suddenly serious, as was his way: 'Bach has done it. No man has

[1] See Percy Young (ed.), *Letter to Nimrod* (1965), p. 3.
[2] R. Vaughan Williams, *The Vocalist*, May 1902.
[3] *Op. cit.*, p. 31.

a greater reverence for Bach than I . . . [but] I don't write in the
Bach style.' Then, after saying that the old theorists were not
entitled to lay down hard and fast rules for all composers to the end
of time, he walked out into the garden of Forli and continued:
'There is music in the air, music all around us, the world is full of
it and [here he raised his hands and made a rapid gesture of
capture] and—you—simply—take as much as you require!' He
was both inspired and eclectic at this time. He would listen with
grave and courteous attention to skilled comment on his work
but was inclined to make patronizing or incompetent critics wish
that they had never opened their mouths.

Travel at the time was mainly by various horse-drawn vehicles.
If you read Winifred Norbury's diary for 3rd May 1897 you will
see that 'Lady Mary Lygon called on horseback'. Bicycles were
also used extensively: Dora Penny (Dorabella) thought nothing
of the forty miles from Wolverhampton in 1899.[1] And there was
much slogging on foot.

A certain amount of material success and eventual promotion
followed some 'occasional' music: the *Imperial March* and *The
Banner of St George*, both performed in 1897. Then Elgar's mother
got him interested in the story of the British chieftain who defied
the Romans, and thus *Caractacus* was conceived. In the spring of
the next year the Elgars took over Birchwood Lodge in the
country (at the opposite end of the Malvern range to Alice's old
home, Redmarley) and there he finished *Caractacus*, which was
dedicated to the Queen and performed at the Leeds Festival in the
autumn. Elgar's patriotic outlook, as shown in these works, was
perfectly natural in an Englishman of the time, as was also a
reticent lack of showiness, because 'we are too strong to need it'
(see his letter to Jaeger of 5th November 1899). There was much of
the typical countryman's outdoor life too, ranging from bicycling
and kite-flying to beagling and fox-hunting. Birchwood adjoins
the Norbury estate and Winifred Norbury (soon to be in the

[1] Mrs Richard Powell, *Edward Elgar. Memories of a Variation* (2nd ed.,
1947), p. 17.

Enigma Variations) helped with the copying of the parts. 'Do *not* trouble,' he wrote on 10th September 1898, 'if you are at all

1 busy
2 tired
3 ill
4 lazy
5 unwilling.'

A very typical letter. Lifting her long Victorian dress above her brightly buttoned boots, Winifred would sometimes show her elegant ankles—quite a bold move in those prim days. In February 1899 Lady Mary Lygon and she came to tea when Elgar had just finished his *Variations*. The next month the Elgars moved to Craeg Lea at Malvern Wells nearer 'Caractacus' hill, and in June Richter conducted the new work at St James's Hall, London. The most important period of Elgar's creativity had arrived when he was already in his forties. He is known still in every corner of the globe, even by the most 'insular' of nations, by the *Enigma Variations*, Op. 36, if by nothing else. Dedicated to his friends 'pictured within', the work's enigma was never disclosed (for a discussion see Chapter VIII). W. H. Reed, one of his closest friends, thought that it was probably a joke,[1] and Diana McVeagh pertinently remarks that 'Elgar, who, when the work came out, seemed almost to want his secret to be guessed . . . in later years replied to questions about it with answers as enigmatical as the enigma'.[2] What was not fully realized at the time was that the orchestration was masterly far beyond anything that had come out of England.

After *Sea Pictures* (one with words by Alice), his active mind soon became engaged in one of his greatest religious compositions: *The Dream of Gerontius*. This tremendously personal setting of Cardinal Newman's poem was finished early in 1900 and the full score completed in August. The performance at Birmingham in October was not a great success. Stanford was reported to have

[1] *Op. cit.,* p. 53.
[2] *Op. cit.,* p. 26.

said: 'My boy, it stinks of incense'—a dig at Elgar's Catholic con-victions rather than at the musical style of the work. However, he did arrange for Elgar to receive an honorary doctorate of Cam-bridge University, where he himself was Professor of Music. Later Elgar, the English Catholic, and Stanford, the Irish Protestant, did not get on so well.

In retrospect we can see the Wagnerian influences which had been quietly accumulating, so that the use of leading motives is understandable—though Elgar himself said he got this idea from Mendelssohn's *Elijah*.[1] The Wagner cult was spreading: such books appeared as Freda Winworth's *The Epic of Sounds: An Elementary Interpretation of Wagner's Nibelungen Ring* (1898), and others were to follow on the 'ethics' and the 'symbolism' and many other aspects since lost sight of. Strange though the con-tinental musical language of *Gerontius* might have been to the average English musician, there was a chance that a sympathetic hearing might be found for it in Germany. And so it turned out. Jaeger saw it as a second *Parsifal*[2] and got in touch with Julius Buths, in whose German translation it was performed at the Lower Rhine Festival at Düsseldorf in December 1901. When the work was repeated in May the following year Richard Strauss referred to Elgar as the first English progressive musician. Strauss's very different treatment of a similar theme, *Tod und Verklärung*, had been given in England for the first time in 1897. *Gerontius* waited a further two years before being accepted for a full performance in its native land. Some popular works were written, however: the first two *Pomp and Circumstance* marches and the overture *Cockaigne* (London Town). Of the trio to the first march King Edward VII is said to have remarked: 'You have composed a tune which will go round the world.' With the words 'Land of Hope and Glory' added (despite Jaeger's objection: see letter of 6th December 1901) it has certainly done that. The words were added when it was put into the *Coronation Ode*, Op. 44 (1902). 'It was no disgrace,' said Elgar, referring to the time of the troubadours and bards, 'for a

[1] *Musical Times*, October 1900.
[2] McVeagh, *op. cit.*, pp. 29 and 32.

9

man to be turned on to step in front of an army and inspire them with a song.'[1] He had reached the hearts of the people, as Sir Hugh Allen said later to Hubert Parry—or perhaps Parry said it.[2] There were to be a total of five *Pomp and Circumstance* marches, wherein we do indeed 'hear the Nation march Beneath her ensign as an eagle's wing' (Lord de Tabley).[3]

If the word 'imperial' is in the mind when we contemplate one side of Elgar's nature, so the word 'dream' represents the other. After some incidental music, Op. 42, to *Grania and Diarmid* by Yeats and George Moore, we note a characteristic title for Op. 43, *Dream Children* (inspired by an essay of Lamb). Indeed by the time of *The Music Makers* ten years later one almost suspects that his references to dreamers and dreaming have become an obsession. At the least we are reminded of the introspective lonely artist in a predominantly extrovert world. Even *King Olaf* had stood and dreamed (vocal score, p. 19) to characteristic music. No doubt Michael Kennedy was right to say that Elgar's music was 'at its first peak of popularity when Britain's greatness was uncontested', but to hear it now as 'the funeral march of a civilization . . . which was decaying' is being somewhat wise after the event.[4] Purcell also transcended his age and there was plenty of 'Rule, Britannia' to come.

Elgar's mother died in September 1902. Within ten days he had the solemn satisfaction of conducting *The Dream of Gerontius* in its entirety in the Three Choirs Festival at Worcester, where his subtly blended scoring had the benefit of the fine acoustics of the Cathedral.[5] He was now thoroughly in the mood for a truly biblical oratorio and had already started to compile the text for *The Apostles*, on which he worked during most of the following year. The majestic reverberation of a great cathedral is even more part of

[1] *Strand Magazine*, May, 1904.

[2] McVeagh, *op. cit.*, p. 55.

[3] Ernest Newman, *Elgar* (1904), p. 150.

[4] *Op. cit.*, p. 151.

[5] For a full account of the early performances of *Gerontius* see Kennedy, *op. cit.*, pp. 86–108.

the designed orchestration and, as *Gerontius* was a nineteenth-century work, so the new oratorio looks forward stylistically to the twentieth. The very opening bars, *Lento* and *solenne*, anticipate the style of Vaughan Williams, while the unrelated root position chords ('Christ's Prayer') of the second section, 'In the Mountain —Night', do so even more. There are still the echoes of Wagner and Franck—'render therefore unto César the things that are Franck's,' said one wag—and other composers, but here is Elgar's most mature and individual language in all its richness and with an unmistakable personality. He did not of course write specifically to a commission. As he himself said: [1] 'A composer worthy the name never waits for an order before setting to work. He is always thinking out works, always making sketches.' Indeed the idea of writing about the apostles dated back to his schooldays.

After the first performance at the Birmingham Festival in October 1903, Myles B. Foster wrote that Elgar 'appears to have shaken off all models and become a law and idiom to himself'.[2] It is doubtful, even so, if Foster had more than an inkling of the significance of the 'mosaic' building of material—for example, one page of 'In the Mountain' contains five separate elements, or 'motives', which can occur later in the oratorio in any different order. After all, it has taken people more than fifty years to appreciate this method of construction in Debussy, whose *La Mer* was written at this time. While Debussy was considered as hopelessly incomprehensible, Elgar was being judged by post-Beethoven sonata-form criteria. As he advanced, therefore, he met new forms of incomprehension, and he was influenced by Brahms usually only when at his worst. There are now no long, gay, sweeping scherzo movements like the last of the *Bavarian Highlands* or many parts of *King Olaf*. Yet after the ancient Jewish shofar has heralded the morning psalm and before the laconic statement 'and when it was day, He called unto Him His disciples', there is such a sunrise for orchestra alone as only Elgar could write. This again combines various elements—even a suggestion of Brahms—and makes

[1] See Buckley, *op. cit.*, p. 73.
[2] Reed, *op. cit.*, p. 72.

shattering use of the three chords representing Christ, the Man of Sorrows, in the texture of those unrelated chords.

Ex.1

'Christ, the Man of Sorrows'

Not even the dawn of Debussy's *La Mer*, finished at Eastbourne in 1905, is more orchestrally colourful. Elgar was original also in his libretto, particularly when he took the view that Judas wished only to force Christ to display his miraculous powers to save himself from death. Buckley [1] was perspicacious enough to consider this work an advance on *Gerontius* in technique, conception and originality of invention. Later commentators have not followed him, because mostly they have been mesmerized by the traditional 'unity' of the earlier work.

[1] *Op. cit.*, p. 79.

CHAPTER III

MATURITY: THE CONCERT HALL

ELGAR had now 'arrived'. An all-Elgar festival at Covent Garden took place in 1904, which included the new exuberant overture *In the South*, written after a visit to Alassio in Italy. In July he was knighted and the Elgars moved once more, this time further west to a house outside Hereford named Plas Gwyn. Elgar was further honoured in many ways both at home and abroad, including a doctorate at Oxford University. Still not wealthy, he reluctantly accepted the Peyton Professorship of Music at Birmingham University, but was glad to hand over to Bantock after he had given a series of controversial lectures during two sessions (he resigned formally in August 1908). He had had misgivings and some ill-health throughout, but still had compositions to occupy him, the most important being the *Introduction and Allegro* for strings, which was finished early in 1905. Despite his military appearance, says Diana McVeagh,[1] his physique was by no means robust and he did not enjoy travelling, although it became increasingly necessary. In June he went with Lady Elgar to America (one of several visits) where he received an honorary degree from Yale University and formed a friendship with the Professor of Music, S. S. Sanford.

The second subject of the sonorous *Introduction and Allegro* (dedicated to Sanford) was inspired by hearing a group of Welsh singers at a distance in Cardiganshire in 1901 [2] and perhaps again later nearer the Wye.[3] Though the falling third occurs in many Welsh hymn tunes, the most likely theme here, as Mr Alan Webb, curator of the Birthplace, has suggested, is 'Land of my Fathers',

[1] *Op. cit.*, p. 46.
[2] Percy Young, *Elgar O.M.*, p. 293.
[3] Reed (*op. cit.*, p. 85) is wrong when he says Malvern.

13

the Welsh National Anthem (second half). The middle section of
the work is one of the things the composer enjoyed: 'A devil of a
fugue . . . with all sorts of japes and counterpoint.' 'Jape' was a
characteristically Elgarian word. In the main, however, the work
is sadly grand, with a tremendous feeling for sound, without
theorizing.

When Elgar was given the freedom of the city of Worcester on
12th September 1905 he walked in procession wearing the Yale
University gown and hood, while his father, now unable to leave
his room (he died early the next year), watched from an upstairs
window. Elgar turned and saluted him as he passed.

During the latter part of the year and early in 1906 Elgar was
busy on a second oratorio to follow *The Apostles*, using some of the
same material: *The Kingdom*. He intended that there should be
three works but was too discouraged to complete the third part of
the trilogy. When he had overcome initial inertia he worked
extremely hard: his concentration and utter detachment from the
world while on the soprano passage, 'The sun goeth down', are
well described by Dorabella.[1] This was also the time when he
enjoyed his chemistry experiments, which were a relaxation from
composition. *The Kingdom* was produced at the Birmingham
Festival in October, conducted by the composer in New York in
March 1907 and then in other parts of the United States.

In June 1907 Lord Northampton came to stay at Plas Gwyn
and he sometimes played the pedal parts of Bach's organ music at
the piano while Elgar played the rest.[2] He was another encouraging
friend for whom Elgar 'felt better'. In a letter of 15th August 1904
the former had written: 'You have in you a special power of
bringing upon others the strongest influence for good. . . . You
have moved men's souls to the highest truths of Christianity',[3] but
even Northampton could not get Elgar to write the third oratorio,
of which there were sketches waiting to be used. Others tried, and

[1] Powell, *op. cit.*, pp. 69–72.
[2] Young, *op. cit.*, p. 136.
[3] Quoted by Kennedy, *op. cit.*, p. 165 (see also pp. 168 and 169).

he made half-hearted attempts right up to his seventieth birthday, but with no result.

Apart from small pieces and a fourth *Pomp and Circumstance* march, Elgar next became absorbed in some of his early sketches dating back to 1867 and wrote two suites based on them called *The Wand of Youth*, though his mind had long been working on a symphonic project, with the idea of characterizing Gordon in it. Ultimately he used no character in the Symphony for Full Orchestra, Op. 55,[1] which was first performed under Richter in Manchester in December 1908. Only four days later it was given in London. Richter, to whom it was dedicated, addressed the orchestra: 'Gentlemen, let us now rehearse the greatest symphony of modern times, written by the greatest modern composer,' and he added, *'and not only in this country.'* [2] (One sign of Elgar's continuity of thought has been pointed out by Reed: the motto theme with which this Symphony opens is foreshadowed in the first violins at the very end of the *Enigma Variations*, fig. 82,[3] though he was sketching it, as if new, in Italy in December 1907.[4]) The work was received with enormous enthusiasm and there were nearly a hundred performances of it in Britain during its first year. During the next two years it went all over Europe. Jaeger, ill and now with less than a year to live, when he had looked at the score wrote that it had the greatest slow movement since Beethoven. It was, as Kennedy has noted, not only Elgar's but England's first symphony.

The beginning of 1909 was somewhat fallow, but another visit to Italy produced the part-songs 'Angelus (Tuscany)', Op. 56, and 'Go, Song of Mine', Op. 57. In May 1909 Elgar wrote some of his tiniest pieces: two single and two double chants. At least one of the former (in the *New Cathedral Psalter*) has an Elgarian touch—not easy in such an apparently simple medium. An *Elegy*, Op. 58, for string orchestra followed the news of the death of his great

---

[1] See letter to Walford Davies, 13th November 1908.

[2] Reed, *op. cit.*, p. 97.

[3] *Ibid.*, pp. 156, 157.

[4] McVeagh, *op. cit.*, p. 49.

champion, Jaeger, though it was not actually in his memory. Richter's performance of 'Nimrod' was a greater tribute—the first of many funeral occasions on which this solemn variation has been played. Most of Elgar's works were dedicated to his friends but usually the composition had started some time before the dedica'tion, or—if one allows the absurd idea of the variation 'G.R.S.' representing not the organist Sinclair but his bulldog Dan—re'dedication.

Another puzzle arose over the Violin Concerto, Op. 61 (on which he had started work in February 1910), although it was clearly dedicated to Fritz Kreisler, who gave the first performance in November 1910. W. H. Reed had been with the composer, giving technical advice as violinist both in London and in 'The Hut' near Maidenhead belonging to another friend, Frank Schuster. On the score is the inscription in Spanish: 'Aquí está encerrada el alma de . . . . .' (Here is enshrined the soul of . . . . .). The five dots were thought to be the Christian name of an American friend, Julia Worthington.[1] Dunhill [2] does not even bother to copy out more than three dots, while Reed actually uses eight.[3] It was not 'Fritz' or 'Frank' because, according to Ernest Newman,[4] Elgar had assured Basil Maine that it was feminine. According to Percy Young [5] it could have been Adela Schuster or many others. According to Kennedy [6] it is much more likely to have been Alice Stuart'Wortley, daughter of Millais and second wife of Lord Stuart of Wortley, who was closely associated with Elgar and his music at this time. In fact between 1909 and 1931 he wrote her more than four hundred letters; all the sketches of the concerto went to her; the second subject is quoted on the occasion of the anniversary of starting work; and it, and others, are called 'windflower themes', since he always referred to her by this drooping wood'anemone's

[1] Powell, *op. cit.*, p. 86; McVeagh, *op. cit.*, pp. 53 and 54.
[2] Thomas Dunhill, *Sir Edward Elgar* (1938), p. 138.
[3] W. H. Reed, *Elgar as I knew him* (1936), p. 154.
[4] In the *Sunday Times*, 21st May 1939.
[5] *Op. cit.*, p. 335.
[6] *Op. cit.*, p. 129.

A FAMILY GROUP, WHEN EDWARD ELGAR WAS ABOUT
TWENTY-ONE.
Left to right: *back* Dot, Frank, Polly
front Lucy, Edward

name. When Reed went to Schuster's, he met many Elgar worshippers and the first he named was Mrs Stuart-Wortley.[1] A granddaughter of Millais, Mrs Perrine Moncrieff, recalls that once when she visited her aunt Alice a stiff servant stopped her with: 'Yes, her Ladyship is in. But you can't go up, Miss: Sir Edward Elgar is with her.'

The maturing man and the changing relationship is shown if one compares a very early, typically 'silly' letter of 10th June 1903 with one of 23rd February 1920. In the former, he 'flirts' as he did with most of the ladies of the *Variations*, and says how sorry he was that 'goodnight' was not said and wanting forgiveness for '(A) not saying "goodnight" prettily (B) for sending such a long letter (C) for not knowing your name; it must be a "nice" one . . .'. Brought up sharply by the harsh realities of the world six weeks before his beloved wife's death, he wrote the following very different letter seventeen years later:

My dear W. [Windflower]

It seems weary ages since I saw or heard of you: things are very dull and my poor dear Alice does not really improve in strength, so after all I did not go to Stoke; it seemed too lonely for her. Carice will be back indoors a fortnight and we shall see what can be done.

I have just been down to the club a few times and tried a lonely theatre on occasion but everything seemed dreadfully commonplace and awful! I go to the Gramophone tomorrow and have several silly meetings, etc.—it is a brainless soulless existence and I wonder very often what it is all about and why it is so—but so it is. Do ring up sometime—I want to go to *Pygmalion* one day—wd that do for you?

Felix was here yesterday eveg and delighted at the prospect of going to you.

Have you played the Sonata with Reed yet or again?

Love yours
E.

Many writers have apologized for Elgar's vocal compositions, and he was clearly a man who thought first of instruments, although at this time he did work with Ivor Atkins, organist of Worcester, on a new and excellent edition of Bach's *St Matthew Passion*. Jaeger objected to several things in *The Apostles* connected with word-setting, none of which was altered by the obstinate composer. Typical was the repeated 'cometh' on p. 135 of the vocal score, in a typically orchestral thought during Judas's betrayal scene. A purely orchestral work would show Elgar at his best; a work, moreover, with solo violin was to show him at the height of his powers. Some composers write with caution and even tameness for the instrument that they themselves have played. Not so Elgar. The solo part is fiendishly difficult. But it is violinist's music and full of intense emotion—a portrait rather than a landscape.

George V succeeded Edward VII in 1910; 1911 was Coronation Year. Alice was delighted to watch her husband enter the temple of fame and at the same time to see him climbing even higher up the social ladder. Five days before the coronation Elgar received the Order of Merit and his Symphony No. 2, Op. 63, was produced. Much time had been spent on its composition in different places: most years in this period of his life he visited Italy and the U.S.A. It was dedicated to the memory of Edward VII and the score is prefaced with some lines from Shelley: 'Rarely, rarely, comest thou, Spirit of Delight!' Although the symphony contains some of Elgar's finest music—particularly the intimate slow movement—it did not appeal to the public as the Symphony No. 1 and the Violin Concerto had done. This was noticed with disappointment by the composer.

Early in 1912 the Elgars moved to a Hampstead house (which they called Severn House) because they felt the need to be in London to cope with the large number of engagements and to be near many influential people. Also Edward liked the theatre and his clubs in London. Using up some old material and breaking off from time to time to play billiards or use his microscope, he completed the music for the masque *The Crown of India,* which was performed at the London Coliseum in March. The occasion was George V's visit to India. The next work, also using old material, was *The Music Makers*; the difference was, however, that this time the listener could recognize an almost embarrassing number of well known themes from the composer's greatest works. Charles Proctor, who has given sympathetic performances of this setting of O'Shaughnessy's ode, suggests that one should think of these self-quotations as one thinks of a small boy who invites you up to his bedroom to show you his 'treasures': string, penknife and so on. Some ear trouble which had interfered with Elgar's work was treated and cleared up by the end of May and *The Music Makers* was first performed in Birmingham on October 1st.

While in Italy early in 1913 Elgar started seriously accumulating sketches for a musical study of Shakespeare's Falstaff: the knight, gentleman and soldier of Henry IV, not the buffoon of *The Merry Wives of Windsor*, as already treated by Nicolai and Verdi. His views are given in an analytical essay in the *Musical Times*, 1913. Elgar was extremely well-informed on Shakespeare: see, for example, his letter on 'Scott and Shakespeare' to *The Times Literary Supplement* of 21st July 1921. He conducted the first performance in October at the Leeds Festival and thought it to be his best orchestral work. This was his last major contribution to composition before the outbreak of World War I when, at the age of fifty-seven, he was a great and respected figure throughout the musical world. He was toying not only with the idea of a third oratorio but also with the possibility of writing an opera and—less enthusiastically—with a piano concerto, but to no effect. The Elgars were holidaying in Ross-shire when war was declared. When they returned 'Land of Hope and Glory' had become once more the composer's most popular piece.

CHAPTER IV

THE THIRD PERIOD: THE CHAMBER

IN THE earlier part of 1914 Elgar wrote some small orchestral pieces—*Carissima* (the first of his works to be recorded), *Rosemary* and (more seriously) *Sospiri*—and a setting of Psalm xxix, 'Give unto the Lord', performed at St Paul's in April. Soon, however, he had to exchange his conductor's baton for that of a special constable. He was too old to be a soldier but he was willing to serve his country. Most biographers have quoted either with no comment or with embarrassment a letter he wrote to Frank Schuster on 25th August 1914. Since, however, I share Elgar's view that it is more sinful to torture animals than humans, I have some sympathy with the feelings expressed in the following extract from that letter: 'The only thing that wrings my heart and soul is the thought of the horses—oh! my beloved animals—the men—and women can go to hell—but my horses; I walk round and round this room cursing God for allowing dumb beasts to be tortured— let Him kill his human beings but—how CAN HE? Oh, my horses.' With very few exceptions this was to be the last time that horses were actually to be used in cavalry action (as opposed to ordinary pack duties), though Elgar was not to know this.

In Rome in December 1907 his horror of pain and suffering had showed itself in a strangely tortured part-song called 'Owls', for which he wrote the words himself. Frightened of being laughed at, he made not only the words and the music obscure but also the dedication, which was to 'my friend Pietro d'Alba' (his daughter's white Peter Rabbit): 'A wild thing hurt but mourns in the night. ... What is it? Nothing,' he says. The following April, in a letter to Jaeger, he laughed it off as only a fantasy, but obviously it was not.

During the war Elgar wrote a number of patriotic pieces, songs,

choral and orchestral works and several settings of recitations by the
Belgian poet, Émile Cammaerts. After Belgium, he turned his
attention to Poland, again to help refugees, together with his friend
Paderewski, the great pianist who later became Prime Minister of
Poland. Themes from Paderewski and Chopin are quoted in
Polonia, Op. 76, first performed at the Queen's Hall, London, in
July 1915. In 1915 Elgar resigned from the Special Constabulary
and joined the Hampstead Volunteer Reserve: now he had a rifle
instead of a baton. Alice and Carice were also doing war work,
but they had time for entertaining and Edward still enjoyed art,
drama and old books.

The settings of Binyon started in 1915 with 'To Women' and
'For the Fallen'. With the addition of the weaker 'The Fourth of
August', they were put together under the title of *The Spirit of
England* and performed collectively in London in November 1917.
There had been a misunderstanding with Cyril Rootham, who
also set and published 'For the Fallen', and it may well be that the
lack of enthusiasm for Elgar's music in Cambridge—already
Stanford had cooled—increased at this time. 'The academics who
held Elgar down until he had reached his forties had fortunately no
stronger weapon than a common dislike which found vent in
systematic disparagement,' said Sir Richard Terry.[1] In 1930
Edward Dent, Professor of Music at Cambridge, contributed a
distinctly cool appraisal of Elgar to Adler's *Handbuch der Musikgeschichte*.[2]

A complete contrast in these grim times was the writing of
incidental music to a fanciful play, *The Starlight Express* by Violet
Pearn, based on a book by Algernon Blackwood and first performed in December 1915. Another work of this kind was a
ballet, *The Sanguine Fan*, first performed in March 1917, after
which Elgar returned to the war with *The Fringes of the Fleet* in
June. This also involved a good deal of conducting, both in
London and in the provinces.

[1] See Cecil Gray, *Peter Warlock* (1934), p. 268.
[2] See Kennedy, *op. cit.*, p. 261, and Basil Maine, *Elgar: his Life and
Work* (1933), vol. i, pp. 277 foll.

Among those who died in 1917 were Elgar's uncle, Henry, and his old friend of Hereford Cathedral, George Sinclair. Lady Elgar noted that her husband thought much about the latter, as he contemplated his last letter. Now came a withdrawal from the hurlyburly of the metropolis to Sussex to write chamber music. There was even a withdrawal from his former self.[1] Brinkwells is a thatched cottage off a secluded winding lane which runs from Fittleworth to Wisborough Green. From a studio in the garden there was a beautiful view. Fifty years later the roof was leaking badly and there was a threat of demolition but, thanks to the generosity of a lady who wishes to remain anonymous, the roof was re-thatched in the autumn of 1967 and so the cottage has been saved for a further spell in a setting still remarkably unchanged and unspoilt. Lady Elgar and Carice did not always enjoy the remoteness and the lack of amenities, but for Edward the stimulus came to write new and more intimate music.

Early in 1918 Elgar had a tonsil operation and while in the nursing home started sketches for a string quartet; then at Severn House he started planning a violin and piano sonata. Ultimately, at Brinkwells, he was working on three chamber works: Sonata in E minor, Op. 82, for violin and piano, String Quartet in E minor, Op. 83, and Piano Quintet in A minor, Op. 84. All three works were performed in London the following year. The woods at Flexham Park, with a legend of impious Spanish monks who were turned into withered trees, exercised a strange power over him as he wrote (but see page 77).

There was alternatively serenity and psychic disturbance, sometimes producing what Reed aptly describes as 'languid melancholy'[2] in the second subject of the Piano Quintet, where the austere first subject, converted, seems to take on an almost Spanish flavour—not, I think, a 'semi-oriental mood' as Reed suggests, unless one accepts the Moorish influence in Spain. Elgar also enjoyed his pipe and other compensations. 'You will be amused to learn,' he writes, 'that I get Beer here in "plural quantities" as O.

[1] Young, *op. cit.*, p. 191.
[2] *Op. cit.*, p. 125.

Henry says. It seems strange after the difficulties in London. . . . It is lovely to hear the birds—nightingales abound and their song is really the most lovely thing in nature. . . .' [1] While still completing the chamber works he started composing the Cello Concerto, and carried on with its composition at Severn House in October.

Reed first played the Sonata with, as pianist, Landon Ronald, who at the time was one of the finest conductors of Elgar's orchestral music.[2] Then he played second violin to Albert Sammons (the British String Quartet) when all three chamber works were splendidly performed on 21st May 1919 at the Wigmore Hall. The cellist was Felix Salmond, who not only later tried over the new concerto with the composer but was the soloist for the first performance with the London Symphony Orchestra at the Queen's Hall in October. A nineteen-year-old cellist, John Barbirolli, was in the orchestra. The public did not show great excitement about this strange melancholy work, with its frequent strainings towards optimism but equally numerous moments of resignation—in the long drawn-out slow passage just before the end of the finale, in particular. The work was also under-rehearsed.[3]

Elgar's close association, if not infatuation, with Alice Stuart-Wortley, a lady five years younger than himself, the discreet supper-parties, the visits to the opera, the fishing expeditions, were borne with a politician's indifference by Lord Stuart of Wortley. They were tolerated also by Lady Elgar, but at this time can hardly have increased her will to live. Earlier biographers seem to have been totally unaware of, or singularly discreet about, this strange episode. One can only suppose that Lady Stuart of Wortley inspired the Violin Concerto as Mathilde Wesendonck did *Tristan*; it is possible for a composer to be inspired by a woman who is not his wife, without the suspicion of a dishonourable liaison. Jelly D'Aranyi, not only a fine violinist but also an attractive young lady

[1] Letter to Lady Stuart of Wortley, 7th May 1918.
[2] Dorabella (Mrs R. Powell) wrote to E. A. Butcher on 26th January 1955: 'Landon Ronald was certainly a very fine conductor and interpreter of Elgar and there is not his equal now in England.'
[3] Kennedy, *op. cit.*, p. 235.

23

of twenty-six in 1919, did not much enjoy Elgar's company or attention [1] and consequently, it seems, she did not like his concerto.

Back in Severn House, which they were finding expensive to run, Elgar became occupied again with his microscope and with visits to the zoo. There were more honours, more conducting, being filmed for the first time, the appreciation of Bernard Shaw and the thrill of Symphony No. 2 under a new conductor, Adrian Boult, who was to be identified with Elgar's music as no one else. 'How beautiful to have this and the Symphony success—so thankful,' wrote Alice, for the last time, in her diary. There was no new composition. Instead there was foreboding. After a short illness, Alice died on 7th April 1920, at the age of 71. Sammons, Reed, Jeremy and, for Salmond, Patterson Parker [2] played the slow movement of the String Quartet at the funeral, which took place at St Wulstan's Roman Catholic Church, Little Malvern, near the pre-Cambrian volcanic rocks of the Herefordshire Beacon and not far from Craeg Lea. It seems that Reed was so upset that he did not know who was playing with him. He said in his first book [3]: 'I hurriedly arranged this: and Sammons, Tertis, Salmond and I went to Malvern and played.' In fact Tertis sent his talented pupil, Raymond Jeremy, which was noted by Reed in his second book,[4] and Parker was substituted for Felix Salmond.

Added to Elgar's personal sense of loss was the bitterness in knowing that his daughter Carice [5] would inherit nothing from the 'awful aunts': 'a wretched lot of old incompetents simply because I was—well—I.' [6] Alice, it may be remembered, had married the son of a mere tuner, a tradesman who had called at the back door of her upper-class family, some of whom had actually disinherited her on her marriage. What an ironic situation that

[1] Joseph Macleod, *The Sisters D'Aranyi* (1969), pp. 116–19.
[2] McVeagh, *op. cit.*, p. 69.
[3] *Elgar as I knew him* (1936), p. 67.
[4] *Elgar* (1939), p. 131.
[5] She was married to Samuel Blake on 16th January 1922.
[6] Letter to Frank Schuster, 17th April 1920.

when she died Elgar was a friend of royalty and at the top of the social hierarchy!

After the war the revived Three Choirs Festival at Worcester in 1920 included the Elgar-Atkins edition of the *St Matthew Passion*. There were few other occasions on which the conditions of the original performance, at Leipzig with two organs, had been reproduced, observes Watkins Shaw.[1] A Wagnerian touch was added by playing a chorale before each part by brass from the top of the Cathedral tower, as in Elgar's arrangement of 1911. Elgar now buried himself in his hobbies as much as he could but creatively his life was empty. 'I feel like these woods [Brinkwells] —all aglow,' he wrote in July 1921, 'a spark wd. start a flame— but no human spark comes.'[2] But a more cheerful letter of the same date to Lady Stuart of Wortley quoted a German in his '*best English*': '"the celestial unearthly Quintet that to hear I had the occasion only *one meal*"—meaning, of course, *ein mal*'.

He enjoyed recording for H.M.V. at Hayes and in April 1921, a year after his bereavement, he orchestrated Bach's organ Fugue in C minor, the fulfilment of a promise made to Richard Strauss in 1902. Later he added the Fantasia, to demonstrate how the modern orchestra could be used to show off these works. To Eugene Goossens, who conducted the first performance of the Fugue at the Queen's Hall in October 1921, he confessed that now only the works of J. S. Bach inspired him to think musically.[3] He left Severn House and lived in a London flat for two years, going the rounds of his clubs, which now included Brooks's. He went on a cruise to South America and a thousand miles up the Amazon in November 1923, after having already leased a new house back in his own county of Worcestershire.

Elgar conducted his *Empire March*, not as planned at the opening ceremony of the British Empire Exhibition at Wembley in April 1924, but later in the year at the Pageant. In June he had a strenuous tour of central and north Wales. At the fifth Aberystwyth

[1] *Op. cit.*, p. 94.
[2] Letter to Sir Sidney Colvin, 27th July 1921.
[3] Eugene Goossens, *Overture and Beginners* (1951).

Festival the Cello Concerto was played by Joachim-trained Arthur Williams, who was particularly good in the slow movement (he had played it before in 1923); two days later Elgar was conducting *The Apostles* at Harlech. He had to stop a little man who started to make a speech and it needed all the tact and charm of Walford Davies to soothe him.[1] He noted with regret the deaths of Fauré and Puccini this year. On the death of Sir Walter Parratt the position of Master of the King's Musick fell vacant and Elgar was appointed in May 1924 to this important but not exacting post. The next year he received the gold medal of the Royal Philharmonic Society.

His love of animals, especially dogs, was so strong in this retirement period that it was said that he used to ring up his Worcestershire house from Brooks's just in order to hear his dogs barking.[2] He was happy if he could see the wild birds feeding within thirty yards of his window, as he wrote from Scotland to Lady Stuart of Wortley in 1914, and resented it if 'progress' made it no longer possible for birds to nest in the eaves of his house. 'I think I could turn and live with animals,' wrote Whitman in a poem of which Elgar was particularly fond. He was in most respects a Conservative. Politically he opposed the beginning of Socialism, while he loved and romanticized the past both in his behaviour and, as can be seen, in his works. He seemed to know every inch of his native county and never tired of re-exploring it.[3] With silvery hair and moustache he roamed the countryside looking, but not feeling, like a local squire. He still conducted from time to time, with an 'uneasy wilful beat',[4] yet 'he could make you feel exactly what he wanted if you were in sympathy with him'[5] and he had an expressive left hand. He did not like other people's interpretations,[6]

[1] Ian Parrott, *The Spiritual Pilgrims* (Llandybie, 1969), p. 62.

[2] Charles Graves, *Leather Armchairs* (1963).

[3] W. H. Reed, *Elgar as I knew him* (1936).

[4] 'C' in the *Musical Times*, June 1926.

[5] John Barbirolli, 'A Personal Note' in the L.P. recording of *Gerontius*, E.M.I., 1965.

[6] See his letter of 1st June 1903 to Jaeger.

he seemed 'frigid' when compared with Henry Wood,[1] and yet he astonished with the 'magic powers of his personality . . . all performers are controlled by a great mind from the moment he raises his baton'.[2] His only compositions at this time were either slight, 'occasional' or arrangements, although he thought of writing an opera. Between 1927 and 1929 he moved twice to other houses not far away before settling down in the last one, Marl Bank, on the edge of the city of Worcester.

[1] *Sheffield Telegraph*, 3rd October 1902.
[2] *Birmingham Post*, 10th September 1931.

CHAPTER V

THE LAST YEARS: RETIREMENT

IN THE year 1928 Elgar was created K.C.V.O., and received the Cobbett Medal for Chamber Music. Also his oboe-playing brother, Frank, died. When Elgar left the Theatre Royal, Birmingham, after conducting the first performance of the *Beau Brummel* incidental music on 5th November 1928, a reporter asked him, 'Have you any faith in Choral Singing in this country in the future?', to which he replied, 'I have no faith in anything,' and slammed the taxi door.

A new pleasure for him was the gramophone, while an old one was going to the races. He saw an increasing amount of Bernard Shaw at about this time and it was through him that the B.B.C. was persuaded to commission a third symphony for £1,000. For many years Shaw had expressed himself forcibly as an anti-vivisectionist and his protest was particularly strong at this time; [1] thus he gained a bond of sympathy with Elgar, animal-lover as well as play-goer. He also recommended osteopathy for Elgar's lumbago.

The lonely composer really loved his dogs. Mr Wulstan Atkins, son of the organist of Worcester Cathedral, remembers the dogs at mealtimes sitting on chairs on either side of the composer. In human company the composer was sometimes moody and impolite. The first appearance of the New York Philharmonic Orchestra in London under Toscanini was a memorable occasion for all who can remember it. After a thrilling performance of the *Enigma Variations* on 2nd June 1930 Harriet Cohen went up to Elgar at the Savoy Grill and burst out with 'Wasn't it mar-

[1] See 'The Shavian Approach to Medical Reform', *Medical News*, 13th November 1964.

vellous?' 'What was marvellous?' he asked, stonily. 'The concert,' she faltered. 'What concert?' he said, and sat down without a further word.[1]

In 1930 there were signs of a new lease of life, however, when in April the *Severn Suite*, Op. 87, was completed for the annual brass-band contest held at the Crystal Palace. This work, dedicated to Shaw, was later arranged by the composer for orchestra. Shaw advised him to drop the polite Italian indications and suggested bandsman's language: 'Remember that a minuet is a dance and not a bloody hymn; or Steady up for artillery attack; or Now— like hell.'[2] The *Severn Suite* contains passages marked to be played muted for euphoniums, but at the time no euphonium mutes existed:[3] they had to be made specially for the Crystal Palace contest. The results were not very satisfactory and the experiment has not been repeated. With the military band the composer was completely at ease. Many were the times when he would drive to Kneller Hall with the Duke of Connaught, whose estate at Rich-mond was near by. He enjoyed in particular listening to the students playing the wind version of *Cockaigne*. The next work, finished the following year, was dedicated to the Princesses Elizabeth (later Queen) and Margaret and their mother, then the Duchess of York. The *Nursery Suite*, first performed in June 1931, also made use of old sketches; it was later made into a ballet by Ninette de Valois.

Another thing gave the ageing composer a new zest for life: his friendship with the fifteen-year-old violinist, Yehudi Menuhin, who gave a historic performance of the Violin Concerto, with Elgar conducting, in November 1932. Elgar's seventy-fifth birth-day (June) was celebrated by the B.B.C. with three concerts in December and he started work on the third symphony and on an opera: Sir Barry Jackson[4] helped to compile a libretto from a book

[1] Harriet Cohen, *A Bundle of Time* (1969), p. 166.
[2] Letter of 28th September 1930.
[3] Denis Wright, *The Complete Bandmaster* (1963), p. 148.
[4] See his article in *Music and Letters*, January 1943.

of Elgar's choice, Ben Jonson's *The Devil is an Ass*, and the work was to be called *The Spanish Lady*. In May 1933, Menuhin performed the Violin Concerto again in Paris; Elgar travelled for the first time by plane and before the concert visited the paralysed Delius at Grez. Both composers had only one more year to live. 'To me,' wrote Elgar,[1] 'he seemed like the poet who, seeing the sun again after his pilgrimage, had found complete harmony between will and desire.' The recording made at this time of Menuhin's performance of the concerto remained in the catalogues until January 1955, and it was to appear later on an L.P. disc. The boy's understanding was remarkable not only because of his age but also because of his completely different background.[2] He was able to impress even the most insular of nations, the French, although he was partly helped by the selfless preparation of the resident conductor in Paris, Georges Enesco.[3]

In October 1933 Elgar went to a nursing home in Worcester and was found to be suffering from a malignant tumour which pressed on the sciatic nerve; from now on he was to have periods of intense pain, in between which he thought about his third symphony. However this, like the opera, was to be merely sketches. Although he recovered somewhat and returned to Marl Bank after Christmas, he grew steadily weaker. Just as he enjoyed the gramophone—his bedroom was connected by microphone with a London recording studio—so he also enjoyed the radio. In particular, unlike most people, he liked to turn the controls down for the softest possible sounds. He had written a little essay (found among his papers) called 'H.M.V.' in which he extolled the 'marvel' of the gramophone, which 'makes study so much easier and makes the waste of so much time and energy [his early journeys to London] unnecessary'. On 23rd February 1934 he died.

Since some doubt has been expressed on Elgar's faith at the end

[1] In the *Daily Telegraph*, 1st July 1933.

[2] Maine, *op. cit.*, i, p. 264.

[3] H. A. Chambers (ed.), *Edward Elgar, Centenary Sketches* (1957), p. 30.

of his life, a letter from his daughter to the *Musical Times* of January 1969 needs quoting: 'Father Gibb S.J. from St George's, Worcester, was asked to attend, and to him my father re-affirmed his faith in the Roman Catholic Church.' Peter J. Pirie, in a letter in the same issue, confirms this, adding the significant comment that Elgar 'would utter extravagant things under provocation or pain'. After the disastrous first performance of *Gerontius*, for example, he wrote that his heart was now 'shut against every religious feeling and every soft, gentle impulse *for ever*'.[1] But if he had moved away from 'orthodoxy' it was, thought Percy Young,[2] not because he had too little faith but because he had too much. Ernest Newman wrote in the *Sunday Times* of 13th November 1955 that he had visited Elgar a few days before his death: 'Then, after a brief silence, he made a single short remark about himself which I have never disclosed to anyone and have no intention of ever disclosing, for it would lend itself too easily to the crudest of misinterpretations at the hands of thick-fingered psychologists.' As a last effort in 1970 I asked Newman's widow if she had been told but, alas, Newman had been as enigmatic as Elgar, so the reader must continue to speculate. The comment may have concerned Elgar's relationship with his wife, I venture to think, but it may equally well have been about his music or his religious doubts.

He was buried as he had wished, beside his wife at St Wulstan's Church, Little Malvern, and not near the junction of the rivers Teme and Severn which had also been considered. A memorial service was held in Worcester Cathedral. The same year his birth-place was bought by Worcester Corporation, the first step in the establishment of a museum, and on the first day of the Three Choirs Festival of 1935 a cathedral window, designed by A. K. Nicholson, was dedicated to Elgar's memory. Written tributes to him were not always consistent. Constant Lambert declared that Elgar was 'the first English composer since the eighteenth century who was the technical equal of his foreign contemporaries', whilst

[1] Letter of 9th October 1900 to Jaeger.
[2] *Op. cit.*, p. 255.

Arnold Bax commented [1] that 'He may be described as the last of the classics' and Kreisler said: [2] 'Elgar was great—the last, perhaps, of the great romantic composers.' Most of his belongings, heirlooms, honours and paraphernalia are still to be seen at the cottage birth-place, which was reopened in May 1967 by Yehudi Menuhin.

[1] *Daily Telegraph*, 26th February 1934.
[2] *Daily Telegraph*, 1st March 1934.

THE WAND OF YOUTH. A Faery Fantasy, rewritten by Winifred Barrows with Elgar's approval and performed in 1930, and again in 1957, by Lawnside School, Malvern.

CHAPTER VI

CANTATAS AND OTHER CHORAL WORKS

LUDWIG UHLAND (1787–1862), though not one of Germany's greatest poets, had his verses set by such composers as Mendelssohn, Schumann and Brahms. The 'horrific' romanticism of his *Der Schwarze Ritter* appealed to the young Elgar who, like many another enthusiastic young composer, did not wait to decide what impact any musical setting would have but simply used the lines to release his creative energy. Even at this early stage (1890–2) his feeling for instruments was ahead both of his sense of the appro-priate and of his personal individuality. Not surprisingly he describes *The Black Knight* (in Longfellow's 'broken-backed, spavined' [1] translation) as a 'Symphony for Chorus and Orchestra' and not a 'Choral Ballad'. Though Reed admired much of the dramatic chromatic writing [2] it is nearly all derivative, and the word-setting is sometimes awkward. Schumann, Mendelssohn, Chopin and others have their echoes. Some of the most elegant music is what has later been called 'light'—e.g. in sc. 3—and this is sturdily un-Wagnerian. Does the second dance here, with its curious Spanish rhythm, anticipate the odd motive later not very well adapted to Gerontius on his death-bed (see No. 4)? A wholly delightful pastiche of 1895 is the set of 'choral songs' *From the Bavarian Highlands*, in which the composer and his wife collaborated in music and words to imitate Bavarian *Volkslieder* and *Schnadahüpfler*, which they did with gusto and brilliance.

Not only in its use of an orchestral introduction but in other ways too *The Light of Life* (*Lux Christi*, early 1896) anticipates *Gerontius*. Although Elgar seems still to treat the chorus as an appendage, he is developing a most sensitive Italianate attitude

[1] Ernest Newman, *Elgar* (1905), p. 10.
[2] *Op. cit.*, p. 38.

towards the solo voice. He is not yet using very small units but he displays his material in the opening 'Meditation'—quite short ideas of eight to a dozen bars each—immediately and he is rich in invention; there is little padding or marking time. An Elgarian habit is soon noticed: the two inner parts move in octaves. The story of Jesus healing the blind man was adapted by the Rev. E. Capel-Cure and Elgar seems to identify himself to some extent with the blind man's suffering in a way that he was to again with the death throes of Gerontius. If he writes in eight parts and if he manages a four-square fugue (in No. 9)—to the rather appropriate words, 'The wisdom of their wise men shall perish'—without adding to his stature today, it must be remembered that at that period this was expected of any respectable oratorio writer. Elgar was to be dogged for many years by the taunts that he was not as good at this sort of thing as Parry, Stanford and others. After a while he went his own way as a composer, but he never forgot the taunts.

The unaccompanied part-song 'As torrents in summer', already in print, was pasted into the manuscript full score of *Scenes from the Saga of King Olaf*, after which the practical composer wrote the significant words: 'Pause for lost pitch'. Before this somewhat Sullivanesque epilogue there is some powerful music despite the lame, tame verses of Longfellow, which are helped out by some of H. A. Acworth's. The vigour of the tales of the Norsemen is a challenge to the composer as Thor is a challenge to Olaf and there is much that is pictorial in the music, much of it hearty in a pagan way, though at 'Olaf bore the cross to the folk at Nidaros' (Acworth), there is a chorale-like motive, later used to represent the Christian influence. More striking harmonically is the motive associated with Odin the Goth, forebear of Ironbeard, who is slain by Olaf; yet Christianity, with its weaker music, ultimately prevails. The work is divided into some well-constructed separate choral numbers and the composer's invention runs high, especially attractive being the ballad 'A little bird in the air' (Thyri, No. 13), which is like a scherzo; and much of the writing generally is prophetic of the greater Elgar to come. It was intended, said the com-

34

poser, that the performers should be looked upon as a gathering of *skalds* (bards)—all in turn taking part in the narration of the saga and occasionally, at the more dramatic points, personifying for the moment some important character. This, not really operatic thinking, became Elgar's general method. (The relics of the historic Olaf, King of Norway, killed 1030, are enshrined in the cathedral at Trondhjem—in 1930 the ancient name of Nidaros was re-introduced.)

The cantata *Caractacus*, written for the Leeds Festival of 1898, although exhibiting some fine moments, does not show as much development of Elgar's individuality as one would expect. The last stand of the British chieftain offers as much dramatic stuff as before, but Caractacus is still a Wagnerian hero and when his daughter, Eigen, enters (fig. 33) the music, losing its Siegfried-like, flat-keys panache, softens to G major as if it were Gutrune who steps upon the stage (see *Götterdämmerung*, Act I, sc. 2, her second appearance). Much of the chorus work in the second scene is devised on lines which Sullivan used more than once in his operas: the men sing their theme, then the women, then both together. Eigen's betrothed lover, Orbin, moreover, has a feeble *leitmotiv* reminiscent of 'I have a song to sing-O',[1] which is not very inspiring. The work is peppered with stage directions such as 'He casts down his harp and rushes off', but these are normally purely imaginary. Once, however, the work was actually staged as an opera, serving, as Percy Young [2] has noted, to show that it lacks 'compulsive dramatic movement'. It is surprising how unoriginal much of *Caractacus* is. Scene 5, the lament at the chief-tain's capture, is very Brahmsian, but fortunately scene 6 recovers, although Caractacus is now paraded ignominiously before the Emperor Claudius in Rome, who pardons him. Final choral praise not for the Roman Empire but for the British was described by Maine as 'incongruous' [3] and by Newman as 'a serious blot on the dramatic scheme' and 'the cantata is thus made to end in a

[1] *The Yeomen of the Guard*, 1888.
[2] *Op. cit.*, p. 299.
[3] *Op. cit.*, ii, p. 32.

sputter of bathos and rant'. However, patriotic sentiment at this time was something very real. Elgar had already shared in it in the short 'ballad' of 1897, *The Banner of St George*, and he was to express it again in the *Coronation Ode* of 1902.

Some of the broader, lyrical middle sections of his vigorous choral set pieces impressed themselves on the styles of such men as Bax and Ireland, for example the part at No. 4, *cantabile e larga* mente, in the splendid Triumphal Procession which opens sc. 6 of *Caractacus*. Elgar made the Romans see into the future in a very odd way by anticipating the British Empire, but Ireland wrote similar *cantabile* music in *These Things Shall Be* (1936), and his view of international brotherhood was anything but imperialistic.

After the three great oratorios (see Chapter IX), Elgar wrote very little substantial choral music. The ode *The Music Makers*, a setting of O'Shaughnessy, dates from 1912, although sketches go back more than four years, while the three Binyon settings called *The Spirit of England* date from war-time 1916. Although these works with their assured technique are effective in performance, they do not materially add very much to the composer's reputation; indeed the former serves to remind the listener of his greater works by extensive use of self-quotation. These, eight in number, are listed by Kennedy.[1]

[1] *Op. cit.*, p. 298.

CHAPTER VII

THE 'ENIGMA VARIATIONS': THE MUSIC
AND THE PROBLEM

FROM the earliest days Elgar showed an inclination towards the tonality of G major-minor. His earliest surviving work is probably an unfinished Fugue in G minor of about 1870. The alternation of a minor key with its tonic major was not a particulare featur of the practice of the classical masters before Schubert, but it does happen to be the scheme of the Menuetto and Trio of Mozart's Symphony No. 40 in G minor. In 1878 Elgar started to write a paraphrase of this work. That he apparently broke off before reaching the Minuet need not concern us; the pattern was established [1] and he used the key of G, fluctuating between minor and major in such large works as *King Olaf, Lux Christi* and the Organ Sonata, employing or suggesting also a *tierce de picardie* at the end.

A short, irregular, 'rather unpromising',[2] 'very odd' tune [3] of an 'a b a' shape, first improvised at the piano in the autumn of 1898, forms the basis of the *Variations on an Original Theme* for Orchestra, Op. 36, of 1899. On an inner page is inscribed 'Dedicated to my friends pictured within' and over the first page of the score is the word 'Enigma'. Lady Elgar thought that the composer was doing something that had never been done before—but it is not clear in what way:

---

[1] See Young, *op. cit.*, p. 275.
[2] See Buckley, *op. cit.*, p. 55.
[3] See Powell, *op. cit.*, p. 12.

Ex.2 Andante

Although Elgar originally mapped out eight bars for the middle major section and reduced it, the first part consists of the unusual number of six bars (followed by a double bar). Mozart's minuet, be it noted, starts with two three-bar phrases and not with the more conventional two or four bars. This theme is certainly stilted as it stands: a rest followed by two quavers and two crotchets alternating with a rest followed by two crotchets and two quavers for no less than twelve bars—and in the remaining four bars, in the middle, the same rhythmic pattern throughout:

There follow fourteen variations with initials or nicknames to designate the composer's friends. In a letter to Jaeger of 24th October 1898, he said: 'I have sketched a set of Variations (orkestra) on an original theme . . . labelled 'em with the nick-names of my particular friends—*you* are Nimrod. That is to say I've written the variations each one to represent the mood of the "party" —I've liked to imagine the "party" writing the var: him (or her) self and have written what I think they wd. have written—if they were asses enough to compose.' In another letter to Jaeger [1] he said

[1] See *Musical Times*, October 1900.

he 'looked at the theme through the personality (as it were) of another Johnny': 'it's a quaint idea and the result is amusing to those behind the scenes and won't affect the hearer who "nose nuffin".' In fact in the programme note for the first performance on 19th June 1899 he stated that their idiosyncrasies 'need not have been mentioned publicly'. Dunhill says: 'Great musical works ... often owe their existence to exterior influences with which the public has no concern. When a composer takes his prospective audience into his confidence ... he creates, perhaps, an added zest in listening. But when he stops short of telling them the whole story ... he starts tongues wagging.'[1]

Because of the many misleading comments arising from his tantalizing 'Enigma' subtitle, it has become necessary to subject his musical pictures to further scrutiny. His most important pronouncement, in the programme note, was: 'The enigma I will not explain—its "dark saying" must be left unguessed, and I warn you that the apparent connection between the variations and the theme is often of the slightest texture; further, through and over the whole set another and larger theme "goes", but is not played.' From this it can be seen that the problem must be divided into two parts. Referring to the Finale in a letter to Jaeger of 30th June 1899, Elgar crosses out the words, '1st theme' and substitutes, 'principal motive (Enigma)', so there is a hint that the enigma is attached in some way to the theme. As early as 1904 Buckley, without any obvious grounds, categorically stated that 'the theme is a counterpoint on some well-known melody', while Dunhill in 1938, again without any grounds, said that the 'larger Theme ... only existed in the composer's mind'. It is important to notice carefully how Elgar's views on the original stimuli changed through the years; for this purpose I give overleaf a summary of what has been deduced or said on each movement.

[1] Thomas F. Dunhill, *Sir Edward Elgar* (1938), p. 83.

Elgar

What Elgar (Jaeger Memorial Concert, 1910, & Pianola Rolls, 1913) *& others subsequently wrote.*

Do = Mrs R. Powell (Dorabella), 1937
Du = T. F. Dunhill, 1938
E = Elgar (as above)
N = Ernest Newman, 1904
Y = Percy Young, 1954

I ('C.A.E.') *The Composer's Wife*

Alice, who became Elgar's pupil in 1886, had an instinctive faith that her husband-to-be was a genius. They were married in May 1889.

Alice did not literally help her husband with the composition (Do) but 'those who knew C.A.E. will understand this reference to one whose life was a romantic & delicate inspiration' (E).

II ('H.D.S.-P.') *Hew David Steuart-Powell*

Pianist in trio with Elgar and Basil Nevinson; his finger-loosening exercises were diatonic.

'His characteristic diatonic runs over the keys . . . here humorously travestied . . . chromatic beyond H.D.S.-P.'s liking' (E).

III ('R.B.T.') *Richard Baxter Townshend*

The story goes back to 1895 (Do) that he had to act, against his will, the part of an old man in which he used a high falsetto. An eccentric, he rode about Oxford on a tricycle with a bell continually ringing. His voice fascinated Mrs Elgar Blake as a child.

'. . . The low voice flying off occasionally into "soprano" timbre' (E).

IV ('W.M.B.') *William Meath Baker*

A Wagnerian. He liked to lay down the law. One of his sisters married the father of Dorabella

'. . . Read out the arrangements for the day and hurriedly left the music-room with an inadvertent

and the other married Richard Townshend.

bang of the door . . . some suggestions of the teasing attitude of the guests [figs. 13–14 in canon]' (E).

V ('R.P.A.') *Richard Penrose Arnold*

Son of the poet, Matthew Arnold, a 'gentleman of the old school' (Do).

'Whimsical & witty' (E).

VI ('Ysobel') *Isabel Fitton*

Viola-player who had to practise leaps across the strings. Very serious, sombre and contemplative (N).

Years afterwards, when conducting a performance of the work in Worcester, Elgar was astounded that Miss Fitton, despite 'Ysobel', still made the errors that he had sought to overcome (Y).

VII ('Troyte') *Arthur Troyte Griffith*

Not as noisy as this one-in-a-bar variation would suggest. Perhaps it represented an invigorating walk (N) over the Malvern Hills in blustery weather. He was a quiet man, a painter, designer and architect.

Mrs Elgar Blake reminded me that there were (friendly) arguments, her father being a strong Conservative and Troyte Griffith a very strong Liberal.

'The uncouth rhythm of the drums and lower strings was really suggested by some maladroit essays to play the pianoforte' (E), but 'I never heard E.E. try to make him play the piano' (Do) and 'it is impossible to believe that E. really meant what he said. . . . May we not believe that Elgar (like another famous composer) delighted to indulge in "leg-pulling" when people became over-inquisitive?' (Du).

VIII ('W.N.') *Winifred Norbury*

Winifred and her sister Florence lived at Sherridge, near Elgar's house, Birchwood. She met Troyte for the first time in March 1898. She had a trilly laugh which Elgar deliberately used to encourage.

'Really suggested by an eighteenth-century house' (E), the music is connected to the next variation but in fact Miss Norbury and Mr Jaeger only met on two or three occasions (Do).

Elgar

IX ('Nimrod') *August Johannes Jaeger*

Beethoven, Pf. Sonata, Op. 13. Adagio cantabile (transposed)

Elgar. Notes that correspond to Beethoven are starred.

'I have omitted your outside manners & have only seen the good, lovable honest SOUL in the middle of you,' Elgar wrote on 13th March 1899 to Jaeger (German for Hunter, thus 'Nimrod'). His 'outside manner' was in fact amusing and almost racy (Do). This represents Elgar's gratitude to Jaeger who, when Elgar wanted to give up writing altogether, preached the example of Beethoven.

'No one could approach Beethoven at his best in slow movements (said Jaeger), a view with which I cordially concurred. . . . Jaeger was for years the dear friend, the valued adviser & the stern critic of many musicians beside the writer; his place has been occupied but never filled'. (E).

X ('Dorabella') *Dora Penny*

Probably subtitled Intermezzo because of its slight connection with the theme. Elgar first called Miss Penny 'Dorabella' in September 1898, explaining that it was a quotation from Mozart's *Così fan tutte*. She had a stammer.

Not in the least theatrical (Du); 'suggests a dance-like lightness' (E).

XI ('G.R.S.') *George Robertson Sinclair*

Dr Sinclair, organist of Hereford Cathedral from 1889, had the reputation of never playing a

'We jumped to the conclusion that this represented the musician's skill on the pedal-board of

wrong pedal note (evidence of E. C. Broadhurst given to the author). The scoring of bar 2 for bassoons (mf) and double basses (p) *without* cellos should make this obvious point. The addition of tuba (ff) two bars after fig. 50 gives the effect of an organist drawing a stop.

'G.R.S. will be no mystery to anyone who knows the names of the "Three Choir" organists' (N). Elgar started visiting him about 1896 and wrote in the Visitors' Book musical quotations called 'The Moods of Dan'. (Sir Percy Hull to Do, 13th June 1944.)

Sinclair died in 1917 and yet another so-called 'growl' appears in the String Quartet the following year (last movement: five bars before fig. 39). (See opposite column.) In any case at the same point in *King Olaf* the violins anticipate 'Dorabella' (not shown in vocal score).

his instrument, only to be corrected by the composer' (Du). (See also Maine, ii, p. 112.)

'The variation has nothing to do with organs or cathedrals, or, except remotely, with G.R.S. The first few bars were suggested by his great bulldog Dan (a well-known character) falling down the steep bank into the river Wye (bar 1); his paddling up stream to find a landing place (bars 2 & 3); and his rejoicing bark on landing (second half of bar 5). G.R.S. said, "Set that to music". I did; here it is' (E).

Dorabella had a 'growl' (bar 5) written into her vocal score of *King Olaf* ('watchdog', sc. 9) by Elgar in October 1896 (Do.). True, the full score of *King Olaf* has a similar viola motive, and again for 'foot print', so this *may* be taken as a touch of Dan. Tovey [1] asking 'Mr G.R.S. for his dog-licence' is just being wise after the event.

XII ('B.G.N.') *Basil Nevinson*

Cellist (see Var. II).

'A tribute to a very dear friend' (E).

XIII ('***') *Lady Mary Lygon*

Subtitled 'Romanza', the first sketches were marked 'L'. Elgar

'The drums suggest the distant throb of the engines of a liner over

---

[1] Sir Donald Tovey, *Essays in Musical Analysis*, vol. iv (1936).

intended to get Lady Mary's permission for the use of initials, but
she was already on the high seas
bound for Australia.

In the score the timpani roll is
marked 'with side-drum sticks'.
In fact, in June 1899, Charles
Henderson of Richter's orchestra
played with two coins. This
pleased the composer and it is now
always done that way.

which the clarinet quotes a phrase
from Mendelssohn's "Calm Sea
and Prosperous Voyage"' (E).

In 1905 Lady Mary Lygon was
married to Major the Hon. Henry
Forbes-Trefusis.

XIV ('E.D.U.') *Finale*

This is the composer himself,
Edu, short for Eduard, being the
name by which he was known to
Alice. Elgar used to give a whistle
to announce his return (four bars
before fig. 73; also in ob. & fag.
of Var. I) to Alice (Do).

'Written at a time when friends
were dubious and generally dis-
couraging ... the work is summed
up in the triumphant, broad
presentation of the theme in the
major' (E).

A study of these double columns will reveal several inconsis-
tencies, the grossest concerning 'Troyte' and 'G.R.S.'—both fast
and noisy variations. If Dunhill had exercised his incredulity
about the latter rather than about the former, we might have had
confirmation of a vital link in the mystery. When Elgar specifically
says 'G.R.S.' has 'nothing to do with organs or cathedrals' he
sounds like the boy who said he did *not* throw the little girl's hat
out of the window. Has he something to hide? Did Elgar and his
wife constantly divert attention from the truth? It was Sir Jack
Westrup who first suggested that the original form of the theme
was possibly such a sequence of notes as is presented in 'G.R.S.' [1]
Indeed how many classical masters would start with a theme in
which rests in the melody line come at the beginning of bars? Only,

[1] Professor J. A. Westrup, 'Elgar's Enigma', *Proceedings of the Royal
Musical Association*, 23rd April 1960.

44

perhaps, if one were thinking as a violinist, as Elgar would, but even the Bach *Chaconne* for unaccompanied violin does not exploit this across-the-strings technique in the theme. Surely the theme, as it stands, is more like a variation. Here are examples from other composers for comparison:

Composer and Title	Number of Variations	First Use of Rests at Beginning of Bar
Purcell		
Grand Dance (King Arthur)	Theme & 15	Var. 8 = ♩ ♩ ♩	× 6
Bach		
Organ Passacaglia	Theme & 20	Var. 1 = ♩ ♩ ♪ ♪♪
Mozart		
Sonata in A ma, K.331	Theme & 6	Var. 4 = ♪ ♫ ♫♪	
Beethoven		
32 Variations	Theme & 32	Theme = ♩ ♩.. ♪ (first bar)
Diabelli Variations	Theme & 33	Var. 2 = ♪ ♪ ♪ ♪ ♪	× 32
Eroica Symphony	Theme & 8	None
Schumann		
Études Symphoniques	Theme & 12	None (Appendix 4 has some)
Brahms		
Symphony No. 4	Theme & 30	Var. 1 = ♩ ♩ ♩	× 8

From this random list only Beethoven once seems to start the theme with a rest (in the *32 Variations*) and that for only one bar.

CHAPTER VIII

THE ENIGMA: A SOLUTION

WHEN we consider that more than seventy fruitless years have passed, it may seem surprising that it should now be possible to offer a solution to the enigma—and indeed to both parts. For help with the first part, unravelling the enigma's 'dark saying', I am much indebted to the Rt Rev. John Richards, Bishop of St Davids.

Elgar was a Roman Catholic, helped his father as organist and was familiar with the language of the Roman Mass. Were not his friends to see themselves through these variations as in the Vulgate version of I. Cor. xiii. 12: 'Videmus nunc per speculum in aenigmate',[1] words which come in the Quinquagesima Mass in the Epistle?[2] The last word is from the Greek αἴνιγμα, which is translated in the Revised Version margin as 'in a riddle'. The passage in the Authorized Version is: 'For now we see through a glass, darkly; but then face to face: now I know in part; but then shall I know even as also I am known.' Elgar gave a clue by his use of the word 'dark', in the meaning of obscure, literally or figura- tively. The *New English Bible* has: 'Now we see only puzzling reflections in a mirror, but then we shall see face to face. My knowledge now is partial; then it will be whole, like God's knowledge of me.' For further confirmation of how Elgar felt about himself—his reaching maturity as a composer but massive lack of

---

[1] Βλέπομεν γὰρ ἄρτι δι᾽ἐσόπτρου ἐν αἰνίγματι, τότε δέ πρόσωπον πρὸς πρόσωπον· ἄρτι γινώσκω ἐκ μέρους, τότε δὲ ἐπιγνώσομαι καθὼς καὶ ἐπεγνώσθην.

[2] Elgar knew his Vulgate (letter of 11th April 1902 to Jaeger) and his liturgy (ditto, 1st March 1903); he quoted Titus I. 12 (ditto, 22nd March 1903).

recognition—we may read the verses of the Bible before and after verse 12:

> 11. When I was a child, my speech, my outlook, and my thoughts were all childish. When I grew up, I had finished with childish[1] things.
> 13. In a word, there are three things that last for ever; faith, hope, and love; but the greatest of them all is love.

If the above solution is correct, Elgar's remark of November 1899 to Dorabella fits into place: 'Haven't you guessed it yet? Try again.' 'Are you quite sure I know it?' 'Quite.' And on another occasion: 'Well I'm surprised. I thought you of all people would guess it.'[2] This could now be interpreted as meaning that the daughter of a clergyman (Dorabella's father was Rector of St Peter's Collegiate Church, Wolverhampton, from 1895) should know her Bible.

Elgar orchestrated the work during early February (the autograph bears the inscription: 'Ended Feb. 19th 1899'). In a letter of this date to Jaeger he calls it just *Variations*, and on another occasion 'symphonic variations'; the word 'enigma' is not used until May, so it seems. The score was sent to Richter's manager on 21st February[3] and the great conductor's acceptance of it proved to be a turning-point in Elgar's career.

In 1899 Quinquagesima Sunday fell on February 12th. So the reading of I. Cor. xiii must have been in the composer's mind during the final week's scoring. The Bishop adds, for the thought underlying the *Variations*, that the previous chapter, I. Cor. xii, has as its main theme 'Diversity in Unity': one spirit, but a diversity of gifts; one body, but a diversity of limbs; one Lord, but a diversity of ministries. Love alone can maintain the diversity in true unity. And I. Cor. xiii is a chapter divided into thirteen verses: an interesting coincidence when one thinks of the thirteen friends 'pictured within' the *Variations*. According to Mrs Elgar

---

[1] In a letter of 4th July 1901 to Jaeger Elgar refers to Gerontius's 'memory (remembrance) of the soul—an utter childish (childlike) peace'.

[2] Powell, *op. cit.*, p. 119.

[3] Young, *op. cit.*, p. 87; McVeagh, *op. cit.*, p. 27.

Blake,[1] her mother's diary for Sunday 12th February 1899 has the
entry: 'E. to S. Joseph's.' Elgar, therefore, did go to Mass that day
—at the nearest Roman Catholic church in Malvern. So, from
Quinquagesima 1899, Elgar and his thirteen friends were to see
each other in a new way.

We may now turn to the second and harder part of the problem:
the larger theme that 'goes'. If your friend is a viola player or a
cellist, you are free to pay gracious tribute to his playing, but if an
organist you are not? Why not? Is Elgar playing an extravagant
confidence trick on us? Or is he trying to divert our attention? I
am compelled at last to the view that he is trying to take our minds
away from 'G.R.S.' The bulldog may never have put a paw wrong
in the Wye. The fact is that E. C. Broadhurst was assistant to
Sinclair from 1892 to 1896 and, like his master, never played a
wrong pedal note. I myself was a pupil of Broadhurst and can
vouch for the fact that both players were proud of their pedalling.
The Bach Gesellschaft edition was available in the mid-nineteenth
century and both Sinclair and Elgar were enthusiasts. Elgar
presented the complete edition to Birmingham University in 1905.
Three works of Bach, all in G minor, anticipate much of Elgar's
style: the chorale at the end of the motet, *Komm, Jesu, komm* (see the
Angel's Alleluia in *Gerontius*, after fig. 12); the chorale variations for
organ on *Sei gegrüsset*, where ten out of eleven movements end with
a *tierce de Picardie*; and the unfinished pedal *Exercitium* for organ:

Ex. 3

where most of the intervals of 'G.R.S.', bar 2, can be noticed (note
also the orchestration):

Ex. 4

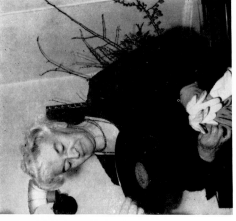

'DORABELLA'
(MRS R. POWELL), 1956.

WINIFRED NORBURY, 1923.

DR G. R. SINCLAIR WITH HIS
BULLDOG, DAN.

THREE FRIENDS 'PICTURED WITHIN'

The Enigma: a Solution

Elgar did not like to be told that his music was like anyone else's. Dorabella had her head snapped off more than once;[1] so did Jaeger and others. To mention Bach to him as someone from whom he 'cribbed' would have produced either a peppery outburst or a hurt withdrawal—or a cover-up in the form of a puzzle, so that he could laugh at his friends' failure to solve it.

It is unnecessary to try to fit in such tunes as 'Home, Sweet Home', 'Ta-ra-ra-boom-de-ay', 'Auld Lang Syne'[2] or Chopin's G minor Nocturne; all have been suggested, but their 'greatness' must be questioned.[3] Elgar was familiar with Wales; and in the traditional art of *penillion* singing a counterpoint of *words* and music is fitted to a harp air *after* the latter has started. The opening six-bar phrase followed by an apparently redundant double-bar would lend itself admirably to this treatment,[4] which none of the many ingenious contrapuntists has yet tried. However this also seems to be a dead end. I think it best to say simply that Bach was the inspiration behind the theme of the *Variations*, not as the writer of exact counterpoint but as a great and powerful imaginative writer whom Elgar admired probably more than any other composer (he did, after all, travel more than 150 miles from Düsseldorf in May 1902 to visit Bach's birthplace). Here, surely, is the greater *canto fermo* that 'goes' with Elgar's music which, on its own, starts as a variation.

Mrs Elgar Blake wrote to me on 7th July 1969 after reading the above, to say that she found it 'very interesting and a perfectly original point of view, not, so far as I know, put forward by any-one else. And most ingenious—I can't see *why* it could not be the answer, though I fear we shall none of us ever know for certain'.

[1] Powell, *op. cit.,* p. 52.

[2] Roger Fiske pursues this one in 'The Enigma: a solution' (*Musical Times*, November 1969, p. 1124) and confirms that Elgar some-times intentionally misled.

[3] Elgar said, 'No. *Auld Lang Syne* won't do. E.E.' on a postcard to Fox Strangways's friend, Dyneley Hussey, in 1929 (*Music and Letters*, January 1935).

[4] See Ian Parrott, *The Enigma: A New Slant* (Worcester, 1968).

CHAPTER IX

THE GREAT ORATORIOS

'I HAVE not seen or heard anything since "Parsifal" that has stirred me and spoken to me with the trumpet tongue of genius as has this part of your latest, and by far greatest work,' wrote Jaeger in May 1900. 'I except, perhaps, the Pathetic Symphony,[1] although that is but worldly, pessimistic, depressing, whereas your wonderful music is inexpressibly and wonderfully elevating, "aloof", mystic, and heart-moving, as by the force of a great compassion.' Thus, a fortnight before its completion, did Jaeger appreciate the quality of *The Dream of Gerontius*. In the centenary edition of the *Musical Times* (June 1957) at least five out of twenty-one distinguished contributors put *Gerontius* at the top of their list of masterpieces (with *Falstaff* the favourite in second place), while Miss McVeagh[2] categorically calls it his greatest work. Future generations may not agree. Writing to Jaeger in August, Elgar said he imagined Gerontius as a sinner, a worldly man and so he did not fill '*his* part with Church tunes & rubbish but a good, healthy full-blooded romantic, remembered worldliness'. 'It is,' he imagined, 'much more difficult to tear one's self away from a well to do world than from a cloister': and thus he characterized Gerontius in the music.

Maine thought that the average reader in the thirties would consider it as either an 'incomprehensible exposition of dogma or else as a Jesuitical attempt to make him swallow a theological pill hidden in the jam of a human story'.[3] Now, another thirty years on, much of the theology has fallen away, leaving only the music.

[1] The reference to Tchaikovsky is omitted in Kennedy, *op. cit.*, p. 79.
[2] *Op. cit.*, p. 129.
[3] *Op. cit.*, vol. ii, p. 37.

Cardinal Newman's verses were selected with much care and understanding by the composer. An interesting comparison between the treatment of death and judgment by two Catholics is given by Norman Suckling when writing of Fauré's *Requiem* of 1887.[1] In Fauré there is passionless peace, ending in Paradise; while in Elgar there is the torment of the composer as well as of the subject. Much of *Gerontius* is like the Pathetic Symphony (introduced to Hereford by Sinclair in 1897): the opening theme; the wild exultation; the snarling trombones; the demons; and the final resignation, although this last is musically perhaps more like something between Wagner's 'Liebestod' in *Tristan* and the 'Good Friday Music' in *Parsifal*. And the composer thinks of instruments before voices. Even Walford Davies (*Radio Times*, 16th March 1934) says, in characteristic vein: 'Listen intently to the instruments rather than to the voices'—something that the general public is usually loath to do.

The opening bars have an awe-inspiring solemnity, but I feel a certain unease at the appearance of the fourth motive (at fig. 4), labelled by Jaeger in his complete Analytical Notes as 'the weary, troubled sleep of a sick man'. All the themes in the Prelude are striking and varied, but this one seems to have been designed for some languid secular occasion, where a *habanera* may have been half-abandoned. Incidentally, the now traditional silent pauses which halt the full orchestra so dramatically in the Prelude between figs. 9 and 10 were not in the original sketches. The treatment of the solo voice is fully Italianate. The composer even wrote two syllables to one note, as follows:

Ex. 5

With and through the an - gel - ic host

---

[1] N. Suckling, *Fauré* (1946), pp. 175–6.

This was later printed as 'th'angelic'. In the first half, Gerontius, still alive, is guided towards his God. The chorus, his 'assistants' or, in the German edition, 'Freunde', produce the first wholly Elgarian sound with their Kyrie eleison (fig. 29). This is a motive which makes a magical reappearance (Part II, fig. 115) when the soul of Gerontius, to the accompaniment of harp, bass drum and lower strings and sustained organ, marked *pppp*, goes before its Judge.

In the introduction to Part II a feeling of other-worldliness is achieved by *legato* strings; the conservative but discerning Professor Kitson says that 'the consecutives, i.e. the octavos in bar 5, actually provide the means of suggesting the conditions of a soul wandering in space'.[1] The soul 'hears' the sound of singing, though he cannot 'rightly say Whether I hear or touch or taste the tones'. First appearing in 5/8 time in the orchestra three bars before fig. 11, this theme becomes the lovely and later impassioned 'Alleluia' of the Angel, underlined in the bass three octaves below. The soul passes demons, 'Low-born clods of brute earth', who make a terrifying ironic din with clanging orchestra, and then angelicals who sing another memorable Elgar melody, 'Praise to the Holiest' (fig. 61). Considerable momentum is built up, spoilt momentarily by a Gounod-like chromaticism for 'O loving wisdom of our God' (fig. 75); there is nothing else in all of Elgar's works quite like this long pounding episode, culminating in a paean of praise (ending at fig. 101). The Angel of the Agony leads the soul to God for a short glimpse, where Elgar instructs every instrument for one moment to exert its fullest force (fig. 120). Finally a half-chorus, a double chorus and the Angel bring the work to an end with something approaching the serenity of Fauré, though it is the peace after torment and the passion of someone who has attempted to solve the riddle of death.

I have referred above (Chapter II) to the solemn opening of *The Apostles*, which immediately proclaims a new and compelling musical language. For Edmund Rubbra this work was 'a major

[1] C. H. Kitson, *The Evolution of Harmony* (1914), p. 452.

experience',[1] but only by a minority is it still considered one of the greatest. 'It has long been my wish,' wrote the composer as a preface to the score, 'to compose an oratorio which should embody the Calling of the Apostles, their Teaching (schooling) and their Mission, culminating in the establishment of the Church among the Gentiles'. With his considerable knowledge of the Bible and with much interest in theology at the time, Elgar was ready to compile his own text. The music from the dawn, with shofar and integrated ancient Hebrew melody, to the end of the first section is powerful. Observe how the unaccompanied 'Mission' music at fig. 3 is similar to but stronger than the passage at fig. 51 in the *Coronation Ode*. 'By the Wayside', with the Beatitudes, is more gentle, somewhat in the manner of Walford Davies (at that time a composer to be reckoned with). The third section, 'By the Sea of Galilee', combines various elements with considerable imagina-tion: Mary Magdalene and her memories (chorus: 'Let us fill our-selves with costly wine') and a great tempest (chorus: 'He walketh on the waters'). Mary Magdalene, a genuinely repentant sinner, takes her place as a soloist beside Peter and the other disciples, and her characteristic music is added to theirs. In Caesarea Philippi they are joined by the Virgin Mary. Criticisms by Jaeger of this part were all ignored by the composer: the phrase 'ye shall lie down' (vocal score, p. 83) was like 'God save the King'; 'And I will give you the keys of the kingdom of heaven' (p. 102) was 'too jolly'; and 'Turn you to the stronghold' (p. 109) was 'crude'. This last indictment hurt Elgar enough for it to stay in his mind; often he joked to Jaeger about it, signing himself 'Crood' or 'Cruuuuuuud'.

Almost certainly the finest single episode is the first of Part II, 'The Betrayal'. Not only is Judas a strongly drawn character, but the use of the chorus (within the Temple) has a very compelling effect, as the drama, from the pieces of silver to his suicide, unfolds. Note the hard silvery effect of the 'price of blood', with cymbals, triangle, glockenspiel and, especially macabre, organ manual

[1] *Musical Times*, June 1957.

triplets with two, four and sixteen foot stops. After the Crucifixion and Ascension a beautiful amalgam of angels singing Alleluias with earthly chorus and soloists, including a touch of 'Is it nothing to you?' in the eighteenth section of Stainer's *Crucifixion* (1887) at 'They mocked Him' (2 bars before fig. 227), brings the oratorio to an end.

The intention, however, is that *The Kingdom* should be performed on the following evening. Here the apostles, filled with zeal, go out into the world to preach, and the composer's music has the same urgency and exaltation, particularly in the optimistic opening Prelude, which involves the *nota cambiata* plainsong 'Constitues eos', used as a motive representing the apostles. Many themes from the other oratorio reappear and sometimes develop. The organ is often used in its own right as an orchestral instrument with its own characteristics and not as a continuo or mere stiffener. At fig. 6 appears the dignified 'New Faith' motive, serenely Elgarian with its rising sequences and diatonic discords. The language of the second oratorio is ripe—unmistakably characteristic is the music for the two Marys, 'At the Beautiful Gate', or 'the tongues parting asunder, like a fire' (fig. 78) at Pentecost, when the composer seems himself filled with the Holy Spirit—but the structure is looser. The arrest of the apostles gives way to one of Elgar's greatest single compositions: the soliloquy for the Virgin Mary, 'The sun goeth down'. Hebrew melodies are again woven into the texture [1]; to Adela Schuster he wrote on 17th March 1933, 'The Jews have always been my best and kindest friends'. If he had written nothing else, this aria would be memorable in its original harmony, subtle changes of tempo and in its fastidious orchestration. Sir Adrian Boult has rated *The Kingdom* higher than *Gerontius*. 'It maintains throughout,' he says, 'a stream of glorious music,' [2] and in April 1969 he made for E.M.I. the first complete recording. The last section represents the Fellowship in the Upper Room, and includes the insertion of the Lord's Prayer; one

[1] Jaeger, Analytical Notes (1906), p. 39.
[2] See Alec Robertson, *Radio Times*, 31st July 1969, p. 35.

cannot help wondering whether the confidence of the opening has slipped a little in this serene ending. Elgar did not complete a third oratorio for the trilogy. He probably would have called it not 'The Judgement', but 'The Saints'.[1] The last theme he ever wrote, however, was called 'The Judgement' and as he gave it to W. H. Reed, he said, 'This is the end, Billy'.

[1] Young, *op. cit.*, p. 255.

CHAPTER X

MISCELLANEOUS INSTRUMENTAL WORKS

ELGAR was first and foremost an instrumental composer, even when he used the human voice. Thanks to his early practical experience, he soon outstripped all his contemporaries in his technique even before a personal style had evolved. The almost wholly unoriginal *Sursum Corda*, Op. 11, of 1894, with its almost sanctimoniously complacent and expected phrases, is yet extremely carefully orchestrated for the combination of two trumpets, four horns, three trombones, tuba, timpani, organ and strings. The organ is an integral part but there is no sign as yet of the composer using it in his constant efforts to produce a more sonorous bass line. The treatment of the strings is already masterly and almost every note is carefully marked with phrasing, bowing, accents, *tenuto*, fingering, the string to be used, and so on. As he said later to Reed,[1] any sets of notes without nuances, accents or stress marks, etc., were 'naked' and the passage 'tame'. It may be added that this work is not improved in Max Leistner's ingenious transcription for piano, published in 1901, in which the introduction is reduced, while five extra bars are gratuitously inserted in the middle and the Gounod-like barley-sugar at the end is drawn out by a further eight bars. Elgar was not the victim when, while adding parts for Heinrich Esser's transcription for orchestra of Bach's *Toccata* in F major,[2] he restored the original strong ending in place of an outrageous coda.

The composer had already completed a good deal of miscellaneous orchestral composition, mostly without more than a flair for pulling off an effective trifle, and he continued thus. 'Contrasts: The Gavotte A.D. 1700 and 1900', the third of *Three Pieces for Small Orchestra*, Op. 10 (some dating back to 1882), is typical.

[1] *Elgar as I knew him*, p. 141.
[2] Young says D minor (*op. cit.*, p. 424).

One of his early pieces with real charm and delicacy as well as popularity was *Salut d'Amour*, Op. 12, which, although available in many forms, is worth looking at again in score for the impeccable placing of notes. It was dismissed by Walker as 'West-End drawing-room' music.[1] Also popular were *Chanson de Nuit* and *Chanson de Matin*, Op. 15, No. 1 and No. 2, of 1897 and 1899 respectively, violin and piano pieces later arranged for orchestra.[2]

Since they made effective use of very early material, the two *Wand of Youth* suites may be considered at this stage, although they were not published until 1907 and 1908. Here is shown Elgar's great skill in getting 'out of himself' in order to entertain rather than to uplift. Both suites are subtitled 'Music to a child's play' and this indicates the intention though no actual play is provided. A 'Faery Fantasy' to the music, rewritten by Winifred Barrows with Elgar's permission, was performed at Lawnside School, Malvern, in 1930. Elgar himself wrote some 'notes':

> Some small grievances occasioned by the imaginary despotic rule of my father and mother (The Two Old People) led to the devising of 'The Wand of Youth'. By means of a stage-allegory—which was never wholly completed—it was proposed to show that children were not properly understood.

> The scene was a Woodland Glade, intersected by a brook; the hither side of this was our fairyland; beyond, small and distant, was the ordinary life which we forgot as often as possible. The characters on crossing the stream, entered fairyland and were transfigured. The Old People were lured over the bridge by the 'Moths and Butterflies' and the 'Little Bells', but these devices did not please; the Old People were restive and failed to develop that fairy feeling necessary for their well-being. While fresh devices were making 'The Fairy Pipers' charmed them to sleep; this sleep was accompanied by 'The Slumber Scene'. To awaken the Old People glittering lights were flashed in their eyes by means of 'Sun Dance'. Other episodes—'The Fountain Dance', etc., whose character can be deduced from the titles, followed, and the whole concluded with the March.

> March 1929.

[1] Ernest Walker, *A History of Music in England* (1907), p. 304.
[2] These are listed by Young in the reverse order.

These 'notes', found in the school album at Lawnside, were printed when *The Wand of Youth* music was recorded. Elgar had hoped to conduct the reconstructed play but was prevented by illness. How gaily this early carefree music trips along! And what a characteristic clarinet tune appears in the 'Serenade', and how vividly pictorial are the 'Fairies and Giants' (first sketched when the composer was only ten and thus preceding Tchaikovsky's *Nutcracker* music of 1892 in composition if not in orchestration) of the first suite! Not until the second subject of 'The Little Bells' in the second suite does the introspective composer begin to dominate. In his youth Elgar must have been moved to compassion by the sight of a chained bear shuffling along, for the onomatopoeia of percussion in 'The Tame Bear' is instinctively right, matching the pathos of the music, as is the similar clanking of 'The Wagon Passes' in the later *Nursery Suite*; the latter was, incidentally, the favourite movement, when recorded in 1931, of the Duke and Duchess of York and their daughters, the Princesses Elizabeth and Margaret. Deriving seemingly from one of Mussorgsky's *Pictures at an Exhibition*, it has the flavour of an old Worcestershire carter whistling a tune on his way through Broadheath.[1] 'The Tame Bear', however, takes one more to the Kremlin square of *Boris*.

Elgar's earliest concert overture of substance was *Froissart*, Op. 19. Full of youthful vigour, with a quotation from Keats, 'When Chivalry lifted her lance on high', at the head of the score, it is now seen to be somewhat derivative, though the scoring is assured, with its subtle placing of string parts and beautiful distribution of wind lines. Not for nothing had the young composer started making his visits to Germany. More modest in conception but more lasting has proved the *Serenade* for string orchestra, Op. 20, in which the authentic voice of the composer can be heard, especially in the slow movement.

Separate consideration is given in this book to the *Enigma Variations* (see Chapter VII). In addition to the five extrovert *Pomp*

[1] See Reed, *Elgar*, p. 2.

and Circumstance military marches (preceded by the bright but formal *Imperial March* of 1897) there is a splendid piece in the same tradition, the concert overture *Cockaigne*, with an abundance of good tunes descriptive of London Town—the soldiers, the urchins, the lovers, the Salvation Army, the churches—a London, said Edwin Evans, on the threshold of that period of social splendour which we know as Edwardian.[1] Music of Elgar's prime includes also the delicate *Dream Children* and the boisterous, episodic *Introduction and Allegro* for string quartet and string orchestra.

Nothing could be more typical of the composer at the beginning of his 'second period' than the exuberant first subject of the latter. Equally typical is the speed with which it gives way to the dreamy second subject (six bars after fig. 2), inspired first by the sound of distant Welsh voices at Ynys Lochtyn in Cardiganshire (see Chapter III). John Horton has suggested the Welsh folk tune *Bugeilio'r gwenith gwyn*,[2] but the more likely theme, as already stated, is *Hen Wlad Fy Nhadau*, though members of the Welsh Folk Song Society continue to imagine that they hear other tunes. What transforms the 'Welsh' tune, in any case, is the slide-slipping accompaniment, which develops four bars after fig. 3; compare it with the lovely subsidiary idea in *Cockaigne* five bars before fig. 5. It is easy to say that this great work for string quartet and string orchestra derives from the old *concerto grosso*, but in fact this is what Elgar hardly ever lets it do: there is never a true alternation of soloists and *ripieno* players. Take, for example, the appearance of the quartet at fig. 3. They are not playing on their own (as they might at first imagine), their lines being blurred by a fuzzy touching-up of odd notes on the orchestral violas and the addition of double basses. Elgar never leaves his parts clear, as a classical composer would (compare his scoring of Handel's Overture in D minor with Handel's own orchestral writing). Even when writing a fugue, as he does in the middle of the present work, the whole quartet is used at the unison to reinforce the bass line for two beats

[1] Pocket score note.
[2] 'Two Possible Elgar Allusions', *Musical Times*, August 1960.

(four bars before fig. 20). Another curious idea completes the material of this work: the throbbing syncopated chords at fig. 10, which seem to have something Spanish about them—more over-heard music, perhaps, on a hot evening in a sunnier clime? [1]

Elgar's favourite 'sunnier clime' was in fact Italy, though one feels at the beginning of the concert overture *In the South (Alassio)* that he had stopped short in Munich, since the first subject is so strongly Straussian. The most arresting idea is that associated with the past might of Imperial Rome—the historic past often impressed him more than the present—though there is a gentle *canto popolare* too. This sort of 'folk-tune' atmosphere, incidentally, was recap-tured in October 1905 with one of his quite distinguished short piano pieces, *In Smyrna*.

Short works worthy of note—and revival—are the *Romance* for bassoon and orchestra of 1910 and the sadly beautiful *Sospiri* of 1914. Not only is the latter in Elgar's most mature manner but in some ways it breaks the new ground that Bloch was on, with its dissonances moving not by step but by thirds (see, for example, the third bar) and a melodic line not only with sevenths but with agonized ninths (see bar before fig. 3).

The 'symphonic study' *Falstaff*, on which the composer had been working for more than ten years, was first performed at the Leeds Festival in 1913. For it Elgar published his own 'analytical notes', and in some ways he demanded more imagination from the listener than was reasonable. His own knowledge of Shakespeare was encyclopaedic (see Chapter III) and his delineation of the central figures is sumptuous, beautifully set off by two delicately nostalgic 'interludes' or 'dream-pictures', in which Jack Falstaff reminisces about his youth. The changing and deteriorating rela-tionship between Falstaff and Henry V is treated deftly and the metamorphosis of themes (e.g. from fig. 96 to fig. 103) is often very subtle. The theme for Falstaff starts, rightly, to swagger—gay, easy, corpulent—and later becomes gargantuan. The theme for the King

---

[1] Could Bartók ever have heard this? See 'Concerto for Orchestra', II, fig. 116 foll.

while still a prince is regal: in fact it seems to be a youthful relation of King Mark:

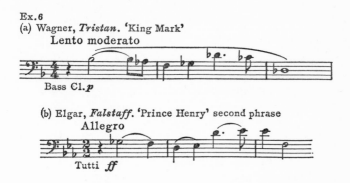

Ex. 6
(a) Wagner, *Tristan.* 'King Mark'
Lento moderato
Bass Cl. *p*

(b) Elgar, *Falstaff.* 'Prince Henry' second phrase
Allegro
Tutti *ff*

The work as a whole is bubbling over with tunes and there is much 'working out' of them though, as Miss McVeagh notes, it is often more fugal than symphonic.[1] There is indeed some amusing fuguing at fig. 44: but the treatment is also to some extent symphonic. For example, when Falstaff leads his 'scarecrow army' to battle, there is a shuttle-cocking of material from bass to treble (fig. 93) somewhat like the development section of the first movement of his early valued model: Mozart's G Minor Symphony. As is frequent in Elgar, the brash new sounds (the alternating chromaticisms at fig. 19 or the clashing brass at fig. 83) are now less memorable than such things as the diatonic theme at fig. 32—which Elgar called 'cheerful out-of-doors ambling'. After those personal outpourings, the great oratorios, the symphonies, and the Violin Concerto, *Falstaff* appears somewhat detached, and yet this work is autobiographical, from the optimistic loyalty expressed in the opening to the sad repudiation at the end. The 'loyalty-motive' (fig. 119) appears, in fact, as a sketch labelled 'Farewell to the Hut', July 1913, *espressivo,* and 'Written on Thursday after you left and

[1] *Op. cit.,* p. 174.

now Good night. E.E.' (Lord Northampton and Julia Worthington had died in the previous month and there is no doubt that Elgar was in solemn mood.) To show whether one is in Eastcheap, Gadshill, the Boar's Head, Westminster Abbey, or Gloucestershire, etc., and who are present, the Hostess, Doll Tearsheet, Pistol, etc., would it not be good to perform Elgar's *Falstaff* to a film some time?

The orchestration of Hubert Parry's *Jerusalem* dates from the time of the Leeds Festival of 1922, when the first half of one concert was devoted to Parry's music.[1] It was used again by Sir Hugh Allen, to whom it was dedicated, and it was performed under Elgar's baton at the Aberystwyth Festival of 1923, with Walford Davies trying to add to the noise by playing an unauthorized piano duet, with the lid open, with Charles Clements. The scoring does not ask for piano, but characteristic use is made of the organ, the basses sometimes have ♫♩♫ instead of ♩, so as to keep pressing out the tone, and in the second verse 'Bring me my spear' has elaborate figuration for strings and sharp ejaculations for brass. Altogether it is a worthy example of what Elgar could do but Parry could not: orchestrate.

[1] See letter from Sir Jack Westrup in the *Musical Times*, October 1969.

CHAPTER XI

INCIDENTAL MUSIC, SONGS AND PART-SONGS

W. B. YEATS was not given to flattering musicians. In fact he usually objected strongly to music being associated in any way with his poetry. Nevertheless, he said of Elgar's incidental music to *Grania and Diarmid* (1901), a play by himself and George Moore, that it was 'wonderful in its heroic melancholy'. There is incidental music and a fine Funeral March as well as a lovely song for the first act; all of them show character. After this one has to wade a long way through a number of trivial and uninspired occasional pieces, searching in vain for the true Elgar. One of these, the masque *The Crown of India*, dates from the composer's ripest period, 1912, but it contains little of value. The sumptuous orchestration may deceive some into feeling that there is originality in, say, the 'March of the Mogul Emperors'; in fact there is only a tremendous technique. The war-time music was stirring at the time. The effect of *Carillon* in 1914, when Germany invaded Belgium, was like the 'brandishing of a sword'.[1] Of the later works most are unimportant: *The Fringes of the Fleet* and the ballet *The Sanguine Fan*, both of 1917, the music to a production of *King Arthur*, 1923, the *Pageant of Empire* for the 1924 Wembley Exhibition, the music for *Beau Brummel*, 1928. There is one exception: most of the music which he lavished on a comparatively unworthy play in 1915 has a lightness and charm which are wholly delightful. This was for the fanciful children's play *The Starlight Express* by Violet Pearn, based on a book by Algernon Blackwood. There is at least one waltz song with a technique and imagination worthy of the Johann Strauss family: 'The Blue-Eyes Fairy'. Some other movements such as the 'Dance of the Pleiades' go through the

---

[1] Maine, *op. cit.*, vol. i, p. 204.

motions of contemporary light opera and musical comedy, and the 'Sunrise Song' takes one back to Sherridge, where one can see W.N. looking out of the window. The strongest effect comes with a quotation from the *Wand of Youth*, 'Little Bells', which is used throughout the play as a leading motive and is worked into and developed in the Finale with real gusto and even put alongside 'The First Nowell'. Clearly an escape to the stars with children released some creative energy in Elgar, which other topics failed to do, although *Carillon* the previous year had produced a strong *ostinato* figure.

Although he had thought of opera on many occasions, he finally got down to the idea too late. He was already a sick man when Bernard Shaw politely refused to be his librettist and passed him on to Sir Barry Jackson. Jackson's first reaction [1] was astonishment that Elgar should want to take not one of Ben Jonson's better-known plays, but *The Devil is an Ass*, which he thought quite moribund. 'Nothing,' he said at first, 'could be done with it.' Later, prodded by the enthusiastic Elgar, he found a 'splendid story for an opera . . . fined down to the uttermost dramatic limits in my version', after which Elgar added incidents and complications over which they fought, Barry Jackson with his vast stage experience and Elgar perhaps not so practical. The opera project, called *The Spanish Lady*—again a pull towards Spain—did not come to fruition, although much detailed planning went on [2] (see page 78).

Writing bitterly to Jaeger after the first and unsuccessful performance of *Gerontius*, Elgar said (12th October 1900): 'All my best friends including the highest thinkers only made one remark during my "exaltation": now you must write a few popular songs . . . that will make up for this.' As is often the case, the worst music may sometimes make more money and, by trying to carry out his friends' advice, Elgar put his name to some very feeble, dated rubbish of which we can now only feel ashamed. When on

[1] See Reed, *Elgar as I knew him*, p. 90.

[2] Young, *op. cit.*, pp. 360–75.

THE FIRST PAGE OF THE SKETCH FOR SYMPHONY NO. 2.

occasion he rises above the trivialities of fashion he seems to copy previous song-writers: in 'In the Dawn' it is Schumann and Schubert; in 'Is She not Passing Fair?' it is Brahms; and so on. This is not the stuff of which a new school of British song-writing is made. In fact it was left to composers like Peter Warlock to establish this with a truly new and original approach in the twenties.

One song, however, stands out. Significantly it was originally an instrumental item. The trio tune of the first *Pomp and Circumstance* march (1901) became in the following year 'Land of Hope and Glory' in the *Coronation Ode*. The splendid broad lines, which grew out of Elgar's love of the pageantry associated with imperial Britain, were split up with many repeated notes to accommodate A. C. Benson's words. A glance at the following sample will show how this was done and it will be seen further that the general public, who have taken the tune to their hearts, do not now in fact follow Elgar's rhythmic pattern in many places.

Ex.7

Elgar

Older readers must have regretted the announcement in *The Times* of 6th June 1969 that 'Rule, Britannia' and 'Land of Hope and Glory', following the death of Sargent in 1967, were to be dropped from their traditional position on the last night of the London 'Proms'. The B.B.C. relented a month later, however, after a storm of protests from all sides, and the two patriotic songs were restored once more.

Returning to the minims of the original, Elgar arranged the tune himself for cello and piano: a 'Duet for two nice people by another (nice) Person, op. x' and at the end, 'Repeat ad infinitum, ad nauseam'. He thinned out some of the chords, as the pianist's hands were very small. The piano writing for his songs is usually quite easy and effective—he does not, as has been claimed, write awk-wardly for the instrument—but he sometimes does odd things. For example he writes like an organist on occasion. In the early song 'Through the Long Days' of 1885 some notes are irritatingly tied over from one chord to the next. This was the way in which pro-fessional organists were taught to play hymns and it is unsuitable for the piano. But this habit gradually disappears; Elgar's own piano arrangement of 'Dorabella', with Jaeger's help, is a brilliant transformation of an unyielding orchestral thought. In one case his use of the pedal is strangely insensitive over nearly two bars of introduction to the second verse of 'The Pipes of Pan.' However, when his songs have orchestral accompaniments, as this one does, we are in a world of tone-colour of a very different order. The five songs in the cycle known as *Sea Pictures* are not in fact all consistently good, but the ebb and flow of the sea and wind is so beautifully portrayed that we are deceived. Note the tranquil heaving of the swell in the first song, 'Sea Slumber-Song', at the words 'I, the Mother mild' (letter B), with the strings three octaves deep and a sponge stick on the gong. This theme (which foreshadows Vaughan Williams), and the lovely opening bars, suggesting sleeping sea-birds, are used again in the third song. His wife's own words provide an utterly simple second song in this cycle, which completes Elgar's 'first period'. Here and there the words are ineffectively, indeed incorrectly, set.[1]

Although encumbered frequently by the different conventions of his environment both in songs—popular ballads and patriotic airs—and in part-song—insipid sentiments—Elgar unexpectedly rises to the challenge of writing for unaccompanied chorus, with several telling results. Unexpected it seems, because he manages the solo voice so much more naturally than the chorus in his oratorios. He rarely strains the voices in their upward reaches, though he frequently takes the second basses too low for effective balance, e.g. the final chord, *fortissimo*, of 'O Wild West Wind', where, after a fine progression of harmonies, the whole structure rests on a bottom E flat. A similar ending comes to 'Love's Tempest', where the thinking is strong and passionate but somehow instrumental. Of the earlier part-songs, 'The Snow', with the happy idea of piano and two violins to go with the voices, is one of the best, while the five part-songs for unaccompanied male voices, from the Greek Anthology, contain some good ideas, especially the popular 'After many a dusty mile'. The eight-part chorus setting of Tennyson, 'There is Sweet Music' (Rome, December 1907), is in two keys at once. The female voices are written consistently in the key of A flat while the male voices are in G major. There is a good deal of ingenious alternation (including the final bars) and some modification, which produce a comparatively harmonious result, but pitching is difficult. Holst faced the same challenge with his six bitonal 'Canons' twenty-five years later. One of Elgar's joyous inspirations from Italy is 'Angelus' (Careggi, April 1909), where the imitation of bells and the cross rhythms arise easily from the voice parts.

[1] See Newman, *op. cit.*, pp. 121–6.

CHAPTER XII

THE SYMPHONIES

SOME wines, often the best, do not 'travel'. They used to need to be 'fortified' for the journey. It also often happens that only music which has been artificially 'spiced up' makes its mark in foreign countries. Certainly Elgar made few concessions to any alien tastes in spite of his predominantly 'continental' language. Hence the curious concept of his 'Englishness' which has apparently applied to his aloofness. One of the most persuasive advocates of the 'English' Elgar has been David Cox of the B.B.C., who gives three main headings: imperialist pageantry, the choral tradition and a 'particular kind of restraint'.[1] He continues by quoting the 'most passionate music', Gerontius's declaration of faith, 'Sanctus fortis', and then refers to Elgar's scoring with its meticulous detail. Taking the last point first, I must say that the almost fussy over-marking of parts which is such a feature of Elgar's orchestration cannot possibly be 'English'. Regarding the three main features, the only one which I would have accepted is the 'restraint', and only then if I believed that Elgar had it in the true 'English' sense—that is, as understatement—but Elgar usually wore his heart on his sleeve in a very un-English way, it seems to me. Assuredly, like some fine vintages, his music has never until very recently 'travelled' well; certainly not to the countries, Italy and America, which the composer so frequently visited. Like Mahler, this melancholy individual never came to terms with the particular way of life in which he grew up. But if, superficially, we can identify Mahler with the Austrian Empire it is because we recognize the sounds of the brilliant Vienna of an earlier epoch, whereas if Elgar's two symphonies fit into the splendid pageantry

[1] In *The Symphony*, vol. ii, ed. Robert Simpson (1967).

of the Edwardian era, there is yet nothing English about the actual sounds they make: no echo even of Elizabethan or folk music. What there is comes from abroad. The first magnificent sound, the motto theme of Symphony No. 1 in A flat (1908), has a phrase which almost certainly comes from Wagner:

Ex.8
(a) Wagner, *Parsifal.* End of first phrase *(Liebesmahl)*

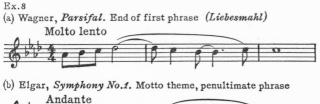

(b) Elgar, *Symphony No.1.* Motto theme, penultimate phrase

In theory, therefore, this fine first symphony should have become a favourite work in Germany at least, but it has not done so. For this rejection I still cannot happily accept any 'Englishness' unless it be the subtle 'non-academic' approach, which so often was Elgar's starting point. In this instance it was the text-book rule that A flat major and D minor could not possibly be combined. Thus the introduction in the former key, *Andante, Nobilmente e semplice*, gives way to the first subject group, *Allegro*, in the latter; and the movement, looking as if it is to finish in A minor, strangely and beautifully settles down in A flat. Moreover the composer starts the Finale in D minor and later re-introduces his first idea in a splendid setting as a motto. The last bars of the symphony, marked *Grandioso*, give the final glitter. Another motive which is common to the first and last movements is made up of notes (see fig. 29) and seems like an incomplete note-row. It is so odd that one suspects that it is made out of the letters of someone's name:

Ex.9

Elgar

The two inner movements are linked since the fast pelting notes of the scherzo, *Allegro molto*, become the serene opening sequence of one of Elgar's sublimest slow movements. One of the composer's most unmistakable rising sequences (fig. 96) is followed by some of his loveliest chromatic harmony (two bars before fig. 98) and chains of arabesques. This is much stronger than a similar passage near the beginning of Charles Griffes's *The White Peacock*, 1915,[1] and more positive than the soft-edged floating driftwood of Delius, whose chromatically surging *Sea Drift* was first published in 1906. A profound movement is brought to an unforgettable close with alternating phrases on muted strings and muted trombones. The orchestration throughout the work has been virtuosic —note, for example, the rising chromatic scale on all four horns while the three trumpets hold a high G flat *crescendo molto* and *vibrato*, after fig. 46. This would have been a great symphony even if the second had not followed it three years later. Only one year after its production Lady Elgar wrote from Careggi, near Florence, to Lady Stuart of Wortley: 'My dearest Namesake. I have been wanting to send you a few lines from this lovely place and to tell you Edward is looking well and rested. I trust you will hear E's impressions, tonally, some day.' The new symphony, it seems, was on the way, as well as some part-songs.

There is something hectic about Symphony No. 2. Small figures treated sequentially dominate much of the intense writing of the first movement, *Allegro vivace e nobilmente*, and even the slow movement seems restlessly tragic rather than at peace. A constant battering at the ears of the listener pervades the third and apparently scherzo movement. The opening theme of the finale, *Moderato e maestoso*, originally designed to suit the tuba, suggests calm, but later drooping sequences soon tinge the movement with sadness. On the first page, in ink, Elgar wrote, 'Rarely, rarely, comest thou, Spirit of Delight!', but in pencil he drew another of his odd devils alongside. The autograph, on twenty-six-line manuscript paper, includes the writing-in of smudgy passages in blank spaces in red, and sometimes patches are stuck on. Lady Elgar, as usual, would

---

[1] Griffes returned to the United States from Berlin in 1907.

prepare the pages for full orchestra, but at fig. 33 he had to alter her lay-out for four pages so that there would be fewer staves for wood-wind, leaving room for divided strings. Even so the side-drum and bass drum get added below the bottom stave. The passage between fig. 46 and fig. 49 is not in his hand; it is copied from fig. 8 a tone down, and Elgar added the altered timpani figure.

How did Elgar compose? The slow movement of this sym-phony offers an interesting example. From the sketches, which were sent to Lady Stuart of Wortley in March 1911 and be-queathed by her to the Birthplace, we can see that a certain single 'clash' sound came first in his mind for this movement (originally marked *Adagio*). There were also some rejected ideas not sent to her but found after his death by his daughter and sent to Lady Stuart of Wortley's daughter. He writes of 'clashes', 'later' and 'together', but does not in fact do what he had in mind. Here is one of the relevant sketches, in which the first chord is the 'clash', which was finally used with such restraint:

Ex. 10

crossed out
and marked
'later'

etc.

The published version, in fact, contains the following poignant phrase at the beginning and ending of the movement only, and it will be seen that the 'clash' chord, marked with an asterisk, is now the seventh:

Ex. 11

strings
(Violas
at top)

pp

71

It is not even marked with any sort of *sforzando* and yet the sketches had constantly harped on it. It is as if the black despair, akin to Tchaikovsky's in his sixth symphony, has been purged and refined. The sketches also included the combination of this idea with the first subject proper (at fig. 67)—a brass theme which comes back later (at fig. 79) with some of the most impressive full orchestra decoration written by any composer, through which a plaintive oboe weaves its solitary, but clearly audible, way.

The scherzo movement, *Rondo: presto*, is mainly a fierce *moto perpetuo* with cross rhythms, but a lovely middle-section tune, associated with Lady Stuart of Wortley, as 'Windflower' is written on the sketch, appeared first in this weaker form (a). The final version (b) has the stronger drop from F sharp to C.

Ex.12

(a)
Sketch

(b)
At fig.106
woodwind

Like the *Enigma*, the first subject of the last movement employs a severely restricted rhythmic pattern. Later it becomes, as Harriet Cohen put it, 'like a molten blaze of sunlight across a great sky'. 'One can't hear anything at all after it,' Lawrence of Arabia said to her, 'it kills all other music.' [1] Was it the string of sequences that grows out of the end of the second subject after fig. 140 that Miss Cohen and Walton were thinking of when they joked about Elgar's descending sequences? The composer wrote out the initial phrase, they decided, and then went out for a walk, leaving Lady Elgar to complete them, right down to the last one in the bass.[2] It

[1] Cohen, *op. cit.*, p. 149.
[2] *Ibid.*, p. 167.

was, of course, a joke. Sequences had flowed throughout Elgar's artistic career like life-blood. They only cheapened the stereotyped music which already had little value; they enriched those finer passages which were already pulsating with originality. Here they seem to have the tragic last word.

Just before the recapitulation (four bars before fig. 156), the composer wrote in the autograph over a static passage: 'Art made tongue-tied by authority.' The ending is like a sunset. Some would suggest that it represents the sunset of the British Empire. Elgar, at any rate, knew that values were changing and a way of life was going. Music to elevate, exalt and ennoble would no longer be required. A glance at Appendix A at the end of this book will show that the first writers of the 'new music' were already active at this time: Schönberg was thirty-seven, Bartók thirty, while Hindemith, Hába and Křenek were in their teens and Dallapiccola was seven. Music was soon to lose nationality; the question of 'Englishness' would fade away for ever, while music, like architecture, became not even international, but rather non-national. Even Wilfrid Mellers was sufficiently disturbed by listening to a performance of the Second Symphony after a weekend of experimental music to be astonished at what had happened in sixty years.[1] Is there a patronizing tone in 'Elgar's heroic, noble, prideful, tender, frenzied, melancholy (*etc.*) assertion of human will and consciousness' compared with the 'de-humanizing mutterings and mumblings' of the present day, and does his sociological approach solve this problem? Our culture, he claims, has been responsible also for the horrors behind Elgar's jingoism.

[1] *Musical Times*, October 1968, p. 922.

CHAPTER XIII

CONCERTOS

ELGAR destroyed a youthful violin concerto in 1890 and from 1909 to 1932 toyed on and off with the idea of a piano concerto. There remain then only two complete concertos in his output: the Concerto for Violin and Orchestra, Op. 61, of 1910 and the Concerto for Violoncello and Orchestra, Op. 85, of 1919. Basil Maine suggested that the symphonies 'make us aware of life primarily in terms of conflict and action; [but the Violin Con-certo] carries us to the safe retreat of the contemplative life'.[1] Like other commentators, he seemed unaware of the intense inner con-flict in Elgar which went into the Violin Concerto, which is as *unsafe* a retreat as any, although the musical language has become more refined. The move backwards to Schumann, the *fons et origo* which was to become so pronounced in the 'third' period, has already started. Schumann's influence is at its most powerful in the first movement—for example the groups of four chords repeated many times after fig. 12; and yet by the time the music has reached fig. 15, little more than a minute later, its angular leaps already anticipate Walton. The most telling part of the opening structure is that the orchestral *tutti* leads one to the point where one would expect the soloist's entry, but the soloist slips in unobtrusively two bars late and then blandly finishes the phrase on the tonic, as if the concerto had ended before it started. By a series of rhapsodic phrases, alternately faltering or urgent, the soloist lifts the work off the ground and it soars. By its opulent yet balanced scoring this work is like the symphonies, but by its constant changes of tempo (what Miss McVeagh calls 'minute quickenings and dallyings'[2]) it is

[1] *Op. cit.*, vol. ii, p. 140.
[2] *Op. cit.*, p. 167.

74

like the sort of piece that an Italian would have written for a sensitive *prima donna*.

No genuine old-fashioned *prima donna* would be very pleased in the slow movement, however, to discover that the main theme, in the mood of Brahms's Violin Concerto, is given to the orchestra; and the soloist, when he enters, is always given a counter-melody. The flowing music, suggesting perhaps Puccini and Tchaikovsky on the way, reaches a sublime moment six bars after fig. 53, where the violinist plays demi-semiquaver arabesques but the orchestra is significantly marked *nobilmente*. Elgar must have known instinctively that this was the 'best of him', since he quotes this phrase again in the finale (at fig. 94). The intensely personal middle part of the slow movement rises to an impassioned climax at fig. 56, after which the music falls away as if exhausted, the first horn repeating a falling sixth and the soloist playing slow *appoggiaturas* until the recapitulation—where, again, the soloist is still not permitted to play the theme.

Back again from B flat major to B minor, the last movement, *Allegro molto*, takes us into the world of the great virtuosos—the cascading chromatic chords between figs. 65 and 66, so up-to-date in 1910, were very much the stock-in-trade of Elgar's experimenting but less talented contemporaries. He understood the violin as no other great composer and he needed no Joachim to edit his music, although one is reminded of Brahms in the phrase which first appears one bar after fig. 72. The most unexpectedly magical feature of this movement is the *cadenza accompagnata* where the strings are told that the *pizzicato tremolando* should be 'thrummed' with the soft part of three or four fingers, while the soloist muses at length, recalling ideas from the first movement.

Nine years later Elgar has changed: perhaps now there is a retreat from the world, and this I have called the 'third' period. It includes the three chamber music pieces and also the Violoncello Concerto. Apart from the elasticity in the motto theme which appears at the beginnings of the first, second and fourth movements, there is less of that Elgarian eager hurrying and shy holding back; there is considerably less weight in the orchestra too, though it may be argued that this arises naturally from the problem of balance that every cello concerto presents. More striking still, the harmonic language has retreated strangely so that there is hardly a progression in the short third movement, *Adagio*, that Schumann would not have enjoyed. In fact, had it appeared nearly a century earlier, he might have reviewed it in his *Neue Zeitschrift* and said, 'Hats off, gentlemen. A genius.' Even so, there is a newness here every bit as personal as the more obvious later French influence in the fleet and fleeting *scherzo*, the second movement. Tucked away in this movement, indeed, is one of Elgar's stray thoughts that no one else could have written—a sort of tiny second subject.

The mood of the whole work is subdued and resigned; and although the Finale, *Allegro non troppo*, looks like being a hearty reminder of happier days, this movement gives way to a melancholy as deep as anything the composer has yet expressed (at fig. 66). The drooping sequences which follow (at fig. 69) manage to avoid the commonplace in much the same way that Verdi's beautiful motive in *Otello* does—by the chromatic raising of the expected last note by a semitone. The note is marked with an asterisk in each case:

Ex.13

(a) Verdi, *Otello*, End of Act I

(b) Elgar

Although the two concertos dovetail with the two symphonies in time, that for cello is a work apart, by a lonely man in war-time who sees that artistic criteria have altered irreversibly.

When the soloist is for the second time exulting in the swaggering tune of the finale at fig. 59, it may come as a shock to him to discover that a dozen or so cellists of a full symphony orchestra are playing with him at the unison. Except while playing in the *tuttis* of a Baroque concerto, soloists do not expect this: it is typical of Elgar's 'not leave well alone' scoring. The idea of constantly touching up, smoothing over, blending and blurring colours and strengthening tone is much like the contemporary brass-band scoring: Elgar naturally took to the scoring of his *Severn Suite* with an easier grace than many of the other 'serious' composers who ventured into that unfamiliar field at the time and later. We may also think back to the cadenza of the Violin Concerto. Again he will 'not leave well alone' and the soloist has attendants, though producing a lovely mysterious discreet thrumming which is like a Spanish serenade, especially the guitarist's chords six bars after fig. 103.

A word or two on the Spanish influence on Elgar may now be appropriate. He never visited Spain and yet time and time again a Spanish flavour affects his music. Many of his early trifles, from *Sevillaña*, reveal it in the harmony and rhythm, while semi-Moorish melodic inflexions are to be found in the 'Sérénade Mauresque' as well as in the weird dance in *The Black Knight*. But what of the rhythm for the ill Gerontius (at fig. 4), what of the swaying chords in the *Introduction and Allegro* (at fig. 10)? These chords move, by the way, to a syncopated rhythm which Elgar seems unconsciously to have repeated in the solo line of the second movement of the Cello Concerto (cf. *Introduction and Allegro*, fig. 10, and the concerto, one bar after fig. 20). Gervase Hughes [1] thinks that the Gerontius motive may owe something to Sullivan's *The Rose of Persia* (1899). Also Elgar had contemplated setting Belloc's 'Spanish' poem 'Tarantella' (later set by Francis Toye). Then there is the strange influence of the legend of the impious Spanish monks at Flexham Park, which must have affected both harmony and rhythm of the second subject of the Piano Quintet. [2]

[1] *The Music of Arthur Sullivan* (1960), p. 72.

[2] The story is apparently a modern myth. For a detailed discussion see the foreword by Michael Pope to the Eulenberg miniature score of the Piano Quintet (London, 1971).

Finally the composer tried to complete an opera which had been on his mind for a very long period, *The Spanish Lady*. It seems as if he had been drawn as by the memory of a previous existence. An interesting radio programme, using the 180 fragments, edited by Percy Young, was broadcast by B.B.C. 4, Midland, on 15th December 1969. Dr Young had fully scored many of the items, some of which made quite a strong impression: only one page, of four bars, had been written in full score by the composer. Of course a fugue was used for the 'diabolical behaviour' of Meercraft, a plausible rogue. The final 'Bolero' is exciting, if more like a polonaise than anything Spanish. The opera was gradually dropped by the end of 1932, and it is very difficult to decide whether the work would have held the stage as the composer had earlier wished.[1]

[1] A whole chapter is devoted to the work in Percy Young's *Elgar O.M.*

CHAPTER XIV

CHAMBER MUSIC AND KEYBOARD MUSIC

THE main paradox of Elgar's three mature chamber music works is that in one sense the composer has too few instruments yet in another he has too many. His thought, like Haydn's, was often in two or three parts: a melody, a bass and sometimes a counter-melody—and this may account for his sometimes doubling alto and tenor lines. But much of his orchestral writing 'blows up' the texture so that, most important, he cannot refrain from demanding a large number of instruments to colour, to thicken, to underline, to highlight and, in innumerable ways, to touch up all three basic lines. Thus writing for a string quartet alone was an unusual experience and a challenge for him.

Another curious feature is his apparently unadventurous style in 1918. It appears that he left his sketches in London when he went down to Brinkwells.[1] This may be the reason why the style has become so refined, though the war obviously affected him also. Gone are the brash, brassy modernisms. He is content instead to play about with formal differences in a more conservative idiom, being avowedly out of touch with new music. There are mannerisms, of some of which he was fond, which to later ears are rather tiresome. The progression deriving from Wagner in the Piano Quintet is referred to below in the chapter on harmonic language. The melancholy doodling on a dominant minor ninth or a dreary series of diminished sevenths in the same work, in the second movement at fig. 32, shows Brahms all too clearly as its inspiration. The stronger series of *arpeggios* in the Violin Sonata at fig. 5, thought by Reed to come from listening to the wind rustling an Aeolian harp,[2] has a more Slavonic origin. The constant pedal

[1] Young, *op. cit.*, p. 345.
[2] *Elgar as I knew him*, p. 149.

idea (low G) with changing harmonies runs through all the Russians from Balakirev to Tchaikovsky.

It seems that, instead of breaking away from the procedures of the past, Elgar now prefers to take sonata form with its system of keys and gently to break its rules—with a quiet chuckle to himself as he does so. Seventeen years before this he had chuckled that his first *Pomp and Circumstance* march, although in D major, had started on E flat. Now, for those who are sympathetic to him, there are some beautiful but gentle surprises. Not only does the Violin Sonata start in the 'wrong' key—A minor instead of E minor—but it maintains the deception right up to the penultimate bar of the movement. The second movement alternates a fancy, which is like a grave dance from an unwritten ballet, with a strongly lyrical second subject. This first idea is in Elgar's best *salon* manner. The finale, more solemn, is somewhat disappointing, but it does quote the lovely second subject of the second movement: Elgar here, as in the Violin Concerto, had a knack of knowing what was the best of him.

Simultaneously the other two compositions were being worked on and the creative flame was burning high. The idea which had delighted him before in the exposition of the Violin Concerto is now exploited in the Piano Quintet: that of coming to a full stop in the home key at the ends of opening phrases. He boldly plays this dangerous game at the sixth bar and again at the seventeenth. Moreover, when the introduction is over, the following *Allegro* also crashes to a halt almost before it has got under way. One cannot help believing that Elgar actually wanted to see the old fogies of the Germanic school wagging their heads ruefully at his misdeeds. This work uses the Franckian idea of a motto theme returning in the finale in a somewhat conventional way, but it also uses diverse ideas in juxtaposition, rather as the great oratorios had done. A peculiar 'Spanish' idea in the first movement (after fig. 4) gives way to a jaunty tune (fig. 6) before returning to the original idea (in the *Allegro* there is a metamorphosis of the introductory bars). There is some ordinary 'working out' which does not add much, and ordinary bass notes become busy, as they have done so

197

EXAMPLE 5*b*

THE SECOND SUBJECT FOR THE FIRST MOVEMENT OF THE
UNFINISHED SYMPHONY NO. 3.

many times before: for example, in *Pomp and Circumstance*, March
No. 1, two bars before E, and even in his edition of 'God Save the
King'—a phrase from the first bar of *Froissart*. But he does also
sometimes use the newer technique of short repeated units which
do not develop in the old classical way. Typical of this are the one-
bar motives at fig. 25 in the slow movement of the String Quartet.
There are less obvious sequences—but what is Elgar without this
essentially classical device? It is clear here that with the four string
players Elgar welcomes the idea of returning to the world of
classical Vienna: the interplay of intimate voices as in Beethoven.
Just as cadences in late Beethoven become increasingly back-to-
front and strangely consonant, so do Elgar's, e.g. this from the
Quartet:

Ex.14

The String Quartet's last movement, starting as if from Eastcheap
with Falstaff, ends in a gay rhythmic cavalcade in which it seems
that hordes of 'Little Bells', 'Bears' and 'Bavarians' invade the
score. In the last bar but two in the manuscript Elgar has crossed
out the upper octaves for the first violin. It is as if he had told
himself that a good quartet must not have a concerto part for the
leader—again part of the paradox.

What of Elgar's supposed awkwardness when writing for the
keyboard? It is certainly there in the Piano Quintet, and Young
makes a good point when, concerning the Sonata, he thinks he
might have learnt from Brahms—and 'Brahms might very well
have been glad to have written so miraculously for violin'.[1] Be this

---

[1] *Op. cit.*, p. 349.

as it may, Elgar had had considerable experience. He successfully made his own piano arrangements of the orchestral part in many choral works and of such essentially instrumental textures as the Violin Concerto. 'I have no opinion,' he said to Basil Maine,[1] 'of the composer who can only think in terms of the keyboard.' There is nothing awkward in the many early piano accompaniments, while most of the solos for piano from *May Song* (1901), with its Schubertian changes of key, to the delightfully easy *Sonatina* (1932) for May Grafton, his niece, are completely professional. As one would expect, there is not the brilliance that one finds in the unaccompanied violin *Études Caractéristiques* (published in 1892), but the composer can manage the keyboard and he can manage manuals and pedals too. The Organ Sonata, Op. 28 of 1895, is superior to the Eleven Vesper Voluntaries of 1889 not in competence but in personality. In fact the sonata is one of the first early works of Elgar which has the character of the great composer stamped all over it, and which must still be assessed in his total output.

On 9th January 1969, *The Times* announced that John Ogdon would give the first public performance for sixty years of the 'lost' Concert Allegro at the Cardiff Festival on March 2nd. Although influenza in fact prevented Ogdon from playing on this occasion he had edited and in February broadcast the work, which had been written for Fanny Davies in 1901. The manuscript was discovered by Mrs Bernard in August 1968 in the library of her late husband, the conductor Anthony Bernard. But although a certain excitement has attached to the discovery after over sixty years and though Ogdon declares the work is well written for the medium, there is very little in it that proclaims the master hand.

[1] *Op. cit.*, vol. i, p. 212.

CHAPTER XV

ELGAR'S HARMONIC LANGUAGE

ALTHOUGH Elgar naturally fell in with the Germanic chromati-cized major-minor system of the late nineteenth century, it is true to say that some of his most characteristic utterances were in conflict with these influences. Much of his music is non-Germanic; much of his very finest music is diatonic; and frequently he uses an impure form of the minor key—Percy Young thinks the 'whimsical treatment of minor tonality' comes from Mendelssohn.[1] To take the last point first, it would not be true to say of his minor writing that it is modal, any more than it would be true of that of Dvořák or Grieg; but from a sketch of 1878,[2] through the opening bars of *King Olaf* (the saga motive), through the song published in 1900, 'The Pipes of Pan', the *Grania and Diarmid* funeral march, 'The Tame Bear' in the second *Wand of Youth* Suite, etc., to the first interlude in *Falstaff*, Page to the Duke (see Ex. 23 below), the 'Nineveh' section of *The Music Makers* (fig. 28), the *Serenade* Op. 73, No. 2 for unaccompanied voices, and the opening of the *Piano Quintet*, etc., there is a strangely personal use of the flat seventh. It is neither the correct 'descending form of the scale' of the text-book nor the more 'folky' modal treatment which was later to be exploited by Vaughan Williams and his followers. The opening motive of *King Olaf* is described by Newman—rightly—as 'extremely effective',[3] but nowadays we can look back at some of Elgar's most admired passages and see them as somewhat

[1] *Op. cit.*, p. 277.
[2] *Ibid.*, p. 383.
[3] Newman, *op. cit.*, p. 18.

derivative. Did Newman in 1904 not see that the end of the
Introduction (used again at the end of the Cantata) is much more
individual than the beginning?

And what of the very first bass note in the Violin Concerto? Is
this not almost perversely flat, almost like a misprint to the unini﹣
tiated? Bars 3 and 4 of *Pomp and Circumstance*, No. 2, go through
the same motions.

Elgar frequently alternated the minor key with the tonic major
rather than the relative major. The only classical composer to make
a serious feature of this was Schubert. Elgar also preferred the
minor tonality—and it might even be said that in particular he
liked G minor: the key of one of his earliest pieces, a Fugue for
organ of about 1870 (see Chapter VII). 'Fugue was a form which
often curiously and fantastically fired his imagination,' said Percy
Young [1]—but Elgar was always unorthodox.

The self﹣taught Elgar has often been contrasted with the
'academic' Englishman, Irishman and Scotsman: Parry, Stanford
and Mackenzie. Sometimes, however, he is indistinguishable.[2]

---

[1] *Op. cit.*, p. 269.

[2] See 'Allusiveness in Musical Composition', a lecture delivered at
Cardiff by H. A. Harding, Mus.D., F.R.C.O., 13th April 1909.
Printed for the R.C.O., 1910.

Ex.16

(a) Mackenzie. *The Dream of Jubal* (Funeral March) 1889

Molto maestoso

(b) Elgar *Sea Pictures* (No.5 The Swimmer) July 1899

Allegro di molto

Elgar conducted the Mackenzie work in Worcester on 4th May 1899.

And what are those formerly admired chromatic passages but new toys that had already been played with? Wagner, who changed the face of the musical map, included in his innovations the 'weak' resolution of chords, as seen in the 'Liebestod' from *Tristan* and the 'Reine Thor-motive' in *Parsifal*, but one of these devices occurs as early as *Tannhäuser*, completed in 1845 and an opera which Elgar knew as early as 1883, when he arranged a part of it for piano.

This not only got into *King Olaf*, the arresting wailing of the wind and dashing of the foam (vocal score p. 21) which comes again at Olaf's death (p. 153), but it gets into *Gerontius* in many new forms. The first striking example of this sliding harmony here is at 'Go, in the name of Angels and Archangels' (fig. 72) and a later one is when Gerontius goes before his Judge (after fig. 115):

Ex.17

Although it is the 'leading note' (starred in both examples) which limply falls instead of rising in both Wagner and Elgar, it can be seen that the latter is now writing something different and distinctly personal.

The middle part of the 'Agnus Dei' of Fauré's *Requiem* (1887) is also Wagnerian but yet different. For the technically minded some of it can be put thus: whereas Wagner uses an irregular second inversion (marked $\frac{6}{4}$), Elgar introduces a 'weak' suspension on a first inversion (marked $\frac{6}{4}$–3), which is new. Elgar loathed the rules of the theorists. Is it coincidence that they always call the 7–6 and the $\frac{5}{4}$–3 (but not this $\frac{6}{4}$) 'strong'? These Wagnerian harmonies in different guises became a mannerism: e.g. 'Owls' (bar 5) and the

Piano Quintet, first movement at fig. 1. The theory of suspensions comes ultimately from the practice of the sixteenth century; and Elgar, like Beethoven, used in his own way only such ideas from antiquity as he liked. When he writes the more usual suspensions or *appoggiaturas*, he usually involves the 'forbidden' tritone. Climaxes of phrases frequently use this almost as a fingerprint, as in some of the loudest parts of the orchestral *tutti* of the Violin Concerto (between figs. 3 and 4), for example; but surely never in a more evocatively lovely way than with the softest insistence in the slow movement (between figs. 56 and 57) before the recapitulation. In so far as the former climactic chord, with high-lying strings and punching trombone entry, is virtually identical with a similar moment (three bars before fig. 4) in the second of the *Enigma Variations*, 'C.A.E.', one might even suppose that the 'soul' of the Violin Concerto was, after all, that of the composer's beloved wife. The 'Et incarnatus' from Beethoven's *Missa Solemnis* suggests that the composer studied the older counterpoint and then forgot it, just as the 'Apostles' motive—see the Prelude to *The Kingdom*, bars 7 to 9—is a *nota cambiata* only in general shape, not in treatment.

For the non-Germanic—let alone non-English—sound in Elgar's language, we may take a further look at the Violin Concerto. The opening theme, with its optimistic outburst soon to be tinged with melancholy, is not typical of Tchaikovsky, but the reappearance of this theme on the horns in the major key during the work's final seven bars most surely is. In fact it is just the sort of thing that the Russian composer does with one of the principal themes, also in B minor, in *Swan Lake*. The mixed-colour scoring (fig. 10), furthermore, in the first movement of the Violin Concerto is thoroughly un-German. It again recalls *Swan Lake*: the famous waltz in Act I. It is, of course, un-English, because there was no such thing as English scoring (notice the different nuances: solo violin *ff*; three horns *pp*; and basses *p*), and the only composer who had recently written anything at all like this work in harmonic language was MacDowell, in the last movement of his *Sonata Tragica* for piano (1893).

Elgar

But, much though Elgar seems to have shared Tchaikovsky's melancholy, so also was he able to share the spirit of the lighter and more cheerful *salon* pieces. The dancing of 'Dorabella' and the brass of 'E.D.U.' (himself) also owe something to the Russian. If he had been a Russian, said Elgar much later on, the *Enigma Variations* would have been a ballet. And in 1968 they were finally made into one by Frederick Ashton. If Ravel thought that Elgar's language was 'in effect Mendelssohn',[1] then Ravel must have been thinking of the very earliest *salon* pieces (did he know the *Romance*, Op. 1, 1878?); if not, he was indeed very insensitive to stylistic detail or perhaps just deliberately ignorant.

Of course Elgar does not slavishly follow Tchaikovsky. For instance, when he has just had the instruments the right way round, you will find an inversion of violin parts such as this from the *Introduction and Allegro*:

Ex. 18
bar after ⑤

Tempo primo

Strings

Reminding one possibly of the nervous twisting of string lines in the final movement of Tchaikovsky's *Pathetic Symphony*, this nevertheless represents the practical Elgar: he gives the second fiddles the limelight. In the Symphony No. 1 he goes even further: he gives the last desks of all the strings the tune (in the last movement at fig. 146). This is tremendously practical and original. It is also diatonic, like the quotation above, which has cascading

[1] In Vaughan Williams's 'Musical Autobiography', quoted fully in H. Foss, *Ralph Vaughan Williams* (1950), p. 35.

clashes more in the tradition of Bach (the organ *Toccata* in F major, for example) than that of the Romantics:

Ex. 19

(a) Bach, *Toccata* in F, BWV. 540

(b) Elgar, *Pomp & Circumstance* March No. 1, bar 15.

(c) Elgar, *Gerontius* Part II (before ③):

But the later Romantics had been exploiting new progressions. Another 'new look' had been coming in: a major sub-dominant chord, often with seventh or ninth added (Elgar plays with it in fig. 5 of the *Light of Life*, 1896)—*see* Examples 20*a* and 20*b* below.

Ex. 20

(a) Sullivan, *The Golden Legend*, Sc. VI (1886)

(b) Puccini, *Manon Lescaut,*
Act III (1893)

In his ding-dong use of two chords, Elgar follows Sullivan, is paralleled by Puccini and Fauré and anticipates the Vaughan Williams of *On Wenlock Edge* (third song, 1911). These chords, somewhat extended, are exploited at the end of Fauré's song 'Clair de Lune' (1887), for example. Elgar makes use of these sounds as small units and he also likes to move them up and down:

Ex. 21

Elgar, *The Kingdom*, Sc. IV (1906)

repeated and transposed

Similar four-chord units, deriving ultimately from Wagner, form a rather tiresome feature of *Falstaff* (figs. 19–21). Elgar was sufficiently 'taken' by his own sequences here to ink in the sketches (? August 1913). The extraordinary thing is that these seemingly 'modern' effects are now forgotten. The most lasting Elgar—and therefore the most true Elgar—is not to be found here, nor in the Debussyan consecutive fifths of *Gerontius* (fig. 108), and still less in the even lusher slide-slipping of the later oratorios, culminating with the ninths and thirteenths of *The Music Makers* (fig. 43). These sounds have become dated. As one might expect, it is the 'still small voice' of unpretentiousness which has given Elgar the stamp of genius. And the two-chord units which are now remembered are either wholly diatonic (*The Wand of Youth* and the Organ Sonata) or nearly so, with the supertonic imaginary root being used (*Chanson de Matin*):

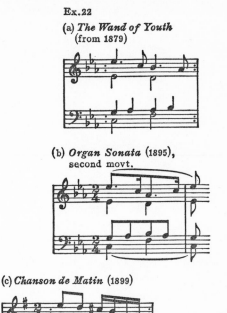

Ex.22

(a) *The Wand of Youth*
(from 1879)

(b) *Organ Sonata* (1895),
second movt.

(c) *Chanson de Matin* (1899)

melody repeated at
different octave

Sometimes the two-chord unit is expanded sequentially, as in *Caractacus* (1898), sc. 3 (at fig. 1).

Just as the Russian Nationalists had the problem of fitting their tunes into the obsessively uniform bed of German harmony, which never comfortably accepted their falling fourths, so Elgar's melodic line never really lent itself either to the main stream. Typical of this is what Elgar himself called the 'cheerful, out-of-doors, ambling theme' in *Falstaff*. His treatment is naturally in two parts—and he does not really care about orthodox treatment—and then he adds a holding note (figs. 36 and 53 for example). A student of Tovey's suggested that, although for full orchestra, *Falstaff* consisted entirely of two-part harmony.[1] This may be exaggerated, but much of Elgar's thinking is initially of two lines: a melody and a bass.

[1] *Op cit.*, vol. iv.

CHAPTER XVI

ELGAR'S STRUCTURE, COLOUR AND INFLUENCE

IF ELGAR has been criticized for the detail of his writing, the chromaticism and the sequences, etc., he has been criticized even more for his structures. What he enjoyed was in the music. At his zenith he was as prodigal with his material as Sullivan had been. He would certainly have echoed Sullivan's advice to Dame Ethel Smyth: 'We composers have to make a shillingsworth of music for a penny—and here you go throwing away guineas.' But, like the Sullivan of *The Mikado*, Elgar was brimming with ideas: putting them together was a skilled occupation but a secondary matter to the urgent business of creating. Elgar would also have agreed with Sibelius: 'Preserve the themes of your youth; they are the best you will ever invent.' He was not content with the con-cocted abstractions of dullards but, when needing ideas for a new work, he constantly turned and re-turned the pages of his old sketch-books. Extremely well-read in the literary classics, he was also an enthusiast for the great classical composers. It is not sur-prising, therefore, that his music should so often be unashamedly full of sequences. Percy Young may be right to say that the use of sequence as early as 1871 is 'straight from the text-book',[1] but Elgar would never have retained such a device if he had not found it also in living music. What 'came off' in Bach also suited Elgar, and it was frequently a structural device for propelling the music forward. Even so, using ideas from his sketch-books, he also employed the method of integrating small original units into his music. I have already described this as a more modern device and, looking back now, we can see the older, conservative classical building process being frequently thrust aside. Newman did not

[1] *Op. cit.*, p. 271.

understand this when he thought some of *The Apostles* was built
as if by children 'putting together painted blocks of wood'.[1]

These 'units' were nearly always instrumental rather than vocal.
When they are used in the big choral works, it is easy to see how
notes are twisted or repeated to suit voices. Even with such
significant lines as 'They shall grow not old, as we that are left
grow old' ('For the Fallen', fig. 19), the voice parts are an obvious
addition to the texture. Only the solo voice, with 'we will remember them', has its natural line and its characteristic Italianate
pause, which halts the orchestra. Elgar is kind to his soloists. To
some extent, he started where Wagner finished: the main thought
was usually in the orchestra.[2] He was, however, a portrait painter
(dedicating most of his works to sympathetic people, despite his
favouring of 'absolute' music in his Birmingham lectures). The
Variations are a gallery of friends, the oratorios are about New
Testament characters, the Violin Concerto enshrines someone's
soul, and the *Sea Pictures* are not empty seascapes. The ultimate
achievement in this respect is his 'study' of *Falstaff*, where he sees
no need for singers; almost certainly he is happier without their
personification. Richard Strauss, on the other hand, did the
opposite; he left his earlier symphonic poems and turned to opera
during the course of his prolific career. Modern though he sounded
then, Strauss is now seen as less original and lasting than Elgar. We
may be thankful that Ken Russell, who produced such a fanatically
hostile fantasy-portrait of Strauss, *The Dance of the Seven Veils*, on
B.B.C. Television on 15th February 1970, gave us a comparatively
down-to-earth, sane and friendly picture of Elgar in his film first
shown on B.B.C. Television on 11th November 1962.

Falstaff is a curious work also in that the two Interludes actually
sound like reminiscences from an earlier world. And yet, with their
'static' and non-symphonic quality, they are remarkably modern;
the only older composer who comes to mind is the untaught, crude
but vivid Mussorgsky—Elgar must often have wanted to escape
from the main stream by parading his lack of formal training. The

[1] *Op cit.*, p. 102.
[2] See Reed, *op. cit.*, p. 150.

94

first, the 'Dream Interlude' at fig. 76, consists almost entirely of one tune, a most characteristic one, repeated over and over again. All the composer does to it, as with many others, including the *Enigma* theme (first six bars) and the opening of Symphony No. I at its first repeat appearance, is to add a scrap of counterpoint (in *Dream Children*, No. 2, it is the middle section tune which gets this treatment):

Ex. 23   **Poco Allegretto**

I know few people who do not find themselves constantly humming this tune—not the countersubject, although no Elgarian can fail to note the stamp of personality here—when it has recently been played. The sheer repetitiveness has an almost hypnotic effect, more akin to Eastern music than the European tradition. The second episode, likewise, is just an alternation of ideas. Perhaps, with Hans Keller, we may talk of 'conservative progressiveness' [1] here.

Another really progressive quality which cannot be overlooked is Elgar's masterly concern with colour. If the second subject of the 'Romance' movement of the mature Sonata for Violin and Piano, Op. 82, sounds superficially like something from the Germanic past, the one feature which marks it out as belonging to Elgar's world (and the later twentieth century) is the composer's continual preoccupation with heard sound as opposed to academic development. Whether the violin soars (fig. 32) or dips down to the G string (four bars before fig. 31), the composer is utterly absorbed in the sonorities of the instrument. It goes without saying that Elgar will contrive that a recapitulation in the Violin Concerto will give him the same opportunity for double-stopping with an open string (cf. two bars before fig. 22 with two bars before fig. 41)—although he writes significantly on the sketch: 'These passages must lead "on".' Very few composers, if any, have been more fastidious in indicating their exact intentions with such loving care. As early as 1898 Elgar knew his own orchestration was good, and he described Parry's as 'dead and never more than an *organ part arranged*'.[1] Once Elgar's was written he never changed a thing. Meyerbeer's plan of writing alternative scorings in different coloured inks to find out how they sounded was a favourite subject of derision with him.[2]

Elgar's influence has not at first been apparent. Some minor composers have absorbed something from him; the biggest followers have been Vaughan Williams, Bliss and Walton. Vaughan Williams said modestly: 'I am astonished . . . how much I cribbed from him, probably when I thought I was being most original.'[3] Which of these extracts would strike one as Elgar and which Walton?

Ex. 24

[1] Letter to Jaeger, 9th March 1898.
[2] Reed, *Elgar as I knew him*, p. 149.
[3] *Music and Letters*, xvi, No. 1.

SIR EDWARD ELGAR CONDUCTING IN THE H.M.V. RECORDING
LABORATORY, ABOUT 1915.

The first, from *Gerontius* (two bars before fig. 106), contains what was known as a 'certain appalling chord' (letter to D. Ffrangcon-Davies, 30th December 1902) [1]—though the progression had actually occurred in *Caractacus*, sc. 3, after fig. 12. The second extract is from *Belshazzar's Feast* (at fig. 11) which appeared thirty-one years later. Gerald Finzi is one of the minor composers who gets as near as anyone to the true nobility of an Elgar slow movement in his own Cello Concerto. William Wordsworth's sad-voiced Symphony No. 1 of 1944, with its ambiguous tonal centres and angular leaps, uses to some extent a post-*Falstaff* idiom. Finally, 'light music' would never have been what it is without the *Pomp and Circumstance* marches—for example Eric Coates's popular *Knightsbridge* march from the *London Suite* of 1933.

What was Elgar's greatest achievement? One school of thought, including the composer's leading biographers, says it was *Gerontius*, which, they claim, has unity. For the composer, at the time, 'this is the best of me . . . this, if anything of mine, is worth your memory'. I can find no more unity in the small sections which are fitted together here than in Elgar's other great works; and the poem is no more unified than the many inferior verses also set by him, though it does certainly have classical continuity. Another school of thought, preferring a more secular and less tragic subject, chooses *Falstaff*. Again the composer is with them and frequently said he thought it the 'highest point he had reached in the production of a purely orchestral work'.[2] Again I beg to suggest that the composer may not be the best judge. A third school, a minority,

[1] Marjorie Ffrangcon-Davies, *David Ffrangcon-Davies* (1938), pp. 33-4.
[2] Reed, *op. cit.*, p. 113.

makes a plea for the chamber music, but this cannot in all seriousness be supported. I will end by making what may seem a more extravagant claim: not only did Elgar accept Jaeger's challenge, but he actually wrote four or five superb slow movements which really do measure up to the greatest in Beethoven. These, the greatest of him in spite of his own modesty about them, are surely:

1899   'Nimrod'
1908   The slow movement of Symphony No. 1
1910   The slow movement of the Violin Concerto
1911   The slow movement of Symphony No. 2

To which we might add:

1906   'The Sun goeth down' (from *The Kingdom*)

These movements contain his most mature and personal musical thoughts—and they can move to tears.

APPENDICES

APPENDIX A

(Figures in brackets denote the age reached by the person mentioned during the year in question.)

Year	Age	Life	Contemporary Musicians
1857		Edward William Elgar born Broadheath, June 2, son of W. H. Elgar, tuner, organist and later music dealer in Worcester (business established 1841). Siblings: Harry aged 7, Lucy aged 4, Pollie aged 2.	Glinka (54) dies, Feb. 15; Auber 75; Balakirev 20; Balfe 49; Sterndale Bennett 41; Berlioz 54; Berwald 61; Bizet 19; Boito 15; Borodin 24; Brahms 24; Bruch 19; Bruckner 33; Chabrier 16; Chausson 2; Cowen 5; Cui 22; Dargomizhsky 44; Delibes 21; Duparc 9; Dvořák 16; Fauré 12; Franck 35; Gade 40; Gounod 39; Grieg 14; Halévy 58; Humperdinck 3; d'Indy 6; Janáček 3; Lalo 34; Liadov 2; Liszt 46; Mackenzie 10; Marschner 62; Meyerbeer 66; Mussorgsky 18; Offenbach 38; Hubert Parry 9; Raff 35; Rheinberger 18; Rimsky-Korsakov 13; Rossini 65; Saint-Saëns 22; Smetana 33; Spohr 73; Stainer 17; Stanford 5; Johann Strauss 32; Sullivan 15; Tchaikovsky 17; Verdi 44; Wagner 44; S. S. Wesley 47.

Appendix A—Calendar

Year	Age	Life	Contemporary Musicians
1858	1		Leoncavallo born, March 8; Puccini born, June 22; Ethel Smyth born, April 23.
1859	2	Family moves back into Worcester. Brother, Joe, born.	Spohr (75) dies, Oct. 22.
1860	3		Albéniz born, May 29; Charpentier born, June 25; Mahler born, July 7; Wolf born, March 13.
1861	4	Brother, Frank, born.	Arensky born, Aug. 11; MacDowell born, Dec. 18; Marschner (66) dies, Dec. 14.
1862	5		Debussy born, Aug. 22; Delius born, Jan. 29; E. German born, Feb. 17; Halévy (63) dies, March 17.
1863	6		Mascagni born, Dec. 7; Somervell born, June 5.
1864	7	Goes to school. Sister Helen (Dot) born. Brother Harry dies of scarlet fever.	Meyerbeer (72) dies, May 2; Richard Strauss born, June 11.
1865	8		Dukas born, Oct. 1; Glazunov born, Aug. 10; Sibelius born, Dec. 8; Nielsen born, June 9.
1866	9	Helps in father's shop in Worcester. Brother Joe dies.	Busoni born, April 1; Satie born, May 17.
1867	10	First known composition, 'Fairies and Giants' (later used in *Wand of Youth* Suite)	Granados born, July 27.
1868	11	Attends Littleton House school.	Bantock born, Aug. 7; Berwald (71) dies, April 3; Rossini (76) dies, Nov. 13.
1869	12	He learns to play violin, viola, cello and bassoon as well as piano and organ.	Berlioz (65) dies, March 8; Dargomizhsky (55) dies, Jan. 17; Walford Davies born, Sept. 6; Roussel born, April 5.

Year	Age	Life	Contemporary Musicians
1870	13		Balfe (62) dies, Oct. 20; Lekeu born, Jan. 20; Novák born, Dec. 5; Florent Schmitt born, Sept. 28.
1871	14		Auber (89) dies, May 12.
1872	15	Song, 'The Language of Flowers'. Apprenticed to solicitor, but gives up after about a year.	Skriabin born, Jan. 6; Vaughan Williams born, Oct. 12.
1873	16	Assistant organist at St George's Roman Catholic Church.	Rakhmaninov born, April 1; Reger born, March 19.
1874	17	Violinist in orchestra of Worcester Festival Choral Society.	Holst born, Sept. 21; Schönberg born, Sept. 13; Suk born, Jan. 4.
1875	18		Sterndale Bennett (59) dies, Feb. 1; Bizet (36) dies, June 3; ColeridgeTaylor born, Aug 15; Ravel born, March 7.
1876	19		Falla born, Nov. 23; S. S. Wesley (66) dies, April 19.
1877	20	Violin lessons with Adolphe Pollitzer in London.	Dohnányi born, July 27; Dunhill born, Feb. 1; Quilter born, Nov. 1.
1878	21		Boughton born, Jan. 23; Holbrooke born, July 6.
1879	22	Appointed Band Instructor to the County and City of Worcester Pauper Lunatic Asylum at Powick. Sister Pollie married to William Grafton.	Frank Bridge born, Feb. 26; Ireland born, Aug. 13; Respighi born, July 9; Cyril Scott born, Sept. 20.
1880	23		Bloch born, July 24; Medtner born, Jan. 5; Offenbach (61) dies, Oct. 5; Pizzetti born, Sept. 20.

Year	Age	Life	Contemporary Musicians
1881	24	Sister Lucy married to Charles Pipe.	Bartók born, March 25; Mussorgsky (42) dies, March 28.
1882	25		Kodály born, Dec. 16; Malipiero born, March 18; Raff (60) dies, June 24-5; Stravinsky born, June 17; Szymanowski born, Oct. 6.
1883	26	'Intermezzo Moresque' (later 'Sérénade Mauresque', Op. 10, No. 2) performed by W. C. Stockley's Birmingham Orchestra.	Bax born, Nov. 8; Berners born, Sept. 18; Casella born, July 25; Wagner (69) dies, Feb. 13; Webern born, Dec. 3.
1884	27	Resigns from asylum post.	van Dieren born, Dec. 27; Griffes born, Sept. 17; Smetana (60) dies, May 12.
1885	28	Organist at St George's Roman Catholic church.	Berg born, Feb. 9; Varèse born, Dec. 22; Wellesz born, Oct. 21.
1886	29	Caroline Alice Roberts (born Oct. 9, 1848) first becomes pupil.	Liszt (74) dies, July 31.
1887	30		Borodin (53) dies, Feb. 28; Villa-Lobos born, March 5.
1888	31		Durey born, May 27.
1889	32	Marries Caroline Alice Roberts at Brompton Oratory. They move to London. *Liebesgruss* (later *Salut d'Amour*) published.	Shaporin born, Nov. 8.
1890	33	*Froissart* first performed at Worcester Festival. Daughter Carice Irene, born Aug. 14.	Franck (67) dies, Nov. 8; Gade (73) dies, Dec. 21.
1891	34	Still virtually unknown as a composer, settles in Malvern.	Bliss born, Aug. 2; Delibes (54) dies, Jan. 16; Prokofiev born, April 23.
1892	35		Honegger born, March 10; Howells born, Oct. 17; Kilpinen born, Feb. 4; Lalo

Year	Age	Life	Contemporary Musicians
			(69) dies, April 22; Milhaud born, Sept. 4; Sorabji born, Aug. 14.
1893	36	*The Black Knight* performed at Worcester.	Eugene Goossens born, May 26; Gounod (75) dies, Oct. 18; Hába born, June 21; Tchaikovsky (53) dies, Nov. 6.
1894	37		Chabrier (53) dies, Sept. 13; Lekeu (24) dies, Jan. 21; Moeran born, Dec. 31; Pijper born, Sept. 8; Warlock born, Oct. 30.
1895	38	Composes Organ Sonata, Op. 28.	Hindemith born, Nov. 16.
1896	39	*From the Bavarian Highlands* and *Lux Christi* (*The Light of Life*) performed at Worcester. *King Olaf* performed at Hanley.	Bruckner (72) dies, Oct. 11; Sessions born, Dec. 28.
1897	40	*Imperial March* and *The Banner of St George* composed for Queen Victoria's Diamond Jubilee.	Brahms (63) dies, April 3.
1898	41	First performance of *Caractacus*, Leeds.	Roy Harris born, Feb. 12.
1899	42	First performances of the *Enigma Variations*, London, and *Sea Pictures*, Norwich.	Auric born, Feb. 15; Chausson (44) dies, June 10; Johann Strauss (73) dies, June 3.
1900	43	*The Dream of Gerontius* first performed at Birmingham, without success. Hon. Mus.D., Cambridge.	Copland born, Nov. 14; Křenek born, Aug. 23; Sullivan (58) dies, Nov. 22.
1901	44	First performance of *Cockaigne*, London. *Gerontius* performed at Lower Rhine	Rheinberger (62) dies, Nov. 25; Finzi born, July 14; Rubbra born, May 23;

Year	Age	Life	Contemporary Musicians
		Festival, Düsseldorf, with success.	Stainer (61) dies, March 31; Verdi (87) dies, Jan. 27.
1902	45	Mother's death, Sept. 1.	Walton born, March 29.
1903	46	*The Apostles* first performed at Birmingham.	Berkeley born, May 12; Blacher born, Jan. 3; Wolf (42) dies, Feb. 22.
1904	47	Knighted July 5. Overture *In the South* first performed in Elgar Festival, Covent Garden.	Dallapiccola born, Feb. 3; Dvořák (62) dies, May 1.
1905	48	Professorship at Birmingham University. Visit to U.S.A. *Introduction and Allegro* first performed, London.	Constant Lambert born, Aug. 23; Tippett born, Jan. 2.
1906	49	Father's death, April 30. *The Kingdom* first performed at Birmingham.	Shostakovich born, Sept. 25.
1907	50		Grieg (63) dies, Sept. 4.
1908	51	First performance of Symphony No. 1 in Manchester.	MacDowell (46) dies, Jan. 23; Rimsky-Korsakov (64) dies, June 21; Messiaen born, Dec. 10; William B. Wordsworth born, Dec. 17.
1909	52		Albéniz (48) dies, May 18.
1910	53	First performance of Violin Concerto in London, with Kreisler as soloist.	Balakirev (73) dies, May 29; Samuel Barber born, March 9; William Schuman born, Aug. 4.
1911	54	First performance of Symphony No. 2 in London. O.M. conferred.	Mahler (50) dies, May 18.
1912	55	*The Music Makers* first performed at Birmingham.	Coleridge-Taylor (37) dies, Sept. 1; Massenet (70) dies, Aug. 13.
1913	56	*Falstaff* first performed at Leeds.	Britten born, Nov. 22.
1914	57		Liadov (59) dies, Aug. 28.

Appendix A—Calendar

Year	Age	Life	Contemporary Musicians
1915	58	Incidental music to *The Star-light Express*.	Skriabin (43) dies, April 27. Searle born Aug. 26.
1916	59		Granados (48) dies, March 24; Reger (43) dies, May 11; Parrott born, March 5.
1917	60	All three parts of *The Spirit of England* first performed at Albert Hall, London.	
1918	61		Boito (76) dies, June 10; Cui (83) dies, March 24; Debussy (55) dies, March 25; Parry (70) dies, Oct. 7.
1919	62	First performances of Violin Sonata, String Quartet, Piano Quintet and Cello Concerto, London.	Leoncavallo (61) dies, Aug. 9.
1920	63	His wife (71) dies, April 7.	Bruch (82) dies, Oct. 2; Griffes (36) dies, April 8.
1921	64		Humperdinck (67) dies, Sept. 27; Saint-Saëns (86) dies, Dec. 16.
1922	65		Lukas Foss born, Aug. 15.
1923	66		
1924	67	Appointed Master of the King's Musick.	Busoni (58) dies, July 27; Fauré (79) dies, Nov. 4; Puccini (65) dies, Nov. 29; Stanford (71) dies, March 29.
1925	68	Receives Gold Medal of Royal Philharmonic Society, Nov. 19. Sister Lucy dies.	Boulez born, March 25; Satie (59) dies, July 1.
1926	69		Henze born, July 1.
1927	70		
1928	71	K.C.V.O. Brother Frank dies.	Janáček (74) dies, Aug. 12.
1929	72		
1930	73	*Severn Suite* first performed at	Warlock (36) dies, Dec. 17.

Appendix A—Calendar

Year	Age	Life	Contemporary Musicians
		Crystal Palace Brass Band Festival.	
1931	74	Created baronet.	d'Indy (80) dies, Dec. 2; Nielsen (66) dies, Oct. 2.
1932	75	Works on sketches for an opera, *The Spanish Lady*.	
1933	76	Works on sketches for Symphony No. 3. First signs of illness. G.C.V.O.	Duparc (85) dies, Feb. 13.
1934	76	Dies at Worcester, Feb. 23.	Delius (72) dies, June 10; Holst (59) dies, May 25; Auric 35; Bantock 66; Barber 24; Bartók 53; Bax 51; Berg 49; Berkeley 31; Berners 51; Blacher 31; Bliss 43; Bloch 54; Boughton 56; Boulez 9; Frank Bridge 55; Britten 21; Casella 51; Charpentier 74; Copland 34; Cowen 82; Dallapiccola 30; Walford Davies 65; van Dieren 50; Dohnányi 57; Dukas 69; Dunhill 57; Durey 46; Falla 58; Lukas Foss 12; German 72; Glazunov 69; Goossens 41; Hába 41; Roy Harris 36; Henze 8; Hindemith 39; Honegger 42; Howells 42; Ireland 55; Kodály 52; Křenek 34; Lambert 29; McEwen 66; Mackenzie 87; Malipiero 52; Mascagni 71; Medtner 54; Messiaen 26; Milhaud 42; Moeran 40; Novák 64; Parrott 18; Pijper 40; Pizzetti 54; Poulenc 35; Proko-

fiev 43; Quilter 57; Rakh-
maninov 61; Ravel 59;
Respighi 55; Roussel 65;
Rubbra 33; Florent Schmitt
64; Schönberg 60; William
Schuman 24; Cyril Scott 55;
Searle 19; Sessions 38;
Shaporin 45; Shostakovich
28; Sibelius 69; Ethel Smyth
75; Somervell 71; Sorabji
42; Richard Strauss 70;
Stravinsky 52; Suk 60;
Szymanowski 51: Tippett 29;
Varèse 49; Vaughan Wil-
liams 62; Villa-Lobos 47;
Walton 32; Webern 51;
Wellesz 49.

APPENDIX B

CATALOGUE OF WORKS

ORCHESTRAL WORKS

Op.		Date
1A	*The Wand of Youth.* First Suite	1867–1907
1B	*The Wand of Youth.* Second Suite	1879–1908
3	*Cantique*	1879–1912
7	*Sevillaña* (Scène Espagnole)	1884–9
10	*Three Pieces for Small Orchestra*	1882–8
	1. Mazurka	
	2. Sérénade Mauresque	
	3. Contrasts	
11	*Sursum Corda* (brass, organ and strings)	1894
12	*Salut d'Amour* (*Liebesgruss*)	1888
	(also many arrangements)	
19	*Froissart.* Concert overture	1890
20	*Serenade.* Strings	1892
32	*Imperial March*	1897
36	*Variations on an Original Theme* (Enigma)	1898–9
39	*Pomp and Circumstance.* Marches	1901–30
	1. D ma 1901 2. A mi 1901	
	3. C mi 1904 4. G ma 1907	
	5. C ma 1930	
40	*Cockaigne.* Overture	1901
43	*Dream Children.* Two pieces for piano or small orchestra	1902
47	*Introduction and Allegro.* String quartet and string orchestra	1901–5
50	*In the South* (Alassio). Overture	1899–1904
55	Symphony No. 1 in A flat ma	1907–8
58	*Elegy.* String orchestra	1909
63	Symphony No. 2 in E flat ma	1903–10
65	*Coronation March*	1902–11
68	*Falstaff.* Symphonic Study	1902–13

Appendix B—Catalogue of Works

Op.		Date
70	*Sospiri*. Strings, harp and organ	1914
75	*Carillon*. Reciter and orchestra	1914
76	*Polonia*. Symphonic prelude	1915
77	*Une Voix dans le Désert*. Reciter and orchestra	1915
79	*Le Drapeau Belge*. Reciter and orchestra	1917
87	*Severn Suite*. Brass band	1930
	Arranged for orchestra	1932
	Arranged by Ivor Atkins for organ (Sonata No. 2)	1933
88	Symphony No. 3. Fragments only	1933
—	*Rosemary*	1882
—	*Sérénade Lyrique*	1899
—	*Carissima*	1914
—	*Nursery Suite*	1931
—	*Mina*. Small orchestra	1934

INCIDENTAL MUSIC

42	*Grania and Diarmid* (George Moore and W. B. Yeats). Funeral March, song and incidental music	1901
66	*The Crown of India*. Masque in 12 movements for 6 soloists, chorus and orchestra (Henry Hamilton)	1902–12
78	*The Starlight Express* (play by Violet Pearn based on book, *A Prisoner in Fairyland*, by Algernon Blackwood)	1915
81	*The Sanguine Fan*. Ballet	1917
—	*The Fringes of the Fleet*. Four songs by Kipling and one by Gilbert Parker	1917
—	*King Arthur*. (L. Binyon) MS.	1923
—	*Pageant of Empire* for Wembley Exhibition in 8 movements	1924
—	*Beau Brummel*. (Bertram P. Matthews) MS.	1928

SOLO INSTRUMENT AND ORCHESTRA

61	Concerto for Violin in B mi	1909–10
62	*Romance for Bassoon*	1910
85	Concerto for Violoncello in E mi	1919
90	Concerto for Piano. Fragments only	1909–32

Appendix B—Catalogue of Works

Appendix B—Catalogue of Works

Op.		Date
—	Piece for Organ. MS. 'For Dot's nuns'	1906
—	*Sonatina*. Piano	before 1932
—	*Adieu*. Piano (transcribed for violin by Szigeti)	before 1932
—	*Serenade*. Piano (transcribed for violin by Szigeti)	before 1932

SONGS

5	'A War Song' ('A Soldier's Song') (C. F. Hayward)	1884
16	1. 'Shepherd's Song' (Barry Pain)	1892
	2. 'Through the Long Days' (John Hay)	1885
	3. 'Rondel' (Longfellow from Froissart)	1894
31	1. 'After' (Philip Bourke Marston)	1895
	2. 'A Song of Flight' (Christina Rossetti)	before 1900
37	*Sea Pictures*. Contralto and orchestra	1897–9
	1. 'Sea Slumber Song' (Hon. Roden Noel)	
	2. 'In Haven' ('Love alone will stay') (C. Alice Elgar)	
	3. 'Sabbath Morning at Sea' (Elizabeth Barrett Browning)	
	4. 'Where Corals Lie' (Richard Garnett)	
	5. 'The Swimmer' (Adam Lindsay Gordon)	
41	1. 'In the Dawn' (A. C. Benson)	before 1901
	2. 'Speak, Music' (A. C. Benson)	
48	'Pleading' (Arthur L. Salmon) (also with orchestra)	before 1908
59	Song cycle with orchestra (Nos. 1, 2 and 4 not composed) (Gilbert Parker)	1909–10
	3. 'Oh! Soft was the song'	
	5. 'Was it some golden star?'	
	6. 'Twilight'	
60	Folk Songs (from Eastern Europe) (Pietro d'Alba) with orchestra	
	1. 'The Torch'	1909
	2. 'The River'	1910
—	'The Language of Flowers' (Percival)	1872
—	'Is she not passing fair?' (Charles, Duke of Orléans, trans. Louisa Stuart Costello)	1886

Appendix B—Catalogue of Works

Op.		Date
—	'As I laye a-thinking' (Thomas Ingoldsby)	c. 1888
—	'The Wind at Dawn' (C. Alice Roberts)	1888
—	'Queen Mary's Song' (Tennyson)	1889
—	'Like to the Damask Rose' (Simon Wastell)	1892
—	'A Song of Autumn' (A. Lindsay Gordon)	1892
—	'The Poet's Life' (Ellen Burroughs)	1892
—	'Love alone will stay'. See *Sea Pictures*, No. 2	1898
—	'Dry those fair, those crystal eyes' (Henry King)	1899
—	'Pipes of Pan' (Adrian Ross)	c. 1899
—	'Come, gentle night' (Clifton Bingham)	c. 1901
—	'Always and everywhere' (Krasinski, trans. F. E. Fortey)	c. 1901
—	'Land of Hope and Glory' (A. C. Benson, arranged from *Coronation Ode*)	?1901
—	'Speak, my heart' (A. C. Benson)	?1902
—	'The Kingsway' (C. Alice Elgar)	1909
—	'A Child Asleep' (Elizabeth Barrett Browning)	1909
—	'Arabian Serenade' (Margery Lawrence)	before 1914
—	'The Chariots of the Lord' (John Brownlie)	1914
—	'Fight for Right' (William Morris)	1916
—	'Big Steamers' (Rudyard Kipling)	1918
—	'It isnae me' (Sally Holmes)	1930
—	Unison songs (words by Charles Mackay):	
	'The Rapid Stream' (also 2-part, 1933)	1932
	'When Swallows fly'	1932
	'The Woodland Stream' (also 2-part, 1933)	1933

Choral Music

Cantatas, Oratorios and Odes, etc.

25	*The Black Knight* (Uhland trans. Longfellow)	1890–2
27	*From the Bavarian Highlands* (C. Alice Elgar); also for orchestra alone (3 Dances)	1895
29	*The Light of Life* (*Lux Christi*) (E. Capel-Cure)	1896
30	Scenes from the *Saga of King Olaf* (Longfellow and H. A. Acworth)	1894–6
33	*The Banner of St George* (Shapcott Wensley)	c. 1897
35	*Caractacus* (H. A. Acworth)	1897–8

Appendix B—Catalogue of Works

Op.		Date
38	*The Dream of Gerontius* (John Henry Newman)	1899–1900
44	*Coronation Ode* (A. C. Benson)	1901–2
49	*The Apostles* (Elgar)	1902–3
51	*The Kingdom* (Elgar)	1905–6
69	*The Music Makers* (Arthur O'Shaughnessy)	?1902–12
80	*The Spirit of England* (Laurence Binyon)	
	1. 'The Fourth of August'	1917
	2. 'To Women'	1915
	3. 'For the Fallen'	1915

CHURCH MUSIC

Op.		Date
2	1. *Ave Verum Corpus*	1887
	2. *Ave Maria*	
	3. *Ave Maris Stella*	
	Also with English words for C. of E.	
34	*Te Deum* and *Benedictus*	1897
64	*Coronation Offertorium*, 'O hearken thou'	1911
67	'Great is the Lord' (Psalm 48)	1912
74	'Give unto the Lord' (Psalm 29)	1914
—	Music for St George's Roman Catholic Church	*c.* 1875–85
—	*O Salutaris Hostia* (4-part)	*c.* 1880
—	*O Salutaris Hostia* (Tozer's *Benediction Manual*)	before 1898
—	*Ecce Sacerdos Magnus*	1888
—	'Lo! Christ the Lord is born'. Carol (Shapcott Wensley)	*c* 1897
—	'O mightiest of the mighty.' Hymn (S. Childs Clarke)	*c.* 1901
—	Two Single Chants and Two Double Chants	1909
—	'They are at rest.' Elegy (John Henry Newman)	1909
—	'Fear not, O land.' Harvest anthem	1914
—	'I sing the birth.' Carol (Ben Jonson)	1928
—	'Good morrow.' Carol (George Gascoigne)	1929

PART-SONGS (accompanied)

Op.		Date
23	'Spanish Serenade' ('Stars of the summer night': Longfellow). With orchestra	1891

Op.		Date
26	For women's voices with 2 vi. and piano (C. Alice Elgar):	1894
	1. 'The Snow'	
	2. 'Fly, singing bird'	
52	'A Christmas Greeting' (C. Alice Elgar) 2 sop., male chorus ad lib., 2 vi. and pf.	1907

PART-SONGS (unaccompanied)

(for mixed voices unless otherwise indicated)

18	1. 'O happy eyes' (C. Alice Elgar)	1890
	2. 'Love' (Arthur Maquarie)	1890
45	*Part-songs from the Greek Anthology* for male voices	1902
	1. 'Yea, cast me from heights' (trans. Alma Strettell)	
	2. 'Whether I find thee' (trans. Andrew Lang)	
	3. 'After many a dusty mile' (trans. Edmund Gosse)	
	4. 'It's oh, to be a wild wind' (trans. W. M. Hardinge)	
	5. 'Feasting I watch' (trans. Richard Garnett)	
53	Four Part-songs	1907
	1. 'There is sweet music' (Tennyson)	
	2. 'Deep in my soul' (Byron)	
	3. 'O wild west wind' (Shelley)	
	4. 'Owls' (an epitaph) (Elgar)	
54	'The Reveille', male voices (Bret Harte)	1907
56	'Angelus (Tuscany)' (from the Tuscan)	1909
57	'Go, song of mine,' 6 parts (Calvacanti, trans. Rossetti)	1909
71	Two Part-songs (Henry Vaughan)	before 1914
	1. 'The Shower'	
	2. 'The Fountain'	
72	'Death on the Hills' (Maikov, trans. Rosa Newmarch)	1914
73	Two Part-songs (Maikov, trans. Rosa Newmarch)	1914
	1. 'Love's Tempest'	
	2. 'Serenade'	

Appendix B—Catalogue of Works

Op.		Date
—	'My love dwelt in a northern land' (Andrew Lang)	1890
—	'Grete Malverne on a Rock'	1897
—	'To her beneath whose steadfast star' (F. W. H. Myers)	1899
—	'Weary wind of the west' (T. E. Brown)	1903
—	'Evening Scene' (Coventry Patmore)	1905
—	'How calmly the evening' (T. T. Lynch)	1907
—	'The Birthright' (George A. Stocks)	c. 1914
—	'Marching Song' (Capt. de Courcy Stretton)	c. 1908
	(also for male voices as 'Follow the colours')	1914
—	'The Wanderer', male voices (from Wit and Drollery, 1661)	c. 1923
—	'Zut, zut, zut', male voices (Richard Marden)	c. 1923
—	'The Herald', male voices (Alexander Smith)	c. 1925
—	'The Prince of Sleep' (Walter de la Mare)	c. 1925

OPERA

89	The Spanish Lady (Ben Jonson adapted by Elgar and Barry Jackson). Planned in two acts, but incomplete.	1878–1933

ARRANGEMENTS

—	Orchestration of Emmaus by Herbert Brewer	published 1901
—	'God Save the King', soloists, chorus and orch.	published 1902
—	Edition of St Matthew Passion by Bach with Ivor Atkins	published 1911
—	Chorales from above arrangement for 3 tpts., 4 hns., 3 tbnes. and tuba	MS. 1911
86	Fantasia and Fugue in C mi by Bach, arranged for full orchestra	1921–2
—	Toccata in F by Bach, arranged Esser, rearranged Elgar	?
—	Orchestration of 'Jerusalem' by Parry	MS. 1922
—	Orchestration of Jehova quam multi sunt by Purcell	MS. 1929
—	Overture in D mi by Handel, arranged for full orchestra	published 1923

Op.   *Date*
— Funeral March by Chopin, arranged for full
    orchestra   published 1933
    Juvenilia include paraphrase of Mozart's Sym-
    phony in G mi (1878); and arrangements of
    Beethoven (1880) and Wagner, part of *Tann-*
    häuser for piano (1883) and Good Friday music
    from *Parsifal* for small orchestra (1894)
    Also orchestrations of works by S. S. Wesley,
    Battishill, hymns, etc.

WRITINGS

Programme notes for Worcestershire Phil. Soc.   1898–1904
Preface to *The Singing of the Future* by D.
    Ffrangcon-Davies   1904
Lectures, Birmingham University   1905–6
'Analytical Notes on *Falstaff*', *Musical Times*   1913
My Friends Pictured Within   1913
'Gray, Walpole, West and Ashton', *Times Literary*
    Supplement   4 Sept. 1919
'Notation', *Musical Times*   1920
'Scott and Shakespeare', *Times Literary Supplement*   21 July 1921
Foreword to *Forgotten Worcester* by H. A. Leicester   1930

APPENDIX C

Allen, Sir Hugh Percy (1869–1946), born at Reading, organ scholar of Christ's College, Cambridge, organist at various cathedrals; a bluff, vigorous and generous character. He left little in writing, but his many friends and pupils have testified to his varied enthusiasms in music and musicians, and his influence was considerable. In 1918 he combined the post of Director of the Royal College of Music with the Chair of Music at Oxford and two years later was knighted. Sir Thomas Armstrong delivered an informative centenary address at Oxford in June 1969.

Atkins, Sir Ivor Algernon (1869–1953), from 1897 to 1950 organist at Worcester Cathedral and Three Choirs Festival conductor, he was knighted in 1921. A composer, he collaborated with Elgar in preparing a new edition of Bach's *St Matthew Passion*.

Bantock, Sir Granville (1868–1946), born in London, a prolific composer whose larger scores include the complicated *Omar Khayyám*, he succeeded Elgar as Peyton Professor of Music at Birmingham University in 1908. He also ran the School of Music in Birmingham until 1934 and later became chairman of the corporation of Trinity College of Music, London. He was knighted in 1930.

Blake, Mrs Carice Irene (1890–1970, née Elgar), Elgar's only child, she was educated in Malvern and Italy. Married in 1922 to Samuel Blake (d. 1939), she helped her father in many ways after the death of Lady Elgar and for many years had a great deal to do with looking after the Birthplace Museum at Broadheath.

Broadhurst, Edgar C. (1877–1967), chorister at Hereford Choir School at the age of seven; Dr Sinclair's assistant at Hereford Cathedral from 1892. He was appointed organist at St Michael's College, Tenbury, in 1896. From 1907 to 1947 he was Assistant Music Master at Harrow School and organist of Harrow parish church. In 1952 he became organist at St George's Church, Worcester.

Appendix C—Personalia

Buths, Julius (1851–1920), German conductor in Düsseldorf from 1890; directed the Lower Rhine Festival there, where he introduced Elgar's *Gerontius* in December 1901 and again in May 1902.

Cohen, Harriet (*c.* 1898–1967), pianist, famous for being a champion of modern British music, especially that of Bax; she recorded with the Stratton Quartet the Elgar Piano Quintet and in spite of a severe hand injury received in 1948 played the slow movement of Elgar's unfinished Piano Concerto with the Boyd Neel Orchestra in 1956. During the last seven years of her life she devoted much time to her Harriet Cohen International Awards for composers, performers and music scholars.

Colvin, Sir Sidney (1845–1927), a great personal friend of the Elgars, he was appointed Keeper of the Department of Prints and Drawings at the British Museum in 1884 and was knighted in 1911. The Cello Concerto was dedicated to him and his wife. They lived near the Elgars in Sussex at that time.

Davies, Sir Henry Walford (1869–1941), organist at the Temple, then Professor of Music at the University College of Wales, Aberystwyth, from 1919 to 1926, made Master of the King's Musick on the death of Elgar; popularizer of music, he was famous for his broadcast talks in the twenties and thirties. In the early days of the century his music, taken up by Wood at the Proms and by other organizations including the Three Choirs Festival, was thought to be important—the Novello printing may have helped. Now the pretentious works have faded and only miniatures such as the *Solemn Melody* and 'God be in My Head' remain.

Griffith, Arthur Troyte (1864–1942), of Welsh extraction, No. 7 in the *Enigma Variations*, a Malvern architect and water-colourist, he was a life-long friend and correspondent of Elgar (see also in Chapter VII).

Hall, Marie (1884–1956), a violinist who made her début in Prague in 1902; in 1916 she was the first soloist to record Elgar's Violin Concerto. The Stradivarius violin which she bought in 1905 for £1,600 was sold at Sotheby's in 1968 for £22,000 (*The Times*, 8th November 1968). Married in 1911 to Edward Baring. Vaughan Williams wrote *The Lark Ascending* for her.

Hull, Sir Percy Clarke (1878–1968), in 1896 succeeded Broadhurst as Dr Sinclair's assistant at Hereford Cathedral. As a prisoner of war in

Germany, he was in the same internment camp as fellow-musicians Benjamin Dale (1885–1943), composer, and Arthur Williams (1875–1939), the cellist of whom Elgar spoke highly as soloist in his Cello Concerto in 1924. He was organist of Hereford from 1918 until 1949 and knighted in 1947.

Jaeger, August Johannes (1860–1909), from Düsseldorf, No. 9 in the *Enigma Variations* and one of Elgar's greatest inspirers. A dozen years after his arrival in England, he joined the firm of Novello in 1890 and, although in a junior position, he became chief negotiator between Elgar and the firm, as well as an enthusiastic private correspondent and writer of analytical notes (see also in Chapter VII).

Kreisler, Fritz (1875–1962), Viennese violinist, made his London debut with Richter in 1901 and received the gold medal of the Royal Philharmonic Society in 1904. He gave the first performance in 1910 of Elgar's Violin Concerto, which was dedicated to him. His own compositions, mainly trifles imitated from light classical models, were very popular when brilliantly performed by himself.

Maine, Rev. Basil Stephen (b. 1894), from Norwich, a music critic and author who wrote two volumes on Elgar, one on his life and one on his work, both published in 1933. He was ordained in 1939.

Manns, Sir August (1825–1907), from Germany, became first sub-conductor and then, in 1855, conductor to the Crystal Palace Company (Secretary: Sir George Grove), converting a brass band into a full symphony orchestra. He introduced to London the music of Sullivan in 1862 and that of Elgar in 1884.

Menuhin, Yehudi (b. 1916), American-born Jewish concert violinist of distinction, he was associated with Elgar's Violin Concerto first as a boy of fifteen. Resident in London since 1960, he founded the Yehudi Menuhin School for musically gifted children in 1964 and was made an Honorary Knight Commander of the Most Excellent Order of the British Empire in 1965. Festivals in many places from Bath to Gstaad have owed much to his direction.

Newman, Ernest (1868–1959), one of the most famous music critics of his time, he was first noticed in Liverpool where he met Elgar in 1900. He was critic of the *Manchester Guardian* in 1905, the *Birmingham Post* in 1906, the *Observer* in 1919 and then for many years from 1920 the *Sunday Times*. He wrote books and programme notes about many composers, including Elgar, but his greatest achievement was the four volumes on the life of Wagner (completed in 1947). His critical writings on Elgar were frequently frankly harsh but the Piano Quintet's dedication to him proved a personal friendship.

Norbury, the sisters *Florence* (1858–1937) and *Winifred* (1861–1938), both commemorated in the *Enigma Variations* (see Chapter VII) though only the latter's initials appear at the head of the movement. They lived at Sherridge, adjoining Birchwood, which Elgar used as a summer cottage from 1898 to 1903. Winifred helped with the copying of parts on several occasions. She was also Joint Secretary of the Worcestershire Philharmonic Society.

Parry, Sir C. Hubert H. (1848–1918), an important English composer who succeeded Sir George Grove as Director of the Royal College of Music in 1894 and six years later became also Professor of Music at Oxford University. One of his best-known works is *Blest Pair of Sirens*. Elgar came to know his music when performed at the Three Choirs Festival and he orchestrated 'Jerusalem' for the Leeds Festival of 1922.

Pollitzer, Adolf (1832–1900), Hungarian violinist, with whom Elgar studied as a young man; he came to London in 1851 and led first the orchestra of Her Majesty's Theatre, then that of the New Philharmonic Society and then that of the Royal Choral Society. He introduced Elgar to Manns (q.v.).

Powell, Mrs Richard (1874–1964, née Dora Mary Penny), of Wolverhampton, No. 10, 'Dorabella', of the *Enigma Variations*, first met Elgar in 1895. A woman of strong views, author in 1936 of *Edward Elgar: Memories of a Variation*, in characteristic vein she wrote to Mr E. A. Butcher in March 1955: 'Did you hear M. Sargent *dirge* "Nimrod" the other night? It made me ill! Yes, and then he plays "Troyte" like a whirlwind. . . .' She was inclined to over-emphasize the happy side of Elgar (see also in Chapter VII).

Reed, William Henry (1876–1942), violinist who studied at the Royal Academy of Music, and became leader of the London Symphony Orchestra in 1912. He helped Elgar with the Violin Concerto and the chamber music, playing over much of the music while it was still in only sketch form. A great personal friend of the composer, he played in many performances and wrote two books on him.

Richter, Hans (1843–1916), Austro-Hungarian conductor who studied in Vienna, where he was a horn player at the opera. First to conduct Wagner's *Ring* at Bayreuth in 1876, he came to London the following year. From 1897 to 1911 conductor of the Hallé Orchestra in Manchester, he was a great champion of Elgar, whose Symphony No. 1 was dedicated to him, 'true artist and true friend'.

Ronald, Sir Landon (1873–1938), London-born conductor who became an important interpreter of Elgar's music. 'He wants to make more of every passage than you do', wrote Bernard Shaw to Elgar on 7th January 1932. Principal of the Guildhall School of Music from 1910 to 1937, Landon Ronald was knighted in 1922.

Schuster, Leo Francis (Frank) Howard (1852–1927), of German-Jewish extraction, a patron of the arts. He and his sister Adela entertained various artists at 'The Hut' at Bray, three miles from Maidenhead, and took considerable interest in Elgar. Another friend of similar blood and wealth was *Alfred Rodewald* (d. 1903), a Liverpool businessman, who had a villa at Betws-y-Coed, in North Wales, called Minafon, where Elgar wrote some of *The Apostles*.

Shaw, George Bernard (1856–1950), great Irish playwright and also a most discerning critic of music, as his observations on London concerts in the eighties and nineties show. While Elgar grew to like his plays, Shaw in his turn became an enthusiast for Elgar's symphonic works. The *Severn Suite* was dedicated to him.

Sinclair, George Robertson (1862–1917), Irish musician, No. 11 in the *Enigma Variations*. After being assistant conductor at Gloucester Cathedral, he was appointed organist at the Cathedral of Truro in 1880 and at that of Hereford in 1889. He had a strong influence in widening the repertoire of the Three Choirs Festival. Between 1897 and 1903, Elgar wrote 'The Moods of Dan, Illustrated' in his Visitors' Book. Although ostensibly referring to Sinclair's bulldog, some of these seven musical snippets anticipated motives in *Gerontius*, *In the South*, *The Apostles* and *For the Fallen* (see also in Chapter VII). Dan is buried in Hereford Conservative Club garden.

Stanford, Sir Charles Villiers (1852–1924), Irish composer who, with Parry, was considered to have helped bring about a 'renaissance' in British music. Elgar and Stanford did not always get on together but the latter, as Professor of Music at Cambridge from 1887, did see that the former was awarded an honorary doctorate in 1900. Later he had Elgar nominated for membership of the Athenaeum.

Strauss, Richard (1864–1949), Munich-born composer, at one time considered to be Elgar's greatest contemporary. Elgar met him at Garmisch in 1897. After the repeat performance of *Gerontius* at Düsseldorf in 1902, Strauss toasted Elgar as the 'first English progressive musician'. Elgar's orchestration of the Fugue (1921) and Fantasia (1922) in C minor of Bach was said to be the outcome of a wager with Strauss, who, like Elgar, was admired for his masterly orchestration.

Stuart of Wortley, Lady (Alice Stuart-Wortley, 1862–1936), third daughter of Sir John Millais. Her husband, Charles Stuart-Wortley, was created Baron in 1916. A friendship with Elgar grew from his visits to Sheffield and developed in London. A considerable correspondence, starting in about 1903, lasted for more than twenty years. Musical and sympathetic, she was involved to some extent in inspiring the composition of parts of Symphony No. 2 and more particularly the Violin Concerto.

Wood, Sir Henry Joseph (1869–1944), London-born conductor, became famous for his Promenade Concerts which started at the Queen's Hall in 1895. 'I suppose there will be a chance for English composers some day at Queen's Hall', wrote Jaeger to Elgar on 8th March 1898. The 'Meditation' from *The Light of Life* was given in May the following year and later Wood took up Elgar's music with enthusiasm. The *Grania and Diarmid* music is dedicated to this conductor, who did much for many living British composers in his time.

Young, Dr Percy Marshall (b. Cheshire, 1912), author on various subjects, was educated at Christ's Hospital and Cambridge. Director of Music at Wolverhampton College of Technology from 1945 to 1966 and expert on football. Young has written on many composers but has made a speciality of Elgar. Also a composer and recently appointed adviser on music in Nigeria, he published a substantial *History of British Music* in 1967. Songs and a string orchestra suite from Elgar's unfinished opera, *The Spanish Lady*, have been edited and published by him.

APPENDIX D

BIBLIOGRAPHY

Anderson, W. R., 'Introduction to the Music of Elgar' (London, 1949).

Barber, Cecil, 'Enigma Variations: the Original Finale' (*Music and Letters*, April 1935).

Bax, Sir Arnold, 'Farewell my Youth' (London, 1943).

Bennett, Joseph, '*King Olaf*, Analytical Notes' (London, 1896).

Bonavia, Ferruccio, 'Elgar' in *Lives of the Great Composers*, vol. iii (London, 1935), *The Symphony* (ed. Ralph Hill, London, 1949), and *The Music Makers*, vol. iii (London, 1952).

Brent Smith, A. E., 'The Humour of Elgar' (*Music and Letters*, January 1935).

Buckley, R. J., 'Sir Edward Elgar' in *Living Masters of Music* (London, 1905).

Byard, Herbert, in *The Concerto* (ed. Ralph Hill, London, 1952).

Cardus, Sir Neville, 'Elgar' in *Ten Composers* (London, 1945), and *A Composer's Eleven* (London, 1968).

Chambers, H. A., ed., 'Edward Elgar: Centenary Sketches' (London, 1957), contributors: *Sir John Barbirolli, Carice Elgar Blake, Sir Adrian Boult, H. A. Chambers, Bernard Herrmann, Alan J. Kirby, Yehudi Menuhin, Dora M. Powell, Stanford Robinson, David Willocks* and *Percy M. Young.*

Colles, H. C., Analytical Notes (*Musical Times*) on Symphony No. 1 (December 1908), Piano Quintet (November 1919) and Cello Concerto (February 1920).

——, Article on Elgar in Grove's *Dictionary of Music and Musicians* (London, 1927, revised 1954).

Cox, David, 'Edward Elgar' in *The Symphony*, vol. ii (ed. Robert Simpson, London, 1967).

Cumberland, Gerald, 'Elgar' in *Set Down in Malice* (London, 1919).

Dann, Mary G., 'Elgar's Use of Sequence' (*Music and Letters*, July 1938; part of degree thesis at Rochester, U.S.A.).

Dent, Edward J., article in Adler's *Handbuch der Musikgeschichte* (1931).

Dunhill, Thomas F., 'Sir Edward Elgar' (London, 1938).

Appendix D—Bibliography

Fiske, Roger, 'The Enigma: a solution' (*Musical Times*, November 1969), a plea for 'Auld Lang Syne' as Enigma, but see below.

Fox Strangways, A. H., 'Elgar' (*Music and Letters*, April 1934).

——, letter to editor (*Music and Letters*, January 1935), rejecting 'Auld Lang Syne' as Enigma.

Gaisberg, Fred, 'Music on Record' (London, 1946).

Gorton, Canon C. V., 'Interpretation of the Librettos of the Oratorios' (the three in Chapter IX) (London, 1907).

Gray, Cecil, 'Edward Elgar' in *A Survey of Contemporary Music* (Oxford, 1924).

Grew, Sydney, 'Sir Edward Elgar, O.M.' in *Our Favourite Musicians* (London, 1924).

Hadden, J. Cuthbert, 'Modern Musicians' (London, 1913).

Howes, Frank, 'Edward Elgar' in *The Heritage of Music*, vol. iii (Oxford, 1951).

——, 'The Two Elgars' (*Music and Letters*, January 1935).

——, 'The English Renaissance' (London, 1966).

——, 'Nimrod on Strauss' (*Musical Times*, June 1970).

Hurd, Michael, 'Elgar' (London, 1969).

Jackson, Sir Barry, 'Elgar's *Spanish Lady*' (*Music and Letters*, January 1943).

Jaeger, A. J., Analytical Notes on *Gerontius* (1900), *The Apostles* (1903), *In the South* (1904) and *The Kingdom* (1906), (London).

Johnstone, Arthur, 'Musical Criticisms' (Manchester, 1905).

Jose, Everard, 'The Significance of Elgar' (London, 1934).

Keeton, A. E., 'Elgar and Quotations' (*Musical Opinion*, August 1942).

——, 'Elgar's Music for *The Starlight Express*' (*Music and Letters*, January, 1945).

Kennedy, Michael, 'Portrait of Elgar' (London, 1968).

Lambert, Herbert, 'Modern British Composers' (London, 1923).

Langford, Samuel, 'Musical Criticisms' (ed. Neville Cardus, London, 1929).

LISTENER, THE (30th July 1942), *Carner, Mosco,* 'Elgar as Symphonist'.

——, (4th November 1943), *Hutchings, Arthur,* 'Elgarian Oratorio and its Background'.

McVeagh, Diana M., 'Edward Elgar: his life and music' (London, 1955).

——, 'Elgar: an Appreciation' (Elgar Society, 1955).

——, 'Elgar's Birthplace' (*Musical Times*, June 1957).

——, 'Ashton's Enigma Ballet' (*Musical Times*, December 1968).

——, 'Elgar's Concert Allegro' (*Musical Times*, February 1969).

Maine, Basil, 'Elgar: his Life and Work' (2 vols., London, 1933).

Mason, Daniel Gregory, 'Contemporary Composers' (New York, 1918).

MONTHLY MUSICAL RECORD (March–April 1947), *Wood, Ralph W.,* 'Enigma Derivations'.

—— (October 1948), *Gregory, Robin,* 'Elgar's use of *nobilmente*'.

Moore, Jerrold N., 'Elgar as a University Professor' (*Musical Times,* October and November 1960).

——, 'An Elgar Discography' (London, 1963).

MUSIC AND LETTERS (January 1935), contributors to special issue: *Donald Tovey, Hubert Foss, Vaughan Williams, Brent Smith, Frank Howes* and *W. H. Reed.*

—— (April 1942), *Dickinson, A. E. F.,* 'The Drama behind Elgar's Music'.

MUSIC IN EDUCATION (May–June 1944), *Wood, Frederic,* 'Edward Elgar'.

MUSIC SURVEY (June 1951), *Dickinson, A. E. F.,* 'The Isolation of Elgar'.

MUSICAL OPINION (April 1945), *Hunt, Reginald,* 'Elgar and the Common Touch'.

MUSICAL STANDARD (13th October 1900), 'Edward Elgar's Hobbies'.

MUSICAL TIMES (October 1900), biographical, portrait, analysis, etc.

—— (April 1934), contains list of articles on Elgar published in the magazine during his lifetime.

—— (January 1938), *Judd, Percy,* 'Elgar's Part-Songs'.

—— (July 1949), *Godman, Stanley,* 'The Elgars of Dover'.

—— (August 1949), *Jacobs, Arthur,* 'Elgar's Solo Songs'.

—— (June 1957), contributors to Centenary Number: *Vaughan Williams, John Ireland, Julius Harrison, Sir Arthur Bliss, Herbert Howells, Gordon Jacob, Edmund Rubbra, Patrick Hadley, J. A. Westrup, Sir Steuart Wilson, Herbert W. Sumsion, Eric Blom, Frank Howes, Sir George Dyson, Thomas Armstrong, Sir Ernest Bullock, W. Greenhouse Allt, Edric Cundell, R. J. F. Howgill, Maurice Johnstone, Eric Warr, Alec Robertson, Diana McVeagh* and *Harold Rutland.*

—— (March 1960), *Wykes, David,* 'Elgar's Cello Concerto: A Query'.

Newman, Ernest, 'Elgar' (*The Music of the Masters,* London, 1905).

——, 'Edward Elgar' (*The Speaker,* 22nd December 1901).

——, 'Elgar and his Enigma' (*Sunday Times,* 16th, 23rd, 30th April, 7th May, 1939).

——, 'Elgar and his "Stately Sorrow"' (*The Listener,* 11th March 1954).

Newman (cont.), 'The Artist and the Man' (*Sunday Times*, 13th November 1955).

——, Analytical Notes (*Musical Times*) on Violin Concerto (October 1910), Symphony No. 2 (May 1911) and *The Spirit of England* (May 1916).

PALL MALL GAZETTE (21st March 1904), 'Elgar in London'.

Parrott, Ian, 'Variation for a Dog?' (*Music Teacher*, January 1956).

——, 'Was Elgar's Orchestration Impeccable?' (*The Chesterian*, 1957).

——, 'The Enigma: A New Slant' (Elgar Society, 1968).

——, 'Elgar's Associations with Wales' (*Anglo-Welsh Review*, Summer 1969).

Porte, John F., 'Sir Edward Elgar' (London, 1921).

Powell, Richard C., 'Elgar's Enigma' (*Music and Letters*, July 1934).

Powell, Mrs Richard (Dorabella), 'Edward Elgar: Memories of a Variation' (London, 1937, 1947 and 1949).

——, 'The First Performances of *The Apostles* and *The Kingdom*' (*Musical Times*, January 1960).

Reed, W. H., 'Elgar as I knew him' (London, 1936).

——, 'Elgar' (London, 1939 and 1943).

——, 'Elgar' (*Cobbett's Cyclopaedic Survey of Chamber Music*, 1929).

——, 'Elgar's Violin Concerto' (*Music and Letters*, January 1935).

——, 'Elgar's Third Symphony' (*The Listener*, 28th August 1935).

Sams, Eric, 'Elgar's cipher letter to Dorabella' (*Musical Times*, February 1970).

——, 'Variations on a Original Theme (Enigma)' (*Musical Times*, March 1970).

——, 'Elgar's Enigma: A Past Script and a Postscript' (*Musical Times*, July 1970).

Shaw, George Bernard, 'Sir Edward Elgar' (*Music and Letters*, January 1920).

Sheldon, A. J., 'Edward Elgar' (London, 1932).

Shera, F. H., 'Elgar: Instrumental Works' (*Musical Pilgrim*, London, 1931).

Shore, Bernard, 'Elgar's Second Symphony' (*Sixteen Symphonies*, London, 1949).

Stone, Irving J., 'Edward Elgar' (*The Musical Record*, Philadelphia, 1933).

STRAND MAGAZINE (May 1904), 'Dr Elgar' (interview by Rupert de Cordova).

Streatfeild, R. A., 'Un Musicista Inglese' (*Rivista d'Italia*, October 1912).

Appendix D—Bibliography

Thompson, Herbert, Analytical Notes on *Caractacus* (London, 1898).

Tovey, Sir Donald F., Analytical Notes on *Enigma Variations, Cockaigne, In the South, Introduction and Allegro,* Violin Concerto, Symphony No. 2, *Falstaff* and Cello Concerto (*Essays in Musical Analysis,* London, 1935-9 and *Some English Symphonists,* London, 1941).

——, 'Elgar, Master of Music' (*Music and Letters,* January 1935).

Turner, E. O., 'Tempo Variations with Examples from Elgar' (*Music and Letters,* July 1938).

Vaughan Williams, Ralph, 'What have we learnt from Elgar?' (*Music and Letters,* January 1935).

Webb, Alan, 'A Curator's Notebook' (Worcester, 1969 and 1970).

Westrup, Professor Sir Jack, 'Elgar's Enigma' (*Royal Musical Association,* April 1960).

Wood, Sir Henry J., 'My Life of Music' (London, 1938).

WORLD, THE (11th December 1901), 'Dr Edward Elgar at Malvern'.

—— (22nd October 1912), 'Sir Edward Elgar O.M.'.

Young, Percy M., 'Elgar O.M.' (London, 1955).

——, 'Letters of Edward Elgar' (London, 1956).

——, 'Letters to Nimrod from Edward Elgar' (London, 1965).

——, 'A History of British Music', Chapter 12 (London, 1967).

——, ed., 'A Future for English Music', Birmingham University Lectures (London, 1968).

APPENDIX E

(With information compiled by Alan Webb for the Elgar Society)

1857–9	The Birthplace at Broadheath, some three miles from Worcester, stands between the Tenbury and Bromyard roads, and is signposted at both junctions. The three museum rooms are open daily (except Wednesdays), 1.30 to 6.30 p.m., or by special appointment. Broadheath Common, to which Elgar often returned in boyhood, was probably the place where the *Wand of Youth* music germinated.
1860–6	1 Edgar Street, Worcester (now Tower House, Severn Street). The family lived here until about 1864, removing then to new business premises at 10 High Street, almost opposite St Helen's Church (now engulfed in Messrs Russell and Dorrell's extensions).
1866–79	With his family over their music shop (10 High Street, Worcester).
1879–83	With married sister Pollie at Loretto Villa, 12 Chestnut Walk, Worcester.
1883–9	With married sister Lucy at 4 Field Terrace, Bath Road, Worcester.
1889–90	After his marriage, at 3 Marloes Road, Kensington, and Oaklands, Fountain Road, Upper Norwood.
1890–1	51 Avonmore Road, West Kensington.
1891–9	Forli, Alexandra Road, Malvern (named after Melozzo da Forli, who painted angels playing instruments). *Enigma Variations.*
1898–1903	Birchwood Lodge, Storridge, near Malvern (as a summer cottage). *The Dream of Gerontius.*

Appendix E—Houses where Elgar lived

1899–1904   Craeg Lea, Malvern Wells (the name is an anagram of C A E Elgar). *Gerontius, Cockaigne, The Apostles.*

1904–11   Plas Gwyn, Hampton Park Road, Hereford. *Introduction and Allegro, The Kingdom,* Symphony No. 1, Violin Concerto, Symphony No. 2.

1912–21   Severn House, Netherhall Gardens, Hampstead (this house no longer exists). *Falstaff, The Music Makers, The Spirit of England.*

1917–21   Brinkwells, near Fittleworth, West Sussex (as a summer cottage). Violin Sonata, String Quartet, Piano Quintet, Cello Concerto. Re-thatched in 1967.

1921–3   37 St James's Place, London.

1923–7   Napleton Grange, Kempsey, near Worcester.

1927–8   Battenhall Manor, Worcester. This house (said to have been haunted) now no longer exists.

1928–9   Tiddington House, Stratford-on-Avon (now demolished).

1929–34   Marl Bank, Rainbow Hill, Worcester. Elgar died here on 23rd February 1934. Demolished, 15th October 1969, to make room for flats.

Several of the above houses have a plaque bearing the words 'Sir Edward Elgar lived in this house', with the dates.

INDEX

INDEX

Index

Index

Index

Powick, 3

Proctor, Charles, 19

Puccini, Giacomo, 26, 75, 90

Purcell, Henry, 10, 45

Ravel, Maurice, 88

Reed, W. H., vii, 3, 5, 8, 11, 13, 15–17, 22–4, 26, 33, 55, 56, 58, 64, 79, 94, 96–7, 122

Richards, Rt Rev. John, Bishop of St David' vii, 46–7

Richter, Hans, 8, 15–16, 44, 47, 121, 123

Roberts, Caroline Alice. *See* Elgar, Caroline Alice

Roberts, Major-General Sir Henry Gee, 4

Robertson, Alec, 54

Rodewald, Alfred, 123

Romance, Op. 1, 88

Romance for bassoon and orchestra, 60

Rome, 20, 67

Ronald, Sir Landon, 23, 123

Rootham, Cyril, 21

Rosemary, 20

Royal Philharmonic Society, 26, 121

Rubbra, Edmund, 52

'Rule, Britannia', 10, 66

Russell, Ken, 94

Rutherford, Ernest, 3

Salmond, Felix, 17, 23–4

Salut d'Amour, 4, 57

Sammons, Albert, 23–4

Sanford, S. S., 13

Sanguine Fan, The, 21, 63

Sargent, Sir Malcolm, 66, 122

Schönberg, Arnold, 73

Schubert, Franz, 37, 65, 82, 84

Schumann, Robert, 4, 33, 45, 65, 74, 76

Schuster, Adela, 16, 54, 123

Schuster, Frank, 16–17, 20, 24, 123

Scott, Sir Walter, 19

Sea Pictures, 8, 66, 94

Serenade for strings, 5, 58

Serenade for unaccompanied voices, 83

Sérénade Mauresque, 77

Severn House, 18, 22–5

Severn Suite, 29, 77, 123

Sevillaña, 4, 77

Shakespeare, William, 19, 60

Shaw, A. T., vii

Shaw, George Bernard, 24, 28–9, 64, 123

Index